Commercial and Economic Law in India

Commercial and Economic Law in India

K.B. Agrawal
Neha Dixit

This book was originally published as a monograph in the International Encyclopaedia of Laws/Commercial and Economic Law.

Founding Editor: Roger Blanpain
General Editor: Frank Hendrickx
Volume Editors: Jules Stuyck & Evelyne Terryn

Wolters Kluwer

Published by:
Kluwer Law International B.V.
PO Box 316
2400 AH Alphen aan den Rijn
The Netherlands
E-mail: international-sales@wolterskluwer.com
Website: lrus.wolterskluwer.com

Sold and distributed in North, Central and South America by:
Wolters Kluwer Legal & Regulatory U.S.
7201 McKinney Circle
Frederick, MD 21704
United States of America
Email: customer.service@wolterskluwer.com

Sold and distributed in all other countries by:
Air Business Subscriptions
Rockwood House
Haywards Heath
West Sussex
RH16 3DH
United Kingdom
Email: international-customerservice@wolterskluwer.com

Printed on acid-free paper

ISBN 978-94-035-0285-4

e-Book: ISBN 978-94-035-0174-1
web-PDF: ISBN 978-94-035-0260-1

This title is available on www.kluwerlawonline.com

Printed in the United Kingdom.

The Authors

Professor K.B. Agrawal is the Director of the Indian Institute of Comparative Law, Jaipur, Rajasthan, India. He has been the Dean of the Faculty of Law, University of Rajasthan, Jaipur. He has experience of teaching LLB and LLM classes for the last thirty-eight years. He has been Editor-in-Chief of the renowned *Indian Socio Legal Journal* for the last thirty-nine years. He has written more than 150 research papers published in various law journals of the world. He has written many books; the most important of them are *Some Thoughts on Modern Jurisprudence* (1976); *Random Thoughts on Family Law* (1981); *Writings on Legal Education* (1982); *Comparative Constitutionalism* (1992); and *Legal Pluralism in India* (2006). He wrote a monograph on *Indian and Inter-country Adoption Law,* Published by the Kluwer Law International, London. He has also written monographs on India for the *Encyclopedia of Family Law and Children-Indian Section* (in German Language), International Encyclopedia of Laws on *Family and Succession Law*, *Private International Law* and *Insurance Law*, *Commercial and Economic Law, Corporations and partnerships*. He also revised the Indian section of the *International Encyclopedia on Civil Procedure* 2006 and 2009, *Family and Succession Law, Private International Law, Insurance Law*, 2012. Professor Agrawal has also been an advocate for several years. He worked for the Scandinavian Institute of African Studies, Uppsala, Sweden in 1979. He was at the Max Planck Institute for Foreign and International Private Law, Hamburg, Germany in 1981. He also did research work at the Christian Albrechts University, Kiel, Germany under the German Academic Exchange Programme (DAAD) in 1995 and at the International Institute for Unification of Private Law (popularly known as UNIDROIT), Rome, Italy in 2001.

The Authors

Dr Neha Dixit is working as an Assistant Professor in Department of Law, University of Rajasthan, Jaipur, Rajasthan. She did her PhD from University of Rajasthan, Jaipur. She has completed LLM and LLB from Government Law College, Ajmer, Rajasthan. She has written many research articles, which have been published in various reputed legal journals. She has participated in various national and international seminars, conferences and workshops. She is an active member of various committees including legal aid committee in the University Law College, University of Rajasthan, Jaipur, Rajasthan.

Table of Contents

List of Abbreviations

AC	Appeal Cases
ACJ	Accident Claims Journal
AIC	All India Cases
AIHC	All India High Court Cases
AIR	All India Reporter
ALJ	Allahabad Law Journal
All	Allahabad High Court
All E R	All England Reports
ALT	Allahabad Law Times
AP	Andhra Pradesh High Court
App Cas	Appeal Cases
Arb L R	Arbitration Law Reports
ASSOCHAM	Association of Chamber and Commerce and Industries in India
AWR	Andhra Pradesh Weekly Law Report
Bom	Bombay High Court
BSE	Bombay Stock Exchange
Cal	Calcutta High Court
CCI	Competition Commission of India
CII	Confederation of Indian Industry
CLA	Central Listing Authority
CLJ	Civil Law Judgments
CLP	Commercial Law Practice
CLT	Calcutta Law Times
Com Cas	Company Cases
Comp LJ	Company Law Journal
CPA	Consumer Protection Act, 1986
CPJ	Consumer Protection Journal
CPR	Consumer Protection Reports
CWN	Calcutta Weekly Notes

Del	Delhi High Court
DIS	Direct Investment Scheme
DLT	Delhi Law Times
ECA	Essential Commodities Act, 1955
ER	England Reports
FDI	Foreign Direct Investment
FEMA	Foreign Exchange Management Act, 1999
FICCI	Federation of Chamber of Commerce and Industry
GIC	General Insurance Corporation
Guj	Gujarat High Court
HLC	House of Lords Cases
Hyd	Hyderabad High Court
IA	Indian Appeals
IC	Indian Cases
ICADR	International Centre for Alternative Disputes Resolution
ILR	Indian Law Reports
Ind Dec	Indian Decisions
IR	Indian Reports
ISE	Inter-connected Stock Exchange of India
JBCs	Joint Business Council
Jhar	Jharkhand High Court
Kant	Karnataka High Court
KB	King's Bench
Ker	Kerala High Court
KLT	Kerala Law Times
Lah	Lahore High Court
LIC	Life Insurance Corporation of India
Lloyd's Re	Lloyd's Reports
Luck	Lucknow High Court
MIA	Moore Indian Appeals
Mad	Madras High Court
MHCR	Madras High Court Reports
MLJ	Madras Law Journal
MNCs	Multinational Companies

List of Abbreviations

MP	Madhya Pradesh High Court
MRTP Act	Monopoly and Restrictive Trade Practices Act, 1969
MWN	Madras Weekly Notes
Mysore	Mysore High Court
Nag	Nagpur High Court
NC	National Commission
NEDFC	North Eastern Development Financial Corporation
NH Act	National Highway Act, 1956
NRI	Non-resident Indian
NSDL	National Stock Depository Limited
NSE	National Stock Exchange
Ori	Orissa High Court
OTC	Over the Counter
OTCEI	Over the Counter Exchange of India
Oudh	Oudh High Court
P&H	Punjab and Haryana High Court
Pat	Patna High Court
Pb	Punjab High Court
PC	Privy Council
PIS	Portfolio Investment Scheme
Punjab Reco	Punjab High Court Records
QB	Queen's Bench
QBD	Queen's Bench Division
Raj	Rajasthan High Court
Rang	Rangoon High Court
RBI	Reserve Bank of India
S.	Section
SC	Supreme Court
SCC	Supreme Court Cases
SCR	Supreme Court Reports
SCRA	Securities Controls (Regulations) Act, 1956
SEBI	Security and Exchange Board of India
SEZ	Special Economic Zone
Sind	Sindh High Court

TP Act	Transfer of Property
Trav LJ	Travancore Law Journal
UNCITRAL	United Nationals Commissions for International Trade Law
UTI	Unit Trust of India
VCF	Venture Capital Fund
WLC	Western Law Cases
WLR	Weekly Law Reports

Preface

The subject of Commercial Law has always been a matter of great interest to the business community all over the world. International trade and commerce, as being learnt from the history and scriptures, has been since the beginning of the society. The complexity of modern contractual relationships and, in general, of the social and economic environment, requires similar weight to be given to values other than the classical values of freedom, security and certainty.

Commercial Law is a body of rules that regulates and controls business transactions in the society. These are those rules that ascertain uniformity in the procedure and principles in the mercantile transactions. They determine the standards that are essential to observe in trade and business. Besides this, the governmental policy is also being enforced by these laws.

Not only in early society, but also even in modern society, customs, conventions, usages and traditions have played major roles in commerce and industries all over the world. In India, however, with the development of society, a need for codification of commercial law arose. During the nineteenth and twentieth centuries, a number of laws concerning commerce and business were enacted on the recommendations of various law commissions appointed by the then British Government and also the present Law Commission of India.

In this monograph on Commercial Law, descriptions on many laws have been made dealing with, e.g., Indian Contract Act, 1872, Insurance Act, 1938, Transfer of Property Act, 1882, Indian Evidence Act, 1872, Negotiable Instruments Act, 1881, Companies Act, 2013, Banking Companies Act, 1949, Banking Regulation Act, 1965, Consumer Protection Act, 1986, Indian Arbitration and Conciliation Act, 1996, Essential Commodities Act, Monopolies and Restrictive Practices Act, 1969, Copyright Act, 1957, Trade Marks Act, 1999, Limitation Act, 1963, Partnership, 1932, Workmen's Compensation Act, 1923, Industrial Disputes Act, 1948, Payment of Wages Act, 1936, Registration Act, 1908, Indian Designs Act, 2000, Indian Patents and Designs Act, 1970, Presidency Town Insolvency, Act, 1909, Provincial Insolvency Act, 1920, Negotiable Instrument Act, 1881, Capital Issues (Control) Act, 1947, Sale of Goods Act, 1930, Carrier Act, 1865, Indian Carriage by Air Act, 1972, Railways Act, 1989, Foreign Exchange Management Act, 1999, Financial Corporation Act, 1974, Competition Act, 2002. In this monograph, attempts have been made to update these Acts by inserting latest Parliament amendments Acts and latest possible judgments of the Supreme Court and different High Courts of the country.

Relevant parts of other non-commercial laws, which are necessary for the details of the various Acts on commercial, have also been dealt with. Philosophical aspects of business law have not been lost sight of.

Prof. K.B. Agrawal
Dr Neha Dixit

General Introduction

§1. General Background of the Country

I. General

1. The Indian subcontinent occupies a strategic position in the world, looking across the seas of Arabia and Africa on the West and to Myanmar, Malaysia and the Indonesian Archipelago on the East. Geographically, Himalayan ranges keep India apart from the rest of Asia. Occupying a highly favorable situation for the purpose of international trade and commerce, India stands almost at the centre of the Eastern Hemisphere and the head of the Indian Ocean. She commands all the sea routes for trade between old and new worlds, towards the Middle East, Africa and Europe in the West, Australia in the South and Indonesia, Malaysia, China, Japan and America in the East.

II. The Natural Regions

2. A region of such vast extent is naturally of diversified configuration, viz., plains, plateaus and mountains. Geographically, India presents four natural divisions, e.g., the mountainous regions each of which is quite unlike the other. These divisions are based on physical conditions:

(a) the Mountain Regions of the North;
(b) the Indo-Gangetic plain;
(c) the Peninsular India; and
(d) the Desert.

A. Mountain Regions of the North

3. They are seven, viz., (1) the Himalayas; (2) the Patkai and other ranges bordering India in the North and Northeast; (3) the Vindhyas, which separate the Indo-Gangetic plain from the Deccan Plateau; (4) the Satpura; (5) the Aravali; (6) the Sahyadri, which covers the eastern edge of the West Coast plains; and (7) the Eastern Ghats, irregularly scattered on the East Coast and forming the boundary of the East Coast Plains from the Deccan Plateau.

B. The Indo-Gangetic Plain

4. The plain of India occupies the greater part Northern India and covers more than 5,000 km, from east to west with a width of 500 km. This plain is formed by the basins of the rivers Ganga, the Indus and the Brahmaputra with their tributaries, and has been the cradle of Indo-Aryan civilization from the earliest times. The geographical advantages are: (1) fertile soil; (2) favourable climate; (3) the surface making possible the construction of roads and railways; (4) rivers; and (5) mineral products, etc. In the Gangetic plain, rainfall is heavy and agriculture is the chief occupation of the people. It contains more than 40% of the total population of India. Agriculture is practiced with the help of a well-developed system of irrigation.

C. Peninsular India

5. Peninsular India lies within the tropics. It is bounded on three sides by mountains: on the north by the Vindhya and Satpura ranges, including the Malwa and the Arvali plateau; on the west by the Western Ghats and on the east by the Eastern Ghats. Two coastal strips of flat land exist on the outer edge of both the Western and Eastern Ghats. The western coastal strip is known as the 'Konkan Ghats' in the north and 'Malabar' in the south, and the Eastern coastal strip is known as the 'Coromondal Coast'.

D. The Desert

6. The desert region can be divided into two parts, the great desert and the little desert. The great desert extends from the edge of the Rann of Kachha beyond the Luni River northward. The whole of the Rajasthan-Sind Frontier runs through the Luni between Jaisalmer and Jodhpur up to the Northwest.

III. Watersheds

7. There are mainly three watersheds, viz., (1) Himalayan range with its Karakoram branch in the north; (2) Vindhya and Satpura ranges in Central India; and (3) Sahyadri or Western Ghats on the West coast. All the major rivers of India originate in one or the other of these watersheds.

IV. Rivers

8. The main rivers of the Himalayan group are the Indus, the Ganga and the Brahmaputra. The rivers are both snow-fed and rain-fed and, therefore, continuously flow throughout the year. About 70% of the Himalayan Rivers flow into the central Indian rivers. They join Ganga and drain into the Bay of Bengal.

A. The Indus

9. The Indus, which the Aryans called the Sindhu, has lent its name to India. Its valleys on both sides have been the seat of civilization. This historic river has five major tributaries: the Jhelum, the Chenab, the Ravi, the Beas and the Sutlej. These in turn have inspired the name 'Punjab'. The Indus rises from Mount Kailash in Tibet and traverses many miles throughout the Himalayas before it is joined by its tributaries in Punjab. Thereafter it passes into Sind (Pakistan) to fall into the Arabian Sea.

B. The Ganga

10. The Ganga, famous both in legend and history, is considered the most sacred river by the Hindus. It covers, what is called the heartland of India, which was the main centre of the ancient Aryan culture. It rises near the glacier, Gangotri in the Himalayas and flows through the states of Uttaranchal, Uttar Pradesh, Bihar and Bengal, to fall into the Bay of Bengal. The Ganga and its tributaries, viz., Jamuna, Gomti, Ghagra, Sarda, Gandak, Chambal, Soni and Kosi, spread out like a fan in the plain of India thus forming the largest river basin in India, with an area, one-quarter of the total area of India.

C. The Brahmaputra

11. The Brahmaputra, rising in western Tibet, flows for some 1,300 km through the Himalayas, then turns south west and then south joining the eastern most branch of the Ganga, the Padma and falls together with Ganga into the Bay of Bengal.

D. The Deccan Rivers

12. The major Deccan rivers are the Godavari, the Krishna, Cauvery, the Pennar, the Mahanadi, the Damodar, the Saraswati, the Netravati, the Bharatapuzha, the Periyar, the Pamba, the Narmada and the Tapti. These rivers are entirely rain-fed with the result that many of them shrink into rivulets during the hot seasons. These rivers contribute about 30% of the total outflow in India. Of this, rivers those flow from west to east account for 20% and those from east to west about 10%.

V. Climate

13. The Climate in India is so vast that the climatic conditions are much varied. India has mainly three seasons a year, viz., rainy (June–September: southwest monsoon, October–November: northeast monsoon); summer (April–July) and winter (mid-October–February). In south India, however, there is no winter as such is evidenced by the clear sky, hot days and cool nights. This type of weather condition prevails from September to March. The rainy season sets in with the onset of southwest monsoon over Kerala, usually on 1 June. It progresses northward and covers the whole country by the end of July. The eastern coastal belts – coasts of Andhra Pradesh and Tamil

Nadu, experience north east monsoons during October and November, when it is winter in north India. Along the east coast, this period is also marked by cyclones, which cause widespread destruction of crops, lives and property. It develops due to severe atmospheric depression in the Bay of Bengal and Indian Ocean and moves towards the mainland often hitting at high speed. Rarely does the west coast experience such cyclonic effects.

VI. People

14. India being a vast country equal in area to the whole of Europe excluding Russia. It has a population of more than 1,210 million embracing a medley of most varied racial elements. The Indian population is polygenetic and is said to be the melting pot of various racial mosaics. Few, if any, can claim to belong to any particular stock. Nevertheless, many Indians pride themselves on their Aryan descent.

15. The species is known as Ramapithecus was fund in the Siwalik foothills of the north-western Himalayas. This species believed to be the first in the line of hominids (human family) lived some 14 million years ago. Researches have found that a specie resembling the Australopithecus lived in India some 2 million years ago. Even this discovery leaves an evolutionary gap of as much as 12 million years since Ramapithecus.

VII. Political and Legal System

A. General

16. The Constitution of India came into effect on 26 January 1950. It was drawn up by Constituent Assembly, initially summoned on the 9 December 1946. The Constituent Assembly was summoned initially for undivided India, but when Pakistan separated from India in June 1947, her delegates ceased to be members of the same. A draft Constitution of India was published in February 1948, but it was finally adopted on the 26 November 1948 and came into effect on the 26 January 1950.

17. The Constitution of India, a written document containing 392 Articles and 10 schedules, came into force on 26 January 1952. It is partly rigid and partly flexible, i.e., some provisions can be amended by simple majority of Parliament while others require a two-thirds majority of Parliament besides a majority of the state legislatures. According to its preamble, India is a sovereign democratic republic, which assures its citizens social, economic and political justice; liberty of thought, expression, belief, faith and worship, equality of status and of opportunity. India is a Union of states, i.e., it is a federal state but the Indian Constitution has the unique distinction that it contains an inbuilt mechanism, which enables Parliament to convert the federal constitution into a unitary system under certain circumstances, e.g., declaration of emergency due to war or internal disturbances,[1] breakdown of the constitutional machinery of the

1. Indian Constitution, Art. 352 also *Manilaxmi Patel v. Hindustan Coop. Insurance Society*, AIR 162 Cal 625.

state;[2] or financial emergency.[3] But this is only a temporary phase. Parliament, however, has also been empowered to make laws on the subjects of the states during proclamation of emergency or if the Rajya Sabha (Council of States) by two-thirds of the members present and voting passes a resolution that it is expedient to do so in the national interest,[4] or for the implementation of international treaties, agreements or covenants.[5]

18. The Constitution of India introduces universal adult franchise and accords voting rights for all its citizens above 18 years of age. However, for being elected member of Lok Sabha (House of People) and Vidhan Sabha (state legislatures), he/she should be of 25 years of age and that of Rajya Sabha, 35 years.

19. There are special provisions in the Constitution for minorities, scheduled castes, scheduled tribes, other backward classes, etc.

20. The Constitution of India, though a federal state, recognizes single citizenship for the whole of India. The Indian Constitution provides citizens many fundamental rights, which are inalienable. They form one of the basic structures of the Constitution of India and as such they cannot be amended by Parliament. Part IV of it prescribes directive principles of state policy. They are no doubt unenforceable by any court but the principles laid down therein are nevertheless fundamental in the governance of the country and it is the duty of the state to apply these principles in making laws.

21. In India, there is a parliamentary system of government. Parliament consists of two houses, viz., Lok Sabha (House of People) and Rajya Sabha (Council of States). All bills except financial bills can be initiated in either house but they have to be passed by both houses. In the case of deadlock, a joint sitting of both houses considers the bill, which may or may not be passed. After being passed by both houses, the bill is sent to the President for his consent. After the consent, the bill becomes an act. A financial bill can originate only in Lok Sabha. After being passed by Lok Sabha, it is sent to Rajya Sabha. Whether or not the latter house approves it, the bill is sent to the President for his/her assent after the passage of fourteen days.

22. The Constitution of India has established a secular state, i.e., there is no state religion and the state is completely detached from religious dogma. The state cannot levy any tax on any religion. However, there is religious freedom to all the persons in India including freedom to profess, practice and propagate his/her own religion.

23. The Constitution of India provides an independent judiciary, which ensures that the government operates according to the provisions of the Constitution and it also protects the fundamental rights of the people. In a federal democratic polity, the judiciary is the sole arbiter and interpreter of the will of the people. The Constitution of India, though a federal one, provides a single system of court for the whole of India. At the apex, there is a Supreme Court for the whole of India. In every state, there are High Courts and a network of subordinate courts. Besides these courts, the Gram Nyayalaya Act, 2008 has been enacted to establish gram nyayalayas (village courts) in order to provide access to justice to the citizens at their doorsteps and to ensure

2. Indian Constitution, Art. 356.
3. Indian Constitution, Art. 360.
4. Indian Constitution, Art. 249.
5. Indian Constitution, Art. 253.

opportunities for securing justice are not denied to any citizen by reason of social, economic or other disabilities and for matters connected therewith or incidental thereto.

24. There is a multi-party system in India. There are a number of political parties. Prominent among them are Bharatiya Janata Party, Indian National Congress, Communist Party of India, Samajwadi Party, Janata Party (U), Bahujan Samaj Party, etc. At present, there is ruling party, viz., National Democratic Alliancerty Party consisting of Bharatiya Janata Party and some smaller parries.

VIII. Cultural Composition

25. India is a multi-religious country. Hindus, Muslims, Christians and Parsis are the major religious communities. Parsis are, no doubt, numerically insignificant, but they are important in other ways. In India, at present, the Hindus are 997,174,853, Muslims are 174,198,270, while Christians are 27,080,216. Parsis are only 71,000. For the first time, a no religion category was added in the 2011 census and 2.87 million were classified as people belonging to 'No Religion' (approximately 0.24% of the India's population of 1.28 billion).[6]

A. Hinduism

26. Hinduism was not founded by any one sage or teacher in the way that, for instance, Christianity was founded by Jesus Christ, or Islam by the Prophet Mohammed, neither was it planned in the socio-political sense as a means of public control or order. It grew out of the ancient Vedic scriptures, interpreted by many sages including an early intellectual, Manu. He translated the meanings of Vedism (the worship of nature), compiled the existing rules of conduct meant for human beings as Manava Dharma Shastra (i.e., code of law application to human beings). The whole Hindu society even much before Manu was broadly divided into four classes or varnas, viz., Brahmin, Kshatriya, Vaishya and Shudra. These classes have been wrongly termed as castes. The classification was done according to the responsibility of the class owed towards the society. Brahmins belonged to the elite class of the society, and also to a priestly class. They were the intellectuals who cultivated learning and spiritual ideals. Brahmins are the most interesting social phenomena of India's history. Their claims became extravagant in later times, but it cannot be denied that a very high moral standard was prescribed for them. Their special privileges were really due to their learning. Unlike Christian and Muslim clergy, they were an intellectual hereditary aristocracy who directed the thought of India, whatever form it took. Many Brahmins used to run schools of military science, diplomacy and political education of the royal princess.

27. The Kshatriyas or warriors Class: They used to defend the kingdom from external attacks and protect from internal disturbances. Under the orders of the king, they were required to maintain law and order in the kingdom. Instances, however, are not lacking when they made notable contributions to later Vedic literature, and it is also said that the Upanishads reflected the literary and philosophic efforts of Kshatriyas

6. Available on http://www.censusindia.gov.in/2011-Common/CensusInfo.html.

compared to the ritual literature of Brahmins. They, along with the Brahmins, constituted the elite class of the Hindu society.

28. The Vaishyas are the trading and agriculturist class. They mostly belonged to a rich class and as such were required to contribute financial assistance to the state in times of need especially during wars.

29. The Shudras are at present considered to belonging to the lowest class. It is only at present there is a wrong notion that their duty was to serve the higher classes. Further, politicians have termed them as the dregs of the Hindu society, as also the aboriginals who had submitted to conquerors and had adopted Hindu customs. In fact, the duty of this varna was to do the remaining work of the society, that is, the works not done by the people of the three varnas as mentioned above. There used to be so many other functions in the society. For example, there used to be office of works of many kinds in the then governments, i.e., office assistants, peons, physicians, medical surgeons, engineers, artisans, artists, painter, carpenters, cobblers goldsmiths, watermen, washermen, tailors and so many. Before the advent of British's rule, before the revolution of 1857, they were never considered as dregs of the Hindu society. even during the Muslim period, they were never treated as downtrodden. The Britishers in order to divide the Hindu society, they with the help of some traitors spread the hatred against this class and these shudras have been termed as people belonging to lower social strata.

30. The varna system or classification of the society in the original form was a simple affair and based on the basics of capacity, intellect, labour, responsibility and racial distinctions. This original basis of classification was constantly extended. The non-Aryans who adopted the main principles of Aryan culture were admitted within the pale without being required to abandon their own social customs and popular deities.

31. This classification of society was elastic and transfer from one class to another was not difficult. Some of the great Hindu sages revered by Hindus were half-castes and hybrids. For example, Vashistha was born of the prostitute, Vyasa of a fisher-woman, Parashara of a chandala girl. Instances are ample when many sages of Vedic period were promoted from Kashtriyas to Brahmin hood. Form of conduct was what counted and not the state of birth. This healthy rule of life disappeared over time.

32. Over time, the Aryan thinkers did not encourage indiscriminate racial fusion. Marriages were idealized. Marriages of men of higher class with women of lower class (anuloma) were tolerated but marriages of women of higher class with men of lower class (pratiloma) were strongly condemned.

33. Over time, Varnas were further divided into castes. This caste system became rigid and hereditary. Change from one varna to another became increasingly difficult and eventually impossible. The number of castes and further sub-castes multiplied rapidly till the Hindu society was divided into thousands of mutually exclusive groups. In its present form, caste may be considered as a group of families closely knit to each other and effectively separated from all other groups by strict rules of purity of life, especially relating to diet and marriage. Each caste is now a kind of close corporation equipped with an independent tradition, social code and organization.

34. There are three important sects within the Hindu religion viz., Buddhism, Jainism and Sikhism. The followers of these three sects claim themselves as religions different from Hinduism. Article 25 of the Constitution of India while providing religious freedom, permits the state under its sub-clause (b) of clause 2 to provide 'for social welfare/and reform or the throwing open of Hindu religious institutions of a public character to all classes and sections of Hindus'. In Explanation II, it clarifies that this sub-clause, referring to Hindus shall be construed as containing a reference to persons of the Sikh, Jain or Buddhist religion. It is, therefore, necessary to write something about these sects.

B. Buddhism

35. The rise of Buddhism in the sixth century BC. was a turning point in the history of Hindu culture. It was founded by a great genius Gautam Buddha. At his time, the rituals of Brahmin priests became complicated and expensive. The belief in divine power of sacrifice was fully exploited by these priests. Elaborate sacrifices were not within the easy reach of an average man. Hindu religion became cold and formal and had lost living touch with the masses. The Brahmin priests became all powerful and had established themselves as an exacting and unscrupulous monopoly. Superstition had become a burden on the spiritual outlook of the masses. Obviously, there was a reaction against all this. At this time, Buddha's teachings played a major role in the minds of great masses. 'Never perhaps in the history of the world has there been a personality that has wielded such a powerful influence over the thoughts of humanity.'

36. Gautam Buddha was born in 624 BC and died in 544 BC His real name was Sidharth. Renouncing all worldly pleasures at the age of 29, Buddha left home and his wife, whom he had married at the age of 16 years, with his hair cut off and poorly dressed. He was tormented by memories of the indulgent living of others while so many had so little, and he was determined to find a means of relieving the suffering of less privileged people. He travelled from place to place to find mental solace and enlightenment. For seven years, he wandered in the forest in search of truth. He approached many Brahmin philosophers but their cold theories could not satisfy him. Once, while he was passing through the banks of the river Niranjara near Gaya, he sat down under a tree, closed his eyes and started meditating. Suddenly enlightenment came to him, a momentous happening for him. His future at once became clear. He came to be known as Buddha, the one who is awakened to the truth, and immediately began to preach his way of life, the way that had been revealed to him when meditating. He first preached his first sermon at Sarnath, 6 km from Varanasi. He told his listeners stories much in the same way as did Jesus Christ and soon attracted a strong following. There were no social degrees. All men were (and are) equal on becoming a part of Buddhism. Anyone giving up material values, or the lack thereof would automatically be a follower of this sect. Gautam Buddha died at the age of 80 years. He preached nirwana, i.e., free from the cycle of rebirth.

37. In India, Buddhism developed swiftly. Many kings embraced Buddhism. Ashoka was the most prominent among them. The Ashoka empire extended everywhere except in south India. He erected huge pillars of stone wherever he went. The virtues of Buddhism were written down. These edicts of Ashoka were his personal law. One such pillar can be seen at Sarnath. There are at present only 5 million Buddhists throughout India as compared to its 1 billion population. The reasons for such a small number of people of this sect are many. Hindus could not tolerate this new sect. Many Hindu religious leaders e.g., Shankaracharya, etc. and their followers with the help of Hindu kings opposed and destroyed Buddhism. Further, at several places especially in vihars (places of stay of Buddhist saints or monasteries) corruption spread. Foreign invasions, the loss of royal patronage, internal dissensions and the revived vigour of its great rival and repeated onslaughts of Hindu philosophers sapped the vitality of Buddhism. With the Muslim conquest of Bihar, Bengal, Buddhism disappeared altogether.

C. Jainism

38. Early religion of Aryans was very simple both to understand and to practice. Gradually it became complex. Instead of truth, emphasis was placed on the empty rituals instead of purity of heart and conduct. Religious practices became not only complex but also very expensive. The introduction of animal sacrifice further alienated the people. Superstition prevailed in the society. Many progressive thinkers were not ready to believe in such practices blindly.

39. Jainism came as a reform to the Hindu religion and gave solace to those annihilated by the existing Hindu religious order. Jainism is generally believed as being founded by Mahavira. According to Jain traditions, however, Mahavira was only the last of a line of illustrious preachers known as 'teerthankars' who appeared at regular intervals and were always born among kshatriyas, the warrior class, and never among Brahmins. There were twenty-four teerthankars. The first one was Rishabh Dev, who is said to be the son of Ayodhya. Not enough literature about the first twenty-two Jain 'teerthankars' is available. Parshava Nath, the 23rd teerthankar, lived about 250 years before Mahavira. He began his religious life as a reformer in the then Hindu society and reviver of Parshava Nath sect.

40. Parshva Nath was the son of King Ashvasena of Varanasi. Vardhamana, popularly known as Mahavira, the 24th teerthankar is considered to be the real founder of Jainisim. About his early life, much information is not available. He was born in 599 BC at Kudalgram, near Vaishali (in modern Bihar) and belonged to a highly aristocratic kshatriya family. He led the life of an ordinary house-holder for thirty years. He married a princess and also got a daughter. He left his house and became ascetic at the age of 30 years. He wandered from place to place in search of truth and knowledge for twelve continuous years. At the age of 42, he acquired the highest knowledge (kevalyanana), and began to be known as Mahavira, i.e., the great hero and Jina, the conqueror. From this later term, Jina, the sect came to be known as Jainism. He travelled for the remainder of his life, i.e., for more than thirty years throughout East India, spreading this new faith, i.e., Jainism. At the age of 72, i.e., in 527 BC, he passed away, leaving behind 14,000 disciples. Jainism emphatically denies the belief in God. They reject the authority of vedas and Brahmins with scorn. The theory of karma and rebirth is recognized. Jain philosophy is full of subtle theories. Its main purpose is to free the soul from its fetters by means of three pillars, i.e., right faith, right knowledge and right action. In ethics or practical morality, the first place is given to ahimsa (non-violence) or not hurting any kind of life, however low it is on the evolutionary scale. According to Jainism, not only men and animals, but also plants and inanimate objects possess a degree of consciousness. Austerity and severe discipline of the body are essential for the attainment of the highest spiritual state. One of the important teachings of Jainism is adopting aparigirahi, i.e., non-accumulation of wealth by any means even by lawful earning. It was one step towards socialism. Santhara, i.e., voluntary suicide by slow process is highly approved by Jains. At certain age, especially when the body does not remain active, it is advised to take santhara. This has not been declared illegal by the courts in India.

41. Jainism never became a dominant sect in India, but so far it continues to be a powerful sect for over 2,500 years. Jains mostly belong to affluent class and have more than 94% literacy. After the death of Mahavira, Jainism was divided into digambara, i.e., those who are clothed by air and regard absolute nudity as an essential of saint-ship, and in shvetambara, the saints are dressed in white clothes. Digambaras are idol worshipers whereas in Shvetambaras, they are both i.e., idol worshipers and non-idol-worshipers. The digambaras are divided into a further four divisions and shvetambaras into eighty-four which are said to date from the tenth century A.D. Evidence from inscriptions and literature indicates that the early success of Jainism was more remarkable then those of Buddhism. It made headway in south India; before the end of the fourth century B.C. Jainism gradually made its way in all parts of India. Jains have not ousted themselves from Hinduism, and many priests in their temples are Brahmins. Marriage relations between Hindus and Jains take place. Jains are basically vegetarians.

D. Sikhism

42. Guru Nanak, the founder of the Sikh sect, was born in 1469. He belonged to the Kshatriya class. The caste system had become rigid and oppressive by the fifteenth century from cradle to grave one was compelled to live within one's caste. Guru Nanak was not alone in opposing the caste system, but he had a powerful enough personality to become a religious teacher. He taught in the local dialects of his people and accepted disciples irrespective of caste. He was born at Talwandi, a village 64 km south-west of Lahore, now in Pakistan. Throughout his life, he attempted to unite Hindus and Muslims, and all the religions then practicing in India. Guru Nanak travelled all over India and conveyed his message. He died in 1539. He practiced that there is one God, whatever the method of worship.

43. The Sikhs continued in the steps of their first Guru for centuries adding to the prayers and songs – hymns – until all those prayers and worshipers were gathered into one volume, and has now become the scripture for all Sikhs. It is called the Guru Granth Sahib.

44. The Sikhs have a reputation for being volatile, war-like and hot-tempered. Most of the Sikhs bear five essentials, viz., kesh (long uncut hair), the kangha (comb), the kirpan (sword), the kacha (short cotton trousers worn under long trousers) and kara (steel bracelet). Intermarriages between Sikhs and Hindus still take place. In spite of this and also the provisions of Article 25 of the Constitution of India, Sikhs claim to be a different religion from Hinduism.

E. Islam

45. The founder of the Islamic religion was the Prophet Mohammad who was born in Mecca, Saudi Arabia in AD 570. During that time, Arabs lived under miserable conditions. They were divided into a number of tribes that were always at war with each other. They worshiped many gods and goddesses. They were idol worshippers. Indo-Greek and Jewish cultures prevailed in Middle East countries during those days, this condition was not tolerated by Prophet Mohammad. He taught people of Saudi Arabia many wisdoms that are the principles of Islam. He said that there is one God and he is His messenger. He asked his followers to pray five times a day and to fast during Ramadan. He preached equality and universal brotherhood among his followers. He declared that pilgrimage to Mecca is an essential duty of every Muslim. All his teachings are contained in the holy Koran.

46. The Arabs, after embracing Islam, began to spread Islam all around. They entered India in AD 712 and conquered Sind, now in Pakistan, but they were held back by the strong and powerful rulers of Rajasthan. They however continued their political occupation of Sind. The Arabs did not come to India only to conquer, but to spread Islam and also trading. On the west coast of the country, they established their trading settlements. At that time, they lived in peace and even married Indian women. Islamic religion, in reality, however, came to India in AD 1000 and gained ground gradually, either by self-generating or by voluntary or compulsory conversion. From AD 1000 to 1026, Sultan Mahmood Gaznavi became the ruler of Gazni in Central Asia. He made seventeen plundering raids in India from the north-western side but did not settle in India. After his death, Muhammad Ghori turned his attention to India and conquered Punjab and Sind from 1175 to 1182. He established his kingdom in Delhi and left it in the hands of his trusted slave, Qutub-ud-din. From this period begins the Muslim rule in India. It continued till 1857, when the British declared India as part of the British Empire. In their treatment of the conquered Hindus, the Muslim rulers adopted by and large a policy of partial toleration. They Muslim rulers normally used to allow Hindus free exercise of their religion, provided they submitted to Muslim rule and agreed to pay Jajiya or poll tax. The Jajiya and land tax formed the principal sources of revenue. The collection of revenue and the details of administration were placed with the local Hindus. All local institutions of Hindus were maintained and merchants and artisans were exempted from molestation. In Islam, there are no priests, but each mosque has in charge of a Mullah, a fairly powerful figure in the community, as can be seen in Iran even at present. Muslims believe that each person is responsible for his own actions and will answer for them on the Day of Judgment. The whole life of a Muslim should be dedicated to God. The compulsory duties of a Muslim are to perform prayers five times a day, to give alms, to fast during the month of Ramadan and to make pilgrimage to Mecca at least once during his lifetime. He must worship according to the tenets of the holy Koran. Muslims believe that to worship God through idols or any form of representation of the human form is blasphemous. It is this belief more than any other that brought about the desecration of most of the Hindu architecture during Muslim rule in India.

F. The Parsis

47. The Parsi religion is one of the oldest religions of the world. Their believers are the followers of the Prophet Zorastra of the sixth century B.C. Their God is Mazda, i.e., the God of Light. They worship in Fire Temples where the flame is kept burning. It is considered as the symbol of God i.e., it is God that is worshipped, not the fire. It is said that sacred fire is brought from heaven by Zorastra himself. After the advent of Islam in the Middle East, Parsis were continually prosecuted by the Muslims. They had no other alternative but to leave for India along with sacred fire in AD 632. The Parsis landed on the coast of Gujarat in western India and settled amicably with the local population. As Parsis did not and do not convert Hindus, they did not come into religious conflict. They became businessmen in India and most of them do it from Mumbai where they developed commercial, cultural and charitable buildings. They, thus, to a great extent have influence in India.

48. Parsis, like Hindus, believe that their behaviour in this life directly affects their next life. They do not marry with the people of other communities. They marry within their own community. Their population is on the verge of decline because they only recognize a child of their religion, if he is born of two Parsi parents and not that of a mixed marriage. Parsis do not believe in conversion of other religions to their own religion. In spite of Parsis being peace-loving and small in number, they are powerful and influential. They take a very active part in the commercial activities of India. Large number of Parsis are holding big business houses in India. They own big businesses in the country. They do not normally participate in the political life of India.

G. Christians

49. Christians form a very small part of the population in India. They number about 30 million and consist of people from every denomination of Christianity. Christianity, by tradition, is said to have arrived in India with Saint Thomas, one of the apostles of Jesus Christ, during the first century AD. Saint Thomas is said to have spent some years in south India and possibly died there. It is also said that the first Church was established in the state of Kerala. There are people who believe that the first missionary activity started with Saint Francis Xavier in 1544. He was followed by Portuguese missionaries at first and eventually missionaries from other countries like Denmark, Holland, Germany and Great Britain. Throughout the eighteenth and nineteenth centuries, Catholic as well as Protestant missionaries preached Christian doctrines in India and also made important contributions to social improvements and education in India. Much of the modern influences in the Indian society can be attributed to the role of Christianity in India. Christian missionaries helped in setting up schools, colleges and hospitals all over India and also spread the message of faith and good will in the country. Christianity and its teachings influenced a number of intellectuals and thinkers in India. After the independence of India, these missionaries, in order to spread Christianity in India, converted people mostly from the downtrodden society and tribal areas of India. Because of rampant poverty in India, they have been successful in attracting, or even sometime forcefully converting, the people of lower social strata.

IX. The Population

50. The world's second-most-populous country, India, is the home of 16% of the world population. The country, however, accounts for only 2.42% of the total world area. According to 2011 census the total population of India is 1,210,854,977. Out of which 62,37,24,248 are males and 58,64,69,174 are females. The density of population is 382 per km square. The sex ratio is 943 females per 1,000 males and child sex ratio is 918 per 1,000 males.

51. India, with 2.4% of the world's surface area, accounts for 17.5% of its population. India is one of the few countries where males significantly outnumber females, and this imbalance has increased over time. There is rampant unemployment in the county. However the effective literacy rate increased to a total of 74.04% with 82.14% of the males and 65.46% of females being literate.

52. However, India was the first country to announce an official planning programme in 1952. Its population grew from 361 million in 1951 to 844 million in 1991 and over 1.21 billion in 2011 with sex ratio 940 females as against 1,000 males in 2011.

§2. Economic System

53. It is a well-known fact that India is a developing country and has a mixed economy. India is basically an agrarian economy. Its dependency on agriculture is substantial. More than 60% of the working population is engaged in agriculture. Compared to developed countries, this is very high. The structure of employment has not changed drastically during the last fifty years.

54. India's per capita income was Indian Rupees (INR) 255 in 1950–1951 only and has increased to about INR 40,141 in 2009–2010. India's per capita income was USD 1,497 in 2013, ranked at 120th out of 164 countries by the World Bank. The economic activities of the government are carried out through a planning process. India prepared plans for every five years and involved all public sector enterprises, and its administrative machinery to allocate all income and resources it possessed to different segments and sectors of the Indian economy. In 2011, the 15th Indian Census was conducted in two phases, house listing (involving the information about all building, etc.) and population enumeration.

55. The public sector is playing a dominant role in the Indian economy. After independence, i.e., 1947, the government of India adopted the concept of a mixed economy, with public and private sectors playing complementary roles and remaining active partners in the common task of development. At the time of independence, the private sector had neither the resources nor the will to undertake the task of industrial development on a massive scale. Since 1991, there has been a drastic change in the government policy. It has tilted towards privatization, liberalization and globalization. Even then, public sector enterprises play a crucial role not only in infrastructure facilities for the people, but also in industries in the private sector. However, at present, the emphasis on the public sector is less pronounced and the current thinking on planning the country, in general, is that it should increasingly be of an indicative nature.

56. Fifty years of economic planning in India has resulted in a remarkable improvement in social sectors such as education and health. Literacy is one of the important measures of social development. Statistics released by Union ministry of Health and family welfare show that life expectancy in India has gone up by five years, from 62.3 years for males and 63.9 years for females in 2001–2005 to 67.3 years and 69.6 years respectively in 2011–2015.

57. The income and wealth in India is not distributed equally among all the people. Wealth and other resources are concentrated in the hands of a few. Technological advancement is a prerequisite for the development of the economy. In India, technologies used in the production of goods and services are quite backward, particularly in agriculture. The majority of the farmers are still following outdated methods of production. In the case of manufacturing and service sectors, and despite using modern technology, the country is still far behind as compared to developed countries.

I. Financial Institutions

A. Banking

58. Banking is an institution that deals with money and credit. These days, banks perform a large variety of functions in the modern society. A bank is an institution that borrows and lends money. In modern times, bank performs numerous functions that throw light on the variety of the services it renders to the modern civilized society. These functions may be divided into three classes viz., (1) Primary Functions; (2) General Utility Functions; and (3) Agency functions.

1. Primary Functions

59. The primary and essential functions of a bank are two, viz., (a) the borrowing and lending of money business i.e., banks borrow money through receiving deposits. (b) The small deposits received by banks together constitute a huge amount. This is lent out by the banks to capable agriculturists, industrialists and businessmen, who utilize it in their venture of their own profit and to the economic advancement of the country. In India, the great service rendered by banks in converting huge idle resources into active capital by acting as a sort of standing brokers between the quiet saving money and the active employment such money into agriculture, industries and business. The banks utilize this money in the discounting of the bills of exchange and the granting of overdraft on current accounts.

2. General Utility Functions

60. Modern banks perform many miscellaneous functions, which are of great general utility. Some of them are as follows: (a) Issue of currency notes: The issue of currency notes in India is entrusted solely to the Reserve Bank of India, which is the central bank of the country. (b) Issue of Credit Instruments: Banks create credit instruments like bank drafts, cheques, letters of credit, etc. which economize the use of metallic currency, currency notes, make the transmission of money over long distances convenient and cheap, and remove the want of medium of exchange felt by modern communities currency alone being inadequate to meet the entire need. (c) Foreign Exchange Business: Bankers even today useful business of changing one kind of money into the other kinds. Different countries possess currencies and banks play important role of purchasing and selling foreign currencies, foreign bills of exchange and other instruments in exchange of the currency of the country in which they are situated. They facilitate foreign trade to an appreciable degree. (d) Safe custody of valuables: Banks undertake to keep in safe custody valuables and important documents in specially constructed strong rooms, which are sure safeguards against fire and theft.

3. Agency Functions

61. (a) Banks also render many 'agency business' in various capacities. They collect and pay cheques, realize dividends and interest and pay subscriptions and insurance premiums in the capacity of special agents to their customers. (b) These days Banks do the business of registrarship of the floating of companies. (c) They conduct stock and share transactions on behalf of their customers. They deal with selling and buying the business of shares of the companies. The banks these days also deal with the mutual fund schemes. Some of the Banks are dealing with the insurance business of the Insurance companies. (d) Further, they also act in various other agency capacities such as those of trustees, attorneys and executors.

Further details about banking *see* Part II, Chapter 2.

B. Insurance

62. One of the modern institutions of law fast developing in response to the increasing complexities and uncertainties of life is insurance. The hazards of trade and commerce and the increasing complexities of life in recent years have made a precise knowledge of laws of insurance, as codified in India, very important. Urge to provide protection against the loss of life and property prompted people/groups to make some sort of sacrifice willingly in order to achieve security through 'collective cooperation'.

63. The subject of insurance has been perceived differently by different persons. It does perform multiple functions all of which contribute in varying degrees to social and economic management today. Insurance offers security to individuals and transactions; it is a growing business to many others; and it is a legal device to distribute risks and make development possible to the society at large. Given the expansion to insurance into almost all aspects of life in recent times, one can expect the subject to assume great importance in the spheres of commerce, law, management and government. State control of insurance has been a subject of controversy in India after some times of the Independence of the country. However, provision of adequate security to life and property is a fundamental duty of civilized society. This has been well considered by the Indian government. Present day conditions have made it necessary for man to face many hazards and undertake risks in day-to-day life. Different types of private and public organizations including the governments themselves have undertaken, in different countries, the responsibility of providing many forms of cover to the individual from the possible results of accidents to his person involving even death and to his property.

64. In India, the majority of the population is far from affluent. Therefore, the benefits, which good insurance schemes can provide, are of vital importance to the Indian people. Insurance is a comprehensive work susceptible of varied meanings. It is a contract of indemnity for the benefit of the insured and those in privity with him. The word 'assurance', which formerly did duty for 'insurance' in its modern sense, particularly in English maritime law, has now fallen into desuetude. Insurance now covers multitude of risks and, therefore, there are many kinds of insurance. It is, however, mainly of four kinds: life, marine, fire and accident. The first Act in Indian dealing with insurance was the Indian Life Assurance Companies Act, 1912, which was based mainly on the English Assurance Companies Act, 1909. It was applicable only to the life insurance companies and left untouched companies doing the other kinds of insurance business. The need for a comprehensive Act relating to the business of insurance was answered by enacting the Insurance Act (IV of 1938). This Act of 1938 was subjected to several amendments from time to time, the most extensive of the, being the Insurance (Amendment) Act, 1950. Next came the Life Insurance Corporation Act, 1956, providing for the nationalization of life insurance business. This was later followed by the Marine Insurance Act, 1963, dealing with the marine business. Before 1956, the whole of the insurance sector was in the hands of private sector companies. A number of life insurance companies became bankrupt and could not meet out the public obligations. Moreover, there was the temptation for takeover of life insurance business of ghost companies. While public was saved from the burden of bubble companies, the people had to put up with loss of bonus and low dividend at the hands of the government insurer. On the formation of the Life Insurance Corporation, the provisions of the Insurance Act, 1938 applied to life insurance business only as modified by section 43 of the Life Insurance Corporation Act, 1956. These provisions apply to regulate the working of the Life Insurance Corporation, e.g., (A) Accounts and Return: All receipts in respect of life insurance business shall be carried out and form a separate fund called the 'life insurance fund' which shall not be applied directly or indirectly for any purpose other than those of the life insurance business.[7] The Life Insurance Corporation of India (LIC) shall prepare a balance sheet and profit and loss account every year in a prescribed manner.[8] Once at least in every three years, an investigation into financial condition of the business including the valuation of its liabilities by an actuary shall be made.[9] Once in every two years, the LIC shall submit the copies of statements, abstracts referred to in sections 11, 13 and 18 of the Insurance Act, 1938 and also a return of investments made out of the controlled fund under section 27A of the said Act to the Insurance Regulatory Authority.[10] Every such return furnished to the Authority is open to inspection by the public and one may obtain a copy thereof on payment of fee.[11]

---

7. Insurance Act, 1938, s. 10.
8. Insurance Act, 1938, s. 11.
9. Insurance Act, 1938, s. 13.
10. Insurance Act, 1938, s. 28A.
11. Insurance Act, 1938, s. 28.

65. Controller of Insurance and his powers: The central government constituted under section 3 of the Insurance Regulatory and Development Authority Act, 1999. It shall appoint a Controller under section 2B of the said Act. The IRDA administers the functions assigned to it under the Act. This Authority may require LIC to supply it with any information relating to the insurance business.[12] If any return furnished appears to the Authority to be inaccurate or defective, may decline to accept it unless it is rectified or any deficiency is made good, and for that purpose may call for and inspect any books of account or other document or examine any officer of the insurer on oath.[13] The Authority may also order an investigation and valuation to be made again at the expenses of the insurer, by an actuary appointed with its approval, if it finds that a faulty basis has been adopted in the valuation already made. The Authority or an officer authorized by it can grant licences for persons to act as insurance agents.

66. Powers of Authority: The Authority is empowered to order investigation of the affairs of an insurer by an investigating authority and to take suitable action.[14] The central government is required to publish every year a summary of the various returns furnished to the Controller during the previous year.[15]

C. *General Insurance*

67. In 1960, there were ninety-nine Indian and nearly the same number of non-Indian companies, which were, engaged in general insurance business. In 1957, the first Indian Reinsurance Corporation of India was established. It was formed with a view to stop the heavy drain on the India's foreign exchange resources, as all reinsurance was being effected with foreign concerns. In 1968, drastic amendment of the Insurance Act, 1938 provided for more effective supervision and control over insurers doing general business, requiring increased deposits from them, giving the Controller of Insurance more powers to inspect and issue directions to the insurers on all matters including the appointment and removal of their directors, constituting a Tariff Advisory Committee (TAC) to fix, control and regulate the premium rates and conditions of policies, etc. In spite of such control, there was persistent demand for the nationalization of general insurance business, so that there could be no concentration of wealth in the hands of a few insurers. In order to meet with the demands of the people, the General Insurance Business (Nationalization) Act, 1972 was passed. The Act was to provide for the acquisition and transfer of shares of Indian Insurance companies and undertakings of other existing insurers in order to serve better the needs of the community and to ensure that 'the operation of the economic system does not result in the concentration of wealth to the common welfare, for the regulation and control of business to the common detriment' as is required by Article 39(C) of the Indian Constitution. By sections 4 and 5 of the 1972 Act, all shares in the capital of every Indian insurance company free from all trusts, liabilities and encumbrances affecting them and the undertaking of every existing insurer which was not an Indian insurance company stood transferred to and vested in the central government from 1 January 1973. The

12. Insurance Act, 1938, s. 110C.
13. Insurance Act, 1938, s. 21.
14. Insurance Act, 1938, s. 33.
15. Insurance Act, 1938, s. 116-A.

central government under section 9 of the Act formed General Insurance Corporation (GIC) as a government company. There is a difference between LIC and the GIC the former is a statutory corporation whereas the GIC is a company registered under the Companies Act. By section 10 of the Act, on the formation of the Corporation, all shares that stood vested in the central government, excepting a few shares, vested in the GIC All the insurance companies were thereafter merged into four 'acquiring companies', viz., the New India Assurance Co. Ltd., United India Fire and General Insurance Co. Ltd., the Oriental Fire and General Insurance Co. Ltd. and the National Insurance Co. Ltd. from 1 January 1974.

D. Functions of GIC

68. The functions of the GIC according to section 18 of the Act includes to carrying on any part of the general insurance business if it thinks it is desirable to do so; aiding and advising the acquiring companies in the matter of setting up standards of conduct and sound practice in general insurance business and rendering efficient service to their policy-holders; advising them in the matter of controlling their expenses including payment of commission and other expenses; advising them in the matter of investment of their funds; and issuing directions to them in relation to the conduct of general insurance business. In all these functions, the corporation should keep in mind the desirability of encouraging competition among the acquiring companies as far as possible in order to render their services more efficient.

69. The amendment of 2002 has added a provision to section 18 of the Act, whereby the functions of the corporation shall be performed by the central government. At present, the corporation is undertaking reinsurance business in India and also underwriting general insurance business in civil aviation and crop insurance.

E. Functions of Acquiring Companies

70. Section 19 of the Act lays down the functions of the acquiring companies to be: (a) to carry on general insurance business and to develop it to the best advantage of the community, subject to the rules if any made in this behalf by the central government under section 39 of the Act and subject to its memorandum and articles of association; and (b) to act so far as may be on business principles and in conformity with any directions that may have been issued to it by the GIC Section 19(4) clarifies that the GIC and the acquiring companies may enter into reinsurance contracts or treaties for the protection of their interests, subject to rules if any made by the central government in this behalf.

F. Powers of Central Government over GIC

71. Section 23 of the Act lays down that the GIC and every acquiring company shall be guided in the discharge of its functions by such directions as the central government may give in regard to matters of policy involving public interest. Rule 6 of the General Insurance Business (Nationalization) Rules, 1972 in exercise of the powers conferred by section 39 of the Act requires the GIC to prepare and submit to the central government a report reviewing the working and administration of the Corporation during the year, as soon as may be after the end of each calendar year, and also append to the report similar report relating to each of its subsidiaries for the same year. The central government under section 35 of the Act is empowered to specify by notification the exceptions, restrictions and limitations, if any, subject to which the Insurance Act, 1938 shall apply to or in relation to the GIC and every acquiring company. Section 39 of the Act empowers the central government to make rules to carry out the provisions of the Act.

G. Status of LIC and GIC

72. LIC is a statutory corporation, whereas the GIC is a government company, which is registered under the Indian Companies Act. Rules and regulations framed by LIC have the force of law. Their employees, though have a statutory status and are entitled to a declaration of being in employment when their dismissal or removal is in contravention of statutory provisions, but will not be the servants of the Union of India or the state. The employees of GIC do not get the benefit of the protection available to the government servants.

H. Insurance Act, 1938 and GIC

73. The elimination of many private insurance companies caused the elimination of many provisions of the Insurance Act, 1938 redundant. Thus, under section 35 of the Act, the Government of India by notification on 29 December 1972, the four acquiring insurance companies on 1 January 1973, have been required (a) to keep separate accounts in respect each class of insurance business under section 10 of the Act; (b) to prepare, at the expiration of each calendar year, with reference to that year audited balance sheet, profit and loss account, revenue account, etc. in prescribed forms under sections 11 and 12; (c) to maintain register of policies and of claims and of insurance agents under sections 14 and 43; (d) to furnish to the Controller, printed copies of revenue accounts, etc. as returns and of every report made to the members or policy-holders as well as a report of all general meetings held under sections 15, 18 and 19; (e) not to pay by way of remuneration or reward for soliciting or procuring business to anyone other than an insurance agent under section 40; (f) not to make any investment other than in approved investments under section 27B and within thirty-one days of the beginning of a year make a return to the controller, of all investments and the changes made therein during the previous year.

74. The Controller of Insurance (now authority) under section 21 of the Act may have any return which appears to him to be incorrect or defective, duly corrected and supplemented and may inspect any books of the insurer or examine any officer in connection with the return or decline to accept any return for sufficient reasons. All returns submitted to the Controller are open to inspection by the public and they can obtain certified copies thereof on payment of prescribed fees. Under section 42 of the Act, the authority or any other officer authorized by him may grant and renew licences for persons to act as insurance agents. The central government may direct the authority or any other specified person to investigate the affairs of the insurer and make a report, and make suitable orders thereon. The manager and every officer of the insurer must provide all facilities for such investigation.

I. Tariff Advisory Committee (TAC)

75. The TAC was established by an amendment in 1968 to the Insurance Act, 1938 to control and regulate the rates, advantages, terms and conditions that may be offered by insurers in respect of general insurance business. The committee under section 64U is a body corporate having perpetual succession and a common seal and with power to hold and dispose of property and to contract and to sue and be sued. TAC consists of fifteen members nominated by GIC with prior approval of the central government. Under section 64UA, its chairman was to be the chairman of the Authority or a member of the TAC to be nominated by him and the secretary of the committee is an officer of the office of the authority nominated by the authority. The TAC is empowered to constitute regional committees and sub-committees and to make regulations for their working. Each regional committee shall consist of not more than seven persons nominated by the TAC under section 64UJ on questions connected with the fixation of rates, advantages, etc. for risk in its region and perform such other functions as may be assigned to it. The TAC under section 64UE may require the insurer to furnish such information or statements periodically or ad hoc as may be necessary to discharge its functions and the insurers are bound to comply with such requirements. The TAC may from time to time and to the extent it deems expedient control or regulate the rates, advantages, etc. in respect of risks or classes of risks which in its opinion is proper to control and regulate. Any such rates, etc. regulated by the TAC are binding on the insurers and its contravention is punishable under section 64UC. In fixing or modifying the rates, etc. the TAC should regard and make suitable allowances for past loss, expenses and for future fluctuations and unforeseen future contingencies including hazards or catastrophes.

76. The TAC constituted under section 64U of the Insurance Act, 1938 is a statutory body empowered to fix rates, etc. from time to time. Its instructions have the force of law and binding on all the insurers and their contravention is punishable.[16]

16. *K.M.D Association v. Union of India*, AIR 1992 SC 1616.

Part I. Commercial Law

Chapter 1. Concepts and Sources of Commercial Law

§1. Meaning of Mercantile Law

77. Mercantile law is a body of rules, which regulate and control the commercial transactions in the society. These are the rules, which ascertain uniformity in the procedure and principles in the mercantile transactions. They determine the standards, observations of which are essential in the trade and business. Besides this, the governmental policy is also being enforced by these laws.

78. Business or mercantile law bring certainty in the commercial behaviour and they determine the validity of contracts an also the mode of their execution and thus, this branch of law creates a mechanism of dispute settlement among the business community. This Branch of law, thus, relates to the contracts regarding partnership, sale of goods, agency, bailment, indemnity and guarantee, insurance, negotiable instruments. Mercantile law also relates to the joint stock companies, carriage of goods, insolvency and arbitration and so on. In the Indian legal system, there is no separate system of mercantile law as it exists in France, Germany, etc. but it is a part of the civil law. In India, thus, the mercantile law is a branch of civil law.

§2. Law Anterior to the Contract Act, 1872

79. The Charters[17] of the eighteenth century, which established courts of justice,[18] viz., Supreme Courts for the Presidencies of Calcutta, Bombay and Madras. These Supreme Courts introduced into their jurisdiction the English common and statute

17. The Charters, for example, are as follows: the Charter of 1661, Charter of 1726, Charter of 1753, Charter of 1774 etc.
18. The Charter of 1661 constituted court consisting of the Governor and Council of each factor. The Charter of 1726 constituted Mayor's Courts in all the three Presidencies of Calcutta (now Kolkata), Bombay (now Mumbai) and Madras (now Chennai). The Charters of 1774 and the Indian High Courts Act, 1861 established Supreme Court and High court at Calcutta respectively. Recorders' Courts at Madras and Bombay were established in 1797. In place of Recorders' Courts, Supreme Courts were established in 1799 and 1823 in Madras and Bombay respectively. They were replaced by the High Courts in 1862.

laws in force there at that time so far as it was applicable to the Indian circumstances and conditions and so far as they regulated private rights among parties.

80. The Charter of 1781 was issued to do away the ill effects of above Charters and particularly to 'maintain and protect the inhabitants in the enjoyment of all their ancient laws, usages, rights and privileges'. By the Charter of 1781, the courts in Calcutta and Bombay were empowered to apply Hindu law and customs in cases of Hindus and Muslim law and usages in cases of Muslims and where parties to the suit belong to different religions, the law and usages of the defendant was to be applied.

81. The High Courts, before the passage of Indian Contract Act, 1872 used to apply the law and usages of Hindu in cases the parties were Hindu and Muslim law and usages of Muslims where the parties were Muslims.

82. In the courts beyond Presidency Towns, known as mufassil courts, the section 21 of the old Bengal Regulation III of 1793 directed the judges where no specific rule or law existed, they could impart justice in accordance with the principles of 'equity, justice and good conscience'. Similar provisions were provided in section 17 of the Madras Regulation II of 1802. These Regulations have long been repealed but the direction to act in the absence any specific law or rule, custom, etc. to act in absence of any specific rule according to justice, equity and goods conscience is still retained in section 37 of the Bengal Civil Courts Act, 1873 and section 16 of the Madras Civil Court. Similarly, in the mufassil courts of Bombay, section 26 of the Bombay Regulation Act of 1827, that is still in force, provides the law to be observed in the trial of suits shall be Acts of Parliament, Regulations of the government and in the absence of such Acts and Regulations, the usages of the country wherein the suit arose, and in the absence of these above any specific law and usages, principles of 'equity, justice and good conscience'.

83. In the Supreme Courts in the Presidency Towns and the diwani adalats (civil courts), most of the judges used to be lawyers from England. They were well trained in English law. They, therefore, interpreted the concept of 'justice, equity and good conscience' in the light of English law when applying it in India.[19]

§3. Sources of Indian Mercantile Law

84. Indian mercantile law is mostly based on English law and its principles. Certain changes, however, have been made in accordance with the local usages, business customs in the Indian mercantile law.

85. Disputes relating to the business transactions, as already stated, before the enactment of the Indian Contract Act, 1872, were resolved in accordance with the personal law of the parties, i.e., in the case of disputes between Hindus, Hindu law and its customs and usages ere applied; similarly in cases of disputes between Muslims, Muslim Law customs and usages were applied. In cases, however, where the parties belonged to different religions, personal law of the defendant was applied. In cases, where no law or usage was available, the judges used to decide the cases accordingly

19. *See Waghela Rajsonji v. Shekh Masludin* (1887) 14 I.A 89; *Dada v. Babaji* (1885) 2 BHC 36; *Naresh Chandra v. Ram Chandra* (1852) Cal 93 etc.

with the concept of justice, equity and good conscience, which in effect meant application of English law.

86. Mercantile law before codification was in a chaotic condition. The courts found many times difficulty in applying the law to the parties in disputes. There were number of problems faced by the judges in the courts. The practice of the then Supreme Court in the Presidency of Calcutta was very peculiar. In one case[20] the Supreme Court of Calcutta said that although the clause in the Charter directed that matter of contract between Hindus be decided by the law, customs and usages of Hindus, the fact is that in every question that arose, it was the English law of contract alone was referred to. The reason was that both laws were founded upon the same broad principles of good faith and that very little difference existed between them.

87. In the Presidency Towns of Bombay and Calcutta, the Hindu law of damdupat was applied to the Hindus under which a Hindu could not claim an interest more than the amount of the principal lent. These courts felt bound to apply this rule amongst the Hindus in accordance with section 17 of the Settlement Act of 1981[21] In Madras, however, the rule was not applied.[22]

88. The first time attempt was made for codification of commercial law in order to resolve many difficulties, controversies, uncertainties, etc. some of them have been described above, in the existing commercial laws. Codification was considered as the only solution for the above difficulties, uncertainties, etc. Indian Contract Act, 1972 was enacted. After the enactment of this Act, many other Acts relating to commercial laws were enacted, viz., the Negotiable Instruments Act, 1881, the Transfer of Property Act, 1882, the Indian Railways Act, 1890, the Sale of Goods Act, 1930, the Partnership Act, 1932, the Companies Act, 1956, Companies Act, 2013, the Specific Relief Act, 1964, Banking Regulation Act, 1965, the Arbitration and Conciliation Act, 1996, the Competition Act, 2002, Unlimited Liability Act, 2009, etc.

89. Even before the enactment of Contract Act, 1872, there were many enactments already in force in this area. These enactments have neither been expressly repealed nor declared unenforceable by any competent courts. These enactments are, e.g., the Conveyance of Land Act, 1854, Usury Law Repeal Act, 1855, Bills of Lading Act, 1856, Merchant and Shipping Act, 1859, Common Carriers Act, 1865, etc. these various Acts are still in force.

§4. The Main Sources of Commercial Law in India

I. English Mercantile Law

90. The English mercantile law, though a considerable body of Indian laws in this field have been codified, still remains an important source of law because basically the Indian law is based on English law and principles. The common law of England,

20. *The Opium Case*, 4 Ind Dec (O.S), 205.
21. *Nobin Chunder Banerjee v. Rameshchunder Ghose*, ILR 14 Cal 781; also *Shah Mukhum v. Baboo Sri Kishen*, 12 MIA 157.
22. *Annaji v. Ragubai*, 6 MHCR 400(1871).

the law merchant, principles of equity and statutory law are the main sources of English law.

II. Statutes of Indian Legislatures

91. The larger part of the corpus juris of India in the area of commercial law is in the form of legislative enactments. Parliament of India is the central legislative body and the states have also been empowered to enact laws in their jurisdiction.

III. Judicial Decisions

92. Judicial decisions have played an important role in the development and source of commercial law in India. Law laid down by the superior courts, by virtue of theory of precedent, is binding and is to be followed by the inferior or subordinate courts. The law laid down by the High Court of a state is binding on all the subordinate courts situated in that state. Similarly, decisions of the Supreme Court are binding on all the High Courts and subordinate courts throughout the territory of India. In fact, law laid down by the Supreme Court is the law of the land according to Article 141 of the Constitution of India. Prior to Independence of India, Privy Council in England was the highest Court and as such its decisions were binding on all the courts in India. After the establishment of the Supreme Court, appeals to Privy Council were stopped. Besides Privy Council, question arose about the applicability of the decisions of the House of Lords in England.

IV. Customs and Usages of Commercial Transactions

93. Customs and usages have always played a very important role in the commercial transactions in India. In India today majority of commercial law is based on statutory provisions and enacted laws, but there is recognition of customs and usage by the courts in India. But such customs and usages should not be inconsistent with the enacted law. Section 1 of the Indian Contract Act, 1872, declares, 'Nothing herein contained shall effect … any usage or custom of trade … not inconsistent with the provisions of this Act.' Similarly, section 1 of the Negotiable Instruments Act, 1881, provides that 'Nothing herein contained … effects any local usage relating to an instrument in an oriental language.' The provisions of section 1 of the Indian Contract Act, thus, implies that where parties have based their contract on the local usages, then such contract shall be beyond the scope of the Act, provided such usages are not contrary to the statutory provisions. For example, in the states of West Bengal and Maharashtra customary rule of 'damdupat' in Hindu law is recognized. It was recognized by the Calcutta High Court,[23] because this custom was not inconsistent with any enacted law. The custom of 'damdupat' means that such interest money which is more than

23. *Nobin Chunder Banerjee v. Rameshchunder Ghose*, ILR 14 Cal 781; also *Shah Mukhum v. Baboo Sri Kishen*, 12 MIA 157.

the principal amount, cannot be recovered. The customs were recognized by the Statutes of 1781 and 1797. 'Custom of trade' means such specific customs, which can be proved by evidence, and they are different from such general customs of trade, which have already become part of the law. Section 190 of the Indian Contract Act, 1872 provides that an agent cannot lawfully employ another to perform act, which he has expressly or impliedly undertaken to perform personally, unless by the 'ordinary custom of trade' a subagent may, or from the nature of the agency, a subagent must be employed. Similarly, under section 211 of the Indian Contract Act, 1872, it has been provided that in the absence of express direction from his principal the agent shall be entitled to act in accordance with the 'custom', which prevails in doing business of the same, kind at the place where the agent conducts such business. Section 1 of the Negotiable Instrument Act, 1881, similarly, expressly saves from its operation local usages in respect of all instruments in an oriental language unless an intention is expressed in any such instrument that it would be governed by the Act.[24] It must, however, be noted that what is excluded from the operation of the Act is the local usages relating to the instruments themselves.[25] Thus, the various usages and customs of trade in force in India in commercial community have been recognized in the statutory provisions of different Acts and therefore, have been accepted as source of commercial law.

A. *Share Capital*

94. Share capital as has been previously state, may be divided into preference shares, and ordinary shares, and from this it is obvious, rights attached to one class of shares may be different from those attached to the other class.

B. *Alteration of Capital of Capital*

95. A limited company with share capital can alter the structure of its share capital by issuing new shares; or by consolidating the whole or any part of share capital into shares of larger amount; or by converting shares into stock or vice versa; or by sub-dividing the whole or any part of its share capital in smaller amount; or by cancelling unallotted shares and reducing accordingly.[26] For this the company will pass a resolution in the general meeting, but do not require to be confirmed by National Company Law Tribunal.[27] Within thirty days the notice must be given to the Registrar who will record the same and make the necessary alteration in the company's memorandum and articles.[28]

96. Subject to confirmation by the Tribunal on an application by the company, a company limited by shares or limited by guarantee and having a share capital may, by a special resolution, reduce the share capital in the following ways: (i) by extinguishing or reducing the liability on any of its shares in respect of the share capital not paid-up;

24. *Kamal Singh v. Rambaroza*, AIR 1943 Nag. 99(F.B.). Section 80 of the Negotiable Instruments Act, 1881 was not applied to *hundis* (a kind of demand draft).
25. *Chandulal v. Ram Chnadar*, ILR 1955 Hyd 20.
26. Companies Act, 2013, s. 61.
27. Companies Act, 2013, s. 60(2).
28. Companies Act, s. 64.

or (ii) either with or without extinguishing or reducing liability on any of its shares, (a) cancel any paid-up share capital which is lost or is unrepresented by available assets; or (b) pay off any paid-up share capital which is in excess of the wants of the company, alter its memorandum by reducing the amount of its share capital and of its shares accordingly.[29]

C. Loan Capital

97. Every trading company has implied power to borrow from others. It should, however, make use of the power in the manner mentioned in the memorandum of association. It can arrange loan capital in various ways, e.g., by issuing debentures, by mortgage and pledge, and by inter-corporate loans and investments, etc. A debenture is a certificate of loan issued by a company. A company may issue debentures convertible in shares either fully or partly. Debentures are secured by the assets of the company. It is, therefore, usual for debentures to create on its assets. A company issuing debentures is required to maintain a register of debenture holders. Any charge or mortgage created on certain assets of the company must be registered with the registrar of companies under the Act.

98. Parties may agree to share profits and losses in any proportion. A partner may join the partnership only for earning profit.[30] He may not to participate in losses.[31] However, such arrangement does not absolve a partner from the liability against the third parties or outsiders,[32] because all partners are liable for the acts of the firm individually and collectively. If there is no provision in the partnership agreement relating to sharing of profits and losses, all partners shall share profits and losses equally.[33] Profit in the business basis and commission are not profit.[34]

V. Mutual Agency

99. The partnership business is to be carried on for sharing profits 'by all or any of them acting for all'.[35] This implies that partnership is the extension of law of agency. According to the Act, a partner is the agent of the firm for the purpose of business of the firm.[36] Thus, for determining the existence of partnership among persons, sharing of profit is not true test but mutual agency is real test of partnership.[37]

29. Companies Act, 2013, s. 66(1).
30. *Raghunandan v. Harmansji*, AIR 1927 Bom 187.
31. *Ibid.*
32. *Ibid.*
33. Indian Partnership Act, 1932, s. 13(b).
34. *Raghumal v. Official Assignee, Calcutta*, AIR 1924 Ca. 424.
35. Indian Partnership Act, 1932, s. 4.
36. Indian Partnership Act, 1932, s. 18.
37. *Cox v. Hickman*, 8 HLC 268.

A. Registration of Partnership Firms

100. There was no provision for the registration of partnership prior to passing of the Partnership Act, 1932. However, in 1932, Chapter VII containing provisions relating to registration was included for the first time.[38] Each state, however, in India is empowered to direct by notification in the official gazette that provisions of that chapter shall not apply to that state or any part thereof.[39] Each state, therefore, is empowered to appoint a Registrar of Firms and to define his jurisdiction. Registrar of firms shall maintain a 'Register of Firms'.[40] Procedure for registration is simple when application form containing required information and signed and verified by each partner or his agent is submitted to the Registrar of Firms and when he is satisfied that the provisions of the Act are duly complied with, he shall make an entry of the application in the Register of Firms and shall file the same.[41] Registration is completed when the Registrar files the application.[42] Registration of partnership firm is not compulsory. The Act, however, denies certain rights to the firm and partners of an unregistered firm, e.g., a partner of unregistered firm cannot file a suit against the firms or past and present fellow partners for enforcing contractual or statutory rights, similarly an unregistered firm cannot file suit to enforce contractual rights against third parties.[43] Non-registration of a firm does not, however, affect the right of a partner to sue for dissolution of the firm or for accounts, and right to realize the property of his share of the dissolved form. The right of official assignee to realize property, or an insolvent, or right to sue for set-off in which claim does not exceed one INR 100, or the right of a third party to proceed against the unregistered firm or its partners shall not be affected.[44]

B. Time of Registration

101. Partnership firm may be registered at any time before dissolution. But it must stand registered on the date of the institution of the suit, otherwise the suit shall be dismissed. Registration of the firm after institution of the suit will be of no avail[45] Relations of partners to one another is a contract of utmost good faith and the partners stand in a fiduciary relationship with each other. In the absence of any express contract between them, the Partnership Act lays rules, which govern their relations.[46] These rules have been summed up in the following paragraph dealing with the rights and duties of the partners.

38. Provisions for registration are from ss 56 to 71 of the Indian Partnership Act.
39. Indian Partnership Act, 1932, s. 56.
40. Indian Partnership Act, 1932, s. 57.
41. Indian Partnership Act, 1932, s. 59.
42. *Jayalakshi Rice and Mills v. I.T. Commissioner*, AIR 1967 AP 99.
43. Indian Partnership Act, 1932, s. 69(1) and 69(2).
44. Indian Partnership Act, 1932, s. 69(3)(a), 69(3)(b), 69(4)(a) and 69(4)(b).
45. *Prithvi Singh v. Haji Hassan Ali*, AIR 1951 Bom 6.
46. Indian Partnership Act, 1932, ss 17 and 25 dealing with mutual rights and liabilities of partners.

C. Rights of the Partners

102. Rights of the partners includes the right to take part in management, right to consult all matters affecting the business of partnership, right to have access to books of accounts and other record, right to share profits of business, right to receive interest on capital, right to receive interest on loans given to the firm; right to be indemnified in respect of payment made and liabilities incurred by him in ordinary and proper conduct business of the firm and acts done in emergency to protect the interest of the firm; right to use property of partnership for partnership business; right to do all acts in emergency to protect the interest of the firm; right to disallow new partner to be included in the firm; right to retire according to the Act, right to carry on competiting business; right to share subsequent profits after retirement.[47]

D. Duties of Partners

103. Sections 9 and 10 of the Act lay down absolute duties of the partners, all other provisions, all other provisions relating to duties may be changed by agreement between the parties. Duties of the parties may be summed up as follows:

> Partners are bound (a) to carry on the business of the firm to the greatest common advantage; (b) to be just and faithful to each other; and (c) to render true accounts and full information of all things affecting the firm to any partner or his legal representative[48] Every partner shall indemnify the firm for any loss caused to it by this fraud in the conduct of the business of the firm[49] Every partner is bound to attend diligently to his duties in conducting the business of the firm.[50] Every partner is liable to the firm for any loss caused to it by his wilful neglect.[51] In the absence of contract to the contrary partner is bound to share losses. Partner should hold and use firm's property only for the firm's business. Partners shall be liable to account for and pay to the firm any private profit desired from the transactions of the firm. Partner is liable to account for the profits of the competing business. Partners are bound to act within the scope of his actual or apparent authority. A partner cannot assign his rights or interests in a partnership firm. A partner, similarly, cannot assign his rights or interests in a partnership firm to an outsider, so as to make the outsider a partner in the firm's business. The Act also declares that every partner is liable jointly and severally for all the acts of the firm done while he is a partner.[52]

47. Indian Partnership Act, 1932, ss. 12(a), 12(c), 12(d), 13, 13(a), 13(e), 14, 15, 21 and 31(1), 31(2), 32(2), 33(1), 36 and 37.
48. Indian Partnership Act, 1932, s. 9.
49. Indian Partnership Act, 1932, s. 10.
50. Indian Partnership Act, 1932, ss 12(a) and 13(A).
51. Indian Partnership Act, 1932, s. 13(f).
52. Indian Partnership Act, 1932, ss 13(b), 16(a), 29 and 25.

E. Relations of Partners to Third Parties

104. Partnership Act provides that a partner is the agent of the firm.[53] Each partner, thus, is a principal for the self and an agent for his co-partners. Each partner is an agent of other partners in matters connected with the partnership so far as outsiders are concerned, and therefore, his acts will bind the firm irrespective of any other private arrangement between them. The authority of the partner to bind the firm by his acts done in the usual course of the business carried only by the firm is called the implied authority of a partner.[54] In the absence of any usage or custom of trade to the contrary, the implied authority of a partner does not empower him, submit a dispute relating to the business of the firm to arbitration, to open a bank account of the firm in his own name, to compromise any claim of the firm, to withdraw any suit filed by the firm, to admit ant liability in a suit or proceedings against the firm, to acquire, transfer any immovable property belonging to firm, and to enter into partnership on behalf of the firm.[55]

105. Implied Authority and Third Party: Partners are individually and jointly liable to the third parties for all of their acts, which come within their implied authority. Such acts are termed as 'acts of the firm'. Section 2(a) of the Act defines an 'act of the firm' as an 'act or omission by all the partners or by any partner or agent of the firm, which gives rice to a right enforceable by or against the firm'. The liability of partners to third parties for such acts may be summed up as follows: (a) The firm can be held liable for all wrongful acts, torts committed by a partner that has caused loss or injury to third party.[56] (b) The firm shall be liable to make good for the losses where a partner receives money or property from third party and misapplies it.[57] (c) Any information obtained by a partner in the course of partnership business shall be taken to be obtained by all partners except in the case of fraud played by a third party in collusion with that partner.[58] (d) An admission or representation made by a partner concerning the affairs of the firm is valid evidence against the firm if made in the usual course of the business of the firm.[59]

F. Dissolution of the Partnership Firm

106. Indian Partnership law makes difference between dissolution of partnership and dissolution of the firm. Any change in the relationship. In all these cases, where a partnership is reconstituted, there is a dissolution of partnership. For example, if a new partner is admitted or existing partner dies or adjudged as insolvent or expelled, there is dissolution of partnership. The dissolution of partnership between all the partners if a firm is called the dissolution of the firm.[60] In that case, the business of the

53. Indian Partnership Act, 1932, s. 18.
54. Indian Partnership Act, 1932, s. 19.
55. Indian Partnership Act, 1932, s. 19(2).
56. Indian Partnership Act, 1932, s. 26.
57. Indian Partnership Act, 1932, s. 27.
58. Indian Partnership Act, 1932, s. 24.
59. Indian Partnership Act, 1932, s. 23.
60. Indian Partnership Act, 1932, s. 39.

firm is closed down and the affairs are wound up. The assets are realized and liabilities are paid off. The dissolution of a partnership may or may not result in the dissolution of a firm but a dissolution of a firm will necessarily result in the dissolution of the partnership. In India, partnership may be dissolved without the intervention of the court:

(a) *Dissolution without the intervention of the court*: A partnership firm may be dissolved without intervention of the court in any of the following ways:

(1) *Dissolution by agreement*: A firm may be dissolved by the mutual consent or in accordance with the contract between the parties. Consent must be of all the partners.[61]
(2) *Compulsory dissolution*: Partnership firm will have to be dissolved compulsorily: (a) by the adjudication of all the partners or all the partners, but one as insolvent; or (b) by the business of the firm becoming unlawful due to happening of any such event. Where the firm carried on more than one separate businesses, the illegality of one or more shall not of itself cause the dissolution of the firm.[62]
(3) *Dissolution on the happening of certain contingencies*: In the absence of any contract to the contrary a firm will be dissolved on the happening of the following contingencies: (a) on the expiry of the fixed period for which the firm was constituted; (b) on the completion of the adventure or undertaking for carrying out of which the firm was constituted; (c) on the death of a partner; (d) on the adjudication of a partner as insolvent.[63]
(4) Even in those cases where the partnership was constituted for a fixed term or for carrying out a particular adventure, death or insolvency would have the effect of dissolving the firm, unless it can be shown the existence of the fixed term or adventure coupled with particular circumstances of the case amounted to a contract to the contrary.[64]
(5) *Dissolution by Notice:* Where a partnership is at will the firm may be dissolved by any partner giving notice in writing to all partners.[65] Notice must be unconditional, unambiguous and certain. The firm will be taken to be dissolved from the date as specified in the notice, if no date is mentioned from the date of the communication of the notice to the last of the partners.[66]

(b) Dissolution of the Firm by the Court: On a suit of a partner, the court may order for the dissolution of the firm on any of the grounds provided in the Act.[67] These grounds are:

61. Indian Partnership Act, 1932, s. 40.
62. Indian Partnership Act,. 1932, s. 41.
63. Indian Partnership Act, 1952, s. 47.
64. *Abdul Azeez v. M.K.P. Kadar Mohideen*, AIR 1963 Mad 428.
65. Indian Partnership Act, 1932, s. 43.
66. *Banarsidas v. Kansi Ram*, AIR 1963 SC 1165.
67. Indian Partnership Act, 1932, s. 44.

(1) *Insanity:* On a suit filed by the next friend of the partner of unsound mind, court may order for dissolution of the firm. Lunacy need not be permanent.[68]
(2) *Permanent Incapacity:* Permanent incapacity in performing duties as a partner is a ground for dissolution of a firm.[69]
(3) *Misconduct:* misconduct of the partner should have prejudicially affect the carrying on of the firm's business[70]
(4) *Breach of Agreement*: Wilfully, persistently breach of partnership agreement, particularly provisions relating to accounts of the firm, management of the firm gives a right to the other partner of the firm.[71]
(5) *Transfer of Interest:* When a partner, other than the partner suing, has transferred the whole of his interest in the firm to a third party.[72]
(6) *Loss of business:* When the *business* of the firm cannot be carried on except at a loss, court may order for dissolution.[73]
(7) *Just and Equitable:* When the court considers any other ground to be just and equitable for the *dissolution of the firm*, e.g., deadlock in the management or disappearance of the substratum of the business, etc. the court may order for the dissolution of the firm.[74]

107. As a result of dissolution of partnership, partners shall have equitable lien on the property of the firm, right to return of premium, right to restrain use of firm's name or property of the firm.[75] After dissolution, partners shall be liable for the acts of the firm till they give a public notice of the dissolution.[76]

68. Indian Partnership Act, 1932, s. 44(a).
69. Indian Partnership Act, 1932, s. 44(b).
70. Indian Partnership Act, 1932, s. 44(c).
71. Indian Partnership Act, 1932, s. 44(c).
72. *Ram Singh v. Ram Chand* ILR (1923) 5 Lah 23.
73. Indian Partnership Act, 1932, s. 44(e).
74. Indian Partnership Act, 1932, s. 44(f).
75. Indian Partnership Act, 1932, ss 46, 51, 52 and 53.
76. Indian Partnership Act, 1932, ss 48–55.

Chapter 2. The Economic Operators

§1. Personal Status of Merchants (Capacity to Contract)

I. General

108. In India, the provisions of the Indian Contract Act, 1872, provide the legal framework for formulation of business and commercial transaction. Section 10 of the Contract Act, 1872, requires that the parties to the contract must be competent to contract. Section 11 of the said Act states that every person is competent to contract who is of the age of majority according to the law to which he is subject, and who is of sound mind and is not disqualified from contracting by any law to which he is subject. Thus, there are classes of persons who have been declared as incompetent to enter into a contract, viz., (1) minors; (2) persons of unsound mind; (3) persons disqualified by law by any law to which they are subject.[77]

109. Every person domiciled in India shall be deemed to have attained the age of majority when he shall have completed the age of 18 years and not before, or 21 years in the case of a person who is under the guardianship of a person appointed by the court according to the Indian Majority Act, 1875.[78] Such person is entitled to contract in Indian laws.

A. Void Agreements

110. According to section 11 of the Contract Act, 1872 a contract with the minor is void. The Judicial Committee of the Privy Council in *Mohori Bibi v. Dharmodas Gosh*,[79] held that section 11 makes it essential that all contracting parties should be competent to contract and as a minor is incompetent to make a contract, it is absolutely void ab initio. In the case that a minor, through misrepresentation induces another into a contract, thereafter, the minor is not stopped from using the defence of being a minor. Thus, the rule of estoppel is not enforceable against a minor as there can be no estoppel against a statute.[80] A contract cannot be specifically enforced by or against a minor, as the minor's agreement is void. But in the case that a competent guardian along with minor contracts with another party for the benefit of the minor, such contracts can be specifically enforced by or against the minor.[81] If a minor, by misrepresenting his age, obtains property or goods in a contract and it can be traced to him, the minor can be

77. *Ashok Kumar J. Pandya v. Suyog Coop Housing society Ltd.*, AIR 2003 Guj 118 (NOC): 2002 AIHC 3401, a housing society agreed to sell land before it became a legal person by registration. The contract was not enforceable.
78. Indian Majority Act, 1875, s. 3.
79. (1930) 30 IA.114.
80. *Jagarnath Singh v. Lalta Prasad*, (1908) 31 All 21.
81. *Manik Chand v. Ram Chandra*, AIR 1981 SC 591.

compelled to restore it. If, however, the minor has converted the goods into money or has obtained money under a contract of loan, the money will not be restored as restitution of money will amount to enforce a void agreement.[82] However, under section 33 of the Specific Relief Act, 1963, a minor may be required to restore such benefits received under a contract, when a void or voidable contract is cancelled at his instance.

111. If a person on attaining majority ratifies an agreement made by him during his minority, such an agreement will still be void because an agreement made by him during his minority is void ab initio and as such, it cannot be made valid by subsequent ratification.[83] A minor cannot become a member of a company as he is not competent to enter into a contract.[84] In the case that a minor inherits certain shares, the name of his lawful guardian shall be entered into a register of members of the company.

B. Valid Contracts

112. Two kinds of transactions with the minor are valid, viz., (1) contracts for the supply of necessities, which include goods as well as services; and (2) contracts for loans taken for purchasing articles for necessities. Section 68 of the Indian Contract Act, 1872 provides for the liability for necessities supplied to persons incompetent to contract. The term 'necessities' is not defined in the Act. However, an illustrative statement of the meaning of the term is to be found in *Chappel v. Cooper*[85] wherein it says, 'things necessary are those without which an individual cannot live reasonably'. Things that are 'necessities' include food, entertainment, lodging and the like, again as the proper cultivation of the mind is a necessity similar to the support of the body, therefore, instruction in art or trade, or intellectual, moral or religious education may be 'necessities' also. What is necessary is a relative term to be determined according to the facts and circumstances of the particular minor. Example where funds are supplied to the minor for the marriage of a minor female in the family. The lender can get his loan reimbursed from the property of the minor.[86] The debt incurred for performing the funeral obsequies of the father of a minor is necessary.[87] Where a minor is involved in a litigation threatening his property[88] or liberty, expenses reasonably incurred for his defence are necessary.[89] A minor will not be personally liable for necessities, only his property is liable.[90] However, to render the property of the minor liable for necessities, two conditions must be satisfied, viz., (1) the contract must be for goods necessary for his support in life; and (2) he must not already have a sufficient supply of those necessities.[91]

82. *Gokeda Latcharao v. Viswariadhan Bhimayya*, AIR 1956 AP 182.
83. *Suraj Narain v. Sukhu Ahir*, ILR (1928) 51 All 164.
84. *Palaniappa v. Pasupati Bank*, (1942) 1 MLJ 425.
85. (1844) 13 LJ (Ex) 286.
86. *Tikkilal v. Komal Chand*, AIR 1940 Nag 327.
87. *Bechu Singh v. Baldeo Prasad*, AIR 1933 Oudh 132.
88. *Kedar Nath v. Ajudhia Prasad* (1883) Punj. Reco 165 at p. 522, money advanced to save a minors' estate from execution sale was held to be necessary.
89. *Shyama Charan Mal v. Chaudhary Deby Singh*, ILR (1884) 21 Cal. 872.
90. Indian Contract Act, 1872, s. 68.
91. *Nash v. Inman* (1908) 2 KB 1, 12.

113. Section 68 of the Contract Act, 1872, under which transactions relating to the supply of the necessities to the minor or any other person incapable of entering into contract, or any one whom he is legally bound to support is supplied by another person suited to his conditions in life, the person who was furnished such supplies is entitled to be reimbursed from the property of such incapable person. Such a person besides minor may be a lunatic or his wife and children. These transactions relating to the necessities of the minor or any other such person are not a contract in a strict sense. There is no recognized category of voidable contract in India where contracts are made with the minor or such persons. However, certain beneficiary contracts in which a minor is only a promisee or he has already given consideration, are enforceable by the minor only and not the other party. Such contracts can be reasonably considered voidable contracts at the option of the minor.

C. Voidable Contract

114. Agreements, which are re-enforceable by law at the option of one or more of the parties thereto, is a voidable contract.[92] Voidable contracts are, thus, valid and enforceable by the minor unless he repudiates them within reasonable time. The other party is bound by the contract, if the minor wishes to continue with it.

115. Other matters in relation – partnership arises from contract and since a minor is incompetent to contract, a contract of partnership cannot be entered into with a minor.[93] Section 30 of the Indian Partnership Act, 1932, however, provides that a minor may be admitted to the benefits of an existing partnership firm. His liability is limited to the extent of his interest in the partnership. He has no right to take part in the management of the firm. He cannot inspect such documents, which are available to the partners only. At any time within six months of his attaining majority or of his obtaining knowledge that he had been admitted for the benefit of the partnership, whichever date is later, such a person may give public notice that he has elected to become or that he has elected not to become a partner of the firm and such notice shall determine his position in regard to the firm. In the case that he fails to give such a notice, he shall become partner at the expiry of six months.[94] When such person becomes partner, his rights and liabilities as a minor continue up to the date on which he becomes a partner, but he also becomes personally liable to third parties for all acts of the firm done since he was admitted to the benefits of partnership.

II. Aliens

116. An alien is a person who is not an Indian citizen. In peaceful times, an alien is capable of entering into legally enforceable contracts. In times of war, however, no alien enemy can enter into a valid contract as such agreements are unlawful, as they are against public policy under section 23 of the Indian Contract Act, 1872. An alien can become a partner with an Indian firm. But such an alien becomes an enemy

92. Indian Contract Act, 1872, s. 2(i).
93. *Lacchmi Narain v. Beni Ram*, AIR 1931 All 327; ILR 53 All 479 (1931).
94. Indian Partnership Act, 1932, s. 30(1), (2), (3), (4), (5), (6), (7), (8), (9).

following the outbreak of a war. Such partnership will be illegal and is thereby dissolved.[95]

III. Persons of Unsound Mind

117. A person, under section 12 of the Contract Act, 1872, is said to be of sound mind for the purpose of making a contract if, at the time when he makes it, he is capable of understanding it and of forming a rational judgment as to its effect upon his interests. A person who is usually of unsound mind, but occasionally of sound mind, may make a contract when he is of sound mind. However, a person who is usually of sound mind, but occasionally of unsound mind may not make a contract when he is of unsound mind.

IV. Unlawful Agreements

118. An agreement under section 10 is valid, if it has been made fulfilling other conditions with free consent and under section 13, two or more person are said to consent when they agree upon the same thing in the same sense. However, it will not be held free, if it has been caused by: (i) coercion; (ii) undue influence; (iii) fraud; (iv) misrepresentation; or mistake of fact.

119. Coercion: Section 14 of the Contract Act defines 'coercion' as omitting or threatening to commit, any act forbidden by the Indian Penal code or the unlawful detaining, or threatening to detain, any property, to the prejudice of any person whatever, with the intention of causing any person to enter into an agreement.

120. Undue Influence: According to section 16 of the Contract Act, a contract is said to be induced by 'undue influence' where the relations subsisting between the parties are such that one of the parties is in a position to dominate the will of the other and uses that position to obtain an unfair advantage over the other. A persons is deemed to be in a position to dominate the will of another, (a) where he holds a real or apparent authority over the other, or where he stands in a fiduciary relation to the other; or (b) where he makes a contract with person whose mental capacity is temporarily or permanently affected by reason of age, illness, or mental or bodily distress.

121. Fraud: According to section 17 of the Act, fraud is committed by a party to a contract with intent to deceive another party to induce him to enter in to contract: (a) the suggestion of a fact that which is not true by one who does not believe it to be true; or (b) the active concealment of a fact by one having knowledge or belief of the fact; (c) a promise made without any intention of performing it; (d) a promise made without any intention of performing it; (e) any other act fitted to deceive; (f) any such act or omission at the law specially declares to be fraudulent.

122. Misrepresentation: Section 18 of the Contract Act defines 'misrepresentation' as means and includes: (a) the positive assertion, in a manner not warranted by the information of the person making it, of that which is not true, though he believes it to be true; (b) any breach of duty which, without an intent to deceive, gains an advantage

95. Indian Partnership Act, 1932, s. 41(b).

to the person committing, or any one, claiming under him, by misleading another to prejudice or to the prejudice of any one claiming under him; (c) causing innocently, a party to an agreement to make a mistake as to the substance of the thing which is the subject of the agreement.

V. Voidable Agreements

123. Voidable agreements without free consent: When consent to an agreement is caused by coercion, fraud or misrepresentation, the agreement, according to section 19, is voidable contract at the option of the party whose consent was so caused.

124. Contract induced by undue influence: Such an agreement under section 19A of the Act is a voidable contract at the option of the party whose consent was so caused. However, such a contract may be set aside absolutely or, if the party who was entitled to avoid it has received any benefit thereunder, upon such terms and conditions as to the court may seem just.

125. Where both the parties to an agreement are under a mistake of fact essential to the agreement, the agreement is void under section 20 of the Act. However, under section 21 of the Act, a contract is not voidable because it was caused by a mistake as to any law in force in India, but a mistake as to a law not in force in India has the same effect as a mistake of fact. But a contract is not voidable merely because it was caused by one of the parties to it being under a mistake as to a matter of fact.

VI. Validity of Considerations and Object

126. A valid contract is that the parties must contract for a lawful object. Section 23 of the Indian Contract Act, 1872 renders certain considerations and objects as unlawful, which are: (i) forbidden by law; (ii) is of such nature that if permitted, it would defeat the provisions of any law; (iii) is fraudulent; (iv) involves injury to the person or property of another; or the court regards it as immoral; or (v) opposed to public policy. In each of these cases, the consideration or object of an agreement is said to be unlawful and such agreements are void. All contracts with the inhabitants of the enemy's country after the declaration of war are illegal. However when a commercial contract or partnership is lawful in the beginning but subsequently, on account of some change in law or outbreak of hostilities, the contract or business becomes unlawful, if there is a partnership, such partnership will become illegal and the firm will be, by force of law's dissolved.[96] In case any part of a single consideration for one or more objects, or any one or any part of any part of any one of several considerations for a single object is unlawful, the agreement is void.[97] An agreement without consideration is void, unless it is in writing and registered, or is a promise to compensate for something done, or is a promise to pay debt, barred by limitation of law.[98] The provisions of section 25 of the Act will not affect the validity as between

96. Indian Partnership Act, 1932, s. 41(b).
97. Indian Contract Act, 1872, s. 24.
98. Indian Contract Act, 1872, s. 25.

donor and done or any gift actually made.[99] Inadequacy of consideration would not make the agreement void.[100] Inadequacy of the consideration is a fact, which the court should take into account in considering whether or not the consent was freely given.

VII. Void Agreements

127. The certain kinds of agreements are considered as void. For example: Agreement in restraint of marriage;[101] Agreement in restraint of trade, lawful profession or business[102] except when there is an agreement for the sale of goodwill of a business; Agreement in restraint of legal proceedings[103] except where there is an agreement for referring the disputed before the arbitration;[104] Agreements, the meaning of which is not certain, or capable of being made certain, are void;[105] Agreements by way of wager are void.[106] However, this provision shall not render unlawful a subscription, or contribution, or agreement to subscribe or contribute, made or entered into for or toward any plate, prize or sum of money, of the value or amount of INR 500 or upwards, to be awarded to the winner of any horse-race.[107]

VIII. Convicts

128. While undergoing a sentence, a convict is incapable of entering into a contract. This inability terminates at the expiry of the sentence or if he has been pardoned.[108]

IX. Corporations

129. A corporation or a company is a legal person and has a separate legal existence from its members[109] and, therefore, a corporation has a capacity to contract after it has been incorporated.[110] The Companies Act, 2013 does not define a company in terms of its features. 'Company' means a company incorporated under the Company

99. Indian Contract Act, 1872, s. 25, Expl. 1.
100. Indian Contract Act, 1872, s. 25, Expl. 2.
101. Indian Contract Act, 1872, s. 26.
102. Indian Contract Act, 1872, s. 27.
103. Indian Contract Act, 1872, s. 28.
104. Indian Contract Act, 1872, s. 28, Except. 1.
105. Indian Contract Act, 1872, s. 29.
106. Indian Contract Act, 1872, s. 30.
107. Indian Contract Act, 1872, s. 30, Exception.
108. R.P. Maheshwari & S.N. Maheshwari, *Mercantile Law* 44 (3d rev. ed., National Publishing House 1975).
109. Companies Act, 1956, s. 34; *see also Electronics Corporation of India v. Secretary Revenue Department, Government of Andhra Pradesh*, AIR 1999 SC 1734.
110. Companies Act, 1956, s. 149(4).

Act, 2013 or under any previous Company Law.[111] Two or more persons who are desirous of joint business enterprise can form a company or partnership. A company is the beneficial owner of its own property[112] and it does not hold it as trustee for its shareholders. Further, shareholders are not proprietors of the company but merely investors and are entitled to participate in the profits of the company when the company declares dividend and they have also got further rights to participate in the assets of the company, which would be left over after winding up, but not in the asset as a whole.[113] An incorporated company, being a legal person, can sue and be sued in its own name. But if on the date of filing suit the company's name has been struck from the Register of Companies and as a consequence dissolved, then it cannot initiate any legal proceedings so as to be valid in law.[114] The powers and capacity of the company, however, is determined by its document called a 'Memorandum of Association'. Contracts, which are beyond the powers of corporation granted by the memorandum of association, may be ultra vires[115] Ultra vires acts are void ab initio. Ultra vires acts are merely void.

130. The promoters of the company may, prior to its incorporation, enter into contracts on behalf of the company. They are called 'pre-incorporation contracts'. Such contracts are generally made where a company is formed to buy an existing business because in such an instance, there must be a person to enter into a contract on behalf of the intended company with the vender. A company is not bound by the contracts made on its behalf prior to its incorporation just as a person is not liable for the contracts or acts done before its birth. Similarly, the company is not entitled to enforce such contracts. The ratification of pre-incorporation contract by the company is, however, possible. Under sections 15(h) and 19(e) of the Specific Relief Act, 1963, a company after its incorporation is fully entitled to accept a pre-incorporation contract. Thus, the pre-incorporation contracts are enforceable by or against the company after its incorporation.[116]

§2. Partnerships and Corporations

I. Partnerships

A. General

131. The concept of partnership is ancient in India. Kautilya in his Arthashastra has elaborately discussed this concept of partnership is in no way be termed as an import from Britain. It is contented that the Indian Partnership, Act, 1932 is based,

111. Companies Act, 2013, s. 2(20).
112. *Deputy Commissioner v. Cherian Transport Corp.* (1992) 74 Com Cas 563.
113. *National Textiles Workers' Union v. P.R. Krissanan and Ors*, AIR 1983 SC 75 ; *K.S.Mothilal v. K.S. Kasimaris Ceramique (p.) Ltd.*[2003] 113 Com Cas 562(Mad.).
114. *Floating Services Ltd. v. M.V. San Fransceco Dipalola* (2004) 52 SCL 762 (Guj).
115. *A.L. Mudaliar v. Life Insurance Corporation of India*, AIR 1963 SC 1185.
116. *See* Specific Relief Act, 1963, ss 15(h) and 19(e).

though not wholly, on the analogous English Act of 1890, the provisions of which again are in most instances merely declaratory of the previous law, as such, the English decisions which form the basis of various sections of the Act, as well as those which interpret the different sections of the Act themselves must be of great value even in this country for the purpose of understanding the Indian Act. The comments and explanations of the meaning of the various sections of the Act are extracted mainly from the judicial decisions of the various courts in England, especially of the Judicial Committee of the Privy Council.

132. The law relating to partnership in India is in the Indian Partnership Act, 1932, came into force on 1 October 1932, except section 69 which relates to the effects of non-registration of partnership firms was enforced a year later. Most of the provisions of the Act are based upon the provisions of the English Partnership Act, 1890. Prior to the Partnership Act, 1932, the provisions of law relating to a partnership was contained in sections 239–266 of the Indian Contract Act, 1872. Section 3 of the Partnership Act, 1932 provides that the unrepealed provisions of the Indian Contract Act, 1872, save in so far as they are inconsistent with express provisions of the Act shall continue to apply to firms. Apart from this, principles of equity and common law are also applicable to partnership firms. Section 1 of the Act also provides that all statutes, Acts, regulations not repealed by the Act, usage or custom of trade, or any incident of any contract, not inconsistent with the provisions of the Contract Act, 1872 or Partnership Act, 1932, shall also continue to be in force.[117]

B. Definition and Characteristics of a Partnership

133. Partnership firms are a very common form of business organization in India. They are particularly suited to the small associations of business persons and family enterprises. In comparison to the joint stock companies, they require a small number of persons, a small amount of capital. They have the benefit of inexpensiveness of creation and freedom from the regulations of governmental controls. The major disadvantage is that every partner is liable, jointly and severally with other partners for acts of the firm done while he is a partner in the firm. Every partner may face unlimited liability for debts and obligations of the partnership firm.

134. Section 4 of the Partnership Act, 1932 defines the 'partnership' as the relation among persons who have agreed to share the profits of business carried on by all or any one of them acting for all persons who have entered into the partnership with one another and are called individually 'partners' and collectively 'a firm' and the name under which their business is carried on is called the 'the firm name'.

1. Association of 'Persons'

135. Partnership is the relation between two or more persons. The term 'person' includes natural person as human beings and artificial person or legal person as incorporated company[118] a partnership is not a legal person,[119] wakf is also not a legal

117. *Irrawaddy Flotilla Co. v. Bhagwan Das* (1891) 18 IA 121, p. 127.
118. *Jagdish Chand Gupta v. Kazaria Traders*, AIR 1964 SC 1882.
119. *Duli Chand v. C.I.T.* AIR 1956 SC 354.

person.[120] Similarly, a Hindu joint family trade is also not a legal person.[121] Thus, only two natural persons or one natural and one company may create a partnership, or two joint stock companies may form a partnership. Any two people capable of contracting can form a partnership. Though a partnership is an association of persons, but in spite of that unity among themselves every person can have his own separate existence from the firm. Any right, which a partner has over any property, other than partnership property would remain as his individual asset. The mere fact that the particular person has chosen to include himself as a partner of a firm will not result in incorporation of all his individual properties as the assets of the partnership.

136. In order to create a partnership, a minimum of two persons are required. There is no provision for a maximum number in the Act.

2. A Partnership is Created by Agreement

137. The partnership relationship arises from the contract and not from status.[122] Contract may be express or implied, written or oral.

138. A provision in the partnership deed that the heirs of the deceased partner would be entitled to become partners in the firm was held as not making them partners automatically. They had to express their desire to become partners.

139. There are different kinds of partnerships. Sections 7 and 8 of the Partnership Act refer to different kinds on the basis of formation, management, representation, circumstances, dissolution, taxation, etc.

140. Section 7 of the Partnership Act provides that where no provision is made by contract between the partners for the duration of their partnership, or for determination of their partnership, it is a 'partnership at will' where no period or duration is fixed, the rim can last only as long as the partners are willing to continue as partners. Its survival depends upon the willingness of the partners. There are, however two exceptions[123] to a partnership at will, viz., (i) where there is a provision in the contract for the duration of the partnership; (ii) the where there is a provision for the determination of partnership. In either of these cases, the partnership is not a t will. Even if there is no express provision of duration, the partnership will not be a will if the duration is implied. In case a partnership is for carrying on a specific job, the partnership will come to an end on the completion of the job.[124] However, where the partnership firm is for a fixed period and after the expiry of the term and without making any new agreement, the original contract is prolonged by tacit consent, the partnership will be termed as partnership at will.[125] A partnership is dissolved by any partner giving a notice in writing to all the other partners of his intention to dissolve it. The firm is dissolved from the date mentioned in the notice.[126]

---

120. *Hussain Kazi v. C.I.T.* (1941) CWN 629.
121. *Rasik Lal & Co. v. C.I.T.* AIR 1998 SC 401.
122. Indian Partnership Act, s. 5.
123. *Karumuthu Thiagarajan Chettiar v. E.M. Muthappa Chettiar*, AIR 1961 SC 1225.
124. *Deok, Rajgariah v. Anar Dai Poddar*, AIR 1999 PaT 22.
125. *Nelson v. Mossend Iron Co.* (1886) 11 App.Cs 298 HL.
126. *Banarsidas v. Knsiram*, AIR 1961 SC 1165.

141. Section 8 of the Partnership Act, 1932 provides a partnership in a particular adventure or undertaking, for example, for construction of bridge or production of a film. It is not necessary there should be permanent bond between the partners. There can be as much a partnership in a single and brief business venture as in a business of particular adventure. In a partnership between two persons for entering into certain wagering transactions for particular season only. It was held to be a particular partnership.[127] Partnership for a particular period of time is called fixed partnership. After the expiry of the period, the partnership comes to an end. When a partner in the firm includes only other person to share the benefits derived from the firm, such included person is called sub-partner. This partnership exists between the transferor partner and transferee person. Transferee is not a partner in the firm. Transferee is not entitled to take part in the management and conduct of the business of the firm.

3. A Partnership for Carrying on Some Business

142. In order to create a partnership, carrying on business is essential. The term 'business' means every kind of trade, occupation and profession. Benefits derived from co-ownership do not constitute partnership. For partnership, 'business' must be in existence. It is not an agreement alone, which creates a partnership. A partnership comes into being with the commencement of the business.[128] No partnership can be formed to carry on a future business.[129] When a partnership is created to carry on a business that depends upon approval of a tender submitted for some work, if the tender is not approved, no partnership is created.[130] A business may be of a permanent nature or a partnership may be formed to carry out a single enterprise such as construction of a bridge or making of a film only.

4. Business of the Firm to Be Carried on Is to 'Share the Profits'

143. There must be provisions to share the profits in the business of the firm. Profit means net profit. Agreement to share losses by the partners is not necessary. Partners may make an agreement that all partners shall share profits, but only a few will share the losses.[131]

144. Parties may agree to share profits and losses in any proportion. A partner may join the partnership only for earning profit. He may not participate in losses.[132] However, such an arrangement does not absolve a partner from the liability against the third parties or outsiders,[133] because all partners are liable for the acts of the firm individually and collectively. If there is no provision in the partnership agreement

127. *Gherulal Parekh v. Mahadevdas*, AIR 1959 SC 781.
128. *Khan v. Miah*, (2000),1 WLR 2123.
129. *R.R. Sarna v. Ruben*, AIR 1946 Oudh 68.
130. *Ram Priya Saran v. Ghanshyamds*, AIR 181 All 1843. *Minck v. Roshan Lal shore*, AIR 1931 Lah; *K. Jaggi v. K. Venkat Satnarain*, AIR 1984 AP 149.
131. *Raghunadhan v. Harinasji*, AIR 1927 Bom. 187.
132. *Ibid.*
133. *Ibid.*

relating to the sharing of profits and losses, all partners shall share profits and losses equally.[134] Profit in the business is the basis and commissions are not profit.[135]

5. Mutual Agency

145. The partnership business is to be carried on for sharing profits 'by all or any of them acting for all'.[136] This implies that partnership is the extension of the 'law of agency'. According to the Act, a partner is the agent of the firm for the purpose of business of the firm.[137] The act of a partner alone to carry on the firms' usual business binds the firm.[138] Thus, for determining the existence of a partnership among persons, sharing of profit is not true test but mutual agency is real test of partnership.[139]

146. The existence of the partnership depends upon their intention as shown by their agreement or conduct or both put together. Where the self-same partners formed several firms, the Supreme Court held that each firm, though not a juristic person, is identifiable on the basis of the respective agreements.[140]

C. Registration of Partnership Firms

147. There was no provision for the registration of a partnership prior to the enactment of the Partnership Act, 1932. However, in 1932, Chapter VII containing provisions relating to registration was included for the first time.[141] Registration, though, is not one of the essential requirements for coming into existence of a partnership, but there are certain consequences attached to non-registration, which seem to put a non-registered firms at disadvantage vis-à-vis registered firms. Each state, however, in India is empowered to direct by notification in the official gazette that provisions of that chapter shall not apply to that state or any part thereof.[142] Each state, therefore, is empowered to appoint a Registrar of Firms and to define his jurisdiction. The Registrar of firms shall maintain a 'Register of Firms'.[143] Procedure for registration is simple whereby the application form containing required information, signed and verified by each partner or his agent is submitted to the Registrar of Firms and when satisfied that the provisions of the Act are duly complied with, it shall make an entry of the application in the Register of Firms and shall file the same.[144] Registration is completed when the Registrar files the application.[145] Changes in the membership of the firm does not affect the registration once made. It is not required that every time a new partner is introduced, a fresh registration has to be applied for and obtained. However, the omission to give

134. Indian Partnership Act, 1932, s. 13(b).
135. *Raghumal v. Official Assignee, Calcutta*, AIR 1924 Cal. 424.
136. Indian Partnership Act, 1932, s. 4.
137. Indian Partnership Act, 1932, s. 18.
138. Indian Partnership Act, 1932, s. 19.
139. *Cox v. Hickman*, 8 HLC 268.
140. *CST v. K. Kelukutty*, (1985) 4 SCC 35 at p. 41: AIR 1985 SC 1143.
141. Provisions for registration are from ss 56–71 of the Indian Partnership Act.
142. Indian Partnership Act, 1932, s. 56.
143. Indian Partnership Act, 1932, s. 57.
144. Indian Partnership Act, 1932, s. 59.
145. *Jayalakshi Rice and Mills v. I.T. Commissioner*, AIR 1967 AP 99.

notice will effect that the ability of the firm and its partners for legal proceedings will become affected in the same manner as if the firm was not registered[146] failure to inform registrar of partner's death did not affect the registration of the firm. It merely results in imposition of penalty under section 69A.[147] Registration of a partnership firm is not compulsory and there is no penalty The Act, however, denies certain rights to the firm and partners of an unregistered firm, e.g., a partner of unregistered firm cannot file a suit against the firms or past and present fellow partners for enforcing contractual or statutory rights. The firm cannot, for example, sue any person for the price of the goods supplied by it.[148] Similarly, an unregistered firm cannot file suit to enforce contractual rights against third parties.[149] Non-registration of a firm does not, however, affect the right of a partner to sue for dissolution of the firm or for accounts, and right to realize the property of his share of the dissolved form. The right of official assignee to realize property, or an insolvent, or right to sue for set-off in which a claim does not exceed INR 100 or the right of a third party to proceed against the unregistered firm or its partners shall not be affected.[150] Even the arbitration proceedings shall be barred.[151] The action of unregistered firm is liable to be dismissed and it cannot be rectified by registration section 69(b) of the Act permits an official assignee, receiver or court acting for an insolvent partner may bring an action for realization of the insolvent's share, whether or not registered. Similarly, third parties can always sue a firm whether or registered. The disability is that of the firm and not of persons outside it.

D. *Time of Registration*

148. A partnership firm may be registered at any time prior to its dissolution. But it must stand registered on the date of the instituting of the suit. Otherwise, the suit shall be dismissed. Registration of the firm after instituting of the suit will be of no avail.[152] Relations of partners to one another is a contract of utmost good faith and the partners stand in a fiduciary relationship with each other. In the absence of any express contract between them, the Partnership Act lays down rules, which govern their relations.[153] These rules have been summed up in the following paragraphs dealing with the rights and duties of the partners.

149. Rights of the partners includes: (a) the right to take part in management; (b) the right to be consulted in all matters affecting the business of the partnership; (c) the right to have access to books, accounts and other records of the firm; (d) the right to share business profit; (e) the right to receive interest on capital; (f) the right to receive interest on loans given to the firm; (g) the right to be indemnified in respect of payment

146. *Sharad Vasant Kotak v. Ramniklal Mohanlal Chawda*, (1998) 2 SCC 171.
147. *Pawan Nandlal Agarwal v. Asian Dye Chemicals*, AIR 2008 (NOC) 804 (Bom).
148. *Ram Adhar v. R.K. Tiwari*, AIR 1981 All 405.
149. Indian Partnership Act, 1932, s. 69(1) and 69(2); *Sriram Finance Corp. v. Yasin Khan*, AIR 1989 SC 1769.
150. Indian Partnership Act, 1932, s. 69(3)(a), 69(3)(b), 69(4)(a) and 69(4)(b).
151. *Jagdish Chandra Gupta v. Kajaria Traders (India) Ltde.*, AIR 1964 SC 1882.
152. *Prithvi Singh v. Haji Hassan Ali*, AIR 1951 Bom 6.
153. Indian Partnership Act, 1932, ss 17 and 25 dealing with mutual rights and liabilities of partners. *E. Rights of the Partners.*

made and liabilities incurred by a partner in ordinary and proper conduct of firm business and acts done in an emergency to protect the firms interests; (h) the right to use property of the partnership for partnership business; (i) a partner has authority in an emergency, to do all such acts which are essential to do to protect the interest of the firm; (j) the right to disallow a new potential partner to be included in the firm; (k) the right to retire according to the provisions of the Act or special contract; (l) the right not to be excepted; (m) the right to carry on competing business; (n) the right to share subsequent profits after retirement.[154]

E. *Duties of the Partners*

150. Sections 9 and 10 of the Act lay down absolute duties of the partners. All other provisions, as well as provisions relating to duties may be changed by agreement between the parties. Duties of the parties may be summed up as follows.

151. Partners are bound: (1) to carry on the business of the firm to the greatest common advantage; (2) to be just and faithful to each other; and (3) to render true accounts and full information of all things affecting the firm to any partner or his legal representative.[155] Every partner shall indemnify the firm for any loss caused to it by his fraud in the conduct of the business of the firm.[156] Every partner is bound to attend diligently to his duties in conducting the business of the firm.[157] Every partner is liable to the firm for any loss caused to it by his wilful neglect.[158] In the absence of a contract to the contrary, a partner is bound to share losses. Partners should hold and use the firms' property only for the firms' business. A partner shall be liable to account for and pay the firm any private profit desired from the transactions of the firm. A partner is liable to account for the profits of the competing business. Partners are bound to act within the scope of his actual or apparent authority. A partner cannot assign his rights or interests in a partnership firm. Partners are bound to act within the scope of their actual or apparent authority. A partner cannot assign its rights or interests in a partnership firm to an outsider, so as to make the outsider a partner in the firms' business. The Act also declares that every partner is liable jointly and severally for all the acts of the firm done while he is a partner.[159]

F. *Relations of Partners to Third Parties*

152. The Partnership Act provides that a partner is the agent of the firm.[160] Each partner, thus, is a principal for the self and an agent for his co-partners. Each partner is an agent of other partners in matters connected with the partnership, so far as outsiders are concerned, and therefore, his acts will bind the firm irrespective of any other private

154. Indian Partnership Act, 1932, ss 12(a), 12(c), 12(d), 13, 13(a), 13(e), 14, 15, 21 and 31(1), 31(2), 32(2), 33(1), 36 and 37.
155. Indian Partnership Act, 1932, s. 9.
156. Indian Partnership Act, 1932, s. 10.
157. Indian Partnership Act, 1932, ss 12(a) and 13(a).
158. Indian Partnership Act, 1932. s. 13(f).
159. Indian Partnership Act, 1932, ss 13(b), 16(a), 29 and 25.
160. Indian Partnership Act, 1932, s. 18.

arrangement between them. The authority of the partner binds the firm by his acts done in the usual course of the business carried on by the firm and this is called the implied authority of a partner.[161] In the absence of any usage or custom of trade to the contrary the implied authority of a partner does not empower him to submit a dispute relating to the business of the firm to arbitration, to open a bank account of the firm in his own name, to compromise any claim of the firm, to withdraw any suit filed by the firm, to admit any liability in a suit or proceedings against the firm, to acquire or transfer any immovable property belonging to the firm, and to enter into a partnership on behalf of the firm.[162]

153. Implied Authority and Third Party: Partners are individually and jointly liable to third parties for all of their acts done within their implied authority. Such acts are termed as 'acts of the firm'. Section 2(a) of the Act defines an 'act of the firm' as an 'act or omission by all the partners or by any partner or agent of the firm, which gives rise to a right enforceable by or against the firm'. The liability of partners to third parties for such acts may be as follows:

(a) The firm can be held liable for all wrongful acts, torts committed by a partner which have caused loss or injury to third party.[163]
(b) The firm shall be liable to make good for the losses where a partner receives money or property from a third party and misuses it.[164]
(c) Any information obtained by a partner in the course of partnership business shall be taken to be obtained by all partners except in the case of fraud perpetrated by a third party in collusion with that partner.[165]
(d) An admission or representation made by a partner concerning the affairs of the firm is valid evidence against the firm if made in the usual course of the firm business.[166]

G. *Dissolution of the Partnership Firm*

154. The Indian Partnership law differentiates between dissolution of partnership and dissolution of the firm. Where a partnership is reconstituted, there is a dissolution of partnership. For example, if a new partner is admitted or an existing partner dies or adjudged as insolvent or expelled, there is dissolution of partnership. The dissolution of partnership between all the partners of a firm is called the dissolution of the firm.[167] In that case, the business of the firm is closed down and the affairs are wound up. The assets are realized and liabilities are paid off. The dissolution of a partnership may or may not result in the dissolution of a firm but a dissolution of a firm will necessarily result in the dissolution of the partnership. In India, a partnership may be dissolved without the intervention of the court.

161. Indian Partnership Act, 1932, s. 19.
162. Indian Partnership Act, 1932, s. 19(2).
163. Indian Partnership Act, 1932, s. 26.
164. Indian Partnership Act, 1932, s. 27.
165. Indian Partnership Act, 1932, s. 24.
166. Indian Partnership Act, 1932, s. 23.
167. Indian Partnership Act, 1932, s. 39.

155. Dissolution without the intervention of the court: A partnership firm may be dissolved without intervention of the court in any of the following ways:

(a) *Dissolution by agreement*: A firm may be dissolved by mutual consent or in accordance with a contract between the parties. Consent must be received from all the partners.[168]
(b) *Compulsory dissolution*: A partnership firm must be dissolved compulsorily: (i) by the adjudication of all the partners, or all the partners but one is insolvent; or (ii) by the business of the firm becoming unlawful due to occurrence of any such event. Where the firm carried on more than one separate business, the illegality of one or more shall not of itself cause the dissolution of the firm.[169]
(c) *Dissolution on the occurrence of certain contingencies*: In the absence of a contract to the contrary, a firm will be dissolved at the occurrence of any of the following contingencies: (i) at the expiry of the fixed period for which the firm was constituted; (ii) at the completion of the activities or undertaking for which the firm was constituted; (iii) at the death of a partner; (iv) at the adjudication of a partner as insolvent.[170]

156. Even in those cases where the partnership was constituted for a fixed term or for carrying out a particular activity, death or insolvency would have the effect of dissolving the firm, unless it can be shown that the existence of the fixed term or activity coupled with particular circumstances of the case amounted to a contract to the contrary.[171]

157. (d) Dissolution by Notice: Where a partnership is at will, the firm may be dissolved by any partner giving notice in writing to all the partners.[172] Notice must be unconditional, unambiguous and concrete. The firm will be considered dissolved at the date specified in the notice; if the date for dissolution is not entailed in the notice, then from the date of the communication of the notice to the last of the partners.

158. Dissolution of the firm by the court: If a lawsuit is brought by a partner, the court may order the dissolution of the firm on any of the grounds provided in the Act.[173] These grounds are:

(a) *Insanity*: When a lawsuit is filed by the next relative or friend of the partner of unsound mind, the court may order the dissolution of the firm. Lunacy need not be permanent.[174]
(b) *Permanent Incapacity*: Permanent incapacity in performing duties as a partner is ground for dissolution of a firm.[175]

168. Indian Partnership Act, 1932, s. 40.
169. Indian Partnership Act, 1932, s. 41.4.
170. Indian Partnership Act, 1952, s. 47.
171. *Abdul Azeez v. M.K.P. Kadar Mohideen*, AIR 1963 Mad 428.
172. Indian Partnership Act, 1932, s. 432. *Banarsidas v. Kansi Ram*, AIR 1963 SC 1165.
173. Indian Partnership Act, 1932, s. 44.
174. Indian Partnership Act, 1932, s. 44(a).
175. Indian Partnership Act, 1932, s. 44(b).

(c) *Misconduct*: Misconduct of the partner should have prejudicially affected the carrying on of the firm's business.[176] Misconduct complained of should be directly connected with the business,[177] e.g., conviction of a partner for travelling on the railway without ticket with intention to defraud.[178]
(d) *Breach of Agreement*: Wilfully, persistently breach of partnership agreement, particularly provisions relating to accounts of the firm, management of the firm and this gives the other partner of the firm a right.[179] However, where partnership is at will, the guilty partner is not denied the right to sue the other partner for dissolution on the ground that he himself was guilty of misconduct.
(e) *Transfer of Interest*: When a partner, other than the partner suing, has transferred the whole of his interest in the firm to a third party.[180]
(f) *Loss of business*: When the *business* of the firm cannot be carried on except at a loss, the court may make an order for the dissolution of the firm.[181]
(g) *Just and Equitable*: When the court considers any other ground to be just and equitable for the dissolution of the firm, e.g., deadlock in the management or disappearance of the substratum of the business, etc. the court may make an order for the dissolution of the firm.[182]

159. As a result of dissolution of partnership, partners shall have equitable lien on the property of the firm, a right to return of the premium, a right to limit the use of the firms' name or firm property.[183]

160. After dissolution, the partners shall be liable for the acts of the firm until they give a public notice of the dissolution. Accounts shall be settled among the partners as per provisions of the Act.[184]

H. Limited Liability Partnership

161. The limited liability partnership (LLP) is a hybrid form of business. It has features of both a body corporate as well as a general partnership. The Limited Liability Partnership Act, 2008 came into effect in the year 2009. The LLP has Separate Legal Entity, i.e., the LLP and the partners are distinct from each other. Minimum of two partners are required to form a LLP. However, there is no limit on the maximum number of partners. No requirement of Minimum Capital Contribution. The LLP Act does not restrict the benefit of LLP structure to certain classes of Professionals only and it would be available for use by any enterprise. Though it cannot come out with its IPO and raise money from the public, which a 'company' form of organization can do. Benefits of forming an LLP is that the liability of partners is limited to his share as written in

176. Indian Partnership Act, 1932, s. 44(c).
177. *Snow v. Milford* (1868) P&LT 142.
178. *Karmicale v. Evansa* (1904) 1 Ch. 986S.
179. Indian Partnership Act, 1932, s. 44(c).
180. *Ram Singh v. Ram Chand*, ILR (1923) 5 Lah 23.
181. Indian Partnership Act, 1932, s. 44(e).
182. Indian Partnership Act, 1932, s. 44(f).
183. Indian Partnership Act, 1932, ss 46, 51, 52 and 53.
184. Indian Partnership Act, 1932, ss 48–551.

the agreement filed at the time of creation of LLP. It has low cost of formation and easy to form. The partners are not liable for the act of each other and can be held liable for their own acts. The partners are not liable to be sued for the dues of LLP. It being a separate legal person can sue and be sued in its own name. Foreign Direct Investment in LLP is allowed with the specific approval of the government, in those sectors where 100% FDI is otherwise allowed. On 19 October 2015, the Central Government in exercise of the powers conferred by subsections (1) and (2) of the section 79 of the Limited Liability Partnership Act, 2008, amend the rules (now called 'Limited Liability Partnership (Amendment) Rules, 2015').

II. Corporations

A. General

162. Corporations are not novelties, they are the institutions of very old date. It finds its roots in English company law and has been following the English Companies Acts, with certain modifications to suit the Indian legal system. In England the earliest business associations during the eleventh to thirteenth centuries, were known as 'merchant guilds'. The primary purpose of these guilds was to obtain Royal Charters from the Crown so as to create a monopoly in respect of a particular trade or commodity for their members. The word 'company' finds mention during the fourteenth century, and was adopted by merchants for their overseas trade. Thus, a 'company' at that time was a foreign trading extension of the merchant guild. In the sixteenth century, the crown passed Royal Charters by which members of the company were granted monopoly of trade over a specific portion of territory held by the Crown. Such companies came to be known as 'regulated companies'. The East India Company, the first British entity to establish a lasting presence in India, was also regulated company, established by Royal Charter in 1600. It had a monopoly to trade in India and its members divided the profits among themselves after the completion of each voyage. As the company grew however, it introduced a 'joint fund' or stock of the company, in 1653. By this, a permanent subscribed fund was introduced and members contributed to the total capital reserves of the company and were shareholders in respect if the profits earned by the use of such contribution, which were shared after the completion of each voyage. This is the genesis of a joint stock company.

163. Towards the seventeenth century, however, trade had risen substantially, and all regulated companies created permanent fixed capital. This capital was represented by freely tradable shares of the company. The companies were under the control of their board of governors or directors. A company, however, could be created only by Royal Charter or Act of Parliament, which required a lot of time and money. As a result, in order to save resources, people began to form companies by an agreement without incorporation. Such practice was often considered illegal. The South Sea Company, which was floated as a chartered company in 1711, ultimately failed. During this period, there was great rise in speculation of shares and securities. To check this, the English Parliament passed the Bubble Act, 1720 and prohibited all other forms of corporations unless they were incorporated by an Act of Parliament or Royal charter.

This caused abolition of many companies existing that time. This led to the formation of number of partnerships. In 1825, the Bubble Act was repealed. And joint stock companies were recognized for the first time by the Joint Stock Companies Act, 1844.

164. The company law in India emerged and developed through the English Companies Acts. Immediately following the enactment of the Joint Stock Companies Act, 1844 in England, the first Companies Act was passed in India in 1850. This Act provides for the registration of the companies and the transferability of shares. The Act of 1850 was amended in 1857 and conferred the right of registration with or without limited liability. Subsequently, this right was granted to banking and insurance companies by the Act of 1860. In 1866, another amending Act was enacted repealing previous Acts. This Act was recast in 1882, embodying the amendments, which were made in company law in England up to that time. This Act remained in force up to 1913. In this year, a comprehensive enactment was enacted based on the English Companies Act, 1908. The Companies Act, 1956 came into force by repealing the Act of 1913. The main features of this Act are: Full and fair disclosure of various matters in a prospectus, information of financial affairs of the company to be disclosed; powers of the government to intervene and investigate into the affairs of a company, restrictions on the powers of managing agents and other managerial personnel, protection of minority shareholders, etc. The Indian Parliament has amended the company law from time to time and has stayed in sync with the times in order to accept the challenges of the business world. The Companies Act, 1956 has, thus, been amended several times. Some of the important amendments have been in 1960, 1962, 1963, 1965, 1966, 1969, 1977, 1988, 1996, 1999, 2000, 2002, 2006 and the latest in 2011. Out of two amendments in 2002, the second one, i.e., the Companies (Second Amendment) Act, 2002 amended the law relating to insolvencies and winding of companies. It provided for repeal of Sick Industries Companies Act, 1985 (SICA) and dissolution of the Board for Industrial and Financial Reconstruction (BIFR) and seeks to establish a National Company Law Tribunal providing it with powers for expediting the winding up procedure. Unfortunately, this provision has not yet been enforced. Companies (Amendment) Act, 2006 introduced provisions for Directors Identification Numbers (DIN) and electronically filing of returns and forms. This amendment was brought on the recommendations of the Ministry Company Affairs who decided to enable the operations carried out by the Ministry and its field officers to be performed more efficiently and effectively through the use of contemporary information technology and computers. The Amendment of 2006 inserted new sections 610B, 610C and 610D and 610E in the Companies Act, 1956 so as to make provision for electronic filing system and for payment of fees through electronic form under the said Act. The Company Act, 1956 could not keep pace with the changes and many provisions became outdated. Therefore, the recent Companies Act, 2013 has been enacted to fulfil the need of flexible law that can address the challenges faced in the dynamic business environment taking into account the national and international economic scenarios. The Companies bill as passed by Lok Sabha on 18 December 2012 (Company Bill, 2012) and passed by Rajya Sabha on 8 August 2013 (Company Bill, 2013). Section 1 came into effect from 30 August 2013, i.e., the date of notification in the official Gazette after it received assent of President of India on 29 August 2013 and became the Company Act, 2013. The ministry of Corporate Affairs notified 98 sections of the Companies Act, 2013 vide its notification dated 12 September 2013 the effective date of which is 12 September 2013. On 27 February 2014, the provisions of section 135 i.e., Corporate Social Responsibility were notified to come into force w.e.f. 1 April 2014 along with Companies (Corporate Social Responsibilities Policy) Rules, 2014 and Schedule VII. On 26 March 2014, 183 sections of the Companies Act, 2013 and 6 Schedules were notified by the Ministry of Corporate Affairs and came into effect from 1 April 2014. It contains 470 sections and 7 Schedules. The significant part of the legislation will be in the form of rules. The Government of India (GOI) had received several representations from industry stakeholders for amending various provisions of Companies Act, 2013 to ensure ease of doing business in India. Towards this, the Companies (Amendment) Act, 2015 received the assent from the President of India on 25 May 2015 after both the houses of the Parliament approved the Companies (Amendment) Act, 2015. The Companies (Amendment) Act, 2015 has been published in the Official Gazette on 26 May 2015 and is a welcome step towards addressing some of the concerns under Company Act, 2013. The Central Government is authorized to appoint different dates for implementation of different provisions in the Companies (Amendment) Act, 2015. Accordingly, while most provisions have become effective from 29 May 2015. Further, on 29 May 2015, in order to align Company Act, 2013 and the rules thereunder with the Companies (Amendment) Act, 2015, the Ministry of Corporate Affairs (MCA) has also issued amendments to relevant Rules under Company Act, 2013 (namely, the Companies (Share Capital and Debenture) Second Amendment Rules, 2015, the Companies (Declaration and Payment of Dividend) Secondment Amendment Rules, 2015, the Companies (Incorporation) Second Amendment Rules, 2015, the Companies (Registration of Charges) Amendment Rules, 2015 and Companies (Registration offices and Fees) Second Amendment Rules, 2015), Some of the key amendments and clarifications in the Company Act Amendment 2015 are as follows:[185]

- **No Minimum Paid-up Share Capital**: The minimum paid-up share capital requirement of INR 100,000 (in case of a private company) and INR 500,000 (in case of a public company) under Company Act, 2013 has been done away with. Consequently, the definitions of private and public companies stand amended. Therefore, no minimum paid-up capital requirements will now apply for incorporating private as well as public companies in India.
- **Relaxations *vis-a-vis* Related Party Transactions:** Section 188 of Company Act, 2013 lists out such related party transactions, which require approval from the board of directors and/or the shareholders, as prescribed. The Companies (Amendment) Act, 2015 has relaxed the approval requirement from a special resolution (i.e., requiring approval of three-fourth majority of shareholders) to an ordinary resolution (i.e., requiring approval of simple majority of shareholders) in case of related party transactions which require shareholders' approval.
- **Inspection of Resolutions, etc. filed with the Registrar:** The Companies (Amendment) Act, 2015 has limited public access of such resolutions relating mainly to strategic business matters.

185. Available on http://www.indiacode.nic.in/acts-in-pdf/2015/201521.pdf.

- **Common Seal Optional**: The use of common seal has been made optional. All such documents which required affixing the common seal may now instead be signed by two directors or one director and a company secretary of the company.
- **No declarations for commencement of business, etc.**: The Companies (Amendment) Act, 2015 has removed the above requirements and deleted section 11 of Company Act, 2013. This reduces the filings to be made by companies in India.
- **Violation of Acceptance of Deposits, etc.**: A new section 76 A has been introduced for the above non-compliances. The defaulting company will be liable for fine of a minimum amount of INR 10,000,000 and a maximum of INR 100,000,000 in addition to the amount of deposit or part thereof, along with interest. Further, every officer of the company in default is punishable with imprisonment which may extend upto seven years or with a fine amounting to a minimum of INR 2,500,000 and maximum of INR 20,000,000 or both. Such officer may attract additional penalty for fraud under Company Act, 2013 if the non-compliance was done knowingly or with the intention to deceive the company, shareholders, depositors, creditors or tax authorities.
- **Reporting by Auditors in respect of Fraud:** The Companies (Amendment) Act, 2015 has provided that thresholds will be prescribed for reporting of frauds to the Central Government, or the audit committee or the board of directors. All such instances of frauds falling below prescribed thresholds will be reported to the board or the audit committee and will need to be disclosed in the annual report of the company, instead of mandatory reporting to the Central Government.
- **Exemptions to section 185:** Section 185 includes restrictions on loans by a company to a director or other interested persons/entities. However, the rules prescribed under section 185 exempted any loans/guarantee/security by a holding company to its wholly-owned subsidiary, and any guarantee or security by a holding company to a financial institution for loan availed by its subsidiary, provided the loan in each of these cases is utilized by the subsidiary for its principal business.
- **Dividend**: The Companies (Amendment) Act, 2015 has introduced a new proviso which states that a company cannot declare dividend for a financial year, unless the losses and depreciation carried over from past years have been set-off against the profits of the company.
- **Special Courts**: Section 435 read with section 436 provides the Central Government the power to set up special courts to try offences under Company Act, 2013. Thus, the special courts may now only try offences punishable under Company Act, 2013, with imprisonment for two years or more. All other offences are to be tried by a Metropolitan Magistrate or a Judicial Magistrate of the First Class.

B. Application of Company Act, 2013

165. The Companies Act, 2013 has replaced the Companies Act, 1956. The Company Act, 2013 has widely expanded the ambit and scope of applicability to corporations, boards, authorities, bodies and other entities established under several statutes. The Company Act, 2013 has finally been enacted to become a new corporate regulatory framework. The Company Act, 2013 is more of a ruled-based legislation.

It has been enacted after taken into account the national and international economic scenarios with the view to incorporate the international best practices. This Act not only applicable to companies incorporated under this Act but covers companies, body corporate, statutory bodies incorporated under statutes. The provisions of this Act shall apply to Companies incorporated under this Act or under any previous company law or insurance companies (except where the provisions of the said Act are inconsistent with the provisions of the Insurance Act, 1938 or the IRDA Act, 1949) or Banking Companies (except where the provisions of the said Act are inconsistent with the provisions of the Banking Regulation Act, 1949) or the Companies engaged in the generation or supply of the electricity (except where the provisions of the said Act are inconsistent with the provisions of the Electricity Act, 2003) or such Body corporate which are incorporated by Act time being in force, as the central Government may by notification specify in this behalf. The Act has been made flexible as in the case provisions of the Company Act, 2013 are inconsistent with the provisions of the Acts under which the aforesaid Companies are incorporated, the provisions of said Acts shall apply. The New Act strikes a reasonable balance for serving the interest of industry. It introduced the new concepts supporting enhanced disclosure, accountability, better Board governance, better facilitation of business, etc. Thus, the Company Act, 2013 is a principal legislation which will govern companies. Although the companies will be governed by other Acts, Rules and Regulations like Security and Exchange Board of India (SEBI), SCRA, RBI depending on the type and nature of the company. The Government is empowered to issue orders for removing any difficulty that arises in the implementations of this Act. The Company Act, 2013 acknowledges the technological development and incorporate the use of technologies for empowerment of stakeholders and effective dissemination of information.[186]

C. Administration of Company Law

166. In India, the company law is to be carried out through various administrative authorities under the Company Act, 2013. The new Act has created separate civil and criminal mechanism to deal with the corporate commercial matter. Great emphasis has been given in the new Act on the protection of the rights of shareholders and other stakeholders. Many changes have been introduced to detect and prevent frauds and cast the duty of reporting frauds on professionals. It provides the provisions for prevention of Insider trading and thus it enhanced disclosures. The Act provides mechanism for compensating aggrieved persons and for disgorgement of illegal gains.[187] The provisions for protecting the public funds including the funds of public financial institutions as well as funds raised from the public has also been introduced in the new Act. The corporate governance has been strengthened by Company Act, 2013 to improve transparency and accountability. The provisions are included for disclosure additional information like board report, mandatory disclosures on company websites, audit rotation, consolidation of accounts even of associate company. With the new Company Act, more stringent provisions are included for governing setting up and functioning of enterprises, structure for sharing risk and reward, governance and

186. Prachi Manekar, *Insights into the New Company Law* 5 (Lexis Nexis 2013).
187. Prachi Manekar, *Insights into the New Company Law* 4 (Lexis Nexis 2013).

accountability to the investors and other stakeholders and structural changes to comply global standards.

D. Incorporation and Consequences

167. The Company Act, 2013 provides first time included many new provisions like Associate Company, One Person Company (OPC), Small Company, Dormant Company, Independent Director, Women Director, Resident Director, Secretarial Standards, Secretarial Audit, Special Courts, Class Actions, Registered Valuer, Rotation of auditors, Vigil Mechanism (Whistle Blowing), Corporate Social Responsibility, Cross Border Mergers, Prohibition of Insider Trading, Global Depository Receipts.

168. Limited liability companies can be companies: (i) limited by shares; (ii) limited by guarantee; and (iii) limited by guarantee having share capital.[188] The liability of the members, in case of a limited company, may be limited with reference to the nominal value of the shares, respectively held by them or to the amount which they have respectively guaranteed to contribute in event of winding up of the company. 'The company limited by shares' means a company having the liability of its members limited by the memorandum to the amount, if any, unpaid on the shares respectively held by them. A 'company limited by guarantee' means a company having the liability of its members limited by the memorandum to such amount as the members may respectively undertake to contribute to the assets of the company in event of its wound up.[189] The 'company limited by guarantee' may also be called a 'Guarantee Company'. A Guarantee company must suffix the words 'Ltd.' or 'Pvt. Ltd.' As the case may be, in its name and register its Articles along with the Memorandum. It may be seen that the liability of the members of the unlimited company appears to be similar to that of partners but it is unlike the partners, the members of the company cannot be directly proceeded against. The claim can be enforced only against the company as it is a separate legal entity. An unlimited company may or may not have share capital.

169. The company is a separate legal entity, different from its members. Its assets and liabilities are not the assets or liabilities of members. Any change in membership of the company does not mean a change in the company itself.[190] A company has perpetual succession,[191] it can own separate property of its own, movable or immovable.[192] The greatest benefit of the incorporated company is that its shares are directly transferable. A company being an artificial person cannot sign its name on a contract. A common seal is used as a substitute for its signature. The principle of separate entity is considered as a veil between the company and its members, protecting its members from the liability of the company. But in certain circumstances, the court may identify a company with its members when the motion of legal personality is misused to justify wrong or defend crime or protect fraud, and the court may look behind the artificial person. The company may take account of the personalities of

188. Companies Act, 2013, s. 3(2).
189. Companies Act, 2013 , s. 2(21).
190. *J.H. Rayner (Mincing Lane) Ltd. v. Deptt. of Trade and Industry* (1989) 3 WLR 969 HL.
191. *Gopalpur Tea Co. Ltd. v. Penhok Tea Co. Ltd.* (1982) 52 Com Cas 238 Cal.
192. *M.V. 'Dong Do' v. Ramesh Kumar & Co. Ltd.* (2002) Com Cas 450 Cal.

natural persons, the corporate. This is called 'lifting the company's veil'.[193] The veil may be lifted for determining the enemy character of the company.[194] The court may pierce the veil in the case that a company is formed to defeat or to defraud creditors or to avoid legal obligations.[195] Where a company is acting as the agent of the shareholders or of another company, it will be liable for its acts.[196] The court will lift the veil where the company is a mere sham, i.e., when the device of incorporation is used for some illegal or improper purpose.[197]

170. The company differs from partnership in many ways. The company is a distinct legal person, but the partnership is not distinct from the persons who form it. A partnership firm cannot be formed, with more than ten members in case of banking business and twenty members in case of any other business, whereas in a public company there must not be less than seven members and in case of a private company the minimum number is two. There is no restriction as to maximum number of members of a company in case of a private company which cannot have more than fifty members, excluding past and present employees.

E. Types of Companies

171. Section 2(20) of the Company Act, 2013 states that a 'company' means a company incorporated under this Act or under any previous Company Law. 'Existing company' means a company formed and registered (1) under any Act or Acts relating to companies in force before the Indian Companies Act, 1866; (2) under the Indian Companies Act, 1866; (3) under the Indian Companies Act, 1882; (4) under the Indian Companies Act, 1913; (5) under the registration of transformed Companies Ordinance, 1942; (6) under any law, Act or ordinance in force in the merged territories. The following are the kinds of companies:

(a) Statutory companies: a company incorporated by a special Act of Parliament or any state legislature. They are called statutory companies, e.g., Reserve Bank of India, LIC; State Bank of India; Unit Trust of India, etc. Each statutory company is governed by the provision of its special Act.
(b) Registered companies: companies registered under the Companies Act, 2013 or the earlier companies Acts. A registered company may be limited by shares; or limited by guaranty; or an unlimited company. Further, they may be incorporated as private companies or public companies. The company comes into existence from the date of incorporation, and it has perpetual succession.
(c) Private companies:[198] those companies which have minimum paid-up capital of INR 100,000 or as may be prescribed by its capital such higher paid-up share capital as may be prescribed by Company Act, 2013, and which (i) restricts the right to transfer its shares, if any; or (ii) limits the number of members to fifty

193. *Daemler Co. v. Continental Tyre and Rubber Co.* (1916) 2 AC 307.
194. *Dinshaw Maneckjee Patil, Re*, AIR 1927 Bom 371.
195. *SEBI v. Libra Plantation Ltd.* (1989) Com Cas 373 Bom.
196. *Dy. Commr. I.T. v. Cherian Transport Corpn. Ltd.* (1992) 74 Com Cas 563 Mad.
197. *Delhi Development Authority v. Skipper Construction Company Pvt. Ltd.* (1997) 11 SCC 430.
198. Companies Act, 2013, s. 2(68).

two hundred, thus it will increase the ability of private companies to raise capital; or (iii) prohibits any in invitation or acceptance of deposits from persons other than its members, directors of their relatives. Existing private companies have to increase to INR 100,000. If it fails do so, it would be liable to be struck off the Register of Companies in the manner of a defunct company. While calculating the limit of 200, the persons who are in employment of the company, persons who having been formerly in the employment and have continued to be members after the employment ceased shall not be included in the number of members. Shareholders holding shares in joint names shall be treated as single members. A private company is compulsorily required to have articles of association. Under Company Act, 2013, the private companies are prohibited to issue securities to public and prohibition on deposits is specified in Chapter V of Companies Act, 2013. Even under new Act there are restrictions from accepting deposits from members.

(d) Public company:[199] A company which is not a private company, has a minimum paid-up capital of INR 500,000 or such higher paid-up capital as may be prescribed, and is legally formed and registered under the Companies Act. If it is not registered, it would be considered an illegal association. A public company can also be converted into a private company, by passing a special resolution amending the articles of association according to the Company Act, 2013. Under old Act, only public financial institution, public sector bank or rescheduled banks whose main object is financing were able to raise funds by self-prospectus but the new Act extended this benefit to such companies as the SEBI prescribe. Now under the new Company Act, 2013, the government can specify norms for public issue for all securities.

(e) One Person Company (OPC):[200] The One Person Company is a company which has only one person as member. It is a private limited company unless otherwise specified in the Act or Rules. Only a natural person shall be eligible to incorporate a one person company. Thus a company or body corporate or foreign company or government company cannot incorporate One Person Company. Such company is entitle to all advantages of a private company. The capital raising capacity of the OPC is limited as maximum number of member is restricted to one. Thus it can accept deposits only from one member. Such Company cannot carry out Non-Banking Financial investment activities including investment in securities of any body corporate. Such company cannot voluntarily into any kind of company unless two years have expired from date of incorporation of One Person Company (OPC), except threshold limit (paid up capital) is increased beyond INR 50 lakh or its average annual turnover during the relevant period exceeds INR 2 crore.

(f) Small Companies:[201] The Small Company is a status. The Company Act, 2013, defines the small companies as the company whose paid up share capital does not exceed INR 50 lakh or such higher amount that is prescribed. However, it cannot be more than INR 5 crore; or a company whose turnover as per its last profit and loss account does not exceed INR 2 crore but a higher amount not more

199. Companies Act, 2013, s. 2(71).
200. Section 2(62) Comp. Act, 2013.
201. Section 2(85) of Comp. Act, 2013.

than INR 20 crore can be prescribed. Thus the company can be meet any of the two amount. Thus all companies like Private, One person Company or Company other than public company can be small company but this does not include public company, Holding company, subsidiary company, charitable company registered under section 8 or a company or a body corporate governed by any special Act. All liabilities which are applicable on the private company or OPC, except those who are exempted, will be applicable to a small company. A small company can enter into contractual merges without approaching the tribunal.

(g) Charitable Companies:[202] The concept of the charitable companies is retained in Company Act, 2013. Basically such companies can be incorporated for charitable objects including sports, education, research, protection of environment, etc. Such company may be private, public or one man company. The Central Government may grant a licence for incorporating a charitable company. The Government can grant exemption from using the words 'Limited', or 'Private Limited' as case may be. The New Act also permits conversion of charitable companies into the company of any other kind after complying with such conditions as may be prescribed. Such companies will also enjoy the tax benefit under the Income Tax Act, 1961.

(h) Dormant Companies:[203] Company Act, 2013 recognized a new set companies called 'Dormant Companies'. According to the Act where a company is formed and registered under this Act for a future project or to hold an asset or intellectual property and has no significant accounting transaction, such a company or an inactive company may make an application to the registrar in such manner as may be prescribed for obtaining the status of a dormant company. The registrar on consideration of the application shall allow the status of a dormant company to the applicant and issue a certificate in such form as may be prescribe to that effect.[204] If the company has not filed financial statements or annual returns for two financial years consecutively then the registrar shall issue a notice to that company and enter the name of such company in the register maintained for Dormant Company.[205] The Registrar shall strike off the name of a Dormant Company from the register of Dormant companies, which failed to comply with the requirements of the Act.[206]

172. Under the Company Act, 2013, the term 'Government company' is defined under section 2(45). The new Act has extended the concept of deemed Government company and includes all those companies which are directly or indirectly owed by government or its company. For the purpose of the Act the 'Government company' means any company in which not less than 51% of paid-up share capital is held by the Central Government, or by any State Government or Governments, or partly by the Central Government and partly by one or more State Governments, and includes

202. Section 8 of Comp. Act, 2013.
203. Section 455(1) of Comp. Act, 2013.
204. Section 455(2) of Comp. Act, 2013.
205. Section 455(4) of Comp. Act, 2013.
206. Section 455 (6) of Comp. Act, 2013.

a company which is a subsidiary company of such a Government company.[207] However, takeover of the management of a company by the central government under the provisions of the Industries Development and Regulation Act, 1951 does not have the effect of converting the company into a Government company.[208] Under the old Act, the government was empowered to modify the Act with respect to Government companies. This power was exercised and many Government companies were enjoying significant exemptions under the old Act. Now this power has been withdrawn in the new Act.

F. *Foreign Companies*

173. The term 'Foreign Company' has been defined under section 2(42) of Company Act, 2013. A foreign company means company incorporated outside India, but for the purposes of section 591, it means a company, which, though incorporated outside India, has a place of business in India. The 'place of business' has not been defined and therefore the courts have judicially construed. The court considered the extent of business, which has to be carried on to make 'a place of business' for the purpose, in that case, to establish a sufficient presence within the jurisdiction for service of process. Where a foreign company posted its representative in India only for the purpose of eliciting orders for the company's customers, that was held to be not establishing a place of business in India. The new Act requires the registration within thirty days of establishment of its place of business in India. A foreign company has to furnish the following information to the registrar:

(1) a certified copy of the charter, statutes or memorandum, articles or any instrument containing the constitution of the company;
(2) the full address of the registered or principal office of the company abroad;
(3) a list of directors of the company; in case of individuals their names, usual residential addresses, nationality of origin, business, occupation, etc.; in case of a corporate body, the particulars of its directors individually;
(4) the name and address of the person resident in India authorized to accept on behalf of the company to accept service process and other documents;
(5) full address of the office of the company in India, which is to be principal or registered place of business in India;
(6) the company shall conspicuously exhibit of every office, its name and the country of incorporation;
(7) the name and country of incorporation to appear on its letters, bill-heads, notices and other official publications of the company with inscription whether the liability of members being limited;
(8) the obligation of a foreign company in respect of accounts is almost the same as those of a company registered under the Indian Act.

207. Companies Act, 2013, s. 2(45).
208. *Kulbir Singh v. Union of India* (1997) 88 Com Cas 586 (Del).

G. Guarantee Company

174. The company limited by the guarantee may also be called a Guarantee Company. The liability of the members of a guarantee company is limited by a fixed sum which is specified in the memorandum and beyond which they cannot be called upon to contribute. Thus, the fourth clause of Memorandum of Association provides for the nature of liability.[209] If it is proposed to register the company limited by guarantee, this clause will state the amount which every member undertakes to contribute to the assets of the company in the event of its winding up. A guarantee company must include the word 'Limited' or the words 'Private Limited' as part of its name, and must register its articles and it shall adopt the provisions of the Table 'G' and 'H' of Schedule I. The Memorandum and Articles of a guarantee company not having the share capital be in Form provided in Table C of Schedule I of the Act while that of a company having share capital, should be in Form as provided in Table D. The right of a guarantee company to refuse to accept the transfer by a member of his interest in the company is on a different footing than that of a company limited by shares.[210]

H. Company Capital

175. According to Indian company law, a company makes its capital from two sources, viz., share capital and loan capital.

1. Share Capital

176. A share is not a sum of money but is the interest of the shareholder in the company measured by a sum of money for the purpose of liability and interest but also consisting of a series of mutual covenants entered by all the shareholders inter se. Share capital is not a necessary condition of incorporation. A large number of companies, however, are registered with capital rather than without capital. A company registered for carrying on business for gain is required to be registered with capital where capital is necessary. The amount stated in the memorandum is the authorized capital of the company. The amount of capital issued for public subscription is the issued capital and the amount of the issued capital subscribed by the public is the subscribed capital. The actual amount of subscribed capital received is called paid-up capital.[211] Uncalled capital of the company can be converted into reserved capital, which shall not be called except in the event of the company's winding up.

177. The Act permits only two kinds of shares to be issued,[212] viz., (1) Equity share capital,[213] that is, ordinary shares all share capital which is not preference share

209. Companies Act, 2013, s. 4 (1)(d).
210. *Narendra Kumar Agrawal v. Saroj Maloo*, (1995)6SCC 114. The court pointed out the difference in the set of articles in Sch.1 which are applicable to guarantee companies and companies limited by shares.
211. Section 2(64) of Comp. Act, 2013.
212. Private companies are exempted and, therefore, they enjoy the freedom of having any other kind also.
213. Companies Act, 2013, s. 43(a).

capital. There are two types: (a) with voting rights; or (b) with differential rights as to the dividend, voting or otherwise subject to conditions as may be prescribed. (2) Preference share capital,[214] having (a) a preferential right to take from the dividend, and (b) in the case of winding up, a company has preferential rights to be paid back, before anything is paid to the ordinary shareholders. Public limited companies can also issue cumulative convertible preference share. However, under SEBI Act, 1992 any security convertible into equity shall be subject to SEBI (Issue of Capital and Disclosure Requirements) Regulations 2009. With respect to issue of equity shares with differential voting rights, the Department of Company Affairs has notified Companies (Issue of Share Capital with Differential Voting Rights) Rules, 2001. Every share in a company having a share capital shall be distinguished by its distinctive number.[215] The New Act defined the concept of 'Employee Stock Option'(ESOP).[216] According to which the option given to directors, officers or employees of a company or of its holding company or subsidiary company or companies, if any, which gives such directors, officers or employees, the benefit or right to purchase, or to subscribe for, the shares of the company at a future date at a pre-determined price. A company, other than a listed company, which is not required to comply with SEBI's ESOP guidelines shall not offer shares to its employees under a scheme of employees stock option unless it complies with certain requirements as per Act.

178. Derivative:[217] The definition of derivative is provided under section 2(33) of Company Act, 2013. According to which 'Derivatives' means the derivative as defined in clause (ac) of section 2 of the Securities Contracts (Regulation) Act, 1956.[218] The term 'Derivative' indicates that it has no independent value, i.e., its value is entirely 'derived' from the value of the underlying asset. With Securities Laws (Second Amendment) Act, 1999, derivatives have been included in the definition of securities. The term derivative has been defined in Securities Contracts (Regulations) Act, 1956 as: (a) a security derived from a debt instrument, share, loan, whether secured or unsecured, risk instrument or contract for differences or any other form of security; (b) a contract which derives its value from the prices, or index of prices, of underlying securities.

179. Share holding: A person may become a shareholder of a company in many ways, i.e.: (a) by allotment,[219] the acceptance by the company of the offer to take shares in accordance with the requirements of the Act. A large number of shareholding is by way of allotment. (b) By transfer, i.e., in India, a share is a movable property,[220] section 2(7) of the Sale of Goods Act, 1930 defines goods to mean any kind of movable property, other than actionable claim and money and includes shares and stocks) transferable in the manner and subject to the restrictions as provided under the articles of association of the company. Articles of association of private companies contain

214. Companies Act, 2013, s. 43(b).
215. Companies Act, 2013, s. 45.
216. Section 2(37) of Comp. Act, 2013.
217. Securities Contracts (Regulation) Act, 1956, s. 2(a), (c).
218. Companies Act, 2013, s. 2(33).
219. *Shri Gopal Jalan & Co. v. Calcutta Stock Exchange*, AIR 1964 SC 250 wherein meaning of allotment was explained.
220. Companies Act, 2013, s. 44.

more rigorous restrictions on the right of transfer of shares. As per section 58(2) of Act, the securities or other interest of any member in a public company shall be freely transferable. Section 44 of the Companies Act, 2013 provides that the shareholders are free to transfer their shares in a manner prescribed by the Act and by the articles of association of the company. Section 56 of the Companies Act, 2013 requires that unless a proper instrument of transfer duly stamped and executed by or on behalf of the transferor and by or on behalf of the transferee and specifying the name, address and occupation, if any, of the transferee has been delivered to the company along with certificate relating to shares or debentures or if no such certificate is in existence, along with the letter of allotment of the shares or debentures, a company shall not register a transfer. A company shall have power to register on receipt of an intimation of transmission of any right to securities by operation of law from any person to whom such right has been transmitted.[221] Every company delivers the certificates of all securities allotted, transferred or transmitted, within a period of one month from the date of receipt by the company of the instrument of transfer or as the case may be of the intimation of transmission, in case of transfer or transmission of shares.[222] The transfer of any security or other interest of a deceased person in a company made by his legal representative shall, even if the legal representative is not a holder thereof, be valid as if he had been the holder at the time of the execution of the instrument of transfer.[223] When any default is made in complying with the provisions of section 56 of the Act, the company shall be punishable with fine which shall not be less than INR 25,000 but which may extend to INR 5 lakh and every officer of the company who is in default shall be punishable with fine which shall not be less than INR 10,000 but which may extend to INR 1 lakh.[224] Section 222(1) of the Companies Act, 2013 empowers the tribunal to impose restrictions on the transfer of any share for a period exceeding three years. Such order may be made by the tribunal either on a reference made by the Central Government in connection with investigation of the ownership of any company under section 216; or on a complaint by any person made in this behalf and there is necessity to find out the relevant facts by imposing restrictions on transfer of shares. The permission of RBI (Reserve Bank of India) is necessary for transfer of shares of a company registered in India where the transferee is a person residing outside India even though he may be Indian citizen or where the transferee is not an Indian citizen,[225] whether resident or non-resident, or where the transferee is a company in which NRI interest is more than 40%,[226] or where the transferor is a person resident outside India or is a foreign national, irrespective of the fact whether transferee is a resident of India or outside India.[227] Transmission of securities has not been defined by Companies Act, 2013. Transmission of shares takes place by operation of law when a shareholder dies or is adjudged insolvent or is lunatic or if the shareholder being a company goes into liquidation. Section 101 of the Companies Act, 2013 provides that

221. Companies Act, 2013, s. 56(2).
222. Companies Act, 2013, s. 56(4)(c).
223. Companies Act, 2013, s. 56(5).
224. Companies Act, 2013, s. 56(6).
225. Sections 19(1)(b) and 29(1)(b) of FERA (Foreign Exchange Regulation Act),1973.
226. Section 9(1)(a) of FERA (Foreign Exchange Regulation Act), 1973.
227. Section 9(5) of FERA (Foreign Exchange Regulation Act), 1973.

the legal representative of any deceased member or the assignee of an insolvent member are entitled to receive notices of general meetings of the company even though he is not registered as member.[228]

180. In India, a minor can also be allotted shares. His name may remain on the company's register of members, but during the age of minority, he incurs no liability.[229] A company being a legal person can become a shareholder in another company. It can hold shares of another company in the name of the nominee appointed for the purpose. As per section 19 of Company Act, 2013, a subsidiary company cannot become a member of its holding company. A trade union registered under the Trade Unions Act, 1926 can hold shares.[230] A partnership firm is not a legal person and as such it cannot, in its own name, become a member of a company except in company registered under section 8 of Companies Act, 2013. A non-profit making company licensed under section 8 of the Companies Act, 2013 can become a member of another company if it is authorized by its Memorandum of Association to invest into shares of the other company.

181. A person ceases to be a shareholder in a company in the event of transfer of shares, forfeiture of shares, surrender of shares or death of the shareholder and otherwise in accordance with the provisions of the company's articles of association. By virtue of section (68)(ii) of the Companies Act, 2013, the maximum number of members of a private company except in the case of One Person Company is limited to Two Hundred excluding the present and past employees of the company who continue to be members of the company. There is no restriction with regard to the Maximum number of members of a public company.

182. Every company in India is bound to keep a register of shareholders containing information as to the name, address and occupation of each shareholder, number of shares held by each shareholder, date on which his name was entered into the register and date on which any person ceased to be a shareholder in the company.[231] Section 94 of the Companies Act, 2013 fixes the place for maintaining a company's registers, returns, etc. and for allowing their inspection.

183. Share capital may be divided into preference and ordinary shares. Rights attached to one class of shares may be different from those attached to the other class. The share capital of a company limited by shares shall be of two kinds only, namely: equity share capital with voting rights; or equity share capital with differential rights as to dividend, voting as otherwise in accordance with such rules and subject to such conditions as may be prescribed and other one is preference share capital.[232] Every member of a company limited by shares and holding equity share capital therein shall have a right to vote on every resolution placed before the company and his voting right on a poll shall be in proportion to his share in the paid-up equity share capital of the

228. Companies Act, 2013, s. 101(3)(a).

229. *Palaniappa v. Official Liquidator*, AIR 1942 Mad 470.

230. *All India Bank Officers Confederation v. Dhanlakshmi Bank Ltd.* (1997) 90 Com Cas 225.

231. Under s. 88, every company is bound to maintain such register, otherwise there is provision of fine Which shall not be less than INR 50,000 but which may extend to INR 3 lakh and where the failure continuing one, with a further fine which may extend to INR 1,000 for every day, after the first during which the failure continues.

232. Companies Act, 2013, s. 43.

company.[233] Where a share capital of the company is divided into different classes of shares, the right attached to the shares of any class may be varied with the consent in writing of the holders of not less than three-fourths of the issued shares of that class or by means of a special resolution passed at a separate meeting of the holders of the issued shares of that class if the provision with respect to such variation is contained in the memorandum or articles of the company; or if such variation is not prohibited by the terms of issue of the shares of that class.[234]

184. Alteration of capital: A limited company with share capital may alter the structure of its share capital in the following ways:[235]

(1) by increasing the share capital by issuing new shares;
(2) by consolidating the whole or any part of the share capital into shares of a larger amount;
(3) by converting shares into stocks or *vice versa*;
(4) by sub-dividing the whole or any part of its share capital into smaller amounts;
(5) by cancelling unallotted shares and reducing the capital accordingly. Such cancellation of shares shall not be deemed to be reduction of share capital within the meaning of the Act.

185. A company limited by shares or a guarantee company having share capital may reduce its share capital by a special resolution. The reduction of capital has then to be confirmed by the court. The company may reduce its share capital in the following ways:[236]

(1) extinguish or reduce the liability on any of its shares in respect of share capital not paid-up;
(2) by cancelling any paid-up share capital, which is lost or is unrepresented by any available assets;
(3) by paying off any paid-up capital which is in excess.

186. Under the section 62 of the Company Act, 2013 a company can at any time by passing an ordinary resolution at its general meeting resolve to increase its capital by such amount as it thinks expedient by issuing new shares. A company may increase its capital by allotment of new shares or by conversion of debentures or loans into shares. By the amendment of 1963 the central government has taken a new power of converting into shares any debentures issued to or loan taken from the government by a company.[237] The power is to be exercised only if such conversion appears to be necessary in the public interest. Regard shall be given to the financial position of the company, the original terms of issue, the rate of interest, the capital of the company, its liabilities, its reserves, its profits during the preceding five years and the current market value of the company's shares. The government must exercise the power at a

233. Companies Act, 2013, s. 47(1).
234. Companies Act, 2013, s. 48(1).
235. Companies Act, 2013, s. 61.
236. Companies Act, 2013, s. 66(1).
237. Companies Act, 2013, s. 62(3).

time when it will not cause undue violent fluctuations in the market value of shares. If the terms and conditions proposed by the government are not acceptable to the company, it may within sixty days prefer an appeal to the tribunal and the decision of the tribunal shall be final.

187. In a certain sense, they are also the trustees of the company,[238] in respect of their powers to apply funds and property of the company and where there is a misuse of their powers, they can be held liable as a trustee, and on their death, their legal representatives. Directors are sometimes described as managing partners because like partners of a firm, they manage the affairs of the company and they usually hold a large shareholding in the company. They are not the servants of the company. They can, however, work as an employee in a different capacity, e.g., manager, secretary or financial advisors to the company.[239] Where the affairs of a company were manipulated as to deprive a shareholder of his sizable amount of rights shares, the remedy open to him is before the Company Law Board and not before the High Court. The company court would not as a general rule interfere with internal management of a company. It is for the board of directors to decide the manner in which the affairs of the company are to be carried on. Courts determine questions of law and not questions of business management. The company court shall not interfere with the lawful decision of the board of directors of a company. Even a commercial misjudgment would not amount to oppression or mismanagement. The board of directors may err, every error cannot be a ground for action and the company court is not a correctional court for all errors.[240]

2. Appointment of Directors

188. Section 149(1) provides that every public company (other than a public company which has become such by virtue of section 43A) must have at least three directors, every private company must have at least two directors and one director in case of a One Person Company. A company can appoint maximum fifteen directors but the company may appoint more than fifteen directors after passing passing a special resolution in general meeting and approval of Central Government is not required. A period of one year has been provided to enable the companies existing on or before the commencement of Companies Act, 2013 to comply with requirement. Maximum number of directorships, including any alternate directorship a person can hold is twenty.[241] Any person holding office as a director in more than twenty or ten companies as the case may be before the commencement of this Act shall, a period of one year from such commencement, have to choose companies where he wishes to continue or resign as director and intimate his choice to concerned company as well as concerned registrar Company Act, 2013 mandates the appointment of independent directors by listed companies and other class of companies. It also prescribes the aspects such as maximum tenure of independent directors, separate meeting of independent directors,

---

238. *Kuriakos v. P.K.V. Group Industries* (2002) III Com Cas 826 Ker.

239. *Ramaswamy Iyer v. Brahmayya & Co.*, (1966) 1 Comp LJ 107S.

240. *Cochin Malabar Estates And Industries Ltd. And Anr. v. P.V. Abdul Khader And Anr.* (2003) 114 Com Cas 777 Ker: 2003 45 SCL 170 Ker.

241. Section 165 of Comp. Act, 2013.

tenure, their qualifications, liability, appointment, remuneration and other aspects.[242] Such independent director will be the director other than a managing director or a whole time director or a nominee director, who in opinion of the board, is a person of integrity and possess relevant expertise and experience and who is or was not promoter of the company or its holding, subsidiary or associate company and who has not no pecuniary relationship or transaction with the company. Every listed public company shall have at least one-third of the total number of directors as independent directors and Central Government may prescribe the minimum number of independent directors in case of any class or classes of public companies.[243] Chapter XII provides that an independent director shall possess appropriate skills, experience and knowledge in the field of finance, law, management, sales, marketing, administration, research, corporate governance, technical operations or other disciplines related to company's business. The Company Act, 2013 first time mandates the appointment of at least one Women Director in certain classes of companies like every Listed company, every Public Company having paid-up share capital of INR 100 or more; or turnover of INR 300 crore or more.

189. The success of a company depends, to a large extent, upon the competence and integrity of its directors. It is, therefore, necessary that management of companies should be in proper hands.[244] There are special provisions for preventing management by undesirable persons. Every person proposed to be appointed as a director shall furnish his Direct Identification Number and a declaration that he is not disqualified to become a director under the Act. The Central Government shall, within one month from the receipt of the application under section 153, allot the DIN to an applicant.[245] No individual shall apply for or obtain or possess another DIN who has already been allotted a DIN under section 154.[246] Every company shall, within fifteen days of receipt if intimation under section 156, furnish the DIN of all its director to the Registrar or authorized officer by the Central Government, every such intimation shall be furnished in such form and manner as may be prescribed.[247] If the company fails to furnish DIN under section 157(1), before the expiry of the 270 days period from the date by which it should have been furnished with additional fee, the company shall be punishable with fine which shall not be less than INR 25,000 but which may extend to INR 1,00,000.

190. Section 2(34) of the Company Act, 2013 prescribed that 'Director' means a director appointed to the Board of a company. The appointment of directors is accordingly strictly regulated by the Act. According to section 149, only an individual can be appointed as a director. Thus according to the new Act no company or a firm can act as director. Every company is to have a Board of directors consisting of individuals as directors.[248] The Rule 4 of Companies (Appointment and Qualification of Directors) rules 2014, provides that the public companies having paid up share

242. Section 149(6) of Comp. Act, 2013.
243. Section 149(4) of Comp. Act, 2013.
244. *Indian States Bank Ltd. v. Kunwar Sardar Singh*, AIR 1034 All 855.
245. Companies Act, 2013, s. 154.
246. Companies Act, 2013, s. 155.
247. Companies Act, 2013, s.157(1).
248. Companies Act, 2013, s. 149.

capital of INR 10 crore or higher, the public companies having turnover of INR 100 crore, public companies which have, in aggregate, outstanding loans, debentures and deposits, exceeding INR 50 crore.

191. The concept of 'Qualification Shares' has been dropped by Company Act, 2013.

192. The general power of appointment, no doubt, is vested in the general meeting of shareholders. There are other cases when the board can also appoint new directors.

193. Right to increase the number of directors: A company may increase the number of directors by passing an ordinary resolution at a general meeting. The increase, however, shall not exceed the limits fixed by the articles of the company. Second, an increase shall not have any effect unless approved by the central government. Approval of the central government is not necessary, in cases: (1) a company in existence on 21 July 1951, for an increase which was within the permissible maximum under its articles as in force on that date; (2) in the case of other companies an increase which is within the permissible maximum under the articles of a company as first registered; (3) Where permissible maximum is twelve or less and the proposed increase does not make the total number of directors more than twelve. However, this provision is not applicable to a private company unless it is a subsidiary of a public company. Increase would require approval of the central government.[249] An agreement among groups of shareholders not to increase the number of directors and capital of the company and also not to do anything disturbing the existing pattern of management was held to be not binding on the company so as to prevent it from doing any of those things.[250]

3. Qualification of Directors

194. Share Qualifications: Articles of a company may require certain number of shares to be held by each director. Such shares are called the qualification shares. A director is required to acquire the required number of shares within two months of his appointment. There is no compulsion to have those required number of shares before his appointment as director. The value of the qualification shares cannot exceed INR 5,000 except when the nominal value of a single share exceeds that amount. In case a director fails to acquire qualification shares within prescribed period, his office falls vacant[251] and he is liable to a penalty, if he continues to act as the director. The Company Act, 2013 provides that residence of a director must be in India for a total period of not less than 182 days in previous calendar year.[252]

4. Disqualifications of Directors

195. Section 164[253] lays down the minimum eligibility requirements. A person is not capable of being appointed a director in the following cases:

249. *Vinod Kumar Mittal v. Kaveri LimeIndustries Ltd.*(2000)2 Comp LJ 154 CLB.
250. *Rolta India (P) Ltd. v. Venire Industries Ltd.* (2000) 100 Com Cas 19.
251. *Coal Products v. R.A. Jalan*, (1968) 1 ComL J 311.
252. Section 149(2) of Comp. Act, 2013.
253. Companies Act, 2013.

i. where he is of unsound mind as certified by a court of competent jurisdiction;
ii. where he is an undischarged insolvent;
iii. where he has applied to be adjudicated as an insolvent;
iv. where he has been sentenced to at least six months of imprisonment for an offence involving moral turpitude and five years have not elapsed from the date of the expiry of the sentence;
v. where he has not paid for six months any call of his shares;
vi. where he has been disqualified under section 203 of the Act of the purpose of preventing fraudulent persons from managing companies;
vii. he has not paid any calls in respect of any shares of companies held by him, whether alone or jointly with others, and six month elapsed from the last day fixed for the call;
viii. he has been convicted of the offence dealing with related party transactions under section 188 at any time during the last preceding five years; or he has not got the DIN;
ix. where such a person is already a director of public company.

5. Remuneration to the Directors

196. The Companies Act, 2013 has brought important changes in respect of remuneration of directors. Section 197 of the Companies Act, 2013 prescribed the maximum ceiling for payment of remuneration by public company to its managing director, whole-time director and manager which shall not exceed 11% of the net profit of the company in that financial year computed in accordance with section 198 except the remuneration of the directors shall not be deducted from the gross profits.[254] The company in general meeting may, with approval of the Central Government, authorize the payment of remuneration exceeding 11% of the net profits of the company, subject to the provisions of Schedule V.[255] The remuneration payable to any one managing director; or whole-time director or manager shall not exceed 5% of the net profits of the company and if there is more than one such director remuneration shall not exceed 10% of the net profit to all such directors and manager taken together.[256] The remuneration payable to directors who are neither managing directors nor whole-time directors shall not exceed 1%. of the net profits of the company, if there is a managing or whole-time director or manager,[257] 3% of the net profits in any other case.[258] A director or manager may be paid remuneration either by way of a monthly payment or at a specified percentage of the net profits of the company or partly by one way and partly by the other.[259] An independent director is not to be entitle to any stock option and may receive remuneration by way of fees provided under subsection (5) of section 197, reimbursement of expenses for participation in the Board and other meetings and profits related

254. Companies Act, 2013, s. 197(1).
255. Companies Act, 2013, s. 197(1).
256. Companies Act, 2013, s. 197(1)(i).
257. Companies Act, 2013, s. 197(1(ii)(A)).
258. Companies Act, 2013, s. 197(1)(ii)(B).
259. Companies Act, 2013, s. 197(6).

commission as may be approved by the members.[260] If any director draws or receives, directly or indirectly, by way of remuneration any sums in excess of the limit prescribed or without the prior sanction of the Central Government, where it is required, he shall refund such sums to the company and until such sum is refunded, hold it in trust for the company.[261] Section 198 of the Act lays downs the manner of calculations of net profits of a company in any financial year for the purpose of section 197. Subsection (2) specifies the sums for which credit shall be given and subsection (3) specifies the sums for which credit shall not be given while calculating the net profit.

197. The following shall not include in the 11%:

(i) any fee that may be payable to directors for attending meetings or the board or of committees of the board;

(ii) payment of guarantee commission to directors on their guarantees for the company's loans is not a part of the remuneration so as to require government approval;

(iii) any commission or other remuneration payable to any officer or employee (other than directors) or a manager of the company is fixed by way of percentage or otherwise based on the net profits of the.

198. It is a rule of equity that a director who is having a fiduciary relationship with the company cannot enter into any transaction, which would conflict with the company's interest. Directors and key managerial personnel are prohibited from buying in the company, or in its holding, subsidiary or associate company a right to call for delivery or right to make delivery at a specified price and within a specified time, of a specified number of relevant shares or a specified amount of relevant debentures, or a right, as he may elect, to call for delivery or to make delivery at a specified price and within a specified time, of a specified number of relevant shares or a specified amount of relevant debentures.[262] If they contravene the provisions of section 194 they shall be punished with imprisonment for a term which may extend two years or with fine which shall not be less than INR 1 lakh but which may extend to INR 5 lakh, or with both.

199. Directors of the company exercise most of their powers in the board meetings. The Company Act, 2013 provides for the meetings of Board.[263] It provides that the first Board meeting should be held within thirty days of the date of incorporation.

200. The board of directors is the working organ of the company. Some powers are specially reserved for the Board, e.g., appointing directors in casual vacancies, appointing officers including CS, CEO, CFO and determine their remuneration, the power to issue debentures, to constitute the committee and select its members, to provide the direction to the company, etc. Board can take temporary loans without the approval from the shareholders. It can also grant political contribution upto 7.5% of the average net profit. It oversees the management of the company and also act as advisory Board.

260. Companies Act, 2013, s. 197(7).
261. Companies Act, 2013, s. 197(9).
262. Section 194 of Comp. Act, 2013.
263. Companies Act, 2013, s. 173.

201. The Companies Act, 2013 aside from powers and duties, imposes civil and criminal liabilities on the directors. Civil liabilities towards a company arises as a result of negligence, misfeasance, breach of trust and for ultra virus. Under section 195 of the Company Act, 2013 the insider trading is strictly prohibited. If any person contravenes the provision of section 195 and communicate or procure directly or indirectly any non-public price-sensitive information to any person, he shall be punishable with imprisonment for a term which may extend to five years or with fine which shall not be less than INR 5 lakh but which may extend to INR 25 crore or three times the amount of profits made out of insider trading, whichever is higher, or with both.

6. Other Managerial Personnel

202. The Companies Act, 2013 has first time recognized the concept of Key Managerial Personnel As per the section 2(51) 'Key Managerial Personnel', in relation to a company means the Chief Executive Officer or the Managing Director or Manager, Company Secretary, Whole-time director, Chief Financial officer and such officer as may be prescribed. Chapter XIII of the Company Act, 2013 read with Companies (Appointment and Remuneration of Managerial Personnel) Rules, 2014 deal with the legal and procedural aspects of appointment of Key Managerial Personnel. The Board of Directors is a representative body of the company, which directs and controls its affairs. A day-to-day administration has to be delegated to professional management.

203. A 'managing director' is a director who, by virtue of the articles of the company or an agreement with the company or a resolution passed in its general meeting, or by its Board of Directors, is entrusted with substantial powers of management of the affairs of the company and includes a director occupying the position of managing director, by whatever name called. The 'substantial powers' of management may be conferred upon him by virtue of an agreement with the company, or by a resolution of the company or the Board or by virtue of its memorandum and articles.[264] Section 2(94) of the Companies Act, 2013 defines 'Whole-Time Director' as a director in the whole-time employment of the company. A 'Manager' is an individual who, subject to the superintendence, control and direction of the Board of Director, has the management of the whole, or substantially the whole, of the affairs of a company, and includes a director or any other person occupying the position of a manager, by whatever name called, whether under a contract of service or not.[265] Section 196 of Company Act, 2013 provides that no company shall appoint or employ at the same time a Managing Director and a Manager. Further, a company shall not appoint or reappoint any person as its Managing Director, Whole Time Director or Manager for a term exceeding five years at a time and no reappointment shall be made earlier than one year before the expiry of his term. Section 196(4) of the Comp. Act, 2013 provides that subject to the provisions of section 197 and Schedule V, managing director, whole-time director or manager shall be appointed and terms and conditions of such appointment and remuneration payable be approved by the Board of directors at a meeting which shall be subject to approval by a resolution at the next general meeting of the company and

264. Avtar Singh, *Company Act* 332 (16th ed., Eastern Book Company 2015).
265. Companies Act, 2013, s. 2(53).

by the Central Government in case such appointment is at variance to the conditions specified in Schedule V. A company shall file a return of appointment of a Managing Director, Whole-Time Director or Manager, Chief Executive Officer (CEO), Company Secretary and Chief Financial Officer (CFO) within sixty days of the appointment with the Registrar in Form No. MR. 1 along with such fee as may be specified for this purpose.[266] An important difference between the position of a managing director and that of a manager is that the managing director is a part of the company board and not subordinate to it, whereas a manager is a paid executive of the company subject to the overall control of the board of directors. Section 196 of Company Act, 2013 provides that no company shall appoint or employ at the same time a Managing Director and a Manager. Further a company shall not appoint or reappoint any person as its Managing Director, Whole Time Director or Manager for a term exceeding five years at a time and no reappointment shall be made earlier than one year before the expiry of his term. Section 196(3) of the Company Act, 2013 provides the prohibitory provision with regard to the appointment of managing director, whole-time director or manager. It lays down that no company shall appoint or continue the employment of any person as its managing director, whole-time director or manager who:

(a) is below the age of twenty-one years or has attained the age of seventy years, provided that appointment of a person who has attained the age of seventy years may be made by passing a special resolution in which case the explanatory statement annexed to the notice for such motion shall indicate the justification for appointing such person; or
(b) is an undischarged insolvent or has anytime been adjudged as an insolvent; or
(c) has at any time suspended payment to his creditors, or makes, or has at any time made, a composition with them; or
(d) has at anytime been, convicted by a court of an offence and sentenced for a period of more than six months.

7. 'Sole Selling Agent'

204. The term 'Sole Selling Agent' has not been defined in Companies Act, 2013. The appointment and terms of a sole selling agent are regulated by section 188 of the Companies Act, 2013. The company may appoint a sole selling agent for any area by approval of a special resolution in the general meeting if the proposed sole selling agent does not have substantial interest in the company. Within thirty days of passing of the resolution a copy of the resolution and the Explanatory Statement annexed to the notice for the general meeting is to be filed with the concerned Registrar of Companies with the required fee as prescribed. The section 188 does not prohibit the reappointment or extension of the term of any sole selling agent. There is no need for approval of the Central Government in the appointment of sole selling agent under the Companies Act, 2013 nor the Central Government has any power of investigation under the Act. The Act does not specify any limit of the remuneration payable to the sole selling agents.

266. Rule 3 of Companies (Appointment and Remuneration of Managerial personnel) Rules, 2014.

8. Protection of Investors' Interest

205. Protection of investors' interest is one of the primary themes of the Companies Act, 2013. The Companies Act provides the shareholders a forum of protection and leaves them to a large extent to care for them. The Companies Act, 1956 contained provisions relating to statutory meeting and statutory report under section 165 of the said Act but this section has been omitted in the Companies Act, 2013 and therefore, there is no provision for statutory meeting under the new Act. Chapter VII of the new Act deals with management and administration and covers all the provisions relating to convening, constituting and conducting of general meetings of a company. Under the new Act, the concept of electronic voting has been introduced. The procedure for the e-voting shall be determined by the Central Government. The meeting of members of a company may be categorized into two broad heads, namely: (1) General meeting; and (2) Class meetings. General Meeting signifies any meeting in which all those members of a company who have a right to vote are entitled to attend. The General meeting is further divided into two kinds, namely: (a) Annual General Meeting; (b) Extraordinary General Meeting. A General meeting of a company may be called by giving not less than twenty-one days' notice either in writing or through electronic mode and a general meeting may be called after giving a shorter notice, if consent is given in writing or electronic mode by not less than 95% of the members entitled to vote at such meeting.[267] Every company, whether public or private, has to hold a periodical general meeting of its members annually for the purpose of transacting its routine ordinary business. Such meeting is called the 'Annual General Meeting'. Every company other than one person company must, in each year, hold an Annual General Meeting and shall specify the meeting as such in the notices calling it, and not more than fifteen months shall elapsed between the date of one annual general meeting of a company and that of next.[268] It is also provided that first Annual general meeting, should be held within a period of nine months from the date of closing of the first financial year of the company and in other case, within a period of six months, from the date of closing of the financial year.[269] Every annual general meeting shall be called during business hours, that is, between 9 a.m. and 6 p.m. on any day that is not a National Holiday either at the registered office of the company or at some other place within city, town or village in which the registered office of the company is situated.[270] The business to be transacted at an Annual General Meeting of a company has been classified into two heads, namely: (1) Ordinary Business; and (2) Special Business.[271] All business to be transacted shall be deemed to be Special, other than the consideration of financial statements, reports of Board of Directors, declaration of dividend, appointment of directors in place of those retiring, appointment of, and the fixing of the remuneration of, the auditor.[272] Clause 42 of Table F (Schedule 1) provides that all general meeting other than annual meetings shall be known as extraordinary

267. Companies Act, 2013, s. 101.
268. Companies Act, 2013, s. 96(1).
269. Companies Act, 2013, s. 96(1) proviso.
270. Companies Act, 2013, s. 96(2).
271. Companies Act, 2013, s. 102.
272. Companies Act, 2013, s. 102(2).

general meetings. Section 100 of the Companies Act, 2013 provides for calling of extra ordinary general meeting. Extraordinary meetings may either be called by the Board of Directors voluntarily or on the requisition of a specified number of members. The requisition must be signed by holders of at least one-tenth paid-up capital of the company having the right to vote on the matter of requisition.[273] The meeting can be called by giving not less than twenty-one days' notice in writing by the requisitionists and the meeting should be actually held within forty-five days from the date of requisition.[274] The Articles of a company may provide that certain matters affecting the interests of the holders of a particular class of shares shall be subject to the consideration and decision of a meeting of those holders only. Such meetings are called 'Class Meeting'. An extraordinary general meeting may be convened by the Board of Directors or by the directors on requisition of the shareholder, or Company Law Tribunal. Class meetings of shareholders of different classes of shares are also held where a company has more than one class of shares, for the reason that different classes of shares have different kinds of interest in the company. Directors' meetings include: (a) board meetings; and (b) committee meetings. Meetings of the creditors and debenture holders are usually held: (a) during the lifetime of the company; and (b) on the winding up of the company.

206. A valid meeting can be called by proper authority through a proper notice. For the conduct of business at a meeting, required quorum must be present and the meeting should be held by the chairman, who shall be elected by the members themselves. The court also has power to appoint an independent chairman to preside over a meeting of a company in a case of dispute.[275]

207. The business of the meeting is done in the form of resolutions passed at the meeting through votes. Voting right means the right of a member of a company to vote in any meeting of the company or by means of postal ballot.[276] Every holder of equity shares has the right to vote.[277] Under the New Act a company cannot prohibit any member from exercising his voting right on the ground that he has not held his shares for specified period before the meeting or on any other ground.[278] The only ground on which the right to vote may be excluded is non-payment of calls by a member or other sums due against a member or where the company has exercised the right of lien on his shares.[279] A preference shareholders has the right to vote only on resolution which directly affect the rights attached to preference shares.[280] An insolvent shareholder is entitled to exercise the right to vote provided his name appears on the register of members and no payment is due against him. The official receiver, however, should have his name first entered in the register of members and only then does he become eligible to vote. Every listed company or a company having five hundred or more

273. Companies Act, 2013, s. 100(2).
274. Companies Act, 2013, s. 100(4).
275. *Swadeshi Chemicals Ltd. v. Kothari Industrial Corpn. Ltd.* (1995), 18 Corpt L A 23 Mad.
276. Companies Act, 2013, s. 2(93).
277. Companies Act, 2013, s. 47.
278. Companies Act, 2013, s. 106, *A. Ananthalakshmi Ammal v. Hindustan Investment and Financial Trust*, AIR 1951 Mad 927.
279. Companies Act, 2013, s. 106(1).
280. Companies Act, 2013, s. 47.

shareholders may provide to its members facility to exercise their right to vote at general meetings by electronic means, a member may exercise his right to vote at any general meeting by electronic means and company may pass any resolution by electronic voting system.[281] The central government may prescribe the class or classes of companies also the manner in which a member may exercise his right to vote by electronic means.[282] The voting right of a member on a poll shall be in proportion to his share of the paid-up equity capital of the company.[283] A member may vote either in person or by proxy. But unless the articles of association otherwise provide, a proxy shall not be allowed to vote except on a poll.[284] Section 110 of Act provides the passing of resolution by postal ballot.[285] Section 2(65) of Act provides that postal ballot means voting by post or through any electronic mode. The President of India or the Governor of a State, if he is a member of a company, may appoint such person, as he thinks fit, to act as a representative at any meeting of the company or at any meeting of any class of members of the company.[286] Where a company or a corporation is a member of another company, it may attend the meeting of the other company a representative and such representative must be appointed be a resolution of the Board of Directors or the other Board of directors or the other governing body.[287]

208. Decisions of the company are made by resolutions of its members passed at meetings. Resolutions are of two kinds viz. (1) ordinary resolutions; (2) special resolution.[288] A resolution is said to ordinary when the votes cast in favour of it at a general meeting of a company exceeds the votes, if any, cast against the resolution. Thus such resolution is passed by a simple majority of shareholders present and voting. While the special resolution requires the support of three-forth majority of shareholders present and entitled to vote at a meeting. A typed or printed copy of every resolution must be registered with the Registrar within thirty days of its date.[289] The Company Act, 2013 clearly mentioned the rights of shareholders and Board of directors. A company takes its decision by majority of members of the company. Therefore, the majority of members enjoy the supreme authority to exercise the power of the company and the minority of the shareholders have to concede to the majority decision. There may be possibility that the members having majority vote may tend to be oppressive towards the minority shareholders by misusing their powers and this may result in the mismanagement in the company. With the view to protecting the rights of minority shareholders and safeguard the interests of the investors from oppressive decisions of the majority shareholders, adequate provisions are provided in the Company Act, 2013 for controlling the misuse of powers by majority shareholders. These provisions are incorporated in sections 241–243 of the Company Act, 2013.

281. Section 108 of Comp. Act, 2013.
282. Companies Act, 2013, s. 108.
283. Companies Act, 2013, s. 47(1)(b).
284. Companies Act, 2013, s. 105.
285. Companies Act.
286. Companies Act, 2013, s. 112(1).
287. Companies Act, 2013, ss 112, 113.
288. Companies Act, 2013, s. 114.
289. Companies Act, 2013, s. 117(1).

I. Winding Up of a Company

209. A company is brought into existence by a legal process and when for any reason, it desires to end its existence, it must again do so by way of a legal process. In India, the Companies Act distinguishes between dissolution of a company and the winding up of a company. Dissolution means the existence of the company is put to an end. On the dissolution of the company, the company is no more in existence, and its name is struck off from the register of companies, whereas the winding of a company is a process of putting an end to the life of a company. It is a proceeding by means of which a company is dissolved. Thus, in between the winding up and dissolution, the legal status of the company continues and has corporate powers until dissolution.[290] Winding up is the first stage in the process whereby assets are realised, liabilities are paid off and the surplus, if any, distributed among its members while the dissolution is the final stage whereby the existence of the company is ended by the law. Dissolution is brought by any of the following methods: (a) by removal of the name of the company from the Register when it becomes a defunct company under section 248; (b) by an order of the court, without winding up, under a scheme of arrangement as provided by section 241; (c) by winding up when the purpose of the company has been accomplished or may have become impossible or in the event of insolvency or liquidation of the company. There are two kinds of winding up orders under the Companies Act, viz., (1) compulsory winding up by the Tribunal as initiated by petition to the Tribunal; (2) voluntary winding up initiated by a resolution of the company. The Company Act, 2013, does not acknowledge the distinction between member's voluntary winding up and creditor's voluntary winding up.

210. A company may be wound up by an order of the Tribunal.[291] This is called a compulsory winding up. Circumstances under which a company may be wound up by Tribunal are stated in section 271. They are as follows: (a) company is unable to pay its debts; (b) if the company has, by special resolution, resolved that the company be wound up by the Tribunal; (c) if the company has acted against the interests of the sovereignty and integrity of India, the security of the state, friendly relations with foreign states, public order, decency or morality; (d) if the Tribunal has orders the winding up of the company under Chapter XIX; (e) if the tribunal is of the opinion that the affairs of the company have been conducted in a fraudulent manner or the company was formed for fraudulent and unlawful purpose or the persons concerned in the formation or management of its affairs have been guilty of fraud, misfeasance or misconduct in connection therewith and that it is proper that the company be wound up; (f) default in filing profit and loss account, financial statements or annual returns for immediately preceding five consecutive financial years; or (g) for just and equitable reason.[292]

211. Every company shall file a statement of affairs with the tribunal along with the petition for winding up.[293] A petition may be presented under section 272 by any of the following persons: (a) the company; (b) any creditor or creditor, including any

290. *Hari Prasad Jayantalal & Co. v. I.T.O. Ahmedabad* 1966 Comp LJ 320.
291. Companies Act, 2013, s. 271.
292. Companies Act, 2013, s. 271(1)(a)(b)(c)(d)(e)(f)(g).
293. Companies Act, 2013, s. 272.

contingent or prospective creditor or creditors; (c) any contributory or contributories; (d) all or any of the parties specified above in clauses (a), (b), (c) together; (e) the registrar; (f) any person authorized by the Central Government in that behalf; (g) by the Central Government or State Government in case falling under clause (c) of section 271(1) i.e., the company is against the interest of the sovereignty and integrity of India. On a winding up order being made in respect of a company by the tribunal, the tribunal shall forthwith notify the official liquidator and the registrar. On the receipt of a petition for winding up of a company under section 272, the Tribunal may pass order either to dismiss the petition with costs; or make any interim order as it deems necessary; or appoint a Provisional Liquidator of the company till the making up of a winding up order; or any other order as it thinks fit.[294]

212. Dissolution of company by Tribunal:[295]

(1) When the affairs of a company have been completely wound up, the Company Liquidator shall make an application to the Tribunal for dissolution of such company.
(2) The Tribunal shall on an application filed by the Company Liquidator under subsection (1) or when the Tribunal is of the opinion that it is just and reasonable in the circumstances of the case that an order for the dissolution of the company should be made, make an order that the company be dissolved from the date of the order, and the company shall be dissolved accordingly.
(3) A copy of the order shall, within thirty days from the date thereof, be forwarded by the Company Liquidator to the Registrar who shall record in the register relating to the company a minute of the dissolution of the company.
(4) If the Company Liquidator makes a default in forwarding a copy of the order within the period specified in subsection (3), the Company Liquidator shall be punishable with fine which may extend to INR 5,000 for every day during which the default continues. Arrest of person trying to leave India or abscond.

It has been further provided that tribunal may declare the dissolution of company void if:[296]

(1) Where a company has been dissolved, whether in pursuance of this Chapter or of section 232 or otherwise, the Tribunal may at any time within two years of the date of the dissolution, on application by the Company Liquidator of the company or by any other person who appears to the Tribunal to be interested, make an order, upon such terms as the Tribunal thinks fit, declaring the dissolution to be void, and thereupon such proceedings may be taken as if the company had not been dissolved.
(2) It shall be the duty of the Company Liquidator or the person on whose application the order was made, within thirty days after the making of the order or such further time as the Tribunal may allow, to file a certified copy of the order with the Registrar who shall register the same, and if the Company Liquidator or the person

294. Companies Act, 2013, s. 273.
295. Companies Act, 2013, s. 302.
296. Companies Act, 2013, s. 356.

fails so to do, the Company Liquidator or the person shall be punishable with fine which may extend to INR 10,000 for every day during which the default continues.

213. Voluntary winding up of a company is entirely different from the compulsory winding up. Section 304 of the Companies Act, 2013 provides that a company may be voluntarily wound up. In voluntary winding up, the members of the company, instead of presenting a petition to the tribunal for winding up of the company, pass a resolution in the general meeting that the company should be winding up. The object of voluntary winding up is to leave company and its creditors free to settle their affairs without going to Tribunal, although they may apply to the tribunal for directions or orders if and when necessary.[297] The Company Act, 2013 has abolished the distinction between members' voluntary winding up and creditors; winding up. The requirement now is that after members meeting for winding up a meeting of creditors must also be called. A meeting of the creditors of the company shall be convened either on the day when the meeting of the company is convened under section 304 or on the next day. The notice of the meeting shall be sent by registered post to the creditors with the notice of the member's meeting requiring the company to be wind up under section 304.[298] A list of creditors with the estimated amount of claim, a copy of declaration that the company is not being wind up to defraud any person any person and full statement of the position of affairs of the company shall be presented by the Board. One of the directors, as appointed by the Board, shall preside at the meeting.[299] If two-third in the value of creditors of the company are of the opinion that it is in the interest of all parties that the company be wind up voluntarily, the company's voluntary winding up is to proceed. If they are of opinion that the company may not be able to pay its debts from the proceeds of its assets sold in voluntary winding up. In such case they may pass a resolution to wind up the company by the tribunal. If such resolution is passed the company shall within fourteen days thereafter file an application before the tribunal.[300] The notice of any resolution passed at the meeting of the creditors in pursuance of section 306 shall be given by the company to the Registrar within ten days of the passing of the resolution.[301] If a company contradicts the provision of section 306, it shall be punishable with fine which shall not be less than INR 50,000 but which may extend to INR 2 lakh and director of the company who in default shall be punishable with imprisonment for a term which may extend to six months or with fine which shall not be less than INR 50,000 but which may extend to INR 2 lakh or with both.[302] The general meeting at which a resolution for voluntary winding up is passed, a company liquidator has to be appointed from the penal prepared by the central government for winding up the company's affairs and distribute its assets and recommend the fee to be paid to the company liquidator.[303] In case a resolution has been passed

297. Companies Act, 2013, s. 322.
298. Companies Act, 2013, s. 306(1).
299. Companies Act, 2013, s. 306(2).
300. Companies Act, 2013, s. 306(3).
301. Companies Act, 2013, s. 306(4).
302. Companies Act, 2013, s. 306(5).
303. Companies Act, 2013, s. 310(1).

by the creditors under section 306(3) the appointment of company liquidator will need to be approved by the majority of the creditors in value. Where such creditors do not approve the appointment, the creditors have to appoint another company liquidator.[304] They have also to pass a suitable resolution fixing the fee of the company liquidator.[305] On appointment as company liquidator, such liquidator shall file a declaration in the prescribed form within seven days of the date of appointment disclosing conflicts of interest or lack of independence in respect of his appointment, if any, with the company and the creditors and such obligation shall continue throughout the term of his appointment.[306] The powers to remove and fill the vacancy of company liquidator are contained in section 311 of the Company Act, 2013, that a company liquidator appointed under section 310 may be removed by the company where his appointment has been made be removed by the company where his appointment has been made by the company where his appointment has been made by the company and, by the creditors where he is appointed by creditors with their approval.[307] The company liquidator proposed to be removed is entitles to receive a notice in writing stating the grounds of his removal. On receipt of his reply to the notice, the removal shall require resolution passed with consent of three-fourth of creditors in value to give effect.[308] If the vacancy occurs by death, resignation, removal or otherwise in the office of any company liquidator appointed under section 310, the company or creditor may fill the vacancy in a manner specified in section 310 of the Company Act, 2013.[309] The company must give the notice to the registrar regarding the appointment of a company liquidator within ten days of his appointment.[310] In case of contravention with these requirements render the company and every officer of the company who is in default shall be punishable with fine which may extend to INR 500 for every day till the default continues.[311] The company liquidator shall perform such functions and discharge such duties as may be decided from time to time by the company or the creditors, as the case may be.[312] Liquidator shall settle the list of contributories.[313] The liquidator shall prepare the quarterly statement of accounts, get it audited within thirty days from the close of each quarter and file it with registrar and any failure to file the statement of accounts shall make him punishable with fine which may extend to INR 5,000 for every day during which the failures continues.[314] He shall pay the debts of the company and adjust the rights of the contributories among themselves.[315] He shall observe due care and diligence in the discharge of his duties.[316] If the company liquidator fails to comply with the provisions the section 314 he shall be punishable with fine which

304. Companies Act, 2013, s. 310(2).
305. Companies Act, 2013, s. 310(3).
306. Companies Act, 2013, s. 310(4).
307. Companies Act, 2013, s. 311(1).
308. Companies Act, 2013, s. 311(2) & (3).
309. Companies Act, 2013, s. 311(4).
310. Companies Act, 2013, s. 312(1).
311. Companies Act, 2013, s. 312(2).
312. Companies Act, 2013, s. 314(1).
313. Companies Act, 2013, s. 314(2).
314. Companies Act, 2013, s. 314(5).
315. Companies Act, 2013, s. 314(6).
316. Companies Act, 2013, s. 314(7).

may extend to INR 10 lakh.[317] The company liquidator has to report quarterly on the progress of winding up to members and creditors. He shall also call their meetings as and when necessary but at least one meeting in each quarter and apprise them of the progress of the winding up.[318] The company liquidator can make a report to the tribunal stating that in his opinion a fraud has been committed by some person in the promotion or formation of the company or by an officer of the company after its formation. The Tribunal may subject such person to a public examination.[319] As soon as the affairs of a company are fully wind up, the company liquidator shall prepare a report of the winding up showing how the winding up has been conducted and the property and assets of the company has been disposed of and its debt fully discharged to the satisfaction of the creditors and thereafter call a general meeting of the company for the purpose of laying the final winding up accounts before it and giving any explanation thereon.[320] At the meeting after considering the report of the company liquidator, the members of majority may resolve to wind up the company.[321] Within two weeks, after the meeting, the company liquidator must send to the registrar copy of the final winding up accounts and make a return in respect of each meeting and its date and copies of the resolutions passed in the meetings. The company liquidator shall make an application to the tribunal for passing an order of dissolution. The application for the tribunal shall be supported by the report and also books and papers relating to winding up.[322] Within sixty days of receiving the application, the tribunal if satisfied that the process of winding up was just and fair, shall pass an order dissolving the company.[323] Within thirty days the liquidator has to file a copy of the order with the registrar.[324] On receipt of the order, the registrar will immediately publish a notice in the official gazette that the company is dissolved.[325] In case of default on the part of the company liquidator in calling general meeting of the company or a meeting of creditors after the company is wind up, he shall be punishable with fine which may extend to INR 1 lakh.[326] The assets of the company on its winding have to be applied in satisfaction of its liabilities paripassu and distributed among its members in accordance with their rights and interest in the company.[327] A company liquidator or any creditor or contributory may apply to the tribunal to determine any question arising in the course of the winding up of a company, or to exercise in respect of enforcing of calls, staying of proceedings or any other manner, in which the tribunal could exercise its power, if company were wind up by the tribunal.[328] The company liquidator or any creditor or contributory may apply to the tribunal for an order to set aside any attachment, distress, or execution put into force against the estate or effects of the company after commencement of

317. Companies Act, 2013, s. 314(8).
318. Companies Act, 2013, s. 316(1).
319. Companies Act, 2013, s. 317(1).
320. Companies Act, 2013, s. 318(1).
321. Companies Act, 2013, s. 318(3).
322. Companies Act, 2013, s. 318(4).
323. Companies Act, 2013, s. 318(5).
324. Companies Act, 2013, s. 318(6).
325. Companies Act, 2013, s. 318(7).
326. Companies Act, 2013, s. 318(8).
327. Companies Act, 2013, s. 320.
328. Companies Act, 2013, s. 422(1).

winding up.[329] A copy of the order staying the proceeding in the winding up shall immediately be forwarded by the company to registrar who shall make a minute of the order in his books relating to the company.[330] All the costs, charges and expenses properly incurred in the voluntary winding up of a company, including the fee of the company liquidator, are subject to the rights of secured creditors, payable out of the assets of the company and shall receive priority to all other claims.[331]

III. Limited Liability Partnership

214. The limited liability partnership is a hybrid form of business. It has features of both a body corporate as well as a general partnership. The Limited Liability Partnership Act, 2008 came into effect on 31 March 2009.

329. Companies Act, 2013, s. 422(2).
330. Companies Act, 2013, s. 422(4).
331. Companies Act, 2013, s. 323.

Chapter 3. The Economic Institutions

§1. Professional Organizations, Chambers of Commerce

215. There are numerous professional organizations and chambers of commerce that play a leading role in the development and practice of commercial law in India. Most participate effectively in developing, or at least influencing, governmental policy, while many also have in-house dispute resolution bodies applying commercial law. Described below are some of the prominent Indian institutions.

216. The Federation of Indian Chambers of Commerce and Industry (FICCI) is the 'rallying point for free enterprises in India'. It has empowered Indian businesses, in the changing times, 'to shore up their competitiveness and enhance their global reach'. With a nationwide membership of over 1,500 corporations and over 500 chambers of commerce and business associations, the FICCI advocates directly and indirectly for over 250,000 business units. It has an expanding direct membership of enterprises drawn from large, medium, small and tiny segments of manufacturing, distributive trade and services. The FICCI maintains the lead as the proactive business solution provider through research and interactions at the highest political level and global networking.

217. Among the most prominent of the FICCI's member chambers of commerce is the Confederation of Indian Industry (CII). It is India's premier business association, with a direct membership of over 5,800 organizations from the private as well as public sectors, including SMEs and MNCs (Multinational Companies) and indirect membership of over 95,000 companies from around 325 national and regional sectoral associations.

218. Apart from FICCI and CII, there are at least seventeen other prominent, influential chambers of commerce. These include, the Punjab, Haryana and Delhi Chamber of Commerce and Industry; the East India Cotton Association Limited; the Iron Steel Chamber of India, The Mill owners' Association, the Bombay Chamber of Commerce and Industry; Cotton Textiles Export Promotion Council; the Bengal (and Bengal National) Chamber of Commerce and Industry; the Indian Chamber of Commerce; the Calicut Chamber of Commerce and Industry; the Cochin Chamber of Commerce and Industry; the Coimbatore Chamber of Commerce; the Goa Chamber of Commerce and Industry; the Tuticorin Chamber of Commerce and Industry; the Madras Chamber of Commerce and Industry; the Southern Indian Chamber of Commerce and Industry; and, the Travancore Chamber of Commerce. These chambers of commerce regularly resolve disputes between members, and even between non-members by providing the services of expert individual arbitrators and conciliators, or by providing infrastructural facilities for dispute resolution. Some of these seventeen prominent chambers are promoters of the Associated Chambers of Commerce and Industry in India (ASSOCHAM) which is another premier chamber covering a membership of over 100,000 companies across the country. Formed in 1920, ASSOCHAM 'represents the interests of industry and trade, interfaces with the government on policy issues and interacts with counterpart international organizations to promote bilateral economic issues'.

219. In addition, these chambers of commerce are also represented by numerous governmental panels and committees so that they may effectively convey industry viewpoints. Since their members include prominent individuals from trade and industry, as well as lawyers, chartered accountants and other professionals, such members are often called upon by the government to advise on commercial law and policy.

§2. Advisory Bodies and Committees

220. The premier advisory body on legislative reform in this country is the Law Commission of India. The Law Commission have been constituted by the Government of India from time and again with a view to clarify, consolidate and codify particular branches of law where the government felt then necessity for it. Since the first such Law Commission in 1834 which recommended codification of the Penal code, the Code of Criminal Procedure, and a few other important matters, to the present day, 188th Report published in 2003 which put forth 'Proposals for Constitution of Hi-Tech, Fasttrack Commercial Divisions in High Courts', the present Law Commission of India has contributed a great deal to enrich the Indian Statute Book.

221. Apart from the Law Commission of India, the government regularly solicits the advice of prominent chambers of commerce, professional institutions, as well as reputed industrialists and experts, and seeks their representation on various committees and working groups on commercial laws. As a result, the government is able to draw from a vast array of resources drawn, for example, from FICCI, CII, ASSOCHAM, and the Institute of Company Secretaries of India.

222. For instance, on 2 December 2004, the Government of India appointed the J.J. Irani Committee under the chairmanship of Shri J.J. Irani, Director, and Tata Sons with the task of advising the government on the proposed revisions to the Companies Act, 1956. The committee had presented its report to the government on 31 May 2004. Similarly, the Narayana Murthy Committee presented its Report of the SEBI Committee on Corporate Governance in 2003. The Committee was constituted by the SEBI to review the performance of corporate governance in the country as well as to determine the role of companies in responding to rumour and other price sensitive information circulating in the market in order to enhance the transparency and integrity of the market.

223. Amongst the other well-known committees has been the one under the Chairmanship of Naresh Chandra. In the aftermath of the controversial global meltdowns of many prominent trans-national companies based in the United States, the Department of Company Affairs, Government of India, set up the Naresh Chandra Committee to examine various corporate governance issues to avoid similar incidences in India. This committee presented its Report on Corporate Audit and Governance in 2002. An earlier committee under the chairmanship of Kumar Mangalam Birla also reported on improving corporate governance in this country. The Birla Committee was set up by SEBI and its terms of reference included suggesting suitable amendments to the listing agreement executed by the stock exchanges with the companies in order to enhance corporate governance standards of listed companies, drafting a code of corporate best practices; and suggest safeguards to be instituted within the companies to deal with insider information and insider trading. This committee presented its report in 1999.

224. The Government of India has also appointed numerous high-level committees to examine emerging and problematic areas in commercial law. Members of the High Level Committee on Competition Policy and Competition Law were therefore involved in the actual drafting of the [Indian] Competition Act.

§3. Commercial Arbitration and Commercial Courts

225. Most, if not all, of the professional organizations and chambers of commerce and industry mentioned in the previous paragraphs provide facilities for arbitration and conciliation of disputes. They may be engaged either by members of the respective organizations, or by entities depending on their region or field of operation.

226. Particular mention must be made of the Indian Council of Arbitration (under the aegis of FICCI) and the International Centre for Alternative Dispute Resolution (ICADR). Both these institutions attract a majority of disputants due to the impressive array of specialist arbitrators on their panels, and due to their reputations built over numerous years.

227. Undoubtedly, commercial arbitration in India has received a fillip over the past few years with the introduction of the Arbitration and Conciliation Act, 1996. With arbitration laws in India now being harmonized with those in all developed countries that adopted the UNCITRAL Model Law, it is becoming increasingly apparent that corporate bodies and those engaged in commercial transactions prefer to resort to arbitration rather than court adjudication. Judicial opinion in the last few years has also seen a phenomenal transition, with courts now allowing the parties the greatest freedom to choose governing laws of the arbitration agreements and the applicable rules. It is therefore not inconceivable today to have parties wholly based in India choosing to be governed substantively by Indian law, while adopting the arbitration conduct rules of the International Chamber of Commerce and holding the arbitration proceedings in London. The enforcement of arbitral awards, both domestic and foreign, has also become easier with the Arbitration and Conciliation Act, 1996, narrowing the scope of challenges as well as of judicial interference.[332] Additionally, self-imposed restrictions by courts through judicial principles have also given greater sanctity to awards of arbitral tribunals. For example, it has been held that in applications challenging an award, courts would not inquire into the merits of the dispute to reopen the matter or reappraise the evidence. Only the grounds of challenge would be considered and tested to see if they are satisfied.[333] The Arbitration and Conciliation Act, 1996 has been amended on 31 December 2015. The major salient features of the Arbitration and Conciliation (Amendment) Act, 2015 are:[334]

332. Arbitration and Conciliation Act, 1996, ss 34 and 48. Also *see* , for example, *Municipal Corporation of Greater Mumbai v. Pesticides Products (India)*, (2003) 4 RAJ 363 (Bom).
333. *Satellite Cables (P.) Ltd. v. Union of India*, (1999) 1 Arb L.
334. Available on http://lawmin.nic.in/la/Arbitration.pdf.

(1) Amendment of section 2 including the definition of 'Court' & 'International Commercial arbitration'.
(2) Amendment of section 7 by which the word 'communication through electronic means' has been added.
(3) Amendment of sections 8, 9, 11, 12, 14, 23, 24, 25, 28, 31, 34, 37, 47, 48, 57 of The Arbitration and Conciliation Act, 1996.
(4) Insertion of new section 11A 'power of the central government to amend the fourth Schedule'.
(5) Substitution of new Section for section 17 'Interim measures ordered by arbitral tribunal'.
(6) Insertion of new section 29A and 29B that are 'Time limit for arbitral award' and 'Fast Track procedure'.
(7) Insertion of new section 31A 'Regime for cost'.
(8) Insertion of Forth Schedule relating to 'Sum in Disputes'; Fifth Schedule relating to 'The grounds giving rise to justificable doubts as to independence or impartiality of arbitrator'; sixth Schedule 'relating to details of arbitrators'; seventh Schedule relating to 'arbitrator's relationship with parties and counsel'.

228. Insofar as commercial courts are concerned, with the exception of the Delhi High Court, the other High Courts do not identify and dispose of commercial cases separately. Instead, such cases are heard along with the non-commercial cases, leading to avoidable delays and prolonged adjudication. In almost all instances, the formal court-system also does not make allowance for specialist judges to adjudicate such disputes.

229. The Delhi High Court Rules designate certain cases as 'commercial' for purposes of adjudication and appeal. These are contained in Chapter III of the Delhi High Court Rules, and define 'commercial causes' to include causes arising out of the ordinary transactions of merchants, bankers and traders, such as those relating to the construction of mercantile documents, export or import of merchandise, affreightment, carriage of goods by land, insurance, banking and mercantile documents, mercantile agency, mercantile usage and infringements of trademarks and passing off actions.[335]

230. These rules further clarify that all cases under the [Indian] Companies Act, 2013, and those affecting the responsibility of the Indian Railways as carriers are to be treated as 'commercial causes'.[336] Part VI of the Delhi High Court Rules provide further provisions for designating original suits as commercial causes. The definition of a 'commercial cause' is similar to that in Part V described above, and such suits are marked separately by the Registrar of the High Court for disposal.

231. Considering the lack of specialist commercial divisions in the High Courts across the country, the Law Commission of India has recommended establishment of such divisions along with 'fast track' procedures.[337] The Law Commission has also

335. Delhi High Court Rules, Ch. III, Part V.
336. Delhi High Court Rules, Ch. III, Part V, Rule 3(a).
337. Law Commission of India. *The Proposals for Constitution of Hi-Tech Fast-Track Commercial Divisions in High Courts*, 188th Report, 2003. For a study on the advantages and potential risks of a specialized court system *see* Edward Cazalet, *Specialized Courts: Are They a 'Quick Fix' or a Long-Term Improvement in the Quality of Justice?* (World Bank 2001).

made clear that it does not favour the creation of separate commercial courts, debars the High Court itself.

232. If established, these commercial divisions of existing High Courts would function in tandem with specialist tribunals established under Parliamentary legislation to hear commercial disputes in various fields, including, securities,[338] labour,[339] consumer disputes,[340] and taxation.[341]

§4. Miscellaneous

233. In conclusion, it would also be worthwhile to touch upon various international commitments in trade and commerce. Globalization has made it imperative to revise the workings of our economic institutions and commercial laws. In this respect, there has been a marked gravitation towards giving our economic institutions a much-needed trans-national reach. The Government of India has therefore established Bilateral Chambers of Trade / Joint Business Councils (JBCs) to promote international trade and commerce with particular countries or regions. At present there are approximately seventy-four JBCs with developing and developed countries, including, the US-India Business Council, Indo-African Chamber of Commerce and Industries, the Indo-Australian Chamber of Commerce, Canada-India Business Council, and the Indo-EU Chamber of Commerce.[342] In addition, these JBCs are also given impetus by way of various bilateral trade treaties and agreements, such as the Indo-Mauritius Double Taxation Avoidance Convention 1983,[343] which have been entered into by the Government of India.

234. Similarly, influential international committees have also shaped the growth of commercial laws in India. An outstanding example is the International Chamber of Commerce's Commission on Commercial Law and Practice (CLP), which facilitates international trade and promotes a fair and balanced self-regulatory and regulatory legal framework for international business-to-business (B2B) transactions in member countries. India has been represented in the CLP and its views and concerns are regularly expressed in that forum. Consequently, India has also agreed to execute from time to time various consensual decisions made at the CLP to bring its commercial laws and institutions at par with global standards.

338. The Securities and Exchange Board of India (SEBI) Act, 1992 establishes the Securities Appellate Tribunals.
339. The Industrial Disputes Act, 1947 establishes Labour Courts.
340. Consumer Protection Act, 1986, s. 9 establishes Consumer Disputes Resolution Commissions.
341. The National Tax Tribunal Act, 2005 proposes to establish National Tax Tribunals across the country.
342. For more information, visit the website of the Ministry of Commerce and Industry, Government of India at www.commerce.nic.in.
343. Famously upheld by the Supreme Court in *Union of India v. Azadi Bachao Andolan*, 2003 (56) CLA 344.

Chapter 4. General Obligations and Economic Operators

§1. In General

235. Economic liberalization, including industrial privatization of state-owned enterprises, and reduced controls of foreign trade and investment, began in the early 1990s has served to accelerate the country's growth causing new problems in obligations of economic operators. In India, there are many statutory laws of specific nature govern the various business institutions. They include the obligations of registered societies, companies, partnership firms, etc. They are required to submit information, returns, etc. to the concerning authorities of the registered societies, banking companies, i.e., they are required file returns and information to the Registrar of societies, Reserve Bank of India respectively. Similarly, companies are required to file returns and other information to the Registrar Joint Stock Companies, SEBI, etc. All these bodies are also required to file returns to the income tax authorities. Besides these authorities, there is internal audit and control system commensurate with the size and nature of business to ensure operational efficiency, accuracy and promptness in financial reporting and compliance of various laws and regulations. There are also authorities for the protection of the rights of the employees against the business organizations. They have been dealt with below in details.

§2. Registration of Business Names

236. In India, an economic operator which is doing business has to select such name which has not been adopted by another business, otherwise, it may cause confusion. Section 58(3) of the Partnership Act, 1930 as amended by the state of Maharashtra in 1984, says that a firm shall not have of any name of any other firm on account of similarity, or any name, which in the opinion of the Registrar is undesirable. To avoid confusion, it is necessary for a firm to register.

§3. Companies

237. The subject of companies has not been a new subject but it is the large partnerships from which the modern business company originated. In England during the eighteenth century companies were created either by Royal Charters or Act of Parliament. This way creation of companies was very expensive and dilatory, therefore, unincorporated partnerships came into existence so as to meet the growing commercial needs of the country. The membership of such type of the partnership was large and was left in the hands of a few persons, entitled them as trustees. These trustees were playing with the money of other people. Fraudulent practices were begun causing exploitation of public money. Parliament of England, thus, passed Bubbles Act of

1720. This Act was repealed in 1825. In 1844, Joint Stock Companies Act was enacted. This Act registration and incorporation of large partnerships was made compulsory. The Joint Stock Companies was the first legislative measure in England but the principle of unlimited liability was maintained. It was only in 1855, right to trade with limited liability was granted and in 1856 the whole law relating to such companies was consolidated under the Joint Stock Companies Act, 1856. Since then Companies Acts have been considerably amended, enlarged and improved upon till the English Acts of 1948, 1985 and 1989 were enacted.

238. In India, it was only in 1850, Joint Stock Companies Act was enacted. Since then number of amendment Acts were passed. After several amendments Company Law Act, 2013 came into force on 1 April 2014.

239. The subject of company law is a Union subject and as such only Parliament can enact the law for the regulation of the companies. Accordingly, Parliament enacted Indian Companies Act, 2013. The central government was conscious about revival and rehabilitation of sick industries. It, therefore, enacted Sick Industries Companies (Special Provisions) Act, 1985 under which Board of Industrial and Financial Reconstruction was constituted. This Board makes efforts for salvaging of such companies by providing protection from the devouring state of liabilities by adopting scheme of revival. Later on Parliament realized that instead of creating duplicity of authorities, the corporate industrial sickness should be encountered through a single Act. The fate of such companies is to be handled by the National Company Law Board. Moreover, the adjudication of company matters will not basically going to be done by the National Company Law Tribunal. Appeals from the decisions of this Tribunal are to go to the Appellate Tribunal and further appeals to the Supreme Court. Unfortunately, this provision relating to the National Company Law Board have not been enforced.

240. The central government may also consult the Registrar of the Trade Marks Act before declaring a name to be undesirable. Thus, the name of the company should not be identical with or should not be nearly resemble, the name of another registered company, for such a name may be declared undesirable by the central government. Further, the other company can also apply for an injunction to restrain the newcomer from having an identical name. The resemblance between the two names must be such as to be 'calculated to deceive'. A company can also apply for injunction to restrain the newcomer from having an identical name. A name is calculated to deceive when it suggests that the corporation adopting it is in some way connected or associated with the existing corporation. The Department of Economic Affairs has issued a guideline that a company should be allowed to use, as part of its name, expressions like venture capital / venture capital company / venture capital fund / venture capital finance company, etc. or such similar expression only when the company or its promoters have obtained approval from the said department or any other nominated authority.

241. This exemption is intended to encourage the incorporation of associations societies of public utility with the members having to incur no liability. The licence, however, is revocable at the discretion of the central government when fundamental conditions of the licence are contravened.

242. Change of name: A company may change its name only by passing a special resolution and with the written approval of the Central Government.[344] The powers of

344. Section 13(2) of The Companies Act, 2013.

the Central Government to accord approval to the change of name have been delegated to Registrar of Companies. Once a name has been allotted to a company it cannot be normally further change. But if, it is subsequently found that through inadvertence or is identical with or too nearly resembles the name of a company which is already in existence, the Central Government have power to direct the company to change or to rectify its name by passing an ordinary resolution.[345] When a company has changed its name, the registrar shall substitute the new name in the Registrar of Companies and issue a certificate of incorporation in the new name. The change of name shall become effective only on the issue of such a certificate.[346] The proviso to section 12(3) of the Companies Act, 2013 provides that in case of 'One Person Company' the words 'One Person Company' shall be mentioned in brackets below the name of such company wherever its name is printed, affixed and engraved.

243. Licence to drop 'Limited' clause in Company Act, 2013: Where it is proved to the satisfaction of the Central Government that a limited company registered under this Act or under any previous company law has been formed with any of the objects specified in clause (a) of subsection (1) and with the restrictions and prohibitions as mentioned respectively in clauses (b) and (c) of that subsection, it may, by licence, allow the company to be registered under this section subject to such conditions as the Central Government deems fit and to change its name by omitting the word 'Limited', or as the case may be, the words 'Private Limited' from its name and thereupon the Registrar shall, on application, in the prescribed form, register such company under this section and all the provisions of this section shall apply to that company.[347] The Objects provided in clause (a) of subsection (1) of section 8 are:

(a) has in its objects the promotion of commerce, art, science, sports, education, research, social welfare, religion, charity, protection of environment or any such other object;
(b) intends to apply its profits, if any, or other income in promoting its objects; and
(c) intends to prohibit the payment of any dividend to its members, the Central Government may, by licence issued in such manner as may be prescribed, and on such conditions as it deems fit, allow that person or association of persons to be registered as a limited company under this section without the addition to its name of the word 'Limited', or as the case may be, the words 'Private Limited', and thereupon the Registrar shall, on application, in the prescribed form, register such person or association of persons as a company under this section.[348]

244. The Central Government may, by order, revoke the licence granted to a company registered under this section if the company contravenes any of the requirements of this section or any of the conditions subject to which a licence is issued or the affairs of the company are conducted fraudulently or in a manner violative of the objects of the company or prejudicial to public interest, and without prejudice to any other action against the company under this Act, direct the company to convert its status and change

345. Section 16(1) of The Companies Act, 2013.
346. Section 16(2) of The Companies Act, 2013.
347. Section 8(5) of The Companies Act, 2013.
348. Section 8(1) of The Companies Act, 2013.

its name to add the word 'Limited' or the words 'Private Limited', as the case may be, to its name and thereupon the Registrar shall, without prejudice to any action that may be taken under subsection (7), on application, in the prescribed form, register the company accordingly:

> Provided that no such order shall be made unless the company is given a reasonable opportunity of being heard:
>
> Provided further that a copy of every such order shall be given to the Registrar.[349]
>
> Where a licence is revoked under sub-section (6), the Central Government may, by order, if it is satisfied that it is essential in the public interest, direct that the company be wound up under this Act or amalgamated with another company registered under this section:
>
> Provided that no such order shall be made unless the company is given a reasonable opportunity of being heard.[350]
>
> Where a licence is revoked under sub-section (6) and where the Central Government is satisfied that it is essential in the public interest that the company registered under this section should be amalgamated with another company registered under this section and having similar objects, then, notwithstanding anything to the contrary contained in this Act, the Central Government may, by order, provide for such amalgamation to form a single company with such constitution, properties, powers, rights, interest, authorities and privileges and with such liabilities, duties and obligations as may be specified in the order.[351]

§4. Partnership

245. Indian Partnership Act, 1932 deals with partnership in India. Section 4 of the Act defines 'partnership' as the relation between persons who have agreed to share the profits of business carried on by all or any of them acting for all. The relation among partners is contractual and not status. Persons who have entered into partnership with one person are called individually 'partners' and collectively 'a firm' and the name under which their business is carried on is called the 'firm name'. Thus, a firm is a collection of the partners. According to section 5 of the Partnership Act, the relation of partners arises from contract and not from status; and, in particular, the members of a Hindu undivided family carrying on a family business as such. Section 6 of the

349. Section 8 (6) of The Companies Act, 2013.
350. Section 8(7) of The Companies Act, 2013.
351. Section 8(8) of The Companies Act, 2013.

Act deals with the mode of determining existence of partnership. It says regard shall be had to the real relation between the parties, as shown by all relevant facts taken together. Under section 7 of the Act, where no provision is made by contract between the partners for the duration of their partnership, or for the determination of their partnership, The partnership is a 'partnership at will'. Under section 7 of the Act, a person may become a partner with another person in particular adventures or undertakings.

246. A partnership firm is not a legal person or a separate legal entity having any independent or distinct existence. It is nothing but partners bracketed together under one name. When a partner dies or becomes insolvent the firm is dissolved. The assets of the firm are joint property of the partners and the partners are personally liable for all the business obligations of the firm. A firm is not recognized as a person.

247. The name in which the partners of a firm carry on their business is called, as stated, 'firm name'. The selection of the name is a matter entirely for the partners, but even certain matters have to be kept into mind in making the choice. One of the primary considerations in the selection of a name is that it should not be misleading, which means that it should not be identical with or too closely resembling the name of the other firm, or with the trademark of the goods produced by another firm. A new coming firm can be restrained from adopting a similar name or giving a similar name to its product, which is already in the use of another firm. A really tough problem arises when a firm wants to adopt the name of a partner as its business name and, there being so many repeated names, that name is already the name of an established firm. Generally, a person cannot be restrained from carrying on business in its real or reputed name simply because its name being similar to the same of an existing firm is likely to cause confusion. Any newly formed partnership firm cannot have a name resembling to any existing form. There is no statutory law preventing the use of similar name by a firm. The right, however, is under un-statutory common law. In *Virendra Dresses v. Virendra Garments*.[352] Delhi High Court held that a registered or unregistered firm can be allowed to sue for a permanent injunction to prevent passing off. This is a civil wrong of infringement of trademark or name. A better safety, however, can be attained by getting one's product registered under Trade and Merchandise Marks Act, 1958 (now Trade Marks Act, 1999). Such registration enables the person who first gets his product registered under a trade name to exclude others from adopting a similar name.[353]

248. Under section 28(1), anyone who words spoken or written or by conduct represents himself, or knowing himself to be represented, to be a partner in a firm, is liable as a partner in that firm to anyone who has on the faith of any such representation given credit to the firm, whether the person representing himself or represented to be a partner does or does not know that the representation has reached the person so giving credit. However, under section 28(2), where after a partner's death the business is continued in the old firm name, the continued use of that name or of the deceased partner's name as a part thereof shall not of itself make his legal representative or his estate liable for any act or of the firm done after his death.

352. AIR 1982 Del 482.

353. For example, *J.L. Mehta v. Registrar of Trade Marks* AIR 1962 Bom 82. In this case the Registrar was restrained from allotting the mark 'Sulekha' to a new maker of pens.

I. Registration of Firm

249. Under section 57 of the Partnership Act, 1932, the state government is empowered to appoint registrar for the registration of firms. Registration of a firm may be effected at any time by sending by post or delivering to the registrar of the area to which any place of business of the firm is situated or proposed to be situated, a statement in the prescribed form and accompanied by the prescribed fee, stating: (a) the name of the firm; (b) the place or principal place of business of the firm; (c) the names of any other places where the firm carries on business; (d) the date when such partner joined the firm; (e) the names in full and permanent addresses of the partners; and (f) the duration of the firm. The statement has to be signed by all the partners, or by their authorized agents.[354] A firm shall not contain any of the following words: 'crown'; 'emperor'; 'Empire'; 'imperial'; 'king'; 'queen'; 'royal'; or words expressing or implying the sanction, approval or patronage of government, except when the state government signifies that consent to the use of such words as part of the firm name by order in writing.[355] When the registrar is satisfied that the provisions of section 58 have been duly complied with, He shall record an entry of the statement in a register called the Register of Firms, and shall file the statement.[356] When an alteration is made in the firm name or in the location of the principal place of business of a registered form, a statement may be sent to the registrar accompanied by the prescribed fee, specifying the alteration and signed and verified in the manner required by the registrar under section 58 of the Act.[357] When any partner in a registered firm alters his name or permanent address, an intimation of the alteration may be sent by any partner or agent of the firm to the registrar under section 63 of the Act. When a change occurs in the constitution of a registered firm any incoming, continuing or outgoing partner and when a registered firm is dissolved any person who was a partner immediately before the dissolution or the agent of any such partner or person specially authorized in this behalf, may give notice to the registrar of such change or dissolution, specifying the date thereof; and the registrar shall make a record of the notice in the entry relating to the firm in the register of firm.[358]

250. Effect of Non-registration. No suit to enforce a right arising from a contract or conferred by this Act shall be instituted in any court by or on behalf of any person suing as a partner in a firm against the firm or any person alleged to be or to have been a partner in the firm unless the firm is registered and the person suing is or has been shown in the register of firm as a partner in the firm.[359] Similarly, no suit can be instituted against any third party unless the firm is registered.[360] However, these provisions will not effect the enforcement of any right to sue the dissolution of a firm or for accounts of a dissolved firm, or any right or power to realize the property of a dissolved firm[361]

354. Indian Partnership Act, 1932, s. 58(1).
355. Indian Partnership Act, 1932, s. 58(3).
356. Indian Partnership Act, 1932, s. 59.
357. Indian Partnership Act, 1932, s. 60(1).
358. Indian Partnership Act, 1932, s. 63(1).
359. Indian Partnership Act, 1932, s. 69(1).
360. Indian Partnership Act, 1932, s. 69(2).
361. Indian Partnership Act, 1932, s. 69(3)(a).

or the powers of an official assignee, receiver or court under the Presidency Towns Insolvency Act, 1909 or the Provincial Insolvency Act, 1920 to realize the property of an insolvent partner.[362]

§5. Limited Partnership

251. In England, the Limited Partnership Act, 1907 permits formation of partnership firms with limited liability, but this institution is not much in use because the institution of private limited company offers a more advantageous choice. In India, there was no concept of limited partnership because people were going for private limited company. However Parliament enacted the Limited Liability Partnership Act, 2008 with a view to enabling small entrepreneurs, professionals and enterprises providing services of any kind or engaged in scientific and technical disciplines, to form commercially efficient vehicles suited to their requirements. This came on Statute Book as the Limited Liability Partnership Act, 2009 (6 of 2009). Limited liability partnership (amendment) rules, 2015 which came into effect on 19 October 2015 has substituted Rule 33:[363]

> where the firm has been converted into limited liability partnership, an intimation of such conversion to the concerned Registrar of Firms shall be given in Form 14 within fifteen days of the date of registration of the Limited Liability Partnership.

252. Limited Liability Partnership (LLP), as per section 3 of the Act, is to be a body corporate having perpetual succession and a legal entity separate from the partners and any change in the partners of such partnership shall not affect its liability. Further under section 4 of the Act, unless otherwise provided, provisions of Partnership Act, 1932 are not applicable to a LLP. Under section 5, if an LLP consists of at least two partners and also provides that in a situation where the number of partners is reduced to one and such LLP carries on business with such sole partner for more than six months and then such partners, if having knowledge of such a situation, shall be liable personally for the obligations of LLP. Section 7 of the Act deals with designated partner, i.e., an individual shall not become a designated partner in any LLP unless he has given prior consent to act as such to the LLP in the prescribed form and manner. Particulars of every designated partner who agrees to act as such shall be filed with the registrar. It also provides that any partner may become or cease to be designated partner in accordance with LLP agreement. It also seeks to empower the central government make rules for prescribing conditions and requirements for an individual to be designated partner. It further provides that every designated partner shall obtain a designated partner identification number from the central government.

253. Provision under sections 11 and 12 of the Act have been made for the registration of the LLP. On being registered, an LLP under section 14 of the Act becomes a body corporate entitling that body to sue or to be sued, acquire, own, hold and develop or dispose of property. According to section 23 of the Act, mutual rights

362. Indian Partnership Act, 1932, s. 69(b).

363. Available on http://www.mca.gov.in/MinistryV2/llpact.html.

and duties of the partners of the LLP inter se and that of LLP and its partners shall be governed by the LLP agreement and in the absence of any such agreement, such mutual rights and duties shall be determined as set out in the First Schedule of the Act. This section empowers the central government to prescribe by rules, the form, manner and fees of filing the LLP agreement and informing changes therein. Further it is provides that any agreement, made before the incorporation LLP, between the partners who subscribed their names to the incorporation document may impose obligation on LLP, if ratified by the partners after its incorporation.

254. Cessation of Partnership interest: Under section 24 of the Act, a person ceases to be a partner of the LLP either according with the agreement with the other partner; or by giving a notice in writing of not less than thirty days to the other partners; or on his death or dissolution of LLP; or if declared to be of unsound mind; or if he is declared as an insolvent.

255. Every partner of the LLP, under section 26 of the Act, is for the purpose of the business of the LLP, an agent of the LLP, but not of other partners. Further under section 27 of the Act, the LLP is not bound by anything done by a person dealing with a person if that partner has no authority to act for LLP in doing a particular act and the person with whom is dealing with also knows that the partner has no authority for such act and to provide that an obligation of LLP, whether arising out of contract or otherwise will solely be the only obligation of LLP, It also provides that liability of LLP are to be met from the property of LLP. It further provides that LLP shall be liable for a wrongful act or omission by a partner in the course of the business of the LLP or with its authority. Section 28 of the Act clearly provides that the partner is not personally liable directly or indirectly for an obligation of LLP solely by reason of his being a partner of the LLP. It further provides that the obligation of an LLP shall not affect the personal liability of a partner for his own wrongful act or omission but a partner shall not be personally liable for wrongful act or omission of any other partner.

256. Section 29 of the LLP, provides that any person, who by words spoken or written or by conduct, represents himself, or knowingly permits himself to be represented to be a partner in any LLP is liable to any person who has on the faith of any such repression given credit to the LLP, whether the person representing himself or represented to be a partner does or does not know that the representation has reached the person so giving credit. It also provides that where any credit has reached the person so giving credit. It also provides that where any credit is received by the LLP as a result of such representation, the LLP shall, without prejudice to the liability of the person so representing himself or represented to be a partner, be liable to the extent of credit received by it or any financial benefit derived thereon. It further provides that where after a partner's death the business is continued in the same LLP name, the continued use of the name or of the deceased partner's name as a part thereof shall not of itself make his legal representative or his estate liable for any act of the LLP done after his death.

257. Unlimited Liability in case of Fraud: Section 30 provides unlimited liability of the LLP and its partners in case LLP or any of its partners carryout an act with intent to defraud creditors of LLP or any other person or if they carry out an act for any fraudulent purpose. It further provides that in case any such act is carried out by a partner, the LLP is liable to the same extent as the partner unless it is established by the LLP that such act was without the knowledge or the authority of the LLP. It also provides that any person who knowingly carries such act shall be punishable with imprisonment for a term, which may extend to two years and with fine which shall not be less than INR 50,000 but which may extend to INR 500,000. It further provides that where an LLP has conducted the affairs of the LLP or any partner or designated partner then without prejudice to any criminal proceedings which may arise under any law for the time being in force, the LLP and any such partner or designated partner or employee shall be liable to pay compensation to any person who has suffered any loss or damage by reason of such conduct.

258. Under section 35 of the Act, every LLP shall file annual return duly authenticated with the Registrar within sixty days of the closure of its financial year in such form and manner and accompanied by such fee as may be prescribed. Failing to comply with this provision is punishable with fine which shall not be less than INR 25,000 extendable to INR 100,000. Similarly, the designated partner of such LLP shall be punishable with fine not less than INR 10,000 extendable to INR 100,000. Under section 36 of the Act, any person can inspect any incorporation document, names of partners and changes, if any made therein, statement of account and solvency, annual return filed by each LLP by paying prescribed fee. If in any return, statement or other documents required for the purposes of any of the provision of this Act, any person makes a statement: (a) which is false in any material particular, knowing it to be false; or (b) which omits any material fact knowing it to be material, shall be punishable for a term up to two years or fine up to INR 500,000 but not less than INR 100,000 under section 37 of the Act. Under section 38 of the Act, the Registrar is entitled to obtain information for the purposes of carrying out the provisions of the Act from any present or former partner, employee of the LLP. In case that persona does not answer such question, the registrar can summon that person and in case that person does not appear is punishable with fine of not less that INR 2,000 which can be extended to INR 25,000.

259. Assignment and Transfer of Partnership Rights: Section 42 provides that the rights of a partner to a share of the profits and losses of the LLP and to receive distributions shall be transferable in accordance with the LLP agreement and such transfer shall not by itself cause the disassociation of the partner or a dissolution and winding up of the LLP. It further provides that such transfer would not entitle the transferee to participate in the management of the LLP.

260. Application for Winding up of Limited Liability Partnership: Section 51 of the Act provides that if any such LLP is liable to be wound up under this Act or any other law and it appears to the central government from the report made by the Inspector under section 49 that it is expedient to do so by reason that the business of the LLP is being conducted with an intent to defraud the creditors, partner or any other person or otherwise for a fraudulent or unlawful purpose or that the affairs of the LLP are not being conducted in accordance with the provisions of the Act, the central government may, cause to be presented to the Tribunal by any person authorized by it, petition for the winding up of the LLP on the just and equitable ground.

261. Foreign Limited Liability Partnership: The central government may make rules for provisions in relation to establishment of place of business by foreign limited liability partnerships within India and carrying on their business therein by applying or incorporating, with such modifications, as appear appropriate, the provisions of the

Companies Act, 1956 or such regulatory mechanism with such composition as may be prescribed.

262. Winding up and Dissolution: Section 63 provides winding up of an LLP may be either voluntary or by the Tribunal and the LLP so wound up may be dissolved. A. LLP may be wound up by the Tribunal under section 64 of the Act in the following circumstances:

(a) if the LLP decides that LLP may be wound up by the Tribunal;
(b) if, for a period of more than six months, the number of partners of the LLP is reduced below two;
(c) if the LLP is unable to pay its debts;
(d) if the LLP has acted against the interests of the sovereignty and integrity of India, the security of the state or public order;
(e) if the LLP has made a default in filing with the Registrar the Settlement of Accounts and Solvency or annual return for any five consecutive financial years; or
(f) if the tribunal is of the opinion that it is just and equitable that the LLP be wound up.

The central government, under section 5, is empowered to make rules for the provisions in relation to winding up and dissolution of LLP.

263. Business Transactions of Partners with LLP: a partner may lend money to and transact other business with the LLP and has the same rights and obligations with respect to the loan or other transactions as a person who is not a partner.

264. Application of other Laws is not barred: The provisions of this Act shall be in addition to, and not in derogation of, the provisions of any other law for the time being in force.

§6. Association

265. Article 19(1)(c) of the Constitution of India provides fundamental rights to the citizens of India to form associations and unions. There are, however, under Article 19(4) certain reasonable restrictions on this right, i.e., nothing in sub-clause (c) of the said clause shall effect the operation of any existing law in so far as it imposes, or prevent the state from making any law imposing, in the interests of the sovereignty and integrity of India or public order or morality, reasonable restrictions on the exercise of the right conferred by the said sub-clause. Societies Registration, 1958 provides registration of associations and the Trade Union Act, 1926 provides registration of trade unions of the employees.

I. Trade Union Act, 1926

266. Trade unionism in India began in India in 1890 when for the first time an association of mill workers was formed in Mumbai so as to redress the grievances of the mill workers. But its mode of working is not very much known. However, increase in cost of living and country wide political upsurge found its way in economic discontent among mass, particularly in industries led to a number of strikes. Success of these strikes led to impetus to the trade unionism in India. In 1920 the Madras High Court in a suit filed against the officials of the Madras Textile Labour Union by Binny & Co. granted an injunction restraining the trade union officials to induce certain workers to break their contracts of employment by refusing to return to work. The trade union leaders became liable to prosecution and imprisonment. It was then realized some kind of legislative protection to the trade unions. One M.N. Joshi, the then General Secretary of All India Trade Union Congress moved a resolution in the central legislative Assembly seeking introduction of for the protection of the trade unions by the government and as such Trade Unions Act was enacted in 1926. This Act was amended in 1929 in order to provide for the procedure of appeal against the order of the Registrar. In case the registrar refused to register a trade union or the registration was withdrawn, an appeal could be preferred against any such order. In 1947, an amendment to Act of 1926 was made. Under the Act of 1926 even after fulfilling all the conditions and also registered, the employer was not bound to recognize or deal with the trade union The amendment Act of 1947 enjoined upon the employer to compulsorily recognize the trade union within three months in connection with the employment, non-employment, terms of employment, conditions of work of all or any of the employee. The amendment Act declared certain acts amounting to unfair practices on the part of the trade union and certain others on the part of the employers. This amendment Act further refrains both the trade union and the employer to desist from unfair practices. The recognition of any trade union found guilty of unfair practice can be withdrawn on an application by the employer to the registrar. In case of an employer found guilty of unfair practice, the registrar on an application by the trade union may impose fine. The Amendment Act of 1960 made tremendous changes in sections 2(f), 3, 4,6,14, 16 and 28 of the Trade Union Act of 1926.

267. An individual dispute cannot be per se a trade dispute unless the cause is sponsored by a trade union or by a substantial number of workmen.[364] It is not necessary that it should be supported by all or majority of the workmen, but it should have the support of a substantial section of workmen of the establishment. An industrial dispute may be raised by a group of workmen who may not represent all or even the majority of workmen, and if the dispute is referred to the industrial tribunal for adjudication and an award is made, it binds not only the parties to the dispute, or other parties summoned to appear but all persons who were employed in the establishment, or who would be employed in future are also governed by the award.[365]

§7. Employers' Social Security Obligations

268. Social functions of law is to make adjustments in the society to enable it to fact the changing patterns. This function of law is more evident in the cases of employer-employee relations. Employees' legislation is one of the most important institutions of the modern Indian society. Its origin and growth may be ascribed to

364. *Newspapers Ltd. v. StateIndustrial Tribunal, U.P.*, AIR 1957 SC 532.
365. *Associated Cement Ltd. v. Their Workmen*, AIR 1960 SC 777.

several social forces, the most important of which is the development of organized industry., where large number of men, women and children are employed under conditions which tend to be detrimental to their health, safety and welfare and against which they are often unable to protect themselves.

269. Industrialization in India as in any the country implies the growth of factory system with employers and wage-earners. As a consequence introduction of factory system production became concentrated in a few selected places. People from rural areas migrated to these industrial towns, resulting into the disappearance of the village handicrafts system because they could not compete with the machine-made cheaper products. The village craftsmen became wage-earners. The employers were more concerned with maintenance of machines and improvement of know-how, etc. Workers being illiterate and poor were unconscious of their rights.

270. After Independence of India, basing on the principles of social justice, social equity, international uniformity and national economy, a number of laws were enacted. The earliest law has been Workmen's Compensation Act, 1923 which ensures payment of compensation to the workman or his dependents in case of personal injury caused by an accident arising out of and in the course of employment. The amount of compensation payable depends, in case of death on the average monthly wages of the deceased workman and in the case of an injured workman, both on the average monthly wages and the extent of disablement. The term 'wages' for the purpose of this Act includes overtime pay, and the value of any concessions of benefits in the form of food, clothing free quarters, etc. Whenever the compensation payable to any workman has to be worked out, first of all his monthly wages are determined and then the amount of compensation is decided by reference to schedule IV, where, in a tabular form the amount of compensation for death, permanent, total and temporary disablement in respect of each of the twenty wage level is given. In order to protect the interest of dependants in case of fatal accidents the following provisions are made:

(i) all cases of fatal accidents are to be brought to the notice of the Commissioner;
(ii) if the employer admits his liability to amount of compensation payable is to be deposited with the Commissioner;
(iii) if the employer disowns his liability and at the same time there are grounds for believing compensation to be payable, dependants get the information necessary to enable them to judge if they should make a claim or not.

271. In order to make the employer liable to pay compensation, death or injury must be the consequence of an accident arising out of and in the course of his employment is dependent upon the following conditions:

(i) a casual connection between the injury and the accident; and the accident and the work done in the course of employment is essential;
(ii) the onus lies upon the claimant to establish that the injury or its aggravation was the outcome of the work and the resulting strain;
(iii) it is not necessary that the workman must be actually working at the time of his death or that death must occur while he is working or has just ceased to work;

(iv) if the evidence adduced shows greater probability which satisfies a reasonable man that the work contributed to the causing of personal injury, it would be sufficient ground for the workman to succeed in his claim;

(v) if a workman while doing his employer's work, trade or business engages himself in some other work which he is not ordinarily required to do under the contract of his service and which act involves extra danger, he cannot hold his master liable for the risks arising therefrom; the doctrine of added peril therefore comes into play only when the workman is at the time of meeting the accident performing his duty;

(vi) an injury caused by accident which could have been anticipated or foreseen, or is brought about intentionally or negligently by workman himself does not make the master liable, for it cannot be termed as an injury by accident within the terms of the Act. Accident means any unintended and unexpected occurrence, which produces hurt or loss. If the mishap was designed, intended or anticipated it is self-inflicted injury and not as injury caused by accident.

I. Maternity Benefit Act, 1961

272. Maternity Benefits Act, 1961 was enacted in different states in India. This Act was enacted to regulate the employment of a woman in certain establishments for certain periods before and after child birth and to provide for maternity benefit and certain other benefits. It applies to every establishment which is a factory, mine or. plantation, including any such establishment belonging to the government, etc. excepting those factories or establishments to which Employees State Insurance Act, 1948 applies. Section 4 of the Act the employer is prohibited from knowingly employing any woman in any establishment during six weeks immediately following the day of her delivery or her miscarriage. No woman shall work in any establishment during the six weeks immediately following the day of her delivery or her miscarriage. Further no pregnant woman shall, on a request being made by her, be given any work of the following nature during the period of one month immediately preceding the period of six months before the date of her expected delivery and during the said period of six weeks for which the pregnant woman does no avail of the leave of absence under section 6:

(i) any work which is of arduous nature;

(ii) any work which involves long hours of standing;

(iii) any work which in any way is likely to interfere with her pregnancy or the normal development of foetus or is likely to cause her miscarriage or otherwise adversely affect her health.

273. Section 5 provides that the maternity benefit to which every woman is entitled and her employer is liable for, is a payment to a woman worker at the rate of average daily wages for the period of her actual absence immediately preceding and including the day of her delivery and for six weeks immediately following that day. However no woman shall be entitled to maternity benefit unless she has actually worked for a period of not less than 160 days in the twelve months immediately preceding the date of her expected delivery. Under section 5(3) a woman shall be entitled for maternity benefit for a minimum period of twelve weeks, i.e., five weeks up to and six weeks immediately following that day.

274. If a woman is entitled to maternity benefit under this Act dies before receiving such maternity benefit, her nominee or legal representative under section 7 of the Act shall be granted such benefit or amount Every woman who is entitled to maternity benefit shall be entitled under section 8 medical bonus from her employer. A woman shall also be entitled under section 9 to leave with wages at the rate of maternity benefit for a period of six weeks immediately following the day of her miscarriage.

275. It shall be unlawful for an employer to dismiss or discharge during the period the woman is absent herself from the work in accordance with the provisions of this Act. However, where the dismissal is for any prescribed gross misconduct, the employer may, by order in writing communicate to the woman deprive her of the maternity benefit to medical bonus or both. But an aggrieved woman can appeal to the authority as may be prescribed. In case a woman works in another establishment during the period of her authorized absence, shall forfeit her claim to the maternity benefit for such period under section 18 of the Act. Similarly, if an employer contravenes any provisions of this Act or the rules made thereunder, shall be punishable with imprisonment which may extend to three months or fine which next end to INR 5,000 or with both.

276. The Employees Provident Funds and Family Pension Fund and Deposit-linked Insurance Fund Act, 1952 provides for retirement benefits. The Industrial Disputes Act, 1948, ensures retrenchment and lay-off benefits. The most important of all the legislation is the Employees State Insurance Act, 1948 which provides for medical sickness, dependent, disablement and maternity benefits. The Payment of Wages Act, 1936 provides for the protection of wages of the employees. This Act was enacted for the purpose of regulating the payment of wages to certain classes of employees in an industry. One more important social legislation is Factories Act, 1948 which provides provision for the safety of workers' health, sanitation, cleanliness, disposal of wastes and effluents, ventilation and temperature, lighting, physical safety, welfare, working hours, etc. The payment of Bonus Act, 1965 has acquired importance these days. Bonus is a cash payment made to employees in addition to wages. It is not an ex gratia payment, but is legally due and it does not rest upon contract.

§8. Employees' Taxation Obligations

277. Existence of 'Master-servant' or 'employer-employee' relationship is essential for taxing income under this heading. In case such relationship does not exist income is taxable under some other head as in the case of a partner of a firm, advocates, chartered accountants, etc. Salary of an employee is chargeable to income tax on due or paid basis, whichever is earlier. Under section 15 of the Income-tax Act, any arrears of salary paid in the previous year, if not taxed in any earlier previous year, shall be taxable in the year of payment.

278. Income tax is levied on salary which includes: wages, annuity or pension, any gratuity over and above the exemption limit, any fee, commission, any advance of salary, amount contributed by the employer towards the recognized provident fund, in excess of 12% of the salary, dearness allowance, interest on the balance of R.P.F., in excess of 9.5%, the value of any perquisites and benefits to the employee provided by the employer, any amount or profit in lieu of salary, payment received by the employee in respect of any period of leave not availed of by him, central government's contribution in previous year to an employee's account under notified pension scheme under section 80CCD, salary paid by a foreign government to its employees serving in India, advance salary, arrears of salary, bonus, pension, etc.

279. Section 17(3) of the Income-tax Act lays down that income tax is chargeable on (i) any compensation due to or received by an employee from his employer or former employer at or in connection with the termination of his employment or modification of the terms and conditions relating thereto; (ii) any payment (other than 'receipts exempt from tax' under section 10 due to or received by an employee from his employer or former employer or from a provident or other fund to the extent it does not consist of contributions by the assessee or interest on such contributions received under a Keyman Insurance Policy; (iii) any amount whether in lump sum or otherwise, due to or received by an assessee from his employer, either before his joining employment or after cessation of employment.

280. Income tax is levied on various types of allowances. Allowance has been defined as fixed amount of money given periodically in addition to the salary for the purpose of meeting some specific requirements connected with the service rendered by the employee or by way of compensation for some unusual conditions of employment. It is taxable on due/accrued basis whether it is paid in addition to the salary or in lieu thereof. All such allowances are taxable as these are paid because of direct relationship between an employee and employer. For example, city compensatory allowance, house rent allowance, entertainment allowance, tiffin allowance, meal allowance, refreshment allowance, dinner allowance, health allowance, medical allowance, telephone allowance, holiday allowance, education allowance, special qualification allowance, servant allowance, etc.

281. Certain allowances, however, are exempted subject to certain conditions, e.g., academic allowance granted for encouraging academic research and other professional pursuits, or for the books for the purpose are exempt under section 10(14). Similarly newspaper allowance shall also be exempt. Under section 10(14)(i), conveyance allowance is exempt to the extent it is paid and utilized for meeting expenditure on the travel for official work. Some of the examples of such exemptions are agriculture income, receipt from Hindu undivided family, interest on securities/bonds specified by the government in the official gazette of 31 May 2002, value of leave concession, remuneration to an official of Embassy, High Commission, Legation, Affairs, Commissioner, consulate or trade representative of a foreign state or as a member of staff of any of these officials, remuneration to staff of the ambassador, consulate, trade commissioner, etc. remuneration received by employees of foreign enterprise, salaries to residents employed on a foreign ship, remuneration received by certain foreigners, on training in certain establishments, allowances/perquisites for services rendered outside India, paid or allowed by the government to an Indian citizen, death-cumretirement gratuity under the rules of the central government and state governments, compensation to the workman under the Industrial Disputes Act, 1948, any payment, subject to a limit of INR 500,000, receivable by an employee of public sector company or any other company or any authority established under a central, state or Provincial Act under section 10(10C) of the Income Tax Act, any sum received under a life insurance policy including bonus under such policy under section 10(10D) of the Income Tax Act, any payment of provident fund under the Provident Fund Act, 1925 or Public Provident Fund Scheme, 1968 or such fund established by the central government, reimbursement of medical expenses incurred on medical treatment of an employee or his family member in a hospital (other than hospital maintained by the government or employer in excess of INR 15,000 in the previous year):

There are certain permissible deductions from total income of the whole financial year. They are as follows:

(i) permissible deduction from the entertainment allowance of a sum equal to one fifth of the salary or INR 5,000 whichever is less;
(ii) professional tax;
(iii) deduction in respect of life insurance premium, purchase of national saving certificates, contribution towards provident fund, fixed deposit in a bank under tax saving scheme, etc. up to a limit of INR 100,000 under section 80C of the Income Tax Act;
(iv) contribution to life insurance pension plan under section 80CCC of the Act;
(v) payment of medical insurance premium under section 80D up to INR 10,000 and INR 15,000 to a senior citizen;
(vi) a deduction is allowed to compensate for any expenditure incurred by an assessee, during a year, for the medical treatment including nursing training or rehabilitation of one or more handicapped relatives wholly dependent on him, and for amount deposited in an approved scheme of Life Insurance Corporation or Unit Trust of India, for the benefit of a handicapped dependent up to a limit of INR 50,000 under section 80DD;
(vii) deduction up to INR 40,000 incurred for the medical treatment of specified diseases or ailments for the assessee himself or a dependent relative; in case of senior citizen, it is up to INR 60,000 under section 80DDB;
(viii) repayment of loan taken for higher education from any financial institution or any approved charitable institution for the purpose of pursing his higher education without any limit under section 80E;
(ix) deduction up to 50% is allowable on the donation made to charitable institutions registered under Societies Act, 1957; 100% deduction is allowed for donation to National Defence Fund, Prime Minister National Relief Fund, etc. under section 80G;
(x) deduction of INR 50,000 for disability and INR 70,000 for severe disability, Senior citizens over the age of 80 years are entitled to the exemption from income tax up to the income of INR 500,000 under section 80CCD.

§9. Other Work Related Obligations

282. Employers have number of other obligations in relation to their employees in India. Service conditions of employees, whether private or public or even of the government servants, are important so far as social obligations of the employers are concerned. In 1946, it was considered to be 'expedient to requires employers in individual establishments to define with sufficient precision the conditions of employment under them and to make the said conditions known to the workmen employed by them'. With this object Industrial Employment (Standing Orders) Act, 1946 was enacted. This Act made it compulsory for the establishments to reduce to writing the conditions of employment and get them certified as provided by the certifying officer appointed under the Act.

283. Article 39(e) of the Constitution of India contains a directive that the health and strength of workers, men and women, are not to be abused. Article 43 of the Constitution of India ensures, among other things, that the state shall endeavour to secure to all workers a full enjoyment of leisure. This article further directs the state to secure to the workers opportunities to take part in social and cultural activities, the question of fixation of hours of work is to be covered in any programme of social obligation.

284. Holidays declared under the Negotiable Instruments are usually applicable to the government institutions and they have certain financial and statutory implications envisaged by the Act itself and therefore it is not considered reasonable to insist that the commercial establishments and factories should be made bound to grant holidays as sanctioned by the said Act.

285. Security of service: The conditions of the industrial employees are governed by Standing Orders certified under the Industrial Employment (Standing Orders) Act, 1946 which requires the employers to make the conditions of employment precise and definite e.g., tenure of service, termination of employment, suspension or dismissal for misconduct, etc.

286. The Employees' Provident Funds, Family Pension Fund and Deposit Linked Interest Fund Act, 1952 is very important in connection with the obligation of the employers towards the employees. The object of this Act is to provide for the institution of the funds for employees in factories and other establishments. An employer is under a duty to put the Provident Fund scheme into operation and to make contributions of both the employees' and employers' share to the fund then and there and deduct from the wages of the employees their share. Subsequently by an amendment in 1956, the Act was extended to non-factory establishments. Similarly for the employees serving state governments and the central governments there are provisions in the service rules regarding payment of pension and provident fund. Employers of both private and public establishments are under a duty to provide medical facilities to their employees. Similarly employees of both state governments and central government are also entitled to get medical facilities.

§10. Banking Obligations

287. The banking law as it exists today is the outcome of the gradual process of evolution. Prior to 1949, Indian Companies (Amendment) Act, 1936 dealt with the banking companies. In order to protect the interests of depositors and plug the loopholes, consolidate and amend the law relating the banking companies, Banking Companies Act, 1949 was enacted. In 1965, the Act was renamed as Banking Regulation Act, and made it applicable to certain cooperative societies, the principal business of which was banking. Again in 1968, the Act was amended in order to make social control on the banks by inserting regulatory provisions of far reaching significance. After the enactment of Banking Companies (Acquisition and Transfer of Undertaking) Act, 1970 the banks have been divided into three main categories:

(a) Banking companies which are not nationalized.
(b) Nationalized Banks.
(c) Cooperative Banks.

At present there are twenty-seven Public Sector Banks comprising of nineteen nationalised banks and eight Banks of State Bank group. In January 1993 the RBI issued guidelines for setting up of new private sector banks in India and in 1996 it was decided by the Government of India to allow setting of Local Area banks.

288. The whole of the Banking Regulation Act except section 56 applies to all the banking companies which are not nationalized. It also applies to all the cooperative banks whose capital is not less than INR 100,000. However, the Act applies to all central cooperative and state cooperative banks. Section 9.2 of the Banking Regulation Act, 1965 regulates the following matters:[366]

(1) Accepting of deposits from the public and lending or investing the same:

(i) Control over the management of the banks.
(ii) Prohibition of certain activities in relation to banking companies.
(iii) Acquisition of the undertakings of banking companies in certain cases.
(iv) Suspension of business and winding up of banking companies.
(v) Special provisions for speedy disposal of winding up proceedings.
(vi) The Act prohibits the banking company from engaging directly or indirectly in trading activities and undertaking trade risks. However, a banking company is permitted to do so for the following purposes:

(a) to realize the security given to it or held by it for a loan;
(b) to buy or sell or barter for others in connection with bills of exchange recovered for collection or and for negotiation or with the undertaking of the administration of estate as executor, trustee or otherwise;

366. Banking Regulation Act, 1965, s. 6.

(vii) A banking company cannot hold any immovable property, however, acquired, except for its use, for any period exceeding seven years from its acquisition. The Reserve Bank, however, may extend this period by another five years if it finds that such extension would be in the interest of the depositors of the banking company. But the banking company shall have to dispose of such property within such period or extended period.[367]

(viii) The Act requires the banking companies to submit the following returns:

(a) Monthly return of liquid assets and liabilities.[368]
(b) Quarterly return of assets and liability.[369]
(c) Return of unclaimed deposits.[370]
(d) Return showing assets and liabilities.[371]
(e) Other statements relating to business or affairs of the banking company, e.g., investments and classification of advances, etc.[372]

289. Section 29 of the Banking Regulation Act, 1965 Act provides that at the expiration of each calendar year every banking company incorporated in India, in respect of all business transacted by it and every banking company incorporated outside (India in respect of business transacted through its branches in India), is required to prepare with reference to that year a balance sheet and profit and loss account on the last working of the year.

290. Section 30(1) of the Act requires that the balance sheet and profit and loss account of a banking company must be audited by a person who is duly qualified under any law for the time being in force to be an auditor of the companies.

291. The Reserve Bank of India was established on 1 April 1935 under the Reserve Bank of India Act, 1934. On 1 January 1949, the Reserve Bank of India started functioning as a state-owned Central Banking Institute. The Reserve Bank of India under section 35 of the Reserve Bank of India Act, 1934 is empowered, for safeguarding interests of shareholders and depositors of the banking company, at any time and must on being directed by the central government, cause an inspection to be made by one or more of its officers, in respect of any banking company and its books and accounts and must supply a copy of the inspection report on such inspection to the banking company. At such inspection, every director or other officer of the banking company is bound to produce to the officer making the inspection such books, accounts and other documents and information relating to the affairs of the banking company as such officers may require. The Banking Regulation Act, 1949 empowers the Reserve Bank of India to control the banking institutions of India. Section 17 of the R B I Act, 1934 deals with the functions which RBI is authorized to carry. While section 19 of

367. Banking Regulation Act, 1965, s. 9.
368. Banking Regulation Act, 1965, s. 24(3).
369. Banking Regulation Act, 1965, s. 25.
370. Banking Regulation Act, 1965, s. 26.
371. Banking Regulation Act, 1965, s. 27(1).
372. Banking Regulation Act, 1965, s. 27(2).

RBI Act, 1934 deals with the business which the RBI may not transact. According to section 22 of the RBI Act, 1934, the RBI shall have the sole right to issue bank notes in India. The Reserve Bank of India can issue directions to banking companies generally or to any banking company in particular, if it is satisfied that such directions as it deems fit, are necessary: (a) in the public interest or in the interest of banking policy; or (b) to prevent the affairs of any banking company being conducted in a manner detrimental to the interests of banking company; or (c) to secure the proper management of any banking company; or (d) the banking companies are bound to comply with such directions.

292. Part IIC constituting section 36AE–36AJ was introduced in the Act by an Amendment of the Act in 1968. It lays down that if, upon receipt of a report from the Reserve Bank, the central government is satisfied that a banking company:

(i) has, on more than one occasion, failed to comply with the directions given to it under section 21 or section 35A of the Act in so far as such directions relate to the banking policy; or
(ii) is being managed in a manner detrimental to the interests of its depositors and that:

(a) in the interest of the depositors of such banking company; or
(b) in the interest of the banking policy; or
(c) for the better provision of credit generally or of credit of any particular section of the community or in any particular area.

Chapter 5. Business Assets, Goodwill and Commercial Property Rights

§1. Business Assets

I. General

A. Concept of Property

293. In modern times, apart from its common use, 'property' is used in a wider sense also. In its widest sense it is a bundle of rights which a person has. Thus, a person's life, liberty, reputation and all other claims which he might have against other persons as his property. The term 'property' is used also to denote the proprietary rights of a man as opposed to his personal rights. In this sense it means a person's land, house, his shares in a business concern, etc. In the third sense it means proprietary rights in rem, the law of proprietary rights in personam being distinguished from it as the law of obligations. A freehold or leasehold estate in land or a patent or copyright is property. In the narrowest sense, the term 'property', includes corporeal property only. Business assets, however, can be both real and personal property. Real property refers to land or things affixed to the land. Personal property consists of the property which is other than real property.

B. Registration of Real Property

294. Real property means immovable property, such as cannot be either moved themselves or be removed from one place to another. The Registration Act of 16 of 1864 did not contain any definition of immovable property. The first Registration Act in which the definition appeared was Act, 20 of 1866. 'Fisheries' were added in the definition by the Registration Act XX of 1866, and 'hereditary allowances' by section 3 of Act III of 1877.

295. Immovable property is also defined in at least other two enactments, i.e., Transfer of Property Act, 1882 and the General Clauses Act, 1897.

296. The definition of 'immovable property' given in section 3 of the Transfer of Property Act is not exhaustive. It simply says: 'Immovable property does not include standing timber, growing crops or grass'. The definition of 'immovable property' given in section 3(26) of the General Clauses Act, 1897, is also not exhaustive as it uses the word 'includes'. It provides: 'immovable property shall include land, benefits to arise out of land, and things attached to earth, or permanently fastened to anything attached to earth'. It follows from the overall reading of definitions of immovable property given in section 3 of the Transfer of Property Act and in section 3(26) of the General Clauses Act, and also the definitions in the Transfer of Property Act of 'attached to the earth' that the definition given in section 2(6) of the Indian Registration Act, includes all the ingredients of the immovable property defined above. In addition to it, includes also, hereditary allowances, right to ways, lights, ferries, fisheries as immovable property.[373]

297. In India, according to section 17 of the Registration Act, 1908, a document is compulsorily registrable, if it purports or operates to create, declare, assign, limit or extinguish right of the value of INR 100 and above in immovable property. Therefore, whether or not a deed is compulsorily registrable must be determined with reference to the consideration or the principal money set forth in the deed or at least the amount payable thereunder irrespective of any interest that might subsequently accrue.[374] In the case of *Ghulam Ahmad v. Gulam Quadir*,[375] it was observed that the 'the words documents and instruments used under section 17 are interchangeable'. A person who admitted execution of a document before the Sub-Registrar, cannot raise a question that the initials at the bottom of page 3 of the original were not his.[376] The amount of consideration and the actual value of the property sold has to be taken into account. Thus, for the purposes of the Registration Act, the value of an interest that is conveyed is the consideration mentioned in the sale deed by the parties thereto. Where parties to a deed have chosen to specify therein a value for the property deed, the court will not go into evidence to question that value. But it would be extending the principle to an unreasonable extent to hold that while no value is stated, the court can ignore an obvious inference of the fact that the property dealt with must, in the nature of things, exceed the limit of INR 100 in value.[377] A deed or assignment of a mortgage for over INR 100 for consideration less than INR 100 does not need compulsory registration, but a transfer deed in a hypothecation bond for a consideration more than INR 100, though the amount due under the bond that is less than INR 100 must be registered.[378]

298. Section 18 of the Registration Act, 1908 deals with those documents, the registration of which is optional. Non-registration of a document compulsorily registrable is invalid in evidence under section 49 of the Act. However, under section 50 of the Act, a document whose registration is optional if not registered will not lose all validity, but the effect is that, if it is registered, it shall have effect against and priority over an unregistered document. In the case that a document falls under both sections 17 and 18, it shall be construed as compulsorily registrable and not optional.

C. Registration of Personal Property

299. The provisions of sections 17 and 18 of the Registration Act, 1908 are applicable also in cases other than real property. They are: (a) any composition-deed; (b) any instrument relating to shares in a joint stock company, notwithstanding that the assets of such company consist in whole or in part of immovable property; (c) any

373. *Ram Kumar v. Krishan Gopal* (1046) A.O. 106.
374. *Bikroo v. Anant Bahadur Singh*, AIR 1921 Oudh 167.
375. AIR 1968 J & K 38.
376. *Bina Murlidhar Namdev v. Kanhaiyababu Lokdev*, AIR 1999 SC 2171.
377. *Devidas Jagjivan v. Pirjada Begum*, ILR 8 Bom 377.
378. *Satra Kamaijla v. Visram Hazagavda*, ILR 2 Bom 97; (*see also Ramosami v. Proavadi* 1910 MWN 73).

debenture issued by any such company and not creating, declaring, assigning, limiting or extinguishing any right, title or interest, to or in immovable property except in so far as it entitles the holder to the security afforded by a registered instrument whereby the company has mortgaged, conveyed or otherwise transferred the whole or part of its immovable property or any interest therein to trustees upon trust for the benefit of the holders of such debentures; (d) any endorsement upon or transfer of any debenture issued by any such company; (e) any document other than documents containing contracts to transfer for consideration, any immovable property for the purpose of section 53A of the Transfer of Property Act, 1882 not creating, declaring, assigning, limiting or extinguishing any right, title or interest of the value of INR 100 and upwards to or in immovable property, but not merely creating a right to obtain another document which will, when executed, create, declare, assign, limit or extinguish any such right, title of interest; (f) any decree or order of a court except a decree or order expressed to be made on a compromise and comprising immovable property other than that which is the subject matter of the suit or proceeding; (g) any grant of immovable property by the government; (h) any instrument of partition made by a revenue-officer; (i) any order granting a loan or instrument of collateral security granted under the Land Improvement Act, 1871, or Land Improvement Loans Act, 1883; (j) any order granting a loan under the Agriculturists Loans Act, 1884, or instrument for securing the repayment of a loan made under that Act; (k) any order made under the Charitable Endowments Act, 1890 vesting any property in a treasurer of charitable endowments or divesting any such treasurer of any property; (l) any endowment on a mortgage-deed acknowledging the payment of the whole or any part of the mortgage-money, and any other receipt for payment of money due under a mortgage when the receipt does not purport to extinguish the mortgage; (m) any certificate of sale granted to the purchaser of any property sold by public auction by a civil or revenue-officer; or (n) authority to adopt a son executed after 1 January 1872, and not conferred by a will.

300. As per section 18 of the Registration Act, there are certain kinds of instruments for which the registration is optional like: (a) Instruments relating to the transfer of an immovable property, the value of which is less than INR 100; (b) Acknowledgement of receipt, payment of any consideration for creation, declaration, assignment, limitation or extinction of any right, title or interest in immovable property for a term not exceeding one year; (c) Lease of an immovable property for a term not exceeding one year; (d) Instruments transferring any decree or order of a court where the subject matter of such decree or order is an immovable property whose value is less than INR 100; (e) Instruments other than wills, which purport or operate to create, declare, assign, limit or extinguish any right, title or interest to or in movable property; wills; and (f) All other documents not required by section 17 of the Registration Act to be registered.

301. Oral gift is permitted in Muslim Law. The gift need not be in writing and, consequently, need not be registered. But declaration is necessary.[379] The family arrangement may be even oral in which case no registration is necessary. It is well settled that registration would be necessary only if the terms of the family arrangement are reduced into writing. Here also a distinction should be made between a document containing the terms and recitals of a family arrangement made under the document

379. *Mujeer Ahmed G. v. Mohammed Zafrulla*, AIR 2000 Kant 318.

and a mere memorandum prepared. In such a case the memorandum itself does not create or extinguish any rights in immovable properties therefore, does not compulsorily registrable.[380] To effect a family arrangement all that is necessary is that the parties must be related to one another in some way and have a claim or a possible claim to the property or even a semblance of a claim of spes successionis or even or some other ground as, say, affection or ignorance of the parties of their rights and with the purpose of object of maintaining peace and harmony in the family.[381] Declaration of a right in immovable properties made in decree does not require registered instruments to convey the title. Registration of such decree is optional under the provisions of Registration Act.[382]

D. Refusal of Registration

302. Registration of the documents can be refused in the following cases:

(1) Where the document is in a language not understood by the registering officer.[383]

(2) Documents containing interlineations, blanks, erasures or alterations unless the persons executing the document attest with their signatures or initials such interlineations, blanks, erasures or alterations.[384] Refusal to initial an alteration in the deed by the executant, however, is not a ground to refuse registration if such alteration was made subsequent to the execution of the deed.[385] In case of non-admission of an interpolation, interlineations or alteration in a document, the registering officer can refuse to admit it for registration. He is also competent to accept a deed even though the alterations are not attested.[386] When a document has been refused registration, the sub-registrar shall make an order of refusal and record his reasons for such order and endorsed the words ‘registration refused’ on the document.[387]

E. Description of Property and Maps or Plans

303. No non-testamentary document relating to immovable property shall be accepted for registration unless it contains a description of the property sufficient to identify the same and if the instrument contains a map, a copy or copies of the map shall accompany the instrument when presented for registration[388] In the event that the property is situated in several districts, then there should be a number of true copies

380. *Mohan Lal Duggal v. I.M. Sharma*, 1999 AIHC 4686 Delhi.
381. *A.C. Lakshmipathy v. A.M. Chakrapani Reddiar*, AIR 2001 Mad 135.
382. *Dhaesa v. Bandagisab*, AIR 1999 Kan 190.
383. Indian Registration Act, 1908, s. 19.
384. Indian Registration Act, 1908, s. 20(1).
385. *Bhoneswar Ram v. Ram Khelawan*, 12 CLJ 137.
386. *Veerappa Chettiar v. Viswanath*, AIR 1916 Mad 873; also *Hussain Abdul Rehaman & Co. v. Lakhmichand*, AIR 1925 Bom 34.
387. Indian Registration Act, 1908, s. 71.
388. Indian Registration Act, 1908, s. 21(1).

of the map or plans equal to the number of such districts.[389] Non-compliance of these provisions, does not, however, disentitle the deed to be registered, provided that the description of the property in the deed is sufficient to identify the property,[390] save the rule made by a state government which expressly states that the deed should not be registered.[391]

F. Time for Presenting Documents for Registration

304. No document other than a will shall be accepted for registration unless presented for that purpose to the proper officer within four months from the date of its execution[392] except when: (1) the documents executed by several persons at different times;[393] (2) where delay in presentation is unavoidable;[394] (3) where documents are executed out of India.[395] Wills, however, may be presented or deposited at any time for registration.[396] Period during which award remained with court liable to be excluded in computing limitation of four months.[397]

G. Place of Registration

305. Every document as detailed in sections 17 and 18 of the Registration Act, 1908 shall be presented for registration in the office of a sub-registrar within whose sub-district the whole or some portion of the property to which such document relates is situated.[398] Other documents may be presented for registration either in the office of the sub-registrar in whose sub-district the document was executed, or in the office of any other sub-registrar under the state government in which all the persons executing and claiming under the document the same to be registered.[399] The Registering officer, on special cause being shown attend the residence of any person desiring to present a document or will for registration.[400]

389. Indian Registration Act, 1908, s. 21(4).
390. Indian Registration Act, 1908, s. 22(2).
391. Indian Registration Act, 1908, s. 22(1); *see also Galliora v. U, Thet*, AIR 1929 Rang 117; *Somasundram Mudaliar v. Ranjappa Mudaliar*, AIR 1927 Mad 369.
392. Indian Registration Act, 1908, s. 23.
393. Indian Registration Act, 1908, s. 24.
394. Indian Registration Act, 1908, s. 25.
395. Indian Registration Act, 1908, s. 26.
396. Indian Registration Act, 1908, s. 27.
397. *Madhukar Goel v. M.S. Goel*, AIR 1998 Del. 257.
398. Indian Registration Act, 1908, s. 28.
399. Indian Registration Act, 1908, s. 29.
400. *Cherichi v. Ittianam*, AIR 2001 Ker. 184.

H. *Appeal to the Registrar Against the Orders of Registration by a Sub-registrar*

306. An appeal shall lie against an order of a sub-registrar refusing to admit a document to registration to the Registrar to whom such sub-registrar is subordinate within a period of thirty days from the date of the order.[401]

§2. Protection of Business Names

307. The topic has been covered in Chapter 4.

§3. Intellectual Property

I. Trademarks

A. *General*

308. The origin of trademarks can be traced back a far as the beginning of the circulation of goods. The history of marks is nearly as old as the histories of mankind and religion. Scientists have come across excavated artifacts from places such as ancient Egypt with various symbols carved thereon by religious and superstitious reasons. Potter marks on the earthen pot during and were used to identify the maker, i.e., potter of a particular vessel. They, perhaps, cannot be considered as trademarks in the modern sense.[402] However, over the time, different methods of identification and distinction developed. Proprietary marks in the form of a name or symbol were affixed to goods to enable one person to distinguish their own possessions from those of others. Around the tenth century, a mark called a 'merchants mark' was used to prove ownership rights of goods.[403] The earliest English law on trademarks originated in AD 1266 in the form of Baker's Marking Law, i.e., law required bakers to place a mark on the leaves of bread that they sold, identifying the baker. Any bread offered for sale unstamped was at once forfeited and offending baker was to pay heavy damages. In 1353, an Act was passed where merchants were required to provide proof of their ownership in order to have any good returned to them by registering marks. In 1905, Merchandise Marks Act was enacted. This Act focused on provisions dealing with deceptive indications. Subsequently many amended acts on trademarks were enacted.[404] In India there was no trademark law in India until 1940, though the principles of infringement action had already been embodied in section 54 of the Specific Relief Act, 1887, while registration was secured by obtaining a declaration as to ownership

401. Indian Registration Act, 1908, s. 72.
402. *See* Muragendra B. Tubake, *The History and Development of Trade Marks Law*, 26.9 10 Leg. News & Views 10 (2012).
403. *Ibid.*
404. *Ibid.*, at 13.

under the Indian Registration Act, 1908. However it is surprising to note that there does not appear even a single reported case in India in which section 54 of the Specific Relief Act was relied upon.[405] In 1942 and also in 1943, amendments to the 1940 Act took place. By the Amendment Act of 1943, the Trade Marks Registry, formerly a part of the Patent Office, Calcutta (now Kolkata) was separated from the Patent Office to constitute a separate Trade Marks Registry under a Register of Trade Marks at Bombay (now Mumbai). On the recommendations of Justice Rajagopal Ayyangar Committee, the 1940 Act was replaced by the Trade & Merchandise Marks Act, 1958. This Act consolidated the provisions of Trade Marks Act, 1940 and the Indian Merchandise Marks Act, 1889. The Trade and Merchandise Marks Act, 1958 had been in force for the last four decades, but it was felt that a comprehensive review of the existing law be made in view of developments in trading and commercial practices, increasing globalization of trade and industry, the need to encourage investment flows and transfer of technology, need for simplification and harmonization of trademark management systems and to give effect to important judicial decisions. The Trade & Merchandise Marks Act, 1958 was therefore revised and replaced by the Trade Marks Act, 1999. This Act came into force with effect from 15 November 2003.

309. The concept of trademark is essentially a business concept but is intertwined with legal things as exclusion of all others from using a similar trademark is the fundamental tenet of a trademark. This sort of monopoly is possible with the help of law alone. The object of trademark legislation is intended to provide protection of the interest of the consumers and also protection of the reputation and goodwill of the proprietors of certain marks which are used on the goods. The purpose of the trademarks legislation is also to provide registration and better protection of trademarks and prevention of the use of fraudulent marks on the merchandise. Thus Trade Marks Act recognizes and an important IPR.

B. Meaning of Trademark

310. Section 2(1)(zb) defines 'Trademark' as a mark capable of being represented graphically and which is capable of distinguishing the goods or services of one person from those of others and may include shape of goods, their packaging and combination of colours. Mark includes also the name or word amongst it. Name includes any abbreviation of name.[406]

C. Registration of Trademarks: Procedure for and Duration of Registration

311. A person claiming to be the proprietor of a trademark used or proposed to be used by him, who is desirous of registering it, shall apply in writing to the Registrar in the prescribed manner for registration of his trademark.[407] The application can also be signed by the agent of the applicant. A single application can also be made for

405. *Ibid.*, at 15.
406. *Laxmikant V. Patel v. Chetanbhat Shah*, AIR 2002 SC 275.
407. Trade Marks Act, 1999, s. 18(1).

different class of goods or services included in any one class.[408] The Registrar on receipt of the application with enclosures and fees, will acknowledge their receipt by returning one copy each of the paper submitting. Every application shall be filed in the office of the Trade Marks Registry within whose territorial limits is situated the principal place of business in India of the applicant whose name is first mentioned in the application.[409] The registrar may, however, refuse the application or accept it absolutely, all subject to such amendments, modifications, conditional acceptance or limitations, if any, as he may think fit.[410] He may give the applicant a notice and decide upon the issues whether the application shall be accepted as claimed by the applicant or as proposed by the registrar. The registrar shall record in writing the grounds for the refusal or conditional acceptance of the application.[411]

D. Withdrawal of Acceptance

312. After acceptance, the application is advertised in the form in which it has been accepted in the trademark journal.[412] There are incidental powers vested in the Registrar in sections 19 and 20 to withdraw the acceptance or vary the acceptance or to advertise the application before acceptance if proviso to section 20(1) applies. The advertisement, before the acceptance of the application, may be done in the cases falling in section 9(1) or section 11(1) and (2) or in other cases of exceptional circumstances.

E. Advertisement of Application

313. An application for registration shall be advertised in the trademark journal ordinarily within six months of the acceptance of the application or after the expiry of the period referred to subsection (2) of section 154 whichever is later. If the application has been permitted to be amended under section 22 of the act, the registrar may under section 20(2), at his discretion, cause the application to be advertised again, or give notice of the correction or amendment made in the application.

F. Opposition to Registration

314. Any person may file an application within three months from the date of advertisement of an application for opposition of registration give under section 21(1) of the act notice to the registrar who shall under section 21(2) serve a copy of the notice to the applicant for registration. The applicant shall send the registrar a counter-statement on grounds that he is basing his application on and if he does not do so, according to section 21(3) he shall be deemed to have abandoned his application. In the case that the applicant sends such a counter-statement, the registrar shall serve a copy of the same to the person giving notice of opposition under section 21(4) of the

408. Trade Marks Act, 1999, s. 18(2).
409. Trade Marks Act, 1999, s. 18(3).
410. Trade Marks Act, 1999, s. 18(4).
411. Trade Marks Act, 1999, s. 18(5).
412. Trade Marks Act, 1999, s. 20(1).

act. Both opponent and the applicant may submit any evidence within a prescribed period of time before the registrar, who may give opportunity of being heard. After hearing both parties and considering the evidence submitted, the registrar shall decide whether or not the registration may be granted. The registrar may require security for the costs of proceedings from the opponent or applicant in case that neither reside nor carry on business in India and in default of such security being furnished, he may treat the opposition or application, as the case may be, as abandoned. The registrar under section 21(7) may, upon request, permit the correction of any error or amendment to a notice of opposition or a counter-statement on such terms as he thinks fit.

G. Registration

315. The registrar shall, in the event that the application has not been opposed and the time for opposing it has expired or the opposition to it has been decided in favour of the applicant, register the said trademark under section 23 of the act, unless the central government directs otherwise. The registrar then issues a certificate of registration. The registration of a trademark has to be completed within twelve months from the date of application, otherwise by reason of default on the part of the applicant, the registrar may, under section 23(3) of the act, after giving notice to the applicant, treat the application as abandoned unless it is completed within the time specified in the notice. Under Trade Marks Act the registrar has power to issue registration certificate with retrospective effect. This power is based on the principle of deemed equivalence to public user of such mark.[413]

H. Duration, Renewal, Removal and Restoration of Registration

316. The registration of trademark is only for ten years unless renewed from time to time. The registrar before the expiration of the period shall issue notice to the applicant for renewal. In case the applicant does not apply for renewal, the registrar shall remove the trademark from the register. However, the registration shall be renewed, if the applicant applies within six months of the expiration of the removal order. Furthermore, if a trademark has been removed, after six months and within one year from the expiration of the previous registration, on receipt of an application and on payment of the prescribed fee, the registrar shall restore the trademark and renew it[414] if satisfied that it is just to do so.

I. Effect of Registration

317. Section 28 of the Trade Marks Act, 1999 confers on the proprietor of the trademark, exclusive right to use of the trademark in relation to the goods or services in respect of which the trademark is obtained. In addition to conferring the right of exclusive dealing, the proprietor of a trademark also has a right to file a suit for infringement of his right and obtain: (1) injunction; (2) damages; (3) account of profits.

413. *Meghraj Biscuits Industries Ltd. v. Commissioner of Central Excise, Uttar Pradesh*, AIR 2007 SC 1433.

414. Trade Mark Act, 1999, s. 25.

However, the rights conferred are not absolute. The Act lists out the limitations which can be imposed on the exclusive rights.

J. Infringement of Registered Trademark

318. It takes place in the following ways:

(1) A registered trademark is infringed by a person who, not being a registered proprietor or a person not permitted to use it, uses in the course of trade, a mark which is identical with, or deceptively similar to, the trademark in relation to goods or services in respect of which the trademark is registered and in such a manner as to render the use of the mark likely to be taken as being used as a trademark.[415]

(2) The trademark is also infringed because of its identity with the registered trademark and the similarity of the goods or services covered by such registered trademark; or its similarity to the registered trademark and the identity or similarity to the goods or services covered by such a registered trademark; or its identity with the registered trademark and the identity of the goods or services covered by such a registered trademark, is likely to cause confusion on the part of the public, or which is likely to cause an association with the registered trademark.[416]

(3) A trademark is infringed by a person who uses in the course of trade, a mark which is identical with or similar to the registered trademark, is used in relation to goods or services which are not similar to those for which the trademark is registered; and the registered trademark has a reputation in India and the use of the mark without due cause takes unfair advantage of or is detrimental to the distinctive character or repute of the registered.[417] A registered trademark is infringed by a person if he uses such a registered trademark, as his trade name or part of his trade name, or name of his business concern or part of the name, of his business concern dealing in goods or services in respect of which the trademark is registered.[418]

A registered trademark is infringed by a person, if using a registered trademark, in particular, he:

(a) affixes it to goods or the packaging thereof;
(b) offers or exposes goods for sale, puts them on the market, or stocks them for those purposes under the registered trademark;
(c) imports or exports goods under the mark; or
(d) uses the registered trademark on business papers or in advertising.[419]

A registered trademark is infringed by a person who applies such a registered trademark to a material intended to be used for labelling or packaging of goods,

415. Trade Marks Act, 1999, s. 29(1).
416. Trade Marks Act, 1999, s. 29(2).
417. Trade Marks Act, 1999, s. 29(5).
418. Trade Marks Act, 1999, s. 29(5).
419. Trade Marks Act, 1999, s. 29(5).

as a business paper, or for advertising goods or services, provided such person, when he applied the mark, knew or had reason to believe that the application of the mark was not duly authorized by the proprietor or licensee.[420]
A registered trademark is infringed by any advertising of that trademark if such advertising:

(a) takes unfair advantage of and is contrary to honest practices in industrial or commercial matters;
(b) is detrimental to its distinctive character; or
(c) is against the reputation of the trademark.[421]

(4) Where the distinctive elements of a registered trademark consist of or include words, the trademark may be infringed by the spoken use of those words as well as by their visual representation and reference in this section to the use of a mark shall be construed accordingly.[422] In *Dhotha House v. S. K. Maingi*,[423] it was held that mere application for registration of the trademark of another does not amount to infringement.

K. Limits on Effect of Registered Trademarks

319. Section 30 of the Act specifically excludes certain acts as not constituting infringement. The following uses will not constitute infringement:

(1) The provisions of section 29 shall not be so construed as to prevent the use of a registered trademark by any person for the purposes of identifying goods or services as those of the proprietor, provided the use:

(a) is in accordance with honest practices in industrial or commercial matters; and
(b) is not such as to take unfair advantage of or be detrimental to the distinctive character or repute of the trademark.

(2) A registered trademark is not infringed where:

(a) The use in relation to goods or services indicates the kind, quality, quantity, intended purpose, value, geographical origin, the time of production of goods or of rendering of services or other characteristics of goods or services.
(b) A trademark is registered subject to any conditions or limitations of its use in any manner relating to the goods to be sold or traded in, in any place, or in relation to services for use or available or acceptance in any place or country outside India or in any other circumstances, to which, having regard to those conditions or limitations, the registration does not extend.

420. Trade Marks Act, 1999, s. 29(6).
421. Trade Marks Act, 1999, s. 29(7).
422. Trade Marks Act, 1999, s. 29(8).
423. AIR 2006 SC 730.

(c) A person uses it (i) when dealing with goods in the course of trade with a proprietor or a registered user of the trademark, and in respect to those goods or a part thereof, the registered user has conformed to the permitted use, has applied the trademark and has not subsequently removed or obliterated it, has at any time expressly or impliedly consented to the use of the trademark; or (ii) in relation to services whereby the proprietor or registered user of the mark has conformed to the permitted use and applied the mark where the purpose and effect of the use of the mark is to indicate the fact, that those services have been performed by the proprietor or a registered user of the mark.

(d) The use of a trademark by a person in relation to goods adapted to form part of, or to be accessory to, other goods or services in relation to which the trademark has been used without infringement of the right given by registration under the act or might for the time being be so used, if the use of the trademark is reasonably necessary in order to indicate that the goods or services are so adapted, and neither the purpose nor the effect of the use of the trademark is to indicate, otherwise than in accordance with the fact, a connection in the course of trade between any person and the goods or services, as the case may be.

(e) The use of a registered trademark, being one of two or more trademarks registered under this act which are identical or nearly resemble each other, in exercise of the right to the use of that trademark given by the registration.

(3) Where goods bearing a registered trademark are lawfully acquired by a person, the sale of the goods in the market, or any dealing with those goods by that person or a person claiming under or through him is not infringement of a trademark by reason that:

(a) The registered trademark has been assigned by the registered proprietor to some other person, following the acquisition of those goods.

(b) The goods have been placed on the market under the registered trademark by the proprietor or with his consent. However this provision shall not apply where there exists a legitimate reason for the proprietor to oppose further dealings in the goods, has been changed or impaired after they have been put on the market.

L. Miscellaneous Provisions

320. Acting in Good Faith: Section 122 of the Trade Mark Act, 1999 provides that no suit or other legal proceedings shall lie against any person in respect of anything which is done in good faith or is intended to be done in pursuance of this Act.

321. Bar on Jurisdiction: Section 134 of the Act lays down that a suit for infringement of a registered trademark or relating to any right in a registered trademark or the passing off arising out of the use by the defendant of any trademark which is identical with or deceptively similar to the plaintiff's trademark (whether registered or unregistered) shall not be instituted in a court or the district court they have no jurisdiction to try the suit.

322. To protect the registered trademark, the following remedies can be resorted to: (1) civil remedies; (2) criminal proceedings; and (3) administrative remedies.

(1) *Civil Remedies*: When instances of infringement and passing off occur, the court of competent jurisdiction (court not lower than District Court) can be moved for grant of interlocutory injunction, Anton Pillar Orders, damages and account of profits.
(2) *Criminal Proceedings*: Complaint may be made against the person causing infringement. Both the actions, under the civil law and criminal law can be initiated simultaneously. Under the civil law proceedings, the plaintiff seeks relief for himself while under the criminal law proceedings the complainant seeks award of punishment to the infringer.
(3) *Administrative Remedies*: Opposing the registration of a deceptively similar trademark when the trademark registry is in the process of considering the grant of a trademark, can protect the trademark. The registry can also be moved for removal of a deceptively similar trademark, if registered.

The Court in which action can be filed is the court within the jurisdiction of which the infringement takes place or the place within the jurisdiction of which the plaintiff resides. If there are more than one plaintiff, all the places where the plaintiffs are residing have jurisdiction.[424]

323. Special Provisions for Convention Countries: Sections 154 and 155 of the Act deal with the provisions aimed at providing national treatment to, and withdraw this privilege from, the citizens of other countries with whom India has entered into a convention or a treaty or who are the signatories of global agreements to which India is also a party. This is done on the basis of reciprocity.

324. In order to promote global trade and commerce the agreement of Trade Related Aspects of Intellectual Property Rights also called for the provisions in the member countries to provide the nationals of other member countries the same privileges regarding registration and exploitation of trademarks as the said member country would accord to its own citizens. Section 154 of the act says that India shall apply national treatment to nationals of those countries who give national treatment to Indian nationals under their own laws regarding use of a trademark. The moment India, however, comes to know that a member country has ceased to provide this facility to Indian nationals; it would also under section 155 of the act stop providing the national treatment to the nationals of that country.

325. Amendment Act of 2012 – International Registration – Under the Trade Marks Act, the protection available is limited to India only. If any party wants that his trademark shall be recognized in any other country, he should make a separate application in that country. In order to avoid this difficulty, the Madrid Protocol provides international registration. Accordingly, India being a contracting party to the said Protocol, Amendment Act of 2010 provided a procedure therefore. The advantage of this procedure is that the applications for international registration shall pay only single fees and that the

424. *Uniliver Australia v. Shingar Cosmetics Pvt. Ltd. and Ors.*, AIR 2011 Kant 30.

International Bureau acts as intermediary facilitating due disposal of the applications and further simultaneous registration in several countries becomes easier.

II. Copyright

A. General

1. General

326. Copy right is a foreign concept in India. It came into existence after the advent of British rule. Rustom R. Dadachanji observed:

> There is no trace of any protection of law having been given to be called 'copyright' other than by virtue of the principles of equity and good conscience, till the middle of the eighteenth century.[425]

327. The world and society are divided along the lines of knowledge. Knowledge is power which plays a vital role in the recent liberalized and globalized economy. The concept of knowledge creation and its dissemination has changed with time. A person is gifted with intellect, that is, used for the growth and development of self and society at large.[426]

328. The main aim of the copyright law is to give fair return to an author for his/her labour.[427] The copyright law is the mirror and parallel image of law of tort and traditional common law. The award of damages deters the infringer from repairing the wrongs by the infringer to the owner.[428] The copyright law recognizes and protects the original literary, musical works, dramatic and artistic works, cinematograph films pantomime and choreographic audiovisual pictorial, graphic and sculptural sound recording special artistic work and includes computer programme, table and compilations.

329. Copyright is a set of rights given by law to the creators of literary, dramatic, musical and artistic works and producers of cinematograph films and sound recordings to do or authorize the doing of certain acts with regard to their creations for a fixed time duration. The owners of copyright can protect against unauthorized use of their work for the duration of copyright by their own effort. The nation assists in the same. But it is a private right and has to be protected by owners like all other property which is protected by individuals.

330. The copyright protection was extended after the invention of the printing press in the fifteenth century which enabled the reproduction of books in large number.

---

425. Rustom R. Dadachanji, *Law of Library and Dramatic – Copyright in a Nutshell* 6 (N.M. Tripathi Pvt. Ltd. 1960).

426. W.R. Cornish, *Intellectual Proterty, Patents, Copyright, Trade Marks, and Allied Rights* 258 (2nd ed., Sweet & Maxell Publications 1995).

427. *K. Murari v. Mupala anganayakamma*, 1987(2)ALT 699 at pp. 710–711.

428. Wendy J. Gordon, *A Property Right in Self-Expression: Equality and Individualism in the Natural Law of Intellectual Property*, 102 Yale L.J. 1533 (1993).

The first piece of legislation on copyright came into existence in United Kingdom in the form of Copyright Act of 1709 which was then known as 'Statute of Anne'.

331. The History and development of the concept of copyright is traced back to fifteenth century when the concept was for the first time recognized in the city of Venice. It was only during the sixteenth century, England adopted this concept. In India, the Indian Copyright Act, 1847 was enacted during the East India period. It provided protection for a minimum period of seven years and more than forty-two years. It also provided for compulsory registration of copyright. In 1911, another Copyright Act was enacted. This Act provided copyright for the expression and original works and not for ideas. Registration was not compulsory under this Act. The protection was for the whole life and fifty years after the death. In 1913 provisions of English Copyright Act were enacted in India. In 1957, one more amended Act was enacted. This act is a self-contained law incorporating international commitments of the Berne Convention, 1952. According to this Act, if the work is published outside India and also simultaneously published in India with thirty days it will be treated as published in India and the district courts were empowered to have the jurisdiction to hear copyright cases. In order to take adequate anti-piracy measures, Indian Copyright (Amendment) Act, 1984 was enacted. In this Act, three types of piracy cases were stated, e.g., piracy of printed words; piracy of sound recording; and cinematic films. The Copyright (Amendment) Act, 1994 was enacted in order to incorporate some of the provisions of the Trade Related Aspects of Intellectual Property Rights (TRIPS) l inserting anti-piracy provisions were inserted. The last amendment to this Act took place by an enactment in 2010.[429] This amendment seeks to strengthen the position of persons such as music composers and lyricists.

B. Application of Copyright Act, 1957

332. In order to secure copyright protection what is required is that the author must have bestowed upon the work 'sufficient judgment, skill and labour or capital'. It is immaterial whether the work is wise or foolish, accurate or inaccurate, or whether it has or has not any literary merit.[430] The Indian Copyright Act, 1957 provides the subsistence of copyright to original literary, dramatic, musical and artistic works, cinematograph films, and sound recording.[431]

333. In order to qualify the above work, unless protected under section 40 which empowers the central government to extend copyright to foreign works or under section 41 wherein protection of copyright is accorded to works of certain international organizations when so declared by the central government throughout India, the following conditions should be complied with:

429. *See* J.V. Joshi, *Copyright as an Intellectual Property and Information Technology*, in *Intellectual Property Rights & Copyrights* 385 (S.P. Satarkar, Ess Ess Publications 2003); *see also* Ameer Ahmed Husensab Bagali, *Copyright Law: Its National and International Evolution* in 26.2 2 Leg. News & Views (Feb. 2012).

430. *Walter v. Lane*, 1990 AC 539.

431. Indian Copyright Act, 1957, s. 13.

(1) The work is first published in India. Where the work is first published outside India, the author at the date of publication must be a citizen of India. If the publication was made after the author's death the author must have, at the time of his death, been a citizen of India and in the case of unpublished work the author is on the date of making of the work, a citizen of India or domiciled in India. This however, does not apply to works of architecture.

(2) In case of a cinematograph film, the substantial part of it is not an infringement of the copyright in any other work and in case of sound recording of a literary, dramatic, or musical work, the copyright in these works has not been infringed in the making of the sound recording.

334. As far as a work of architecture is concerned the act extends copyright only in respect of the artistic character and design and not to the processes or methods of construction. In the case of designs, the subsistence of a copyright is guaranteed under the act only if the design in question has not been registered under the Designs Act, 1911. In the case that the design made could have been registered under the Designs Act, 1911 but was not, the copyright shall cease as soon as the article, to which the design has been applied, has been reproduced, through an industrial process more than fifty times, by either the owner of the copyright or his licensee.[432] Finally, there can be no copyright, according to section 16 of the act, except as provided under the Copyright Act, 1957.

C. Meaning of Copyright

335. Copyright is a right given by the law to creators of literary, dramatic, musical and artistic works and producers of cinematograph films and sound recordings. In fact, it is a bundle of rights including, *inter alia*, rights of reproduction, communication to the public, adaptation and translation of the work. There could be slight variations in the composition of the rights depending on the work. The Copyright Act, 1957 sets out the meaning of copyright in section 14 and describes it to mean as the exclusive right subject to the provisions of Copyright Act.

D. Conditions for Protection of Copyright

336. In order to secure copyright protection what is required is that the author must have bestowed upon the work 'sufficient judgment, skill and labour or capital'. It is immaterial whether the work is wise or foolish, accurate or inaccurate, or whether it has or has not any literary merit. There are certain conditions for protection under the copyright law which can be summed up as:

(a) It should be original.

(b) It should be a literary, dramatic, musical work or a cinematograph film or sound recording.

(c) It should be a work of an organization declared by the central government as an international organization under section 41 or one covered under section 40 if it is a foreign work

432. Indian Copyright Act, 1957, s. 15.

(d) In case of design, it should not have been registered under the Designs Act, 1911.

(e) It should be a work, which is covered by the act as regards protection of copyright.

(f) It should be an artistic work.

(g) It may be a computer program.

(h) It may be architectural work.[433]

E. Exceptions

337. There are certain types of matters which are not copyrightable like where the matter is taken out of common place information available to all; or if the matter is not in script form; or if the work has been done during the course of employment; or nobody can claim copyright in a folk song.

F. Rights of the Owner of Copyright

338. The provisions of sections 13 (subject matter of copyright); 14 (meaning of copyright); 15 (ownership of copyright); 18 (assignment of copyright); 20 (transmission of copyright); 21 (relinquishing of copyright); 53A (resale share right in original copies); 58 (recovery of infringed copies) deal with the rights of the owner of copyright, which includes: (a) to reproduce the work for sub-clause (c) of section 14 the Amendment Act of 2012 in any material form including the storing of it in any medium by electronic or other means; or depiction in three dimensions of a two-dimensional work; or depiction in two-dimensions of a three-dimensional work; (b) issue copies of work to the public; (c) to perform the work in public or communicate it to the public; (d) to perform the work in public or communicate it to the public; (e) to make a translation, adaptation or cinematograph film of the work; (f) in the case of computer programs, to do any or all works as mentioned above as also to sell or give on commercial rental or offer for sale or rental any copy of a program; (g) in the case of an artistic work, all or any rights enumerated in (a) and (d) above, besides the right to include whole or part of the work in a cinematograph film; (h) in case of a cinematograph film, to make a copy of the film, to sell or hire it and to communicate the film to the public; (i) in the case of sound recording, to make any other sound recording embodying it, to sell or give on hire or to offer for sale or hire any copy of the sound recording as well as to communicate the sound recording to the public; (j) to assign the copyright; (k) to transmit the copyright; (l) to relinquish the copyright; (m) to grant any interest in the right by licence; (n) to claim the recovery of infringed copies, by instituting necessary proceedings; and (o) to get a share in the resale of original copies, any assignment of copyright therein notwithstanding.

G. Performer's Rights

339. Following conclusion of Uruguay Round of Multilateral Trade Negotiations Parliament enacted the Copyright Act in 1994 to bring the Indian statute in conformity

433. *See* Indian Copyright Act, 1957, ss 13, 14, 15 and 16.

with TRIPS Agreement. One of the objects of the amendment Act was to extend protection to all performers by means of a special right, to be known as the 'performer's right', in respect of the making of sound recordings or visual recordings of their live performances, and of certain related acts. The definition of performance to mean, in relation to performer's right, means any visual or acoustic presentation made live by one or more performers.[434] As per the Indian Copyright Act, a 'Performer' includes an actor, singer, musician, dancer, acrobat, juggler, conjurer, snake charmer, a person delivering a lecture or any other person who makes a performance.[435] Section 38 of the Act provides that where any performer appears or engages in any performance, he shall have a special right to be known as the 'performer's right' in relation to such performance. These rights are following: (a) Right to make a sound recording or visual recording of the performance; (b) Right to reproduce the sound recording or visual recording of the performance; (c) Right to broadcast the performance; (d) Right to communicate the performance to the public otherwise than by broadcast.

340. The term of protection for performer's right is fifty years from the year following the year of performance. Anybody who, without consent of the performer, makes a sound recording of the performance, reproduces a sound recording of a performance, broadcasts the performance or communicates the performance to the public shall be guilty of infringing the performer's right. However, section 39 of the act provides defences and states that it shall not be construed as an infringement if a person, with regard to the performance, either makes a sound recording for personal purposes or bona fide for teaching or research, or uses the excerpts of the performance bona fide for teaching and research, or does any other act which does not constitute infringement of copyright as stated in section 52 of the act.

341. Section 39A provides that sections 18 (assignment), 19 (mode of assignment), 30 (licences), 53 (importation of infringing copies), 55 (civil remedies for infringement), 58 (right of owner against persons possessing or dealing with infringing copies), 64 (power of police to seize infringing copies), 65 (possession of plates kept for the purpose of making infringed copies) and 66 (disposal of infringing copies or plates kept for the purpose of making infringing copies) applicable to copyright shall, with suitable modifications, be applicable in the case of performers' rights as well.

H. Rights of the Broadcasters

342. Section 37 of the act states that every broadcasting organization shall have a special right to be known as broadcast reproduction right in respect of its broadcasts. 'Broadcast' means communication to the public: by any means of wireless diffusion, whether in any one or more of the forms of signs, sounds or visual images; or by wire. The rights of a broadcasting organization with reference to a broadcast includes the right to re-broadcast the broadcast; right to cause the broadcast to be heard or seen by the public on payment of any charges; right to make any sound recording or visual recording of the broadcast; right to make any reproduction of such sound recording or visual recording where such initial recording was done without licence or, where it was licensed, for any purpose not envisaged by such licence; and right to sell or hire

434. Copyright Act, 1957, s. 2 (q).
435. Copyright Act, 1957, s. 2 (qq).

to the public, or offer for such sale or hire, any sound recording or visual recording of the broadcast. During the continuation of a broadcast and reproduction right in relation to any broadcast, it shall be an infringement if the above-mentioned acts are done without the licence of the owner.

343. The duration of a broadcast reproduction right shall be twenty-five years with effect from the calendar year following the year of broadcast. The Copyright Act is silent on the term of repeat broadcast. In absence of any specific provision, no new broadcast reproduction right is conferred on the repeat broadcast.

344. The provisions of section 39 and 39A are equally applicable concerning the rights of the broadcasters as they are concerned with the rights of the performers. Further, no broadcast reproduction rights are infringed by such acts, with any necessary adaptations and modifications, which do not constitute infringement of copyright under section 52.

I. Term of Copyright

345. Sections 22–29 deal with the duration of copyright under the Act. Section 22 of the act declares that in all literary, dramatic, musical or artistic works (other than a photograph) the period will be sixty years from the calendar year next to the year of his death, in case the work had been published during the lifetime of the author. While in the case of joint authorship, the time period will be up to the death of the last of the joint authors. In a case of anonymous or pseudonymous works, the copyright of such works is to subsist either for a period of sixty years following the year of publication, or a period of sixty years following the death of the author or the last of the joint authors as the case may, where their identity has become known.[436] For the works in which there existed a copyright in favour of their authors, single, or joint, immediately before, or at the time of, their death, the copyright, in case of its posthumous publication, shall subsist for a period of sixty years counted from the year next to the year of such posthumous publication.[437] The Act has fixed the term of copyright to subsist for sixty years following the year of publication in case of cinematograph films,[438] sound recordings,[439] government works,[440] works of public undertakings,[441] and the works of international organizations.[442] In the case of government work, where government is the first owner of the copyright therein, copyright shall subsist until sixty years from the beginning of the calendar year next following the year in which the work is first published. Sections 22, 23 and 24 of the act do not apply to photographs. However, section 25 provides the duration of photographs for the period of sixty years from the year following the year of publication.

436. Indian Copyright Act, 1957, s. 23.
437. Indian Copyright Act, 1957, s. 24.
438. Indian Copyright Act, 1957, s. 26.
439. Indian Copyright Act, 1957, s. 27.
440. Indian Copyright Act, 1957, s. 28.
441. Indian Copyright Act, 1957, s. 28A.
442. Indian Copyright Act, 1957, s. 29.

J. Infringement of Copyright

346. Section 51 of the Copyright Act, 1957 enumerates certain situations when the copyright shall be deemed to be infringed Such situations can be summed up as: (a) Making infringing copies for sale or hire or selling or letting them for hire; or (b) Permitting any place for the performance of works in public where such performance constitutes infringement of copyright; or (c) Distributing infringing copies for the purpose of trade or to such an extent so as to affect prejudicially the interest of the owner of copyright; or (d) Public exhibition of infringing copies by way of trade; or (e) Importation of infringing copies into India.

K. Defences

347. Apart from common law exceptions to protection of copyright, statutory exceptions are also available under the Copyright Act, 1957. These exceptions are provided by way of a list of permitted uses in section 52 of the Copyright Act, 1957 which would otherwise be infringement of copyright. These can be summed up as: (a) fair dealing with a literary, musical, dramatic or artistic work (not being a computer program) for the purposes of private use including research, criticism or review; (b) fair dealing for criticism or review; (c) fair dealing for the purpose of reporting current events; (d) reproduction of a work in legislature's work; (e) reproduction of a work in a certified copy made under any law; (f) reading or recitation in public of any reasonable extract from a published literary or dramatic work; (g) anthologies for educational use; (h) use and performance of copyright material/work in the course of education; (i) making sound recording in respect of literary, dramatic or musical work in certain cases; (j) causing of a recording to be heard in public; (k) reproduction of articles on current topic in periodicals, etc.; (l) publication of report of a lecture in periodicals; (m) reproduction for the purpose of research or private study of an unpublished literary, dramatic or musical work kept in a library or museum where public has access; (n) reproduction or publication of any matter in official Gazette, Act of Legislature, Judgments of courts, etc.; (o) publication of translation of acts of legislature; (p) making or publishing of a painting, photograph, etc. of a work of architecture or artistic work; (q) incidental inclusion of artistic work in cinematograph film; (s) performance or communication of a work in official ceremony; (t) ephemeral recording for the purpose of broadcast; (u) reconstruction of a building in accordance with architectural drawings or plans by reference to which the building or structure was originally constructed.

L. International Copyright

348. The central government may by order provide for national treatment of books, published or unpublished, and their authors whether living, domiciled or, if dead, living at the time of death, in a foreign country. Under section 40 of the act, such books shall get copyright protection in the same manner as the works of Indian authors published in India.

349. India, being a member of the Berne Convention, is bound under the treaty to provide national treatment to the works and authors of member countries of the

Convention. The government of India, under this act, has extended the national treatment to other countries also, viz., non-members to international conventions or having a bilateral treaty with India on the basis of reciprocity. The term of copyright so given to foreign works in India, however, shall not extend the term conferred by the law of that country. Section 40A of the act confers the power on the central government to give national treatment to the broadcasters and performers of other nations, not necessarily those nations with whom India has entered into a treaty. Furthermore, section 41 applies to those organizations, of which two or more sovereign powers of governments are members, which the central government may declare by order to be organizations to which it is expedient that this section shall apply.

350. Provisions laid down in section 40 and 40A are based upon the principle of reciprocity. The protection available to foreign work under Copyright Act, 1957 is subject to the provisions of section 32 which provides for the grant of compulsory licence to produce and publish translations of the work.

351. The central government under section 42 of the act has the power to restrict the copyright protection to works of foreign authors first published in India, if the government is of the opinion that that country does not give adequate protection to the Indian works. Similarly, section 42A gives the same power to the central government as regards the restriction of the rights of broadcasters and performers of a foreign country. However such orders have to be laid down before Parliament under section 43 of the act.

M. Remedies and Provisions of Appeals

352. The Copyright Act, 1957 provides for civil, criminal and administrative remedies against infringement of copyright or related rights. It also envisages appeals in suitable cases.

1. Civil Remedies

353. The civil remedies for infringement of copyright are of two kinds: (i) preventive civil remedies; and (ii) compensatory remedies.

354. Where the copyright of any work has been infringed, the owner of the copyright under section 55(1) is entitled to all such remedies by way of an injunction, damages, and accounts and otherwise as are or may be conferred by law for infringement of a right. In case, however, the defendant proves that at the date of the infringement he was not aware and had no reasonable ground to believe that the copyright existed in the work, then the only remedy the plaintiff can get is an injunction in respect of infringement and a decree for the whole or part of profits made by the defendant by the sale of the infringing copies.

355. Section 56 of the act protects separate rights of several persons in a copyright work and states that where the several rights comprising the copyright in any work are owned by different persons, the owner of each such right shall to the extent of that right, be entitled to the remedies provided by the act and may individually enforce any such right by means of any suit, action or other proceedings without making the owner of any other right a party to such suit, etc.

356. Section 57 deals with authors' special rights or moral rights and section 58 deals with the rights of the owner against persons dealing with or possessing infringing copies. Section 59 states that the owner of a copyright in the structure of a building cannot get an injunction against one who is constructing a building which is or which, if completed, is likely to infringe the said copyright. It also declares that section 58 shall have no application in such cases as they are covered by section 59.

357. In case someone is threatened by one claiming to be the owner of a copyright on the ground that the former is guilty of infringement, that former person may, if the charge of infringement is baseless and if the threats keep on coming from the said owner, institute a declaratory suit under section 60 of the act that the alleged infringement was not an infringement at all and may obtain an injunction against the continuance of such threats; and recover damages, if any, as he has sustained by reason of such threats.

358. This provision will not apply in case the person making such threats, with the diligence, commences and prosecutes an action for infringement of the copyright claimed by him.

359. Section 61 provides that unless directed otherwise by the court, an exclusive licensee can make the owner of the copyright a defendant and in this situation the owner of the copyright shall have the right to dispute such claim made by the exclusive licensee. And, if the exclusive licensee succeeds in a civil suit or other proceedings against the copyright owner, no fresh suit or other proceedings with respect to the same cause of action shall lie at the instance of the owner of the copyright.

360. Every suit or other civil proceedings arising out under sections 55–61 shall be applied according to section 62 of the act before the district court will have any jurisdiction.

2. Criminal Remedies

361. In addition to civil remedy, the plaintiff can initiate criminal proceedings against an infringer. These two remedies are distinct and can be involved simultaneously. A person who knowingly infringes or abets the infringement of the copyright in a work or any other right conferred by the Copyright Act except the resale share, right in original copies conferred by section 53A, shall, under section 63 of the act be punishable with imprisonment ranging from six months to three years and a fine of INR 50,000–200,000. However, where the infringement is not for commercial gain, the court may, through a reasoned decision, impose a fine of less than INR 50,000 and an imprisonment of less than six months.

362. Section 63A provides enhanced penalties in the case of a second and subsequent conviction in which case the limits are one year to three years imprisonment and INR 100,000. Furthermore, under section 63B, in case a person knowingly uses an infringing copy of a computer program as an offence with a fine from INR 50,000–200,000 and imprisonment from seven days to three years provided that where the computer program has not been used for a commercial purpose, the court may award fines and imprisonment even less than the prescribed minimum, through a reasoned decision.

363. A police officer not below the rank of sub-inspector under section 64 is empowered to seize without warrant all copies of the work, if he is satisfied that an offence under section 63 of imprisonment of copyright is being or likely to be committed. Such seized material shall be produced before a magistrate as soon as possible. Anybody, however, interested in the seized matter may apply to the magistrate who shall, after hearing both parties, i.e., applicant and complainant and making such further inquiry as he deems fit, make an order on the application.

364. A deliberate possession of plates for the purpose of making infringing copies under section 65 of the act is punishable with two years' imprisonment and a fine. However, under section 66, all copies of the work or all plates in the possession of the offender may be delivered by the order of the court to the owner irrespective of whether the offender is finally convicted or not.

365. The imposition up to one year's imprisonment or fine or both has under section 67 provided for the offence of making false entries in the copyright register, while making false statements aimed at deceiving any authority or officer under section 68 is punishable with imprisonment up to one year or fine or both. Section 68A provides that a person who publishes any material in contravention to section 52A shall be punished with imprisonment which may extend to three years and also a fine.

366. In case an offence is committed by the company, every person who was in charge at the time of the commission of the offence and the person responsible for the conduct of the business of the company as well as the company shall be deemed responsible. Any director, manager, secretary or other officer of the company whose consent, connivance or negligence is proved in that regard shall also be held responsible. The man-in-charge at the time of the commission of offence or the man responsible for the conduct of business of the company at that time, however, can absolve himself of the liability if he proves that: (1) the offence was committed without his knowledge; or (2) he exercised due diligence to prevent the commission of the offence.[443]

367. Section 70 of the act lays down that no court inferior to that of a metropolitan magistrate or a judicial magistrate of the first class shall try any offence under this act. The conduct of the criminal proceedings is governed by the Criminal Procedure Code.

3. Administrative Remedies

368. In order to prevent importation of infringing copies in India, the Copyright Act, 1957 makes available an effective and quick administrative remedy to the owner of copyright. Section 53(1) of the Act empowers the Registrar of Copyright to make an order prohibiting the importation into India of copies of a copyrighted work made outside India which, if made in India would infringe copyright in the work, on the application of the owners of copyright in such work, or his duly authorized agent, after making such inquiry as he deems fit.

N. Appeals

369. Any person aggrieved by the order of the magistrate made under section 64(2) or section 66 may, under section 71 of the act, within thirty days of the date of

443. Indian Copyright Act, 1957, s. 69.

such order, appeal to the court to which appeals from the court making the order ordinarily lie and such appellate court may pass stay order on the execution of the lower courts' order pending appeal.

370. Any person aggrieved by any final decision or order of the registrar of copyrights may, under section 72(1), within three months from the date of the order or decision, appeal to the copyright board. Furthermore, if any person is aggrieved by any final decision or order of the copyright board, not being a decision or order made in an appeal preferred against the order of the registrar or copyrights, may within three months from the date of such decision or order, appeal to the High Court within whose jurisdiction the appellant actually and voluntarily resides or carries on business. This, however, is subject to the provision that no appeal shall lie against the decision of the copyright board under section 6. A three-month period excludes the time spent for getting a certified copy of the order or record of the decision appealed against.

371. In all cases where no appeal is provided the High Court may be approached under its special original jurisdiction under Articles 226 and 227 of the Constitution of India. The High Court also under section 73 is empowered to make rules, consistent with this act, to be followed in respect of appeals made to it from the decision of the copyright board.

O. Copyrights in Computer Programs

372. Section 2(ffc) of the act defines a computer program as 'a set of instructions expressed in words, codes, schemes or in any other form, including a machine readable medium, capable of causing a computer to perform a particular task or achieve a particular result'. Section 2(d)(vi) defines author of a computer generated literary, dramatic, musical or artistic work, as the person who causes the work to be created.

373. Copyright in the case of computer program under section 14(b) means the right to reproduce the program, to communicate to the public, to issue copies of the work to the public, to make any adaptation of the program and to translate as well as to make a cinematograph film in respect of the program; and to sell or give on commercial rental or offer for sale or commercial rental, any copy of the program. The Amendment Act of 2012 added following sub-clauses in section 14. To reproduce the work in any material form including the storing of it in any medium by electronic or other means; or depiction in three dimensions of a two-dimensional work; or depiction in two-dimensions of a three-dimensional work.

374. The following acts under section 52, however, do not infringe the copyright in a computer program:

(1) making the copies or adaptation of a computer program by the lawful possessor of the copy from such copy:

   (a) in order to utilize the computer program for the purpose for which it was supplied; or
   (b) to make backup copies purely as a temporary protection against loss, destruction or damage in order only to utilize the computer program for the purpose for which it was supplied.

(2) the doing of any act necessary to obtain information essential for operating inter-operability of an independently created computer program with other programs by a lawful possessor of a computer program provided that such information is not otherwise readily available;
(3) the observation, study or test of functioning of the computer program in order to determine the ideas and principles which underline any elements of the program while performing such acts necessary for the functions for which the computer program was supplied; and
(4) making of copies or adaptation of the computer program from a personally legally obtained copy for non-commercial personal use.

375. The duration or term of copyright in a computer program, since it is included in the definition of a literary work, is sixty years from the year next to the year of making of the program.

III. Design

A. General

376. The word 'new design' is often used to refer to many things, which may refer to construction, novel principles of functioning or operations, but in the field of intellectual property, 'design' is used to refer exclusively to features of appearance as occurs in dress designs or in interior designs. Thus the designs are concerned with 'how the articles looks' or the features which create eye-appeal. The reasons for protecting industrial design are manifold. A strong design protection leads to increased innovation and creativity by providing designers with an economic incentive to develop better products. This increased creativity and design innovation produces other benefits and in turn results in higher quality products.

B. History and Development of Law

377. The first legislation in India for protection of Industrial Designs was The Patents & Designs Protection Act, 1872. It supplemented the 1859 Act passed by Governor General of India for granting exclusive privileges to inventors and added protection for Industrial Design. The 1872 Act included the term – any new and original pattern or design, or the application of such pattern or design to any substance or article of manufacture. The Inventions & Designs Act of 1888 re-enacted the law relating to protection of inventions and designs and contained provision relating to Designs in a separate part. The Patents & Designs Act enacted in 1911 also provided for protection of Industrial Designs. The Patents Act, 1970 repealed the provisions of the Patents and Designs Act, 1911, so far as they related to patents. However, the provisions relating to designs were not repealed and continued to govern the designs law. India joined the WTO as a – Member State in 1995. Consequently, the Patents & Designs Act, 1911 was repealed and the Designs Act, 2000 was enacted, to make the designs law in India TRIPS compliant. The Design Rules have been amended and came into effect from 31 December 2014. Beside revising the forms and fees, the amendment introduce the two main categories of applicants, namely: 'Natural person' and 'other than natural person(s)' categories. Second category of applicants has been further divided into two sub-categories: (1) 'Small Entity'; (2) 'others except small entity'.

C. *Meaning of Design*

378. Section 2(d) of the Indian Designs Act, 2000 defines 'design' as only features of shape, configuration, pattern, ornament or composition of lines or colours applied to any article whether in two dimensional or three dimensional or in both forms, by any industrial process or means, whether manual, mechanical or chemical, separate or combined, which in the finished article appeal to and are judged solely by the eye. The Act further clarifies that the said meaning of the word 'design', however, does not include 'any mode or principle of construction or anything which is in substance a mere mechanical devices'. It does not include a trademark or property mark or an article work either, when used under the Designs Act, 2000.

D. *Kinds of Designs*

379. In view of the modern life, designs can be looked at in various ways, e.g., industrial design, product design, stage design, costume design, fashion design. Similarly, depending upon the way they are legally protected, the designs may be classified as registered designs, unregistered designs, copyright designs, patentable designs, etc.

E. *Criteria of Registrability of a Design*

380. The Indian Designs Act, 2000 provides the only form of protection of design through registration. A design to be registered must fulfil the certain criteria like it must be a design, i.e., it must belong to the subject matter of a design which the Designs Act, 2000 aims to protect; it must be new or original; It must not be one that is excluded from registration; it should not be disclosed to the public anywhere in India or in any other country; is not significantly distinguishable from known designs or combination of more designs and comprises or contains scandalous or obscene matters.

F. *Article*

381. An 'article' according to section 2(a) of the Designs Act, 2000 means 'an article of manufacture and any substantial, artificial or partly artificial and partly natural; and includes any part of an article capable of being made and sold separately'.

1. Novelty or Originality

382. Section 4 of Designs Act imposes the conditions for registration that the design must be 'new or original'. The word 'original' has been defined in section 2(g) as: 'original, in relation to a design, means originating from the author of such design and includes the cases which though old in themselves yet are new in their application'. The design should be new or original. The novelty may reside in the application of a known shape or pattern to new subject matter. A design would be new and original, if the features of shape or pattern constituting the design are new in the sense that they were invented or created for the first time and were hitherto unknown. A design need not be new in the sense that it is 'completely new'. Such a design may be new, or rather original, in the sense that its application to the article is new.

383. Similarly, the exhibition of a design at an industrial or other exhibition or publication of its description during or after the exhibition, or the exhibition of the design or the article during or after the period of the holding of the exhibition by any person without the privity or consent of the proprietor, shall not be taken to be publication for purposes of registrability of the design concerned if the provisions of section 21 of the Act are extended by the central government to the said exhibition, by notification in the official gazette; the exhibitor exhibiting the design or article or publishing a description of the design, gives the controller previous notice in the prescribed form; and the application for registration is made within six months from the date of first exhibiting the design or article or publishing a description of the design.

2. Excluded Subject Matter

384. The third criterion for registrability of a design is that it should not form part of the excluded subject matter, in other words, a design is registrable if it does not come under that class of designs which are excluded from registrability on the ground specified in the act. A design which is not new or original, or forms part of the state of the art (either due to prior publication or being similar to a known design or a combination of known designs); or comprises or contains scandalous or obscene matter shall not be registered.[444]

G. Design Rights

385. The term 'design right' means the rights which the owner of a design may lawfully exercise. Procedure for acquiring design rights, i.e., registration of a design, nature of design rights, right of design owners, infringement and defences, consultation and restoration of design rights in that order shall be described as follows.

1. Registration

386. The design office is headed by the controller of designs who is assisted by a number of examiners and officers appointed by the central government. Since the Controller General of Patents, Designs and Trade Marks is the ex-officio controller of designs, the applications for registration of designs are filed in the prescribed form and manner in the patent office accompanied by the prescribed fee. The controller

444. Indian Designs Act, 2000, s. 4. The Controller of Designs under s. 35 of the act is empowered to refuse to register a design of which the use would, in his opinion, be contrary to public order or morality. Such a decision, however, may be challenged before the High Court.

may, under section 5 of the act, get the application examined to ensure whether the design is new or original or is not covered by excluded subject matter; if the design complies with the requisite criteria for registrability, the controller shall register the design.

387. Following the registration of a design, the proprietor of the design shall have a copyright in the design for ten years from the date of registration which may, under section 11 of the act be extended by the controller, on application and payment of a prescribed fee, for another term of five years.

2. Nature of Design Rights

388. The exclusive right conferred on a design is termed as 'copyright in design', anted for literary and artistic work also termed a 'copyright' in the literary and artistic work. There is an overlapping area of the applicability of the Designs Act and the Copyright Act but they cannot be applied co-terminously (at the same time) for protection of the same subject matter. The Designs Act provides the design protection allowing the proprietor a copy to the registered design for ten years commencing from the date of registration. This is further extendable for a further period of five years and if a design can qualify as an artistic work, under sections 16(c) and 22 of the Copyright Act, 1957 it shall enjoy legal protection for a period equal to the life of the author plus sixty years thereafter, provided that the artistic work, i.e., design is published during the lifetime of the author or creator of the design. For a design registered under the Designs Act, the protection of the Copyright Act does not extend, meaning thereby that the legal protection guaranteed under the latter (which is longer) will not be applicable towards a design registered under the former (which provides protection for a shorter duration). The copyright in any design which is registrable under the Designs Act, but has not been so registered, shall come to an end after the said design has been reproduced for more than fifty years by an industrial process by the owner of the copyright or with his licence or by any other person.[445]

389. A design may have three types of protection, all in the nature of a copyright, depending upon whether they are registered or unregistered or artistic designs such that where a design is registered under the Designs Act, 2000, the legal protection in the nature of a copyright may be availed for a maximum period of fifteen years; or where a design is registerable under the Designs Act, 2000 but not registered as such, the legal protection, again in the nature of a copyright, shall last so long as the design has been industrially reproduced for fifty times either by the copyright owner of the design or any other person working under the licence; or where a design, which qualifies as a totally artistic work, legal protection shall be given in the nature of a copyright for the lifetime of the author plus sixty years thence.

H. Who Can Claim a Right

390. Section 2(j) of the Design Act lays down the person who can claim a right. It provides that the author of the design can claim the right, for good consideration, who executes the work for some other person for whom the design is so executed; or

445. Indian Copyright Act, 1957, s. 16.

where any person acquires the design or the right to apply the design to any article, either exclusively of any other person or otherwise; or in any other case, the term 'proprietor' means 'the author of the design; and where the property in, or the right to apply the design has devolved from the original proprietor upon any other person, it includes that other person'. There is no express provision in the Designs Act which bars foreigners from applying for registration. However, the convention followed is that if a country does not offer the identical registration right to Indian citizens for their designs in their country, its citizens would not be eligible to apply for registration of design in India.

I. Rights of a Design Owner

391. The Indian Designs Act, 2000 nowhere mentions the rights of a design owner. These rights, however, have been gathered from sections 22 and 30 of the act. These rights includes: right to apply the designer class thereof in which the design is registered, for the purpose of sale or anything with the intention to enable the design to be so applied; right to import for the purpose of sale any article belonging to the class in which the design has been registered and to apply the design to such an article; to publish or cause to be published or exposed for sale the article in which the design is registered; and to authorize any other person, either through him, i.e., the proprietor's written consent or licence to use the design.

392. The purpose of the Design Act, 2000 is to protect novel designs devised to be applied to particular articles to the manufactured and marketed commercially.

J. Infringement

393. Infringement of a copyright in design is termed as 'piracy of a registered design'. It is not lawful for any person during the existence of a copyright to do the above-mentioned acts without the consent or licence of the registered proprietor of the design. Section 22(2) states that a person who infringes a registered design right shall be liable, for each infringement to pay the registered proprietor of the design a sum not exceeding INR 25,000 recoverable as a contract debt; or if the proprietor elects, to sue for recovery of damages for any such contravention, and for an injunction against the repetition thereof, to pay such damages as may be awarded and to be restrained by injunction accordingly. But the total sum recoverable as damages in respect of one design shall not exceed INR 50,000, and that no suit or any proceedings for relief shall be instituted in any court below the court of district judge.

394. In any suit or any other proceeding for relief by the registered design owner, the alleged infringer may use as a defence every ground for cancellation of the registration of the design under section 19 of the Design Act, 2000.

395. A suit under section 22 is to be instituted in a district court or a High Court depending upon the quantum of damages claimed. The burden of proof is on the plaintiff who brings an action to establish the fact of piracy of his design.

K. Grounds of Defence Against Allegations of Infringement

396. The alleged infringer can use the following grounds of defence: (a) that the design has been previously registered in India; (b) that it has been published in India or elsewhere prior to the date of registration; (c) that the design is not new or original; or (d) it is not registrable under the Act; (e) that it is not a design as defined under section 2(d) of the act.

L. Cancellation and Restoration

397. Section 19 of the Design Act, 2000, deals with cancellation of registration of design. It provides that any person can present a petition to the Controller for the cancellation of the registration of the design on above-mentioned ground. However, the order of the controller for cancelling the registration under section 19(2) of the Act can be challenged in an appeal before the High Court. If the controller finds to his satisfaction that the failure to pay the fee for the extension of the period of the copyright was unintentional and there has been no undue delay in the making of the application, he shall, upon the payment of any unpaid fee for the extension of the period of copyright, together with the prescribed additional fee, re-register the design under section 13 of the Act. Under section 14 of the act, however, restoration of the design rights as stated above by the controller will be made with certain conditions, if necessary to protect the interest of those persons who had, in the meantime, started using the said design.

M. Miscellaneous Provisions

398. The following are the miscellaneous provisions:

(1) Any interested party under section 17 of the act can inspect the register of designs with the permission of the controller or to know, under section 18 whether the copyright of a registered design is still in force.
(2) A registered design under section 20, shall have for all intents and purposes, the like effect as against the government as it has against any person.
(3) The remedy of passing off is available for the protection of unregistered design.
(4) An appeal before the High Court from the decision of the controller can be preferred within three months of the date of the order passed by the controller under section 36 of the act.
(5) The central government, under section 44 is empowered to make a reciprocal arrangement, as regards the registration of a design, with the United Kingdom and other Convention countries or group of countries or inter-governmental organizations.
(6) The controller under section 34 is empowered to apply for the directions of the central government in case of doubt or difficulty arising in the administration of any of the provisions of the act.
(7) The central government under section 47 of the act is empowered to make rules for carrying out the provisions of the act.

(8) Under section 34 the discretionary power is given to the controller, however, he shall not exercise that power adversely to the applicant for registration of a design without giving the applicant an opportunity of being heard.

(9) Any person found guilty of infringement of a layout design under section 18 of the Act shall be punishable with imprisonment of up to three years, or a fine between INR 50,000 and 1,000,000, or both. The penalty for falsely representing a layout design as registered which in reality is not registered is imprisonment up to six months, or a fine of up to INR 50,000. Where the offence is committed by a company as well, the company shall be deemed guilty of the offence proceedings should be taken against it. The person in charge of the affairs may, however, not be held liable if he proves that the offence was committed without his knowledge, or that he exercised all due diligence to prevent the commission of such an offence.

IV. Patents

A. General

399. An invention is the creation of intellect applied to capital and labour, to produce something new and useful. Such creation becomes the exclusive property of the inventor on grant of patent. The patentee's exclusive proprietary right over the invention is an intellectual property rights. The owner of the 'patent', i.e., patentee is entitled to deal with his such property in the same manner as owner of any other movable property deals with his property. The Patent law recognizes the exclusive right of a patentee to gain commercial advantage out of his invention. This is to encourage the inventors to invest their creative faculties, knowing that their inventions would be protected by law and no one else would be able to copy their inventions for certain period during which the respective inventor would have exclusive rights. India being a signatory to the Paris Convention for the protection of Industrial property, 1883 and the Patent Cooperation Treaty (PCT), 1970, therefore, a foreign entity can file application for grant of patent in India.

400. In the case of *Bishwanath Prasad Radhey Shyam v. Hindustan Metal Industries*,[446] it has been held by the Supreme Court that, 'the object of patent law is to encourage scientific research, new technology and industrial progress. Grant of exclusive privilege to own, use or sell the method or the product patented for a limited period, stimulates new inventions of commercial utility. The price of the grant of the monopoly is the disclosure of the invention at the patent office, which after expiry of the fixed period of the monopoly, passes into the public domain'.

401. The existing Indian Patents and Design Act was enacted in 1911 and since then there have been substantial changes in the political and economic conditions of the country. The first Act for protection of inventions in India, i.e., Act VI of 1856 on protection of inventions, was based on the British Patent Law of 1852. The Act was modified in 1859 and certain exclusive privileges were granted to inventors for making, selling and using inventions in India, and authorizing others to do so for fourteen years

446. AIR 1982 SC 1444.

from the date of filing specifications. The Patens and Designs Protection Act was enacted in 1872, and in 1883, the protection of Investment Act was enacted. The Indian Patents and Design Act came into effect in 1911. Two committees headed by Bakshi Tek Chand and N. Rajagopal Ayyangar JJ led to the emergence of the new patents Act. In 1970, the Patents Act, 1970 was enacted. On 20 April 1972, the Indian Patents Act came into force. This act has been amended in 1974, 1985, 1999 and 2002 and recently in the year 2005 by the Patents (Amendment) Act, 2005. The Indian Patents Rules, 2003 has been amended by way of Patents (Amendment) Rules, 2016. The amendment comes into effect on 16 May 2016. Prior to the amendment, India recognized three types of applicants, such as natural persons, small entity and other than small entity with the amendment, a fourth type of applicant, 'Startup', is being recognized. An entity will be considered a startup as long as the following conditions are met by the entity:

(a) Entity has to be a Private Limited Company (as defined in the Companies Act, 2013), or a registered partnership firm registered under section 59 of the Partnership Act, 1932 or a limited Liability Partnership under the limited Liability Partnership Act, 2002.
(b) Five years should have not lapsed since the date registration or incorporation of the entity.
(c) Turnover in any of the financial year should not be more than INR Twenty Five Crores.
(d) Entity should not have been formed by splitting up or reconstruction of a business already in existence and it is working towards innovation, development, deployment or commercialization of new products, processes or services driven by technology or intellectual property.

The patent office fees for startup, even though a legal entity, is same as the fees charged for natural persons.

B. Nature and Kinds of Patents

402. Patents are monopoly rights for a specified time span granted to one who has come out with some novel and innovative idea capable of industrial application. In India it is twenty years for an inventor. Patents are of various kinds depending upon the subject matter and specialty attached to it. On the basis of the subject matter, patent may be of three types, viz., (1) patent product; (2) patent process; and (3) hybrid patents. As regard patents specialties attached to them, the patents may be divided into several categories, e.g., patents of addition, dependent patents, secret patents and petty patents, etc.

1. Product Patents

403. They are claims on a product per se and hence, they cover all possible uses of the product. Thus, a product patent gives monopoly rights over a physical thing or product and all other possible uses of the product irrespective of the method through which the thing is produced.

2. Patent Process

404. A patent process gives protection only for a specific process or method by which a thing is produced or for a specific use of it. The patent process, therefore, may be sought and granted for any particular process or method of production or use of a physical thing or product. The patent process is generally applicable in an atmosphere where the product in question is already known, or a few methods of its production are known, or some uses of it are already familiar to society. In such a situation this is all that a person can claim in any particular process or method of its production or any specific use of it.

3. Hybrid Patents

405. They are in between a product and a process patents. For example, it is a product by process of a patent. In such a patent, the scope of protection is defined in term of the steps by which the product is produced.

4. Patents of Addition

406. They are granted to the owner of a patent to enable him to make an alteration, addition or improvement to his patented invention. Normally the term of such a patent is the remaining period of the term of original patent. Patents of addition are granted under section 54 of the Indian Patents Act, 1970. The controller of patents, however, may either grant it as patent of addition or an independent patent, and either for a full term of twenty years or for the remainder of the term of the basic patent under section 55 of the Act. In case a patent of addition is granted as an independent patent, the requisite fee will have to be paid with effect from the date of such a grant, i.e., when the latter patent has been granted. Under section 56, the grant of a patent of addition shall not be refused, and a patent granted as a patent of addition shall not be revoked or invalidated on the ground only that the invention claimed in the complete specification does not involve any inventive step. Nor shall the validity of a patent of addition be questioned on the ground that the invention ought to have been the subject of an independent patent. In determining the novelty of the invention claimed in the complete specification filed in pursuance of an application for a patent of addition, under section 56(2), regard shall also be given to the complete specification for which the main invention is described.

5. Secret Patents

407. If the government is of the opinion that the applicant is seeking a grant for a patent for an invention which is important with the view point of safety or defence of the country, the government may direct the person authorized to grant patents, to keep the application and all documents pertinent thereto as a secret until after such time as the government deems fit. Such patents are called secret patents. Section 35 of the Act empowers the central government to notify the controller of patents with a list of those subjects whereby the inventions are important for defence purposes and shall by way of an application put the application on hold until such time as the central government has had a chance to give the secret patent proper consideration. If the government finds that a secret patent is justified, the controller will proceed accordingly. Otherwise, he shall treat it as any other application and proceed likewise. The government is also empowered to notify the controller to reserve for the consideration of the government, any application which does not fall under the notified, but which now in the opinion of the government seems important for defence purposes. Section 36 provides for a periodical review of secrecy directions at intervals of six months or upon an applicant's request to the controller, and if it is found that the publication of the invention would no longer be prejudicial to the defence of India or in case of an application by a foreign secrecy cover will be lifted. If the government makes use of the said invention all the provisions of the act regarding the use of an invention by the central government under section 37 shall be applicable as if the patent had been granted for the invention. In case the applicant faces any hardship due to the treatment of his invention as a secret patent the central government may give him reasonable payment by way of a solatium. After the secrecy directions are revoked, the applicant under section 38 shall not be treated in any way as a time barred one and shall be proceeded with in a normal fashion. Section 39 makes the permit granted by the controller a precondition if one wants to apply for a patent in a foreign country for an invention except where (1) an application for a patent for the same invention has been made in India, not less than six weeks prior to the application outside India; and (2) either no secrecy direction has been given under section 35(1) in relation to the application in India, or all such directions have been revoked. In granting the said permit, the controller has to seek the prior consent of the central government. The provisions of section 39, however, do not apply to a person residing outside India and making a patent application in a country outside India even if the invention is one that is relevant for the defence or atomic energy purposes. A contravention of provisions of section 35 or 39 will result in treating the application as abandoned or, in the case of a patent grant, the patent under section 40 is to be revoked.

408. The orders of the controller or the government in connection With secrecy are final and non-appealable and unquestionable under section 41 of the Act in any court of law. section 42 provides that in the case of secret patents nothing in the act should be construed as preventing the controller from disclosing an application or specification thereof to the central government for the purpose of getting the consent of the said government either to apply secrecy directions or to revoke them.

6. Dependent Patents

409. A patent which cannot be worked unless infringing an existing patent needs a licence from the patent office to use the existing patent. The patent office may grant the said licence, independently. However, if the proprietor of the existing patent also wants a licence to use the latter patent, the patent office shall grant a similar licence for him to use the latter patent. Such a patent which cannot be exercised independently, and needs the use of an earlier patent for its successful working is known as a dependent patent. Section 91 provides that the patentee or licensee of a dependent patent may apply for the grant of a licence from an earlier patent if he is prevented or hindered without such a licence from working on the other invention, i.e., the dependent patent, efficiently or to the best advantage possible. However, before granting the said licence the controller shall be satisfied that the proprietor of the dependent patent is willing to grant a licence to the earlier patentee or his licensee a similar licence on reasonable terms. The other invention, in the opinion of the controller, should be such as having made a substantial contribution to the development of commercial or industrial activities in India.

7. Petty Patents

410. In case the application of some advanced technology results in some other form of that patented product which is useful in some way or the other, one can get, in some countries, a patent for the said new configuration or design of the patented product. Since the term for such a protection is smaller than an independent patent, such protections are often termed as petty patents. In India, however, there is no protection by way of petty patents.

C. Criteria of Patentability

411. There are certain criteria as laid down by section 2 of the Indian Patents Act, 1970 like: (a) novelty; (b) inventive step; (c) industrial applicability; (d) forming of subject matter.

1. Novelty

412. The element of novelty in an invention is dependent upon the state of prior art, i.e., the existing knowledge and similar inventions already known in the particular field. According to section 2(1)(1), an invention is new if it has not been anticipated by publication in any document or used in the country or elsewhere in the world before the date of filing the patent application with the complete specification. The Indian Patents Act, further provides that an invention shall not be deemed to have been anticipated if: (a) the publication of the invention has been made either without the consent of the true and first inventor or in contravention of his rights.[447] (b) The communication of the invention has been made to the government or to any person authorized by the government to investigate the invention or the merits.[448](c) With the consent of the true and first inventor the invention or its description in full or in part is displayed at an exhibition or published or used there, or is read before a learned society or published as part of a transaction of that society, provided that the application for the patent is made by the true and first inventor not later than twelve months after the said events, i.e., opening of exhibition or reading or publication.[449](d) Within one

447. Indian Patents Act, 1970, s. 29.
448. Indian Patents Act, 1970, s. 30.
449. Indian Patents Act, 1970, s. 31.

year before the priority date of the relevant claim of specification, the invention was publicly worked on in India and such working was for reasonable trial and was reasonably necessary.[450](e) The invention is used or published after provisional specification.[451](f) The circumstances are only as described in sections 29, 30, 31 or 32.[452]

2. Inventive Step

413. In order that a patent be granted for an invention, it should either involve an inventive step or be non-obvious to a person skilled in the art. An inventive step and non-obviousness are used interchangeably.

3. Utility, i.e., Industrial Application

414. For an invention to be patentable, it is required that it should be useful. To decide whether an invention is useful or not is, however, a matter of fact. Therefore an invention cannot be useful if it does not appear to be introducing a sufficient improvement over that which is already known to the public.

4. Subject Matter

415. The first and foremost requirement for an invention to be patentable is that it belongs to the field or fields as law does not grant patents for reasons of maintaining morality, public order, public health, public safety, national defence, unity and integrity of India or the like. If the invention qualifies on the above counts, it is said to be regarded as the subject matter of the patent. Only such an invention as this can form the subject matter of a patent. Section 3 of the act enumerates a long list of substances, articles, methods, etc. which it regards as no invention for the purposes of patentability. The Act provides one very wide criterion for non-patentability. An invention which is frivolous or which claims anything obviously contrary to well-established natural law is not an invention within the meaning of section 3(a) of the act. Another significant criterion is provided by section 4 of the act which says that 'no patent shall be granted in respect of an invention relating to atomic energy'. Further, section 3 of the Act also prohibits from being patentable an invention which is prejudicial to animal or plant life, or to the environment, or is based on traditional knowledge, or is a method of agriculture or horticulture, or is a topography of integrated circuits, or is merely an arrangement or re-arrangement or duplication of known devices. The drafter defined patent eligibility in the negative excluding the certain inventions, namely discoveries, scientific theories and mathematical methods; aesthetic creations; schemes, rules and methods for performing mental acts, playing games or doing business and programs for computers; and presentation of information.[453]

450. Indian Patents Act, 1970, s. 32.
451. Indian Patents Act, 1970, s. 33.
452. Indian Patents Act, 1970, s. 34.
453. EPC, Art. 52.

D. Requirements for the Grant of a Patent

1. Application

416. Sections 6–11 require that the application should be in proper form accompanied by a complete specification which makes a proper disclosure of the claimed invention. It should be made by the person who claims to be the true and first inventor of the invention or his assignee or, in the case of a deceased person who before his death was entitled to make such an application, the legal heir of the deceased person. Sections 9 and 10 list the contents of provisional and complete specification to be filled with the application describing the invention, method of performing, claim of invention and the provision for technical information, along with the provision for the international application for invention.

2. Publication and Examination

417. The application in accordance with sections 11A–21 should undergo publication and examination stages. According to section 13, the examiner to whom an application for a patent is referred under section 12 shall make investigation for the purpose of ascertaining whether the invention so far as claimed in any claim of the complete specification. The examiner shall, in addition, make such investigation for the purpose of ascertaining whether the invention has been anticipated by publication in India or elsewhere in any document before the date of filing of the applicant's complete specification. The controller, however, may not allow the details of an application to be open to the public for a prescribed period of time during which he is free to ascertain in consultation with the central government whether the invention is one which should be kept secret. After that period has expired, the application may be allowed by the controller to be made public only upon request from the applicant. From the date of publication until the grant of the patent, the applicant shall have all the rights and privileges as if the patent had been granted on the date of publication. The applicant cannot institute infringement proceedings against anybody until after the actual grant of the patent.

3. Opposition

418. When the application for a patent has been published, but a patent has not been granted, any person may, in writing, represent to the controller to oppose the grant of the patent on the ground that:

(1) the applicant wrongfully obtained the invention or a part thereof from him or from a person under or through him; or
(2) the invention has already been made public in the specification of an earlier application published on or before the priority date of the application in question. The representation opposing the grant of the patent may also be made to the controller within one year from the date of the grant of the patent on similar grounds. In case the controller finds that the invention is really an 'obtained' one,

he may, on request from the opponent to this effect, grant the patent in favour of the opponent, revoking the grant, if it has been made in favour of the applicant. If the controller is satisfied, upon a request or claim made in respect thereof, he may cause a person to be mentioned as an inventor in any patent granted in pursuance of the application in the complete specification, and in the register of patents.

4. Amendment

419. The controller may, on an application by the applicant for a patent, allow him to amend his application for the patent or complete specification or any document related thereto. The application for leave to amend the application for a patent may be published, and any person can, within a prescribed period of time give notice to the controller of opposition thereto. The controller shall, after properly hearing the applicant as well as the opponent, decide the case. In any proceedings before the appellate board or the High Court for revocation of a patent, the board or the court, as the case may be, may allow the patentee to amend his complete specification in such manner and under such terms as to costs which the board or court think fit. However, in any proceedings for revocation where the patent is found invalid, the board or the court may allow the specification to be amended instead of revoking the patent. In such cases the person filing the suit shall give notice to the controller and also under section 58 be entitled to appear before and be heard by the board or the court. The amendment allowed by the controller or the appellate board or the High Court has to be subject to the provisions of section 59 which does not allow an amendment or which may: (1) describe any matter not already described; or (2) make any claim not already made, in the original specification. Where the amendments are allowed after the grant of patent, they shall form the part of the original specification and this shall be published as soon as possible.

5. International Convention

420. A country who is a member of any international, regional or bilateral treaty to which India is also a party is called a convention country. For grant of a patent, applicants from convention countries are accorded national treatment in India only if the same treatment is accorded to the Indian applicants in those countries. When a person has made an application for a patent in respect of an invention in a convention country (it is called a basic application) and, within a period of one year, makes an application under the Indian Patent Act also, the priority date here shall be regarded the same as that of the basic application. Every convention application shall be accompanied by a complete specification and shall mention the date on which, and the convention country in which, the application for the patent was first made. In case two or more applications for patents in respect of inventions, have been made in one or more convention countries, and the inventions are so related as to constitute one invention, one application under the Indian Patents Act, may be made by any or all the applicants of the said interrelated inventions. Applicants of convention applications shall be bound to provide, in addition to complete specification, any other document which the controller may require for his satisfaction as to grant protection. Barring the relevant exceptions provided under the act, all the provisions of the Act shall apply to a convention application and the patent granted in pursuance thereof, in the same way as they apply to an ordinary application and a patent granted in pursuance thereof.

6. Patent Agents

421. To practice as a patent agent under the Act, a person has to get his name registered as a patent agent by making an application in Form 22 as specified in the Patent Rules 2003 at the Head Office of the Patent Office. Every patent agent shall be entitled to practice before the Controller and prepare all documents, transact all business and discharge such other functions as may be prescribed by the Controller.[454] Patent agent is authorized to sign all application and communication to the Controller on behalf of the person concerned, upon his being authorized in writing to do so by that person. Under section 129, no person shall practice, describe or hold himself out as a patent agent unless he is duly registered under the Act. Patent agent must be: (a) citizen of India; (b) completed the age of 21 years; (c) has obtained a degree in science, engineering or technology; (d) an advocate; (e) has paid such fee as may be prescribed.[455]

7. Grant of Patent

422. If the application for the grant of a patent is found in order and if neither the controller has refused it nor does it violate any other provision of the act, the patent shall be granted, and published by the controller. Section 53 of the Patent Act lays down that the term of patent after the commencement of the Patent (Amendment) Act, 2002 or the term of every patent which has not expired and has not ceased to have effect, on the date of commencement of the said Act, shall be twenty years from the date of filling of the application for the patent. After the grant of the patent, the controller can amend it if the patent owner has died and replace the deceased's name with the name of the person who, in absence of the deceased, ought to have been granted the patent. A patent is granted for one invention only and ordinarily the date for filing the application is regarded as the date of the patent. A grant of patent is always made subject to the condition that the patentee shall have no right to prevent the exploitation of patent either by the government for its own use or by the institutions for the purpose of instruction or teaching and research.

a. Rights of the Patent Owner

423. Rights conferred on a patentee under the Patent Act are following: (i) to exploit the patent; (ii) to licence the patent to another; (iii) to assign the patent to another; (iv) to surrender the patent; (v) to sue for the infringement of the patent. The owner of a patent has a right to exclude others from the act of making, using, offering for sale, selling or importing for those purposes that product in India, if the patent is for a product. Where the patent is not a product patent but instead a process patent,

454. Indian Patents Act, 1970, s. 125.
455. Indian Patents Act, 1970, s. 126.

the owner has the right to exclude others, without their consent, from using that process, and from the act of using, offering for sale, selling or importing for those purposes the product obtained directly by that process. However, if a patented article is used, either temporarily or accidentally on a foreign vessel in the territory of India, it shall not be an infringement of the patentees' rights.

b. Revocation of Patents

424. A patent can be revoked if, on a petition to the appellate board or High Court, it is found that another patent had been granted for the same invention before the patent in question; or that the invention claimed therein is not an invention by reason of being already in use in India, or being obvious to a person skilled in the state of the art; or that the invention is not patentable under the provisions of the act. There is a detailed list of the grounds under section 64 of the Act on which a patent may be revoked on a petition from an interested party or the central government. The Act also provides revocation of a patent by the central government itself, if: (a) patent relates to atomic energy which is not patentable under the Act; or (b) the government is of the opinion that the patent goes against the public interest. Under section 63 of the act, a patent can also be revoked after it has been surrendered. For this, the patentee has to give notice to the controller. Thereupon the controller will publish notice to this effect inviting opposition from a person interested in it. Such a person should be one whose name, other than the patentee, appears in the register of patents, as having an interest in the patent. The Controller after hearing the opposition and the patentee is satisfied that the patent may properly be surrendered, may accept the patentees' offer and by order revoke the patent.

c. Restoration of Patents

425. Where a patent has ceased to have effect by reason of non-payment of fee as prescribed, the patentee or his legal heir, or any of the co-owners with the permission of the controller, as the case may be, may apply within a period of eighteen months after the cessation of the patent. The applicant has to justify the delay in payment of the fee which led to the cessation of the patent. The controller, after hearing the applicant, may allow the application if he is convinced that the delay in the payment of the fee was not intentional. After this, the controller shall publish the application which may be opposed and if after hearing the applicant and the opponent, the controller deems fit, may allow the restoration of the patent and require that it be entered into the register of patents.

d. Compulsory Licence

426. The term of patent can, however, be cut short by the grant of 'compulsory licence' or 'license of right' to any person to work the invention when the patentee fails to work the invention in public interest. Under section 84 of the Patent Act stipulates that at any time after the expiration of three years from the date of grant of patent, any interested person may make an application to the Controller for grant of compulsory licence on any of the patent. In Geigy SA's Patent[456] case it was held that three elements should be taken into account in calculating the licence fee: an allowance for research and development costs, an allowance for promotional costs and appropriate uplift.

8. Infringement and Defences

427. A patent confers the exclusive right on the patentee to make, distribute or sell the invention in India. An infringement would be when any of these rights is violated. The person in whom this right is vested, be it the owner of the patent or an assignee or a licensee or anybody else who lawfully has an interest in the patented invention, can bring infringement proceedings against the unauthorized user. In case of a product patent, the rights of the patentee are infringed by anyone who makes or supplies that substance commercially. In case of a process patent, the use of such a method or process in India by anyone other than the patentee amounts to infringement.

428. The defences available are that the invention is not really an invention under the meaning of the act, that it had been obtained wrongfully in contravention of the rights of somebody else who really claimed it, that it was obvious and that it had been the subject matter of an earlier patent, etc. According to section 107, all the grounds on which a patent may be revoked may be the grounds of defence in a suit of infringement.[457] The basic requirement is that the product or process should be an inventive one; otherwise it shall not withstand infringement proceedings or, equivalently, revocation proceedings.

9. Geographical Indications

429. Geographical Indication (GI) is a relatively new but important instrument in intellectual property protection. Articles 22–24 of Part II, Part III of the TRIPS Agreement prescribes minimum standard of protection for GIs that WTO members must provide. The TRIPS[458] Agreement defines GIs as: Indications which identify a good as originating in the territory of a member of the WTO, or a region or locality in that territory, where a given quality reputation or other characteristic of the good is essentially attributable to its geographical origin.[459] The Geographical Indications of Goods (Registration and Protection) Act, 1999 was passed in December 1999 to comply with India's with India's international obligations under the TRIPS Agreement to provide legal means for the protection of GI.

456. 1964 RPC 391.

457. *The Pilot Pen Co. (India) Private Ltd. Madras v. The Gujarat Industries Private Ltd., Bombay*, AIR 1967 Mad. 215.

458. The Trade Related Aspects of Intellectual Property Rights (TRIPS),Under the WTO TRIPS Agreement, protection is provided for GI in terms of Art. 22. It draws from the definition of appellation of origin in Lisbon Agreement.

459. TRIPS Agreement, 1994, Art. 22.I.

10. Definition of GIs

430. The Act defines 'Geographical Indication'[460] in relation to goods, means an indication which identifies such goods as agricultural good, natural goods or manufactured goods as originating, or manufactured in the territory of country, or a region or locality in that territory where a given quality, reputation or other characteristic of such goods is essentially attributable to its geographical origin and in case where such goods are manufactured goods, one of the activities of either the production or of processing or preparation of the goods concerned takes place in such territory, region or locality, as the case may be. Tequila, Scotch, Cogac, Roquefort cheese are examples of GI. GI in relation to goods, means an indication which identifies such goods as agricultural goods, natural goods or manufactured goods as originating, or manufactured in the territory of country, or a region or locality in that territory where a given quality, reputation or other characteristic of such goods is essentially attributable to its geographical origin and in case where such goods are manufactured goods, one of the activities of either the production or of processing or preparation of the goods concerned takes place in such territory, region or locality, as the case may be. The terms goods and indications are defined as Goods means any agricultural, natural or manufactured goods or any goods of handicraft or of industry and includes food stuff. Indication includes any name, geographical or figurative representation or any combination of them conveying or suggesting the geographical origin of goods to which it applies. Darjeeling Tea became the first GI tagged product in India, in 2004–2005, since then by November 2015, 272 had been added to the list.[461]

431. Under the Act, a GI is an indication originating from a certain geographical territory used to identify agricultural, natural or manufactured goods that have a special quality, reputation or other characteristics essentially attributable to its geographical origin. The manufactured goods must be produced, or processed or prepared in such territory, region or locality. Furthermore, any name, which is not the name of a country, region or locality of that country shall also be considered as GI if it relates to a specific geographical area and is used in relation to particular goods originating from that country or region or locality.

11. Registration

432. The registration of a GI is necessary. Registration confers certain rights, as discussed later, on the registered proprietor or authorized user in cases of infringement of registered GI.

12. Application for Registration and Its Acceptance

433. Any association of persons or producers or organization or authority established by or under the law representing the interest of the producers can apply for the registration of a GI.

---

460. GI Act, 1999, S.2(I)(g).

461. GI Tag in India, Geographical Indications Registry, Intellectual Property Office, Chennai, Retrieved 28 Dec. 2013.

434. The application must be done in writing in the prescribed form addressed to the Registrar of Geographical Indications along with the prescribed fees The Controller-General of Patents, Designs and Trade Marks is the Registrar of Geographical Indications. The application for registration of a GI must contain a statement describing how the GI serves to designate the goods as originating from the concerned region in respect of the specific quality or reputation or other characteristics due exclusively or essentially to the geographical environment, with its inherent natural or human factors and the production of which takes place in such territory or locality or region; class of goods to which the GI shall apply; particulars regarding the appearance of the GI as to whether it is comprised of the words or figurative elements or both; and a statement containing such particulars of the producers of the concerned goods, if any, proposed to be initially registered with the registration of the GI as may be prescribed.[462] Every application shall be files in the office of the Geographical Indication Registry within whose territorial limits, the territory of the country or the region or locality in the country to which the GI relates is situated.

13. Withdrawal of Acceptance

435. Where the application for registration has been accepted by the Registrar but before its registration, the Registrar is satisfied that the acceptance has been in error, or in the circumstances such that the GI should not be registered or should be registered under conditions different from the conditions or limitations mentioned in the application, the Registrar may withdraw the acceptance.

14. Advertisement of Application

436. Once the application for registration has been accepted, the Registrar shall advertise the application as accepted together with conditions of acceptance. After the advertisement, the registration can be opposed, as described in the next subsection.

15. Opposition

437. Any person who wants to oppose the application for registration may file a notice of opposition within three months from the date of advertisement or re-advertisement of an application for registration or within a further period not exceeding one month, in writing to the Registrar; and on payment of prescribed fees.[463]

438. The Registrar will serve a copy of the received notice on the applicant. The applicant must send a counter-statement of the grounds on which he relies in support of the registration application within two months of the receipt of the notice of the opposition. The Registrar will send a copy of the counter-statement made by the applicant to the opponent and after hearing the parties and considering the materials on record and evidence adduced by them, decide the matter. If the applicant fails to file a counter-statement within two months, the application shall be deemed to have

462. GI Act, 1999, s. 11.
463. GI Act, 1999, s. 14.

been abandoned. The Registrar is empowered to make correction of any error and amendments in an application.

439. In case of opposition to the application, if the opponent or the applicant neither resides nor carries on business in India, the Registrar may require a security to cover cost of proceedings before him. In the absence of such security, the opposition, or the application, as the case may be, may be treated as abandoned.

16. Registration

440. Once an application has been accepted, opposed or unopposed, the Registrar shall, unless otherwise directed by the Central Government, register the GI and the authorized users, if any, mentioned in the application. The date of registration shall be the date of filing of the application for registration. The Registrar will then issue a certificate in the prescribed form sealed with the seal of the Geographical Indications Registry to the applicant. In case the registration of a GI is not completed within twelve months from the date of application due to applicant's default, the application shall be treated as abandoned after giving notice to the applicant. The Registrar has the power to amend the register or the certificate of registration for correcting any clerical error or an obvious mistake.

17. Authorized User

441. Any person can apply in writing in prescribed manner, accompanied by required statements and documents for registration as an authorized user in respect of a registered GI, if the person claims to be a producer of goods covered under the registered GI. The persons dealing with the following three specified categories of goods would be held to be producer:

(i) In the case of agricultural goods, if the person produces the same, including the one who processes or packages such goods.
(ii) In the case of natural goods, if the person exploits such goods.
(iii) In the case of handicrafts or industrial goods, if the person makes, manufactures, trades or deals in such production or exploitation or making or manufacturing of the goods.

18. Register

442. The Register of Geographical Indications is a record kept at the head office of the Geographical Indications Registry. In this register, all registered GI with the names, addresses and descriptions of the proprietors, the names, addresses and descriptions of authorized user and such other prescribed matters relating to registered GIs are entered. Such registers may be maintained wholly or partly on computer. The Registrar can keep the records wholly or partly in computer floppies or diskettes or in any other electronic form, subject to prescribed safeguards.

443. A copy of the register and such other documents as may be notified by the central government in the official gazette shall be kept at each branch office of the GI

Registrar. The Register has two parts. Part A contains particulars relating to the registration of GIs. Part B contains the particulars relating to the authorized users.

19. Term

444. Registration is required both for a GI as well as an authorized user. A GI is registered for a period of ten years. The registration can be renewed from time to time for further ten years from the expiration of last registration. An authorized user is registered for a period of ten years, or till the date of expiry of the registration of the GI for which the authorized user is registered whichever is earlier. For registration, or renewal of registration an application is to be made in the prescribed format accompanied by the prescribed fee in each case. If the registration is not renewed when due, the GI or the authorized user for it, as the case may be, is removed from the register. However, an application to continue the registration can be made within six months from the expiration of the last registration. Registration of a GI is not mandatory under the Act. However, if a GI is registered, it affords a better legal protection to authorized users in cases of infringement of registered GIs. No infringement proceedings can be launched under the Act, for an unregistered GI, either to prevent infringement or to recover the damages.

445. In case of two or more authorized users, they would have co-equal rights as against other persons and no one will have the exclusive right to the use of any of those GIs. Any right to a registered GI is not the subject matter of assignment, transmission, licensing, mortgage or any such agreement. But on the death of an authorized user, the user's right in a registered GI passes on to his successor.

20. Infringement

446. A registered GI is infringed by a person who, not being an authorized user thereof uses such GI by any means in the designations or presentation of goods that indicates or suggests that such goods originate in a geographical area other than the true place of origin of such goods in a manner which misleads the persons as to the geographical origin of such goods.

Hence the infringement of registered GI occurs if a person:

- uses the GI on the goods or suggests that such goods originate in a geographical area other than the true place of origin of such goods in a manner which misleads the public; or
- uses the GI in a manner that constitutes an act of unfair competition; or
- uses the GI to the goods in a manner, which falsely represents to the public that the goods originate in the territory, region or locality in respect of which such registered GI relates.

21. Suit and Relief

447. A suit for infringement of a registered GI is to be instituted in a district court having jurisdiction to try the suit. The court can grant to the plaintiff relief in the form of injunction and, at the option of the plaintiff, either damages or account of profits together with any order for destruction or erasure of infringing labels and indications, if necessary. However, the court shall not grant relief by way of damages or account of profits, if the defendant satisfies the court that he was unaware and had no reasonable ground to believe that the GI complained of was on the register in the name of plaintiff and that when he became aware of the existence and the nature of the plaintiff's right in the GIs, he forthwith ceased to use it.

22. Appeal

448. Appeals against an order or decision of the Registrar or the rules framed may be prefer by the aggrieved person within three months from the date on which the order or decision is communicated to him to the Appellate Board, established under the Trade Mark Act, 1999.

23. Protection of Certain Trademarks

449. The Act prohibits registration of a GI as a trademark. The GI Act saves the right of a person who had used the mark or who had applied for or registered in good faith under the law relating to trademarks either before the commencement of the GI Act or before the date of filing of the application for registration of the Act.[464] The limitation period for taking the action for infringement of a GI by use or registration of a trade mark is five years from the date on which such use or registration infringes any GI registered under Act or after the date of registration of the trade mark under the Trade Marks Act.[465]

24. Offence and Penalties

450. A person will be considered to have committed offence under section 37 the GI Act, 1999 if he falsely applying GI; or falsifying a GI.

Under the GI Act, applying a GI has specific meaning. A person is deemed to apply a GI to goods in any of the following situations:

- the GI is applied to goods themselves or to any package in which goods are sold, or is possessed for any purpose of trade or manufacture;
- if any goods meant for sale or any purpose of trade or manufacture are enclosed with any package or thing for which a GI has been applied;
- using a GI in connection with goods in any manner likely to lead to the belief that the GI designates or describes the said goods; or
- using a GI in relation to certain goods in any commercial document (including advertisement, invoice, catalogue, business letter, etc.) and delivering the goods to a person following a request made with reference to the GI so used.

464. GI Act, s. 26(I).
465. GI Act, s. 26(4).

A GI is considered to be applied to goods when it is woven in, or impressed on, or otherwise worked into or annexed or affixed to the goods or to any package or other thing.

A person shall be held to *falsify* a GI if he makes that GI or a deceptively similar GI without the assent of the authorized user; or falsifies any genuine GI by alteration, addition, effacement, etc.

Further, a person shall be held to falsely apply a GI to goods if without the assent of the authorized user, he applies such GI or a deceptively similar GI to any goods or any package containing goods; or uses any package bearing a GI which is identical with or deceptively similar to the GI of such authorized user for the purpose of packing, filling or wrapping therein any goods other than the genuine goods of the authorized user of the GI. In a prosecution for falsifying or falsely applying a GI to goods, the burden of proving the assent of the proprietor lies with the accused.

25. Penalty for Offences

451. A person who falsifies GI; or falsely applies to goods any GI; or makes, disposes of, or has in possession, any die, block, machine, plate or other instrument for the purpose of falsifying a GI; or applies to any goods a false indication of country, place, manufacturers name or address; or tempers with an indication of origin applied to any goods shall be punishable with imprisonment for a term between six month and three years and a fine between INR 50,000 and INR 200,000.

452. For selling goods to which false GI is applied: A person who sells or lets for hire, or has in possession for sale, goods or things to which any false GI is applied is punishable with imprisonment for a term, which shall not be less than six months but may extend to three years and with fine ranging from INR 50,000 to INR 200,000. The court may reduce the term of imprisonment or the amount of fine below the minimum as prescribed if adequate special reasons exist.

453. There is a provision of enhanced penalty on second or subsequent conviction for the second and every subsequent offence. The period of imprisonment is between one and three years accompanied by a fine of INR 100,000–INR 200,000. However, the court may, for adequate and special reasons to be mentioned in the judgment, impose a sentence of imprisonment for a term of less than one year or a fine of less than INR 1 lakh.

26. Acts Not Constituting Offence

454. No act or omission shall be deemed to be an offence relating to a registered GI if the act or omission is permitted under the Act, or under any other law in force.

27. Reciprocity and Prohibition from Registration

455. The Act provides for reciprocal treatment of foreign nationals. It gives equal rights to nationals of a foreign country as available to Indian nationals in respect of registration and protection of GIs if their country accords the same rights to Indian nationals as to its own nationals. However, if a country does not give the same rights to the citizens of India as it gives to its own nationals, its nationals are not entitled to apply for registration of, or be registered as the proprietor or an authorized user of a GI. The Act prohibits registration of GI falling into following categories:

- the use of which would be likely to deceive or cause confusion; or
- the use of which would be contrary to any law in force; or
- which comprises or contains scandalous or obscene matter; or
- which comprises or contains any matter likely to hurt the religious susceptibilities of any class or section of the citizens of India; or
- which would otherwise be disentitled to protection in a court; or
- which are determined to be generic names or indications of goods and are, therefore, not protected in their country of origin, or which have fallen into disuse in that country; or
- which, although literally true as to the territory, region or locality in which the goods originate, but falsely represent to the public that the goods originate in another territory, region or locality, as the case may be.[466]

466. GI Act, 1999, s. 9.

Chapter 6. Bankruptcy and Related Institutions

§1. Bankruptcy

I. Introduction

456. In an ordinary meaning bankrupt means one who fails in business or/and insolvent debtor. Bankruptcy means, the state of being an act of becoming bankrupt. However, this word has great economic and legal implications. In India, therefore, two principles underlie the law of bankruptcy. First, the law should provide equitable distribution of the estate of an insolvent in an efficacious manner. Second, in order to prevent a debtor from taking undue advantage, and if an individual is fair, then to allow that person to make a fresh start.

457. The Insolvency Act prevalent in India is, however, primarily based on the Bankruptcy Law of England. Insolvency is a legal concept which exists for the purpose of administering, according to rules of law, the property of a person unable to pay his debts. During the Colonial rule, the British enacted the Presidency Town Insolvency Act, 1909 and Provincial Insolvency Act, 1920 and various rules governing insolvency proceedings. After independence, Parliament has by Article 372 of the Constitution of India[467] practically retained the same laws. The present bankruptcy laws prevalent in India and are still the same with a few minor amendments. The Presidential Town Insolvency Act, 1909 presently applies to the metropolitan cities of Mumbai, Kolkata and Chennai and the Provincial Insolvency Act, 1920 applies to the rest of India. Both the above Acts are based on the English Bankruptcy Act, 1914, and a majority of the provisions are common to both of them. But there are certain procedural differences between the two Acts. The Acts include two procedures for dealing with personal insolvency. The first is realization of the property of a debtor where the divisible property is taken away and applied to the payment of his debt. The second is the scheme of composition and arrangement under sections 28–32 of Part II of the Presidency Town Insolvency Act and sections 38–40 of Part II of the Provincial Insolvency Act. The Insolvency and Bankruptcy Code, 2016 No. 31 of 2016 received the assent of president on 28 May 2016. Certain provisions of has come into force on 5 August and 19 August 2016. The Code seeks to repeal the Presidency Towns Insolvency Act, 19 Act, 1993 and Sick Industrial Companies (Special Provisions) Repeal Act, 2003.[468]

The preamble of the Insolvency and Bankruptcy Code, 2016 provide:[469]

467. Article 372 of the Constitution of India provides that all laws in force in India immediately prior to the commencement of the Constitution shall remain in force until altered, repealed, and amended by a competent authority.

468. Available on http://www.indiacode.nic.in/acts-in-pdf/2016/201631.pdf.

469. *Ibid.*

> An Act to consolidate and amend the laws relating to reorganisation and insolvency resolution of corporate persons, partnership firms and individuals in a time bound manner for maximisation of value of assets of such persons, to promote entrepreneurship, availability of credit and balance the interests of all the stakeholders including alteration in the order of priority of payment of Government dues and to establish an Insolvency and Bankruptcy Board of India, and for matters connected therewith or incidental thereto.

These are following key features of the new Code:[470]

(1) Corporate Debtors: Two-Stage Process.
To initiate an insolvency process for corporate debtors, the default should be at least INR 100,000 (USD 1,495) (which limit may be increased up to INR 10,000,000 (USD 149,500) by the Government). The Code proposes two independent stages:

(a) *Insolvency Resolution Process (IPR)*: The IRP provides a collective mechanism to lenders to deal with the overall distressed position of a corporate debtor.
(b) *Liquidation*: if the insolvency resolution process fails or financial creditors decide to wind down and distribute the assets of the debtor. Under the Code, a corporate debtor may be put into liquidation in the following scenarios:

(i) a 75% majority of the creditor's committee resolves to liquidate the corporate debtor at any time during the insolvency resolution process;
(ii) the creditor's committee does not approve a resolution plan within 180 days (or within the extended 90 days);
(iii) the NCLT rejects the resolution plan submitted to it on technical grounds; or
(iv) the debtor contravenes the agreed resolution plan and an affected person makes an application to the NCLT to liquidate the corporate debtor.

(2) Insolvency Resolution Process for Individuals/Unlimited Partnerships
For individuals and unlimited partnerships, the Code applies in all cases where the minimum default amount is INR 1,000 (USD 15) and above (the Government may later revise the minimum amount of default to a higher threshold). The Code envisages two distinct processes in case of insolvencies: automatic fresh start and insolvency resolution. The eligible debtors (basis gross income) can apply to the Debt Recovery Tribunal (**DRT**) for discharge from certain debts not exceeding a specified threshold, allowing them to start afresh. The insolvency resolution process consists of preparation of a repayment plan by the debtor, for approval of creditors. If approved, the DRT passes an order binding the debtor and creditors to the repayment plan. If the plan is rejected or fails, the debtor or creditors may apply for a bankruptcy order.

470. Available on http://www.indiacode.nic.in/acts-in-pdf/2016/201631.pdf.

(3) Institutional Infrastructure: The code provides the constitution of a new insolvency regulator, i.e., the Insolvency and Bankruptcy Board of India. It also provides for insolvency professionals as intermediaries who would play a key role in bankruptcy process and such professional shall follow the minimum professional and ethical conduct. It also provides for creation of information utilities to collect, collate, authenticate and disseminate financial information of debtors in centralized electronic databases. The adjudicating authority for corporate insolvency and liquidation is the NCLT. Appeals from NCLT orders lie to the National Company Law Appellate Tribunal and thereafter to the Supreme Court of India. For individuals and other persons, the adjudicating authority is the DRT, appeals lie to the Debt Recovery Appellate Tribunal and thereafter to the Supreme Court.

Therefore, it aims to create the time bound processes for insolvency resolution of the companies and individuals. The resolution processes will be conducted by Insolvency professional Agencies (IPA). Information Utilities (IU) will be established to collect, consolidate and to disseminate financial information to facilitate insolvency resolutions. The National Company Law Tribunal (NCLT) will adjudicate insolvency resolutions for companies and Debt Recovery Tribunal (DRT) will adjudicate the insolvency resolutions for individuals.[471]

458. The Insolvency Act lays down two parameters for adjudging a person. First, he should have committed an act of insolvency and second he is subject to the jurisdiction of a court. A non-resident or a foreigner who commits an act of insolvency in India may be adjudged insolvent.[472] It applies to a married woman, partners, partnership firms and joint debtors.[473] But it exempts minors, persons of unsound mind and corporations.[474] Minors and persons of unsound mind are exempted by virtue of sections 11 and 12 of the Indian Contract Act. The liquidation or winding up of a corporation is exclusively covered by The Companies Act, 2013.

II. Constitution and Powers of Courts

459. The powers of Insolvency Courts under both enactments are similar to those exercised by them under their ordinary original civil jurisdiction, civil appellate jurisdiction and revisional jurisdiction.[475] The Presidency Town Insolvency Act empowers the High Courts of Mumbai, Kolkata and Chennai to have jurisdiction in insolvency matters. There is a provision for appeal but there is no further appeal except with the leave of the Court.[476] The insolvency jurisdiction for the whole of India except the Presidency Towns is vested in the District Courts. Appeal lies in High Court under

471. At http://finmin.nic.in/reports/DraftInsolvencyBankruptcyBil2015.pdf & http://www.prsindia.org/billtrack/the-insolvency-and-bankruptcy-bill-2015-.
472. Presidency Town Insolvency Act, 1909, s. 11 and Provincial Insolvency Act, 1920, s. 8.
473. Presidency Town Insolvency Act, 1909, s. 99 and Provincial Insolvency Act, 1920, s. 79(2).
474. Presidency Town Insolvency Act, 1909, s. 107 and Provincial Insolvency Act, 1920, s. 8.
475. Presidency Town Insolvency Act, 1909, s. 90 and Provincial Insolvency Act, 1920, s. 5.
476. Presidency Town Insolvency Act, 1909, s. 3 and s. 8.

section 100 of the Code of Civil Procedure, 1908.[477] Moreover, even a court of Small Causes may have insolvency jurisdiction if specially empowered in that behalf by the state government. An official assignee – official receiver is appointed under the Presidency Town Insolvency Act. The official receiver may be appointed under the Provincial Insolvency Act and these officers are responsible for the equitable distribution of a bankrupt estate.[478]

III. Bankruptcy Proceedings

460. It is the act of insolvency and not the insolvency petition, which gives jurisdiction to the Insolvency Court. Act of insolvency is a creation of statute. There is no common law of an act of insolvency, not even if the consequences of the act are precisely identical to act of insolvency.

461. When a debtor commits an act of insolvency, an insolvency petition may be presented either by the creditor or by the debtor and the court may on such petition adjudge him as an insolvent.[479]

462. The procedure laid down in the Civil Procedure Code 1908 is to be adopted with respect to admission of plaint, service of summons and other proceedings.[480] At the hearing and after perusal of all the proofs and evidences the court may pass the order of adjudication.[481]

463. Upon becoming insolvent, the debtor's property vests in the receiver, official receiver, official assignee.[482]

464. Upon the order of adjudication, all persons alleging themselves to be creditors of insolvents are required to lodge proof of their debts by producing evidence of the amount and particulars. The court shall determine the persons who have proved themselves to be creditors and the amount of debts they owe and the court shall frame a schedule of such persons and debt.[483]

465. The divisible property of the bankrupt is then realized for the benefit of the creditors and on the basis of priority of debts distributed amongst creditors.[484]

466. The debtor may at any time after the order of adjudication apply for discharge. The court may, if it deems fit, grant or refuse an absolute or conditional order of discharge of an insolvent.[485] An order of discharge, however, does not release

477. Provincial Insolvency Act, 1909, s. 3 and s. 75.
478. Presidency Town Insolvency Act, 1909, s. 77 and Provincial Insolvency Act, 1920, ss 56, 57.
479. The Presidency Town Insolvency Act, 1909, s. 10 and Provincial Insolvency Act, 1920, s. 7.
480. Provincial Insolvency Act, 1909, ss 18, 19.
481. Presidency Town Insolvency Act, 1909, ss 13(5), 15(3) and the Provincial Insolvency Act, 1920, s. 27.
482. Presidency Town Insolvency Act, 1909, Part IV, ss 77–87 and Provincial Insolvency Act, 1920, ss 56–59.
483. Presidency Town Insolvency Act, 1909, s. 46(1)(3) and Provincial Insolvency Act, 1920, s. 33.
484. Presidency Town Insolvency Act, 1909, ss 58–76 and Provincial Insolvency Act, 1920, ss 56–68.
485. Presidency Town Insolvency Act, 1909, ss 38(1), 40 and Provincial Insolvency Act, 1920, s. 41.

an insolvent from any debt owed to the government.[486] Section 39 of Presidency Town Insolvency Act, 1909, and section 42 of Provincial Insolvency Act, 1920, enumerates the circumstances under which an insolvent can be given conditional discharge only.

467. As can be seen from this outline a debtor who has committed an act of insolvency can himself present a petition or be compelled to become bankrupt by his creditors on presentation of a petition.

A. Acts of Insolvency

468. The first necessary step to initiate insolvency proceedings against an individual is to prove that he has committed an act of insolvency. This is designed to check frivolous insolvency proceedings. These acts of insolvency include transferring property in order to delay or defeat creditors, transferring property to a third person for the benefit of creditors, fraudulent preference, departure or seclusion, sale of property in execution of a decree, a debtor's petition for insolvency, suspension of payment or imprisonment in execution of a decree by any court for payment of money or non-payment after serving an insolvency notice.[487]

469. In *Gopisetti Venkata Lakshmi Narasimharao v. M/s. Sri Satya Financial Services*,[488] it was held that section 6 of the Provincial Insolvency Act defines acts of insolvency. If a debtor makes a transfer of his property or any part thereof with intent to defeat or delay his creditors, he would be committing one of the acts of insolvency enumerated in the above provision. If an act of insolvency is committed, the remedy of the affected creditor is to present a petition against the debtor within a period of three months from the date of the debtor committing an act of insolvency to get the order of adjudication of debtor as an insolvent. These two remedies are available to the affected creditor.

1. Who Can Be Adjudged Insolvent

470. An individual, a partnership firm can be adjudged insolvent only if all the partners collectively have committed any one or more acts of insolvency. A minor and a joint Hindu family cannot be adjudged insolvent.[489]

B. Debtor's Petition

471. A debtor shall not be entitled to file an insolvency petition unless he is unable to pay his debts and the debt amounts to INR 500 or he is under imprisonment in execution of payment of money or an order of attachment in execution of such a decree has been made against his property. The debtor's petition should contain a plea that he is unable to pay his debts and prove that he is entitled to present the petition

486. Presidency Town Insolvency Act, 1909, s. 45 and Provincial Insolvency Act, 1920, s. 44.
487. Presidency Town Insolvency Act, 1909, ss 9, 9A and Provincial Insolvency Act, 1920, ss 6, 6A.
488. 2010 (3) ALT 325, *see also S. Dalip Singh v. The U.P.F.C. & Ors* decided on 17 Feb. 2010 in the High Court of Delhi.
489. *Vela Partha Garasia v. Ms Kusum M Shah* For decided on 2 Sept. 2011, in the High Court of Gujarat.

on the above grounds. A petition once presented cannot be withdrawn without the leave of the court.[490] The words 'unable to pay his debts' imply that his liabilities far exceeds his assets, that the market value of his realizable assets is less than his whole indebtedness. The burden of proving such inability lies on the debtor.

C. Creditor's Petition

472. A creditor can present a petition to declare his debtor insolvent only if the debt owed by the debtor is at least INR 500. The debt must be a liquidated sum or the Act of Insolvency on which the petition is grounded must have occurred within three months before the submittal of the petition.[491] The creditor's petition must be verified by a person who knows the relevant facts. The court shall also require proof of the debt of the petitioning creditor and the act of insolvency. An insolvency petition cannot be founded on a debt which is time barred at the time when the debtor committed the act of insolvency.

473. In Re Abdul Wahid Khan,[492] it was held that a sole creditor can file an insolvency petition, if a debtor with intent to defeat or delay his creditors departs from his dwelling house or usual place of business, or otherwise absents himself, or secludes himself so as to deprive his creditors of the means of communicating with him.

D. Position of a Secured Creditor

474. If the petitioning creditor is a secured creditor,[493] he shall generally remain outside the bankruptcy process, but if he states in his petition that he will give an account of value of the security, he may be admitted for the difference between the debts and the estimated value of the security, or that he is willing to relinquish the security for the benefit of the creditors in the event that the debtor is declared insolvent.[494] The court may appoint an interim receiver over the property of the debtor directing him to take immediate possession of the property until the petition is heard. The court may also order the attachment and sale of the property, require reasonable security for appearance or issue an arrest warrant.[495] The court after hearing the matter and taking all the evidences and proofs from both the parties may, if not satisfied, dismiss the petition. The court, if satisfied, shall make an order of adjudication and specify the time within which the debtor shall apply for discharge.[496]

490. Presidency Town Insolvency Act, 1909, ss 14, 15 and Provincial Insolvency Act, 1920, ss 10, 13.
491. Presidency Town Insolvency Act, 1909, s. 12 and Provincial Insolvency Act, 1920, s. 9.
492. AIR (1985) N.O.C. 65 (Kant).
493. Secured creditor means a person holding a mortgage, charge, or lien on the property of the debtor as a security for a debt due to him from the debtor. Provincial Insolvency Act, 1920, s. 2(i)(c).
494. Presidency Town Insolvency Act, 1909, s. 12(2), Provincial Insolvency Act, 1920, s. 9.
495. Provincial Insolvency Act, 1920, ss 20, 21.
496. Presidency Town Insolvency Act, 1909, s. 13(5); Provincial Insolvency Act, 1920, s. 27.

475. In *N. Ahmed v. Phool Kunwar*,[497] the court observed that the debt of a secured creditor is not a debt provable in insolvency. Therefore the order of adjudication and the subsequent Order of discharge does not, and cannot affect the legal rights of a secured creditor which flow from the mortgage debt.

IV. Effects of Bankruptcy

A. Effects of Bankruptcy on the Debtor

476. The bankruptcy of an individual will divest the insolvent of his/her property and the property wherever situated shall vest in the official assignee or receiver.[498] The court may stay any insolvency proceeding or suit pending against the insolvent debtor before any court.[499] The bankrupt will be disqualified from being appointed or acting as a magistrate or elected to the office of any local authority.[500] He shall also be disqualified from being the director of a company.[501] Any civil action commenced by the bankrupt will be stayed pending the decision of the assignee or receiver as to whether the action should be continued.[502] The insolvent has to submit a schedule in relation to the property and his affairs to the court and in default he may be sentenced to civil prison.[503] The insolvent may be protected from being arrested or detained if the court passes a protection order.[504] The court shall make an order of public examination of the insolvent as to his conduct, dealings and property.[505] Where a partner in a firm is adjudicated insolvent, he ceases to be a partner in the firm[506] and an undischarged insolvent is disqualified from obtaining credit of more than INR 50 or upward without informing the other person and if he fraudulently obtains credit he shall be liable for imprisonment for up to six months or a fine or both.[507]

477. In *Nalli Textiles v. Minor Krishnan*,[508] it was held that no proceedings could be initiated against the insolvent or in respect of his property except with the leave of the Insolvency Court and such a leave is a necessary precondition to the right of any action.

478. These limitations will continue until the bankrupt is discharged from bankruptcy. This can occur when the bankrupt applies to the court for an order of discharge and the court upon hearing his application may grant an absolute or conditional order of discharge.[509]

497. AIR (1982) All 336.
498. Presidency Town Insolvency Act, 1909, s. 17 and Provincial Insolvency Act, 1920, s. 28(2).
499. Presidency Town Insolvency Act, 1909, s. 18A and Provincial Insolvency Act, 1920, s. 29.
500. Presidency Town Insolvency Act, 1909, s. 103A and Provincial Insolvency Act, 1920, s. 73.
501. The Companies Act, 1956, s. 274.
502. The Code of Civil Procedure 1908; o. XXII, r. 8.
503. Presidency Town Insolvency Act, 1909, s. 24 and Provincial Insolvency Act, 1920, s. 33.
504. Presidency Town Insolvency Act, 1909, s. 25 and Provincial Insolvency Act, 1920; s. 31.
505. Presidency Town Insolvency Act, 1909, s. 27 and Provincial Insolvency Act, 1920, s. 59A.
506. The Indian Partnership Act, 1932, s. 34.
507. Presidency Town Insolvency Act, 1909, s. 102 and Provincial Insolvency Act, 1920, s. 72.
508. (2003) I SCC 476.
509. Presidency Town Insolvency Act, 1909, s. 38 and Provincial Insolvency Act, 1920, s. 41.

B. Effects of Bankruptcy on Creditors

479. Upon bankruptcy, the creditors have a right to participate in the distribution of the bankrupt's estate upon producing proof of debt. As mentioned earlier, a secured creditor shall stand outside the preview of insolvency process.[510] Similarly there are certain debts, which are not provable. These include claims for unliquidated damages, penalties or fines, debts or liabilities that cannot be fairly estimated and debts or liabilities contracted by the debtor after notice of an insolvency petition.[511]

480. Where two parties each owe the other money, the creditor may set-off the two amounts; provided that the transaction arose as a result of mutual dealings[512] and that the creditor has no notice of bankruptcy proceedings against the debtor.[513] The object of a set-off is to do substantial justice between the parties. The right of a set-off being statutory cannot be excluded by an agreement to the contrary.

C. Effects of Bankruptcy on the Debtor's Property

481. Substantially, all of the bankrupts' property will be available to pay off debts owed to creditors. The property includes all property belonging to an insolvent at the commencement of insolvency.[514] All property acquired or devolved on from an insolvent after the commencement of insolvency and before the date of discharge. Such property includes property devolved upon an insolvent by way of succession, inheritance, will, gift, etc.[515] All goods in his possession or which are at his order or disposition at the time of insolvency. Such income or personal earnings as may be required to be given for the benefit of the creditors. Properties, which have been voluntarily disposed of by the insolvent, but the transaction has become voidable by virtue of antecedent transactions.[516] The commencement of insolvency is not from the date of the order of adjudication but from the first act of insolvency.

482. There are some properties which are not available to be realized from the insolvent person. These include certain household properties, the bankrupt's property mentioned in section 52(1) of the Act and includes property held by the insolvent in trust for earning income by personal exertion.

510. Presidency Town Insolvency Act, 1909, s. 12 and Provincial Insolvency Act, 1920, s. 9.
511. Presidency Town Insolvency Act, 1909, s. 46 and Provincial Insolvency Act, 1920, s. 33.
512. Presidency Town Insolvency Act, 1909, s. 47 and Provincial Insolvency Act, 1920, s. 46.
513. Presidency Town Insolvency Act, 1909, s. 47 (proviso).
514. Presidency Town Insolvency Act, 1909, s. 52 and Provincial Insolvency Act, 1920, s. 28.
515. Presidency Town Insolvency Act, 1909, s. 52 and Provincial Insolvency Act, 1920, s. 28.
516. Presidency Town Insolvency Act, 1909, ss 53–57 and Provincial Insolvency Act, 1920, ss 51–55.

V. Property Recoverable Pursuant to the Law Governing Antecedent Transactions

483. The property available to the official assignee or receiver includes all property owned at the commencement of insolvency, pursuant to the doctrine of relation back as well as properties recoverable under the law governing antecedent transactions.[517]

484. After the commencement of insolvency proceedings, the insolvent may be dealing with properties, which have been vested or will be vested in the official assignee or receiver and these transactions are liable to be set aside under the doctrine of relation back. An innocent third party may be affected by this doctrine; therefore, the insolvency law accords protection to bona fide transaction.[518]

A. Provisions Protecting Third Parties

485. An innocent third party who enters into a transaction with the insolvent in good faith, without knowing about the pendency of insolvency proceedings is protected under section 57 of the Presidency Town Insolvency Act, 1909 and section 55 of the Provincial Insolvency Act, 1920. Such transactions include any payment by the insolvent to any of his creditors, any payment or delivery to the insolvent, any transfer by the insolvent for valuable consideration and any contract or dealings for valuable consideration.

486. The burden of proof lies with the person who relies on the validity of such transactions.

487. The crucial terms of the protected transactions are good faith and knowledge of insolvency proceedings and valuable consideration.

1. Good Faith

488. The criteria of determining good faith must be taken with reference to the fundamental aims in bankruptcy law, i.e., to provide expeditious and economic distribution of debtor's property and second to secure release of the debtor.[519] Good faith can be claimed in two circumstances. First, as a bona fide purchaser[520] and second, as a purchaser without notice.[521] A mere knowledge of the proceedings would not be sufficient to negate good faith.

2. Valuable Consideration

489. The party seeking the benefit of bona fide transaction has to prove the fairness of the sale. The purchaser has given a fair price and the transaction has taken

517. Presidency Town Insolvency Act, 1909, ss 53–56 and Provincial Insolvency Act, 1920; ss 51–54.
518. Presidency Town Insolvency Acts 1909, s. 57 and Provincial Insolvency Act, 1920, s. 55.
519. *Cherukuri Venkateswarlu v. Official Receiver, Guntur*, (1970) 2 AWR 185.
520. Presidency Town Insolvency Acts 1909, s. 53 and Provincial Insolvency Act, 1920, s. 51.
521. Presidency Town Insolvency Acts 1909, s. 57 and Provincial Insolvency Act, 1920, s. 55.

place during the pendency of an insolvency petition is protected under bona fide transaction.

B. Avoidance of Preference

490. The law of insolvency tries to prevent fraudulent preference in order to have equitable distribution of property of the insolvent amongst the creditors. Any transaction, which is fraudulent, shall be deemed void.[522]

491. The conditions necessary for avoidance of preference includes there must be some transfer of property or making of payment or an obligation incurred or a judicial proceeding taken or suffered. The person concerned must be, at the time, unable to pay his debts; any of these things must be done with the view of giving preference to a creditor over others and within three months of the transactions, the person concerned is adjudged insolvent.

1. Defences

492. The doctrine of fraudulent preference, however, does not affect the rights of any person who have acquired the title in good faith and for valuable consideration. A creditor shall be deemed not to have been acting in good faith if he knew, or had reason to suspect that the debtor was unable to pay his debt as they became due. However, payments made under compulsion of legal proceedings by a creditor, or under pressure by a creditor, to protect himself from criminal proceedings or to enable him to carry on his business in the ordinary course have been held not to be a fraudulent preference.

493. The intention of the debtor is material, but that of the creditor, the person who alleges that the transaction is fraudulent has to prove fraudulent intention on the part of the debtor.

C. Avoidance of Voluntary Transfer

494. A transfer of property by a person who within two years after the date of transfer becomes insolvent is void, if the property would have been available to creditors if it had not been transferred and the transferor's main purpose in making the transfer was to prevent the transferred property from becoming divisible among the transferor's creditors or was to hinder or delay the process of making the property available for division amongst the transferor's creditors. Defence is provided if the transfer is made in consideration of marriage or the transfer is made in good faith and for valuable consideration.[523]

522. Presidency Town Insolvency Act, 1909, s. 56 and Provincial Insolvency Act, 1920, s. 54.
523. Presidency Town Insolvency Act, 1909, s. 55 and Provincial Insolvency Act, 1920, s. 53.

VI. Realization and Distribution of the Estate

495. Once all the property is recovered and realized, it will vest in the official assignee or the receiver. The official assignee takes possession of all the property, deeds, books and documents of the insolvent.[524]

496. After realization of the property, an onerous duty to distribute the insolvent's property lies on the official assignee/receiver. The general order of payment is that the preferential debts (all debts owed to the government or to any local authority, all salaries or wages of employees, any rent owed to a landlord, costs and charges incurred in management and administration of an insolvent's estate.) should be paid first, then other debts, and finally the partnership debts in the case of an insolvent firm.[525] All other debts are payable rateably without any preference. The insolvent shall be entitled to any surplus remaining after payment in full is made to his creditors.[526]

VII. Termination of Bankruptcy

497. The insolvent may any time after the order of adjudication apply to the court for an order of discharge and the court may after hearing such an application either grant an absolute or conditional order of discharge.[527] The court is also empowered to refuse the discharge of the insolvent if he is guilty under sections 421–424 of the Indian Penal Code. If the insolvent omits to apply for a discharge then he will not automatically be discharged. An order of discharge shall release the insolvent from all debts provable in insolvency and from such liability as the court may specify.[528] However, an order of discharge does not release an insolvent from any debt owed to the government, debt or liability incurred or obtained by any fraud or breach of trust, any liability under order of maintenance[529] or joint debt of partnership.[530] A discharged insolvent, notwithstanding his discharge is required to assist the official assignee in realization and distribution of his property and if he fails to do so, he shall be held guilty in contempt of court and the court may revoke his discharge.[531]

524. Presidency Town Insolvency Act, 1909, s. 58 and Provincial Insolvency Act, 1920, s. 56.
525. Presidency Town Insolvency Act, 1909; s. 49 and Provincial Insolvency Act, 1920, s. 61.
526. Presidency Town Insolvency Act, 1909; s. 76 and Provincial Insolvency Act, 1920, s. 67.
527. Presidency Town Insolvency Act, 1909, s. 38 and Provincial Insolvency Act, 1920, s. 41.
528. Presidency Town Insolvency Act, 1909, s. 45 and Provincial Insolvency Act, 1920, s. 44.
529. Code of Criminal Procedure, 1973, s. 125.
530. Presidency Town Insolvency Act, 1909, s. 45 and Provincial Insolvency Act, 1920, s. 44.
531. Presidency Town Insolvency Act, 1909, s. 43.

§2. Related Institutions

I. Arrangements

498. A debtor who is financially embarrassed may settle the claims of his creditors outside the court by entering into private arrangements, which are quicker and more flexible than the bankruptcy procedure. These private arrangements include composition (compounding of debt) and scheme of assignment of his property to a third person for administering it for the benefit of his creditors so as to ratably distribution of the proceeds of the property.

499. The advantages for the debtor for a private arrangement is that it avoids the stigma of bankruptcy and he will not be subjected to the doctrine of relation back or some or all the provisions relating to antecedent transactions. The advantages for the creditor are that a private scheme is faster and efficacious.

500. An insolvent may through official assignee at any time after the order of adjudication submit a proposal to the creditors for a composition in satisfaction of his debts or a proposal for the scheme of arrangement of his affairs. If on consideration the majority of creditors owed three-fourths of the debt resolve to accept the proposal it shall be deemed to be accepted.[532]

501. The insolvent or official assignee may after the acceptance of the proposal apply to the court for its approval. Upon the approval of the terms of proposal the court shall annul the adjudication and it shall be binding on all the creditors except any creditor who does not assent to the composition or scheme.[533] The effect of annulment will be to re-vest the bankrupt's property with the debtor but the annulment does not affect transactions made prior to the annulment taking effect.

502. Death of a debtor after presentation of an insolvency petition: If a debtor against whom an insolvency petition has been presented dies, the proceedings in the matter are to be continued as if he were alive. Thus death of a debtor after the presentation of insolvency petition makes no difference for the purpose of insolvency law, and his estate can be administered as against his heirs and legal representatives.[534]

532. Presidency Town Insolvency Act, 1909, s. 28 and Provincial Insolvency Act, 1920, s. 38.
533. Presidency Town Insolvency Act, 1909, s. 30 and Provincial Insolvency Act, 1920, s. 39.
534. Presidency Town Insolvency Act, 1909, s. 93 and Provincial Insolvency Act, 1920, s. 17.

Chapter 7. Negotiable Instruments

§1. Introduction

503. The Act applies and extends to the whole of India. However, does not affect any local usage relating to any instrument in an oriental language. However, such usages may be excluded by any words in the body of the instrument, which indicate an intention that the legal relations of the parties thereto shall be governed by this Act.[535] The Negotiable Instruments (Amendment) Act, 2015 came in to force with retrospective effect. According to the notification pub^li^shed in the official Gazette dated 26 December 2015 the Amendment shall be deemed to have come into force on 15 June 2015. Rajya Sabha passed the Negotiable Instrument (Amendment) Bill 2015 on 7 December 2015. Lok Sabha had passed the Bill in August 2015. With this Amendment in the changes have been made in various sections including sections 6, 142, etc. Section 142 A has been inserted by Negotiable Instrument (Amendment) Act, 2015 which states that:[536]

> Section 142A. (1) Notwithstanding anything contained in the Code of Criminal Procedure, 1973 or any judgment, decree, order or directions of any court, all cases arising out of section 138 which were pending in any court, whether filed before it, or transferred to it, before the commencement of the Negotiable Instruments(Amendment) Ordinance, 2015 shall be transferred to the court having jurisdiction under sub-section (2) of section 142 as if that sub-section had been in force at all material times and in subsec (2), it is provided that, where the payee or the holder in due course, as the case may be, has filed a complaint against the drawer of a cheque in the court having jurisdiction under sub-section (2) of section 142 or the case has been transferred to that court under sub-section (1), and such complaint is pending in that court, all subsequent complaints arising out of section 138 against the same drawer shall be filed before the same court irrespective of whether those cheques were delivered for collection or presented for payment within the territorial jurisdiction of that court.

The Negotiable Instruments (Amendment) Act, 2015 provides for retrospective validation for the new scheme of determining the jurisdiction of a court to try a case under section 138 of the Negotiable Instruments Act, 1881. The amendment provides that the offence under section 138 shall be inquired into and tried only by a court within whose local jurisdiction:

535. The Negotiable Instruments (Amendment and Miscellaneous Provisions) Act, 2002 came into force on the 6 Feb. 2003.
536. Available on http://www.indiacode.nic.in/acts-in-pdf/2015/201526.pdf.

(a) if the cheque is delivered for collection through an account, the branch of the bank where the payee or holder in due course, as the case may be, maintains the account, is situated; or
(b) if the cheque is presented for payment by the payee or holder in due course, otherwise through an account, the branch of the drawee bank where the drawer maintains the account, is situated.

504. Scope of the Act: The title of the Act is misleading for it seems to cover a wider field than it actually does. In fact, the Act merely regulates the issue and negotiation of bills, notes and cheques, but does not provide for the transmission of rights in such instruments by operation of law or by transfer inter vivos. It is, therefore, not exhaustive of all matters relating to negotiable instruments.

505. Although there are some points of difference between the Indian and English law which are mainly due to the peculiar conditions prevailing in India. The Act is mainly a codification of the English common law on the subject, which, in turn, is derived from the usages and customs of merchants, commonly known as the law merchant. This is why, in the absence of any special circumstances the India courts are justified in construing the Act conformable with the provisions of English law.

506. The Act, as stated above, saves from its operation any local customs relating to any instrument in an oriental language, such as a hundi. It is only when there is a local usage to the contrary that the local usage overrides the provisions of the Act. In the absence of proof of such usage, the Act applies as much to hundis as to instruments written in the English language.[537] However, such usage may be excluded by any words used in the body of such instruments manifesting an intention that the legal relations of the parties thereto shall be governed by this Act.

§2. Definitions

507. Chapter II of the Negotiable Instruments Act, 1881 primarily deals with definitions. There are many terms which have not been defined by the Act, but they are used meticulously by the parties and are used frequently. They are as follows.

508. Section 3 of the Act provides that the word 'Banker' includes any person acting as a banker and any post office savings bank. Thus, the Act does not define the term 'banker'. In an old English case, it was held that a banker is a person who receives the money of his customer to be drawn out again as the owner has occasion for it, the customer being the lender and the bank the borrower, with the further obligation of honouring the owner's cheque up to the amount of money received by such bank.[538] According to the Banking Regulation Act, 1949 'banking' means the accepting, for the purpose of lending or investment, of deposits of money from the public, repayable on demand or otherwise, and withdrawable by cheque, draft, order or otherwise, and the 'banking company' means any company which transacts the business of banking in India.

537. *Krishnaset v. Hari Valji* ILR 20 Bom 488.
538. *Foley v. Hill*, (1848) 2 HLC 28.

I. Definition of Negotiable Instrument

509. Negotiable instrument in practice means a piece of paper which entitles a person to a sum of money mentioned in it, and which is freely transferable from person to person. It serves as a substitute for money. For the purpose of the Negotiable Instruments Act, a 'Negotiable Instrument' means a promissory note, bill of exchange or cheques payable either to order or bearer.[539] The Act does not give the meaning of the term 'negotiable instrument'. Rather it enumerates the class of instruments considered as negotiable by the statute.

510. Although the Act specifically recognizes only three kinds of negotiable instruments, it includes all other instruments which have the features of negotiability. However, if these other instruments are governed by local custom or usage, law do not intervene there. But in the absence of proof as to the existence of such local usage or custom, the provisions of the Negotiable Instruments Act, 1881 applies.

511. The maker of a bill of exchange or cheque is called the 'drawer'.[540] The person directed to pay is called the 'drawee'.[541] When the name of any person in addition to the drawee is given in a bill or endorsement to be resorted to in case of need, such person is called 'drawee in case of need'.[542] The person named in the instrument to whom or whose order the money is by the instrument directed to be paid is called the 'payee'[543] Any person entitled in his own name to the possession thereof, and to receive or recover the amount due thereon from the parties thereto is 'holder'.[544] Any person who for consideration becomes the 'holder' of a promissory note, bill of exchange or cheque is 'holder in due course'.[545] A promissory note, bill of exchange or cheque drawn or made in India and made payable in or drawn upon any person resident of India is an 'inland instrument'.[546] Any instrument other than an inland instrument is a 'foreign Instrument'.[547]

II. Definition of Promissory Note

512. 'Promissory note' means an instrument in writing (not being a bank note or currency note) containing an unconditional undertaking signed by the maker, to pay a certain sum of money only, or to the order of certain person or to the bearer of the instrument.[548] Thus a promissory note is a written and signed promise to pay a certain sum of money to some person or to his order.

539. The Negotiable Instrument Act, 1881, s. 13.
540. The Negotiable Instrument Act, 1881, s. 7.
541. The Negotiable Instrument Act, 1881, s. 7.
542. The Negotiable Instrument Act, 1881, s. 7.
543. The Negotiable Instrument Act, 1881, s. 7.
544. The Negotiable Instrument Act, 1881, s. 8.
545. The Negotiable Instrument Act, 1881, s. 9.
546. The Negotiable Instrument Act, 1881, s. 11.
547. The Negotiable Instrument Act, 1881, s. 12.
548. The Negotiable Instrument Act, 1881, s. 4.

513. Although no particular form of words is requisite, it must possess the following characteristics:

(1) A promissory note must always be in writing.
(2) It must always contain an express promise to pay. A mere acknowledgement of debt or mere receipt of money is not a promissory note.
(3) The promise to pay the money should be unconditional or subject only to a condition which according to ordinary experience is bound to occur.
(4) The instrument must be payable in money and money only.
(5) The parties to the instrument must be designated with reasonable certainty.
(6) The maker must sign the promissory note.
(7) It must contain a promise to pay a definite sum of money.
(8) Stamp duty must be paid for the promissory note as per the Indian Stamp Act at or before the time of execution otherwise it would not be admissible in evidence.
(9) Lastly, it must be delivered to the payee.

514. If a document is in the form of a letter acknowledging the receipt of a certain sum of money and is affixed with 20 paise stamp, required for a receipt, that does not become a promissory note.[549] Similarly, an instrument is not a promissory note under section 4 of the Act, unless it contains an express undertaking to pay the amount mentioned in the instrument. An implied undertaking would not suffice.[550] Promissory note must indicate with certainty as to who is the payee, i.e., the party who is to receive the money.

III. Definition of Bill of Exchange

515. A bill of exchange is a three-party instrument. The Negotiable Instrument Act a 'bill of exchange' is an instrument in writing containing an unconditional order signed by the maker directing a certain person to pay a certain sum of money only to or to the order of a certain person or bearer of an instrument.[551] A promise or order to pay is not said to be conditional merely because the time for payment of the amount or any instrument thereof is expressed to be on the lapse of a certain period after the happening of a specified event, which according to the ordinary expectation of mankind, bound to happen, though the time of its happening may not be certain.

516. A bill of exchange constitutes a legally binding written promise by the drawer that the person who took it in payment will be paid in cash when he presents the bill for payment at the proper time and place.

517. 'Hundis' though has not been defined, it is, however, is being generally used with reference to native bills of exchange. However, it is at times also used cover native promissory notes. Such hundis are generally governed by the local customs and

549. *Kundan Mal v. Nand Kishore*, AIR 1994 Raj. 1.

550. *Sir Mahomad Akbar Klan v. Attar Chand*, 38 BLR 739, held that an instrument is not a promissory note unless it contains an express undertaking to pay the amount mentioned in the instrument. An implied undertaking would not be sufficient.

551. The Negotiable Instrument Act, 1881, s. 5.

usages of a particular locality or of a particular trade. The Act recognizes such usages, and it is, therefore, provided that if there is any local usage relating to any such instrument, which is inconsistent with the Act, what would prevail is not the provisions of the Act, but such usage.

518. Similarly, the Act does not affect the provisions of section 21 of the Indian Paper Currency Act, 1871, which have now been re-enacted with slight modifications in section 31 of the Reserve Bank of India Act, 1934. This section provides that no private person can issue any instrument which amounts to an unconditional promise to pay a certain sum of money to the bearer on demand. The object of the Paper Currency Act was to prevent private persons and banks for infringing the government monopoly of issuing paper currency in India.

519. Although no particular form for a bill of exchange is specified, it must substantially be complied according to the requirements of section 5. The essence is that a bill of exchange is the order of the creditor upon his debtor requiring him to pay the money to the specified person. The key requirements of a bill of exchange are:

(1) It must be in writing.
(2) The bill of exchange must contain an order to pay. If the language does not show any order to pay the draft will not be a bill of exchange.
(3) The order to pay should be unconditional.
(4) The order must be to pay money and money only.
(5) Usually a bill of exchange requires three parties. First, the person who makes the bill of exchange called the drawer; second the person to whom it is addressed called the drawee and third the payee.
(6) It is necessary that the drawee must be designated with reasonable certainty although the payee does not have to be named.
(7) It must be signed by the drawer.
(8) It must be delivered.

IV. Definition of Cheque

520. A 'cheque' is primarily a bill of exchange drawn on a specified banker and not expressed to be payable otherwise than on demand and it includes an electronic image of a truncated cheque and a cheque in the electronic form.[552]

521. Following are the essentials of a valid cheque:

(1) It must have all the essentials of a bill of exchange. Since the cheque is primarily a bill of exchange drawn on a banker, it must fulfil all the essentials of a bill of exchange discussed earlier. These may be summed up as follows:

   (i) It must be in writing.
   (ii) It must contain an unconditional order to pay.
   (iii) The order to pay must be in terms of money only.
   (iv) The order to pay must mention a definite sum of money.

552. The Negotiable Instrument Act, 1881, s. 6.

(v) It must contain certain parties.
(vi) It must be signed by the drawer.

(2) It must be drawn on a specified banker.
(3) It must be payable on demand.

522. When a cheque bears on it two parallel transverse lines the cheque is said to be a 'crossed cheque'. The cheque is no longer payable to the payee or holder at the counter of the bank. The payment of a crossed cheque can be obtained only through a banker. Crossings are primarily of two kinds, general crossing and special crossing. When there are no words between the lines of a crossing or there are some words but not the name of the bank, it is a general crossing.[553] Where lines of a crossing bear the name of the banker it is a, special crossing.[554] When a cheque is crossed generally then under section 126 of the Act, the banker on whom it is drawn shall not pay it otherwise than to a banker to whom it is crossed or his agent for collection under section 126 of the Act.

523. In *C.T. Joseph v. I.V. Phillip*,[555] it has been held by the Kerala High Court that the cheques do not require any stamp under the Stamp Act. It has also been held that section 20 of the Negotiable Instrument Act, which applies only to inchoate negotiable instruments.

524. Where a cheque is crossed specially to more than one banker (except when crossed to an agent for the purpose of collection), the banker on whom it is drawn shall under section 127 of the Act refuse payment thereof. A cheque bearing more than one special crossing, except in the case mentioned above, is invalid and the banker is prohibited from making payment thereon.

525. A banker, who has, in good faith and without negligence, received payment, for a customer of a cheque crossed generally or specially to himself shall not, in case the title to the cheque proved defective, under section 131 of the Act incur any liability to the owner of the cheque, by reason only of having received such payment. However, a banker receives payment of a crossed cheque for a customer within the meaning of this section notwithstanding the credits his customer's account with the amount of the cheque before receiving payment thereof.[556]

526. Protection to the bankers given by the Act:

(1) Section 85 protects a banker if an endorsement is forged, provided the payment is made in due course. However, it does not protect a banker against a forged signature of the drawer, even if the payment is made in due course, as every banker is supposed to be acquainted with his customer's signature.
(2) Second, section 85(2) gives protection to the bankers, in respect of payment of bearer cheque. When a cheque is drawn payable to bearer, the banker is discharged by a payment in due course, to the bearer thereof, irrespective of any endorsements made on such cheque. Thus, when a cheque is originally drawn payable to bearer,

553. The Negotiable Instrument Act, 1881, s. 123.
554. The Negotiable Instrument Act, 1881 s. 124.
555. AIR 2001 Ker 300.
556. Negotiable Instruments Act, 1881, explanation to s. 131.

later endorsements on it do not convert it into an order cheque, and the drawee-banker, paying the amount to the bearer, in due course, is not affected by such endorsement.

(3) A banker on whom a crossed cheque is drawn is protected under section 128 of the Act, if he makes payment of the amount in due course, it is necessary that he should in good faith and without negligence, if the cheque is crossed, generally, make payment to a banker, and if crossed specially, to the banker to whom it is crossed. If the payment is made out of due course, the banker shall be liable to the true owner of the cheque for any loss he may sustain owing to the cheque have been so paid.[557]

(4) A banker who has, in good faith and without negligence received payment for a customer of a cheque crossed generally or specially to himself shall not, in case the title to the cheque proves defective, incur any liability to the true owner of the cheque, by reason only of having received such payment.[558]

527. Where a banker, on whom a crossed cheque is drawn, has paid the same in due course, the banker paying the cheque and (in case such cheque has come to the hands of the payee) the drawer thereof, shall respectively be entitled to the same rights, and be placed in the same position in all respects, as they would respectively be entitled to, and placed in, if the amount of the cheque has been paid to, and received by the true owner thereof.[559]

528. Any banker, however, paying a cheque crossed generally otherwise than to a banker, or a cheque crossed specially otherwise than to the banker to whom the same is crossed, or his agent for collection being a banker, under section 129 of the Act, shall be liable to the true owner of the cheque for any loss he may sustain owing to the cheque having been so paid. Thus, a banker is not liable to a holder of a cheque, since the contract of the banker is with the drawer only and not with the holder of the cheque. So, a banker can refuse the payment of the cheque to the holder of the same at the direction of the drawer.

529. Liability of the drawee of a cheque: In the drawee, i.e., a bank, having sufficient funds of the drawer properly applicable to the payment of such cheque, must pay the cheque when required so to do, and in default of such payment, must compensate the drawer for any loss or damage caused by such default. The banker is, however, bound to dishonour the customer's cheques in the following cases:

(i) If there are no sufficient funds of the drawer with the drawee.
(ii) Even if the banker has sufficient funds, but they held in trust or the bank has a lien over the funds.
(iii) If the cheque is irregular or ambiguous, or drawn in a form of doubtful legality, or otherwise materially altered.
(iv) When the customer has become insolvent, or an order of adjudication has been made against him, and the banker has notice of the same.
(v) if the customer has died, and the bank has a notice of the same.

557. Negotiable Instruments Act, 1881, s. 129.
558. Negotiable Instruments Act, 1881, s. 131.
559. Negotiable Instruments Act, 1881, s. 128.

§3. Parties to Promissory Notes, Bills of Exchange or Cheques

530. The Negotiable Instruments Act, 1881 recognizes three forms of negotiable instruments, namely, promissory note, bill of exchange, and cheque. The parties to these instruments are following:

> Parties to promissory Note - Maker, payee, indorser, indorsee. Parties to Bill of exchange - Drawer, acceptor or drawee, drawee in case of need, acceptor for honour, indorser, indorsee. Parties to a cheque - Drawer, drawee (always a banker), payee, indorser, indorsee. Out of these parties, some parties are liable to pay upon the instrument, and some are entitled to receive the money on the instrument. The party entitled to receive payment upon the instrument may be a 'holder'[560] or a 'holder in due course'.[561]

531. Every person capable of contracting according to the law of contracts can be a party to a negotiable instrument. He may bind himself or be bound by the making, drawing, acceptance, endorsement, delivery and negotiation of the promissory note, bill of exchange or cheque.[562] If an incompetent person is a party to a negotiable instrument, the instrument is not enforceable against such person. However, the incapacity of one or more parties to a negotiable instrument does not diminish the liabilities of the other parties thereto.

532. Minor: Where a minor is a party to a negotiable instrument, the instrument does not become void merely because of this reason. The instrument is binding on all the parties except minor. This follows that a minor is not liable to pay the instrument but he may operate as a channel to convey title and liability.[563]

533. Corporation: Corporations and companies are artificial juridical persons created by law. A corporation or a company draws power to operate from its respective statute and its special constitution, like memorandum and article of association. The contractual capacity of a company of a corporation depends upon the provisions of its memorandum of association or charter of incorporation. If it is authorized expressly or impliedly, it may become a party to a negotiable instrument in any capacity. Otherwise its contract shall be ultra vires.[564]

534. Agency: Every person capable of binding himself or of being bound by the making, drawing, acceptance, indorsement, delivery, and negotiation of a negotiable instrument, may: (i) so bind himself; or (ii) be bound by a duly authorized agent acting in his name. An agent can bind his principal by acting on his behalf only in the manner in which he is duly authorized to become a party to a negotiable instrument. An agent also has to make clear that he is acting in a representative capacity.[565] The form of signature must show that he intends to act as an agent and does not intend to incur personal liability. If it is not done in this manner, then the agent becomes personally

560. The Negotiable Instrument Act, 1881, s.6.
561. The Negotiable Instrument Act, 1881, s. 9.
562. The Negotiable Instrument Act, 1881, s. 26.
563. The Negotiable Instrument Act, 1881, s. 26.
564. The Negotiable Instrument Act, 1881, s. 26.
565. The Negotiable Instrument Act, 1881, s. 27.

liable except where the parties induced into signing are of the belief that the principal only should be liable.[566]

535. Legal Representative: A legal representative of a deceased person who signs his name on a negotiable instrument, incurs personal liability unless by clear words he limits his liability to the extent of the assets of the deceased received by him as a legal representative.[567] A legal representative may avoid personal liability on a negotiable instrument, by adding to his signature, such words as 'without recourse', or 'without recourse to me personally'. In this way he can limit his liability to the extent of the assets of the deceased received by him.

§4. Negotiation

536. Typically, the term negotiation is used to identify transfers occurring in a particular way after the instrument has been issued. A bearer instrument is transferable by simple delivery.[568] An instrument payable to order can be transferred by endorsement and delivery.[569] An instrument payable to bearer can be negotiated by simple delivery. The person to whom the instrument is delivered becomes the holder. Delivery, though simple, is an important formality, without which a possessor cannot be constituted as a holder of the instrument.[570] An instrument payable by endorsement requires two formalities: First, the holder should endorse it and deliver it to his endorsee.[571] Second, the endorsement is made by signing the name of the endorser, usually on the back of the instrument.

I. Kinds of Endorsements

537. Endorsement is required whenever the instrument being negotiated is classified as an order instrument. Even though no endorsement is required to negotiate a bearer instrument. Even though no endorsement is required to negotiate a bearer instrument, a holder can affix an endorsement while negotiating it. The followings are types of endorsements:

(1) Blank endorsement: Where the endorser signs only his name on the back of the instrument for the purpose of negotiating, it is an endorsement 'in blank'.[572] The effect of a blank endorsement is that an order instrument becomes a bearer instrument.

566. The Negotiable Instrument Act, 1881, s. 28.
567. The Negotiable Instrument Act, 1881, s. 29.
568. The Negotiable Instrument Act, 1881, s. 14.
569. The Negotiable Instrument Act, 1881, ss 15 and 46.
570. The Negotiable Instrument Act, 1881, ss 44 and 47.
571. The Negotiable Instrument Act, 1881, s. 48.
572. The Negotiable Instrument Act, 1881, ss 16 and 54.

(2) Endorsement in full: Where the endorser adds to his signature the name of the person whom or to whose order he wants the instrument to be paid, that is endorsement in full.[573]
(3) Restrictive Endorsement: An, endorsement, which by express words, prohibits the endorsee from further negotiating the instrument or restricts the endorsee to deal with the instrument as directed by the endorser is called the restrictive indorsement.[574]
(4) '*Sans* Recourse' Endorsement: The endorsement by which the indorser excludes his liability on the instrument is known as 'sans recourse' indorsement. The words 'sans recourse' or 'without recourse' are generally used to make such indorsement. In such cases, if the instrument is dishonoured, the indorsee or the subsequent holder cannot ask the indorser for payment of the same.[575]
(5) Conditional endorsement: When payment on the instrument is made dependent on the occurrence of a specified event, the instrument has a conditional indorsement.[576]
(6) Partial endorsement: An endorsement which transfers the rights to receive only a part payment of the amount due on the instrument is known as partial endorsement.[577]

II. Kinds of Delivery

538. The making, acceptance or indorsement of a promissory note, bill of exchange, or cheque is completed by delivery, actual or constructive.[578] The followings are types of delivery:

(1) Actual Delivery – Calls for actual handing over of the instrument by one person to another person, or to an agent on his behalf.
(2) Constructive Delivery – Is affected without any change in actual possession. In this case, the transfer of possession is notional instead of physical.
(3) Conditional Delivery – Is the delivery which is effective on fulfilment of certain condition. When an instrument is delivered conditionally, the negotiation is not complete until the fulfilment of such condition.

§5. Liability of Parties

I. Liability of Acceptor or Maker

539. The maker of a promissory note, and the acceptor is primary in nature. In the absence of a contract to the contrary the maker/acceptor of a bill of exchange is

573. The Negotiable Instrument Act, 1881, s. 16.
574. The Negotiable Instrument Act, 1881, s. 50.
575. The Negotiable Instrument Act, 1881, s. 52.
576. The Negotiable Instrument Act, 1881, s. 52.
577. The Negotiable Instrument Act, 1881, s. 56.
578. The Negotiable Instrument Act, 1881, s. 46.

bound to pay the amount thereof at maturity according to the apparent tenor of the note or acceptance. In case the maker or acceptor defaults in making payment to the holder of the instrument, they are liable to compensate the party to whom the loss is caused by the reason of dishonour of the instrument.[579]

II. Liability of the Drawer

540. The drawer of a bill of exchange or cheque is bound in the case that the cheque is not honoured by the drawee or acceptor thereof to compensate the holder provided due notice of the dishonour has been given to or received by the drawer. However, the liability of the drawer of a cheque is primary and not secondary. The holder of a bill can sue the acceptor but the holder of a cheque has no remedy against the banker. His remedy is only against the drawer.[580]

III. Liability of Drawee of a Cheque

541. The drawee of the cheque is always the banker. A person who keeps an account with the bank is a customer. The banker's contractual duty to pay cheques is owed only to the customer and not to the payee or holder of the cheque. The banker, if having sufficient funds of the drawer available, must pay the cheque when duly required to do so and in default, must compensate the drawer for any loss or damage.[581]

IV. Liability of Endorser

542. Where a negotiable instrument is dishonoured by maker, drawee, or acceptor thereof, any person who has endorsed this instrument before maturity is liable to all the parties who are subsequent to him, provided a due notice of dishonour had been given to him. Thus the endorser stands in the same position as the drawer to all the parties subsequent to him.[582] In *Gadam Venkataraju v. Andhra Bank*, Hyderabad,[583] the payee delivered a cheque to bank without making endorsement and the bank discounted the same. The Bank to whom the payee had delivered the cheque brought an action against the payee for recovery of the amount of the cheque. It was held that payee could not be held liable because he had not made any endorsement.

579. The Negotiable Instrument Act, 1881, s. 32.
580. The Negotiable Instrument Act, 1881, s. 30.
581. The Negotiable Instrument Act, 1881, s. 31.
582. The Negotiable Instrument Act, 1881, s. 35.
583. AIR 2000 AP 379.

§6. Presentment

543. A bill of exchange may have to be presented for acceptance before it is presented for payment. Presentment for acceptance is necessary only where the bill is payable at a given time after acceptance or after sight. The bill expressly stipulates that it shall be presented for acceptance before it is presented for payment. The bill is made payable at a place other than the place of residence or business of the drawee.[584] No presentment is necessary in the following cases:

(1) If the maker, drawee or acceptor intentionally prevents the presentment of the instrument; or (a) if the instrument being payable at his place of business, he closes such place on a business day during the usual business hours; or (b) if the instrument being payable at some other specified place, neither he nor any person authorized to pay it attends at such place during the usual business hours; or (c) if the instrument not being payable at any specified place, he cannot, after due search be found.
(2) As against any party sought to be charged therewith – if he has engaged to pay notwithstanding non-payment.
(3) As against any party – if, after maturity, with knowledge that the instrument has not been presented: (a) if he makes a partial payment on account of the amount due on the instrument; or (b) promises to pay the amount due thereon in whole or in part; or (c) otherwise waives his right to take advantage of any default in presentment for payment.
(4) As against the drawer, if the drawer could not suffer damage from the want of such presentment.[585]

§7. Kinds of Presentment

544. The followings are the kinds of presentment:

(1) *Presentment of bills of exchange for acceptance*, i.e., bills which are drawn payable ‘after sight’ are payable after acceptance. Such bills of exchange must be presented for acceptance in order to fix their date of maturity, but may be negotiated even before acceptance. It is only a bill of exchange which is payable after sight which requires acceptance. Presentment must be made to the drawee or to his duly authorized agent, or if he be dead to his legal representative, or if he has been adjudged insolvent, to his assignee. Where there are several drawees, the bill must be presented to all of them, unless they are partners or agents of one another. If any one of them refuses to accept it, the bill may be considered as dishonoured.
(2) *Presentment of promissory notes for sight*, i.e., in the case or promissory notes, there is no question of acceptance because the maker himself is the person primarily liable in respect of it. A note payable after sight must, however, be presented to the maker of such a note for sight in order to fix its maturity. If the maker cannot

584. The Negotiable Instrument Act, 1881, s. 61.
585. The Negotiable Instrument Act, 1881, s. 76.

be found after reasonable search, such presentment is excused, and as for the dishonoured instrument, a suit may be filed immediately.

(3) *Presentment of negotiable instruments for payment*, i.e., presentment for payment is necessary practically in all cases of negotiable instruments. There are however, cases where the presentment of payment is not required, e.g.: (a) where a bill of exchange or promissory note is payable on a certain date; and (b) where a promissory note is payable on demand and is not payable at a specified place, no presentment is necessary in order to charge the maker thereof.

§8. Discharge from Liability

545. When a negotiable instrument is issued, it carries a liability to pay certain amount to the holder. When this liability is satisfied, the instrument is said to be discharged. They are as follows:

(1) By cancellation – when the holder of a negotiable instrument or his agent cancels the name of any party of the instrument with intent to discharge him.[586]
(2) By release – if the holder of a negotiable instrument discharges the maker, acceptor or indorser of the instrument by any method other than cancellation, such party is said to be released from his liability upon the instrument. For example discharge by making agreement.[587]
(3) By payment – all parties to the instrument are discharged from liability when the amount due on the instrument is paid.[588]
(4) By allowing more than forty-eight hours to accept – if the holder of a bill of exchange allows the drawee more than forty-eight hours, to consider whether he will accept the same, all previous parties not consenting to such allowance are thereby discharged from liability to such holder.[589]
(5) By qualified acceptance – the holder of a bill presenting it for acceptance acquiesces in a qualified acceptance or one part of all previous parties are discharged against the holder unless notice is given by the holder.[590]
(6) By delay in presenting the cheque – if the holder fails to present the cheque within a reasonable amount of time of its issue and something happens which prevents the banker from paying the cheque, then the bearer of the cheque is discharged as against the holder provided that he had a sufficient balance at the time that the cheque was presented.[591]
(7) By material alteration – any material alteration of a negotiable instrument renders the same as void as against anyone who is a party thereto at the time of making

586. The Negotiable Instrument Act, 1881, s. 82(a).
587. The Negotiable Instrument Act, 1881, s. 82(b).
588. The Negotiable Instrument Act, 1881, s. 82(c).
589. The Negotiable Instrument Act, 1881, s. 83.
590. The Negotiable Instrument Act, 1881, s. 86.
591. The Negotiable Instrument Act, 1881, s. 84.

such an alteration and does not consent thereto unless it is made to catty out the common intention of the original parties.[592]

(8) By negotiation back – when a bill of exchange comes back to the acceptor through a process of negotiation, and he becomes its holder, this is known as negotiation back. If it happens at or after maturity all liability of the instrument comes to an end.[593]

(9) By impairing endorser's remedy – where the holder of a negotiable instrument, without the consent of an endorser, destroys or impairs his remedy against a prior party, the endorser is discharged from his liability to the holder.[594]

546. Crossing of the cheque: Where a cheque is uncrossed, the holder may cross it generally or specially. Where a cheque is crossed generally, the holder may cross it specially. Where a cheque is crossed generally or specially the holder may add the words 'not negotiable'. Where a cheque is crossed specially, the banker to whom it is crossed may, under section 125 of the Act, again cross it specially to another banker, his agent, for collection. The crossing of a bill does not, however, amount to a 'material alteration' within the meaning of section 87.

547. A person taking a cheque crossed generally or specially, bearing, in either case, the words 'not negotiable', under section 130 of the Act, shall not have, and shall not be capable of giving, a better title to cheque than to the person from whom he took.

548. Object and Legal Effect of Crossing Cheques 'not negotiable': The object of crossing a cheque 'not negotiable' is to afford protection to the drawer or holder against miscarriage or dishonesty in the course of transit, by making it difficult to get the cheque cashed until it reaches its destination.

549. The only legal effect of the crossing of a cheque 'not negotiable' is that the cheque is deprived of the main feature of negotiability. The transferee of such a cheque can get no better title than that of his transferor, if the cheque happens to be lost or stolen one, though the transferee may have acquired the cheque innocently. Such a crossing, however, does not make the cheque non-transferable. Such a cheque can be transferred, but the transferee does not acquire the rights of a holder by negotiation. His rights are those of an ordinary transferee of a chose in action. He gets no better title than that of his transferor. If the transferor has a defective title, the transferee is affected by such defects, and he cannot claim the right of a holder in due course by proving that he purchased the instrument in good faith and for value.

550. A crossing is merely a direction to the paying banker not to pay the money over the counter, but to pay the money through a bank, or through some particular bank only, so the person who has obtained that amount can easily be traced. It thus compels the holder to present the cheque through a quarter of known respectability and credit, and affords security and protection to the owner of the cheque. But mere crossing of a cheque in no way affects the transferability or negotiability of the cheque. A crossed bearer cheque can be negotiated by delivery. The additional words 'not negotiable' to the crossing will prohibit negotiability, but insertion of the words 'account

592. The Negotiable Instrument Act, 1881, ss 87, 88, 89.
593. The Negotiable Instrument Act, 1881, s. 90.
594. The Negotiable Instrument Act, 1881, s. 40.

payee' do no restrict negotiability. Their object is merely to protect the drawer against theft or loss.

§9. Special Rules of Evidence

I. Notice of Dishonour

551. An instrument is dishonoured when payment or acceptance is refused or is not made within the prescribed time period following the proper presentment of the instrument. A bill of exchange may be dishonoured by: (a) non-acceptance; or (b) non-payment. A promissory note or a cheque may be dishonoured only by non-payment.

552. Dishonour by non-acceptance – When the bill is properly presented for acceptance except where presentment is excused, but the drawee makes default in accepting it or acceptance is qualified or drawee is incompetent to contract, the bill may be treated as dishonoured. Where presentment is excused and the bill remains unaccepted it is dishonoured by non-acceptance.[595]

553. Dishonour by non-payment – When a negotiable instrument is presented to maker, acceptor or banker and he makes default in making payment it is dishonour by non-payment.[596]

554. In both cases, the holder should give notice of dishonour to any prior party whom he wants to hold liable. The effect of not giving notice to the holder is serious. He cannot sue a party to whom he has not given such notice.

555. Noting – When a negotiable instrument dishonoured, the holder of the instrument gets a right of action against the parties to the instrument. The noting works as an official proof of the fact that proper presentment of the instrument was made and that it has been dishonoured. Noting is a minute made on the bill or note by a Notary Public upon the instrument and partly on such paper.[597]

556. Protest – The protest is a formal certificate issued by a Notary Public attesting the fact of dishonour of the promissory note or the bill of exchange. The protest should be done within reasonable time.[598]

557. Both noting and protesting affords authentic and satisfactory evidence of dishonour.

II. Presumptions

558. There is a presumption that every negotiable instrument was made or drawn for consideration. Likewise, there is also a presumption that every instrument, when it has been accepted, indorsed, negotiated or transferred, was accepted, indorsed,

595. The Negotiable Instrument Act, 1881, s. 91.
596. The Negotiable Instrument Act, 1881, s. 92.
597. The Negotiable Instrument Act, 1881, s. 99.
598. The Negotiable Instrument Act, 1881, s. 100.

negotiated or transferred for consideration. Also the time of transfer, order of endorsements, stamps and that holder is a holder in due course.[599]

III. Estoppels

559. In the act there are certain estoppels. These are – estoppel against denial of validity of the instrument,[600] estoppel against denial of payee's capacity at the time to indorse the instrument,[601] estoppel against the endorser to deny the signature or capacity of any prior party to the instrument.[602]

§10. Application of International Law

560. Section 11 of the Act lays down that a promissory note, bill of exchange or cheque drawn or made in India, and made payable in, or drawn upon any person resident in India shall be deemed to be an inland instrument, but any instrument, not so drawn, made or made payable shall be deemed to be foreign instrument under section 12 of the Act.

561. Foreign bills of exchange must be protested for dishonour when such protest is required by the law of the place where they are drawn under section 104 of the Act.

562. In the absence of a contract to the contrary, however, the liability of the maker or drawer of a foreign instrument is regulated essentially by the law of the place where he made the instrument. The respective liability of the acceptor and the endorser is governed by the law of the place where the instrument is made payable.[603]

563. Where the instrument is made payable in a different country from the one where it is made or endorsed, the law of the country where it is made payable shall prevail.[604]

564. If an instrument is made, drawn, accepted or indorsed outside India but in accordance with Indian law, the fact that the instrument is invalid according to that country's law does not invalidate any subsequent acceptance or endorsement of the instrument made within India.[605]

565. The law of any foreign country regarding negotiable instrument is to be presumed to be the same as that of India unless it is proved to be different.[606]

599. The Negotiable Instrument Act, 1881, s. 118.
600. The Negotiable Instrument Act, 1881, s. 120.
601. The Negotiable Instrument Act, 1881, s. 121.
602. The Negotiable Instrument Act, 1881, s. 122.
603. The Negotiable Instrument Act, 1881, s. 134.
604. The Negotiable Instrument Act, 1881, s. 135.
605. The Negotiable Instrument Act, 1881, s. 136.
606. The Negotiable Instrument Act, 1881, s. 137.

§11. Compensation

566. When a negotiable instrument is dishonoured, the party liable to pay becomes bound to pay compensation to the holder or endorsee. Compensation is determined by:[607]

(1) The holder is entitled to recover the amount due upon the instrument together with expenses properly incurred in presenting, noting and protesting it.
(2) The amount can be recovered at a current rate of exchange between the places where the person resides and where the instrument is supposed to be paid.
(3) The endorser who has paid the amount due on the instrument is entitled to recover the amount so paid with 18% per annum from the date of payment until realization.
(4) The party entitled for compensation may draw a bill upon any party liable to compensate him.

§12. Criminal Liability for Issuing Cheques Without Funds

567. Chapter XVII of the Negotiable Instruments Act, from sections 138–147, deals with penalties in case of dishonour of cheques for insufficient funds. These sections impose punishments for issuing cheques with knowledge that they would not be paid. The liability arises when a cheque is not paid on account of insufficiency of funds standing to the credit of the drawer's account or the amount of the cheque exceeds the amount of credit facility allowed to the customer. He shall be punished with imprisonment for a term which may be extended to two years or a fine which may extend to twice the amount of the cheque or both.[608] It is necessary that the cheque should have been presented to the bank within a period of six months from the date on which it is drawn or within the period of its validity whichever is earlier. When the holder of the cheque receives information from the bank that the cheque has been dishonoured he should within thirty days make a demand for payment of the amount of money by giving a notice in writing to the drawer. If the drawer fails to pay the said amount within fifteen days of receipt of such notice the offence is complete and a cause of action begins. The Supreme Court, in its judgment dated on 1 August 2014, in case *Dusrath Rupsingh Rathod v. State of Maharastra* (Criminal Appeal No. 2287 of 2009) held that the territorial jurisdiction for dishonour of cheques is restricted to the court, within whose local jurisdiction the offence was committed, which in present context is where the cheque is dishonoured by the bank on which it is drawn.

568. In the case of a person committing the offence, under section 138, every person who at the time that the offence was committed was in charge of and responsible to the company for the conduct of business of the company shall be deemed to be guilty of the offence.[609] This is provided that no person shall be punished if he proves that the offence was committed without his knowledge or that he had exercised all

607. The Negotiable Instrument Act, 1881, s. 117.
608. The Negotiable Instrument Act, 1881, s. 138 (as amended in 2002).
609. The Negotiable Instrument Act, 1881, s. 141.

due diligence to prevent the commission of such an offence.[610] A director of a company who is holding an office or employment in the central government or state government or financial corporation owned by the central or state government shall not be liable for prosecution.

569. No court shall take cognizance of any offence punishable under section 138 except upon a complaint in writing. Such a complaint must be made within one month of the date on which the cause of action arises. No court inferior to the metropolitan magistrate or judicial magistrate first class shall try such an offence.[611] The court shall try the offence summarily.[612] Every offence shall be compoundable.[613]

§13. Overriding the Provisions of the Negotiable Instruments Act, 1881

570. The law applicable to the negotiable instruments is contained in the Negotiable Instrument Act, 1881. It may, however, be noted that the provisions of the Negotiable Instruments Act are subject to the provisions contained in section 31 of the Reserve Bank of India Act, 1934. The effect of the above provision is as follows:

(1) A bill of exchange, promissory note, or hundi cannot be made payable to 'bearer on demand'. Note that a cheque payable to bearer on demand can be issued.
(2) A promissory note cannot be made payable to bearer. Note that the words 'or to bearer' in the definition of a promissory note given in section 4 of the Negotiable Instrument Act, 1881 become inoperative because of this provision of the Reserve Bank of India Act.

The object of the Reserve Bank of India Act is to prevent banks and private individuals from infringing the Government monopoly of issuing the paper currency in India. The above provisions in the Act are inserted in order to meet this object, and they prevail over the provisions of the Negotiable Instruments Act in case of any contribution.

610. The Negotiable Instrument Act, 1881, s. 141 (proviso).
611. The Negotiable Instrument Act, 1881, s. 142.
612. The Negotiable Instrument Act, 1881, s. 143.
613. The Negotiable Instrument Act, 1881, s. 147.

Chapter 8. Stock and Commodity Exchange

§1. General

571. Regulation of the Indian stock and commodity is intended to ensure that securities are freely marketable and that investors' confidence is retained. Issues of share capital were earlier governed by the Capital Issues (Control) Act, 1947 and controlled by a government wing called the Controller of Capital Issues situated in Delhi, who administered the act until May, 1992. The SEBI Act was enacted in the year, 1992, which was deemed to have come into effect on 30 January 1992. The SEBI was set up as an autonomous apex body under the SEBI Act, 1992 to regulate the securities market in the country. SEBI Guidelines apply to issues of securities to the public and to certain issues of listed companies.

572. With the experience gained, the SEBI has consolidated the said guidelines and clarifications and issued the SEBI (Disclosure and Investor Protection) Guidelines, 2000, which came into effect 27 January 2000. These guidelines have superseded the earlier guidelines and clarifications issued in this regard. The Guidelines have also been amended many times. However, vide circular number. SEBI/CFD/DIL/ICDRR/1/2009/03/09 dated 3 September 2009, SEBI has framed the SEBI (Issue of Capital and Disclosure Requirements) Regulations, 2009 (hereinafter referred to as 'the ICDR Regulations') and that pursuant to the notification of the ICDR Regulations on 26 August 2009, the SEBI (Disclosure and Investor Protection) Guidelines, 2000 had been rescinded.

I. Securities Market: Historical Background

573. The organized stock exchange in India is of a comparatively recent origin. In 1933, there were only three stock exchanges in India. However, trade in securities used to take place much earlier, even in the eighteenth century, and share quotations were published in contemporary newspapers. By the 1830s, there was a noticeable increase in the volume of business as seen through loans and corporate securities, and mainly from banks and cotton presses. The trading list further widened in 1839 and the Companies Act was enacted in 1850, which introduced the principle of limited liability. This along with the development in the means of communication and transport gave a push to the joint stock enterprise. During the share mania of 1860–1865 the share business flourished and the number of brokers increased. In 1874, on a street now called the Dalal Street after their name, a group of people found a place where they could conveniently assemble and transact business in securities. It was in year 1875 that the first stock exchange was formulated in the name of 'The Native Share and Stock Brokers Association' which is presently known as the 'Bombay stock exchange'. It is the India's oldest first stock exchange with more than 6,000 stocks listed. In 1894, following the model of the Bombay Stock Exchange, Ahmedabad

Share and Stock Brokers was established. The Calcutta Stock Exchange Association was founded in June 1908. In India today, there are only twenty-two recognized stock exchanges. The establishment of more stock exchanges in India has called for keeping in view the concentration of business in the Calcutta and Bombay stock exchange only. These two stock exchanges practically dominate the Indian investment market. However with the advancement of technology, this process has almost become redundant. Now, the trading of shares and stock takes place electronically. Another significant development has been corporatization and demutualization of the stock exchanges. 'Corporatization' means the succession of a recognized stock exchange, being a body of individuals or a society registered under the Societies Registration Act, 1860 (21 of 1860), by another stock exchange, being a company incorporated for the purpose of assisting, regulating or controlling the business of buying, selling or dealing in securities carried on by such individuals or society; and 'demutualization' means the segregation of ownership and management from the trading rights of the members of a recognized stock exchange in accordance with the scheme approved by the SEBI. There is an Over The Counter Exchange of India (OTCEI) which allows listing of small and medium sized companies. Pursuant to section 131 of Finance Act, 2015 and central Government notification F.No 1/9/SM/2015 dated 28 August 2015 all recognized associations (Commodity derivatives exchanges) under the Forward Contracts (Regulation) Act, 1952 (FCRA) as on 28 September 2015 are deemed to be recognized stock Exchanges under the Securities Contracts (Regulation) Act, 1956 (SCRA).

II. Background of the Current Regulatory Scheme

574. Because of the importance of the stock exchange, the complexity of the securities market and the inherent potential for improper practice, the Capital Issues (Control) Act, 1947 was passed. In 1956, the Securities Contracts (Regulation) Act, 1956 was passed. It permits only those stock exchanges which have been duly recognized by the central government to function in India. The Act sets up a general framework of control which makes government influence all-pervasive, and, at the same time, by enabling legislative measures, it provides the government with a flexible apparatus for the regulation of the stock market in India. In 1992, SEBI Act was enacted and later the SEBI was set up as an autonomous apex body under the SEBI Act, 1992 to regulate the securities market in the country. By notification No. LAD-NRO/GN/2012-13/07/13546 dated 20 June 2012, in exercise of the powers conferred by sections 4, 8A, and 31 of the Securities Contracts (Regulation) Act, 1956, read with sections 11 and 30 of the SEBI Act, 1992, the SEBI has issued the Securities Contracts (Regulation) (Stock Exchanges and Clearing Corporations) Regulations, 2012 to regulate recognition, ownership and governance in stock exchanges and clearing corporations and matters connected therewith or incidental thereto. Rule 3 of this Regulation states that no person shall conduct, organize or assist in organizing any stock exchange or clearing corporation unless he has obtained recognition from the Board (SEBI) in accordance with the Act, rules and these regulations. Securities Laws (Amendment) Act, 2014 is a legislation in India which provided the securities market regulator the 'SEBI' with new powers to effectively pursue fraudulent investment schemes, especially ponzi schemes. It also provides guidelines for the formation of special fast trial courts.

III. Types of Securities

575. The words 'securities' and 'derivatives' were not defined earlier in the Companies Act, 1956, or in the SEBI Guidelines, 2000, but were defined in the Securities Contracts (Regulation) Act, 1956 (SCRA). The Company Act, 2013 provides the definition of 'securities' in section 2(81), according to which 'securities' means the securities as defined in clause (h) of section 2 of the Securities Contracts (Regulation) Act, 1956.[614] The section 2(h) of SCRA defines 'securities' as follows. The term 'securities' includes:

> (I) shares, scripts, stocks, bonds, debentures, debenture stock or other marketable securities of a like nature in or of any incorporated company or other corporate body;
>
> (ia) derivatives;
>
> (ib) units or any other instrument issued by any collective investment scheme to the investors in such schemes;
>
> (ic) security receipt as defined in clause (zg) of section 2 of the Securitisation and Reconstruction of Financial Assets and Enforcement of Security Interest Act, 2002;]
>
> (id) units or any other such instrument issued to the investors under any mutual fund scheme
>
> (ie) any certificate or instrument (by whatever name called), issued to an investor by any issuer being a special purpose distinct entity which possesses any debt or receivable, including mortgage debt, assigned to such entity, and acknowledging beneficial interest of such investor in such debt or receivable, including mortgage debt, as the case maybe;.
>
> (ii) & (iia) Government securities and any other such instruments as may be declared by the Central Government as a securities; and

614. Available on http://www.mca.gov.in/SearchableActs/Section2.htm.

(iii) rights and interests in securities.

The term 'derivatives' includes[615] (Sec 2(ac) of SCRA:

(A) a security derived from a debt instrument, share, loan (secured or unsecured), risk instrument or contract for differences or any other form of security; and

(B) a contract which derives its value from the prices, or index of prices, of underlying securities.

576. The definition of the term 'securities' was amended by the Amendment Acts from time to time so as to expand the definition of 'securities', the latest being amendment so as to include clause (ie) in section 2(h) of the SCRA.

IV. Definition in the Companies Act, 2013

577. The term 'securities' has been defined under the Companies Act as 'securities as defined in clause (h) of section 2 of the SCRA, 1956 and includes hybrids'. The term 'hybrid' has been defined under section 2(19A) of the Companies Act as 'any security which has the characters of more than one type of security including their derivatives'. Even though the Companies Act, 2013 and the SCRA define instruments such as hybrid, derivative, futures and options in securities, etc. the Indian market has much room for developing and defining the issue and transfer of these instruments. There are basically two types of markets in which derivative contracts trade. These are exchange traded market and over-the-counter (OTC) market.

578. Exchange-traded derivative contracts (ETD): They are instruments that are traded via specialized derivatives exchanges or platforms on other exchanges. A derivatives exchange is a market where individuals' trade standardized contracts that have been defined by the exchange. A derivatives exchange acts as an intermediary to all related transactions, and takes initial margin from both sides of the trade to serve as a guarantee.

579. Over-the-Counter (OTC) derivatives: Due to standardization and fixed contract specifications in exchange traded contracts, financial institutions began to develop non-exchange traded derivatives contracts for sophisticated investors. Indian OTC derivatives markets are well regulated. Only contracts where one party to the contract is an RBI regulated entity are considered legally valid in India. A good reporting system and a post-trade clearing and settlement system, through a centralized counter party, has ensured good surveillance of the systemic risks in the Indian OTC market.

615. Securities Contractors (Regulation) Act, 1956, s. 2(ac).

V. A Wide Range of Shares and Securities Traded on the Stock Exchange

580. Securities are traded on stock exchanges (SEs) commensurate with that which is 'listed' or quoted on them. SEs have their own listing requirements/rules which tend to undergo changes from time to time. Since taking effect on 27 May 1996, the listing requirement on many SEs in India have been made more stringent in order to broaden the shareholder holding in the companies and to avoid a large chunk of shares being held by the few individuals in company management. It is now stipulated that in case of an offer for sale, there will have to be at least ten public shareholders for every INR 100,000 of equity offered to the public. Furthermore, it is stipulated that the minimum equity capital of a company seeking a listing on the Bombay and National Stock Exchange (BSE & NSE) should be INR 1 billion and the capitalization of the applicant equity shall not be less than INR 2.5 billion. For this post issue paid-up equity capital for which listing is sought shall be taken into account. Companies cannot make a public issue unless they have a track record of dividend payments for at least three years out of the five preceding years. In case the Company has not paid dividend in two out of the last three years, the Company is required to provide certificate from the statutory auditors of the company – confirming the net worth of the company for the last three years (providing detailed working for computation of net worth) and distributable profits if any for the last three years computed as per section 205 of the Companies Act, 1956.

VI. Security Groupings

581. The Bombay Stock Exchange Ltd. (BSE) and the National Stock Exchange of India Ltd. (NSE) are the two primary exchanges in India. Most key stocks are traded on both the exchanges and hence the investor could buy them on either exchange. Both exchanges have a different settlement cycle, which allows investors to shift their positions on the bourses. The primary index of BSE is BSE Sensex comprising thirty stocks. NSE has the S&P NSE fifty Index (Nifty) which consists of fifty stocks. The BSE Sensex is the older and more widely followed index. Both these indices are calculated on the basis of market capitalization and contain the heavily traded shares from key sectors. Both the exchanges have switched over from the open outcry trading system to a fully automated computerized mode of trading known as BOLT (BSE Online Trading) and NEAT (National Exchange Automated Trading) System. The scrips traded on the BSE have been classified into 'A', 'B1', 'B2', 'C', 'F' and 'Z' groups. The 'A' group shares represent those, which are in the carry-forward system (Badla). The 'F' group represents the debt market (fixed income securities) segment. The 'Z' group scrips are the blacklisted companies. The 'C' group covers the odd lot securities in 'A', 'B1' & 'B2' groups and Rights renunciations. The classification is on the basis of several factors like market capitalization, trading volumes and numbers, track records, profits, dividends, shareholding patterns, and some qualitative aspects. The non-specified group has been split into a B1 group and a B2 securities group. A B1 group has a weekly settlement; is on par with an A group in every respect except for the fact that carry-over is not allowed; and this also applies in respect of actively traded securities. The B2 group is subject to a settlement procedure, which previously existed in the case of group B securities. Since September 1996, the BSE has started in all debentures listed on it, and they are included in the new group called 'F Group' for this purpose.

VII. Trading Systems

582. Transactions enacted on the Stock Exchange are carried out either on a cash basis or carry-over basis, i.e., through 'clearing'. Exchanges in Mumbai, Calcutta, Chennai and Ahmedabad have their own clearing houses. All transactions made during one account are to be settled by way of payment for purchases and through the delivery of share certificates in the case of sales on notified days of the clearing programme of a given stock exchange. Transactions in non-specified securities have to be settled compulsorily by delivery carry-over which is permitted only in respect of Group A securities.

583. The types of transactions allowed on a cash basis according to the arrangement for delivery (delivery-wise) are:

(1) spot delivery, where the delivery and payment are made on the same day as the day of the contract or the following day;
(2) hand delivery, where the delivery and payment are made when stipulated; and
(3) special delivery, where the delivery and payment are made after fourteen days if so permitted by the stock exchange authority.

VIII. Margins

584. One of the aspects of securities trading is the imposition of margins by the authorities on such trading, particularly on carry-forward transactions. The purpose of margins can be stated in various ways. Margins are required to cover defaults in the event of adverse price movements. They are stipulated on the basis of the risk involved in the securities. They are also required to regulate or restrain forward trading, overtrading and unhealthy, reckless, excessive speculation by putting financial burden or curbs on the traders. In essence, they are meant to reduce the volume of trading.

IX. Ordinary Shares

585. Ordinary shares are ownership securities, which have certain advantages in favour of the issuing companies and investors depending on their attitude for risk-taking. Investment in this financial instrument is permanent but not illiquid. Due to the existence of a fairly active secondary market in shares, investors can turn their shareholding into cash fairly quickly. Because of the high risk, which an investor bears, he may participate in the earning and wealth of the company without limit. In a period of inflation, since the value of a holding increases, ordinary share are expected to act as a hedge against inflation. From the point of view of the company, this is advantageous because dividend payments on ordinary shares are not mandatory and there is no need to refinance the capital raised through the issuance of ordinary shares. As in other countries, this instrument is quite popular with individual investors in India. The face value of ordinary shares in India varies from INR 1 to INR 1,000, but the most common and popular denomination of shares is INR 10.

X. Preference Shares

586. A preference share is a complex financial instrument with a number of modifications to its general characteristics. Strictly speaking it is an ownership security like an ordinary share, but carries a fixed rate of return (dividend) like a debenture. The holders of preference shares are entitled to income after the claims of creditors of the company have been met, but before ordinary shareholders receive any income. Because of these modifications, one comes across the following types of preference shares in the market: (a) cumulative and non-cumulative; (b) convertible and non-convertible; (c) redeemable and non-redeemable; and (d) participating and non-participating.

587. On cumulative preference shares, if a dividend is skipped in any period, it has to be paid subsequently.

588. Convertible preference shares can be converted into ordinary shares on terms and conditions fixed at the time of the issuance of such shares.

589. Redeemable preference shares mature in a fixed period of time and for all practical purposes are regarded as a debt security like debentures.

590. Participating preference shareholders can earn a higher dividend than the fixed one if the company makes good profits.

XI. Debentures or Bonds

591. Debenture or bond is a creditorship security with the following characteristics:

- a fixed rate of return;
- fixed maturity period;
- perfect income certainty; and
- low capital uncertainty.

592. While bonds are secured by tangible physical assets of the issuing company. In the US, debentures are secured only by the general creditworthiness of the company. There is no such distinction in the UK and India where an industrial debenture can be of both types, i.e., secured or unsecured. There are different kinds of debentures: (a) convertible; (b) non-convertible; (c) partially convertible; (d) registered; (e) bearer; (f) redeemable; (g) perpetual; (h) callable; and (i) rights, etc.

XII. Unique Features

593. The dwindling fortunes of Regional Stock Exchanges brought them together to establish the Inter-connected Stock Exchange of India Ltd. (ISE). At a meeting of the Federation of Indian Stock Exchanges held in October 1996, a Steering Committee was formed to evolve an Inter-connected Market System. As a result, ISE, which was promoted by fourteen regional stock exchanges of the country (excluding Calcutta, Delhi, Ahmedabad, Ludhiana and Pune Stock Exchange, apart from NSE, BSE and OTCEI) was incorporated by SEBI under the Securities Contracts (Regulations) Act, 1956 on 18 November 1998. ISE commenced trading on 26 February 1999. ISE was launched with an objective of converting small, fragmented and illiquid markets into large, liquid national-level markets. Unique Advantages for companies to get their securities listed on the Inter-connected Stock Exchange of India Limited (ISE):

(1) ISE is a national-level stock exchange, providing trading, clearing, settlement, risk management and surveillance support to its trading members. It was incorporated as a company limited by guarantee in January 1998. It has 791 trading members, who are located in eighty-four cities spread across eighteen states. ISE is now planning to launch its own trading platform, subject to SEBI approval. Platform testing has already been done and submitted to SEBI for approval in September 2011.[616]
(2) ISE is the only Exchange in the country located in a technology park and the Exchange itself is technology intensive.
(3) It is the only national-level recognized stock exchange granting listing and trading permission to the small and medium sized companies having a post public issue paid-up capital of INR 5 crores. A Company having a post public issue paid-up capital of not less than INR 3 crores can also be listed on the ISE. Minimum 25% of the company's issued capital shall be with Non-Promoter shareholders.
(4) Securities listed on the ISE are available for trading to traders and dealers of the ISE who are spread throughout the country. They permit greater accessibility to retail investors and also more visibility to any scrip.
(5) All the traders and dealers of the ISE have access to the National Stock Exchange (NSE) and BSE through the ISE Securities and Services Ltd. (ISS), a wholly-owned subsidiary of ISE and the traders and dealers of ISE are registered with the ISS as its sub-broker. Thus, the ISE and ISS provide a one stop multiple market solution for trading for the investors in all securities listed on it and the NSE with due safeguards.
(6) The ISE has a very efficient and user-friendly system for listing securities on the ISE.
(7) The ISE intends to decentralize the compliance of listing requirements throughout its five branches situated in three metro cities in India, Coimbatore and Nagpur to assist companies by making compliance more convenient.
(8) The ISE being a national-level stock exchange, listing of shares on ISE provides the company a larger market with nationwide reach amongst millions of investors and would also generate the commitment of the company towards their shareholders

616. *Source*: www.iseindia.com.

by providing them a nationally accessible trading facility and information dissemination facility. This would give greater visibility to the image of the company in times when access by the retail investor is very important for both the primary and secondary market.

(9) The listing of stock with ISE would also have the advantage of being identified as a technology-savvy and investor-friendly company.

(10) India is in an advanced stage of discussion with several good nationally recognized companies for listing their securities on ISE.

(11) India is a technology driven stock exchange with professional management and providing thrust to technological stocks as a highly technological intensive exchange.

(12) The commitment for professional management is displayed from the fact that ISE has decided to have a public representative appointed by SEBI as its Chairman.

(13) ISE is a depository participant of NSDL and CDSL and has established online connectivity with NSDL/CDSL hence trading in demat segment is smoother and it also ensure greater safety of the market and of the small Investors as it eliminates the risk associated with the physical segment.

(14) ISE had setup an 'Investors Grievance & Service cells' which looks after all types of Investor complaints.

XIII. Listed Companies

594. Public limited companies can be broadly classified into a listed company and non-listed company.

595. A 'listed company' means a public limited company, which is:

- listed on any one or more recognized stock exchange(s) in India; and
- securities (i.e., shares, debentures, etc.) of such company are traded on such stock exchanges.

596. 'Unlisted company', therefore, means a company whose securities are not listed on any of the recognized Indian stock exchanges.

597. Some of the advantages of a listed company are:

- securities freely transferable;
- easy liquidity of securities;
- easy availability of prices of securities;
- reputation;
- public awareness;
- more transparency;
- helps in obtaining loans from banks/institutions; and
- helps in marketing its products.

598. In order to list the securities of a company and get its shares traded on any recognized stock exchange, the public limited company may either come out with a public issue (i.e., to offer further securities to the public) or make an offer for sale of existing securities to the public. This can be done through issue of a prospectus and complying with all the provisions of the Companies Act, 1956, rules and regulations issued by the SEBI and other concerned authorities from time to time. SEBI, vide General Order No. 1 of 2012 dated 9 October 2012 has issued 'SEBI (Framework for Rejection of Draft Offer Documents) Order, 2012' wherein it has listed various criterion which could lead to rejection of offer documents filed for the purpose of raising funds from the public. The offer documents may be rejected if SEBI feels that the interest of the investors is prejudiced or inadequate disclosures are made in the offer document or quality of the disclosures are not reasonable or where the risk associated with the issue is high.

599. Each stock exchange has its own criteria for listing securities and must be met. For example, if the company intends to list its securities on the stock exchange of Mumbai, the post issue capital (i.e., paid-up capital after the proposed public issue) of such a company should be at least INR 1 billion.

600. After the successful completion of the issuance, the company finalizes the allotment basis with the regional stock exchange. If the company has proposed to list its securities with more than one stock exchange, then the basis of allotment should be finalized with the stock exchange situated in the state in which the registered office of the company is situated (regional stock exchange).

601. A company enters a listing agreement with the concerned stock exchange and with the approval of the concerned stock exchange(s), the company is listed and its securities are thereafter traded on that stock exchange. Such companies have certain obligations with respect to the stock exchanges where their securities are listed.

602. Nowadays, stock exchanges take serious note if listed companies do not comply with their statutory and listing obligations. The stock exchanges have started penalizing the companies for non-compliances. The Stock Exchange of Mumbai has transferred such companies to a 'Z' category. This creates a very bad reputation for the company and shareholders/investors shy away from such companies. Therefore, it is necessary for listed companies to know what their obligations are so as to enable them to comply accordingly.

§2. Stock Exchanges and Their Regulations

I. Stock Markets

603. A stock market is a market for trading publicly held company stock and associated financial instruments (including stock options, convertibles and stock index futures). The stock market includes all the national stock exchanges of the country. Now stock trading is done in electronic exchange where buying and selling occurs via online real time matching of orders placed by buyers and sellers. In other words it can be said that the stock market is a place where stocks, bonds or other securities are bought and sold.

604. The stock markets provide liquidity and this is provided by speculation and it is this liquidity which allows retail investors to invest money in equity capital. The question may be asked: Why only retail investors? From VCs to institutional investors, everybody looks for an exit option and liquidity. Liquidity ensures easy entry and exit for retail investors. Presently there are twenty-two stock exchanges, which aside from providing a floor for share brokers to buy and sell shares of established companies, also allows direct participation in the flotation of new issues, thus stimulating the financial market. The stock market thus functions like a barometer recording the changing investment moods in the corporate sector.

II. Stock Exchange

605. A stock exchange is an organization of which the members are stockbrokers. A stock exchange provides facilities for the trading of securities and other financial instruments. Usually facilities are also provided for the issuance and redemption of securities as well as other capital events including the payment of income and dividends. According to section 2(j) of the Securities Contracts (Regulation) Act, 1956. 'Stock Exchange' means: (a) anybody of individuals, whether incorporated or not, constituted before corporatization and demutualization under section 4A and 4B; or (b) a body corporate incorporated under the Companies Act, 2013 whether under a scheme of corporatization and demutualization or otherwise, for the purpose of assisting, regulating or controlling the business of buying, selling or dealing in securities. The record keeping is central but trade is linked to such physical place because modern markets are computerized. Foreign Institutional Investors (FII) upon registration with the SEBI and the RBI are allowed to operate in Indian Stock Exchanges subject to the guidelines issued for the purpose by SEBI.

III. Listing Rules

606. Listing means the admission of the securities of a public limited company for trading on a stock exchange. The principle objectives of listing are to provide liquidity and free negotiability to securities; ensure proper supervision and control of dealing therein; and protect the interest of the shareholders and of the general investing public. While there is no statutory obligation that every public limited company should have its securities listed on a recognized stock exchange, section 73 of the Companies Act mandates it to every company intending to offer shares or debentures to the public for subscription. Once a declaration is made as seen on a prospectus, of an intent to apply to list on a stock exchange, the government may use its powers under section 2.1 of the Securities Contracts (Regulation) Act, 1956 in respect of a public limited company, to list its shares on a recognized stock exchange. Financial institutions also require listing. The SEBI also stipulates that companies making a public issuance should have their shares listed on a recognized stock exchange or OTCEI (Over The Counter Exchange of India). The Securities Contracts (Regulation) Act and the Securities Contracts (Regulation) Rules, the by-laws and stock exchange regulations as well as the various guidelines issued by the government from time to time have prescribed a number of requirements which have to be complied with by a company that intends to list its securities on a stock exchange. They mainly relate to the memorandum and articles of association, prospectus, norms about publicity, minimum public offer, basis of allotment and execution of a listing agreement.

IV. Recent Developments

A. Central Listing Authority

607. The SEBI has notified the SEBI (Central Listing Authority) Regulations, 2003 on 13 February 2003 to provide for the setting up of a Central Listing Authority (CLA) to bring about uniformity in the exercise of due diligence in scrutinizing listing applications of companies/mutual funds/collective investment schemes.

608. The CLA was to discharge the following functions:

(1) processing the application made by any corporate body, mutual fund or collective investment scheme; and
(2) making recommendations as to listing conditions.

609. The CLA gave a 'letter of recommendation' to any corporate/mutual fund or collective investment scheme to get itself listed on a particular exchange, after examining its listing application. With effect from 3 January 2007, the SEBI had repealed with immediate effect the SEBI (Central Listing Authority) Regulations, 2003.

610. The process of setting up this authority, in terms of officials who shall man the authority, the location, etc. has been initiated and operating the same shall be a top priority of SEBI and the government.

B. Delisting Guidelines

611. The SEBI has issued the SEBI (Delisting of Securities) Guidelines, 2003 on 17 February 2003. The Guidelines provide that companies can delist from stock exchanges only by offering an exit route to the remaining shareholders through a reverse book building process. This mechanism would leave the option of pricing to the investors and would be totally transparent to the market. Furthermore, the proposer shall offer a floor price on the basis of the average of the previous twenty-six weeks' high and low investor prices. These guidelines seek to protect the interests of the small investor in the wake of any company delisting from the exchange(s). Section 21A was introduced in the Securities Contracts (Regulation) Act, 1956 (SCR Act) effective 12 October 2004. It permitted recognized Stock Exchanges to delist securities on any of the ground or grounds as may be prescribed in this Act. An aggrieved company or investor has right of appeal before the Securities Appellate Tribunal. In furtherance of the above, Rule 21 has now come to be inserted in the Securities Contracts (Regulation) Rules, 1957 (SCR Rules). It deals with delisting compulsorily inflicted by stock exchange as well as voluntary delisting initiated by a company. Simultaneously SEBI has issued the SEBI (Delisting of Equity Shares) Regulations, 2009 (SEBI Regulations) on 10 June 2009. They would prospectively operate in place of erstwhile SEBI (Delisting of Securities) Guidelines, 2003. These regulations replace the SEBI (Delisting of Securities) Guidelines, 2003, as far as delisting of equity shares are concerned. It, however, appears that the 2003 guidelines continue to apply to delisting of other listed securities which are not equity shares as the new Regulations are limited only to equity shares and not all securities. As per the Regulations the floor price shall not be less than, – (a) where the equity shares are frequently traded in all the recognized stock exchanges where they are listed, the average of the weekly high and low of the closing prices of the equity shares of the company during the twenty-six weeks or two weeks preceding the date on which the recognized stock exchanges were notified of the board meeting in which the delisting proposal was considered, whichever is higher, as quoted on the recognized stock exchange where the equity shares of the company are most frequently traded; (b) where the equity shares of the company are infrequently traded in all the recognized stock exchanges where they are listed, the floor price determined in accordance with the provisions of sub-regulation (3); or (c) where the equity shares are frequently traded in some recognized stock exchanges and infrequently traded in some other recognized stock exchanges where they are listed, the highest of the prices arrived at in accordance with clauses (a) and (b) above. Explanation: For the purposes of this sub-regulation, equity shares shall be deemed to be infrequently traded, if on the recognized stock exchange, the annualized trading turnover in such shares during the preceding six calendar months prior to month in which the recognized stock exchanges were notified of the board meeting in which the delisting proposal was considered, is less than 5%. (by number of equity shares) of the total listed equity shares of that class and the term 'frequently traded' shall be construed accordingly. (3) For the purposes of clause (b) of sub-regulation (2), the floor price shall be determined by the promoter and the merchant banker taking into account the following factors: (a) the highest price paid by the promoter for acquisitions, if any, of equity shares of the class sought to be delisted, including by way of allotment in a public or rights issue or preferential allotment, during the twenty-six weeks period prior to the date on which the recognized stock exchanges were notified of the board meeting in which the delisting proposal was considered and after that date up to the date of the public announcement; and, (b) other parameters including return on net worth, book value of the shares of the company, earning per share, price earning multiple vis-à-vis the industry average.

V. Enforceability of Rules of the Exchange

612. The rules of an exchange are enforceable on the following bases:

(1) Contractual Enforceability.
(2) While the Securities Contract Regulation Act is the key enactment concerning the regulation of the security market in India, there are other supporting enactments like the Companies Act, 1956, SEBI, etc. which regulates the incorporation of companies, their periodical financial and other reporting requirements and in the

case of capital issues control, the issuance of securities under SEBI guidelines. The rules of exchange are also enforceable by a few provisions of the Foreign Exchange Regulation Act, the Banking Regulation Act, the Unit Trust of India Act (repealed in 2002), the Indian Trusts Act, the Reserve Bank of India Act, the Income Tax Act, the Wealth Tax Act, the Gift Tax Act, the Public Debt Act and the Indian Stamp Act.

(3) Section 55A of the Companies Act, which reads 'The provision contained in sections 55–58, 59–81 (including sections 68A, 77A and 80A), 108, 109, 110, 112, 113, 116, 117, 118, 119, 120, 121, 122, 206, 206A and 207, so far as they relate to the issue and transfer of securities and non-payment of dividend shall:

(a) in case of listed public companies;
(b) in the case of those public companies which intend to have their securities listed on any recognized stock exchange in India, be administered by SEBI; and
(c) in any other case, be administered by the Central Government'.

613. Explanation – For the removal of any ambiguity, it is hereby declared that all powers relating to all matters including matters relating to a prospectus, statement in lieu of prospectus, return of allotment, issue of shares and redemption of irredeemable preference shares shall be exercised by the central government, the Company Law Board or the Registrar of Companies, as the case may be.

VI. General Law Applicable to Stock Exchange Transactions

A. The Broker-Client Relationship

614. The rapidly changing financial services industry requires an intimate understanding of broker clients in order for brokerage firms to increase and maintain a client base. Just as the technical methods of forecasting price movements, market timing and self-reliance fell by the wayside during the old era, so has the broker/client relationship. With cheap internet trading available and professionally managed accounts and mutual funds promoted by brokerage houses, the relationship between a broker and a client has almost disappeared. Commissions through a broker cost more than an internet transaction and it takes more effort than buying a mutual fund.

615. Under section 2 of SEBI (Stock Brokers and Sub-Brokers) Rules, 1992 the definition is given accordingly. These Rules have been repealed by Ministry of Finance Notification dated 7 September 2006. However, section 2 (gb) and (gc) of the SEBI (Stock Brokers and Sub-brokers) Regulations, 1992 also defines as follows:

(gb) 'stock broker' means a member of a stock exchange; and

(gc) 'sub-broker' means any person not being a member of a stock exchange who acts on behalf of a stock-broker as an agent or otherwise for assisting the investors in buying, selling or dealing in securities through such stock-brokers.

B. Not to Act as Stockbroker or Sub-broker Without Registration

616. No stock broker or sub-broker shall buy, sell or deal in securities, unless he holds a certificate granted by the Board in accordance with the regulations. The stockbroker shall not deal with any person as a sub-broker unless such person has been granted certificate of registration by the Board under sub-regulation (1) of Regulation 12.

617. The above said is provided that such a person has continued to buy, sell or deal in securities and has made an application for such registration till the disposal of such application.

C. Conditions for Granting a Certificate to a Stockbroker

618. An application by a stockbroker for grant of a certificate shall be made in 'Form A' through the stock exchange or stock exchanges, as the case may be, of which he is admitted as a member. The stock exchange shall forward the application form to the Board as early as possible but not later than thirty days from the date of its receipt. The Board may grant a certificate to a stockbroker subject to the following conditions as defined in regulation 6A(1) of SEBI (Stock Brokers and Sub-brokers) Regulations, 1992, namely:

(1) He holds the membership of any stock exchange.
(2) He shall abide by the rules, regulations and by-laws of the stock exchange or stock exchanges of which he is a member.
(3) In case of any change in the status and constitution, the sub-broker shall obtain prior permission of the Board to continue to buy, sell or deal in securities in any stock exchange.
(4) He shall pay the amount of fees for registration in the manner provided in the regulations.
(5) He shall take adequate steps for redressal of grievances of the investors within one month of the date of the receipt of the complaint and keep the Board informed about the number, nature and other particulars of the complaints received from such investors.

D. Conditions for Granting a Certificate to a Sub-broker

619. An application by a sub-broker for the grant of a certificate shall be made in 'Form B'. The application form shall be submitted to the stock exchange of which the stockbroker with whom he is to be affiliated is a member under section 15A, no director of a stockbroker shall act as a sub-broker to the same stockbroker. No fresh certificate needs to be obtained under sub-regulation (1) where a sub-broker merely changes his affiliation from one stockbroker to another stockbroker, being a member of the same stock exchange. The Board may grant a certificate to a sub-broker subject to the following conditions, namely:

(a) he shall abide by the rules, regulations and bye-laws of the stock exchange which are applicable to him;
(b) he shall pay the fees in the manner provided in the regulations;
(c) he shall take adequate steps for redressal of grievances of the investors within one month of the date of the receipt of the complaint and keep the Board informed about the number, nature and other particulars of the complaints received;
(d) in case of any change in the status and/or constitution, the sub-broker shall obtain prior permission of the Board to continue to buy, sell or deal in securities in any stock exchange;
(e) he is authorized in writing by a stock broker being a member of a stock exchange for affiliating himself in buying, selling or dealing in securities.

620. Provided that such a stockbroker is entitled to buy, sell or deal with securities.

E. The Contract and Duty of Brokers

621. A stockbroker shall execute orders at the best available market price and not refuse to deal with small investors.[617] He should promptly inform his client about the execution or non-execution of an order and make payment for sale and delivery of securities purchased. A contract note should be issued promptly. He is expected to maintain confidentiality about his clients' investments. Stockbrokers should not encourage sales or purchases of securities or furnish quotations, information and advice to earn brokerage and commission. Stockbrokers are not expected to deal with clients who are in default with other stockbrokers. Stockbrokers should also disclose to clients whether he is acting as a principal or broker and avoid conflict of interest. Investment advice should not be given unless suitable on the basis of information given by the client about his financial situation, security holdings and investment objectives. Stockbrokers should render fair, prompt and competent services to their clients.

622. A stockbroker should cooperate with other brokers in comparing unmatched transactions, replacing documents declared bad delivery, protection of client's interests, and settlement of transactions. A stockbroker should not advertise his business and induce through unfair means clients from others brokers. Finally, a stockbroker shall not neglect or fail or refuse to submit required returns to SEBI and stock exchange and not make false or misleading statements concerning any such returns.

623. Further, a stockbroker who fails to comply with any of the conditions of registration, contravenes any of the provisions of the SEBI Act, rules or regulations, contravenes the provisions of the SC(R) Act or the rules made thereunder, or contravenes the rules and regulations of the stock exchange is liable to suspension of registration after an enquiry for a specified period, or cancellation of registration.

617. H.R. Machiraju, *The Working of Stock Exchange in India* 32–35 (New Age Intl. Publishers. Ltd. Wiley E. 2000).

624. The penalty of suspension of registration may also be imposed if a stockbroker violates the provisions of SEBI, its rules and regulations, does not follow the code of conduct, fails to furnish information relating to his transactions in securities as required by SEBI, furnishes, etc. are ground for disciplinary action. The penalty of cancellation of registration is imposed if the stockbroker violates the regulations relating to insider trading or takeover is guilty of fraud or convicted of a criminal offence and thereby, his membership to the stock exchange will be cancelled. A suspension or cancellation order is issued only after inquiry with due notice. The stockbroker is given a reasonable opportunity to be heard. It may be preferable to appeal to the Central Government against the order of the SEBI.

VII. Client Agreement

625. The client agreement should cover details of all issues that clearly define the relationship and the extent of liabilities between the client and the trading/clearing member. The following areas are to be included in the agreement. However, the broker/exchange may prescribe additional clauses as necessary.

A. Change in Information

626. In case there is any change in the information provided by the client to the member at the time of opening the account, the client shall immediately notify the member of such change in writing.

B. Client's Understanding of Risks Involved in Derivative Trading

627. The agreement shall clearly specify the client's responsibility for all investment decisions and his complete understanding of the risks involved in trading of various derivatives contracts. The member shall ensure that the client has read and signed the Risk Disclosure Document.

C. Types of Services Offered

628. The agreement shall specify the nature of services provided by the broker, e.g., trading facilities, clearing facilities, advisory services, portfolio management services, etc.

D. Commissions, Brokerage, Other Fees

629. The agreement shall indicate the rate of the brokerage/commission/fee charged by the broker in respect of various services provided by the member.

E. Exposure Limits

630. The client agrees to abide by the exposure limits, if any, set by the trading/clearing member, or exchange or SEBI from time to time.

F. Liquidation/Close-Out of Positions

631. The broker shall have the authority to liquidate/closeout the position of the client for non-payment of margins, outstanding debts, etc. Any amount of loss caused would be charged to the client in such an event.

G. Liability to Reimburse Losses

632. The agreement shall specify the liability of the client to reimburse any losses or financial charges arising from the liquidation/close out of positions by the member as mentioned above.

§3. Marketable Securities Legislation

633. Capital market and securities transactions are regulated by the Capital Markets division of the Department of Economic Affairs.

634. The Indian financial system is regulated and supervised by three governmental agencies under the Ministry of Finance – They are:

(1) the Reserve Bank of India (RBI); and
(2) the SEBI;
(3) forward market commission (FMC) that governs Commodities markets.

635. All elements of the financial system are interconnected with one another and the jurisdictions of the RBI and the SEBI overlap in many fields such as jurisdiction of the interest rate futures market or the currency futures market.

636. Sale and transfer of shares/bonds/debentures.

I. Sale/Transfer of Shares/Bonds/Debentures by NRIs to Residents

637. In order to facilitate the quick transfer of shares/bonds/debentures held by NRIs to residents, the Reserve Bank has granted general exemptions for the sale/transfer of shares/bonds/debentures through the Indian stock exchanges, subject to the fulfilment of certain conditions.

638. No transfer of shares/bonds/debentures of a company registered in India made by a person resident outside India to another person resident in India will be valid unless the transfer is confirmed by Reserve Bank on an application made to it by the transferor or the transferee. Reserve Bank has, however, exempted transfer of shares, bonds or debentures of Indian companies held by persons of Indian nationality/

origin (NRIs) on both repatriation and non-repatriation basis to residents as also transfer of shares, bonds or debentures by way of gift through issue of Notifications, subject to fulfilment of certain conditions. Applications for the sale/transfer of shares/bonds/debentures held by NRIs/OCBs by private arrangement, i.e., other than through the stock exchange shall be made to the Reserve Bank in form TS-1 either by the transferor or by the transferee, attaching therewith the letter of consent of the other party irrespective of whether the shares/bonds/debentures are listed on a stock exchange or not. While conveying its approval, the Reserve Bank shall stipulate the conditions subject to which the sale/transfer should be effected. In the case of the sale/transfer of shares/bonds/debentures acquired on a repatriation basis, repatriation of such proceeds of the bulk holding (i.e., shares/bonds/debentures exceeding INR 1 lakh in face value or 5% of the company's paid-up capital whichever is lower) will be permitted only on production of a certificate from a Chartered Accountant or the concerned company's secretary stating that shares with the necessary transfer form duly signed have been received/lodged with the company for registration in favour of the transferee.

II. Sale/Transfer of Shares/Bonds/Debentures of Indian Companies Through a Stock Exchange Acquired Without Repatriation Benefit

639. The Reserve Bank has exempted the transfer of shares, bonds or debentures of Indian companies made by non-resident Indians (NRIs) through the stock exchange in India in cases where: (a) such transfers are made in favour of an Indian citizen or person of Indian origin resident in India or in favour of a company or other corporate body incorporated in India; and (b) the sale proceeds of shares are credited to the NRO account of the transferor with no right of repatriation outside India. In such cases, authorized dealers may credit the sale proceeds to the seller's NRO account after verifying the contract notes issued by recognized stock exchange brokers, through whom the sale was effected. This exemption is available in respect of shares, bonds, or debentures acquired by NRIs under the Portfolio Investment Scheme as well as under any Direct Investment Scheme.

640. In order to give effect to the sale/transfer of shares, bonds or debentures by OCBs acquired on a non-repatriation basis through a stock exchange in India, a consolidated application giving the full particulars may be submitted to the concerned office of the Reserve Bank. Permission will be granted by the Reserve Bank for a specific period subject to renewal.

III. Sale/Transfer of Shares/Bonds/Debentures of Indian Companies Through a Stock Exchange Acquired Without Repatriation Benefits under the Portfolio Investment Scheme

641. Reserve Bank is exempted from the transfer of shares, bonds, or debentures of Indian companies registered in India previously acquired by NRIs/OCBs with repatriation benefits under the Portfolio Investment Scheme to persons residents in

India or persons of Indian origin resident in India or in favour of companies or corporate bodies, incorporated under any law in force in India under the following conditions:

(1) The transferor had purchased such shares, bonds or debentures from the stock market through a member of a recognized stock exchange in India and the delivery of the shares, bonds, or debentures so purchased has been taken by him or on his behalf by the concerned authorized dealers or its nominee.
(2) The shares, bonds or debentures are sold in the stock market by a member of a recognized stock exchange in India and the sale transaction is effected at the ruling market price as determined on the floor of the stock exchange by the normal bid and offer method and through the same designated branch of the authorized dealer through which the shares, bonds or debentures were earlier purchased.
(3) The sale proceeds are paid to the said designated branch.

642. Consequently, it is not necessary for NRIs/OCBs to obtain the Reserve Bank's permission for sale of shares/bonds/debentures effected in the above manner. As regards the repatriation of sale proceeds received by the designated branches, the Reserve Bank, will while granting approval for the purchase of shares/bonds/debentures, also grant approval for the repatriation of the sale proceeds if and when the shares/bonds/debentures are sold in the above manner. The actual repatriation of the same proceeds or credit thereof to the NRE/FCNR account of the beneficiary will be subject to the payment of Indian taxes.

IV. Sale/Transfer of Shares/Bonds/Debentures Acquired by NRIs/OCBs with a Repatriation Benefit under the Direct Investment Scheme

643. The sale/transfer of shares/bonds/debentures acquired by NRIs/OCBs with a repatriation benefit under the direct investment scheme and sold through the stock exchange in India will require the permission of the Reserve Bank. Applications for the necessary permission should be made by NRIs/OCBs to the central office of the Reserve Bank using the TS 4 Form through the designated bank branch of an authorized dealer.

644. In such cases, permission for the sale/transfer of shares/bonds/debentures acquired with the right of repatriation will be granted by the Reserve Bank to the branch designated by the seller to the authorized dealer, as the case may be, who may sell the holdings at the ruling market price, through a stock exchange at any time within the validity of the permission. While granting permission for the sale/transfer of shares/bonds/debentures, the Reserve Bank shall also authorize the designated branch/authorized dealer to credit the sale proceeds to the NRE or FCNR account of the seller or to remit them abroad subject to payment of capital gain taxes if any. Where the amount of capital gains taxed is not immediately determinable, the designated branch or authorized dealer may allow for the repatriation of sale proceeds or credit thereof to the seller's NRS/FCNR account to the extent that the original cost of investment was immediate on the realization of the sale proceeds. The excess amount, if any representing capital gain should be kept by the designated branch/authorized dealer in a separate NRO account of the seller or in a suspense account. The designated branch/authorized dealer may allow for the withdrawal of this amount for credit to the NRE/FCNR account of the seller or remit it abroad, on production of a necessary tax clearance certificate.

V. Sale/Transfer of Government Securities/Units

645. NRIs/OCBs may freely sell/transfer government securities through a stock exchange in India, provided the sale/transfer of such securities is arranged through an authorized dealer.

646. In addition to the above-mentioned, sections 108–112 of Companies Act deals with the transfer of shares and debentures.

647. Furthermore, to avoid bad deliveries the SEBI has given notice to depositors of the regulations facilitating the setting up of depositories which will provide long-term solution for the problem of bad deliveries and non-transfer of shares. The statutory time limit fixed for registration of transfer of shares is one month (fifteen days with effect from 1 October 2012) as per the Listing Agreement and two months as per the provisions of Companies Act, 1956 after receipt of the necessary documents.

648. It has been suggested to the Government of India to change the denomination of share transfer stamps keeping in view of the present day share value and the increased volume of transactions. At present, share transfer stamps are being printed in denominations of INR 200, 100, 50, 10, 5, 2, 1, and 0.50 paise.

649. The central government has issued various circulars, with regard to the standard denomination for corporate securities, *inter alia*, No. F.1/7/SE/81, dated 17 February 1981, No. F.1/7/SE/81, dated 22 January 1983, No. F.1/7/SE/81, dated 6 October 1983, and No. F.1/7/SE/81, dated 13 December 1983, directing the companies to have a uniform denomination of INR 10 or INR 100 for equity shares. It has been decided to give flexibility to companies to fix any denomination of its equity shares. The companies shall have the freedom to issue shares in any denomination to be determined by them in accordance with section 13(4) of the Companies Act, 1956. While doing so, the companies will have to ensure that shares are not issued in decimal of INR 1. Only companies whose shares are dematerialized shall be eligible to alter the ‘standard denomination’.

VI. Licences

650. According to section 17 of the Securities Regulation Act, subject to other provisions contained in the act, no person may carry on or purport to carry on, either on his own behalf or on behalf of any other person, the business of dealing in securities in any state or area where which section 13 has not been declared to apply and where which the central government may, through notification in the official gazette, declare this Section to apply, except under the authority of a licence granted by the licence granted by the SEBI in this behalf.

VII. Dealers and Representatives

651. The dealers are comprised of a corporate body, partnership firms and individuals having adequate financial strength. Dealers should have adequate knowledge of trading, stock valuation, share transfer rules, etc. Dealers are selected after an interview by the OTC Committee. In both the case of members and dealers, the OTC Committee will prescribe the nature and extent of electronic equipment, which will need to be installed at the members/dealers work place.

VIII. The Business of Primary Dealers

652. In 1995, the Reserve Bank of India (RBI) introduced the system of Primary Dealers (PDs) in the Government Securities (G-Sec) Market, which comprised independent entities undertaking PD activity. In order to broad base the PD system, banks were permitted to undertake PD business departmentally in 2006–2007. It is generally acknowledged that primary dealers have added much needed liquidity to the gilts market and volumes in secondary market in gilts have gone up considerably. As on 30 June 2012, there are eight standalone PDs and thirteen banks authorized to undertake PD business departmentally (source: www.rbi.org.in/scripts/BS_ViewMasCircular details). With a view to putting in place equitable and transparent regulatory guidelines for authorization of PDs and to ensure that the new PDs are adequately equipped to participate meaningfully in all auctions of G-Sec including an underwriting commitment and play an active role in the G-Sec market in the emerging circumstances, the eligibility guidelines has been framed as follows: (1) PD should be registered as a Non-Banking Financial Company (NBFC) under section 45-IA of the RBI Act, 1934 for at least one year prior to the submission of application. (2) It should have minimum net owned funds (NOF) of INR 150 crore/INR 250 crore or as prescribed from time to time. Before commencing PD business, applicant entity has to submit an external auditor's certificate to this effect. (3) it should have exposure, as prescribed, in the securities business and in particular to the G-Sec market for at least one year prior to the submission of application. (4) Applicant entity should submit an annual target along with plan of action for turnover to be achieved on behalf of mid-segment Provident Funds, Urban Cooperative banks, Regional Rural banks, Trusts, etc.) and retail (individual) investors at the time of submission of their application for PD authorization. The annual turnover target on behalf of mid-segment and retail investors should not be less than 75% of minimum NOF for PDs prescribed from time to time. These are, however, major issues which affect the functioning and viability of primary dealers and must be addressed urgently. One issue relates to the source(s) and cost of funding for primary dealers. Given the average yield on assets carried in the books of primary dealers, viz., treasury bills and government dated securities, the only sources of cost-effective funding that primary dealers can consider today are the call money market and RBI's refinance facility.

IX. Investment Advisers

653. Section 205C of the Companies Act deals with the Establishment of the Investor Education and Protection Fund. The Investor Education: SEBI has in the past issued advertisements in newspapers informing investors, inter-alia, of their rights, responsibilities and the key terms used in capital markets. Messages in the interests of investors have been telecast on national and regional channels of Doordarshan. A booklet titled 'A Quick Reference Guide for Investors' has been published by the SEBI and also made available for investors through their website www.sebi.gov.in. Other information for investors is also provided on the SEBI website.

654. Investors' Associations registered with the SEBI were extended financial support by SEBI to organize seminars related to the securities market for educating investors and also to pay for the publication and circulation of investor education material.

X. SEBI Mutual Funds and VCP Department (Grant and Maintenance of Licences)

A. How to Register as a Venture Capital Fund

655. An applicant should follow the procedure given below so as to expedite the registration process. However, the SEBI will also guide the applicant step by step after receiving the application for registration as a venture capital fund. Normally, all replies are sent within twenty-one working days from the date of receiving each communication from the applicant during the registration process. Thus, the total time period for registration depends on how fast the requirements are complied with by the applicant.

656. Main Requirements under the SEBI (Venture Capital Funds) Regulations, 1996.

657. The following are the eligibility criteria for the grant of a certificate of registration as per Regulation 4 of the SEBI (Venture Capital Funds) Regulations 1996.[618]

658. For the purpose of the grant of a certificate of registration, the applicant has to fulfil the following conditions:

(1) If the application is made by a company:

  (a) The memorandum of association has as its main objective, the carrying on of the activity of a venture capital fund.
  (b) The company is prohibited by its memorandum and articles of association from making an invitation to the public to subscribe to its securities.
  (c) The director or principal officer or employee is not involved in any litigation connected with the securities market which may have an adverse effect on the applicants business.

618. *See* SEBI website www.sebi.gov.in.

(d) Its director, principal officer or employee has not at any time been convicted of any offence involving moral turpitude or any economic offence.
(e) The person making the application is a fit and proper person.

(2) If the application is made by a trust:

(a) The instrument of trust is in the form of a deed and has been duly registered under the provisions of the Indian Registration Act, 1908 (16 of 1908).
(b) The main object of the trust is to carry on the activity of a venture capital fund.
(c) The directors of the trustee company, if any, or any trustee are not involved in any litigation connected with the securities market which may have an adverse bearing on the applicants' business.
(d) The directors of the trustee company, if any, or a trustee have not at any time, been convicted of any offence involving moral turpitude or of any economic offence.
(e) The applicant is a fit and proper person.

(3) If the application is made by a body corporate:

(a) It is set up or established under the laws of the central or state legislatures.
(b) The applicant is permitted to carry on the activities of a venture capital fund.
(c) The applicant is a fit and proper person.
(d) The directors or the trustees, as the case may be have not been convicted of any offence involving moral turpitude or of any economic offence.
(e) The directors or the trustees, as the case may be, of such corporate bodies, if any, is not involved in any litigation connected with the securities market which may have an adverse effect on the business of the applicant.

(4) The applicant has not been refused a certificate by the Board or its certificate has not been suspended under Regulation 30 or cancelled under Regulation 31.

B. *Application for Registration*

659. An applicant should apply for registration using form A as prescribed under the First Schedule of the SEBI (Venture Capital Funds) Regulations 1996 along with the requisite fees. All documents should be enclosed as specified in the form.

660. While applying, it is necessary that the main object clause of the memorandum of the applicant company/trust deed, etc. as the case may be, permits the carrying on venture capital fund activities. Section 16(1) of SEBI (Venture Capital Funds) Regulations 1996, the venture capital fund shall: (a) issue a placement memorandum which shall contain details of the terms and conditions subject to which monies are proposed to be raised from investors; or (b) enter into contribution or subscription agreement with the investors which shall specify the terms and conditions subject to which monies are proposed to be raised. (2) The Venture Capital Fund shall file with the Board for information, the copy of the placement memorandum or the copy of the contribution or subscription Throughout the application process, the following additional information must also to be submitted:

(1) a complete list of any associate companies[619] registered with the SEBI, and also the capacity in which they are registered along with the SEBI Registration number;
(2) it has to be stated whether the applicant is registered with the SEBI in any capacity;
(3) a complete list of a group of companies registered with the SEBI, and also indicating the capacity in which they are registered with the SEBI along with their SEBI Registration number;
(4) whether the applicant or the intermediary, as the case may be, or its full time director or managing partner has been convicted by a court for any offence involving moral turpitude, economic offence, securities laws or fraud;
(5) whether any winding up orders have been passed against the applicant or the intermediary;
(6) whether any orders under the Insolvency Act have been passed against the applicant or any of its directors, or persons in management and have not been discharged;
(7) whether any order restraining, prohibiting or debarring the applicant or its full time director from dealing with securities in the capital market have been passed by the SEBI or any other regulatory authority and a period of three years from the date of the expiry of the period specified in the order have not elapsed;
(8) whether any order cancelling the certificate of registration of the applicant on the ground of its indulging in insider trading, fraudulent and unfair trade practices or market manipulation has been passed by the SEBI and a period of three years from the date of the order has not elapsed;
(9) whether any order, withdrawing or refusing to grant any licence/approval to the applicant or its full time director and having a bearing on the capital market, has been passed by the SEBI or any other regulatory authority and a period of three years from the date of the order has not elapsed;
(10) whether the applicant or its group/associate companies are listed on any of the recognized stock exchange(s) in India. If so, the details have to be furnished; and
(11) details of registration of the company/associate/group companies (to be given separately), which are registered/required to be registered with the Reserve Bank of India (RBI) as a Banking company or NBFC or in any other capacity and addresses of any concerned branch offices of the RBI.

661. The applicant can submit a 'no objection certificate' from RBI for registering with SEBI, to expedite the registration process.

C. Other Documents to Be Submitted to SEBI

662. Following documents to be submitted to the SEBI:-

619. *See* Reg. 2(aa) of SEBI (Venture Capital Funds) Regulations, 1996 for the definition of the 'associate company'.

(1) memorandum and articles of association of the applicant company, an executed copy of the trust deed if the fund is being set up as a trust and the main objective of a constitution in the case of a corporate body;
(2) executed copy of the Investment Management Agreement, if applicable;
(3) disclosure in detail of the investment strategy as required under Regulation 12(a) of the SEBI (Venture Capital Funds) Regulations, 1996. Also, it should state the target size of the fund along with the profile of the investors of the fund. Regulation 12(b) states venture capital fund shall not invest more than 25% corpus of the fund in one venture capital undertaking and also in associate company [12(c)]. Section 12A states that the venture capital fund may enter into an agreement with merchant banker to subscribe to the unsubscribed portion of the issue or to receive or deliver securities in the process of market making under Chapter XA of the SEBI (Issue of Capital and Disclosure Requirements) Regulations, 2009 and the provisions of Regulation 12 shall not apply in case of acquisition or sale of securities pursuant to such subscription or market making;
(4) an undertaking to the effect that the fund will not enter into any venture capital activity if it fails to raise a commitment of at least INR 50 million as required under Regulation 11(3) of SEBI (Venture Capital Funds) Regulations, 1996;
(5) copies of letters of commitment from investors supporting the target amount proposed to be raised by the fund;
(6) an undertaking that the venture capital fund will not make an investment in any area listed under the Third Schedule of the SEBI (Venture Capital Funds) Regulations, 1996;
(7) the Venture Capital Fund shall disclose the duration/life cycle of the fund.

XI. Grant of Certificate of Registration

663. Once all above requirements have been complied with and the requisite fees as per the Second Schedule of the Regulations have been paid, the SEBI shall grant a certification of registration as a venture capital fund.

664. Once the company enters into a listing agreement with the concerned stock exchanges, then upon receipt of permission from the concerned stock exchange(s), the company is then listed and securities are thereafter traded on such stock exchange(s). Such companies have certain obligations with respect to the stock exchanges where their securities are listed. Major obligations, which the company is required to perform are given in Chapter III. These obligations arise from the listing agreement which the company enters into with each of the stock exchanges. The standard listing agreement has been given in Chapter IV.

665. Nowadays, stock exchanges are taking serious note if listed companies do not comply with their statutory and listing obligations. The stock exchanges have started penalizing the companies for non-compliances. The Stock Exchange of Mumbai has transferred such companies to 'Z' category. This creates a very bad reputation for the company and shareholders/investors shy away from such companies. Therefore, it is necessary for listed companies to know what their obligations are so as to enable them to comply with them.

XII. Breach of the Licence Provision (Penalty and Liability)

A. Penalties and Adjudication

666. Penalty for failure to furnish information, return, etc. (section 15 of SEBI Act, 1992). If any person, who is required under this act or any rules or regulations made thereunder:

(1) to furnish any document, return or report to the Board, fails to furnish the same, he shall be liable to a penalty of INR 100,000 for each day during which such failure continues or INR 10 million, whichever is less;
(2) to file any return or furnish any information, books or other documents within the time period specified in the regulations, and if he fails to do so, he shall be liable to a penalty of INR 100,000 for each day for which such failure continues or INR 10 million, whichever is less;
(3) to maintain books of accounts or records, and if he fails to maintain them, he shall be liable to a penalty of INR 100,000 for each day during which such failure continues or INR 10 million, whichever is less.

B. Penalty for Failure by Any Person to Enter into an Agreement with Clients

667. If any person, who is registered as an intermediary and is required under this Act or any rules or regulations made thereunder, to enter into an agreement with his client, fails to enter into such agreement, he shall be liable to a penalty of INR 1 lakh for each day during which such failure continues or INR 10 million, whichever is less.

C. Penalty for Failure to Redress Investors' Grievances

668. If any listed company or any person who is registered as an intermediary, after having been called upon by the Board in writing, to redress the grievances of investors, fails to redress such grievances within the time specified by the Board, such a company or intermediary shall be liable to a penalty of INR 100,000 for each day during which such failure continues or INR 10 million, whichever is less.

669. Penalty for certain defaults in the case of mutual funds. If any person, who is:

(1) required under this act or any rules or regulations made hereunder to obtain a certificate of registration from the Board for sponsoring or carrying on any collective investment scheme, and this applies to mutual funds, sponsors or carries on such activities, without obtaining such a certificate of registration, he shall be liable to a penalty of INR 100,000 for each day that he did so or INR 10 million, whichever is less;
(2) registered with the Board under a collective investment scheme, including mutual funds, for sponsoring or carrying on any investment scheme, fails to comply with

the terms and conditions of the certificate of registration, he shall be liable to a penalty of INR 100,000 for each day during which such failure continues or INR 10 million, whichever is less;

(3) registered with the Board under a collective investment scheme including mutual funds, fails to make an application for listing of its schemes as provided for in the regulations governing such listings, he shall be liable to a penalty of INR 100,000 for each day during which such failure continues or INR 10 million, whichever is less;

(4) registered under a collective investment scheme, including mutual funds, fails to dispatch unit certificates of any scheme in the manner provided in the regulation governing such dispatch, he shall be liable to a penalty of INR 100,000 for each day during which such failure continues or INR 10 million, whichever is less;

(5) registered under a collective investment scheme, including mutual funds, fails to refund the application money paid by the investors within the period specified in the regulations, he shall be liable to pay a penalty of INR 100,000 for each day during which such failure continues or INR 10 million, whichever is less; and

(6) registered as a collective investment scheme, including mutual funds, fails to invest the money collected by such collective investment schemes in the manner or within the period specified in the regulations, he shall be liable to a penalty of INR 100,000 for each day during which such failure continues or INR 10 million, whichever is less.

670. There is a penalty in the case that an asset management company fails to observe any rules and regulations binding it. Where any asset management company of a mutual fund registered under this act fails to comply with any of the regulations providing for restrictions on the activities of the asset management companies, the asset management company shall be liable to a penalty of INR 1 lakh for each day during which such failure continues or INR 10 million, whichever is less.

671. Penalty for failure in the case of stockbrokers (section 15F of SEBI Act, 1992). If any person, who is registered as a stockbroker under this act:

(1) fails to issue contract notes in the form and manner specified by the stock exchange of which such broker is a member, he shall be liable to a penalty not exceeding five times the amount for which the contract note was required to be issued;

(2) fails to deliver any security or fails to make payment of the amount due to the investor in the manner or within the period specified in the regulations, he shall be liable to a penalty of INR 100,000 for each day during which such failure continues or INR 10 million, whichever is less;

(3) charges a brokerage amount which is in excess of the brokerage specified in the regulations, he shall be liable to a penalty of INR 100,000, or five times the amount of the brokerage charged in excess of the specified brokerage, whichever is higher.

672. Penalty for insider trading applies to any insider who:[620]

620. SEBI Act, 1992, s. 15G.

(1) either on his own behalf or on behalf of any other person, deals in securities of a corporate body listed on any stock exchange on the basis of any unpublished price sensitive information; or
(2) communicates any unpublished price sensitive information to any person, with or without his request for such information except as required in the ordinary course of business or under any law; or
(3) counsels or procures for any other person to deal in any securities of any corporate body on the basis of unpublished price sensitive information, shall be liable to a penalty of INR 250 million or three times the amount of profits made out of insider trading, whichever is higher.

673. Penalty for non-disclosure of acquisition of shares and takeovers.[621] If any person, who is required under this act or any rules or regulations made thereunder, fails to:

(1) disclose the aggregate of his shareholding in the corporate body before he acquires any shares of that corporate body; or
(2) makes a public announcement to acquire shares at a minimum price, he shall be liable to a penalty of INR 250 million or three times the amount of profits made from such a failure, whichever is higher; or
(3) make a public offer by sending a letter of the offer to the shareholders of the concerned company; or
(4) makes payment of consideration to the shareholders who sold their shares pursuant to the letter of offer.

D. Penalty for Fraudulent and Unfair Trade Practices

674. If any person indulges in fraudulent and unfair trade practices relating to securities, he shall be liable to a penalty of INR 250 million or three times the amount of profits made out of such practices, whichever is higher.

675. Penalty for contraventions where no separate penalty has been provided. Whoever fails to comply with any provision of this act, the rules or the regulations made or directions issued by the Board thereunder for which no separate penalty has been provided, shall be liable to a penalty which may extend to INR 10 million.

676. Power to adjudicate 15I. (1) For the purpose of adjudging under sections 15A, 15B, 15C, 15D, 15E, 15F, 15G, (15H, 15HA and 15HB) and 58 the Board shall appoint any of its officer not below the rank of a Division Chief to be an adjudicating officer for holding an inquiry in the prescribed manner after giving any person concerned a reasonable opportunity of being heard for the purpose of imposing any penalty.

677. (2) While holding an inquiry, the adjudicating officer shall have the power to summon and enforce the attendance of any person acquainted with the facts and circumstances of the case to give evidence or to produce any document which in the opinion of the adjudicating officer, may be useful for or relevant to the subject matter of the inquiry and if, on such inquiry, section (1), he may impose such penalty as he thinks fit in accordance with the provisions of any of those sections.

621. SEBI Act, 1992, s. 15H.

678. Factors to be taken into account by the adjudicating officer: While adjudging the amount of the penalty under section 15J, the adjudicating officer shall have due regard to the following factors, namely:

(1) the amount of disproportionate gain or unfair advantage, wherever quantifiable, made as a result of the default;
(2) the amount of loss caused to an investor or group of investors as a result of the default; and
(3) the repetitive nature of the default.

679. As seen in section 15JA, all sums realized by way of penalties under this Act shall be credited to the Consolidated Fund of India.

XIII. Short Selling

680. The reverse of the usual stock market technique. Short selling is based on the anticipation that a particular security price will go down. The practice of short selling involves borrowing shares of a security from the broker and immediately selling them at the current price. Then, as the price of that security declines, an equal number of shares on the open market can be bought back and used to cover the shares that were borrowed from the broker, and make a profit. For instance, if there is a short sell of 100 shares of XYZ corporation at 50.00 a share and the price of the stock drops to 35.00, the profit is 15.00 a share, or 1500.00. Short sellers lose when the price of the stock ascends rather than descends. Theoretically, there is more risk involved with short selling because a stock price could continue to rise forever. A stock purchased at 10.00 a share can only fall to zero. A stock sold short at 10.00 could go to 20.00, 30.00, 40.00, etc. In March 2001, the SEBI banned short selling in the Indian stock market. The ban was instituted partly because of a crash in stock prices. Shortly after the ban, only retail investors were allowed to short sell in the marketplace. In 2005, the SEBI recommended that institutional investors such as mutual funds be allowed to short-sell shares in the market, as well. In July 2007, SEBI issued short selling guidelines for institutional investors and in early 2008, institutional investors were allowed to start short selling shares again. Short selling can be done by borrowing the stock through Clearing Corporation/Clearing House of a stock exchange which is registered as Approved Intermediaries (AIs). Short selling can be done by retail as well as institutional investors. The Securities Lending and Borrowing mechanism allows short sellers to borrow securities for making delivery.

XIV. Prohibition of Manipulative and Deceptive Devices, Insider Trading and Substantial Acquisition of Securities or Control

681. Prohibition of manipulative and deceptive devices, insider trading and substantial acquisition of securities and control: No person shall directly or indirectly:

(1) use or employ, in connection with the issue, nor purchase or sell any securities listed or proposed to be listed on a recognized stock exchange, or use any manipulative or deceptive device or contrivance in contravention of the provisions of this act or the rules or the regulations made thereunder;
(2) employ any device, scheme or artifice to defraud in connection with any issue or dealing in securities which are listed or proposed to be listed on a recognized stock exchange;
(3) engage in any act, practice or course of business which operates or would operate as fraud or deceit upon any person, in connection with the issue, or have dealings in securities which are listed or proposed to be listed on a recognized stock exchange, in contravention to the provisions of this act or the rules or the regulations made thereunder;
(4) engage in insider trading;
(5) deal in securities while in possession of material or non-public information or communicate such material or non-public information to any other person, in a manner which is in contravention to the provisions of this act or the rules or the regulations made thereunder; or
(6) acquire control of any company or securities, more than the percentage of equity share capital of a company whose securities are listed or proposed to be listed on a recognized stock exchange in contravention of the regulations made under this act.

XV. Finance, Accounts and Audit

682. The central government may, after due appropriation is made by Parliament in this regard, make grants to the Board in such sums of money as the central government may think fit for utilizing the purpose of this act:[622]

(1) There shall be constituted a fund called the SEBI General Fund[623] and there shall be credited thereto:

  (a) all grants, fees and charges received by the Board under this act;
  (b) all sums received by the Board from such other sources as may be decided upon by the Central Government.

(2) The Fund shall be used for covering:

  (a) the salaries, allowances and other remuneration of members, officers and other employees of the Board;
  (b) the expenses of the Board in the discharge of its functions under section 11;
  (c) the expenses on objects and for purposes authorized by this act.

622. *See* SEBI Act, 1992, Ch. VI.
623. SEBI Act, 1992, Ch. 14(1).

(3) The Board shall maintain proper accounts and other relevant records and prepare an annual statement of accounts in such form as may be prescribed by the Central Government in consultation with the Comptroller and General Auditor of India.

(4) The accounts of the Board shall be audited by the Comptroller and General Auditor of India at such intervals as may be specified by him and any expenditure incurred in connection with such an audit shall be payable by the Board to the Comptroller and General Auditor of India.

(5) The Comptroller and General Auditor of India and any other person appointed by him in connection with the audit of the accounts of the Board shall have the same rights and privileges and authority in connection with such audit as the Comptroller and General Auditor generally have in connection with the audit of the Government accounts and, in particular, shall have the right to demand the production of books, accounts, connected vouchers and other documents and papers and to inspect any of the offices of the Board.

(6) The accounts of the Board as certified by the Comptroller and General Auditor of India or any other person appointed by him on his behalf together with the audit report thereon shall be forwarded annually to the central government and that government shall cause the same to be laid before each House of Parliament.

Chapter 9. Commercial Contracts

§1. General Principles of Contract Law

I. Introduction

683. Commercial contracts occupy a significant position in every country of the world where the need of the people is met through a number of business transactions. The principle legislation governing the law of contract in India is 'The Indian Contract Act, 1872'. The Indian Contract Act is based upon the English common law. By virtue of Article 372 of the Constitution of India the legislature has retained the Indian Contract Act almost unamended.

684. An agreement is a promise or set of promises forming consideration to each other.[624] An agreement that is not enforceable by law is a void agreement,[625] while an agreement enforceable by law is a contract,[626] whereby a legal obligation is constituted and defined between the parties to the agreement. All agreements are contracts if they are made by the free consent of the parties, competent to contract, for a lawful consideration, with a lawful object, and not expressly declared void.[627]

II. Principles of Contractual Formation

A. Agreement: Proposal and Acceptance

685. The essence of a contract is the existence of an agreement between the parties to the contract. Agreement is traditionally defined in terms of proposal (offer) and acceptance. The promisor by his proposal signifies his willingness to do or abstain from doing something and when this is accepted, it becomes a promise.[628] Every promise forming consideration to each other is an agreement.[629] The offer and acceptance formula is useful for bilateral agreements but for multi-party agreements contractual intentions are objectively interpreted from circumstances.

686. A proposal and its acceptance is the universally acknowledged process for the making of an agreement. A proposal has two essential elements:[630] First – the offerers' willingness to do something or abstain from doing something. Second – proposal made with a view of obtaining the assent of the offeree. The offer must be

624. The Indian Contract Act, 1872, s. 2(e).
625. The Indian Contract Act, 1872, s. 2(g).
626. The Indian Contract Act, 1872, s. 2(h).
627. The Indian Contract Act, 1872, s. 10.
628. The Indian Contract Act, 1872, s. 2(b).
629. The Indian Contract Act, 1872, s. 2(e).
630. The Indian Contract Act, 1872, s. 2(a).

communicated to the offeree by words, i.e., expressly or by other means, i.e., impliedly.[631] It can be a specific offer or general offer.[632] An offer is distinguishable from an 'invitation to offer' as the latter is a request by a party to others to make an offer to him. The communication of a proposal is complete when it comes to the knowledge of the persons to whom it is made.[633] A proposal may be revoked at any time before the communication of its acceptance is complete, as against the proposer, but not afterwards.[634] A proposal is revoked by communication of notice of revocation, lapse of time, failure to fulfil condition precedent, death or insanity of the proposer.[635]

687. A man may express his desire to do something or to get something done by his conduct. 'Words are not the only medium of expression. Conduct may often convey as clearly as words a promise, or an assent to proposed promise.' An offer which is made by conduct is called an 'implied offer' and the one which is expressed by words, written or spoken, is called an 'expressed offer'. An offer or acceptance can be spelt out from the conduct of the parties which covers not only their acts but also omission.[636]

688. When the person to whom the proposal is made, signifies his assent to the proposal, it is called 'acceptance'.[637] Acceptance must be absolute, unqualified and expressed in a usual and reasonable manner.[638] A conditional acceptance or departure from the term of the offer will become a 'counter offer'. It may be expressed or implied. The communication of acceptance is complete, as against the proposer, when it is put in the course of transmission and is out of power, as against the acceptor, when it comes to the knowledge of the proposer.[639] The Supreme Court in *Bhagwandas v. Girdhari Lal*[640] has held that in instantaneous communication, a contract is only complete when the acceptance is received by the offeror, and the contract is made at the place where the acceptance is received. An acceptance may be revoked at any time before the communication of acceptance is complete as against the acceptor, but not afterwards.[641]

689. There should be some external manifestation (overt act) of acceptance. A mere mental determination to accept unaccompanied by any external indication will not be sufficient. In *New Okhla Industrial Development Authority v. Arvind Sonekar*,[642] earlier offer of a professional site was not accepted, refund of the amount deposited was accepted, and lease deed registered, allottee not allowed to say that the allotment should have been at the earlier price.

631. The Indian Contract Act, 1872, s. 9.
632. *Carlill v. Carbolic Smoke Ball Co.* (1893) 1 QB 256 at 268.
633. The Indian Contract Act, 1872, s. 4.
634. The Indian Contract Act, 1872, s. 5.
635. The Indian Contract Act, 1872, s. 6.
636. *Pure Helium (I) Ltd. v. ONGC*, (2003)8 SCC 593.
637. The Indian Contract Act, 1872, s. 2(b).
638. The Indian Contract Act, 1872, s. 7.
639. The Indian Contract Act, 1872, s. 4.
640. (1966) 1 SCR 656.
641. The Indian Contract Act, 1872, s. 5.
642. AIR 2008 SC 1983.

B. Consideration

690. When, at the desire of the promisor, the promisee or any other person has done or abstained from doing, or does or abstain from doing or promises to do or to abstain from doing, something, such an act or abstinence or promise is called consideration.[643] An agreement made without consideration is void unless it is in writing and registered and made on account of natural love and affection between parties having near relation or it is a promise to compensate a past voluntary service or a time barred debt.[644] An agreement to which the consent is freely given is not void merely on the ground of inadequacy.[645]

691. The provisions as to consideration do not affect as between donor and one the validity of any gift which has actually been made. A gift of movables which has been completed by delivery and gift of immovable which has been perfected by registration cannot be questioned as to their validity only on the ground of lack of consideration. They may be questioned otherwise.[646]

C. Intention to Create Legal Relations

692. There is no provision in the Indian Contract Act requiring that an offer or its acceptance should be made with the intention of creating legal relations. The test of a contractual intention is objective, not subjective and the intention of the parties can be gathered from the terms of the agreement and the surrounding circumstances. The Supreme Court in *Banwari Lal v. Sukhdarshan Dayal*[647] has given limited recognition to intention in business matters.

III. Contractual Capacity

693. Every person is competent to contract who is the age of majority and of sound mind and is not disqualified from contracting by any law.[648] The Privy Council in *Mohoribibee v. Dharamodas Ghose*[649] has held that a contract with a minor is void. There is no estoppel against a minor and a minor has no liability under contract or in torts. However, a minor has to restore the benefits, which he has received under the contract.[650] A person cannot ratify an agreement made by him during his minority. A person who supplies a minor with necessaries is entitled to be reimbursed.[651]

694. A contract for the marriage of a minor is also prima facie for his or her benefit. It is customary amongst most of the communities in India for parents to arrange

643. The Indian Contract Act, 1872, s. 2(d).
644. The Indian Contract Act, 1872, s. 25.
645. The Indian Contract Act, 1872, s. 25 (Expl. 2).
646. *K. Balakrishnan v. K. Kamalam*, AIR 2004 SC 1257.
647. (1973) 1 SCC 294.
648. The Indian Contract Act, 1872, s. 11.
649. (1903) 30 IA 114, *see also Madhusoodhanan v. Kerala Kaumudi (P) Ltd.*, (2004) 9 SCC 204.
650. The Specific Relief Act, 1963, s. 33.
651. The Indian Contract Act, 1872, s. 63.

marriages between their minor children and the law has to adapt itself to the habits and customs of the people. It has, therefore, become well-established, almost without any controversy, 'that while the contract of marriage could be enforced against the other contracting party at the instance of the minor, it cannot be enforced against the minor'.[652]

695. A person is said to be in sound mind when he is capable of understanding the contract and forming a rational judgment.[653] In *Chacko v. Mahadevan*,[654] a sale deed of property was executed at a time when the transferor was suffering from alcoholic psychosis, which was proved by medical certificate. A very valuable land was sold for a paltry amount. The Supreme Court ordered the sale deed to be set aside. The court said that unsoundness of mind is a finding of fact. There could be no interference in it in second appeal.

IV. Vitiation of Contract: Matters Affecting Contractual Assent

696. When two persons agree upon the same thing in the same sense it is called consent.[655] Consent is said to be free when it is not caused by coercion, undue influence, fraud, misrepresentation or mistake.[656] Where consent to an agreement is caused by coercion, undue influence, fraud or misrepresentation, it becomes a voidable contract,[657] i.e., the agreement is a contract at the option of the party whose consent was so caused.[658] When consent is caused by the mistake of both parties, it is a void contract.[659]

697. Coercion is committing or threatening to commit any act forbidden by the Indian Penal Code or unlawful detention or threatening to detain, any property to the prejudice of any person with the intention to force the person to enter into the contract.[660] It is immaterial whether the Indian Penal Code is or is not in force where the coercion is employed. In *Kishan Lal Kalra v. NDMC*,[661] the plea was that the plaintiff was dispossessed of premises forcibly under threat that he would be arrested and detained under the Maintenance of Internal Security Act, the court said that such threats would fall within the mischief of section 15.

698. A contract is induced by undue influence where the relations subsisting between the parties are such that one of the parties is in a position to dominate the will of the other and uses that position to obtain an undue advantage over the other.[662] A person is deemed to dominate the will of the other where he holds a real or apparent authority over the other or he stands in a fiduciary relation to the other or where he

652. *Kumari Shahnoor Md Tahssen v. State of U.P.*, AIR 2007 (NOC) 437 (All).
653. The Indian Contract Act, 1872, s. 12.
654. (2007) 7 SCC 363.
655. The Indian Contract Act, 1872, s. 13.
656. The Indian Contract Act, 1872, s. 14.
657. The Indian Contract Act, 1872, ss 19 & 19A.
658. The Indian Contract Act, 1872, s. 2(i).
659. The Indian Contract Act, 1872, s. 20.
660. The Indian Contract Act, 1872, s. 15.
661. AIR 2001 Del 402.
662. The Indian Contract Act, 1872, s. 16.

makes a contract with a person whose mental capacity is temporarily or permanently affected by reason of age, illness, mental or bodily distress. If a person who is in position to dominate the will of the person enters into contract and the contract seems unconscionable, then the burden of proving that such contract is not by undue influence shall lie with the person who is in a position to dominate the will of the other. In *M. Rangasamy v. Rengammal*,[663] presumption of undue influence only because of near relationship has been held to be not permissible. In contract with pardanashin (veiled) women is presumed to have been induced by undue influence. She can avoid the contract unless the other party can show that it was her 'intelligent and voluntary act'. The burden to prove fairness is on other party.[664]

699. Fraud is an act committed by a party to a contract, or with his connivance, or by his agent, with the intent to deceive or induce another party to enter into the contract. These acts include knowingly suggesting a fact, which is not true, active concealment of a fact by one having knowledge or belief of a fact, a promise made without any intention of performing it, any other act fitted to deceive, any act or omission of law which is specially declared as fraudulent.[665] Mere silence as to a fact is not fraud unless it is the duty of the person keeping silence to speak or his silence is equivalent to speech. A contract of insurance is a contract of absolute good faith because it has to depend on the disclosure made by the assured.[666] where the claimant at the time when he filled his insurance form was suffering from a heart ailment but did not disclose it and having died of heart failure, it was held that the fact not disclosed was very material and crucial to insurance, it could not be regarded as something trivial. The insurer's refusal to pay was held to be justified. The fact that the insured survived for a period of two years was of no consequence.[667]

700. Misrepresentation is a positive assertion of a fact, which is not true, though the person saying believes it to be true. It includes gain by breach of duty, without intent to deceive, gain advantage, by misleading another party. It also includes causing innocently, a party to an agreement, to make a mistake as to the substance of thing, which is the subject of an agreement.[668] Mere commendatory expressions, expression of opinion are not sufficient misrepresentation. There is no misrepresentation if the party whose consent was caused had the means of discovering the truth using ordinary intelligence.

701. A mistake is an erroneous opinion as to the subject matter essential to the agreement. A mistake can be primarily classified as a mistake of fact or a mistake of law. When both parties to the agreement are under mistake as to a matter of fact essential to the agreement, the agreement is void.[669] A contract formed by the mistake of one party as to a matter of fact essential to the agreement, i.e., unilateral mistake, is valid.[670] A contract formed on an erroneous belief of any law prevailing in India,

663. (2003) 7 SCC 683.
664. *Bellachi v. Pakeeran*, AIR 2009 SC 3293.
665. The Indian Contract Act, 1872, s. 17.
666. *P.C. Chako v. LIC of India*, (2008) 1 SCC 321.
667. *LIC v. Permanent Lok Adalat*, AIR 2009 (NOC) 467 (P&H).
668. The Indian Contract Act, 1872, s. 18.
669. The Indian Contract Act, 1872, s. 20.
670. The Indian Contract Act, 1872, s. 22.

i.e., mistake of Indian law, is valid[671] but mistake as to any foreign law will have the same effect of a mistake of fact.[672] Where both parties thought that the letter of allotment issued by the development authority was the document of title, the sale agreement made on that basis was held to be void.[673]

702. The question relating to the facts essential to the agreement depends on facts and circumstances of each case. The judiciary has broadly speaking, classified certain facts, which are essential to every agreement. These are: (1) mistake as to identity of the parties; (2) mistake as to identity and nature of the subject matter of the contract; (3) mistake as to nature and content of promise itself. Apart from this, the statute also lays down that an erroneous opinion as to the value of a thing, which forms the subject matter, is not a mistake of fact.[674] In *Shiv Kant Yadav v. Indian oil Corpn*,[675] it was held that misstatement about income in the application for petroleum dealership, the fact was material about the applicant's financial status, letter of intent allowed to be cancelled.

V. Legality of Object

703. Lawful object is an essential requirement for the formation of a valid contract. A contract, the object of which is opposed to the law of the land may be either unlawful or void, depending upon the provisions of the law to which it is opposed.

A. Unlawful Agreement

704. An agreement is unlawful when the consideration or object is: (1) forbidden by law; (2) of the nature that, if permitted, it would defeat the provisions of law; (3) fraudulent; (4) injurious to person or property of another; (5) considered by court as immoral or opposed to public policy. Every agreement of which the object or consideration is unlawful, is void.[676]

705. In *Chongtuokhawi v. Union of India*,[677] an agreement for sub-division of family pension among family members was held to be void being against pension rules. An agreement is unlawful if the court regards it as opposed to public policy. In *P. Archana v. Varada Siva Rama Krishna*,[678] it was held that a wife who is entitled to maintenance can give up her right in consideration of a lump sum payment, but surrender of the right to claim revision of the amount in the context of rising prices would be opposed to public policy.

671. The Indian Contract Act, 1872, s. 21.
672. The Indian Contract Act, 1872, s. 21.
673. *M. Rathnam v. Susheelamma*, AIR 2009 Kant 79.
674. The Indian Contract Act, 1872, s. 20 (Expl.).
675. AIR 2007 SC 1534.
676. The Indian Contract Act, 1872, s. 23.
677. AIR 2008 Gau 6.
678. AIR 2008 AP 216.

B. *Void Agreement*

706. An agreement not enforceable by law is called a void agreement.[679] The Indian contract Act declares some agreements as void agreements. These are: (1) agreement unlawful in part;[680] (2) agreements without consideration;[681] (3) Agreement in restraint to marriage;[682] (4) agreement in restraint of trade;[683] (5) agreement in restraint of legal proceedings;[684] (6) unmeaning agreement;[685] (7) wagering agreement.[686]

707. An agreement is unlawful in part of any part of a single consideration for one or more objects, or any part of any one of several considerations for a single object, is unlawful. Such an agreement is void.[687]

708. An agreement without consideration is void unless it is in writing and registered and is made on account of natural love and affection between the parties standing in a near relation to each other, or it is a promise to compensate a person who has voluntarily done something for the promisor or it is for the enforcement of a time-barred debt.[688]

709. An agreement in restraint of a marriage of a person, other than a minor is void.[689]

710. Every agreement by which one is restrained from exercising a lawful profession, trade or business of any kind, is void, except when there is sale of goodwill of business where the buyer can reasonably reframe the seller from carrying on similar business within a specified area.[690] Apart from this, under sections 11, 36, 54, 55 of the Indian partnership Act in agreement imposing restraint of trade is validated. The judiciary has also recognized some agreements in restraint of trade. These are: (1) trade combinations; (2) solus or exclusive dealing agreements; (3) restraint upon employees in a limited manner; (4) protection of trade secrets.

711. Every agreement by which a party is absolutely restrained from enforcing his right by legal proceeding is void; except: (1) a contract to refer any matter to arbitration; (2) a contract to refer the matter, which has already arisen to arbitration.[691] Where a clause in the contract conferred upon one party the unilateral right to determine the amount of liquidated damages and that such quantification was to be final and was not to be challenged by the other party, the clause was held to be bad in law.[692] In *Hanil Era Textiles (P) Ltd. v. Puromatic Fitnes(P) Ltd.*,[693] a part of the cause of action arose

679. The Indian Contract Act, 1872, s. 2(g).
680. The Indian Contract Act, 1872, s. 24.
681. The Indian Contract Act, 1872, s. 25.
682. The Indian Contract Act, 1872, s. 26.
683. The Indian Contract Act, 1872, s. 27.
684. The Indian Contract Act, 1872, s. 28.
685. The Indian Contract Act, 1872, s. 29.
686. The Indian Contract Act, 1872, s. 30.
687. The Indian Contract Act, 1872, s. 24.
688. The Indian Contract Act, 1872, s. 25.
689. The Indian Contract Act, 1872, s. 26.
690. The Indian Contract Act, 1872, s. 27.
691. The Indian Contract Act, 1872, s. 28.
692. *B.S.N.L v. Motorola India (P) Ltd.*, (2009) 2 SCC 337.
693. AIR 2004 SC 2432.

at Bombay and a part at Delhi, clause in the agreement provided for proceedings to be taken at Bombay, held not opposed to public policy. Order was placed at Bombay and also accepted there and part payment also made there.

712. Agreements, the meaning of which is uncertain or not capable of being made certain, i.e., unmeaning agreements, are void.[694]

713. Agreements by way of wager are void and no suit shall be brought for recovering anything alleged to be won on any wager, expect in case of horse racing and crossword puzzles.[695] Where the price is left to be fixed by a third by a third party, there is no uncertainty and the agreement will be enforceable. Similarly, if the agreement is totally silent as to price, it will be valid, for, in that case, section 9 of the Sale of Goods Act, 1930 will apply and reasonable price shall be payable.[696]

VI. Discharge of Contract

714. When the object of contract is fulfilled, the liability of either party comes to an end. The contract is said to be discharged. A contract may be discharged by:

- Performance;
- Impossibility of performance;
- Agreement and Breach.

A. Discharge by Performance

715. The performance of the contract must be exactly as specified in the contract, and within the stipulated time. The parties to a contract must either perform or offer to perform their respective promises unless such performance is dispensed with or excused under the provisions of the act, or of any other law. Promises bind the representatives of the promisor in the case of death of such promisor before performance, unless a contrary intention appears from the contract.[697] When in a contract, no time is mentioned for its performance then the contract must be performed within a reasonable time[698] and when time is stipulated then the contract is to be performed during the usual hours of business.[699] Where in a contract time is of an essence, failure to perform at a fixed time makes the contract voidable and where time is not of an essence then the promisee is entitled to compensation.[700] Where the place for performance is fixed in the promise, the performance must be offered at that place. Where, however, no place is fixed and the promisor has undertaken to perform without application by the promise, 'the promise should be performed at the place where it ought to be performed'.[701]

694. The Indian Contract Act, 1872, s. 29.
695. The Indian Contract Act, 1872, s. 30.
696. *M.S.Madhusoodhanan v. Kerala Kaumudi (p) Ltd.*, (2004) 9 SCC 204.
697. The Indian Contract Act, 1872, s. 37.
698. The Indian Contract Act, 1872, s. 46.
699. The Indian Contract Act, 1872, s. 47.
700. The Indian Contract Act, 1872, s. 55.
701. *Varghese Paul v. Narayana Naik*, (1999) 2 Ker LT 571.

B. *Impossibility of Performance*

716. An agreement to do an impossible act is void.[702] In the case of a subsequent impossibility the contract becomes void when the act becomes impossible or unlawful.[703] If the promisor knew or with reasonable diligence could have known and the promisee did not know, that the contract is an impossible contract, then the promisor should make compensation for any loss sustained by the promisee.[704] The doctrine of impossibility of contract is applicable in the following situations: (1) destruction of subject matter; (2) change in circumstance; (3) non-occurrence of a contemplated event; (4) death or incapacity of a party; (5) government or legislative intervention; (6) intervention of war.

717. In *Army Welfare Housing Organisation v. Sumangal Services (P) Ltd.*, contractor was not held liable where they were required to cease work because further work was stopped under Municipal intervention.[705]

C. *Discharge by Agreement*

718. The parties to a contract may agree to substitute a new contract to replace the former contract or rescind or alter the contract, in such a case, the original contract need not be performed.[706] Where the parties to a contract agree to substitute the existing contract for a new contract, that is called novation. In *Nagendra Kumar Brijraj Singh v. Hindustan Salts Ltd.*,[707] the petitioner was appointed in response to an advertisement but placed at a lower scale than that mentioned in the advertisement. He accepted his placement. He then claimed he promised pay scale. He was not allowed to do so. The principle of novation applied. The appointment and acceptance at the lower scale substituted the original proposed scale.

D. *Discharge by Breach*

719. A breach of contract occurs when a party fails to perform or renounces his liability or by his own act makes the contract impossible to perform. The breach is of two kinds, namely: (1) anticipatory breach; (2) present breach. Anticipatory breach occurs when, prior to the promised date of performance, the promisor absolutely repudiates the contract. On acceptance of repudiation the other party is excused from performance and the aggrieved party can sue immediately or can wait till the time of the act was to be done. If repudiation is not accepted then the contract is still valid, so, if the party repudiating the contract chooses to perform, the promisee is bound to accept the same. Certain contracts can be terminated by serving notices for termination

702. The Indian Contract Act, 1872, s. 56.
703. The Indian Contract Act, 1872, s. 56.
704. The Indian Contract Act, 1872, s. 56.
705. AIR 2004 SC 1344.
706. The Indian Contract Act, 1872, s. 62.
707. (2001) 1 Guj CD 532 (Guj).

of the contract. Where one party making unilateral alterations without any intimation to the other and then cancelling the contract, this amounted to breach.[708]

VII. Damages for Breach

720. The party who is injured by a breach of contract can bring an action for damages. Damages means monetary compensation for the loss caused to the injured party. For calculating damages two things have to be seen viz., (1) remoteness of damages; (2) measure of damages.

A. Remoteness of Damage

721. When there is breach of contract, the damages can be: (1) general damages: all reasonable foreseeable consequences of breach; (2) special damages: loss, which arises on account of unusual circumstances affecting the plaintiff. These are not recoverable unless they are specially brought under the knowledge of the other party. When a contract has been broken, the party who suffers by such a breach is entitled to receive, from the party who has broken the contract, compensation for any loss or damage caused to him thereby, which naturally arose in the usual course of things from such a breach, or which the parties knew, when they made the contract, to be likely to result, from the breach of it.[709] No compensation is given to any remote and indirect loss or damage caused by a breach.

B. Measure of Damages

722. Once the extent of recoverable loss is determined, it has to be measured in terms of money. The damages must be compensatory and not penal. In estimating the loss or damages arising from the breach of contract, the means that existed of remedying the inconvenience caused by the non-performance of the contract must be taken into account. When a contract has been broken, if a sum is mentioned to be paid in the case of a breach, the aggrieved party is entitled to receive a reasonable compensation not exceeding the amount mentioned, whether or not actual damages are proved.[710] The courts are given the duty to award compensation and in so doing, it may accept the amount or reduce the amount and make it reasonable. The burden of proof lies on the plaintiff to show that damage has been sustained and what shall be the measure of converting the loss into money. A claim for damages becomes liable to be rejected where this burden is not discharged.[711]

723. A person rightfully rescinding a contract is entitled to compensation for any damage, which he sustained, by non-fulfilment of the contract.[712]

708. *U.P. State Sugar Corpn v. Mahalchand M. Kothari*, (2005) 1 SCC 348.
709. The Indian Contract Act, 1872, s. 73.
710. The Indian Contract Act, 1872, s. 74.
711. *Draupadi Devi v. Union of India*, (2004) II SCC 425.
712. The Indian Contract Act, 1872, s. 75.

724. Apart from these remedies, the court may order for specific performance under the Specific Relief Act, 1963 or it may enforce a prohibitory injunction to restrain a continuing or threatened breach of contract.

§2. Sale of Goods

I. Introduction

725. In India the sale of goods is governed by The Sale of Goods Act, 1930. A contract for the sale of goods is a contract whereby the seller transfers or agrees to transfer the property in goods to the buyer for a price.[713] A transfer of property in goods, that is, to take place at a future time or subject to some condition is called an agreement to sale. An agreement to sell becomes a sale when the time elapses or the conditions are fulfilled. It has to be a bilateral contract where the goods have to pass from one person to another. The consideration should be money. Goods means and includes every kind of movable property other than actionable claims and money.[714]

726. A contract of sale is made by an offer to buy or sell goods for a price and the acceptance of such an offer. A contract may be verbal or written or implied from the conduct of the parties.[715] The subject matter of the contract may be existing or pertain to future goods.[716] Existing goods are goods that are owned or possessed by the seller whereas, future goods are goods to be manufactured or produced or acquired by the seller after the making of a contract of sale.[717] 'Goods' also includes shares and stock. The word is of very general and quite indefinite import, and primarily derives its meaning from the context in which it is used.[718] The price may be fixed at the time of the contract or may be left to be fixed in the manner agreed by the parties. If no price is fixed then the buyer shall pay a reasonable price.[719] Time may or may not be the essence of a contract. Sale also includes transfer of goods on hire-purchase.[720]

727. A stipulation essential for the main purpose of a contract, the breach of which gives the right to treat the contract as repudiated, is called a condition, whereas, a stipulation collateral to the main purpose of the contract, the breach of which gives right to a claim of damages is a warranty.[721] A condition may be treated as a warranty if the buyer may waive the condition or elect to choose the breach of condition as a breach of warranty or where the sale is not severable and the buyer has accepted the goods or it is excused by law by reason of impossibility or otherwise.[722]

713. The Sale of Goods Act, 1930, s. 4.
714. The Sale of Goods Act, 1930, s. 2(7).
715. The Sale of Goods Act, 1930, s. 5.
716. The Sale of Goods Act, 1930, s. 6.
717. The Sale of Goods Act, 1930, s. 2(6).
718. *U.P. Coop Cane Union Federation v. West U.P. Sugar Mills Assn*, (2004) 3 SCC 430.
719. The Sale of Goods Act, 1930, s. 9.
720. *Jay Bharat Credit & Investment Co Ltd. v. CST*, AIR 2000 SC 2860.
721. The Sale of Goods Act, 1930, s. 12.
722. The Sale of Goods Act, 1930, s. 13.

728. Under a contract of sale, there are various implied conditions or warranty. The implied conditions are: (1) The seller has a right to sell the goods. (2) In sale by description, the goods must correspond with the description. (3) Where the buyer makes known the particular purpose and relies upon a seller's skill, then the goods must be in a reasonable condition. (4) Where a sale is done by way of a sample, then the bulk must correspond with the sample.[723] The implied warranties are: (1) the buyer shall enjoy quiet possession of the goods; and (2) the goods shall be free from any charge or encumbrances.[724] In *Shital Kumar Saini v. Satvir Singh,*[725] there was sale of compressor with one year warranty, defect appeared within three months, replaced by the seller without any further warranty, the replaced compressor also proved to be defective, the state commission allowed it to be rejected because there was an implied warranty under section 16 of the Sale of Goods Act that goods should be reasonably fit for the purposes for which they are sold.

II. Effects of Contract

A. Transfer of Property

729. Where the contract is for the sale of specific or ascertained goods, title shall pass when the parties intend for it to pass, as per the terms of the contract. Where the contract is for the sale of unascertained goods, title shall pass when they would be ascertained.[726]

730. The act provides for certain prima facie rules to apply for the passing of title, unless the parties provide evidence to prove the contrary intention. Where there is an unconditional contract for the sale of specific goods in a deliverable state, title passes when the contract is made. It is immaterial whether payment or delivery is postponed. Where there is a contract for the sale of specific goods and the seller is bound to do something to put them in a deliverable state, title does not pass until that thing is done and notice is given to the buyer. Where there is contract for the sale of specific goods in a deliverable state and the seller is bound to measure or test it for the purpose of ascertaining the price of the goods, title does not pass until that thing is done and notice is given to the buyer. Where the goods are delivered to the buyer on 'sale or return' title will pass either when the buyer signifies acceptance of the goods, or when the buyer retains it without giving a notice of rejection to the seller. In the latter case, title will pass upon the expiration of the time specified in the contract for the return of the goods, or where no time has been specified, upon the passing of a reasonable period of time. Where the contract is for the sale of unascertained goods, title passes when the goods are unconditionally appropriated to the contract in a deliverable state by the seller with the assent of the buyer.[727] Where the intention of the parties is not apparent from their contract, their intention will be ascertained in

723. The Sale of Goods Act, 1930, ss 14–17.
724. The Sale of Goods Act, 1930, s. 14.
725. (2005) 1 CPR 401.
726. The Sale of Goods Act, 1930, s. 18.
727. The Sale of Goods Act, 1930, ss 18–24.

accordance with the rules laid down in section 18 and sections 20–24. These sections deal with three kinds of situation: (1) sale of specific goods; (2) sale of goods on approval; and (3) sale of unascertained goods. The law also permits the parties to settle the point for themselves by any intelligent expression of their intention.[728]

B. Risk of Loss

731. The transfer of title determines which of the parties to the contract assumes liability for the loss of the goods. Prima facie risk of loss passes with the title in the goods. Where there is destruction of or damage to the goods after the contract is formed, the seller must bear the risk of loss in circumstances where the title has not passed to the buyer.[729] However where the delivery has been delayed through the fault of either buyer or the seller, the party at fault is liable for the loss, except where the buyer or seller is the bailee of the goods for another party.[730]

732. Where in accordance with the contract 1,500 tents were dispatched by the railways FOR (free on rail), at the place of dispatch and the property thereby having passed to the buyer, the Supreme Court required the Government buyer to pay the price for the full load in spite of the fact that the railways delivered 224 tents short to the buyer. The risk of loss was on the buyer.[731]

C. Transfer of Title by a Non-owner

733. In general, a seller of goods cannot pass to another any better title than that which is possessed by the seller.[732] However; the Sale of Goods Act creates a number of important exceptions to the general rule. These are: (1) sale by the mercantile agent, who is having possession of goods with the consent of the owner and the buyer purchases the goods in good faith and does not have notice that the seller has no authority to sell; (2) sale by one of the joint owners of property; (3) sale by persons in possession under voidable contract; (4) sale by seller or buyer who retains possession of goods after the contract of sale.[733]

III. Performance of Contract

A. Duties of Seller and Buyer

734. The seller is under a statutory duty to deliver the goods and the buyer is under a duty to accept and pay for the goods. The performance of the duties is concurrent, unless the parties intend otherwise.[734]

728. *Sugar Warehousing Corpn v. Pawan Hans Helicopters Ltd.*, AIR 2009 Del 8.
729. The Sale of Goods Act, 1930, s. 18.
730. The Sale of Goods Act, 1930, s. 26.
731. *Marwar Tent Factory v. Union of India*, (1990) 1 SCC 171.
732. *Nemo dat quod non habet.*
733. The Sale of Goods Act, 1930, ss 27–30.
734. The Sale of Goods Act, 1930, ss 31–32.

B. Rules of Delivery of Goods

735. The Sale of Goods Act provides for certain rules of delivery. These may be varied by contract. If no place of delivery has been specified in the contract, the goods must be delivered from the seller's place of business. Where no time of delivery is mentioned, the seller is bound to deliver the goods within a reasonable period of time and at a reasonable hour. Unless otherwise agreed, the incidental expenses are to be borne by the seller.[735]

736. Where there has been delivery of a lesser quantity of goods than specified under the contract, the buyer may reject them. If the buyer accepts the goods so delivered, he shall pay for them at the contract rate. Where the delivery is of a greater quantity, the buyer may appropriate and reject the rest or reject the whole. If he accepts the whole, he shall pay for them at the contracted rate. Where there is wrong delivery of the mixed goods, the buyer may accept the goods within the contract and reject the rest or reject the whole.[736]

737. Unless, otherwise agreed, the buyer is not bound to accept delivery by instalments. Where a contract does provide for such kind of delivery, it depends upon the contract and the circumstances whether a breach in relation to one or more of the instalments will give rise to a right to terminate the whole contract, or the breach gives rise to damages only.[737]

C. Acceptance of Goods

738. The buyer is deemed to have accepted the goods when he intimates to the seller that he has accepted them or when the buyer does something inconsistent with the seller's title after the delivery of the goods or the buyer retains the goods after the lapse of a reasonable time without intimating a rejection to the seller. The buyer has a right to request a reasonable opportunity to examine the goods upon delivery prior to accepting them.[738] Where the buyer received the machine after seeing its demonstration and retained and used it for a long period, that was held to be an effective acceptance. The machine was not allowed to be rejected. The buyer was bound to pay the price. The alleged defect was covered by the warranty clause and the buyer could have made use of it.[739]

IV. Remedies for Breach of Contract

A. Remedies to Seller

739. Under the act, there are various remedies available to the seller against the buyer:

---

735. The Sale of Goods Act, 1930, s. 36.
736. The Sale of Goods Act, 1930, s. 37.
737. The Sale of Goods Act, 1930, s. 38.
738. The Sale of Goods Act, 1930, s. 42.
739. *Kailash Sharma v. Patna Municipal Corpn*, AIR 2009 Pat 60.

(1) Suit for price: Where under a contract of sale, the property of goods has passed to the buyer and the buyer wrongfully neglects or refuses to pay for the goods, the seller may sue him for the price of the goods.[740] If the contract stipulates payment of price on a certain day irrespective of delivery or of passing of property, and if the buyer neglects or refuses to pay on that day, the seller may sue him for the price.[741]
(2) Damages for non-acceptance: Where the buyer wrongfully neglects or refuses to accept and pay for the goods, the seller may sue him for the damages for non-acceptance.[742] Where the carrier lost the seller's goods before he could realize the price, the seller was allowed to recover the price of sale and not merely the replacement value.[743]
(3) Rights of unpaid seller: Where the seller has received only part of the contract price or the negotiable instrument received by him is subsequently dishonoured, the seller may pursue a number of legal remedies, irrespective of the fact that the title may have passed to the buyer:

(a) Seller's Lien: A seller may retain a lien on the goods for the value of the contract price while the seller is in possession of them, or where the goods have been delivered in part, a lien can be over the remainder in possession. The lien is lost when the seller delivers goods to the carrier or other bailee without reserving the right of disposal of the goods or where the agent or buyer lawfully obtains possession of the goods.[744]
(b) Stoppage of Goods in transit: In case of insolvency of the buyer, the seller has a right to stop the goods in transit after the seller has parted with the possession of the goods.[745]
(c) Right of Resale: In case of perishable goods or where the seller has given the buyer the notice of the intention of resale and a reasonable time for payment has passed the seller can exercise his right of resale.[746]

B. Remedies to Buyer

740. Under the act, there are various remedies available to the buyer against the seller:

(1) Suit for damages for non-delivery: Where the seller wrongfully neglects or refuses to deliver the goods to the buyer, the buyer may sue the seller for damages for non-delivery.[747]

740. The Sale of Goods Act, 1930, s. 55.
741. *Charanjit Singh Chadha v. Sudhir Mehra*, (2001) 7 SCC 417.
742. The Sale of Goods Act, 1930, s. 56.
743. *Sony Computer Entertainment U K Ltd. v. Cinram Logistics UK Ltd.*, 2009 Bus LR 529 (CA).
744. The Sale of Goods Act, 1930, ss 47–49.
745. The Sale of Goods Act, 1930, s. 50.
746. The Sale of Goods Act, 1930, s. 54.
747. The Sale of Goods Act, 1930, s. 57.

(2) Suit for specific performance: The buyer may apply to the court to direct that the contract may be specifically performed.[748]
(3) Remedy for breach of warranty: When there is breach of warranty by the seller, the buyer may sue the seller for damages or set up the breach of warranty in diminution or extinction of the price.[749] A buyer who wants to exercise this right has to inform the seller within reasonable time in what respect the goods are defective.[750]
(4) Suit to recover interest or special damages.[751] Interest could be claimed at 6% provided a demand was made.[752]

§3. Commercial Services

I. Distribution

741. Distribution of goods and services from the whole-sellers, manufacturers, etc. to the retailers, or dealers, etc. takes place in various ways. They are all governed by the general principles of the law of contract. The terms and conditions may differ from party to party. However, the terms of contract should not be restraint on trade. This protection is also provided in the Constitution of India. Just as the legislature cannot take away individual freedom of trade, so also the individual cannot barter it away by agreement. Section 27 of the Indian Contract Act, 1872, therefore, declares in plain terms that: Every agreement by which any one is restrained from exercising a lawful profession, trade or business of any kind, is, to that extent void. This restraint from exercising a lawful profession, trade or business, however, does not mean an absolute restriction, and is intended to apply to a partial restriction, and a restriction may be limited to a place only. (1) This interpretation of the section has been generally accepted. The wholesaler can limit the area of operation of a particular dealer, i.e., he will sell the goods in a particular city only. In England a restriction has been held valid if it is reasonable, but in India it could be valid only if it falls within any of the statutory or judicially created exceptions. The Supreme Court in *Gujarat Bottling Co. Ltd. v. Coca Cola Co.*,[753] laid down:

> The question of reasonableness of restraint is outside the purview of Section 27 of the Indian Contract Act and need not be gone into. Therefore, the present case has to be proceeded on the basis that an enquiry into the reasonableness of the restraint of trade is not envisaged by Section 27. On that view, instead of being

748. The Sale of Goods Act, 1930, s. 58.
749. The Sale of Goods Act, 1930, s. 59.
750. *City and Industrial Development Corpn of Maharashtra Ltd. v. Nagpur Steel & Alloys (P) Ltd.*, AIR 1992 Bom 55.
751. The Sale of Goods Act, 1930, s. 61.
752. *Alco Chem Ltd. v. Hyderabad Chemical Pharmaceutical Works Ltd.*, (2003) 3 BC 508 (AP).
753. (1999) 5, SCC 545.

required to consider two questions as in England, the courts in India have only to consider the question whether the contract is or is not in restraint of trade.

742. Section 33(i)(jb) of the Monopolies and Restrictive Trade Practices Act, 1969 provides that an agreement as to making of bids, or excluding a person from bidding, at an auction for sale of goods, shall be a restrictive trade practice and, therefore, void unless it is necessary in the public interest as spelled out in section 38 of that act. Thus, by virtue of this clause, such collusive agreements can be held void unless they are necessary in the public interest within the meaning of section 38. The clause is wide enough to cover cases of secret agreements as to participate in an auction according to pre-planned terms. Though collusive tendering has not been specifically included in the clause, it is often difficult to distinguish an auction from a tender when secret bids are invited in the shape of tenders.[754] Restrictions stipulated in a lease agreement as to the uses to which the premises can be put and what business would be done and in what name and style have been held not to violate section 27.[755]

A. Exceptions

743. There are two kinds of exceptions to the rule, those created by statutes and those arising from judicial interpretation of section 27 of the Indian Contract Act, 1872.

1. Statutory Exceptions

a. Sale of Goodwill

744. The only exception mentioned in the proviso to section 27 of the Contract Act is that relating to sale of goodwill. It is thus stated:

> One who sells the goodwill of a business may agree with the buyer to refrain from carrying on a similar business, within specified local limits, so long as the buyer, or any person deriving title to the goodwill from him, carries on a like business therein: provided that such limits appear to the court reasonable, regard being had to the nature of the business.

745. Apparently the object is to protect the interest of a purchaser of goodwill. It is difficult to imagine that when the goodwill and trade of a retail shop were sold, the vendor might the next day set up a shop within a few doors and draw off all customers. Some restrictions, therefore, on the liberty of the seller becomes necessary. Indeed, the restriction is the only means by which a saleable value is given to the goodwill of a business. The plaintiff and the defendant were carrying on business as carriers of passengers by boats. The plaintiff sold his business to the defendant for a sum of money and agreed to abstain from carrying on a boat business for a period of

754. *Shaikh Kalu v. Ram Saran Bhagat* (1909) 13 CWN 388. Similar opinion was expressed in *Carew & Co. Ltd. v. North Bengal Sugar Mills Co.*, (1951) 2 Cal 386, at pp. 388–389.
755. *Gurjarat Bottling Co. v. CocaCola Co.*, (1999) 5 SCC 545.

three years. The suit was brought for the recovery of a promised sum. Allowing the plaintiff's claim, Lord Haldane of the Privy Council said, 'Their Lordships entertain no doubt that what took place was the sale of goodwill within the meaning put on the expression'.[756] Where the agreement is prevention of competition, it will be void even if its nakedness is concealed behind the 'imposing of façade of a sale' of goodwill. For example, in *Vancouver Malt & Sale Brewing Co. v. Vancouver Breweries Ltd.*,[757] a company was licensed to manufacture liquor and beer but it confined its business to produce only 'sake', a Japanese liquor made from rice. Its only customer was the government. It entered into an agreement with another wine and beer manufacturing company by which it sold its business and goodwill of manufacturing wine and beer, but not the right to produce sake. The agreement was held to be devoid of content. The only business in which it was engaged was the brewing of sake, and the goodwill of its licence so far as relating to sake was expressly excluded from sale. It had no goodwill to sell so far as regards brewing of beer. Nothing has been sold. It is simply a case of the appellant's undertaking to the respondent in consideration of a sum of money that it will not for fifteen years carry on a particular branch of business. If there was any sale, it was a sale by the appellant of its liberty to brew beer and a purchase by the respondent of protection against the possible competition of the appellant in the brewing of beer.

746. Limits of Restraint: The agreement has to specify the local limits of the restraint. The seller can be restrained within certain territorial or geographical limits and the limits must be reasonable. Reasonableness of restriction will depend upon many factors, e.g., the area in which the goodwill is effectively enjoyed and the price paid for it.[758] The seller can only be restrained from carrying on a similar business and also only for such period for which the business sold is actually carried on either by the buyer or by any person deriving title to the goodwill from him.[759]

b. Partnership Act

747. There are four provisions in the Partnership Act, 1932 which validate agreements in restraint of trade. Section 11 of the act, enables partners during the continuance of the firm to restrict their mutual liberty by agreeing that none of them shall carry on any business other than that of the firm.[760] Section 36 enables them to restrain an outgoing partner from carrying on a similar business within a specified period or within specified local limits. Such agreement shall be valid if the restrictions imposed are reasonable. A similar agreement according to section 54 of the act may be made by partners upon or in anticipation of dissolution by which they may restrain

756. *Parasullah Malik v. Chandrakanta Das*, (1917) 21 CWN 979. In appeal *Chandrakanta Das v. Parasullah*, ILR (1930) 48 Cal 1030 PC.

757. AIR 1934 PC 101.

758. *Damodar Laxman Lele v. Kashinagh Waman Lele*, (1906) 9 Bom L R 312; also *Dev Sharmav. Laxmi Narain*, AIR 1956 Punj 49.

759. Avtar Singh, *Law of Contract* 262 (9th ed., E. Bk. Co. 2005).

760. *See Daulat Ram v. Dharam Chand*, AIR 1934 Lah 110, where two ice factory owners constituting a partnership agreed that only one factory will be worked at time and its profits distributed among them. The restrain was held to be justified.

each other from carrying on a business similar to that of the firm. Thus, it is necessary for the validity of a restraint under section 36 or 54 that: (1) the agreement should specify the local limits or the period of restraint; and (2) the restraint imposed must be reasonable. An agreement by a retiring partner not to carry on similar business on the land belonging to him and adjoining the factory of the firm, has been held to be reasonable and binding on the persons buying the land from him.[761]

2. Under Judicial Interpretation

a. Trade Combinations

748. It is now almost universal practice for traders and manufacturers in the same line of business to carry on their trade in an organized way. There are, thus, combinations of ice manufacturers, grain merchants, sugar producers, etc. The primary object of such associations is to regulate business and not to restrain it. Combinations of this kind are often desirable in the interest of trade itself and also for the promotion of public interest.[762] Thus, regulations as to the opening and closing of business in the market, licensing of traders, supervision and control of dealers and the mode of dealing have not been held illegal.[763] The courts, however, would not allow a restraint to be imposed disguised as trade regulations. An agreement, thus, between certain persons to carry on business with the members of their caste only,[764] and an agreement to restrict the business of a sugar mill within a zone allotted to it, have been held void.[765] Agreements as to regulation of prices and output are generally upheld as valid. Thus, where four ginning factories entered into an agreement at a fixed uniform rate for ginning cotton, and pooling their earnings to be divided between them in certain proportions was held valid.[766] In *Bhola Nath Shankar Das v. Lachmi Narain*,[767] the rules of an association of traders and weigh-men provided that the members shall not deal with outsiders and the penalty for such a breach being a fine and expulsion. The legality of the association was assailed on the ground that its objects and methods were unlawful as it aimed for the creation of a monopoly by shutting out all competition and was a defiance of the spirit of section 27 of the Contract Act. Rejecting this contention, it was held that it is the privilege of a trade in a free country in all matters not contrary to law, to regulate its own method of carrying it out according to its own discretion and choice.

b. Solus or Exclusive Dealing Agreements

749. It is a general practice that a producer or manufacturer likes to market his goods through a sole agent or distributor and the latter agrees in turn not to deal with

761. *Hukum Chand v. Jaipur Ice and Oil Mills*, AIR 1980 Raj 155.
762. Avtar Singh, *Law of Contract* 262 (9th ed., Eastern Book Company 2005).
763. *Municipal Committee v. Kalurram Hiralal*, AIR 1944 Nag 73.
764. *Vaithelinga v. Saminada*, ILR (1872) 2 Mad 44.
765. *Carew & Co. Ltd. v. North Bengal Sugar Mills*, ILR (1951) 2 Cal 386.
766. *Haribhai v. Sharaf Ali*, ILR (1897) 22 Bom 461.
767. (1931) 29 ALJ 84.

the goods of any other manufacturer. A producer may, for example agree to sell all his output to one consumer who, in turn, agrees not to buy his requirements from any other source. As long as the negative stipulation is nothing but an ordinary incident or ancillary to the positive covenant, there is hardly anything obnoxious about section 27. For example, an agreement by a manufacturer of dhoti (long cloth born by Indians) to supply 136,000 pairs of a certain description to the defendant and not to sell goods of that kind to any other person for a fixed period.[768] An agreement by a person to send all the mica produced by him to the plaintiff, and not send them to any other firm, nor to keep in stock,[769] and an agreement by a buyer of the goods for Calcutta (now Kolkata) market, not to sell them in Madras (now Chennai), have all been held to be outside the scope of section 27 and therefore valid. However, where a manufacturer or supplier, after meeting all the requirements of a buyer, has surplus to sell to others, he cannot be restrained from doing so.[770] The buyer cannot restrain a seller from dealing with others unless he can acquire the whole stock during the period of agreement. But even so, the court may not countenance an agreement particularly where the buyer intends to corner or monopolize the commodity so that he may resell at his own price or where he binds the seller for an unreasonable period of time. Thus in *Shaikh Kalu v. Ram Saran Bhagat*,[771] a seller of combs entered into an agreement with all the manufacturers of combs in the city of Patna, whereby the latter undertook during their lifetime to sell all their products to the respondent and his heirs and not to sell them to anyone else. Holding the agreement void under section 27, the court said that it binds the manufacturers from generation to generation; it was unrestricted both as to the time and place. It was oppressive and intended to create a monopoly.

c. Franchise

750. Franchising means paying someone for his business strategy, marketing strategy, operations strategy and use of his brand name.[772]

751. These days there is a growing trend to regulate distribution of goods and services through franchise agreements providing for the grant of a franchise by the franchiser on certain terms and conditions to the franchisee. At present, franchising is common in all types of industries and services like fast food centres, hotels, fashion industry, financial services, textile industry, watches, courier services, computer services, publishing industry automobiles, etc. In India the concept of franchising is in its nascent state. So the rights and liabilities of the franchiser and franchisee have not been dealt with elaborately under any law. Such agreements often incorporate a condition restricting the right of the franchisee to deal with competing goods for facilitating the distribution of the goods of the franchiser and it has not been regarded as restraint of trade. The whole franchise agreements are being regulated by the Indian Contract Act, 1872. There is no separate law for the same. In franchising a person establishes a relationship with a successful business firm, i.e., franchiser so that he,

768. *Carliles Nephews & Co. v. Rickauth Budktermull*, ILR (1882) 8 Cal 809.
769. *Subha Naidu v. Haji Badsha Sahib*, ILR (1902) 26 Mad 168.
770. *Har Bilas v. Mahadeo Prasad*, AIR 1931 All 539.
771. (1908) 8 CWN 388.
772. *See* Padala Rama Reddi, *Drafting of Deeds and Documents* (17th ed., Asia L. House 2007).

i.e., franchisee can make use of its system and capitalize on its existing brand awareness in order to get a quicker return on his own investment. Here, a franchisee uses the franchiser's proven system of running the business and name.

752. In *Gujarat Bottling Co. Ltd. v. Coca Cola Co.*[773] an agreement for the grant of a franchise by the Coca Cola Company to Gujarat Bottling Company to manufacture, bottle, sell and distribute beverages under trademarks held by the franchiser contained the negative stipulation not allowing the franchisee to 'manufacture, bottle, sell, deal or otherwise be concerned with the products, beverages of any other brands or trademark/trade names during the subsistence of this agreement including the period of one year's notice'. It was held that the negative stipulation was intended to promote the trade. Moreover, operation of the stipulation was confined only to the subsistence of the agreement and not after termination thereof. Hence the stipulation could not be regarded as a restraint of trade. It was a commercial agreement whereby both the parties had undertaken obligations for promoting the trade in beverages for their mutual benefit. The purpose of the negative stipulation contained in the agreement was that the appellant will work vigorously and diligently to promote and solicit the sale of the product produced on the grade marks of Coca Cola. This would not be possible if the appellant, i.e., Gujarat Bottling Co. were to manufacture, bottle, sell, deal or otherwise be concerned with the products, beverages or any other brands or trademarks/trade names.

II. Contracts with Middlemen (Agency, Commission, Brokerage)

A. Basic Principles of Agency

753. Agency refers to a relationship whereby a person is employed to do any act for another or represent another in dealing with a third party. The person so employed is called the agent and the employer is called the principal.[774] Agent is a person with the express or implied authority to act for the principal with the general object of bringing the principal into legal relations with the third party.[775] The essence of the matter is that the principal authorized the agent to represent or act for him in bringing the principal into contractual relation with a third person.[776] The three basic features characteristic of an agency are: service, representation and the power to affect the legal position of the principal.

754. Any person who is of the age of majority according to the law to which he is subject, and who is of sound mind, may employ an agent.[777] Section 183 follows that a minor cannot appoint an agent. The appointment of an agent involves a contract, and a minor's agreement is void. But in situations where a minor is capable of binding himself by contract he may appoint an agent to contract on his behalf. Whatever a person can do personally he can do through an agent.[778] However, the agent need not

773. (1995) 5 SCC 545.
774. The Indian Contract Act, 1872, s. 182.
775. The Indian Contract Act, 1872, s. 186.
776. *Mahesh Chandra Basu v. R.K. Bhattacharjee*, (1908) 12 CWN 28.
777. The Indian Contract Act, 1872, s. 183.
778. *T.C. Mathai v. District & Session Judge Thiruvananthapuram*, AIR 1999 SC 1385.

be competent to contract. Section 184 lays down very clearly that 'as between the principle and third parsons any person may become an agent'. An agency can also arise by ratification of unauthorized acts by the principal. No consideration is necessary to create an agency.[779]

755. A principal shall be bound by those acts, which are within the scope of the agent's authority. An agent has authority to do every lawful thing, which is necessary in order to do the act.[780] He can do everything necessary for the purpose of doing that which is usually done in the course of conducting such business. In the case of an emergency, an agent can do all acts to protect his principal from loss as would be done by a person of ordinary prudence.[781]

B. Particular Kinds of Agent

756. Agents are of several kinds. The word 'agent' is used to describe various types of activity. The types of agent that are known to the business world are however, fewer:

(1) Factors: An agent employed to sell goods, the possession or control of which is entrusted into the factor's care by the principal. He has ostensible authority to sell, pledge the goods, receive payment for the goods, and sue on a contract in his own name. Where the third party has no knowledge of the factor's status as agent, then he is responsible as if party to the contract.
(2) Brokers: Brokers are employed to sell on behalf of another rather than in their own name. Brokers are not entrusted with the goods or title. Their work is to bring both parties together. They are not responsible to the principal if the purchaser of goods fails to pay the contract price.
(3) *Del Credere* Agents: These agents receive additional commission from the principal in return for an undertaking that the goods sold by him shall be paid for, if not by the buyer, then by the agent himself.
(4) Auctioneers: They are agents employed to sell the property at an auction. They are initially agents of the seller, but when the goods are 'knocked down'; they become agents of both the seller and the buyer for the purpose of settlement of the memorandum.

757. Apart from these; bankers, confirming houses, exclusive agents are also kinds of agents.

C. Duties of the Agent

758. Being a contractual relationship, the duties of an agent depend upon the terms of the contract between the agent and the principal. In absence of any contract, various duties can be conferred upon the agent by the operation of law. These are:

779. The Indian Contract Act, 1872, s. 185.
780. The Indian Contract Act, 1872, s. 188.
781. The Indian Contract Act, 1872, s. 189.

(1) The first and the foremost duty of every agent is to carry out the mandate of his principal. He should perform the work which he has been appointed to do. Any failure in this respect would make the agent absolutely liable for the principal's loss.
(2) Duty to follow instructions or custom: An agent is bound to conduct the business of his principal according to the directions given by the principal and in absence, by the custom.[782]
(3) Duty to take reasonable care: An agent is expected to exercise such care and skill as is necessary for 'the ordinary and proper conduct of the business'. He is also expected to possess as much skill as is generally possessed by persons engaged in a similar business.[783]
(4) Duty to avoid conflict of interest: If the agent deals on his own, without taking consent from the principal and later on, the principal finds out that the agent had concealed some material facts, then the principal can repudiate the contract.[784]
(5) Duty not to make a secret profit: If the agent deals on his own, without knowledge of the principal, then the principal can claim benefits that resulted from the transaction.[785]
(6) Duty to maintain proper accounts: An agent is bound to render proper accounts to his principal on demand.[786]
(7) Duty not to delegate the work. The agent has to perform the act personally and has no authority to delegate the authority to perform the act to another, unless actually empowered to do so by any contract, custom or usage.[787]
(8) Duty to remit sums: The agent is bound to pay principal all sums received on his account.

759. If the agent infringes any of his duties, then the principal is not bound by any contract made by the agent and can recover damages from the agent and can even obtain an account and payment of secret and illicit profit. A defaulting agent can also be dismissed instantly and summarily.

D. Rights of Agents

760. Rights of agent are as follows:

(1) Right of remuneration: The agent has legal right to receive remuneration, provided that the act done was under his authority.[788]
(2) Right of retainer: An agent can retain the money received by him, on account of the principal that any amount is due from the principal.[789]

782. The Indian Contract Act, 1872, s. 211.
783. The Indian Contract Act, 1872, s. 212.
784. The Indian Contract Act, 1872, s. 215.
785. The Indian Contract Act, 1872, s. 216.
786. The Indian Contract Act, 1872, s. 213.
787. The Indian Contract Act, 1872, s. 190.
788. The Indian Contract Act, 1872, s. 219.
789. The Indian Contract Act, 1872, s. 217.

(3) Right of Lien: An agent is entitled to retain goods, papers and other property, of the principal if some amount is due to him.[790]

(4) Right to be indemnified: An agent is entitled to be indemnified against the consequences of all lawful acts done by him in exercise of authority and in good faith.[791]

(5) Right to compensation: The principal must make compensation to his agent in respect of injury caused to such agent by the principal's neglect or want of skill.[792]

E. Termination of Agency

761. The principal can terminate an agency by revoking his authority, or by the agent renouncing the business of the agency, or the business of agency being completed or by death or insanity of either party or insolvency of the principal.[793] The principal may at any time revoke the authority given to his agent. The principal shall be liable for any transaction conducted by the agent with third parties before the revocation and shall also be liable to any third party who acted without notice of revocation.[794] Where there is lawful revocation, the agent can sue for indemnifying for losses suffered and expenses incurred as an agent.[795] An agency comes to an automatic end on the expiry of the term. Where the agency was to run a petrol pump for a specified period, it was held that the agent was bound to vacate the premises on expiry of the period.[796]

III. Insurance

A. General

762. Insurance is a cooperative device to spread the loss caused by a particular risk over a number of persons who are exposed to it and who agree to insure themselves against the risk. The law of insurance has been a subject of considerable importance since its beginning. Parliament is only competent to make law in the field of Insurance. Therefore, the law of insurance in India has been uniform throughout India. The first legislation to regulate the insurance was Indian Life Assurance Act, 1912. Though, currently the principal legislation regulating the insurance business in India is the Insurance Act of 1938. Some other existing legislations in the field are – Employees' State Insurance Act, 1948 the LIC Act, 1956, the Marine Insurance Act, 1963, the General Insurance Business (GIB) (Nationalization) Act, 1972, Public Liability Insurance Act, 1991 the IRDA Act, 1999,. The provisions of the Indian Contract Act, 1872 are applicable to the contracts of insurance, whether for life or non-life. The Transfer of Property Act, 1882, the Hindu Succession Act, 1956 and Indian Succession

790. The Indian Contract Act, 1872, s. 221.
791. The Indian Contract Act, 1872, ss 222 and 223.
792. The Indian Contract Act, 1872, s. 225.
793. The Indian Contract Act, 1872, s. 201.
794. The Indian Contract Act, 1872, s. 208.
795. The Indian Contract Act, 1872, s. 205.
796. *P. Sukhadev v. Commr of Endowments*, (1998) 1 BC 403 (AP) (DB).

Act, 1925, the Indian Stamp Act, 1899, Chapter XI of the Motor Vehicle Act, 1988 and a few others also govern the various contractual aspects of fire and life insurances as also of the many branches that come under accident insurance. Similarly, the provisions of the Companies Act, 1956 are applicable to the companies carrying on insurance business. The subordinate legislation includes Insurance Rules, 1939, and the Ombudsman Rules, 1998 framed by the Central Government under section 114 of the principal Act as also twenty-seven regulations made by the IRDA Act, 1999 (hereinafter referred to as IRDA) Act under section 114A of the principal Act and section 26 of the IRDA Act, 1999.

B. Nature of Insurance

763. Insurance is a contract either to indemnify a person against a loss which may arise on the happening of an event or to pay a sum of money on the happening of some or any event for an agreed consideration. However, it is recognized that to satisfactorily define 'insurance' is a matter of considerable difficulty. The Insurance Act, 1938 nowhere defines the term 'insurance'. It may however be defined as a contract whereby one party (the insurer) promises in return for a money consideration (the premium) to pay to the other party (the insured) money or money's worth on the happening of an uncertain event more or less adverse to the interest of the insured.[797]

764. The nature of contract for insurance is as follows.

1. Unilateral Contract

765. Contracts are ordinarily bilateral in nature, that is, each party to the contract makes enforceable promises to the other party. Thus, where a manufacturer agrees to deliver the goods at an agreed price to the wholesaler who agrees to pay for them when they are delivered, the contract is bilateral in nature. But where the wholesaler pays the price along with the order, then only the manufacturer has something to perform under the contract which is called unilateral. The insurance contract is also a unilateral contract in this sense. Here only the insurer makes an enforceable promise. The applicant for the insurance has to perform his part before the contract comes into effect, viz., payment of the premium or the first instalment of the premium of which the contract comes into force. The insured cannot be compelled to pay the premiums subsequent to the first although if he does not do so, the insurer will be released from the original promise to pay the sum assured. However if he pays the periodic premiums on the terms stated in the policy, the insurer will be obliged to accept the premiums and can be compelled to perform his part of the contract.

2. Conditional Contract or Contingent Contract

766. The insurance contract is also a conditional contract because the promise of the insurer is conditioned on the timely payment of premiums subsequent to the first by the insured. This is a precedent to the continuance of the contract under its original promise. If this condition is not fulfilled, the insurer is relieved of his basic

797. *Prudential Insurance Co. v. Inland Revenue Commrs* (1904) 2 KB 628.

promise contained in the contact, but remains bound to honour other subsidiary promises contained in the contract, viz., the surrender and reinstatement provisions, etc. In addition, the insurer's promise to pay the sum insured is also conditional upon the insured's forbearance during the specified initial period from committing suicide, furnishing satisfactory proof of death of the insured and proof of title of the persons claiming payment of the sum insured and so on. Conditions may be precedent or subsequent. A condition precedent must be satisfied before legal rights and duties are created or continued whereas a condition subsequent must be fulfilled in order to prevent the extinguishment of rights and duties already created by the contract.

3. An Aleatory Contract

767. An aleatory agreement is one in which there is an element of chance or uncertainty, as for instance a wagering contract. Depending upon chance, a party to such an agreement may receive a return out of all proportion to the value which he gives. In ordinary contracts, each party expects to give and to receive from the other party fairly equivalent values in exchange, as for example, in the purchase of goods. In a life insurance contract, however, the full sum insured may become payable even after the insured has paid an initial premium or a few premiums only, though this will not happen in the case of all policies issued by an insurer. Insurers are careful to see that on the whole the sum total of all insurance transaction is also to their advantage. This aleatory nature of insurance has induced many unscrupulous persons to resort to insurance for making fraudulent and illegal gain. It is to counteract this tendency that insurable interest is required in insurance and also the remedies of rescission and repudiation are provided to insurers. However if the insured continues to pay the periodic premiums, the insurer will be obliged to accept the premiums and can be compelled to continue the contract.

4. A Contract of Adhesion

768. A life insurance contract is said to be a contract of adhesion meaning thereby that the terms of the contract are not arrived at by mutual negotiations between the parties as in the case of ordinary contracts. The insured has various types of policies to suit various needs and a person who applies for a policy of life insurance must accept the one, which is most suitable to him. He is not in a position to bargain about the terms of the contract. If he wants a policy he must accept it or adhere to it in the form it is offered. Any negotiation or bargaining is only to do with selecting the one that is most suitable to him, out of the various types of policy that are available with the insurer.

5. Contract for a Certain Amount

769. An insurance contract is a valued contract as against a contract of indemnity. In a life insurance contract a fixed sum is paid whereas in non-life contract, the amount of loss is paid.

6. Not a Contract of Indemnity

770. A life insurance contract is not a contract of indemnity but one to pay a stated sum, while property and casualty insurances can be contracts of indemnity where the insured can recover only the amount of his loss not exceeding the amount of the policy. In life insurance even where the insured has reached a ripe old age and his economic value is not high, the insurers will pay the full sum initially agreed upon.

7. Insurable Interest

771. For an insurance contract to be valid, it is not enough that the parties to it are competent to contract, that it is made with their free consent and that the consideration is lawful. It is necessary in addition that the insured has insurable interest in the subject matter of insurance. According to section 8 of the Marine Insurance Act, 1963, the assured must be interested in the subject matter insured at the time of loss, though he need not be interested when the insurance is effected, and where the assured has no interest at the time of the loss, he cannot acquire interest by any act or election after he is aware of the loss. The Marine Insurance Act, 1963 lays down the requirement of insurable interest in marine insurances. In other branches of insurance, section 30 of the Contract Act, 1872 requires it by implication. The use or driving of a motor vehicle in a public place is sufficient insurable interest for the purpose of effecting insurance in favour of a third party.[798] Insurable interest is the legal right of the insured in insurance. The taking of an insurance policy does not protect the insured property from loss or damage, but protects the insured's interest in the property. Insurable interest is not limited to absolute ownership of property but may arise in other ways also. It may be based on ownership whether absolute, partial or limited, legal or equitable, for example, joint owners, mortgager and mortgagee, trustee or beneficiary. Even mere lawful possession alone such as that of a lessee, bailee or carrier of goods or warehouseman can give insurable interest. It may also be founded upon contract, as in the case of reinsurance by the insurers.[799] Insurable interest is not confined to legal ownership only. The legal liability of common carriers to make good the loss or damage to the goods in transit to the bailor of goods is also an insurable interest.[800]

772. Essentials of Insurable Interest:

(1) There must be some property, right, interest, life, limb or potential liability capable of being insured.
(2) This property, right, interest, etc. which must be the subject matter of insurance.
(3) The insured must stand in a relationship with the subject matter of insurance whereby he/she benefits from its safety, well-being or freedom from liability and would be prejudiced by its loss, damage, or existence of liability.
(4) The relationship between the insured and the subject matter of insurance must be recognized in law.

---

798. *Northern India General Insurance Co. Ltd. v. Kanwarjit Singh Sobti*, AIR 1973 All 357.
799. M.N. Srinivasan, *Principles of Insurance Law*, 77 rev. ed. by Avtar Singh (7th ed., Wadhwa & Company 2002).
800. *Snow White Food Products (P) Ltd. v. Sohan Lal Bagla*, AIR 1964 Cal 204 at 214.

C. Formation of Contract of Insurance

1. General

773. The Indian Contract, 1872 governs the relationship between the parties to an insurance contract generally except in regard to some of its special features. Section 10 of the Indian Contract Act, 1872 lays down conditions which must be followed for the formation of a contract, viz., (1) parties must be competent to contract; (2) the agreement must be with their free consent; (3) it must be for a lawful consideration and for a lawful object; and (4) it should not be expressly declared to be void by any law for the time being in force.

2. Proposal

774. One of the requirements for the formation of an insurance contract is the mutual agreement between the insured and the insurer. There must be an offer on the one hand and an unqualified acceptance of it on the other hand. It is the normal practice of insurance companies to require the applicant for insurance to complete a proposal form containing a number of questions, with the view of ascertaining the exact nature of the risk to be assessed and covered. On the basis of the answers in the proposal form, the insurer relies on the statements in the proposal form, assesses the risk, fixes the premium and informs the applicant that he agrees to enter into a contract if the proposer will pay the premium quoted in the acceptance letter. The date of payment gives rise to the insurance contract. The terms of the contract are then embodied in a policy issued by the insurer.

775. In *General Accident Insurance v. Crank,*[801] the proposal was accompanied with the initial premium and was unconditionally accepted. The insurer was not liable to issue letter of acceptance, but he/she was free to issue only the policy in conformity with the proposal. The proposal form is important because statements in it are the basis of the contract between the parties. However, in *Elsa Tony Philip v. LIC,*[802] where neither acceptance of proposal was communicated, nor policy document issued, it was held that mere encashment of the cheque for payment of first premium was not enough to bring about a contract, insurer not liable to honour claim. In *Pearl life v. Johnson,*[803] it was held that the proposal was the basis of the contract. It was stated that there was no contract between the insurer and insured because misrepresentative statement was there and the proposal was not signed by the assured of his/her authority.

3. Cover Note

776. A contract of insurance is a type of commercial transaction and there is a well A contract of insurance is a type of commercial transaction and there is established commercial practice to send cover notes even prior to the completion of a proper proposal or while the proposal is being considered or a policy is in preparation for

801. (1901) 17 T.I.R. 233.
802. (1909) 2 K.B. 288.
803. AIR 2009 (NOC) 785 (NCC).

delivery. A cover note is a temporary and limited agreement. It may be self contained or it may incorporate by reference the terms and conditions of the future policy.[804] The cover note is a distinct contract of insurance for the short period and should be properly stamped according to the Stamp Act. It automatically expires at the end of the stated period unless it is earlier superseded by the issue of a regular policy or the proposal is declined by the insurer. The cover note usually mentions that the interim cover is under the same terms and conditions of the policy that is usually issued for such proposals. The insurer then examines the proposal and if acceptable issues a policy for the required period or declines the proposal and informs the proposer prior to the expiry of the cover note period. Any claim arising during the currency of the cover note will be determined by reference to the terms of the cover note and not the terms of the subsequent policy. Where the insurer sends a temporary cover note to the insured at the expiry of the insurance coverage for the renewal of the insurance policy, the cover note becomes an enforceable insurance contract only upon acceptance by the insured. Otherwise it has effect only as an offer to insure for the future.

4. The Policy

777. The word 'policy' which is derived from the Italian term polizza is the formal document which evidences the contract of insurance which has been formed by the mutual agreement between the parties. In a contract of insurance, rights and obligations are strictly governed by the policy of insurance. No exception or relaxation can be made on the ground of equity.[805] The mere fact of submission of the proposal form along with first premium did not conclude the contract between the parties. The insurance company has to take steps to underwrite the risk and communicate. The policy document may be issued thereafter.[806]

778. In the case of life insurance, standard policy forms that can be issued should be approved by the controller of insurance (now 'Authority' under the IRDA Act, 1999) with regard to the rates, advantages, terms and conditions as certified to be sound under section 3(2)(f) and 3B of the Insurance Act, 1938. Similarly in the case of general insurance, the rates, terms and conditions of policies to be insured are controlled and regulated by the TAC established under the Insurance Act, 1938. Similarly in the case of general insurance, the rates, terms and conditions of policies to be insured are controlled and regulated by the TAC established under the Insurance Act, 1938. Various standard policy forms are printed in which space is provided in a portion called the schedule where necessary details of the individual contract such as name and address of the insured, the life or property and the sum insured, the premium and the term and any special conditions or warranties can be inserted.

779. In *Atlantic Maritime Co. v. Gibbon*,[807] it was observed that the marine insurance policy which had been in use for more than 200 years with minor changes has been adversely commented upon as archaic, absurd and incoherent and yet adhered to with tenacity. A writ petition seeking an insurance policy covering certain risks not

804. *General Insurance Society v. Chandmull*, (1966) 36 Com Cases 468 (SC).
805. *Deokar Exports (P) Ltd. v. New India Assurance Co. Ltd.*, AIR 2009 SC 2026.
806. *S R Kharidia v. Max New York Life Insurance Co Ltd.*, AIR 2009 Guj 57 (DB).
807. [1954] 1 QB 88, [1953] 2 LL ER 1086.

mentioned in the proposal would amount to a fresh insurance policy. In *Harry & Jenny v. Export Credit Guarantee Corp.*,[808] the proposal and acceptance between the insured and the insurer in the nature of a contract could not be adjudicated under Article 226 of the Constitution of India.

5. Construction of a Policy

780. The following main rules of construction should be adhered to while constructing the policy:

(1) In India, Insurance Regulatory Development Authority wants insurance companies to offer a fair deal, and all the terms and conditions of their offer must be transparent. There should not be any hidden agenda nor should they resort to 'ticketing contract'. Insurance companies cannot either in their prospectus or in the terms of the policy lay down any condition which would be derogatory to the terms and conditions approved by IRDA.[809]

(2) Effect is to be given if possible to every word in the policy. The court should impose a new and reasonable contract, if the parties have not made it themselves.[810]

(3) Words printed or written are equally effective. Where, however, there is a conflict between the printed and written clauses or words, greater consideration has to be paid to the written words as these are words selected by the parties to adapt the policy to their particular case, whereas the printed words are a general formula adapted to apply equally to their case as well as of others in general. Words struck out or deleted from the policy are also significant in ascertaining the intended meaning.

(4) Where a clause in the policy is ambiguous, it is to be construed against rather than in favour of the insurer, because it is the language chosen by the insurer and if he does not use words clearly to express what he means, he is the person who ought to suffer rather than the insured. This rule of interpretation against the insurer and favourable for the assured originates from the rule of *contra proferentem*, which means that a document must be construed against the interest of the person who puts the language into the document upon which he is relying. This rule is not applicable where there is no ambiguity.

(5) Where the language of the clause is taken from an answer in the proposal which is in the wording of the insured it will be construed against him if it is ambiguous.

(6) Warranties are inserted for the protection of the insurers and if the language of a warranty is ambiguous it will be strictly construed against the insurer.

(7) A contract cannot be construed by reference to the subsequent conduct of the parties. But this is only when the clause can have only one proper meaning. When it is not so, but ambiguous and capable of two meanings, it is permissible to look at the way in which the parties themselves have acted upon it.

808. 1999(97) Com Cas 663.

809. *United India Insurance Co. Ltd. v. Manubhai Dharmasinhbhai Gajera*, (2008) 10 SCC 404.

810. *General Assurance Society v. Chandmull*, AIR 1966 SC 1644.

(8) The rule of interpretation as to exceptions is that they are to be taken most strongly against the party for whose benefit they are introduced. The words in which they are expressed are considered as his words.

(9) Where answers given to the questions in the proposal by the insured are true, but evasive, the proper answers should receive a fair and reasonable interpretation. In other words, when the question is reasonably construed, it allows the insurer to benefit from what has been recorded of the insured with regard to claims of the insured.

(10) The policy of insurance evidences a contract and must therefore be construed like any other contract. The intention of the parties must be gathered in the first place from the words used in the policy taking it as a whole and putting a reasonable construction on each clause. In *Yangtze Assurance v. Indemnity Marine*,[811] Farewell J. observed, that the terms themselves are to be understood in their plain, ordinary and popular sense, subject to the rule that technical words must be given their strict technical meaning unless the context indicates otherwise. This was also held in the case of *London and Lancashire Fire Ins*. Co. *v. Bolands*[812] construing the meaning of the word 'riot'.

(11) The rule of construction as to exceptions is that they are to be taken most strongly against the party for whose benefit they are introduced. The words in which they are expressed are considered as his/her words.[813]

(12) A policy of insurance is a contract based on an offer (proposal) and an acceptance if one party made a proposal and other accepted the proposal with a modification. Therefore, it was a counter proposal, in which event there would have been no contract unless other party agreed to such counter proposal. If the appellant did not agree to the policy coverage, it would never create an effective insurance contract.[814]

(13) A document like an insurance proposal form is a commercial document and being an integral part of the policy, reference to the proposal form may not only be appropriate but rather essential. However, the surveyors' report cannot be taken aid of a policy. Such outside aid for construction of insurance policy is impermissible.[815]

6. Duty of Disclosure

781. A contract of insurance is a contract of uberrima fides and as such there must be utmost good faith on the part of the assured. Good faith forbids either party from concealing what he/she privately knows, to draw the other into a bargain, from his/her ignorance of that fact and his/her believing the contrary.[816] A false answer or non-disclosure or concealment of a material fact will avoid the policy, even though

811. (1908) 2KB 504.
812. (1924) AC 836 HL.
813. *Ethirington and Lanclashire and Yorkashire Accident Ins. Co. Re*. (1909) 1 KB 591, *see also Lake v. Simmons*, (1927) AC 487, 508.
814. *Deokar Exports (P) Ltd. v. New India Assurance Co. Ltd.*, (2008) 14 SCC 598.
815. *Vikram Greentech (I) Ltd. v. New India Assurance Co. Ltd.*, (2009) 5 SCC 599.
816. *United India Insurance Co Ltd. v. M.K.J. Corpn*, (1996) 6 SCC 428.

there is no fraud and the concealment is innocent.[817] In insurance contracts, the principle of caveat emptor has no place, as in such cases ordinarily, the risk undertaken by the insurer can only be learnt from the representations made by the intending insured, and non-disclosure of a material fact is regarded as fatal to the validity of the transaction.

782. Upon these principles, there is a legal obligation cast upon the party proposing the insurance, to communicate, not only every material fact of which he/she had actual knowledge, but he/she is also deemed to know every material fact of which he/she ought, in the ordinary course of business, to have knowledge.[818]

783. The duty of good faith is of a continuing nature. After the completion of the contract, no material alteration can be made in its terms except by mutual consent. The materiality of a fact is judged by the circumstances existing at the time when the contract is concluded.[819]

784. Material Facts: Every circumstance is material, which would influence the judgment of a product insurer in fixing the premium or determining whether he/she should take the risk. Therefore, facts regarding age, height, weight, build, previous medical history, smoking, drinking habits, operations, non-disclosure of earlier insurance's 'hazardous' occupation must be disclosed.

785. The above principle has been reiterated in the judgments of the High Courts as well as the Supreme Court of India in the context of challenges by the claimants under a life insurance policy to the decision of the insurer to repudiate such policy.[820] What constitutes a material fact, which affects the risk sought to be undertaken by the insurer, would depend upon the facts and circumstances of a particular case and can be established only by leading evidence. A suppression of a fact or misrepresentation in relation to the health status of the insured, it has been held, will enable the insurer to repudiate a policy.[821]

D. Exceptions

786. The utmost good faith is not required to be fulfilled in the following cases:

(1) The assured is not required to disclose all such facts which diminish the risk, which are known to the insurer or should be reasonably known to him, and the facts to which information are waived by the insurer.
(2) All facts which are superfluous to disclose by reason of a condition or warranty.
(3) Any circumstance whereby the information is waived by the insurer.
(4) Any circumstances which are superfluous to disclose by reason of an express or applied warranty.

---

817. *Rohini Nandan Goswami v. Ocean Accident & Guarantee Corporation Ltd.*, AIR 1960 Cal.696; *see also B.A. Chopra v. New Zealand Insurance Co., Ltd.* AIR 1967 Cal. 35.
818. *Lakshmi Insurance Co. Ltd. v. Bibi Padmawati*, AIR 1961 Punj 253.
819. *Bank of Nova Scotia v. Hollenic War Risks Assn (Bermuda) Ltd.*, (1992) 1 AC 233.
820. *Life Insurance Corporation of India v. Asha Goel* (2001) 2 SC 160.
821. *Life Insurance Corporation of India v. Sosamma Punnam* (1992) 74.

E. Protection of the Policy-holders and the Development of the Insurance Industry

787. In order to protect the interests of policy-holders, regulate, promote and ensure orderly growth of the insurance industry and for matters connected therewith, the Insurance Regulatory and Development Authority Act, 1999 was enacted. Section 14 of the act imposes the following duties, powers and functions applying to the Authorities:

(1) issue to the applicant a certificate of registration, renew, modify, withdraw, suspend or cancel such registration;
(2) protection of the interests of the policy-holders in matters concerning assignment of the policy, nomination by the policy-holders, insurable interest, settlement of insurance claims, surrender the value of the policy, and other terms and conditions of contracts of insurance;
(3) specifying the requisite qualifications, code of conduct and practical training for intermediary or insurance intermediaries and agents;
(4) specifying the code of conduct for surveyors and loss assessors;
(5) promoting efficiency in the conduct of the insurance business;
(6) promoting and regulating professional organizations connected with the insurance and reinsurance business;
(7) levying fees and other charges for carrying out the purposes of this Act;
(8) calling for information from and undertaking the inspection of conducting enquiries and investigations which include auditing insurers, intermediaries, insurance intermediaries and other organizations connected with the insurance business;
(9) control and regulation of the rates, advantages, terms and conditions that may be offered by insurers in respect of the overall insurance business not so controlled and regulated by the TAC under section 64-U of the Insurance Act, 1938;
(10) specifying the form and manner in which books or accounts shall be maintained and a statement of accounts shall be rendered by insurers and other insurance intermediaries;
(11) regulating the investment of funds by insurance companies;
(12) regulating maintenance of margin of solvency;
(13) adjudication of disputes between insurance and intermediaries or insurance intermediaries;
(14) supervising the functions of the TAC;
(15) specifying the percentage of premium income of the insurer to finance schemes for promoting and regulating professional organizations referred to in clause (f) above;
(16) specifying the percentage of life insurance business and general insurance business to be undertaken by the insurer in the rural or social sector; and
(17) exercising such other powers as may be prescribed.

F. Settlement of Disputes and Arbitration

788. There are many forums for the settlement of disputes between insurers and those insured. They may be:

(1) ordinary civil courts;
(2) ombudsman;
(3) arbitration; or
(4) consumer protection.

1. Ordinary Civil Courts

789. The settlement of disputes is available under the normal civil courts established by the Code of Civil Procedure, 1908. The following are the civil courts which have been established according to territorial and pecuniary jurisdictions:

(1) Civil Judge Junior Division.
(2) Civil Judge Senior Division.
(3) Court of the District Judge.
(4) High Court.
(5) Supreme Court.

790. The High Courts and the Supreme Court are the appellate courts whereas the Court of the district judge has both original and appellate jurisdiction, i.e., appeal lies from the judgment of the civil judge junior division and civil judge senior division. The latter two courts have only original jurisdiction.

2. Ombudsman

a. General

791. The Insurance Ombudsman scheme is one more formal grievance and disputes settlement mechanism. It is in addition to the other disputes resolution proceedings. The word 'ombudsman' is a Swedish word, which means the right of an individual to complain against the public authority/establishments/administration. While recommending privatization of the insurance sector, the Malhotra Committee also acknowledged the need to protect the insured's' interests and recommended setting up the institution of the ombudsman, with a view to reduce litigation. The government, therefore, in exercise of the powers conferred by the Insurance Act, 1938, framed the Redressal of Public Grievances Rules, 1998. These rules apply both to life insurance and general insurance in respect of personal life insurance, i.e., insurance taken in an individual capacity. The object of the institution of the ombudsman is to resolve all complaints relating to the settlement of claims on the part of insurance companies in a cost-effective efficient and impartial manner. However, the government has reserved the right to exempt any insurance company from these rules, upon being satisfied that its-in-house grievance redressal machinery fulfils the requirements of these rules. The rules provide appointment of an ombudsman who may be selected from those who have experience in the judicial, civil or administrative service, insurance industry, etc. He shall be appointed for a period of three years and shall receive emoluments equivalent to that of a High Court Judge. The power of the ombudsman is vested on receipt of a written complaint under Rule 13.

792. The ombudsman can also act as a counsellor and mediator, for matters within their terms of reference, if requested to do so by the insurer and the insured. The Ombudsman scheme has been set up at present in twelve centres in India, viz., four in the cities of Delhi, Mumbai, Kolkata and Chennai and eight in some of the state capitals.

b. Presentation of Grievance Before the Ombudsman

793. Any person having a grievance against an insurer may complain in writing to the ombudsman, under Rule 13, within whose jurisdiction the concerned office of the insurer is situated, stating out facts of the dispute and evidence, if any. Before making a complaint, the insured is required to represent his case to the insurer concerned and only upon the rejection of his representation or the failure to reply to the representation within one month, shall a complaint lie with the ombudsman. No complaint made after one year of the cause of action which is the pending subject matter before any court or consumer forum shall be actionable.

c. Maintainability of a Complaint

794. The ombudsman under Rule 12 may receive and consider complaints in respect of:

(1) any partial or total repudiation of claims by an insurer;
(2) any dispute in regard to a premium paid or payable in terms of the policy;
(3) any dispute on the legal interpretation of the policies in so far as such disputes relate to claims;
(4) delay in settlement of claims; and
(5) non-issuance of any insurance document to customers after receipt of the premium.

d. Bilateral References of Disputes

795. Besides the unilateral complaints of the insured persons, the rules also provide for bilateral reference of disputes through mutual agreement between the insurer and the insured, wherein the ombudsman shall act as a counsellor or mediator under Rule 15. The ombudsman shall make his recommendations on the subject, which if acceptable to the insured, shall be satisfied by the insurer. In the case of complaints, the ombudsman passes an award within three months of filing the complaint. The insurer here shall satisfy the award only upon its acceptance by the insured. Thus, the recommendations as well as awards, have been made binding on the insurers, but subject to their acceptance by the complainant.

e. Award

796. The ombudsman under Rule 16 shall make any award which he thinks fair according to the facts and circumstances of a claim, when the complaint is not settled under Rule 15. An award shall be in writing and shall state the amount awarded to the complainant. The ombudsman, however, shall not award any compensation in excess of which is necessary to cover the loss suffered by the complainant as a direct consequence of the insured's' peril, or for any amount exceeding INR 2 million (including ex gratia and other expenses) whichever is lower. This award shall be passed within three months from the date of receipt of the complaint. Under Rule 16(4) a copy of the award shall be sent to the complainant and the insurer. The complainant under Rule 16(5) shall furnish to the insurer within a period of one month from the date of the receipt of the award, a letter of acceptance that the award is in full and a final settlement of his claim. The insurer shall comply with the award within fifteen days of the receipt of the acceptance letter and shall also intimate the compliance to the ombudsman. In case the complainant does not intimate the acceptance, the award may not be implemented by the insurance company under Rule 17. Under Rule 18, the ombudsman, if he deems fit, may award an ex gratia payment.

3. Arbitration

797. Arbitration is a technical term for a person selected with reference to an established system for friendly determination of controversies which, though not judicial, are regulated by law, and his doings may be judicially revised if he has exceeded his authority. Thus, the arbitrator is a private, disinterested person, chosen by the parties to a disputed question, for the purpose of hearing their contentions, and giving judgment between them, and the decision is called an 'award'. The litigants submit themselves to arbitration either voluntarily, or, in some cases, compulsorily, by order of a court. Arbitration, therefore, is the submission for determination of disputed matters to private unofficial person selected in a manner provided by law or agreement. In India, before the promulgation of the present Arbitration and Conciliation Act, 1996, there were a number of Acts, but they have all been repealed. The object has been to consolidate and amend the laws relating to domestic arbitration, international commercial arbitration, enforce foreign arbitral awards and also to define the law relating to conciliation for matters connected therewith or incidental thereto. Section 42C(7) proviso 2 of the Insurance Act, 1938 also provides that in the event of any dispute as to the terms of any new contract, the matter shall be referred to arbitration. Thus, any dispute arising between an insurer and a chief agent or special agent in respect of the terms of any fresh contract must be referred to arbitration according to the provisions of the Arbitration and Conciliation Act, 1966. Surprisingly, only a few insurance companies in India have incorporated in their terms and conditions this provision and not many cases have been found to have been referred to arbitration. Most cases are referred to the law courts, or consumer forum under the Consumer Protection Act, 1986.

4. Consumer Protection Forums

798. Detailed discussions have been made in Part II, Chapter 5.

IV. Financial Services

A. Banking Services

799. Banking services, born in India in the nineteenth century, have played a great role in the commercial market today. It was formerly considered that a banker or bank is a person, firm or company, having a place of business, where credits are opened through the deposits or collection of money or currency or advanced or loaned. The following are the important services that a modern bank in India provides:

(1) depositing money in various forms, e.g., fixed deposit, current deposit, savings bank deposits, etc.;
(2) lending money, i.e., it is the main source of income for most banks. They discount bills, or give funds in exchange for a promissory note, the transaction of which is known as a discount or loan;
(3) agency services. Besides the collection of cheques and bills, the modern bank performs the following other services:

    (a) payment of insurance premiums, rents, subscriptions and collection of promissory acts, coupons, dividends, salaries, pensions, etc.;
    (b) purchase and sale of stocks and shares;
    (c) acting as trustee, executor and attorney;

(4) transferring money from place to place: Modern banks in India transfer funds from one place to another or one country to another by means of drafts drawn upon their branches or agents. They also purchase bills of exchange from the merchants and others to receive money from their debtors in other cities or countries. Thus, the industrial development of the country is accredited for the existence of these banks; and
(5) miscellaneous functions: In addition to the above-mentioned functions, modern banks in India perform miscellaneous services such as:

    (a) the issuance of various forms and credits, e.g., letters of credit, traveller, cheques and circular notes;
    (b) underwriting of capital issues;
    (c) acceptance of bills of exchange;
    (d) safe custody of valuables;
    (e) acting as executor and trustee for customers;
    (f) preparing the income tax return for their customers; and
    (g) furnishing guarantees on behalf of customers, etc.

800. Section 6 of the Banking Regulation Act, 1949 also provides the following forms of business which a bank, can carry out, aside from the above-mentioned functions:

(1) A banking company may also act as the agent for any government, or local authority or any other person or persons, but he cannot act as a managing agent, secretary or otherwise.
(2) A bank may contract for public and private loans and negotiating and issuing them.
(3) A bank may effect, insure, guarantee, underwrite and participate in managing and carrying out any issue of loans or securities made by a state municipality, company, corporation or any other association and may also lend for that purpose.
(4) A bank can carry on and transact any kind of guarantee and indemnity business.
(5) It may acquire, hold and deal with any property or any right, title or interest therein which forms the security for any loans and advances sanctioned.
(6) It may manage, sell and realize any property which may come into its possession in satisfaction of its claims.
(7) It may undertake, and execute trusts as well as administer estates as the executor, trustee or otherwise.
(8) It may establish and support or aid in the establishment of associations, institutions, funds, trusts and conveniences or the benefit of its present or past employees and their dependants and may grant or guarantee moneys for charitable purposes.
(9) It may enquire, construct, maintain and alter any buildings or works necessary for its purposes.
(10) It may sell, improve or manage, develop, exchange, lease, mortgage, dispose of or otherwise deal with any of its properties and rights.
(11) It may take over and undertake the whole or any part of the business of any person or company when much business is of a nature described above.
(12) It may do all other things that are incidental or conducive to the promotion or advancement of its business.
(13) It may engage in any other form of business which the central government specifies to be lawful.

801. Section 8 of the Banking Regulation Act, 1949 prohibits a banking company from trading. A bank shall not deal directly or indirectly in the buying or selling or bartering of goods except in connection with the realization of security for the loans sanctioned or bills of exchange received or collection or negotiation or administration of an estate as the executor and trustee. Section 19(1) of the act further restricts the formation of subsidiary companies.

B. Leasing

802. Leasing is very common in India. It may either be for personal purpose or commercial purposes. In personal dealings, there are a large number leases being made to the lessee. Leasing is concerned with immovable property. Similarly, in commercial transactions, property is being leased for commercial purposes. Sections 105–117 of the Transfer of Property Act, 1882 deals with the subject of leases in India. It defines, a lease of immovable property as a transfer of a right to enjoy such property, made for a certain time, express or implied or in the perpetuity, in consideration for a price paid, or promised or of money, a share of crops, service or any other thing of value, to be rendered periodically or on specified occasions to the transferor by the transferee, who accepts the transfer on such terms. Thus, when the question of transfer on a lease has to be dealt with, automatically the law of contract comes into play. There is, however, no separate law for leasing in India. It is incorporated in the law of agreement. If someone has to give one's own property on lease for a certain period, the lessor and lessee makes an agreement on such terms and conditions which may be laid down in writing. Thus, the concept of lease is governed both by the law of contract as well as section 105 of the Transfer of Property Act, 1882. It may also be pointed out that the transfer of property is a transfer of a right to enjoy the leased property for some consideration. It is different from a sale where there is a transfer of ownership of the property itself for a price and also differs from a gift where the ownership of the thing is transferred without consideration. For a lease, the relation between a transferor and transferee is that of a lessor and lessee, whereby the former does not cease to be the owner of the property and also latter also does not become the owner of such leased property. For example, where the subject matter of the lease is a coal mine, it can only be enjoyed and occupied by the lessee by working in it.[822] The essential characteristic of a lease is that the subject matter is occupied and enjoyed by the corpus of the subject and does not disappear by user. Before a lease, the lessor is entitled to enjoy possession of the land, but according to the lease, he excludes himself during the period of that right. A lease is, therefore, not a mere contract but a transfer of interest in the immovable property.[823] A lease of a house or of a shop is a lease not only of the superstructure but also of its site.[824] A permanent lease providing terms can give rise to tenant-landlord relationship. The only precondition for establishing such relationship is that the landlord should have reserved the right to evict the tenant.[825]

803. Section 106 of the Transfer of Property Act, 1882 lays down that in the absence of a contract or local law or usage to the contrary, a lease of immovable property for agricultural or manufacturing purposes shall be deemed to be a lease from year to year, terminable, on the part of either lessor or lessee, by six months notice expiring with the end of a year of the tenancy; and a lease of immovable property for any other purpose shall be deemed to be a lease from month to month, terminable, on the part of either lessor or lessee, by fifteen days notice expiring with the end of a month of the tenancy. In *Ramkumar v. Jagdish Chandra*,[826] In *Pradeep Oil Corpn. v. Municipal Corpn.* of Delhi,[827] the Supreme Court held that the stipulation in the deed that the grant should not be construed as a lease was held to be inconsequential. The grantee was held liable to pay the Municipal Tax for the land though its ownership

822. *Commissioner of Income tax, Bihar & Orissa v. Ramaksha Narain*, 1940, Pat 633.
823. *Anwarali Bepari v. Jaminilal Roy*, AIR 1940 Cal 89, *see also Nathu Lal v. Union of India, AIR 2007*(NOC) 1863 (Utr).
824. *T. Lakshmipathi v. P. Nithyananda Reddy*, AIR 2003 SC 2427.
825. *Chittoor Chegaiah v. Pedda Jeeyanagar Mutt*, AIR 2010 SC 1278.
826. AIR 1952 SC 22.
827. AIR 2011 SC 1869.

might belong to the administration. the Supreme Court held that the rule of construction embodied in section 106 applies not only to express leases of an uncertain duration but also to leases implied by law which may be inferred from the possession and acceptance of rent and other circumstances exception to the law, and that the lease is applicable only to the immovable property, i.e., under various sales tax laws enacted by the state legislatures in India, with the concept of the lease also applying to movable property, e.g., machinery, instruments, etc. Section 2(23) of the Rajasthan Sales Tax Act, 1994 defines a 'lease' as any agreement or arrangement whereby the right to use any goods for any purpose is transferred by one person to another whether or not for a specified period for cash, deferred payment or other valuable consideration without the transfer of ownership, and includes a sub-lease but does not include any transfer on hire purchase or any system of payment by instalments. It has now become common practice in India to lease even movable property for commercial purposes. In *Johnsen Kanadan v. Patel Saw Mill*,[828] lease was granted for the purpose of running a saw mill but, subject to this right of the lease, the land was always to be deemed in possession of the lessor. The court said that such a clause only indicated that the transaction was a licence and not a lease at all. Another part of the lease permitted the lessor to enter the compound to take usufruct from trees and that the lessee would have no right to the trees or their income. Thus exclusive possession was not given to the lessee any tenement put up by the lessee were to be removable. Where the landlord accepted rent even after quit notice, the court said that the notice to quit had not become ineffective for that reason. It would require acquiescence in the continuation of the tenancy by some overt act on the part of the landlord.[829]

V. Carriage by Land, Sea and Air

A. Carriage by Land

1. General

804. The Carrier Act, 1865 was passed at a time when the profession of carrying goods or passengers was growing and the carriers had an open opportunity to contract out of liability even for negligence or misconduct with the result that the consignors, were left wholly at their mercy. Common carrier has been defined in section 2 of the act as 'common carrier' and denotes a person, other than the government, engaged in the business of transporting property under a multimodal transport document or of transporting for the hire of property from place to place, by land or inland navigation, for all persons indiscriminately.

805. A common carrier may limit his liability by a special contract and he does not thereby cease to be a common carrier, though, of course, the contract would be valid only if it does not offend the provisions of the act.[830] He remains a common

828. AIR 2008 (NOC) 842 (Ker) DB.
829. *Union of India v. ADJ, Kheri*, AIR 2010 (NOC) 742 (All).
830. *Ali Mohamad v. G.P.P. Railway Co.*, AIR 1915 Nag 6; also *Akhil Chandra v. LGN Rly. Co.*, IR 1916 Ca 647, however, by special terms in a contract the liability of the carrier may be varied.

carrier and is liable as such even where he has forwarded the goods to another carrier outside his own system.[831] The nature of the contract entered into must either have the limitation of the liability made expressly in writing, or the facts of the case must show that for the contract in question, the contracting party was departing from his usual business and engaging in a different type of business from that of the common carrier.[832] However, the Indian Carriers Act does not apply to carriage by sea.[833] Carriers by land, except railways or inland navigation carriers, come under the nomenclature of common carriers. Thus, a steamship company carrying goods by a river is a common carrier.[834] Similarly, a licence of a ferry,[835] or a person carrying goods from a jetty to a ship,[836] or the owner of a public lorry is a common carrier.[837] Thus, the legal requirement is the public profession to carry goods or persons indiscriminately and not as a casual operation or for providing the transport service to a particular individual or some individuals. It is on this basis that a licence is issued under the Motor Vehicles Act for the profession of public carrier.[838]

806. In *Nath Bros. Exim International Ltd. v. Best Roadways Ltd.*,[839] the Supreme Court discussed the liability of a common carrier under sections 6, 8 and 9 of the Carriers Act, 1865. The goods were booked by the appellant with the respondent common carrier 'at owner's risk' for transportation. The goods, while stored in godown were destroyed by fire. The respondent contended that the goods were destroyed by fire, which initially broke out in the adjacent godown, and subsequently spread to their own godown, thus, they would not be liable, as they had taken all possible care which was expected of them as carrier. However, the court held them liable and held that 'the liability of a carrier to whom the goods are entrusted for carriage is that of an 'insurer' and is absolute in terms, in the sense that the carrier has to deliver the goods safely, undamaged and without loss at the destination, indicated by the consignor'.

2. Consequence of Rejection

807. Once a person qualifies as a common carrier within the meaning of the definition, he becomes bound to accept the type of goods which he professes to carry on his routes. Any refusal by him is an offence under English law but not under Indian law because it is not made an offence under the Carriers Act. Only a suit for damages for refusal can be filed. He can, however, justly, refuse to carry if there is no room in his vehicle, or the goods are not of the type which he professes to carry, or the destination is not on his routes or if the goods are unlawful, dangerous or improperly packed. He may also refuse if the full and proper price for the carriage has not been paid. A

831. *Tugun Ram v. Dominion of India*, AIR 1966 Nag 260.
832. *India General Navigation & Rly. Co. v. Dekhari Tea Co.*, AIR 1924 PC 40.
833. *Bombay Steam Navigation Co. Ltd. v. Vasudev Babu Rao Kamat*, AIR 1958 Bom 5.
834. *Dekhari Tea Co. v. Assam Bengal Rly. Co.*, AIR 1920 Cal 758.
835. *Maung Po Taw v. Harmdi Missay*, AIR 1919 UB 17.
836. *K.C. Dhar v. Ahmad Bux*, AIR 1933 Cal 734.
837. *Vakil & Co. v. Mahanarain*, 1937 AMLJ 56.
838. *Hussainbhai v. Motilal*, AIR 1963 Bom 208.
839. (2004) 4 SCC 553.

consignment can also be refused if it is offered too much before the time of departure or where the destination can be reached only through areas of disturbance.

3. Government Carriers

808. Government carriers are not generally excluded by the governing statute itself from the category of common carriers. But a carrier of passengers, whether government or private, is likely to be regarded as a common carrier. The very nature of the job is such that they have to offer public services and they cannot pick and choose. A public carrier under the Motor Vehicles Act has been held to mean a common carrier.[840]

4. Private Carrier

809. If a person does not qualify as a common carrier, as stated in the foregoing paragraphs, he is to be regarded as a private carrier. A private carrier occupies the position of a bailee and, therefore, his duty and liability are regulated by sections 151 and 152 of the Indian Contract Act, 1972. These two provisions are as follows.

810. Care to be taken by bailee: In all cases of bailment the bailee is bound to take as much care of the goods bailed to him as a man of ordinary prudence would under similar circumstances take, of his own goods of the same bulk, quality and value as the goods bailed.

811. Bailee when not liable for loss, etc. of thing bailed: The bailee, in the absence of any special contract, is not responsible for the loss, destruction or deterioration of the thing bailed, if he has taken the amount of care of it as described in section 151.

812. The duty of a bailee under section 151 is to exercise reasonable care. So is the duty of a private carrier. He becomes liable when loss of damage is due to his negligence. Since the burden lies on him to account for the goods, any loss or damages is prima facie evidence of negligence. The onus of proving that the loss occurred without negligence is on the private carrier as a bailee. Where a railway administration was not able to explain how the barge carrying the plaintiff's goods sank and was lost, negligence was presumed making the railway liable.[841] The question is whether a bailee can contract himself out of the duty prescribed by section 151, or whether a contract of bailment can exempt a bailee from his liability for negligence. This is due to section 152 of the act which opens with the remark: 'in the absence of any special contract', that is, the legislative intent was to permit him so as to reduce the scope of his liability. In *Bombay Steam Navigation Co. v. Vasudev Baburao*,[842] it was observed, 'in the absence of special contract' as used in section 151 show that a bailee can contract himself out of the obligation under section 151.[843] However, this law laid down by the Bombay High Court was subsequently overruled in *Mahendra Kumar Chandulal v. CBI*,[844] wherein bales of cloth were lost from the bank custody under circumstances

840. *R.R.N. Ramlinga v. V.N. Chettiar*, AIR 1971 Ker 197.
841. *Union of India v. Sugauli Sugar Works*, (1976) 3 SCC 32.
842. AIR 1928 Bom 5.
843. This case was followed in *Chittarmal Anandi Lal v. PNB*, (1969) 10 Guj 480.
844. AIR 1984 Guj (NOC) 53.

showing negligence. The banker was held liable irrespective of a clause which absolved him of all liability. The High Court of Gujarat was of the view that no one can get a licence to be negligent. As an ordinary bailee, railways too have been held bound by the duty imposed by section 151 of the act. The railways were held liable where, instead of keeping the goods in their own go down, they left them at the jetty or a port and they were destroyed by fire.[845]

5. Liability of the Carrier is Not Contractual

813. The Liability arises under the Carriers Act and is not contractual as the carrier is not only a bailee. In *Nath Bros Exim International Ltd. v. Best Roadways Ltd.*,[846] the Supreme Court said that the liability of the carrier to whom goods are entrusted for carriage is that of an insurer and is absolute in terms, in the sense, that the carrier has to deliver the goods safely in an undamaged state and without any loss at the destination indicated by the consigner and so long as the goods are in the custody of the carrier, it is his duty to take as much care as he would have taken for his own goods. He would be liable if any loss or damage was caused to the goods on account of his own negligence or criminal act or that of his agents or servants. The consignor filed a consumer complaint before the National Commission for deficiency in service under the Consumer Protection Act, 1986. The goods were booked in this case at the owner's risk. They were destroyed by a fire while they were stored in a go down. The National Commission dismissed the complaint taking the view that the carrier was not liable as all possible care was taken by it. The Supreme Court held that this was not a correct approach and remanded the case for fresh disposal. The Supreme Court observed that sections 151 and 152 of the Contract Act, 1872 embodies the same rule as to the duty of a bailee as is applicable under the English law, but the liability of the carrier has to be seen under the Carriers Act, 1865 and not under the Contract Act, 1872. The carrier is liable unless it can show that there was no negligence or criminal act on his own part or on the part of his agent and this will be so irrespective of the fact whether the carriage is under a special contract or at the owner's risk.[847] Thus, the position of the common carrier in India is that he is liable for the loss or damage of the goods just like an insurer except where the loss falls within any of the admitted exceptions. His liability is absolute except as modified by the Carriers Act. The modification is that he is permitted by making a special contract with each consignor and not by a general public notice, to limit his absolute liability in any way he likes except that he cannot exclude the liability. In *Transport Corp. of India v. Indian Rayon Corp., Veraval*,[848] it was held that there was no such special contract, and it was no defence to show that there was no negligence on the part of the carrier. In *G.M.*

845. *Union of India v. Hafiz Bashir Ahmed*, 1988 Supp SCC 174.

846. (2000) 4 SCC 553.

847. It was followed in *South Eastern Carriers P. Ltd. v. Oriental Fire & General Insurance Co.*, AIR 2004 Ker 139. In this case the consignment of coconut oil was short delivered. The carrier admitted short delivery because of an accident. No evidence showing application of any exceptions. The printing of a condition at the back of the consignment that the goods were being carried at the owner's risk was not sufficient to constitute a special contract.

848. (1992)1 Guj Law Herald 277 Guj.

Roadways Co. v. P.G. Industries,[849] copper wires were handed over to a transport company at Calcutta to be conveyed to Tatanagar. The contract provided that the goods were received wholly at the risk of the owner. A part of the consignment was stolen en route probably with the connivance of the drivers. This being a criminal act on the part of the carrier's servant, the carrier was held liable notwithstanding that he had agreed to carry the goods only at the owner's risk.

6. Special Contract

814. Where the carrier contended that the carriage was under a special contract but did not come forward to prove his position, the Delhi High Court in *Rolta India Ltd. v. Elbee Services Ltd.*,[850] said that as to the liability of the common carrier for loss of or damage to the goods, it was observed that the position of law is well settled that the liability of the common carrier for loss of or damage to the goods of a common carrier in India is extensive and liability is that of an insurer though the absolute liability of the carrier is subject to two exceptions, viz., an act of God, and a special contract which the carrier may choose to enter into with the customer. Regarding the establishment of negligence for making the carrier liable under the Carrier Act, it was observed:

> From the conspectus of views taken in the decisions of different High Courts it is clear that the liability of a common carrier under the Carrier Act is that of an insurer. This position is made further clear by the provisions of Section 9, in which it is specifically laid down that in a case of claim of damages for loss to or deterioration of goods entrusted to a carrier it is not necessary for the plaintiff to establish negligence. This contention holds even when assuming that the general principle in cases of tortuous liability is that the party who alleges negligence against the other must prove it. The said principle has no application to a case covered under the Carrier Act. This is also the position notwithstanding a special contract between the parties. These principles have held the field over a considerable length of time and have been crystallized into accepted position of law. No good reason has been brought to our notice to persuade us to make a departure from the accepted position. Therefore, we reiterate the position of law noticed above. The consequential position that follows is that the contention, that the respondents herein having failed to establish negligence on the part of the appellant, their claim for damages should be rejected, cannot be accepted.

815. Thus, the only defence available to the common carrier is that the loss or damage was not caused due to its negligence which even otherwise is assumed. In the case before us, the defendant did not come forward to congest the claim of the plaintiff and as such failed to abjure its liability. The scale of proving the negligence is tilted against the defendant as in the opinion of the Supreme Court, negligence of the carrier is assumed.

---

849. AIR 1971 Cal 494; *see also P.K. Kalasami v. K. Pannuswami*, AIR 1962 Mad 44; *Vidya Ratan v. Kota Transport Co*, AIR 1965 Raj 200.

850. AIR 2001 Del 253 at pp. 256–257.

7. Exceptions

a. General

816. Just as the principle of absolute liability is a tradition, the exceptions are also a part of the same tradition. These exceptions do not have statutory force in India because they are not stated in any section of the Carrier Act. They have, however, become part of the law by virtue of the frequent declarations by the courts.[851] These exceptions have been described in the following paragraphs.

b. Act of God and Inevitable Accident

817. A carrier is not liable for any loss or destruction of the goods where such loss or destruction is due to an 'act of God' occurring without the intervention of human forces. A common carrier is not liable for any accident as to which he can show that it is due to natural causes, directly and exclusively, without human intervention, and that it could not have been prevented by any amount of foresight and pains and care reasonably to be expected from him. However, in *R.R.N. Ramalinga v. Narayana*,[852] the plaintiff booked eighteen bags of green gram with the defendant transportation. On the way, goods were robbed. The defendant took the plea of God, but it rejected the argument that all the inevitable accidents must be taken as acts of God. Kerala High Court held that some of the well-known instances of acts of God are the storms, the tides and the volcanic eruptions. Accidents may happen by reason of the play of natural forces or by intervention of human agency or by both. It is only those acts which can be traced to natural forces and which have nothing to do with the intervention of the human agency that could be said to be acts of God. Similarly, road accidents have not been held to be an act of God.[853] An accident due to the bursting of a tyre of the vehicle was held not to be an act of God.[854]

c. National Enemies

818. A carrier is not liable for loss or damage caused by alien enemies, whether they are persons belonging to an enemy country or the enemy state itself. This kind of risk happens during the war. If for example, a ship or a lorry on its way is torpedoed or bombarded, the carrier will not be liable for the consequences. In case war intervenes on account of something wrong on the part of the carrier itself, this will not be allowed as a defence.

---

851. *River Steam Navigation Co. v. Shyam Sunder Tea Co.*, 2 (1962) SCR 802.
852. AIR 1971 Ker 197.
853. *Oriental Road Lines v. Mohammed Hassan Sahib & Co.* (1988) 2 KLT 619; *see also Chitamvara Krishna Iyer v. South Railway Co.*, 21 Trav LJ 1; *General Traders Ltd. v. Pierce Leslie (India) Ltd.*, AIR 1987 Ker 62; *Kerala Transport Co. v. Kunnath Textiles Ltd.* 1983 KLT 480.
854. *State of Rajasthan v. Mehta Transport Co.*, AIR 2002 Raj 17; also *United India Insurance Co. Ltd. v. Mauthulalakshmi*, AIR 2003 Mad 284. This was upheld by the Supreme Court in *Patel Roadways Ltd. v. Birla Yamaha Ltd.*, (2004) 4 SCC 91.

d. Inherent Vice or Defects

819. A common carrier is not liable for an injury to goods caused by an inherent defect or vice in the goods themselves. Thus, where a bullock was consigned with a railway company and it escaped by its own exertions and not due to any negligence was killed, the railway company was held not liable.[855]

8. Carriage by Road Act, 2007

820.

(1) The Carriers Act, 1865 was enacted on 14 February 1865 with a view to regulate the carriage by goods in any form of transport. The main purpose of the Carriers Act, 1865 was to define and limit the liability of the common carriers for loss or damage to consignments entrusted to them owing to their own negligence or fault. The Act envisaged liability of INR 100 only on account of carrier in case of loss of or damage to the goods during transportation owing to his negligence or act of negligence.

(2) Most of the provisions of the Carriers Act, 1865 had become obsolete as the transport trade had undergone a sea change over the last 142 years. A class of middlemen of booking agents/brokers has emerged who play a vital role in the road transportation and trade. They were not covered under the Carriers Act, 1865 since they did not exist at that time. Moreover the other modes of transport such as railways, civil aviation and shipping sector have developed their own sector-wise carriage Act to take care of the liability of the common carrier and other requirements to govern transportation of goods.

(3) The Carriage by Road Act, 2007 was notified on 1 October 2007 with a view to replace the old Act keeping in mind the changes and needs of modern day requirement of trade and transport by road. The Act came into effect from 1 March 2011. The important features of the Carriage by Road Act, 2007 are as under:

- Mandatory registration of common carriers i.e., persons involved in transportation business on roads including goods booking company, contractor, agent, broker, etc. the liability of the common carriers in case of loss or damage to the goods shall be prescribed under the rules. There is also scope for an agreement between the consignor and the common carrier for transport of the consignment on payment of a higher risk rate for higher liability.
- There will be single registration for a common carrier which will be valid for the entire country for a period of ten years initially. Details of branch offices to be reflected in the certificate of registration.
- Common carrier shall be liable for the offence of overloading and shall be penalized in terms of section 194 of the Motor Vehicle Act, 1988 at par with the drivers/owner of the motor vehicle.

855. *Blower v. Great Western Railway*, (1872) LR 7 CP 655.

(4) The Carriage by Road Rules were finalized by a Working Group under Joint Secretary (Transport), MORTH which was also represented by major transport associations such as AIMTC, AITWA, AICGOA.

(5) The Carriage by Road Rules, 2011 were notified on 28 February 2011. The Carriage by Road Rules, 2011 prescribes the following:

- The rules prescribe the form and manner of application/renewal of certificate of registration, eligibility criteria to be fulfilled by the applicant for grant of registration certificate, the form and the conditions for grant of registration certificate, the form and manner of maintaining a Register by the common carrier.
- The manner in which the return is to be filed by the common carrier to the Registering Authority and Transport Research Wing of the Ministry.
- The time period for revocation of certificate of registration due to failure on the part of the common carrier to address certain grievances of the consignor.
- Fee for various purposes.
- The form and manner of submitting Goods Forwarding Note by the consignee, the form and manner of issue of Goods Receipts by the common carrier, liability of the common carrier for loss of or damage to any consignment.

(6) Since Road Transport is a state subject, it is for state governments to make the provisions of Carriage by Road Act/Rule popular and effective through print and electronic media to enforce the provisions in letter and spirit. States/Union Territories were requested to implement the provisions of the Act/Rules and furnish data of agencies/individuals registered under the Act and to facilitate & encourage the common carriers for getting themselves registered.

B. Carriage by Air

1. General

821. The Indian Carriage by Air Act, 1972 applies to international carriage of goods and passengers. The Act replaced the original Act of 1934 (based on Warsaw Convention). This becomes necessary to incorporate the Hague Protocol which made certain changes in the interest of uniformity of rules.

Thus, 1972 Act contains rules of 1934 Act, as amended by the Hague Protocol. The Hague Protocol came into force in 1963. Further, Carriage by Air (Amendment) Act, 2009 revising the Carriage by Air Act, 1972 (the 'Act'), India has ratified the Montreal Convention securing higher levels of compensation and obviating discrimination for Indian passengers.

2. International Carriage by Air

822. An international convention for the unification of the law relating to international carriage was held at Warsaw in 1929 wherein a number of countries, including India, participated. The convention adopted certain rules defining the liability of the carrier for injury or death of passengers or loss of or damage to goods. The rules are binding upon the countries which ratified the convention and for India, the rules were found to be suitable and the Act of 1934 was passed adopting the convention to India. The act has now been replaced by the act of 1972. Section 3 of the act declares that the rules of the convention as stated in the First Schedule of the act shall have the force of law in India in respect of all international carriage by air, irrespective of the nationality of the aircraft performing the carriage. Section 5 of the act, however, lays down that any law in force including the Fatal Accidents Act, shall not apply. Only convention shall apply. According to section 5(1), in the event of death of a passenger, the liability of the carrier shall be determined in accordance with the provisions of the First and Second Schedules. The liability is enforceable for the benefit of the members of the passenger's family to the extent that damage has been sustained as a result of this death. Only one action can be brought in India in respect of a passenger. An action brought by any one of the persons entitled shall be deemed to be for the benefit of all the persons who are domiciled in India or who, not being domiciled, express a desire to take the benefit of the action. The amount recovered, after deducting the expenses, shall be divided among the persons entitled to it in such proportion as the court may direct. The court before whom an action is brought is entitled, at any stage of the proceeding, to make any order which may be just and equitable in keeping with the limits of liability in the First and Second Schedules and in respect of any proceeding that may be brought outside India concerning the same passenger. Where the service is being operated by a foreign national, and though there is no provision for sovereign immunity under the act, it has been held by the Delhi High Court that the provisions of section 86, of the Civil Procedure Code, 1908 would apply and permission of the central government would be necessary.[856]

3. Meaning of International Carriage (Schedule 1(1))

823. The rules apply to all international carriages of persons, luggage or goods performed by aircraft for reward. They also apply to such carriage when performed gratuitously by an air transport undertaking. The rules also bind the 'High Contracting Parties', meaning countries that are party to the convention. An 'international carriage' means any carriage in which the place of departure and place of destination fall in two different countries who have adopted the convention. Where the two places are in the same country, but there is a stop en route in another country, that will also be an international carriage even if that country is not a high contracting party.[857] A carriage without a stopping place in a different country shall not be deemed to be an international carriage.[858] A carriage by several successive air carriers is an international carriage

856. *Deepak Wadhwa v. Aeroflot*, (1983) 24 DLT 1.

857. India and Pakistan, on partition between two different countries, became High Contracting Parties and flights between them were held international flights. *Parasram perumal v. Air India Ltd.*, (1956) 56 Bom LR 944.

858. *Holmes v. Bangladesh Biman Corp.*, (1989) 1 All ER 759 where the flight in which the plaintiff's husband died was purely internal, i.e., Bangladesh flight from Chittagong to Dhaka, and as such compensation according to local laws was allowed. The British laws were held to be not applicable.

even if one part or portion of the journey is to be performed within the territory of a single country. This rule will apply when the parties regard such carriage as a single operation.

4. Documents of Carriage (Chapter II, Schedule I, Part 1)

824. The carrier is required to deliver to the passenger a ticket containing the particulars stated in Part I, Rule 3. The particulars should contain (1) the place and date of issue; (2) the place of departure and of destination; (3) the agreed stopping places in cases of necessity, and that if he exercises that right, the alteration shall not have the effect of depriving the carriage of an international character; (4) the name and address of the carrier or carriers; (5) a statement that the carriage is subject to the rules relating to liability contained in this Schedule. The absence, irregularity or loss of the ticket has no effect, but if the carrier accepts a passenger without a ticket, he will not be entitled to avail himself of the provisions of the schedule which exclude or limit the liability.

5. Luggage Ticket (Schedule 1, Chapter II, Part 2, Rule 4)

825. Excepting the small personal objects which a passenger may keep with himself, a ticket must be issued for every object of his luggage. The luggage ticket has to contain the following particulars: (1) the place and date of issue; (2) the place of departure and of destination; (3) the name and address of the carrier or carriers; (4) the number of the passenger ticket; (5) a statement that the delivery of the luggage will be made to the bearer of the luggage ticket; (6) the number and weight of the packages; (7) the amount of the value declared in accordance with Rule 22(2); (8) a statement that the carriage is subject to the rules relating to liability contained in the schedule. The rule relating to the absence, irregularity or loss of ticket is same as in passenger ticket. These particulars constitute prima facie evidence of the conclusion of the contract and the receipt of the goods, the conditions of the carriage and of all the particulars about the goods as stated above. The carrier can also require the consignor to prepare an air consignment note in accordance with the provisions. If no such note is prepared or the note prepared does not state all the requisite particulars, the carrier will not be entitled to the advantages of the limitation of the liability as stated in the rules.[859] If the consignor supplies incorrect particulars, he will be responsible for the consequences.

6. Air Consignment Note (Schedule 1, Chapter II, Part 3, Rules 5–16)

826. The carriers has been given the right to require the consignor to make out a document called the Air Consignment Note (ACN), and the consignor also has right to ask the carrier to accept it. this will constitute the contract and existence of this contract shall not be affected by the absence, irregularity or loss of CAN. But, if no such note is prepared or the note is incomplete, the carrier will not be entitled to the advantages of the limitation of liability as stated in the rules. The consignee, on arrival

859. *Birdhi Chand v. Assam Travels*, AIR 1954 Cal 170.

of the goods at the appointed destination, is entitled to require the carrier to hand over to him the air consignment note and to deliver the goods to him. The carrier is obliged to do so upon payment of the charges due and in compliance with the conditions of carriage set out in the air consignments note. In case there is loss of goods or if the goods have not arrived at the expiration of seven days after the date on which they ought to have arrived, the consignee or the consignor is entitled to enforce his rights against the carrier.[860] In case the carrier suffers any damage due to any irregularity in the documents the consignor will be liable.

7. Liability of the Carrier (Rule 17, Chapter III, Schedule 1)

827. The liability of the carrier has been detailed under Rules 17–30 in the Third Chapter.

a. Passengers

828. The liability of the carrier arises in the case that death or injury is caused by an accident which takes place on board the aircraft or in the course of any of the embarking and disembarking operations. The question is raised whether or not bodily injury includes mental injury. The general view of the different courts of the United States and the United Kingdom have been against liability, because the adjective 'bodily injury' in Article 17 of the Convention was not intended to cover everything that might possibly be described as an injury to the passenger sustained on board the aircraft or in the course of embarking or disembarking.[861]

8. General Character and Purpose of Hague Rules

829. The general character and purpose of the Hague Rules, which were authorized to be applied to non-international carriage by air were described in *Holmes v. Bangladesh Viman Corp.*[862] They impose liability on the carrier without proof of fault in respect of the death of or injury to passengers, baggage or cargo. They impose limits on the amount recoverable in respect of death, injury, damage, loss or delay. They nullify contractual provisions tending to relieve the carrier of liability or to lower the limits of liability. Actions for damages to enforce the rights given by the rules can only be brought subject to the rules, and they exclude other remedies. The aim has been to achieve certainty and the uniform international code which could be applied by the courts on all the high contracting parties and to exclude domestic law.

9. Baggage Check

830. Some change has been made in respect of baggage. Part II of Chapter II, Rule 4 provides that in respect of the carriage of registered baggage, a baggage check

860. *Agarwalla Air Transport v. Md. Nasarutulla*, AIR 1959 Cal 755.
861. *Rosman v. Trans World Airlines Inc.* (1974) 34 NY 2d 385 at 399; *King v. Bristow Helicopters Ltd.*, (2002) 2 All ER 565 (HL).
862. 1989 AC 1112.

shall be delivered, containing the particulars prescribed. The check shall constitute prima facie evidence of registration of the baggage and of the conditions of the contract of carriage. If the check is not delivered the carrier cannot avail himself of the beneficial provisions of the Schedule.[863]

10. Position of Different Carriers

831. In *Anil & Co. v. Air India*,[864] the carrier was held liable when its agent delivers the goods directly to the consignee instead, as directed, to the bank for collecting payment of the goods. The plaintiff booked certain goods with Air India for carriage to a New York buyer. A New York bank was named as consignee in the airway bill. Air India carried the goods up to Paris and there entrusted them to the Trans World Airlines for carriage to New York. The latter wrongly delivered the goods to the buyer without obtaining payment. Air India accordingly became liable for the loss, because under section 30 of the Carriage by Air Act, 1972 the liability of different carriers with regard to the goods consigned remains joint and several. The present suit is by the consignor and, therefore, the right of action against the first carrier which has been Air India clearly exists. Its agent, the successive carrier, was under the duty to inform the bank so that it may collect payment and deliver the documents to the consignee. This was not done. Instead the goods were delivered without formalities, which is a fraud. The principal is liable for the misconduct of his sub-agent.

11. Liability (Chapter III)

832. The central government by its notification dated 5 July 1980 has laid down that in the event of death of a passenger or any bodily injury or wound suffered by a passenger which results in a permanent disablement, incapacitating him from engaging in or being occupied with his usual duties or business or occupation, the liability of the carrier for each passenger shall be INR 200,000 if the passenger is above 12 years of age and INR 100,000 in case he is below 12 years of age on the date of the accident. In the event of wounding of a passenger or any bodily injury suffered by the passenger which results in a temporary disablement preventing an injured passenger from attending to his usual duties or occupation, the liability of the carrier for each passenger shall be limited to a sum calculated at the rate of INR 200 per day, the period during which he continues to be so disabled or a sum of INR 40,000 whichever is less.

833. In the carriage of registered baggage and of cargo, the liability is limited to 250 francs per kilogram, unless the contract envisages, on payment of extra charges a higher limit. In such a case the carrier will be liable to pay the declared value unless the carrier proves that the declared value is more than the real value. As regards the objects of which the passenger takes charge himself, the liability is limited to FRF

863. *Patricia D'Furlong v. MD, East West Airlines* (2004) 2 CPR 60 (Hyd), action for non-delivery of checked baggage, no complaint was made immediately on termination of journey, nor the complainant filed the baggage taken to show non-delivery of the baggage, complaint was not entertained because requirements of Regulation were not complied with.

864. AIR 1986 Del 312; *see also Rajasthan Handicrafts Emporium v. P.A. World Airways*, AIR 1984 Del 396.

5,000 per passenger. The right to damages stands cease if an action is not brought within two years, reckoned from the date of arrival at the destination or from the date on which the aircraft ought to have arrived, or from the date on which the carriage stopped. The method for calculating the period of limitation shall be determined by the law of the court seized of the case. The Calcutta High Court has pointed out that the effect of this provision is that no plaintiff can be rejected merely by looking at the two year period. In *British Airways v. Art Works Export Ltd.*,[865] though the party had filed the case after two years, British Airways alleged acknowledgement. The court has to see whether the acknowledgement was there for the purposes of the Limitation Act, 1963. It was thus wrong to have rejected the claim merely by looking at two years.

12. Internal Carriage by Air

834. The Carriage by Air Act, 1972 applies to international carriage of goods and passengers by air. There is no act in force relating to home carriage by air. But section 8 of the Act empowers the central government to extend the provisions of the act to carriage by air in India which is not international carriage. Such notification was issued on 17 December 1963 and, therefore, the provisions of the Indian Carriage by Air Act, 1934 became applicable to internal air carriage also. Even under the Act of 1972, the government was empowered to issue such notification which was issued on 30 March 1973. The whole act has thus become applicable.

C. Carriage by Rail

1. The Railways Act, 1989

835. The Railways Act, 1989 deals with carriage by rail. Chapter IX of the said Act deals with the carriage of goods by rail. Section 61 of the act provides that every railway administration shall maintain, at each station and at such other places where goods are received for carriage, the rate books or other documents which shall contain the rate authorized for the carriage of goods. Under section 62, however, conditions in respect of receiving, forwarding, carrying or delivering of any goods can be imposed and a copy of such conditions shall be made available without fee to anyone who needs them. Under section 63, where the owner's risk rates are not in force, goods offered for carriage shall be at the railway risk rate. Where the owner's risk rates and railways risk rates are both in force, there the consignor can exercise his choice for one or the other. If he exercises no choice, his goods would be carried at his risk.

2. Power to Demand Description of Goods

836. For the purposes of calculating the applicable rate for a particular carriage, the consignor, consignee or the endorsee may be called upon to furnish a statement in writing under his signature containing a description of the goods. If he refuses or neglects to do so and refuses to open any package, if so required, the administration has the right to refuse acceptance of such goods unless the person concerned pays for

865. AIR 1986 Cal 120.

such carriage at the highest rate for any class of goods. If a false statement is delivered, double the amount for any class of goods may be charged. In the case of any difference of opinion as to description, the goods may be detained for the purpose of examining them. If the examination shows that the goods are of a different class than the description given, the cost of such detention and examination would have to be borne by the party giving the statement and the railway administration is not to be held liable for any loss, damage or deterioration which may be caused by such detention or examination.

3. Dangerous or Offensive Goods

837. Where the goods belong to any category of dangerous or offensive goods as may be proscribed under the act, every person is charged with the duty of not carrying with him, or requiring the administration to carry such goods unless the procedure prescribed by section 67 is complied with. A person carrying dangerous or offensive goods with him is under an obligation to give a notice in writing to an authorized person of the nature of the goods. Similarly, a person handing over goods to the railway for carriage has to mark on the package that the goods are of a dangerous or offensive nature and also to give a similar notice in writing. If any railway may have reason to believe that the goods contained in a package are of a dangerous or offensive nature but notice of that fact has not been given, he may cause such package to be opened for the purpose of ascertaining their contents. Such goods may be stopped in or removed from transit if notice of their dangerous character was not given. The requirements of this section, however, are not to be construed to derogate from the provisions of the Indian Explosives Act, 1884 or rules or orders made thereunder or goods carried by soldiers, etc. under the government orders. Similarly, under section 68, a railway administration shall not be bound to carry any animal suffering from such infectious or contagious disease as may be proscribed.

4. Delivery of Goods Against Railway Receipt or Otherwise

838. Under section 76, the railway administration is under a duty to deliver the consignment upon the surrender of the relevant railway receipt. Where, however, the railway receipt is not forthcoming and the person who is claiming the goods is able to convince the railway administration that he is entitled to the goods, the goods may be delivered to him in the prescribed manner, i.e., under Rule 3(1) of the Railway (Manner of Delivery of Consignments and Sale Procedure). In the Absence of the Railway Receipt Rules, 1990 and where the railway receipt is not forthcoming, the consignment should be delivered to the person who delivers an indemnity note in the prescribed form. In the case that the railway receipt is not forthcoming, and the goods are claimed by two or more persons, such goods may be delivered or the sale price paid on the execution of the indemnity note as specified in Form I, and required under Rule 4 of the said Rules. As regards perishable goods, the delivery may be given on the production of the railway receipt, but in the case that the railway receipt is not forthcoming, delivery of the goods can be made on the execution of the indemnity bond specified in Form I. In the case that the invoice is not available and the consignment is booked to 'self', such person shall deposit an amount equivalent to the cost of consignment along with the freight and other charges by way of security and take the delivery. The deposited amount shall be refunded on the production of the original receipt within six months. In the absence of the original receipt, a refund may be made on the execution of the indemnity note in Form I or I-A, and I-B as the case may be.

5. Manner of Giving Open Delivery

839. Where any consignment arrives at the destination in a damaged condition or shows signs of having been tampered with, the consignee may make a request for open delivery of such a consignment under Rule 3 of the Manner of Giving Open Delivery and Prescription of Partial Delivery Certificate Form Rules, 1990 framed by the central government under section 87(2)(h)(i) of the Railways Act, 1989. This is subject to the condition under Rule 4 of the said rules, that the extent of the damage shall be assessed by the railway servant granting such open delivery on the basis of visual examination and such other chemical or physical tests as he may deem necessary. Rule 6 of the said rules requires the consignee or the endorsee to produce the original trade invoice or other documents so as to prove the contents and value of the consignment so as to enable the railway servant granting open delivery to compute the shortage or damage. Under Rule 9, where partial delivery is given the railway administration shall furnish to the consignee or endorsee a partial delivery certificate as specified in Schedule II.

6. Railways' General Lien

840. A general lien has been granted to the railways under section 83 of the Act to hold the goods if the charges of freights, etc. are due. Where delivery of the goods was withheld on the ground that reweighment en route showed that the goods were underweighed, it was held that the retention was not proper because the reweighment was not shown to have been done in accordance with applicable rules. The Railways were directed to deliver the consignment and if it had been sold, to refund the sale proceeds to the owner.[866] A consignment held, may be sold at once if it is of a perishable nature. In other cases, it has to be sold through a public auction. The sale should be of any such part of consignment as should be sufficient to realize the sum due. Where a public auction cannot be conveniently organized, the goods may be sold in accordance with the prescribed rules. If a public auction is to be held, the fact of it should be announced through one or more local newspapers. If there are no such newspapers, announcement should be made in accordance with prescribed rules. The railways should retain out of the sale proceeds the amount due including the expenses of organizing the sale and handover the rest of the sale proceeds and the rest of the goods to the person entitled to them. These rules are available under section 84 of the act. An unclaimed consignment includes goods of which delivery has not been claimed by any person or a consignment which has been released from lien or which is the remaining part of the goods after sale of the other part for releasing charges.

866. *Jyoti Enterprises v. Union of India*, (2003) 2 CLT 32 (Jhar).

7. General Responsibility

841. The general principle of liability laid down in section 93 of the act is that the railway is liable for any loss, destruction, damage and deterioration in transit or non-delivery of the goods arising from any cause whatsoever. This is subject to certain exceptions, e.g., act of God, act of war, act of public enemies, orders for restrictions imposed by the central or state governments, fire, explosion or any unforeseen risk, etc. The railways have been equated with common carriers for the purposes of liability. Even in such cases they will be liable unless they can prove that they used reasonable foresight and care in the carriage of the animals or goods.[867] Where a consignment of liquid caustic soda was lost in a train accident occurring because of a defective wagon, and the administration was not able to show when the train was last checked or what caution or foresight was exercised to prevent the happening, they were held liable. Their burden of proving that the accident occurred not on account of their negligence, but on account of some unforeseen risk was not effectively discharged.[868] When a railway receipt shows the contents of the goods, the railways will not be allowed to say afterwards that the receipt was issued recklessly. They will be accountable for the acknowledged contents and weight unless they can show that there was fraud in connivance with the consignor.[869] In *Union of India v. Gajanand Oil and Dal Mill*,[870] a consignment of pulses, after having been accepted but before being loaded into wagons was seized by the police for alleged contravention of Maharashtra Pulses Procurement (Levy) Order, 1973. The Railways did not inform the party of this fact. He was waiting unaware of the arrival of the goods. It was held that the railways could not escape responsibility for non-delivery.

8. Right to Sue

842. A right to sue, ordinarily lies with the consignor.[871] But where the consignee has acquired interest in the consignment, he too gets the right to sue. A Railway receipt is a document of title. It is transferable as such. The bona fide transferee for valuable consideration gets all the rights enshrined in the railway receipt. Under section 2(4) of the Sale of Goods Act, 1930, a railway receipt is a 'document of title of goods'. It is a document useful for proving title, but it is not a negotiable instrument. Unless there is a proof that title has passed to the endorsee according to the terms of the contract, the consignee cannot sue the railway for any loss. It is only the consignor who can sue.[872] When there is negligence and consequent loss of the consigned goods, the railway as bailee is liable to account for the loss to the bailor, the consignor or his representative. The title is with the consignor even when the railway receipt is in the consignee's name unless it is endorsed to him by the consignor whereby no title can

867. *See Punjab National Bank v. Beniprasad Maheshwari*, AIR 1981 MP 95.
868. *Gwalior Rayon Silk Mfg (Weaving) Co. Ltd. v. Union of India*, 1985 ACJ 739.
869. *Mohn Lal v. Union of India*, AIR 1985 Del 209.
870. [1984] 1 ALT 284.
871. *Traders Syndicate v. Union of India*, AIR 1983 Cal 337; *see also Lalchand Madhav Das v. Union of India*, AIR 1986 Del 29.
872. *Ibrahim Ispahan v. Union of India*, AIR 1966 Guj 6.

pass in the goods to him.[873] A pledgee of a railway receipt, however, receives a special interest in the goods. He can enforce delivery of the goods against the railway receipts. This right was recognized by the Supreme Court of India in *Morvi Mercantile Bank v. Union of India*.[874] In this case certain goods were consigned with the railway to 'self' from Bombay for transit to Okhla. The consignor endorsed the railway receipt to the appellant bank against an advance of INR 20,000. As the goods were lost in transit, the bank as an endorsee of the railway receipts and pledgee of the goods sued the railway for the loss. The goods were valued at INR 35,000. The Bombay High Court allowed the recovery of up to INR 20,000 only. On cross appeals the Supreme Court held that the delivery of the railway receipts was the same thing as delivery of the goods; the pledge was, therefore, valid and the pledgee was entitled to sue for the loss. It was further held that the pledgee was entitled to recover the full value of the goods lost and not merely the amount of his advance. Similarly, a commission agent who had paid an amount in advance to secure for himself the selling rights for a consignment of fruits was allowed to sue for the loss caused by damage to the fresh fruits.[875] In the *Union of India v. B. Prahlad & Co.*,[876] the Delhi High court considered the effect of the decision of the Supreme Court in *Union of India v. West Punjab Factories*,[877] as well as several other cases and held that a consignee can if he is a commission agent institute a suit for compensation against the railways if he is able to show that the goods represented by the railway receipt had been transferred to him on sufficient interest therein and created in his favour. An insurer who has paid off the sender is subrogated to the sender's right and, therefore, gets the right to sue.[878]

9. Discharge of the Liability of the Railway

843. A new provision has been added to the Railway Act, 1989, that discharges the railway from any further complication as to the liability if payment is made to the consignee or endorsee who produces the railway receipt. The railway, under section 108 of the act, is discharged from all liability if compensation is paid to the consignee or endorsee who produces the railway receipt. The effect of this statutory discharge is that no application can be made either to the Claims Tribunal or in any other court by way of legal proceeding on the ground that the consignee or the endorsee was not legally entitled to receive such compensation. Subsection (2), however, makes it clear that this discharge of the railway would not affect the rights of any person having any interest in the goods to enforce the same against the consignee or endorsee who has collected the compensation money.

---

873. *Gurden Krishna Reddy v. Union of India*, AIR 1965 AP 263.
874. AIR 1965 SC 1954.
875. *Bhai Mehar Singh Kishan Singh v. Union of India*, 1980 ACJ 110 Del.
876. AIR 1976 Del 236.
877. AIR 1966 SC 395.
878. *Union of India v. Orissa Textiles Mills Ltd.*, AIR 1979 Ori 165, the insurance company filed the case jointly with the sender. *See also Union of India v. Deoria Sugar Mills*, 1980 ACJ 140, where the railway was held liable to pay the full amount including that part of the damage which had been paid by the insurer.

10. Goods Carried at Owner's Risk

844. Section 97 of the act deals with the responsibility of the railways where the goods are consigned at the owner's risk. All goods or animals are presumed to be consigned at the consignors' risk unless the consignor agrees to pay in writing the railway risk rate in which case he will be given a certificate to that effect. Where the goods are consigned at the owner's risk, the railway company is liable only if the loss 'was due to the negligence or misconduct on the part of the railway administration or any of its servants'. In such cases the consignor has to prove negligence.[879] But as the goods are in the hands of the carrier and only he knows how the goods were dealt with within its course, the railways will have to show this, failing which negligence may be presumed. In *Suraj Nath v. Union of India*,[880] silver bars were consigned at Howrah railway station through the passenger carriage to Ballia in U.P. The consignment was wholly at the owners' risk. The goods were never delivered to the consignee. It was held that 'under the law, in case of non-delivery of the consignment the railway administration is bound to make a disclosure showing how the goods or consignment was dealt with at different stages as the same is within the special knowledge of the railway administration'. In case of failure to make such a disclosure an adverse inference can be made against them under section 114(4) of the Indian Evidence Act, 1872.

11. Carriage of Animals

845. Section 101 of the act lays down that the railway shall not be responsible for any loss or destruction of, or injuries to, any animal carried by the railway arising from fright or restiveness of the animal or from the overloading of wagons by the consignor. The amount of liability in respect of different animals is stated in the First Schedule, and that is, of course, the maximum limit of the liability.

12. Carriage of Luggage

846. Section 100 of the act lays down that the railway shall not be responsible for the loss, destruction, damage, deterioration or non-delivery of any luggage unless a railway servant has booked the luggage and given a receipt thereof and in the case of luggage which is carried by the passenger in his charge, unless it is also proved that the loss, destruction, damage or deterioration was due to the negligence or misconduct on its part or on the part of any of its servants.

847. Section 104 of the act provides that where the goods are likely to be damaged if carried in open vehicles, but even if the sender requests in the forwarding note that they may be carried in open wagons, the railway will not be liable for any loss, etc. which may arise only by reason of the goods being so carried.

879. *Union of India v. Universal Traders Corn*, AIR 183 Ker 173.
880. AIR 1972 Cal 203.

13. Responsibility for Delay or Detention

848. Under section 95, the railway is not liable for any loss or damage arising out of delay or detention; unless it is proved that the delay or detention arose without negligence or misconduct. Apparently, the railway is liable for losses arising out of delay or detention and if it wants to escape liability, the burden lies upon it to prove that there was no negligence or misconduct on its part. However, the plaintiff will at least have to prove that the loss in question was caused by the delay or detention.

14. Liability for Deviation

849. Normally under the ordinary principles of the law of carriage, if the carrier deviates from the agreed route or from the customary or usual route, he will be absolutely liable for any loss or destruction of the goods. This rule is also applicable to railways.[881] However, sometimes, a deviation may be quite justified, e.g., if an accident blocked a railway line, the traffic may have to be diverted to other lines. In order, therefore, to protect the railways from the consequences of such justified deviations, section 69 was enacted. This section states that where due to a cause beyond the control of the railway or due to congestion in the yard or other operational reasons, goods are carried over a route other than the route by which such goods are booked, that will not amount to a of breach of contract. The railway, thus, would not be absolutely liable, but would be liable only if the liability would have arisen otherwise, that is, if no diversion had taken place.[882]

15. Termination of Responsibility

850. According to section 96 of the act, the responsibility of the railway as a carrier is terminated with the termination of the transit at the destination and the termination of the free days allowed for clearing away the goods without payment of demurrage. While the liability as carrier terminates with the termination of the transit, the liability as bailee begins and continues up to seven days thereafter. During these seven days the railways will remain liable as bailee under sections 151, 152 and 161 of the Contract Act, 1972. They will be bound to take as much care of the goods as a reasonable person would have taken of his own goods of the same bulk and value and under similar circumstances. They will be liable if the care bestowed by them falls below this standard and they will also be liable for the consequences of their failure to deliver the goods to the owner.

VI. Carriage of Passengers by Railway

851. Chapter XIII of the Railways Act, 1989 deals with the death and injury of passengers due to accidents. Section 123 gives a list of persons who come under the category of dependants for the purpose of claiming compensation for the death of the

881. *Union of India v. Endupadi Narasimhan & Sons*, AIR 1964 Ori 34.
882. *Lakshmi Chand Textiles v. Union of India*, AIR 2005 Del 2.

passenger. Section 124 of the act provides the extent of liability, i.e., in the course of working a railway, an accident occurs, being either a collision between trains of which one is a train carrying passengers or the derailment or other accident to a train or any part of a train carrying passengers, then whether or not there has been any wrongful act, neglect or default on the part of the railway, such that would entitle a passenger who has been injured or suffered a loss to maintain an action and recover damages in respect thereof, the railway administration shall, notwithstanding anything contained in any other law, be liable to pay compensation to such extent as may be prescribed and to that extent only for the loss occasioned by the death of a passenger dying, and for any personal injury and loss, destruction, damage or deterioration of goods owned by the passenger and accompanying him in his compartment or on the train. In *Union of India v. Mulko Bai*,[883] the claimant was found to be a bona fide passenger. The train started all of a sudden without giving any whistle or signal. It resulted in a stampede. The claimant was sitting near the door. She became the victim of pushing and fell down and suffered injuries and this was wholly due to the non-observance of duties. Compensation was awarded to him. Similarly, in *Ulhanan Rajan v. Union of India*,[884] the deceased was getting down from the compartment with her child in her hand. The compartment stopped short of the platform. No warning or signal was given before the train started. The level of the platform was also not raised after converting the rail to broad gauge. It was held that the accident was due to negligence on the part of the railway servants. However, section 154 of the act provides that if any person in a rash and negligent manner does any act, or omits to do what he is legally bound to do and the act or omission is likely to endanger the safety of any person travelling or being on any railway, he shall be punishable with imprisonment for a term which may extend to one year, or with a fine, or with both. Furthermore, under section 159 of the act, if any driver or conductor of any vehicle while on the premises of a railway disobeys the reasonable directions of any railway servant or police officer, he shall be punishable with imprisonment for a term which may extend to one month. Section 175 provides that if any railway servant, while on duty, endangers the safety of any person: (1) by disobeying any rule made under this act; or (2) disobeying any instruction, direction or order under this act or rules made thereunder; or (3) by any rash or negligent act or omission, he shall be punishable with imprisonment for a term which may extend to two years or with a fine which may extend to INR 1,000 or with both.

VII. Carriage by Sea

A. General

852. Carriage of goods by sea is regulated by the Carriage of Goods by Sea Act, 1925. This act applies only in respect of the contract of carriage of goods by sea which are in the form of a bill of lading or any other similar document of title. The Carriage of goods by sea is carried out on the basis of a contract of carriage between the consignor and the carrier. This contract of carriage of goods by sea is called the ‘contract of

883. AIR 2000 MP 22.
884. AIR 1992 Ker 230.

affreightment'. Ordinarily, a carrier by sea is a common carrier, liable absolutely, like all others, for the loss of the goods subject only to a few exceptions, but carriage by sea, being a hazardous job, the carrier usually makes a special contract and, in order to emphasize this special nature of the contract, it is not called the contract of carriage, but rather the contract of affreightment. This contract is of two types, viz., (a) charter-party, i.e., where the ship itself is hired; or (b) bill of lading, i.e., where the goods are delivered to the shipowner for carriage and he issues a bill of lading as a document of title for the goods. In every such contract, there is a certain implied undertaking on the part of the carrier.

B. Seaworthiness, Competent Crew and Requisite Equipment

853. The first and foremost importance of such undertakings is that the ship shall be seaworthy, i.e., the ship should be fit for the journey and also fully equipped for the type of cargo that it contracts to carry. Where a voyage has to run through several stages, it should also be seaworthy at the commencement of each stage. However, a shipowner can rely upon an exclusion clause where the damage in question has not been caused or contributed by un-seaworthiness, but only the excepted peril operating independently. For example, a charter-party excluded liability for collision. The ship arrived with its cargo of bags of sugar safely at the port of discharge, but there she struck the dock wall. The water closet pipes were broken. Water entered inside the decks and damaged the sugar bags stored therein. Water could not have entered further down into the hold but the fact is that some holes there were imperfectly plugged. This defect existed even at the commencement of the voyage and to that extent the ship was un-seaworthy. The shipowner was held liable only for the damage caused by the un-seaworthiness, and for the damage caused by the collision, the exception clause protected him from liability.[885] It also includes cargo worthiness, i.e., in the case that a shipowner contracts to carry animals on the condition that he would not be liable for the death or injury by disease. He did not disinfect the ship after a previous voyage and consequently the cattle were infected with moth and foot disease. He was held liable.[886] Similarly, it is necessary that the ship should be fitted with requisite equipment and a competent crew.

C. Reasonable Dispatch and No Deviation

854. In all contracts for a charter-party, where there is no express agreement as to time, it is an implied condition that there shall be no unreasonable delay in commencing the voyage. It must commence within a reasonable time. It is an important implied warranty that the ship should follow the agreed or customary route. Any departure from such route is called a deviation and this may operate as a breach of the contract making the shipowner absolutely liable like a common carrier and disentitling him from relying on the exception clause, if any. Unjustifiable deviation displaces the bill of lading contract and with it any exceptions included therein; accordingly shipowners are liable for damage which happens after deviation though not caused by it. However,

885. *'Europa', The*, (1904–7) All ER Rep 387.
886. *Fattersal v. National S.S. Co.*, (1884) 12 QBD 297.

this deviation is permitted to save life, but of course, not to save property. In England, in the case that a contract for affreightment is in the form of a bill of lading, then the Carriage of Goods by Sea Act will apply. Article IV (Rule 4) of the said act provides that any deviation in saving or attempting to save life or property at sea, or any reasonable deviation shall not be deemed to be an infringement or breach of these rules of the contract of carriage, and the carrier shall not be liable for any such loss or damage.

D. Not to Load Goods Liable to Cause Danger or Delay a Ship

855. There is an obligation on the part of the shipper not to load the ship with dangerous goods or goods likely to involve unusual danger or delay to the ship without communicating to the shipowner facts which are within his knowledge indicating that there is the risk, provided that the shipowner does not and could not reasonably know those facts. Thus where a shipper delivered casks of what he described as bleaching powder, but they in fact contained corrosive contents which, due to defective packing, escaped and caused damage, the shipper was held liable.[887]

E. Charter-Parties

856. Where a ship is booked to the exclusive use of one shipper either for a particular voyage or voyages or for a certain time, this is a charter-party. It is a contract by which an entire ship or some principal part thereof is let to a merchant, who is called the charter-party, for the conveyance of goods on a determined voyage to one or more place, or until the expiration of a specific period; in the former case it is called a 'voyage charter-party' and in the latter a 'charter-party'. In the latter case, the contract is really one of letting the ship, and subject to the express terms of the charter-party, the liabilities of the owner and the charter-party to one another are to be determined by the law which relates to the hiring of the chattel and not by reference to the liabilities of carriers and shipper. In case the contract was of the nature of a charter-party and the owners were only entitled to payment for the use and hire of the ship and the amount was payable irrespective of what was the ship was put to by the time-charter party, or indeed whether it was put to any use at all and no part of the payment can be said to have been made on account of the carriage of goods.[888] Charter-parties are of two kinds, viz., (1) voyage charter-party; and (2) time charter-party. A time charter-party is also known as a charter-party by demise because the ship is for the time being leased out to the charter-party. Whether it is one or the other depends upon the intention of the parties as shown by their contract. In this kind of charter, the charter-party becomes the owner for the time being not only of the ship but also of the crew and their negligence falls on him.[889] The charter-party becomes responsible for the consequences of the bills of lading signed by the master. In the case that a master signs bills of lading without proper care and consequently the owner will not be able to recover the general average contribution from the cargo-owners. Here the charter-party

887. *Bras v. Maitland*, 119 ER 940.

888. *Union of India v. Gosalia Shipping (P) Ltd.*, AIR 1978 SC 1196.

889. *Epoch Enterprises v. M.V. Won Fu*, AIR 2003 SC 24.

will be liable to the owner under an 'indemnity clause'. However, if it is an ordinary charter-party, the crew being the employees of the shipowner will be just as much liable for their negligence.

1. Payment for Hire

857. The timely payment of hire of the ship is an essential requirement of a charter-party. The shipowner gets the right to withdraw the ship if there is no punctual payment. Where the payment falls due on a holiday or Sunday, it should be made a day before. Payment on the next working day would be too late. The shipowner would be justified in withdrawing the ship. A charter-party, however, can contain an 'anti-technicality clause' requiring the shipowner to give at least a short notice before withdrawing the ship. Such notice must be given after the payment has become due.

2. Section 2 and Sea Carriage Rules

858. It is not clear whether the English Carriage of Goods by Sea Act, 1924 or the Indian Carriage of Goods by Sea Act, 1925 has been applied in India. The rules set out in the Schedule of the Indian Carriage of Goods by Sea Act are applicable only when the starting point or port of loading is a port in India. These rules have no application when the goods are not carried from any Indian post. In *British India Steam Navigation Co. Ltd. v. Shanmugavilas Cashew Industries*,[890] goods were shipped in Africa and carried to Cochin. This act obviously was not applicable. The dispute could not have been decided partly according to municipal law and partly according to English law. The English law was not proven in accordance with the legal requirement of proof. Accordingly, the case was remanded to the trial court for disposal according to the law after giving opportunity to the parties to amend their pleadings and adduce additional evidence.

3. Bill of Lading

859. The Carriage of Goods by Sea, 1925 applies only when the contract of affreightment is evidenced by a bill of lading. The definition in Article 1 of a 'contract of carriage', says that it applies only to contracts of carriage covered by a bill of lading or any similar document of title. The definition also includes any bill of lading or similar document issued under or pursuant to charter-party from the moment in which it regulates the relations between the shipowner and the holder of the bill of lading. A large number of contracts of carriage of goods by sea are made in the form of bill of lading. This is because of the fact that the sender is either a merchant or a manufacturer who wants to have the goods transported and is neither interested nor versed in the management of ships. Ships are usually hired or chartered by those carrying on the profession of carriers. The bill of lading, thus, is a typical document of title. It is one of the key instruments in international trade. The term bill of lading, no doubt, has not been defined in any of the acts of the Indian legislature, but it signifies a number of things.

---

890. (1990) 3 SCC 481; *see also Union of India v. Gosalia Shipping (P) Ltd.*, AIR 1978 SC 1196.

a. Prima Facie it is an Evidence of Receipt of Goods

860. The bill of lading is a prima facie evidence of the receipt by the carrier of the goods as therein described. The date appearing on the bill constitutes evidence of the date of shipment and it is the responsibility of the person preparing the bill and getting it signed to see that the correct date of shipment is entered. Thus, where loading was commenced on the 22nd of a month, and completed on the 27th but the bill showed the date of shipment as the 22nd and this resulted in overpayment because of the fall in prices between the two dates, responsibility fell on those who prepared and got the bill signed from the master.[891] The shipowner is liable for non-delivery or short delivery to the holder of the bill of lading, unless he can show that his agent signed the bill without the goods being put on the board. The whole burden of proof lies upon the shipowner. Thus, a bill of lading as an acknowledgement of the receipt of the goods is twofold, viz., As against the shipper, it is only a prima facie evidence, and as against the consignee or endorsee, the bill is a conclusive evidence, so that if such a person has suffered loss by reason of acting on the bill, he can hold the person signing the bill liable.[892]

b. Bill of Lading as Evidence of Contract of Affreightment

861. The bill of lading is not a contract of affreightment in itself, but it is the evidence of the contract. The terms of contract of carriage are no doubt to be found in the bill, but since the bill is only an evidence of the contract, and not the contract itself, there can be other terms also.

c. Bill of Lading as a Document of Title

862. A bill of lading is a document of title. It is a symbol of the goods, it represents the goods themselves. It is a symbol of the right to property in goods specified in the bill. Its possession is equivalent to the possession of the goods themselves, and its transfer being a symbolic delivery of the goods themselves has by mercantile usage the same effect as to actual delivery.[893] A bill of lading being regarded as a symbol of property or as a document of title is that when the bill is delivered to the buyer or the goods, for example, in cost, insurance and freight (c.i.f.), contract it is considered to be equivalent to the delivery of the goods and the buyer has to pay in the same way as if the goods themselves have been delivered to him.[894] As the bill of lading is not a negotiable instrument, it still has the characteristic of a negotiable instrument that property in the goods represented by the bill passes to the person to whom it is transferred. In the case of a negotiable instrument, a bona fide transferee is not affected by any defect in the title of his transferor, but in a bill of lading, goods pass subject to

891. *The Almak*, (1985) 1 Lloyd's Re 557.

892. *Malabar Steamship Co. v. Central Bank of India*, AIR 1939 Sind 225.

893. *Rudnap Export-Import v. Eastern Associates Co.*, AIR 1984 Del 30.

894. *British India Steam Navigation Co. Ltd. v. Shanmugavilas Cashew Industries*, (1990) 48 ELT 481 (SC); also *Kohinoor Carpet Manufacturers v. Forbes Gokak Ltd.* (2002) 4 Bom CR 295 (Bom).

all previous defects in title. This rule has been incorporated in section 1 of the Indian Bills of Lading Act, 1856. In *New India Assurance Co. Ltd. v. Sanjose Maritime Ltd.*,[895] a contract was for the carriage of 8,750 bags of Tanzanian raw cashew nuts from Dar-Es-Salaam to Cochin. It was found that 11,115 bags were torn and in mouth-burst condition and the shortage was that of 26,442 Kgs. The loss was due to the negligence of the carrier. The goods were imported by the Cashew Corporation of India and they had endorsed the bill of lading in blank to the claimant. The Kerala High Court held that the endorsee had the right to sue. The corporation allotted the goods to him and handed them under the bill of lading and under their blank endorsement. This had the effect of passing the property to him.

d. Bills of Lading in Sets

863. Sometimes bills of lading are made in sets of three or more. One or two of them are sent to the consignee and the rest are kept by the consignor himself so that he can protect his interest in case it becomes necessary. A difficulty was experienced in *Glyn, Mills & Co. v. East and West India Dock Co.* Goods were consigned to C. & Co. The shipmaster signed a set of three bills of lading marked ‘first’, ‘second’, and ‘third’, respectively, and stating that when one of the bills is used in obtaining delivery, the others would stand void. The first bill was pledged by C. & Co. with a bank and with the second they obtained delivery of the goods and sold them to diverse customers. The pledgee sued for his loss. It was held that the delivery was made bona fide and without knowledge or notice of the pledgee and hence the bank should sue the party who committed fraud on them and not the warehouse-keeper. Thus, a pledgee of documents of title should safeguard himself against such risks by insisting on obtaining the complete set of bills.[896]

895. AIR 1983 Ker 98.
896. (1882) 7 App. Cas 591.

Chapter 10. Commercial Securities

§1. General

864. A security indicates an interest based on an investment in a common enterprise rather than direct participation in the enterprise. A security is an interest or investment relating to finances, a note, stock, treasury stock, bond, debenture evidence of indebtedness, transferable share, investment contract, certificate of deposit for a security, guarantee of, or warrants or right to submit, purchase of any of these things, etc. A security, generally, is anything that makes the money more secured in its payment or more readily recoverable as distinguished from bank notes, letters of exchanges, promissory notes and cheques, etc. as securities.

§2. Creation of Securities

I. The Legal Mortgage

A. General

865. A mortgage corresponds to the hypotheca of Roman law. The creditor, on the failure of the debtor to pay the debt, could bring the debtor's property to sale in order to recoup his losses. Both Hindu law and Muslim law recognize this type of mortgage. Section 58A of the Transfer of Property Act, 1882 defines 'mortgage', 'mortgagor', 'mortgagee', 'mortgage-money' and 'mortgage-deed'.

866. Human beings have many needs, and borrowing money for satisfaction for these needs is perhaps as old as civilization itself. Moneylenders needing security for the recovery of the money given on loan originated to the birth hypothecation or mortgage of property. In the beginning. Property was kept as security for the repayment of loan and in case the loan was not repaid, it was forfeited. This was universal practice.

867. A mortgage is defined as the transfer of an interest in a specific immovable property for the purpose of securing the payment of money advanced or to be advanced by way of loan, an existing or future debt, or the performance of an engagement which may give rise to a pecuniary liability.[897] The transferor is called a mortgagor, the transferee a mortgagee, the principal money and interest of which payment is secured for the time being are called the mortgage-money, and the instrument (if any) by which the transfer is effected is called a mortgage-deed.

868. There are the following elements in the transfer of mortgage:

(1) parties to mortgage;

897. *Madan lal Sobti v. Rajasthan State Industrial Development and Investment Corporation*, AIR 2007 (NOC)638(Dwl).

(2) transfer of interest;
(3) in a specific immovable property;
(4) the purpose is to secure the repayment of money advanced or to be advanced or is for performance of an engagement that may give rise to a pecuniary liability.

1. Parties to Mortgage

869. There are two parties to the mortgage, viz., (a) mortgagor and (b) mortgagee.

a. Mortgagor

870. A person who transfers the property on whose security he wants loan is a mortgagor and the one in whose favour it is executed is a mortgagee. A mortgagor must be a competent person to contract and transfer the property. A minor cannot mortgage the property.[898] However a guardian of the minor can make a valid mortgage with the prior sanction of the court.[899] If a karta of a Hindu family makes a mortgage of the joint Hindu family without the consent of other coparcener, the mortgage is voidable at the option of the other coparceners, but if the mortgage is for legal necessity, it will be valid It is not necessary for the mortgagee to see the application of his money. He is to show to the court that he made reasonable enquiries and acted honestly.[900]

b. Mortgagee

871. Mortgagee is a person who can hold the property. It is not necessary that the person is a minor. Only it is enough that he should be capable of holding the property. Even a legal person can become a mortgagee. However, a court, not being a person is not competent to become a mortgagee.[901]

2. Transfer of Interest

872. Transfer of Interest is a necessary element for a mortgage. This interest is dependent upon the nature and type of mortgage. In a simple mortgage, there is a transferor transfers a right to sell the property. In a usufructuary mortgage, there is a transfer of possession and right to enjoyment of the property. In English mortgage, there is transfer of ownership but the mortgagor retains the right of redemption, i.e., the right to get the property back. Interest is a kind of ownership in the property to be mortgage. And ownership is a bundle of rights and when a mortgage is made, he parts with some of the rights in favour of the mortgagee. It may be ownership,[902] or a right to redeem, or a right to transfer the property, may remain with the owner, i.e., mortgagor. There may be some more kind of interests, viz., a right to obtain the timber export quota, a right to receive rents and profits for certain years. A right of redemption, etc.

898. *Sadiq Ali Khan v. Ji Kishore*, AIR 1928 PC 152.
899. *Sinaya v. Munisami*, (1899) ILR 22 Mad 289.
900. *Jugjeewandas v. Ramdas*, (1841) 2 Moo Indian Cases 487.
901. *Mehdi Ali v. Chunni Lal*, AIR 1929 All 834.
902. *State of Punjab v. Labb Singh*, (1985) 4 SCC 52.

According to the Transfer of Property Act, 1882, mortgage is only of immovable property. But in India, mortgage of movable property is also recognized, for example, mortgage of shares,[903] mortgage of stock and trade,[904] paddy boats,[905] floating logs of timber,[906] etc.

3. Specific Immovable Property

873. In a mortgage, the security must be of specific property, i.e., it must be sufficiently identified and description of the same should not be general or ambiguous in character. It should be clearly identifiable. The proper way is describing the same is by its name, if any, with full postal address. In case the property is a land, it should be described clearly and if need be, with reference to the neighbouring description of lands.

4. Purpose of Mortgage

874. A mortgage must have some purpose. Every mortgage, is a debt, but in some cases it may be for the repayment of the debt for that property is to be mortgaged. The primary purpose of the mortgage is to raise a loan and therefore, if there is no consideration, the mortgage is nullity.[907] However, it will not fail merely because the mortgagor did not advance the money.[908] Mortgage-money includes the interest accrued on it and the mortgage is entitled to treat the interest due under the mortgage as a charge on the estate. Unless there is a contract to the contrary.

875. Whether a transaction amounts to a mortgage or not would depend upon the substance of the document. The intention of the parties to be seen.[909] The substance is to be preferred to the form and the determining criterion is not merely the name by which the deed is called. An agreement for mortgage gives rise to only a personal obligation, but it cannot be specifically enforced unless the lender has advanced the money.

In Indian law, there are six different types of mortgages. They are: (a) simple mortgage; (b) mortgage by conditional sale; (c) usufructuary; (d) English mortgage; (e) mortgage by deposit of title deeds; and (f) anomalous mortgage.

a. Simple Mortgage

876. As per section 58(b) of the Transfer of Property Act, where, without delivering possession of the mortgaged property, the mortgagor binds himself personally to pay the mortgage-money, and agrees, expressly or impliedly, that, in the event of his failing to pay according to his contract, the mortgagee shall have a right to cause

903. *Cooperative Bank Ltd. v. Surendra*, AIR 1932 Cal 524.
904. *Backer Khorasain v. Ahmed Ismail*, AIR 1928 Rang 28.
905. *Ko Shway Anug v. StrangSteel co.* (1894) 21 Cal 241.
906. *Ko Kywetnee v. Ko Koung*, (1866) 5 WR 189.
907. *Bsanti Lal v. Phaphi*, AIR 2008 Raj 72.
908. *State of Kerala v. Cochin Chemical Refineries*, 1968 SC 1361.
909. *Kameshwar Singh v. Kaichow Singh*, AIR 1973 Gau 43.

the mortgaged property to be sold and the proceeds of sale to be applied, so far as may be necessary, in payment of the mortgage-money, the transaction is called a simple mortgage and a mortgagee a simple mortgagee.[910] In a simple mortgage, the security for the debt is: (a) personal obligation; and (b) property. Thus, in a simple mortgage, the mortgagor personally binds himself and also at the same time keeps his property as a security for the repayment of loan. In the event of non-payment, the mortgagee can file a suit for recovery against the mortgagor personally and obtain decree against him. He can also move against the property and file a suit for foreclosure and cause the property to be sold and realize the money from the sale of the property. Further, in a simple mortgage, the mortgagor retains the possession of the property. There is no need to deliver the property to the mortgagee.

877. In case money is to be realized from the income of a specific item of property, without any right to have the property sold, it is only a charge. But if the creditor, i.e., mortgagee has the right to have the property sold from the moment the debt is incurred, then it is a mortgage.

b. Mortgage by Conditional Sale

878. According to section 58(c) of the Transfer of Property Act, 1882, the mortgagor ostensibly sells the mortgage property: (a) on condition that on default of payment of the mortgage-money that on a certain date the sale shall become absolute; or (b) on condition that on such payment being made the buyer shall transfer the property to the seller, the transaction is called a mortgagee by conditional sale and the mortgagee a mortgagee by conditional sale, provided that no such transaction shall be deemed to be a mortgage, unless the condition is embodied in the document with effects or purports to effect the sale.

879. A mortgage by conditional sale is an ostensible sale which ripens only on the breach of condition as to payment into an absolute sale. The mortgagor here has no personal liability. Ostensible sale means a sale which apparently looks like a sale but in reality it is not a sale but a security for debt. If there is no relationship of debtor and creditor the question of it being a mortgage by conditional sale does not arise.[911] The mortgage-deed must have been executed containing these conditions as are given in the section. In the case of *Sk. Md. Illiyas v. Narayan Sah*,[912] the condition of repurchase was embodied in the same document. The mortgage value was much less than the actual price. Only possession was handed over and not right or title to the land under deeds. The court said that all these circumstances showed that the transaction was a mortgage by conditional sale and not out sale with right of repurchase. It is mandatory that the condition must be embodied in the document which effects or purports to effect the sale.[913]

910. *Prakash v. Mukhtar*, AIR 1940 Lah 486.
911. *Rama Devi v. Dilip Singh*, AIR 2008 SC 2015.
912. AIR 2009 Pat. 17. *See also Shanti Devi v. Nand Lal*, AIR 2005 Raj 218.
913. *Raj Kishore v. Prem Singh*, IR 2011 SC 382; *see also Simrathmjull v. Nanja Lingiah*, AIR 1963 SC 1182.

c. Usufructuary Mortgage

880. In this kind of mortgage, the mortgagor delivers possession whether expressly or by implication and binds himself to deliver possession of the mortgaged property to the mortgagee, and authorizes him to retain such possession until payment of the mortgage-money, and to receive any amount accruing from the profits derived from the rental of the property and to appropriate partly or as a whole in lieu of interest, or in payment of the mortgage-money. The transaction is called an usufructuary mortgage and the mortgagee is called an usufructuary mortgagee. The essence of the transaction is that the mortgagor is bound to put the mortgagee in possession of the property. If possession is not delivered, the mortgagee may sue for possession or for the recovery of the mortgage-money under section 58(d) of the Transfer of Property Act. In *Pratap Bahadur v. Gajadhar*,[914] the mortgagor covenanted to put the mortgagee in possession of a certain village on a subsequent date, and to pay interest at 24%, until possession was delivered. It was held that the mortgage was a usufructuary mortgage. However, in *Yashwani v. Vithal*,[915] where there was a covenant that the mortgagor would pay interest every year but that if he failed to pay the interest, the mortgagee could take possession, and would appropriate the rents and profits towards interest, it was held that the transaction was a simple transaction. In *Prabhakaran v. M. Azhagiri Pillai*,[916] the Supreme Court held that it is a transfer by the owner (mortgager) of interest in an immovable property for securing an amount advanced by the creditor (mortgagee) under which possession of the property is delivered to the mortgagee with authority to retain possession and enjoy the rents and profits of the property until an amount equal to the debt is realized. In this kind of mortgage, mortgagor is not personally liable to repay the loan and therefore the mortgagee cannot sue him personally for the debt.[917] Further, Delivery of possession of the property is mandatory. In a mortgage, the mortgagee obtains the right to take the rents from the tenant and also acquires the right to evict him so as to act as landlord.[918] Thus, in this kind of mortgage, the mortgagor authorizes the mortgagee to retain possession until payment of the mortgage-money and to receive the rents and profits and appropriate the same in lieu of interest, or in payment of the mortgage-money.[919] A usufructuary mortgagee is entitled to be in possession of the mortgaged property as long as it is not redeemed and where the mortgagee leases the property back to the mortgagor, he can sue the terms of the lease against the mortgagor.[920]

914. ILR (1902) 24 All 521.
915. ILR (1897) Bom 267.
916. AIR 2006 SC 1567. *See also Hastimal v. P. Tej Raj Sharma*, AIR 2007 SC 3246.
917. *Lachhman v. Naina*, AIR 1940 Lah 401; also *Ram Narain Singh v. Adhindra Nath*, AIR 1916 PC 119.
918. *Abdul Aziz v. M. Maniyapa Setty*, AIR 1989 SC 553.
919. Transfer of Property Act, 1882, s. 58(d).
920. *S.B. Abdul Aziz v. M. Maniayappa Setty*, AIR 989 SC 553.

d. English Mortgage

881. Section 58(e) defines an English mortgage as where the mortgagor binds himself to repay the mortgage-money by a certain date, and transfers the mortgaged property into the absolute possession of the mortgagee, but all this is subject to a proviso that he will retransfer it to the mortgagor upon payment of the mortgage-money as agreed. Unlike a mortgage by conditional sale, in the case of an English mortgage there is a personal covenant to repay the amount. In a conditional sale, there is an ostensible sale whereas with an English mortgage, there is an absolute transfer of the property. An English mortgage resembles a mortgage by conditional sale in so far as both of them belong to that class of securities in which the ownership of the property mortgaged is liable to be transferred from the mortgagor to the mortgagee on default of payment. There are, however, two differences, viz., (1) In an English mortgage, the mortgagor ordinarily undertakes to pay the debt personally. But in a mortgage by way of a conditional sale, the mortgagor does not necessarily make himself personally liable for the payment of the mortgage-money and accordingly the mortgagee's only remedy is against the mortgaged property alone; (2) For an English mortgage, the ownership over the mortgaged property is absolutely transferred to the mortgagee, which is, however, liable to be divested by the repayment of the loan as agreed. In a mortgage by conditional sale, the mortgagor acquires only a qualified ownership, which, according to the terms of the agreement, generally ripens into an absolute proprietorship on the case of default by the mortgagor.

882. In a case before the Supreme Court,[921] the mortgage did not bind himself to repay the mortgage-money on a certain date. The sale deed did not even remotely suggest that the transaction was in the nature of a mortgage nor that there was any undertaking or agreement between the parties under which the property sold had to be retransferred to the seller. The seller was not a signatory to the agreement of reconveyance. It was held that the transaction could not be said to be an English mortgage. The suit filed was for a declaration to the effect that the sale deed executed by the plaintiff was void and that he continued to be the owner and in occupation. Hence, the plea that the suit was in substance one for redemption of mortgage was not tenable.

e. Mortgage by Deposit of Title Deeds

883. Section 58(f) of the Transfer of Property Act, states that a person in any of the following towns, namely, the towns of Calcutta (now Kolkata), Madras (now Chennai) and Bombay (now Mumbai), and in any other town whereby the state government concerned may, by notification in the official gazette deliver to a creditor or his agent documents of title to the immovable property, with the intent to create a security thereon. Such a transaction is called a mortgage by deposit of title deeds. In England, a mortgage of this kind is called an 'equitable mortgage' as opposed to a regular 'mortgage' because in this type of mortgage, there is simply a deposit of documents of tile without anything more, and it is without writing or any other formalities. The object of the legislature in providing for this kind of mortgage is to

921. *Raj Kishore v. Prem Singh*, AIR 2011 SC 382.

facilitate the mercantile community in cases where it may be necessary to raise money all of a sudden before the opportunity of preparing the mortgage-deed can be afforded. This mortgage, therefore, is not required to be in writing nor in the form of an oral transaction, and it is not affected by the law of registration. In India, equitable mortgages have been recognized since the decision of the Privy Council in *Verda Seth Sam v. Lauckputty*.[922] The term 'equitable mortgage' and being inappropriate in India on account of the absence of classification or division of estates or rights into legal and equitable classifications, is called a mortgage by deposit of title deed. In this type of mortgage it is not necessary that the transaction should be recorded or registered. But it is usual for the deposit of title deeds to be accompanied by a memorandum in writing that the mortgage has been effected. Supreme Court of India in *Syndicate Bank v. Estate Officer and Manager, APIIC Ltd.*,[923] held that requisites of an equitable mortgage are: (i) a debt; (ii) a deposit of title deeds; and (iii) an intention that the deeds shall be security for the debt.

f. Anomalous Mortgage

884. Section 58(g) of the Transfer of Property Act defines this type of mortgage as a mortgage which is not a simple mortgage, a mortgage by conditional sale, a usufructuary mortgage; an English mortgage by deposit of the title deeds within the meaning of the section is called an anomalous mortgage. The classification of mortgages contained in section 58 is not exhaustive. It only describes certain forms of mortgages which are in common use in India and in the nature of an usufructuary mortgage. These and other types of mortgages have been given the name of 'anomalous' mortgages. Thus, an anomalous mortgage has been defined as a mortgage which does not fall under any of the other five kinds of mortgages mentioned above. An anomalous mortgage includes: (1) a simple mortgage usufructuary mortgage; and (2) a mortgage usufructuary by conditional sale.

885. A simple mortgage usufructuary mortgage is a combination of a simple mortgage and an usufructuary mortgage and consequently an anomalous mortgage. In this transaction, the mortgagee is in possession and pays himself the debt out of the rents and profits and there is also a personal undertaking as well as a right to cause the property to be sold on the expiry of the date fixed for payment.

886. A mortgage usufructuary by conditional sale is another instance of an anomalous mortgage. Here the mortgagee is in possession as a usufructuary mortgagee for a fixed period and if the debt is not discharged at the expiry of the period, he gets all the rights of a mortgagee by conditional sale. In case the debt is not paid within the time fixed, the mortgagee gets the right of the foreclosure, this being the right to deprive the mortgagor's right of redemption. In *Vadalparty v. Appalanarasimhulu*[924] the mortgagee was with possession, the rents and profits were to be set-off against interest and the principal was to be repaid in five years and if not paid, the mortgagee was to procure the sale of the property at the expiry of twenty years. This was held to be mortgage usufructuary by conditional sale. However, where the mortgage in question

922. (1862) 8 MIA 307.
923. (2007)8 SCC 361.
924. (1921) 41 Mad L J 563.

was neither purely simple nor usufructuary exclusively but a mixture of the two then it is an anomalous mortgage within the meaning of section 58(g). The mortgage stipulated that, in the event of failure on the part of the mortgagor to pay up the amount due under the mortgage within the specified period of time, it shall be up to the mortgagee to realize the property through the sale of the property mortgaged.

B. Actionable Claims

887. According to the section 3 of the Transfer of Property Act, actionable claim, means a claim in a debt, other than a debt secured by a mortgage of immovable property or by a hypothecation or a pledge of movable property, to any beneficial interest in movable property not in the possession, either actual or constructive, of the claimant, which the civil courts recognize as affording grounds for relief, whether such debt or beneficial interest be existent, accruing, conditional or contingent. In brief, an actionable claim includes: (1) any unsecured debt; or (2) any interest in immovable property, not in possession of the claimant. The following have been held to be actionable claims.

1. Debt

888. A debt is an obligation to pay a liquidated or definite sum of money. Such debt may be: (1) existing; (2) accruing; (3) conditional; or (4) contingent. If it is not due and owing, it is existent and if it is a present debt but payable in the future then it is accruing. A debt which will be due only if a condition is fulfilled or a certain specified thing happens is a conditional debt. Contingent debts are debts which are payable on a certain contingency, e.g., an amount due under a policy of insurance. Debts secured by a mortgage of immovable property or by a pledge of movable property are excluded from the definition of actionable claim. A claim for damages, i.e., for an unascertained sum of money or a claim for mesne profits, does not come within the definition of actionable claim.

2. Beneficial Interest in Movable Property

889. A claim to any beneficial interest in movable property, not in possession of the claimant, is included in the present definition. Thus, a right to claim the benefit of a contract for the purchase of goods is a beneficial interest in movable property. For example, A agrees to sell to B bales of cotton deliverable on a future day. B has a beneficial interest in the goods and it is an actionable claim.

890. Some of the actionable claims are: (a) the right to claim from a contract for the purchase of goods;[925] (b) a claim money under an insurance policy;[926] (c) a share in a partnership;[927] (d) a claim for arrears of rent;[928] (e) a claim for return of

925. *Jaffar Mehr Ali v. Budge Jute Mills* (1907) 34 Cal 289.
926. *Shamdas v. Saviti*, AIR 1937 Sind 24.
927. *Hiralal v. Tripura Charan*, ILR 40 Cal 650.
928. *Daya Debi v. Chapala Debi* (1959) 63 CWN 976(60) A.C.

earnest money;[929] (f) a claim for return of earnest money;[930] (g) benefit of executor contract for the purchase of goods; (h) claim for a definite sum of money, which a lessee is bound to under the contract with the lessor; (i) claim for future rent; (j) decree that may be passed in a suit for a definite sum of money already filed, because, it is a claim in respect of a debt; (k) right to receive arrears of annuity; (l) sale of lottery tickets amounts to transfer of an actionable claim;[931] (m) usufructuary mortgagor's liability to pay to the mortgagee the balance remaining; (n) right to receive money from a licensee for a licence given to him to remove bark from the tree of the licensor.

891. The following are not actionable claims, though they would be actionable according to English law: (a) a claim to mesne profits;[932] (b) a copyright, because it is capable of possession;[933] (c) a decree already passed, because it is no longer a debt;[934] (d) the right of a person to recover damages by way of interest for the breach;[935] and (e) the right to recover profits from co-sharer.

3. Charges

892. Where immovable property of one person is by act of parties or operation of law made security for the payment of money to another, and the transaction does not amount to a mortgage, the latter person is said to have a share on the property; and all the provisions hereinbefore contained which apply to a simple mortgage shall, so far as may be, apply on such change.

893. Nothing in this section applies to the charge of a trustee on the trust property for expenses properly incurred in the execution of his trust, and save as otherwise expressly provided by any law for the time being in force, no charge shall be enforced against any property in the hands of a person to whom such property has been transferred for consideration and without notice of the charge.[936]

894. Charges on an immovable property is created to secure payment of money 100 says that where immovable property of a person is made security for the payment of money to another and the transaction is not a mortgage, it is said that a charge has been created. In *Subhendu Banerjee v. The CESC Ltd.*,[937] it was held that electricity dues of erstwhile consumer is not a charge on the property. They cannot be recovered from subsequent purchaser. If the charge is attached to the property, the charge for maintenance, present and future, is a recurring charge and is not extinguished by a decree of sale. A recurring charge is not identical to a mortgage. The auction purchaser would not get the purchased property free from the charge. The charge will continue as long as the decree-holder has the right to recover future maintenance. Such can bring the property to sale whenever maintenance becomes due, notwithstanding the

929. *Lal Chand v. Hussaini* (1927) 97 I.C. 257; *Agrenath v. Ram Ratan* (1958) ALJ 854.
930. *Lal Chand v. Hussaini* (1927) 97 I.C. 257; *Agrenath v. Ram Ratan* (1958) ALJ 854.
931. *Sunrise Association v. Govt. of NCT of Delhi*, AIR 2006 SC 1908.
932. *Jai Narayan v. Krishan Dutt*, ILR 3. Pat 575.
933. *Savitri v. Dwarka*, 1929 (ALJ) 575.
934. *Afzal v. Ram Kumar Bhurdra*, ILR S (1886) 12 Cal 610.
935. *Inder v. Raghubir Singh*, ILR (1930) 5 Luck 545.
936. Transfer of Property Act, 1882, s. 100.
937. AIR 2002 Cal 242.

fact that the property is of an auction purchaser, who purchased it in the sale held previously in satisfaction of the decree for arrears of maintenance.

a. Exceptions

895. There are, however, the following two exceptions to the provision.

896. Expenses incurred by the trustee are a first charge upon the trust property but this charge, unlike other types of charges, cannot be enforced by sale of the trust property for it would have the effect of destroying the trust. In this connection, section 32 of the Indian Trust Act says:

> Every trustee may reimburse himself or pay or discharge out of the trust property all expenses properly incurred in or about the execution of the trust. If he pays such expenses out of his own pocket, he has a first charge upon the trust enforced only by prohibiting any disposition of the trust property without previous payment of such expenses and interest.

897. This means the trustee may only reimburse himself for such expenses out of the income of the trust estate and prohibit any disposition of the trust property without previous payment of his expenses.

898. No charge shall be enforced against any property in the hands of a person to whom such property has been transferred for consideration and without notice of the discharge. This exception brings out the distinction between a charge and a mortgage. A mortgage being just in personam can be enforced against the mortgaged property in the hands of any transferee from mortgagor irrespective of notice. A charge, however, is just ad rem and can be enforced against a transferor if he has taken the transfer with notice of the charge.

b. Kinds of Charges

i. Created by the Act of Parties

899. An agreement which designates immovable property as security for the satisfaction of a debt without transferring any interest in the property constitutes a charge by the act of the parties. For example, A inherited an estate from his maternal grandmother and executed an agreement to pay his sister B a fixed annual sum out of the rents of the estate. In this case, B has a charge on the estate. No particular form of words is needed for the creation of a charge. It is sufficient, having regard to all the circumstances of the transaction that the document shows an intention to make the land security for the payment of money mentioned therein. Further, the act nowhere prescribes that any particular instrument must be registered unless the amount involved is less than INR 100 as required under section 17(1)(b) of the Registration Act. In *Dalumbi Devi v. Raghu Raj*,[938] an owner of immovable property executed a power of attorney in favour of 'P' for management of the suit property in which no restriction

938. AIR 2002 HP 99.

was placed on the owner for transfer of property. It was held that the right created in favour of 'P' was only to claim expenses already incurred by him in managing, improving and breaking the lands, if his power of attorney was revoked or cancelled, such right of reimbursement does not amount to creation of interest in property.

ii. A Charge Arising by Operation of Law

900. A charge by operation of law is one which arises irrespective of the agreement of the parties. Such charges are known as equitable in English law. They can be illustrated as follows:

(1) Vendor's charge for unpaid purchase money: This is provided under section 54(4)(b) of the Trades Practices Act as 'Where the ownership of the property has passed to the buyer before payment for it has been made. In this case, the seller is entitled to a charge upon the property that is in the possession of the buyer and this applies in the case of any transaction given without consideration, any transferee with notice of non-payment, or any part remaining unpaid, and for interest on such an amount or part from the date that possession has been delivered'. In *State of Karnataka v. Shreyas Papers Pvt. Ltd.,*[939] a purchase of property cannot be saddled with tax liability of the period before sale where he is not aware of any such outstanding liability. Such tax amount cannot be recovered even as a charge on the property.
(2) Vendee's charge for purchase money paid in advance: Under section 55(6)(b) of the Transfer of Property Act, the vendee is entitled 'to a charge on the property, as against the seller and all persons claiming under him to the extent of the seller's interest in the property, for the amount of any purchase money property laid by the buyer in anticipation of the delivery and for interest on such amount'.
(3) There can be charges arising by operation of law for example, a mortgagee's lien under section 73 of the Transfer of Property Act on surplus sale proceeds, a revenue sale, the right to maintenance under section 39 and the right of a holder of a defective title who makes improvement on the property under section 51 of the Transfer of Property Act.

§3. Guarantee

I. General

901. A contract of guarantee, according to section 126 of the Indian Contract Act, 1872, is a contract to perform the promise or discharge the liability, of a third party in the case of default on the promise. The section further says, 'that the person who gives the guarantee is called the "surety" and the person in respect of whose default the guarantee is given is called the "principal debtor" and the person to whom

939. (2006) 1 SCC 615.

the guarantee is given is called the "creditor"'. A guarantee may be either oral or written.

902. The function of a contract of guarantee is to enable a person to get a loan, or goods on credit or an employment. Some person comes forward and tells the lender, or the supplier or the employer that he may be trusted and in case of any default, 'I undertake to be responsible'.

A. Cases of Bank Guarantee

903. A bank guarantee is a sort of an absolute undertaking on the part of the bank under an arrangement with its customer to pay to the creditor whenever the latter invokes the guarantee. In *State Bank of India v. Prem Dass*[940] it was held that when a borrower and a guarantor both sign an agreement in favour of a bank, they are jointly and severally liable under that contract. The contract of guarantee is no doubt a tripartite in nature but it is not necessary or essential that the principal debtor must expressly be a party to that document. In a contract of guarantee, the principal debtor may be a party to the contract by implication. Thus, there is the possibility that a person may become a surety without the knowledge and consent or the principal debtor. In a case it was argued that the first invocation was not in accordance with the terms of guarantee, such a plea even if accepted, would not prevent the beneficiary from invoking the bank guarantee by a subsequent letter. The reasons for the furnishing of a bank guarantee may still continue to subsist so long as the period of the bank guarantee still continues to subsist and so long as the period of validity of the bank guarantee has not expired and the guarantee continues to remain effective. In this case, the beneficiary could submit a fresh letter of invocation.[941] In another case, the petitioning company had sought to restrain the respondent company from contracting between other parties. The existence or adjudication of the disputes had no bearing on the encashment of the bank guarantee and could not be equated with fraud. The petitioner had failed to make out the case that irretrievable injury would be caused to it if payment is made to the respondent by the bank. The court could not grant the relief sought by the petitioner.[942] In *Gas Authority of India Ltd. v. Official Liquidator*[943] there was a winding up order against a contractor company, whereby the bank had secured the creditor vis-à-vis the contractor company. The Bank had decided to act on the bank guarantee irrespective of whether or not liquidation proceedings were taking place against the contractor company. It was held that the bank does not have the right to claim that it would not honour the bank guarantee. In *Bank of India v. Nangia Construction (I)(P) Ltd.*[944]

904. Sometimes, banks give a 'performance guarantee' on behalf of a party to a contract. The bank giving such a guarantee is bound by the obligation undertaken by it. The performance guarantee is an 'autonomous' contract and imposes an 'absolute

940. AIR 1958 Del 49.
941. *Crown Maritime Co. (I) Ltd. v. ECON Engineering Pvt. Ltd.*, AIR 2003 Bom 163.
942. *Alcove Industries Ltd. v. Oriental Structural Engineers Pvt. Ltd.*, AIR 2005 Del 173.
943. (2004) 4 BC 306 Ibom.
944. (2008) 7 SCC 290.

obligation' on the bank according to its terms.[945] A bank guarantee, for all purposes, should be taken to be a credit note ordinarily, unless the intention of the parties is otherwise.[946] The nature of the obligation of the bank guarantee was, thus, explained in *Hugglunds Drives AB v. National Heavy Engineering Coop. Ltd.*[947]

905. The issuing bank is bound to observe and honour the terms of the guarantee. The beneficiary of a bank guarantee cannot be prevented from paying over the proceeds of the bank guarantee save and except in the case of fraud which vitiates the entire underlying transaction or in case where irretrievable injustice would be caused by the invocation or encashment of the bank guarantee. The issuing bank is not concerned with the terms of the underlying transaction between the beneficiary of the bank guarantee and the person at whose behest the bank guarantee was issued by the issuing bank. The bank guarantee is bipartite a contract between the issuing bank and the beneficiary. The bank is not a party to the underlying contract between the beneficiary and the person at whose behest the bank guarantee is issued. Where the bank assumes an obligation to pay on demand without demur, without reference to the underlying dispute, if any, between the parties, it must honour the terms of its obligation.

906. An unconditional bank guarantee is irrevocable and no injunction can be issued to prevent the enforcement of it. In *Association of Corporation v. State of Bihar*,[948] there was a bank guarantee agreement and the terms incorporated in the agreement indicated that the agreement was irrevocable. The body of the bank guarantee did not mention any condition though some conditions were alleged to exist in the contract between the parties. It was held that it was an unconditional bank guarantee and no injunction can be issued against the encashment of the bank guarantee. In the case that a bank has unconditionally guaranteed the payment of the price on the supply of goods from the seller to the buyer, the bank is bound to honour this obligation, and in the event of any dispute between the seller and the buyer, the buyer cannot obtain an injunction preventing the bank from acting on the guarantee.[949] In *Pesticides India v. State Chemicals & Pharmaceuticals Corp. of India*,[950] the appellants wanted to purchase some goods from the respondents and they gave some earnest money as well as a bank guarantee. On the supply of the goods by the respondents, the appellants were not satisfied with performance and according to them, the supply had been wrongly made on an 'ex go-down' basis instead of a 'high sea' basis. The respondent demanded the amount of the bank guarantee from the bank, but the appellants sought to reason with the bank not to make the payment. It was found that in this case, the bank had undertaken to pay on the 'first demand without protest or demur and without reference to' the appellants, and notwithstanding the 'existence of any dispute whatsoever' between the parties. It was held that the bank was bound to honour the guarantee, and the appellants could not prevent the bank from honouring its promise to pay. Similarly

945. *Banwari Lal v. Punjab State Cooperative Supply and Marketing Federation Ltd., Chandigarh*, AIR 1982 Del 357, 360.
946. *M/s Basanti Polymers v. State Chemical, etc., Corp. of India*, AIR 1986 Raj. 1 at 2.
947. AIR 2002 Bom 305 at 311.
948. AIR 2000 Del 106.
949. *Banwari Lal v. P.S. Coop. Supply, etc. Ltd.*, AIR 1982 Del 357.
950. AIR 1982 Del 78.

was the position in *Vinay Engineering v. Neyveli Lignite Corp. Ltd.*[951] wherein it was held that under a bank guarantee the bank had irrevocably undertaken to pay the purchaser a certain sum of money upon the purchasers' first demand and without demur, provided that the purchaser advised the bank that the contactor had failed to fulfil his delivery obligations under a contract with him. In this case the bank was bound to make the payments based on the necessary advice given by the purchaser. It was further held that the purchaser in such a case need not prove to the bank that the contractor had failed to perform his obligations under the contact, as the fact of the purchaser's advice to the bank was all what was required for the payment of the guaranteed amount. The Supreme Court held that if the bank has issued a letter of credit or given a bank guarantee regarding the performance of a contract, the court cannot grant an injunction to restrain encashment of bank guarantee or letter of credit on the ground that there was a breach of contract between the buyer and seller, meaning that the buyer cannot allege a breach of contract by the seller and obtain an injunction against the bank restraining the bank from acting on the guarantee, and making the payment of the promised amount.[952]

907. In order to obtain an injunction against the bank issuing the bank guarantee it has to be proved that there was a fraud of which the bank had knowledge of such. An unconditional bank guarantee is vitiated by fraud or the likelihood of causing irreparable loss.[953] If a bank guarantee agreement requires fulfilment of certain conditions or requirements necessary for the invocation of the bank guarantee, the guarantee can be invoked if those conditions are fulfilled.[954] The court gave no guidance as to what constitutes 'fraud' except this that it must be 'very clearly established'.[955]

B. Main Features of a Contract of Guarantee

1. A Contract May Be Either Oral or in Writing

908. Section 126 of the Contract Act sets out that a guarantee may be either oral or in writing. The position in India is different from that of England. In England, according to section 4 of the Statute of Frauds, 1677, in the case of a valid contract of guarantee, it is necessary that it should be in writing and signed by the party to be charged therewith but this is not so in India as the contract can also be oral.

2. There Should Be a Principal Debt

909. A contract of guarantee presupposes a principal debt or an obligation to be discharged by the principal debtor. The surety undertakes to be liable only if the principle debtor fails to discharge his obligation. If there is no such principal debt, but there is a promise by one party in favour of another for compensating in a certain situation, and the performance of this promise is not dependent upon the default of

951. AIR 1985 Mad 213.
952. *Federal Bank Ltd. v. V.M. Engineering Ltd.*, AIR 2000 SC 3166.
953. *Rigoss Exports International (P) Ltd. v. Tartan Infomark Ltd.*, AIR 2002 Del 285.
954. *National Telecom of India Ltd. v. Union of India*, AIR 2001 Del 236.
955. *Himadri Chemicals Industries (P) Ltd v. Coal Tar Refining Co.*, (2007) 8 SCC 110.

somebody else, it is a contract of indemnity. For example, when A and B go to a shop, A purchases goods and B tells the seller, 'if A does not pay you, I will', it is a contract of guarantee. However, if A is not the principal debtor but only B makes a promise to the shopkeeper to pay, for instance, B tells the shopkeeper, 'Let him (A) have the goods, I will be your pay master', it is a contract of indemnity.

3. Benefit to the Principal Debtor is Sufficient Consideration

910. As in any other contract, consideration is also necessary for a contract of guarantee. According to section 127 of the Contract Act, 'anything done, or any promise made for the benefit of the principal debtor may be sufficient consideration for the surety for giving the guarantee'. For a surety's promise, thus, it is not necessary that there should be direct consideration between the creditor and the surety. It is enough that the creditor had done something for the benefit of the principal debtor. The benefit to the principal debtor constitutes a sufficient consideration for the surety for giving the guarantee. In a case before Bombay High Court,[956] a guarantee was executed subsequent to release of financial assistance to the borrower. The court held that it could not be said that there was no consideration for the guarantee. In the view of the court, 'past consideration is valid consideration'.

4. Consent of the Surety Should Not Be Obtained by Misrepresentation or Concealment

911. According sections 142 and 143 of the Indian Contract Act, the creditor should not obtain a guarantee either by any misrepresentation or concealment of any material facts concerning the transaction. If the guarantee has been obtained that way, the guarantee is invalid. Silence as regards material circumstances, which would effect the surety's mind to stand as surety or not, would render the guarantee void. If a cashier, thus, has been found guilty of embezzlement, but this fact is not disclosed when a surety has been made to guarantee the future conduct of the cashier, the surety will not be liable as such, under these circumstances. Similarly, if a surety is made to guarantee that an employee is already indebted to an extent more than that of the guarantee, the guarantee is invalid.

5. Guarantor is Bound by Acknowledgement of the Principal Debtor

912. In a suit for the recovery of loans, a suit against a guarantor was time barred and the suit was decreed against the principal debtor. It was held, that the guarantor was bound by the acknowledgement of the principal debtor.[957]

6. Guarantor Cannot Be Made Liable to Pay Interest

913. The liability of a guarantor mainly derives from the terms and conditions of the guarantee bond. Where the amount of interest on the principal amount was not

956. *Sicom Ltd v. Padamshri Mahipatraj J. Shah*, (2005) 3 Mah LJ 125.
957. *Bank of India v. Surendra Kumar Mishra*, (2003) III BC 166 (Jhar).

agreed by the parties, it was held that the guarantor could not be made liable to pay the interest.[958]

7. Surety Can Be Acted on Without First Proceeding Against the Principal Debtor

914. For a loan advanced for an industrial concern, repayment of which has been guaranteed by a surety, the state financial corporation need not first proceed against the borrower (industrial concern) and only when it was unable to recover the dues from the industrial concern can it enforce the liability of the surety. Section 128 of the Indian Contract Act provides that the liability of the sureties is coextensive with the liability of the principal debtor unless it was otherwise provided for by the contract. It will not be necessary for a creditor, before proceeding against the surety to demand payment from the principal debtor or sue the principal debtor unless it was expressly stipulated that the surety may be proceeded against, without first proceeding against the principal debtor.[959]

8. Liability of Surety

915. According to section 128 of the Contract Act, the liability of the surety is coextensive with that of the principal debtor, unless otherwise provided by the contract. This means that the liability is exactly the same as that of the principal debtor, that is, on default having being made by the principal debtor, the creditor can recover from the surety all what he could have recovered from the principal debtor. In case the principal debtors' liability is reduced, e.g., after the creditor has recovered a part of the sum due to him from the debtors' property, the liability of the surety is also reduced accordingly.[960] In *Narayan Singh v. Chattarsingh*[961] it was held that if the principal debtors' liability is scaled down in an amended decree or otherwise extinguished in whole or in part by a statute, the liability of the surety would also pro tanto be reduced or extinguished. If the principal debtor's liability is affected by illegality, so is also that of the surety. Therefore, where the liability of the principal is not held to be enforceable on the ground of the contract being illegal, there is no question of the surety being made liable.[962] In case the principal debtor happens to be a minor and the agreement made by him is void, the surety cannot be made liable in respect of the debt because the liability of the surety is coextensive with that of the principal debtor.[963] Before payment, the surety has no right to dictate terms to the creditor and ask him to pursue his remedies against the principal in the first instance. In the absence of some special equity, the surety has no right to restrain an action against him by the creditor on the ground that the principal is solvent or that the creditor has relief against the

958. *Vyasya Bank Ltd. v. Dy. Director, D.G.F.T. (Enforcement-cum-Adjudication)*, 2004 (13) AIC 7908 (AP).
959. *N. Narasimahaiah v. Karnataka State Financial Corporation*, AIR 2004 Kant. 46.
960. *Harigopal Agrawal v. State Bank of India*, 1956 Mad 211.
961. AIR 1973 Raj 347.
962. *Varadarajulu v. Thavsi Nadar*, AIR 1963 Mad 413 at 419.
963. *Kelappan Nambiar v. Kunhi Raman*, AIR 1957 Mad 164.

principal through some other proceedings. Thus, in *Bank of Bihar v. Damodar Prasad*,[964] where the creditor had obtained a decree against the surety and the principal, it was held that the surety had no right to restrain execution against him. Thus, it is not necessary that there should be a prior action against the principal debtor.

916. The liability of the surety does not depend upon possibility of the surety being able to realize the amount from the principal debtor.[965] The law on this point was settled by the decision of the Supreme Court in a case where it was observed that the right of the creditor to recover from the guarantor arises out of the terms of the deed of guarantee which are not in any way superseded or brought to nullity merely because the creditor may not be able to recover anything from the principal debtor.[966]

9. Limit on Surety's Liability by Contract

917. Section 128 of the act declares that the liability of the surety is coextensive with that of the principal debtor, unless otherwise provided for by the contract. This means that if the contract between the parties so provides, then the surety's liability may not be to the full extent of the principal debtor. In *Yarlagaadda v. Devata China Yerakayya*,[967] the bond executed by the surety limited his liability to the amount of INR 15,000 with a stipulation that he might be liable for any amount finally decreed. It was held that the respondent, i.e., the surety 'had undertaken liability only up to the amount of INR 15,000' and that the clause rendering himself liable for any amount that might be finally decreed should be interpreted as meaning not exceeding INR 15,000. Similarly in *Aditya Narain Chauriasia v. Bank of India*,[968] where the guarantors undertook to be liable up to a maximum of INR 25,000 plus interest payable thereon, it was held that their maximum liability could not exceed that limit. They were, therefore, held liable for only part of the debt.

10. Condition that There Shall Be a Co-surety

918. Sometimes there may be a condition in a contract of guarantee that there shall be a co-surety also. Where a person gives a guarantee upon a contract that the creditor shall not act upon it until another person has joined in it as the co-surety, the guarantee is not valid if that other person does not join.[969] This means that in such a contract, liability of the surety is dependent on the condition precedent that a co-surety will join. The surety can be made liable under such a contact only if the co-surety joins, otherwise not.

964. AIR 1969 SC 297.
965. *Syndicate Bank v. Narayana Iyer*, (2003) 3 Ker LT 726.
966. *Satish Chandra Jain v. National Small Industries Corpn Ltd.*, (2003) All LJ 238 (SC).
967. AIR 1966 AP 151.
968. AIR 2000 Pat 222.
969. Indian Contract Act, 1872, s. 144.

11. Liability of Co-surety

919. The liability of a surety is, as has been explained above, coextensive with that of the principal debtor. The creditor can proceed against the principal debtor or the surety, at his discretion, unless otherwise provided by the contract. The same principle is applicable with regard to the rights and liabilities of co-sureties. Since the liability of co-sureties is joint and several, a co-surety cannot insist that the creditor should proceed against the principal debtor or any other surety before proceeding against him. In the *State Bank of India v. G.J. Herman*[970] it was held that when there is a composite decree against the principal debtor and the sureties, the creditor has the discretion to decide against whom he wants to proceed. Neither the court nor a co-surety can insist that the creditor should first proceed against another surety before proceeding against him. Such discretion would go against the coextensiveness of the liability of the sureties with that of the principal debtor.

12. Discharge of Surety Due to a Variance of the Contract Terms

920. In a suit for recovery, liability of the guarantor was limited to cash credit facility in a bank in favour of the principal debtor up to the extent of INR 250,000 but overdrawn were made by the principal debtor beyond that limit. The guarantor was not bound by the overdrawn allowed by the bank. A plea was made that the guarantee was extended to a series of transactions and, therefore it was not tenable to hold the guarantor liable.[971] In *Industrial Finance Corpn of India Ltd. v. Connanore Spg and Wvg Mills Ltd.*, it was held that nationalization of the borrower mill (textile) did not result in discharge of the contract of guarantee on account of frustration. The guarantee had no co-relationship with the Nationalization Act, 1974. It was an independent contract and had to be honoured to fulfil the contractual obligation between the surety and creditor.[972]

13. Continuing Guarantee

921. A guarantee which, according to section 129 of the Contract Act, extends to a series of transactions is called a 'continuing guarantee'. Such a guarantee may be in respect of a series of transactions during a fixed period, e.g., for one year. The surety may act as the guarantee for the conduct of the principal debtor in respect of a particular transaction, such as guaranteeing the repayment of a loan of INR 50,000, which the principal debtor may have taken from the creditor, or he may undertake to be answerable for the conduct of the principal debtor in respect of a series of transactions. The former guarantee discussed above is known as a 'specific guarantee' whereas the latter is known as a 'continuing guarantee'. In a continuing guarantee, a surety, under section 130, is empowered to revoke it in respect of future transactions, by giving notice to the creditor. His liability in respect of the transactions made continues to exist, whereas his liability for the future transactions comes to an end. According to section 131,

970. AIR 1998 Ker 161.
971. *Bishwannath Agarwala v. State Bank of India*, AIR 2005 Jhar 69.
972. (2002) 5 SCC 54.

unless there is a contract to the contrary, the death of a surety also automatically puts an end to a continuing guarantee, as regards future transactions. It was held by the Bombay High Court that in the case of continuing guarantee, the bar of limitation does not arise as long as guarantee is running.[973]

14. Discharge of Surety from Liability

922. When the liability of surety, undertaken under a contract of guarantee, is extinguished or comes to an end, the surety is discharged from liability. Surety can be discharge by various modes under Indian Contract Act, 1872 like: revocation by the surety under section 130 of the Act; by surety's death under section 131 of the Act; variance in the terms of contract under section 133 of the Act; by release or discharge of the principal debtor under section 134 of the Act; when the creditor compounds with/gives time to/agrees not to sue the principal debtor under section 135 of the Act; by the creditor's act or omission impairing the suretys' eventual remedy under section 139 of the Act; and by loss of the security by the creditor under section 141 of the Act.

923. A surety has certain rights against the principal debtor, the creditor and the co-sureties. They are as follows.

a. Right of Subrogation

924. Under section 140, where a guaranteed debt has become due, or defaulted to the principal debtor to perform, the surety upon payment or performance of all that he is liable for is invested with all rights which the creditor had against the principal debtor. After the surety has made the payment or performed the duty on default of the principal debtor, he is conferred with the same rights which the creditor had against the principal debtor. This means that first, the surety can claim indemnity from the principal debtor for all the sums he has rightfully paid under the guarantee in accordance with section 145 of the Contract Act. Second, under section 141, he is entitled to the benefits of every security which the creditor has against the principal debtor when the contract of surety-ship was entered into, i.e., he would be entitled to the benefit of such securities which the creditor had against the principal debtor at the time when the contract of surety-ship was entered into. In the case that the creditor loses the securities possessed by him at the time of the making of the contract, that results in the discharge of the surety in that respect. Section 141, recognizes and incorporates the general rule of equity as expounded in *Craythorne v. Swinburne*[974] that the surety is entitled to every remedy which the creditor has against the principal debtor, including enforcement of every security. In *State of M.P. v. Kaluram*,[975] the respondent acted as a surety for the payment of the felled trees which were sold by the appellant to another party. The buyer of the trees was to make the payment in four instalments. He only paid one instalment and then defaulted on the rest. The appellant, meaning the surety, had a right to prevent the purchaser from removing the trees when he was in default. The appellant failed to do so. The court held that the appellant by allowing the buyer

973. *SICOM Ltd. v. Harjinder Singh*, AIR 2004 Bom 337.
974. (2002) 5 SCC 54.
975. AIR 1967 SC 1105.

to take away the trees, had allowed the security to be lost, and the surety was, therefore, discharged to that extent.

b. Right of Indemnity Against the Principal Debtor

925. Section 145 of the Contract Act, 1872 lays down that 'in every contract of guarantee, there is an implied promise by the principal debtor to indemnify the surety, and the surety is entitled to recover from the principal debtor whatever sum he has rightfully paid under the guarantee, but not for sums which he has wrongfully paid for'. A surety's right of indemnity is only in respect of the payment rightfully made by him. However, in the case that there is no justification for the surety to make some payment, i.e., he cannot claim indemnity in respect of such payment. In *C.K. Aboobacker v. K.P. Ayishu,*[976] it was held that a guarantee is liable for any payment, or performance, or any obligation only to the extent that the principal debtor has defaulted. If a substantial portion of the loan has been paid by the principal debtor, the guarantor has to pay only the balance due. According to section 145, after the surety has paid the amount, the principal debtor should indemnify the surety for everything the surety has rightfully paid for under the contract of guarantee. Loss of securities by the creditor results in the discharge of the surety, but in the case that hypothecated securities are lost without any fault on the part of the creditor, the surety will thereby not be discharged.[977] A surety also has no right to those securities which the creditor obtained from the principal debtor after making the contract of guarantee and the surety will not be discharged as a consequence of the loss of such securities.[978]

c. Right Against the Co-sureties

926. When two or more persons are co-securities for the same debt or duty, either jointly or severally, and whether under the same or different contracts and with or without knowledge of each other, the co-sureties, in the absence of any contract to the contrary, under section 146 of the Contract Act, are liable, as between themselves, to each pay an equal share of the whole debt, or of that part of it which remains unpaid by the principal debtor. Thus, the duty of the co-sureties is to contribute equally. This is so when they are co-sureties for the same debt. It is immaterial that they have undertaken a duty either jointly or severally, or under the same or different contracts, or with or without the knowledge of each other. The co-sharers are, however free to agree that as between themselves their liability shall not be equal, but according to certain other proportions. Sometimes, one of the co-sureties may have paid more than his share of liability owed to the creditor. When that is so, he can claim contribution from his co-sureties. Sometimes, the sureties may fix the maximum sum that their liability can go. There may be different limits as to the amount for which the sureties are to be liable. According to section 147 of the Contract Act, co-sureties bound by different sums are liable to pay equally in as much as their respective obligations

976. AIR 2000 NOC 29 (Kerala).
977. *R. Lilawati v. Bank of Baroda*, AIR 1987 Kant 2.
978. Indian Contract Act, 1872, s. 141, illustration (c).

permit. It is also possible that one of the co-sureties may be released from liability while the other co-sureties are still liable.

§4. Pledge

I. General

927. A pledge is only a special kind of bailment, and the chief basis of distinction is the object of the contract. Where the object of the delivery of goods is to provide a security for a loan or for the fulfilment of an obligation, that kind of bailment is called pledge. According to section 172 of the Indian Contract Act, 1872, The bailment of goods as security for payment of a debt or performance of a promise is called a 'pledge'. The bailor is called 'pawnor'. The 'bailee' is called the 'pawnee'. The goods pledged or pawned serve as security for the payment of a debt or performance of a promise. The person pledging the goods is known as the 'pawnor' and the person with whom the goods are pledged is known as the 'pawnee' or 'pledgee'.

II. Essentials of a Pledge

928. In order to constitute a valid pledge, the following requirements must be satisfied.

A. Delivery of Possession

929. As a pledge is a bailment, the delivery of the goods, according to section 148 of the Contract Act, from the pawnor to the pawnee is a must. There must be delivery of goods, i.e., the transfer of possession from one person to another. The delivery, however, may be either actual or constructive. Mere agreement to transfer possession from one person to another person in the future is not enough to constitute a pledge. In *Revenue Authority v. Sudershan Pictures*[979] it has been held that an agreement wherein, the producer of a film agreed to deliver the final prints of the film under production, when ready, to the financier-distributor in return for the finance provided by the financier-distributor, is not a pledge because there is no delivery of the goods. Delivery of the goods may either be actual or constructive. Doing something which has the effect of putting the pawnee or his agent in possession of the goods may be treated as delivery.[980] Handing over the key of a godown in which the goods are lying, or a transfer of a document of title, like a bill of lading or a railway receipt, which represents particular goods amount to delivery of the goods.[981] A bill of lading or a railway receipt are documents of title,[982] but not a waybill issued by a public carrier

979. AIR 1968 Mad 319.
980. Indian Sale of Goods Act, 1930, s. 33.
981. *Morvi Mercantile Bank Ltd. v. Union of India*, AIR 1965 SC 1954.
982. Indian Sale of Goods Act, 1930, s. 2(4).

and so these things do not constitute a valid pledge.[983] In *Morvi Mercantile bank v. Union of India*,[984] the delivery of a railway receipt was considered to be enough to constitute delivery of the goods, for the purpose of the pledge. In this case a business firm consigned some goods through a railway from being carried from Bombay to Okhla, near Delhi and to be delivered to 'self'. The firm borrowed a sum of INR 20,000 from the appellant bank and executed a promissory note in favour of the bank and also endorsed the railway receipt as a security for the load. The goods were lost in transit. The appellant bank brought an action against the railway as the pledge of the goods which were lost in transit. The question arose whether through the transfer of the railway receipt, the possession of the goods had been transferred to the bank. The Supreme Court held that according to the prevailing Indian law, a railway receipt is a document of title, and, therefore, delivery of the railway receipt means delivery of the goods represented by the railway receipt. The transaction was held to be a valid pledge and as such the bank was held entitled to a claim against the railway for the value of the loss given against the security of the railway receipt. Possession of goods with the third party will not be deemed to be delivery of the goods unless that party acknowledges to the transferee that he holds the goods on behalf of the transferee.[985] After such an acknowledgement, the third party will be deemed to be the agent of the transferee. In *Bank of Rajasthan Ltd. v. Hajarimal Milap C. Surana*,[986] it was held that the delivery of precious stones to the lending bank for sale and realization of the amount had the effect of creating pledge for securing repayment of the loan.

B. Purpose of a Pledge Should Be Security of Payment of a Debt

930. In a transaction of pledge, the purpose for which the goods are bailed is that the bailed goods should serve as security for the payment of a debt or performance of a promise. When some goods are pledged, the pawnee becomes a secured creditor and he has a prior claim over the goods pledged over the other creditors. In *Bank of India v. Binod Steel Ltd*,[987] it was held that when certain movables were pledged by a company to a bank, they cannot be attached and sold for satisfaction of claims of other creditors of the company without first satisfying the claim of the bank. A pledge or hypothecation, unlike a mortgage, does not transfer any 'interest' in the property in favour of the pledgee or hypothecate. The pledge or hypothecation simply creates a special property in the goods in favour of the pledgee or hypothecate, i.e., it entitles him to have the possession of the goods and dispose of them for the realization of his debt, for which the goods constitute the security. If the pledgee or hypothecate waives his right as mentioned above, his claim in respect of those goods comes to an end. For example, in *Syndicate Bank v. Official Liquidator*,[988] the appellant advanced a loan to Prashant Engineering Co., and the defendant hypothecated all the machines installed in its factory in favour the appellant, as a security for the money advanced by the

983. *Canara Industrial and Banking Syndicate v. Ramchandra*, AIR 1968 Mysore 133.
984. AIR 1965 SC 1954.
985. Indian Sale of Goods Act, 1930, s. 36(3).
986. (2005) 10 SCC 238.
987. AIR 1977 MP 188.
988. AIR 1985 Del 256.

appellant to the company. The appellant brought an action against the said company and obtained a money decree for INR 21,189.20. In this case, the bank neither took possession of the hypothecated property on its own, nor did it request the possession of if through the court. It was held that the fact the bank did not avail of its right to have the possession of the goods, it was deemed to have waived its right as a hypothecate. A subsequent action by the bank to have the right as a hypothecate of those goods could not be entertained.

C. Clause in Agreement Permitting the Financier to Forfeit Non-valid Payments

931. Where a loan agreement was entered into to purchase a vehicle there was default in the payment of the instalments. It was held, that a clause in the agreement permitting the financier to forfeit payments made was void. Any amount paid by the debtor will have to be accounted for and credited to his account and it is the right of the creditor to recover the balance amount only.[989]

D. Who Can Pledge

932. Normally, it is the owner of the goods, or any person authorized by him or acting on his behalf, who can pledge the goods. If a servant has the custody of the goods, or a tenant gets the possession of a finished house, the servant cannot pledge the furnishing materials in his possession. A person obtaining the goods fraudulently does not have any right to pledge them. In *Purshottam Das v. Union of India*,[990] 'A' obtained the possession of certain goods from the railway on the basis of a forged railway receipt and then pledged the goods to 'B'. It was held that the pledge by 'A' was not valid, and 'B' did not get any rights in the goods as a pledgee, and hence the railway authorities could recover the goods from 'B'. In the following cases, a person who is neither the owner, nor has the authority from the owner to pledge the goods, but has possession through the owners' consent can make a pledge and confer rights on the pledgee. The recognized exceptions have been narrated in the following paragraphs.

1. Pledge by Mercantile Agent

933. Under section 178 of the Contract Act, a mercantile agent having possession of the goods with the consent of the owner but having no authority to pledge them can make a pledge provided the pledgee or pawnee is acting in good faith.

2. Pledge by a Person in Possession under a Voidable Contract

934. Section 178-A recognizes another exception to the rule that either the owner or his duly authorized agent can pledge the goods, i.e., a person who has obtained the possession of the goods under a voidable contract, a pledge by him before the

989. *Tarun Bhargava v. State of Haryana*, AIR 2003 P&H 98.
990. AIR 1067 All 549.

contract has been rescinded, to a pledgee acting in good faith and without notice of the pawnor's defect in title, confers a good on the pledgee. A voidable contract is a valid contract until it has been rescinded and becomes void after the same has been rescinded. The pledgee is capable of having a good tile to such goods. Thus, if a person has obtained the possession of goods by fraud, misrepresentation, coercion or undue influence, he could make a valid pledge of the goods, if so done before the contract has been rescinded. If the goods have been pledged before the contract has been rescinded, the rights of the person entitled to rescind the contract are thereby affected. This exception, however, is applicable if the pawnor is in possession of the goods under a voidable contract. If the pawnor has stolen the goods or has obtained possession under a void agreement, the pawnee will get no rights in that transaction. It is, however, necessary that the pledgee must be acting in good faith and without any notice about the pawnor's defect in title.

3. Pledge by a Person with a Limited Interest

935. A person having a limited interest in the goods, for instance, a pledgee, may pledge the goods. According to section 179, where a person pledges goods in which he has only a limited interest, the pledge is valid to the extent of that interest. In such a case, the pawnee's right is limited to the extent of the pawnor's interest in the goods. It is immaterial that the pawnee had no notice that the pawnor had only a limited interest.[991]

4. Pledge by Seller in Possession after Sale

936. After the seller has sold certain goods and the ownership of those goods has passed to the buyer, the seller has no right to deal with such goods. But, according to section 30(1) of the Sale of Goods Act, 1930, if the seller after selling the goods, continues or is in possession of the goods or the documents of title in respect of the goods, then any sale or pledge or other disposition of the goods by him or a mercantile agent acting on his behalf, will convey a good titled to the transferee, provided that the transferee is acting in good faith and without any notice of the previous sale.

5. Pledge by Buyer in Possession after Sale

937. A buyer of the goods, who may have obtained the possession of the goods, but has not yet become the owner of those goods, cannot deal with such goods. According to section 30(2) of the Sale of Goods Act, however, if a buyer has obtained the possession of the goods or the documents of title with the consent of the seller, the delivery or transfer by such a buyer or a mercantile agent on his behalf, by way of a sale, pledge or other disposition will convey a good title to the transferee, provided that the transferee is acting in good faith and without notice of any lien or other rights of the original seller in respect of those goods.

991. *See Belgaum Pioneer Urban Coop. Credit Bank v. Satyapromoda*, AIR 1960 Mays. 48.

E. Rights of Pledgee or Pawnee

1. Right to Retain the Goods Pledged

938. Sections 173 and 174 of the Contract Act deal with the rights of the pledgee. According to these provisions, the right of a pawnee to retain the goods pledged shall be not only for the payment of the debt, or the performance of the promise, but he can also exercise this right for the interest on the debt and all necessary expenses incurred by him in respect of the possession or for the preservation of the goods pledged. Although ordinarily a pawnee can retain the goods pledged only as a security for that debt or promise for which they are pledged, there is a presumption that if there are subsequent advances, they are also part of the original debt, and the pawnee may retain the goods to recover subsequent advances also. This is merely a presumption which could be rebutted by a contract to the contrary.

939. Explaining the nature of the special property in the goods which is acquired by the pledge in *Bank of Bihar v. State of Bihar*[992] the Supreme Court observed: this special property or interest is to be distinguished from the mere right of retention which the holder of a lien possesses, in that it is transferable in the sense that a pawnee may assign or pledge his special property or interest in the goods. In *Bank of Baroda v. Nanital Seeds Corpn.*,[993] perishable items under pledge of bank were damaged due to bank's negligence, the total value of the goods lost was more than the loan amount, bank entitled to no recovery.

2. Right to Recover Extraordinary Expenses Incurred by a Pawnee

940. The pawnee is, under section 175 of the act, entitled to receive from the pawnor extraordinary expenses incurred by him for the preservation of the goods pledged.

3. Right to Sue to Recover the Debt, etc. and Sale of the Pledged Goods

941. Section 176 confers rights on the pawnee, including the right of selling the pledged goods, in case the pawnor makes a default in payment of the debt or performance of the promise at the stipulated time. He can bring a suit against the pawnor upon the debt, or promise, and retain the goods pledged as a collateral security. In case, however, that the pledged goods have been lost or damaged due to the fault of the pawnee, for instance, or he fails to take due care of the goods as required by section 151 of the Contract Act, he will lose his claim against the pawnor to that extent. In the *Central Bank of India v. Grains and Gummy Agencies*,[994] due to the negligence of the pledgee bank, the pledged goods were lost. The bank was requested by the pledgor to sell the goods and realize the balance, but the bank failed to do so. Moreover, the bank was not in a position to redeliver the goods on the satisfaction of the claim.

992. AIR 1971 SC 1210. *See also Konavalov v.* Commander, Coast Guard Region, (2006) 4 SCC 620.

993. AIR 2008 Utt 22.

994. AIR 1989 MP 28; *see also Lallan Prasad v. Rehmat Ali*, AIR 1967 SC 1322.

It was held that the bank was liable for the loss of the goods and, therefore, the bank was not entitled to succeed in the claim against the pledgor.

F. Pawnor's Right to Redeem

942. The pledgor, however, has a right to redeem the goods pledged, i.e., take back the goods from the pawnee on payment of the agreed debt, or performance of the promise in accordance with the agreement as per section 177 of the Contract Act. He can exercise the right to redeem before the pawnee has made an actual sale of the goods.

§5. Lien

I. General

943. Lien is the right of the bailee under which he can retain the goods of the bailor, and refuse to deliver them to the bailor, until his due remuneration for services in respect of the goods bailed, or the amount due is paid. The Contract Act recognizes two kinds of liens: particular lien and general lien.

944. The right of a 'particular lien' entitles the bailee to retain those very goods for the services regarding which the remuneration is due. The 'general lien' entitles the bailee to retain the goods of the bailor for a general balance of account. Then the bailee incurs some expenses for preserving the goods from deteriorating during the lien, and he can recover them from the owner of the goods.[995] When the bailee loses his possession of the goods, the right of lien is thereby lost.

II. Particular Lien

945. Section 170 provides that 'where the bailee has, in accordance with the purpose of the bailment, rendered any service involving the exercise of labour or skill in respect of the goods bailed, he has, in the absence of a contract to the contrary, a right to retain such goods until he receives due remuneration for the services he has rendered in respect of them'. Thus a particular lien means the right of the bailee to retain those goods which have been bailed and in respect of which some service involving the exercise of labour or skill has been rendered but the remuneration for doing so has not been paid. This right can be exercised so long as the remuneration in respect of those goods has not been paid. Once the bailee parts with the possession, his right of lien comes to an end. If the bailee's right of lien has ended by parting with the possession, it is not revived if he happens to get the possession again. In *Eduljee v. Café John Bros.*,[996] the seller sold a second hand refrigerator, and also delivered it to the buyer. After some time there was some trouble with the refrigerator and two

995. *Surya Investment Co. v. S.T.C.*, AIR 1987 Cal 46.
996. AIR 1943 Bag 249.

parts of it were taken out and sent to the seller for repair. The seller, to whom the price had not been paid, wanted to exercise the right of lien over these parts. It was held that the sellers' right of lien had come to an end when he had delivered the refrigerator to the buyer, and this right was not revived by his getting the possession of some parts of it again. The right to a lien contained in section 170 of the Contract Act is available 'in the absence of a contract to the contrary', i.e., the parties by an agreement may exclude the right. The bailee, if he so likes, may waive his right of lien.[997] The right of a particular lien has been recognized not only in favour of a bailee only under section 170 of the Contract but also in other cases, e.g., lien of finder of goods under section 168; pawnees or pledgees lien under sections 173–174; An agents' lien under section 221 of the Contract Act; unpaid seller's lien under section 47 of the Sale of Goods Act, 1930; and a partners' lien under section 52 of the Indian Partnership Act, 1932.

III. General Lien

946. Section 171 of the Contract Act about a general lien lays down the following.

947. A general lien to bankers, factors, wharfingers, attorneys and policy-brokers may, in the absence of a contract to the contrary, retain, as a security a general balance of account of any goods bailed to them; but no other person has a right to retain, as a security for such balance, goods bailed to them, unless there is an express contract to that effect.

948. A general lien, thus, entitles the bailee to retain goods of the bailor 'for general balance of the account'. According to this right, the bailee may retain not only those goods of the bailor in respect of which some particular services are rendered, but also other goods in the possession of the bailee belonging to the bailor. This right of the general lien has been conferred only upon some of the kinds of bailees mentioned in this section and not others. For example, when a banker has advanced money to another, he has a lien on all securities which come into his hands for the amount of his general balance unless there is an express contract or circumstances to the contrary.[998] Therefore, if cheques or other securities have been deposited with a bank, he can exercise a lien over them. A banker can exercise a lien over bills, cheques, and monies entrusted or paid to him in his character as a banker, and this right is not 'prejudiced by any defect in the title of the customer of equities of third parties, provided the banker acts honestly and without notice of any defect in title'.[999] A banker's lien is a general lien and he can retain the goods for the satisfaction of a debt other than the one for which the goods are pledged.[1000] However, if there is an express agreement between the parties contrary to the statutory right of general lien, the right is thereby excluded.[1001] When the goods are given for a special purpose inconsistent with the right of the general lien, the goods can be used only for that special purpose rather than for the general lien.

997. *See* Sales of Goods Act, 1930, s. 49.
998. *Punjab National Bank v. Satyapal*, AIR 1956 Punjab 118 at 120.
999. *Jai Kishan Dass v. Central Bank of India*, AIR 1955 Pb 250 at 251.
1000. *State Bank of India v. Dipak Malviya*, AIR 1966 All 165.
1001. *Krishna Kisohre v. United Commercial Bank*, AIR 1982 Cal 62.

A. General Lien of Factors

949. A factor is a mercantile agent within section 2 of the Sale of Goods Act. A factor is an agent entrusted with the possession of goods of his principal for selling them. He has a right of general lien over the goods belonging to his principal which are in his possession, for the general balance of the account. As already noted, the right of a general lien can be exercised unless there is an express contract between the parties which negatives this right. According to this right, the principals' goods can be retained by the factor until the balance of the account due to the factor from the principal has been paid. In *E.H. Parakh v. King Emperor,*[1002] the appellant was a car dealer with whom one land holder put his car in the possession of. While the car was still in the possession of the appellant, the administration of the landholder was taken over by the court of wards. The manager of the court of wards directed the appellant to deliver the car. The appellant refused to do so in exercise of the power of the right of general lien over it. The High Court held that the appellant was entitled to have a right of general lien over the car.

B. General Lien of Wharfingers

950. Wharf means a loading stage alongside a sea or a river for loading and unloading vessels. Wharfinger means a person who owns, or has the care of, a wharf. A wharfinger has a lien over the goods of his customer, until his wharfage, i.e., the charges for the use of the wharf, is paid to him. His claim of general lien is valid only in respect of those goods which he received in his capacity as a wharfinger.

C. General Lien of Attorneys

951. The attorneys of the High Court, according to section 171 of the Contract Act also have a right of general lien. This right is presumed to be available to advocates and other legal practitioners.[1003] The right can be exercised in respect of documents, etc. belonging to the client which is with him. He can retain them until his fees for professional services and other costs and expenses incurred by him or a client are paid to him. If a solicitor is discharged by the client, the client cannot take back his documents until the costs incurred by the solicitor and his other charges are paid to him.[1004] If he was not discharged by the client, but he otherwise refuses to act on the clients' behalf or is unable to work for him, e.g., he stops his practice, the right of lien does not exist.[1005] This exercise of the right of a general lien in this case, however, is also subject to any contract to the contrary, express or implied. It has been held that if some document, like a promote, which is the foundation of the suit, is given to the advocate for being filed along with the plaintiff or at the first hearing of the suit, the necessary implication in such a case is that the advocate shall file the document as needed, and

1002. AIR 1926 Sind 225.
1003. *Damodardass v. R. Badrilal,* AIR 1987 AP 254; *Lalchand Ramchand v. Pyare Dasrath Chamar,* AIR 1971 MP 245.
1004. *Balkesserbai v. Naranaji,* ILR (1880) 4 Bom 352.
1005. *Basant Kumar Mitter v. Kusum Kumar Mitter,* (1900) 4 CWN 767.

his right of a general lien as regards such a document is excluded by the implied contract.[1006] But in another case, the Supreme Court had held that an advocate has no lien over the files and papers and documents entrusted by his client in connection with litigation.[1007] Section 171 permits a general lien to an advocate in respect of the 'goods bailed'. It has been held that the files and documents entrusted by a client to his advocate are not 'goods bailed' or 'saleable goods' as defined in the Sale of Goods Act, 1930. There is no contract of bailment, which could entitle an advocate to exercise lien over them, because there is neither delivery of goods or a contract that those files, etc. should be returned or otherwise disposed of, etc. as stated in section 148 of the Contract Act.

D. General Lien of Policy-Brokers

952. A policy-broker means a person who acts as an insurance agent to effect marine insurance. He is one of the persons mentioned in section 171 of the Contact Act having a general right of lien. He can exercise such a right until the balance of account due to him from a client has been paid.

IV. Liability of Guarantor for Bank Guarantee for Recovery of Dues by Bank

953. For the exercise of the right of set-off and the right of a general lien by the bank over an amount in a bank account to protect its financial interest. The bank had issued notice before exercising such a right. In *Syndicate Bank v. Wilfred D'Souza,*[1008] it was held that as no element of public law was involved and as the transaction and deed of guarantee did not contain any stipulation governing the recovery of dues, the said right of the bank shall be exercised only after liability was determined by a debt recovery tribunal, hence the impugned action of the bank could not be said to be arbitrary, irrational or a violation of Article 14 of the Indian Constitution.

V. Right of Suit Against a Wrongdoer

954. When the goods have been bailed, if a third party wrongfully deprives the bailee of their use of possession, or causes an injury to the goods, the bailee under section 180 of the Contract Act can sue the third party for any wrong caused to the goods. According to this provision not only the bailee but also the bailor can bring an action against such a third party. If a person fraudulently or forcibly takes away the goods from the bailee, the bailee has a right to recover them. In *Purushottam Das Banarsi Das v. Union of India*[1009] 'A' obtained delivery of certain goods from the

1006. *Lalchand Ramchand v. Pyare Dasrath Chamar*, AIR 1971 MP 245.
1007. *R.D. Saxsena v. Balram Prasad Sharma*, AIR 2000 SC 2912.
1008. AIR 2003 Kant 337.
1009. AIR 1967 All 549.

railway on a forged railway receipt. 'A' pledged the goods to 'B'. It was held that the railway authorities had a right to recover those goods from 'B'.

VI. Position of Finder of Goods

955. A person who finds goods belonging to another and takes them into his custody, according to section 71 of the act, is subject to the same responsibility as a bailee and as such he must take the same amount of care with regard to the goods as is expected of a bailee under section 151. He is also subject to all the duties of a bailee, including a duty to return the goods after the true owner is found. If he refuses to return them, he could be made liable for conversion. Moreover, if by his default in returning the goods, there is some loss, destruction or deterioration of the goods, he will be liable in respect of them under sections 160 and 161 of the Contract Act. There are some rights of the finder of the goods under sections 168 and 169 of the Contract Act. Under section 168, he has no right to sue the owner for compensation for trouble and expenses voluntarily incurred by him to preserve the goods and to find the owner, but he may retain the goods against the owner until he receives such compensation, and where the owner has offered a specific reward for the return of the goods lost, the finder may sue for such reward, and may retain the goods until he receives it. This right is only in respect of lost goods but where it does not pertain to the goods, then this right cannot be used unless there is a contract for the payment of it.[1010] Furthermore, section 169 provides that when a thing which is commonly the subject of a sale is lost, if the owner cannot with reasonable diligence be found or if he refuses upon demand, to pay the lawful charges of the finder, the finder may sell the thing, especially when the thing is in danger of perishing or losing the greater part of its value, or when the lawful charges of the finder, in respect of the thing found, amount to two-thirds of its value.

1010. *See Lalman Shukla v. Gauri Dutt*, (1913) 11 All L J 489.

Part II. Economic Law

Chapter 1. General Principles of Economic Law

§1. State Intervention in Economic Activities

I. Institutional Framework

956. India, a union of states, is a Sovereign Socialist Secular Democratic Republic with a Parliamentary system of Government. The Republic is governed in terms of the Constitution, which was adopted by Constituent Assembly on 26 November 1949 and came into force on 26 November 1950. India has twenty-eight states, six Union Territories and one National Capital Territory in Delhi. The President is the constitutional head of Executive of the Union. Real executive power is vested in the Council of Ministers with the Prime Minister as head. Article 74(1) of the Constitution provides that there shall be a Council of Ministers headed by Prime Minister to aid and advise the President who shall, in exercise of his functions, act in accordance with such advice. The Council of Ministers is collectively responsible to the Lok Sabha, the House of the People. In the states, the Governor is the head of Executive, but real executive power vests with the Chief Minister who heads the Council of Ministers. The Council of Ministers of a state is collectively responsible to the elected legislative assembly of the state. The Constitution governs the sharing of legislative power between Parliament and the State Legislatures, and provides for the vesting of residual powers in the Parliament. The power to amend the Constitution is also vested in the Parliament. Under the Constitution, the Parliament has the power to make laws for the whole of or any part of the territory of India. The State Legislatures have the power to make laws for the states. The subjects on which legislation can be made are specified in the Seventh Schedule of the Constitution.

957. Parliament has the exclusive right to legislate in respect of items appearing in List I, called the 'Union List'. This list includes such matters as defence, foreign affairs, currency, income tax, excise duty, railways, shipping, posts and telegraphs, etc.

State Legislatures have the exclusive power to make laws in relation to items appearing in List II called the 'State List'. This includes items like public order, police, public health, communications, agriculture, lotteries, taxes on entertainment and wealth, sales tax and octroi, etc.

Both Parliament and the State Legislatures have the power to legislate in items appearing in List III of the Constitution which is known as 'Concurrent List'. This list includes items like electricity, newspapers, criminal law, marriage and divorce, stamp duties, trade unions, price controls, etc.

958. The result of this division is that both the governments – Central and State – have powers to regulate economic activities in different fields. The third level of government – local or municipal government – also has power depending upon what is delegated by the state governments.

II. Government Role in the Economy

959. At the time of independence, it was desired that the free flow of trade and commerce in India be promoted in order to achieve economic unity and integration of the economy. For that purpose, Article 301 was incorporated in the Constitution, which provides that 'trade, commerce and intercourse throughout the territory of India shall be free'. In addition to this, the Constitution provides freedom to move throughout the territory of India and to practice any profession or to carry on any occupation, trade or business.

960. At present, the economy of India is one of largest economies in the world and will be ranked first by 2050 on global front. Following strong economic reforms from the socialist inspired economy of a post-independence Indian nation, the country began to develop a fast-paced economic growth, as free market principles were initiated in 1990 for international competition and foreign investment. The economy of India is as diverse as it is large, with a number of major sectors including manufacturing industries, agriculture, textiles and handicrafts, and services. Agriculture is a major component of the Indian economy, as over 66% of the Indian population earns its livelihood from this area. Other areas where India is expected to make progress include manufacturing, construction of ships, pharmaceuticals, aviation, biotechnology, tourism, nanotechnology, retailing and telecommunications. As the free market principles were accepted role of government in Indian economy changed from being a controller to regulator. But still the role of government is relevant as government is the one which decides about the various factors controlling our economy and decides the rules and regulations keeping in mind the welfare of the public. Apart from this government brings new schemes to help person in personal and professional avenues.

961. Notwithstanding the lessening of state ownership, it exercises its control through regulatory mechanism over privately owned industrial units. In addition to this, the state influences private investment through the creation of special economic zones, tax benefits, subsidies, etc. in certain industries and regions.

III. Banking and Finance Sector

962. A Bank is an institution which deals in money and credit or is often styled on credit institution. Bank performs a large variety of functions in the modern society. As such, the word 'bank' has been defined in numerous ways according to the aspect, or aspects, specially emphasized by writers. The borrowing and the lending of money are its essential functions. The modern bank performs numerous functions which throw light on the variety of the services it renders to the modern civilized society. These functions may be divided into three classes: (a) primary functions; (b) General utility functions; and (c) agency functions.

A. Primary Functions

963. The primary and essential functions of a bank, as is evident from the word bank are two: (1) the borrowing; and (2) the lending of money. This essential feature of its business remains the same whether the bank is a vast joint stock organization with a wealth of resources and network of branches and agencies, or a comparatively small private bank or a pioneer bank in a new country, with a stock-in-trade consisting of a tent, a safe, or a trestle table and a revolver.

1. The Borrowing of Money

964. Banks borrow money through receiving deposits. Persons having money but faced with the problem of its proper investment or safe custody, deposit it with banks and in many cases, receive interest. This function of the bank encourages people to save money. When it is known that an easy and convenient means of safe and profitable investment of money in the shape of deposits is available, people who would have otherwise spent all their income or hoard it underground, do not do so.

2. The Lending of Money

965. The small deposits received by banks together constitute a huge amount. This is lent out by the banks to capable agriculturists, industrialists and businessmen, who invest it in their ventures to their own profit and to the economic advancement of the country. Money is lent to industrialists, agriculturists and traders in various ways. The discounting of bills of exchange and granting overdraft on current accounts are two important methods of commercial credit.

B. General Utility Functions

966. Besides the primary functions detailed above, the modern bank; performs many miscellaneous functions which are of great general utility.

1. Issue of Notes

967. It has been entrusted to a duly constituted central or Reserve Bank of India which has the capacity to perform this function more efficiently than the government.

2. Issue of Credit Instruments

968. Banks create credit instruments like bank drafts, cheques, letters of credit, etc. which economize the use of metallic currency, make the transmission of money long distances convenient and cheap, and remove the want of medium of exchange felt by modern communities currency alone being inadequate to meet the entire need.

3. Foreign Exchange Business

969. In old days, each country used to have different parts, and bakers did the useful work of changing one kind of money into the other kinds. This saves them the name of money changers. This function has now become defunct as each country has begun to maintain a uniform currency throughout its length and breadth. The different countries, however, still possess different currencies and banks play the important role of purchasing and selling foreign currency, foreign bills of exchange and other credit instruments in exchange for the currency of the country in which they are situated. They facilitate foreign trades to an appreciable degree.

4. Safe Custody of Valuable

970. Banks undertake to keep safe custody of valuable and important documents in specially constructed strong rooms which are sure safeguards against fire and theft. The small payment charged by them for the purpose is nothing in comparison to the utility of the service rendered.

C. Agency Functions

971. Banks also render many ‘agency services’ by acting as agents to their customers in various capacities. (a) They collect and pay cheques, realize dividends and interest and pay subscriptions and insurance premiums in the capacity of special agents to their customers. (b) Banks conduct stock and share transactions on behalf of their customers. (c) They act in various other agency capacities such as those of trustees, attorneys and executors.

972. The Banking sector in India has emerged as a resurgent sector in the Indian economy. As per the McKinsey report India Banking 2010, the banking sector index has grown at a compounded annual rate of over 51% since the year 2001, as compared to a 27% growth in the market index during the same period. It is projected that the sector has the potential to account for over 7.7% of GDP with over INR 7,500 billion in market cap, and to provide over 1.5 million jobs.

D. Kinds of Banks

973. The financial requirements of the modern community are diverse and various so that different kinds of banks have been set up for specializing in different kinds of requirements. They are as follows:

(1) Indigenous Banking.
(2) Modern Banking.
(3) Foreign Exchange Banks.
(4) Reserve Bank of India.

1. Indigenous Banking

974. Indigenous banking means banking business carried on by the Indians in the old Indian fashion. From the very early times India possessed an efficient system of indigenous banking In fact, money-lending can be traced back to 2,000 BC. and the subsequent history bristiles with definite references to the banking business carried on in the days of yore. The Buddhist works, Kautiliya's Arthshastra, and Darma Shastra make detailed remarks about indigenous banking and show its importance in the economy of the country in those times. Indeed even today indigenous bankers play a much more important part than the more imposing modern banks. They are spread throughout the length and breadth of the country and are to be found in every village, town and even in small and big cities. The firm of indigenous bankers is usually a family concern and is not organized on joint stock principles.

975. Functions: The main business of indigenous bankers is to advance loans on every kind of security – ornaments, land, promissory notes or even verbal promise. In villages, they even finance agriculturists and petty artisans who rarely have any good security to offer. In such areas, indigenous bankers are almost the only source of credit. Their methods are simple and free from formalities and suit the illiterate borrowers eminently. In towns, they finance trade and even big mills and factories. They also deal with hundies (A kind of bills of exchange). They buy or discount hundies offered by their customers and cash those drawn upon them by their agents or by approved firms. They sell hundies drawn upon them by their agents or other firms agreeing to this arrangement. Some of them also receive deposits but all or most of them do not do so. They generally combine trading with the banking or money-lending business. They deal with cotton, grain, gold, etc. while many of them indulge in speculation. Money lending business being a subject, almost all the states in order to regulate these indigenous bankers by enacting money-lending Acts. The Act compels these bankers to maintain proper accounts and charge reasonable interests from the borrowers.

2. Modern Banking

976. With the advent of the Europeans in India, modern Banks began to set up on western lines. There are mainly five kinds of modern banks namely: Commercial banks; Exchange banks; Industrial banks; Land-mortgage banks; and Cooperative banks.

977. Modern banking in India was born in the nineteenth century. Before the banking institutions developed, the business was in the hands of indigenous bankers. The earliest institutions which undertook modern banking business under the British regime were agency houses which carried to banking business in addition to their trading business. Most of these agency houses were closed down in the period 1929–1932, A number of banks which came into existence between the 1830s and 1840s were also in great trouble. Prominent among them were three presidency banks which were later amalgamated into the then Imperial Bank of India in 1919 following a banking crisis. The first bank with limited liability managed by Indians was the Oudh Commercial Bank founded in 1881. Subsequently the Punjab National Bank was established in 1884 and then the Allahabad Bank followed. The Swadeshi (Indianization) movement which began in 1906 encouraged the formation of a number of commercial banks. The banking crisis in 1913–1917 and the failure of 588 banks in various provinces during the decade ending in 1949 underlined the need to regulate and control commercial banks. The Banking companies (Inspection) Ordinance was passed in January 1946 as was the Banking Companies (Restriction of Branches) Act. The Banking Companies Act, was passed in February 1949 and it was subsequently amended to read as the Banking Regulation Act.

978. With a view to bringing big commercial banks into the mainstream of economic development with definite social obligations and objectives, the government issued an Ordinance on 19 July 1969 acquiring ownership and control fourteen major banks in the country, with deposits exceeding INR 500 million each. Six more commercial banks were also nationalized later on. As against public sector banks having 141 branches in twenty-four countries in 1984, there are at resent eight public sector banks and one private bank with ninety-eight branches in twenty-six countries. Besides the branch network, there are at present fifteen representative offices, seven joint ventures and thirteen subsidiaries. The aggregate balance sheet of the overseas branches for the year ended 31 March 1997 was USD 20.872 million.

979. Subsequent to the issue of guidelines in January 1993 for the entry of new private sector banks, the Reserve Bank of India granted 'in principle' approval for the setting up of thirteen new privately owned domestic banks. The number of banks in liquidation as on 20 June 1997 was eighty-eight.

980. There are certain banks and bodies which have been established for special purposes by the government. They are: (i) the Industrial Development Bank of India (IDBI), established primarily for granting assistance to industry in India; (ii) the Small Industries Development Bank of India (SIDBI) primarily established to grant loans to small-scale industries; (iii) the Export-Import Bank (EXIM Bank), with a menu of thirty-five major programmes covering all the stages of the cycle; (iv) the Industrial Reconstruction Bank of India (IRBI), which came into existence on 20 March 1985 under the IRBI Act, 1984; (v) the Board for Industrial and Financial Reconstruction (BIFR) which became operational with effect from 15 May 1987. This looks into the cases of sick industrial companies in the large and medium sectors with a view of achieving, *inter alia*, the objectives of timely detection of sickness and determination of preventive, ameliorative, remedial and other measures in respect of such companies and expeditious enforcement of the measures so determined; (vi) the State Finance Corporations (SFCs) at the state-level form an integral part of the development financing system in the country. They function with the objective of financing and promoting small and medium enterprises for achieving balanced regional socio-economic growth, catalyzing higher investment, generating great employment opportunities and widening the ownership base of industry. At present, there are eighteen SFCs in the country, seventeen of which were set under State Financial Corporations Act, 1951.

981. At present a total of 62,849 branches of scheduled commercial banks are functioning in the country of which 33,092, 1,299, 9,025 and 8,333 branches are located in rural, quasi-urban and metropolitan centres respectively. Local area banks provide an institutional mechanism for promotion of rural savings as well as for the provision of credit of viable economic activities in the local areas. The policy of the government is to allow the establishment of new local area banks in private sectors. The area of operations of these banks is a maximum of three geographically contiguous districts. This is expected to bridge the gap in credit availability and enhance the institutional credit framework in the rural and quasi-urban areas. The minimum paid-up capital for such a bank is INR 50 million, and the promoters' enhancement contribution should be at least INR 20 million. Proposals with diversified share holdings are to be preferred. The promoters of these banks may comprise individuals' corporate entities, trusts and societies.

982. The National Bank for Agriculture and Rural Development (NABARD) as an apex development bank has been charged with the responsibility of promoting integrated rural development in the rural areas. The bank grants loan mostly to state cooperative banks to finance seasonal agricultural operations.

983. Cooperative banks and credit societies are the societies established under the Cooperative Societies Act for providing credit to their members.

984. There are cooperative banks which are working on commercial basis. They are mostly in the cities banking all kinds of commercial business. Cooperative credit institutions fall under three classes:

(a) Primary societies.
(b) Central Banks.
(c) State Cooperative Banks.

a. Primary Societies

985. They are spread throughout the length and breadth of the country and com in direct contact with poor artisans and cultivators whom they finance. They are associations of borrowers and non-borrowers of a particular locality, and the members generally have unlimited liabilities so that they may be very vigilant in making advances. They receive funds mostly in the shape of share capital, grants from the government, deposits and entrance fees. They also get money from the central cooperative banks with which they are affiliated in the shape of loan.

b. Central Cooperative Banks

986. They are incorporated and organized at each district. They unify and direct the primary credit societies affiliated with them and give them financial assistance. Their sources of funds are their own capital, deposits from the public and the funds given by the provincial cooperative banks or rather apex Cooperative Banks. In the beginning there were not many restrictions, control and regulations. This open policy was considered to be harmful to the national interest. The following restrictions and controls were imposed on these banks: (i) licensing of these banks by the government; the licences laid down certain conditions under which these banks are required to work; (ii) asking them to submit their returns to the government and making them liable them for inspection from the government; (iii) asking these banks to obtain permission from the Reserve Bank of India like other joint stock commercial banks and making them liable to the control, regulations and inspection of the Reserve Bank of India; (iv) compelling to publish balance sheets annually and sending copies to the government and also to the Reserve Bank of India.

c. State Cooperative Bank or Apex Bank

987. At the head of the head of the state is the State Cooperative Bank or Apex Bank as it is called. It is the central reserve of the whole movement in the state. It has its members' cooperative credit societies, central banks, mortgage banks, and sometimes primary societies and even individuals. It receives deposits from members and non-members and does all banking business except that in the matter of loans it makes advances only to members. It helps in equitable distribution of funds among banks in different areas for banks with surpluses may keep their money in deposit with the state bank which would advance the same to a bank in need of money.

3. Foreign Exchange Banks

988. Foreign exchange banks, as their name implies, are the result of foreign capital and enterprise and have their head offices in foreign countries. These banks managed to have a foothold in India before the establishment of Indian joint stock banks and when the latter came into the market they found themselves faced with a severe competition from foreign banks which had resources far in excess of those held by the Indian banks and thus could beat their rivals easily. These banks have been established with the sole object of financing the foreign trade of the country. However, many of the Indian banks have now entered in foreign markets and they are doing foreign trade. In the beginning these banks confined their activities to the port towns only, but they began to spread their net in the interior of the country after 1919. They accept deposits as well thus proving formidable rivals to the Indian joint stock banks. These bank, therefore, occupy an important position in the Indian money market. The following are the functions which these foreign banks perform:

(i) they finance the foreign trade of the country by buying, selling and discounting foreign bills of exchange;

(ii) they serve as collecting agents for Indian exporters and collect the proceeds of the bills in foreign countries and hand them over to the exporters;
(iii) they give valuable advice about the credit and standing of the foreign merchants and thus facilitate trade;
(iv) they are freely receiving deposits in India and are thus competing with Indian joint stock banks;
(v) they have begun to take part in the internal trade of the country as well though they also give loans.

989. These banks in the past followed a policy of discrimination and distrust against Indian merchants which crated a deep resentment in the country. By taking part in the internal trade and accepting deposits in competition with Indian banks, they hindered growth of Indian joint stock banks. Thus, the open door policy towards them was thought to be harmful as much to the national interests as to the joint stock banks and the government was asked time and again, to impose restrictions upon their business. Among the restrictions those were proposed to be upon them, the following may be mentioned: (i) licensing of these banking institutions by the government; the licence to be granted should lay down the conditions under which the banks would work; (ii) compelling them to use Indian funds in India; (iii) asking them to convert their capital into rupee capital and have Indian directors on their boards of directors; (iv) restrictions on receiving Indian deposits as is being done in USA; (v) compelling them to publish statement of their Indian business annually.

990. Most of the modern banks in India are commercial banks. They normally finance the internal trade of the country and give short term loans for the purpose. They provide the working capital. On the basis of cash resources and the deposits that they possess they raise a huge structure of short dated credit. Their deposits being mostly demand obligations, They take precautions against getting their fund enmeshed in long term loans. In order to be able to meet the demands of depositors, they have to keep their funds 'liquid'.

4. Reserve Bank of India

991. In India, there is a central bank called the Reserve Bank of India, which was established in 1935 by the Reserve Bank of India Act, 1934. It was established to regulate the issue of bank notes and the keeping of reserves with the view of securing the monetary stability in India and generally to operate the currency and credit system of the country to its advantage. After independence, the Reserve Bank of India was nationalized on 1 January 1949 under the terms of the Reserve Bank of India (Transfer to Public Ownership) Act, 1948. In 1949, the Banking Regulation Act was enacted which empowered the Reserve Bank of India (RBI) 'to regulate, control, and inspect the banks in India'. The Banking Regulation Act also provided that no new bank or branch of an existing bank could be opened without a licence from the RBI, and no two banks could have common directors.

992. The Reserve bank of India Act confers upon the bank all those privileges which are enjoyed by similar banks, called central banks, in other countries. Following the Bank of England which is the central bank of England, the Reserve Bank of India has three functions, viz., (a) Central Banking functions; (b) General Banking functions; (c) Issue of currency notes; and (d) Restrictions on its business.

a. Central Banking functions

993. It acts as banker to the central government, state governments and local bodies. The Reserve Bank of India requires it to accept money for various government bodies and make payments up to the amount standing to the credit of their respective accounts; and carry out their exchange, remittance and other banking operations, including the management of the public debt; It does not pay any interest on the money kept on behalf of the governments. The Bank is authorized to buy and sell government securities maturing within ten years.

It is a bankers' bank: Other banks of the country are required to maintain with it certain cash reserve and eventually the bank is expected to help them in times of financial stringency. All scheduled banks are required to keep 5% of their demand and 2% of their time liabilities with the Reserve Bank. It pays no interest on this amount, but should the balance any bank falls below the prescribed limit, it charges interest on the difference between the balance required and balance maintained.

b. General Banking functions:

994. The Reserve Bank of India is authorized to transact following business:

(i) the acceptance of money on deposit without interest;
(ii) the purchase, sale and rediscount of bills of exchange and promissory notes with certain restrictions;
(iii) the making of loans and advances for not more than ninety days against the security of stocks, gold, bills, etc.;
(iv) the making advances to local governments for a limited period;
(v) the purchase and sale of government securities.

c. Issues of Currency

995. The sole right to issue bank notes is vested in the Reserve Bank. It conducts the issue of bank notes in an Issue Department which is kept wholly separate from the Banking Department. The currency system of India, like that any other country, consists of metallic currency and paper currency. Before the year 1835, there w ere about one thousand coins of different variety and weight in circulation in India issued by various Hindu and Muslim rulers. This bewildering multiplicity of coins greatly hampered trade. Therefore, in 1835, the East India Company minted the present rupee coins, in the beginning of 180 grains of silver, the standard coin of the country. Mints were opened to the free coinage of silver on payment of mintage. A full-fledged silver standard was thus established. The price of silver began to fall from 1873 onwards due to the opening of new and very productive silver mines in America. The gold value of rupee, which normally of two British shillings, fell to the one shilling level. This upset even the basis of trade, in particular, it drastically curtailed imports from foreign countries. Moreover the then government of India had to pay annual home charges to Great Britain in sterling and, in terms of rupees, their commitments almost doubled. The question was, therefore, referred to the Herschell Commission, whose report was published in 1893. This led to the closure of the mints for the unrestricted coinage of silver in 1893, causing demand for rupees. This led to a rise in the value of rupee to the level of one shilling and 4 pence (in the then British currency). In 1898, the Fowler Committee was appointed. It suggested that the British gold sovereign should be made the legal tender and current coin in India and the mints be thrown open to the unrestricted coinage of gold. Thus, the Committee virtually recommended the establishment of gold currency standard. The then government, however, though it is accepted these recommendations, did not put them into practice. This currency policy was greatly criticized by the people of the country and the government of India appointed the Chamberlain Commission in 1913, which gave the gold exchange standard its blessing and recommended its continuance. The report was in the hands of the then government shortly before the First World War. During this period people lost confidence in the government. Deposits were withdrawn from the post office savings banks and currency notes were presented to the government for conversion into gold to such an extent that the government was obliged to suspend the issue of gold. It was difficult for the government to import gold and silver for coinage. The value of silver increased so much that people found it profitable to melt rupee coins and sell them as bullion. An exchange rate of two British shillings and four pence had to be fixed by the government. After World War I the government appointed the Babington-Smith Committee to advise future policy of Indian exchange and currency. The Committee recommended the reintroduction of the gold exchange standard. A high ratio of two shillings was fixed. However, in 1922 the government fixed the price of the rupee as one shilling six pence. In 1931, however, the government had to go off the gold standard. This rate was stabilized even for some time after the Independence of India. At present the rupee is floating independently in the international market. The current price of the rupee is fixed according to its value with the other currencies, e.g., US dollar (USD), the Euro, the British pound, etc.

d. Restrictions of Its Business

996. The bank is not allowed to engage in trade in the ordinary course of business. It is also debarred from advancing money on the mortgage of immovable property. It cannot draw or accept bills payable otherwise than on demand. Nor it is permitted to allow interest on deposits. These restrictions are placed to keep it financially sound and to check it from competing with other banks of the country. It cannot buy or sell its own shares of other companies. It cannot engaged itself in trading directly or indirectly.

997. Metallic Currency: The most important metallic coin in India is the rupee. It is the principal money of the realm, and unlimited legal tender. Hence, it is the standard money of India. However, unlike standard money, its intrinsic value is much less than its face value and it is not open to free coinage. It is as such neither wholly standard money nor wholly token money. It is best described a token standard. Besides the rupee coin, there are following subsidiary coins: 50 paise, 25 paise, 10 paise, 5 paise, 1 paisa. All the coins are made of nickel. However, now Re. one and 50 paise are the only legal tender money. The others have been declared demonetized.

998. Paper currency: Before the Second World War, the Indian paper currency consisted of notes of INR 5, 10, 100, 1,000 and 10,000. During the Second World War, notes worth INR 1 and 2 were also introduced. But later on INR 1,000 and 10,000 notes were not only withdrawn but even declared illegal. A few years ago, INR 500 and 1,000 notes have again been introduced. These notes are promissory notes. They were formerly issued by the government of India, but since the enactment of the Reserve Bank of India Act in 1935, their issue has now been entrusted to the Reserve Bank of India. INR 1 and INR 2 are, however, issued by the government of India. When the issue was in the hands of the government, the profit on paper issue was used to create a paper currency reserve.

999. With the enactment of the Reserve Bank, the paper currency in India entered a new phase. According to this Act, the sole right of issuing notes has been vested in the Issue Department of the Reserve Bank. This issue department is quite separate from the Banking Department and sole liability of the former is with regard to the notes issued. In the beginning, assets of the Issue Department were invariably equal to the value of the total notes issued. Later on this equal amount of assets was gradually reduced to nullity. The Reserve Bank is now no longer required to maintain any amount of reserve below the issue of the notes.

1000. Banking Industry in India functions under the sunshade of Reserve Bank of India – the regulatory, central bank. The commercial banking structure in India consists of: Scheduled Commercial Banks Unscheduled Bank. Scheduled commercial Banks constitute those banks which have been included in the Second Schedule of Reserve Bank of India (RBI) Act, 1934. RBI in turn includes only those banks in this schedule which satisfy the criteria laid down vide section 42 (60) of the Act. Some cooperative banks are scheduled commercial banks although not all cooperative banks are. Being a part of the second schedule confers some benefits to the bank in terms of access to accommodation by RBI during the times of liquidity constraints. At the same time, however, this status also subjects the bank certain conditions and obligation towards the reserve regulations of RBI. For the purpose of assessment of performance of banks, the Reserve Bank of India categorize them as public sector banks (twenty-seven), old private sector banks, new private sector banks and foreign banks.

1001. In order to spread banking to villages, the Regional Rural Banks Act, 1976 was passed through which regional rural banks were established. The purpose of establishing these banks is to develop the rural economy by providing the credit and other facilities for the purpose of development of agriculture, trade, commerce, industry and other productive activities in the rural area. This facility is extended particularly to the small and marginal farmers, agriculture labourers, artisans and small entrepreneurs, etc. Besides, there are cooperative banks established in the metropolitan, urban and semi-urban areas to cater to the needs of local persons. The cooperative banks are registered under the state societies acts of different states in India. At present in India there are eighty-two regional banks.

1002. In addition to public sector banks, certain private banks are also functioning. These banks are given permission to operate as a part of the liberalization process initiated by the central government in the early 1990s in India. The entry into private banks is allowed in view of the recommendations of the Narsimham Committee. These banks are registered as companies under the Companies Act and have to obtain a licence from the Reserve Bank of India. At present in India there are twenty-one private banks.

1003. Taking this liberalization process further, foreign banks too are allowed to operate in India. In this regard, the Reserve Bank of India prescribes the standards, which foreign banks need to comply with. Foreign banks need to obtain a licence from the Reserve Bank of India. At present in India there are thirty-eight foreign banks.

1004. In order to finance the industries, certain financial institutions have also been established viz. the Industrial Finance Corporation of India, the Industrial Credit and Investment Corporation of India Ltd., the Industrial Development Bank of India, Small Industrial Development Bank of India, the Industrial Reconstruction Bank of India, the Export/Import Bank of India, the Securities and Trading Corporation of India, the Stock Holding Corporation of India, the National Housing Bank, etc.

IV. Foreign Investment

1005. Before 1991, foreign investment in India was allowed up to 40% of the equity, provided the investment was accompanied by a technological transfer. This policy has drastically changed after 1991. Now, the Reserve Bank of India has specified high priority industries on an automatic basis that permits foreign equity up to 50%, 51%, 74% and even 100%.

1006. Foreign investment in India by foreign companies is permitted in the following manner. A foreign company may either establish a liaison/representative office or project office or branch office or register a wholly-owned subsidiary or may enter into a joint venture company. For this purpose, financial/technical/techno-financial approval is given through an automatic route through the RBI or the FIPB (Foreign Investment Promotion Board) by the central government. Direct foreign investment is permitted through the manner of financial collaborations, joint ventures and technical collaborations, through capital markets via Euro issues, private placements or preferential allotments. Recently the government of India has permitted foreign direct investment in retail up to 49%.

1007. The areas in which foreign direct investments (FDI) is not permitted are followings:

(i) Retail Trading (except single brand product retailing).
(ii) Atomic Energy.
(iii) Lottery Business.
(iv) Gambling and Betting.
(v) Business of Chit Fund.
(vi) *Nidhi* Company.
(vii) Agricultural (excluding Floriculture, Horticulture, Development of seeds, Animal Husbandry, Pisciculture and cultivation of vegetables, mushrooms, etc. under controlled conditions and services related to agro and allied sectors)

and Plantations activities (other than Tea Plantations) (cf. Notification No. FEMA 94/2003-RB dated 18 June 2003).

(viii) Housing and Real Estate business (except development of townships, construction of residential/commercial premises, roads or bridges to the extent specified in Notification No. FEMA 136/2005-RB dated 19 July 2005).

(ix) Trading in Transferable Development Rights (TDRs).

(x) Manufacture of cigars, cheroots, cigarillos and cigarettes, of tobacco or of tobacco substitutes.

V. Media

1008. The Indian entertainment and media (E&M) industry has out-performed the Indian economy and is one of the fastest growing sectors in India. The E&M industry generally tends to grow faster when the economy is expanding. The Indian economy has been growing at a fast clip over the last few years, and the income levels too have been experiencing a high growth rate. Prasar Bharati, a statutory autonomous body, was established in 1997 by the Prasar Bharati Act. It is the Public Service broadcaster of the country, which aims to empower and enlighten the citizens of India, and audiences outside the country by providing, in the most efficient manner possible, media content of the highest quality. It aims to, through original and relevant programmes, inform, educate and entertain a sizeable audience. This objective of public service broadcasting is purported to be achieved though All India Radio and Doordarshan (Television), which earlier were working as independent media units under the Ministry of Information & Broadcasting.

1009. Growth of TV channels: The total number of TV channels (both private and government owned) grew from 461 in 2009 to 626 in January 2012. The number of News and Current Affairs channels was 312 and that of Non-News and Current Affairs channels was 314 up till January 2012. Foreign Broadcasters: A total of seventy-five channels have been down-linked till January 2012 by a number of foreign broadcasters.

1010. Direct To Home (DTH) Service: DD DIRECT+ is India's first and only FTA Direct-To-Home (DTH) service being provided by Prasar Bharati (a public service broadcaster). Apart from Prasar Bharati, Dish TV India Ltd., Tata Sky Ltd., and Sun Direct TV Pvt. Ltd., Reliance Big TV Pvt. Ltd., Bharti Telemedia Ltd. and Bharat Business Channel Ltd have also been granted licence for operating DTH services.

1011. The eligibility conditions provide for total foreign equity holding, including FDI/NRI/OCB/FII, in the applicant company not to exceed 49%, and within the foreign equity, the FDI component not to exceed 20%. It also provides that Applicant Company must have Indian management control with the majority representatives on the board as well as the chief executive of the company being a resident Indian.

1012. High Definition (HD) Growth Wave: Another trend witnessed in 2010 was the entry of HD channels. Apart from 'Food First', India's first HD food channel, 'Movies Now' was also launched in HD. Doordarshan broadcasted the Commonwealth Games (CWG) in HD format. Sports, Movies and Events are expected to be the key demand drivers for HD content. India currently has channels like NGC HD, Discovery

World HD, Star Plus HD, Zee TV HD, and two Tamil HD channels and others are expected. DTH operators like SUN Direct, Tata Sky, Dish TV and Reliance BIG TV are heavily promoting their HD services in India.

1013. Radio Sector: In 2010, the total size of the Radio Sector was estimated to be about USD 0.22 billion. It is expected to grow at a CAGR of about 20% to USD 0.44 billion.

1014. FM radio: In 2010, total 245 Channels are operational including the 25 channels operationalized in the phase I.

1015. Satellite Radio: At present Worldspace India Private Ltd., a wholly-owned subsidiary of Worldspace Asia Pvt. Ltd. Singapore is providing services under Foreign Investment Promotion Board (FIPB) approval.

1016. Community Radio: The policy on community radio was liberalized during the year 2008 to bring in the civil society and voluntary organizations working on not-for-profit basis under its ambit. Earlier only educational institutions were permitted to set up a community radio. Presently, twenty-nine community radio stations are operating.

1017. Policy Initiatives – DTH Service: Direct To Home (DTH) service is a comparatively recent entrant as compared to cable transmission. DTH is an addressable system and covers the entire country. The programmes transmitted through DTH can be directly be received at homes by installing small dish antennas at convenient locations in the building. DTH transmission does not require any intermediary, since an individual user is directly served by the DTH operator.

1018. Policy on IPTV: The government has put in place the policy on IPTV enabling another mode of distribution of close to 550 permitted satellite TV channels till date through the Telecom and Cable Networks. This is bound to give not only a new digital visual experience to the Indian viewer with various value added and interactive services to cater to the persisting demand of the subscriber for new and interactive services but also for the platform service providers. The policy on IPTV now offers greater clarity on the issues involved and both the telecom operators as well as the cable operators will be able to provide IPTV services and will be regulated as per their respective licensing conditions.

1019. Head-end In The Sky (HITS): To speed up the process of digitalization of cable services located in non-CAS areas of the country, the Government is in the process of taking a view on the recommendations of TRAI on the issue of the proposed policy framework on the Head-end In The Sky (HITS) mode of delivery of content to the cable operators. This system will enable the packaging of content in digital form at the level of HITS operator who will uplink it to a satellite to be received by the cable operators and thereafter distributed in digital mode through cable network.

1020. Mobile TV: Mobile TV is another mode of distribution of TV channels. A joint group of Ministry of Information & Broadcasting (MIB) and Department of Telecommunications (DoT) has considered the regulatory and licensing issues of mobile TV and held that if mobile TV services are to be provided in the broadcasting mode using transmission of terrestrial or satellite broadcast signals, they will come under the domain of MIB and will be governed by the applicable laws. If they are provided by using the infrastructure of telecom service provider, they will fall in the domain of Ministry of Communication and Information Technology (MCIT).

1021. Apart from this public channel, there are plenty of private, news as well as non-news, channels, which are permitted to operate in the process of liberalization. In 2002, the Union Cabinet allowed 26% of foreign direct investment (FDI) in news and current affairs print media and 74% in other print media – non-news and non-current affairs – with 'safeguards' to ensure that the editorial and management control remained in Indian hands. The same pattern is made applicable in respect of the electronic media in 2003.

Chapter 2. Law of the Establishment and Supervision of Economic Activities

§1. Professional and Trade Regulation

1022. The government has prescribed sector and trade specific regulations for different professions and industries, such as, insurance, banking, civil aviation, export-import, etc. It is, therefore, not feasible to state here the generic regulatory rules prescribed by the government. However, details will be proceeded industry wise.

§2. Government Regulation of the Banking Sector

I. General

1023. In India, there are various types of banks viz., commercial banks, regional rural banks and cooperative banks, etc. The commercial banks, which include public sector banks, private banks and foreign banks are regulated by the provisions of the Reserve Bank of India Act, 1934, the Banking Regulation Act, 1949, the State Bank of India Act, 1959 and the Banking Companies (Acquisition and Transfer of Undertaking) Act, 1970 and the Banking Companies (Acquisition and Transfer of Undertaking) Act, 1980.

II. The Reserve Bank

1024. The functions of the Reserve Bank, which was established through the Reserve Bank of India Act, 1935 today can be categorized as follows:

(1) Monetary policy.
(2) Regulation and supervision of the banking and non-banking financial.
(3) institutions, including credit information companies.
(4) Regulation of money, forex and government securities markets as also.
(5) certain financial derivatives.
(6) Debt and cash management for Central and State Governments.
(7) Management of foreign exchange reserves.
(8) Foreign exchange management – current and capital account management.
(9) Banker to banks.
(10) Banker to the Central and State Governments.
(11) Oversight of the payment and settlement systems.
(12) Currency management.

(13) Developmental role.
(14) Research and statistics.
(15) Promotional role.

III. Prudential Supervision under the Banking Act, 1949

1025. The Reserve Bank's regulatory and supervisory domain extends not only to the Indian banking system but also to the development financial institutions (DFIs), NBFCs, primary dealers, credit information companies and select segments of the financial markets. In respect of banks, the Reserve Bank derives its powers from the provisions of the Banking Regulation Act, 1949, while the other entities and markets are regulated and supervised under the provisions of the Reserve Bank of India Act, 1934. The credit information companies are regulated under the provisions of Credit Information Companies (Regulation) Act, 2005.

1026. The banks are registered as banking companies under the Companies Act, 1956. After registration, For commencing banking operations in India, whether by an Indian or a foreign bank, a licence from the Reserve Bank is required under section 22. The opening of new branches by banks and change in the location of existing branches are also regulated as per the Branch Authorization Policy. This policy has recently been liberalized significantly and Indian banks no longer require a licence from the Reserve Bank for opening a branch at a place with population of below 50,000. The Reserve Bank continues to emphasize opening of branches by banks in unbanked and under-banked areas of the country. The Reserve Bank also regulates merger, amalgamation and winding up of banks.

1027. In order to strengthen the balance sheets of banks, the Reserve Bank has been prescribing appropriate prudential norms for them in regard to minimum capital requirement,[1011] creation of a reserve fund,[1012] maintenance of cash reserve,[1013] statutory reserve with a Reserve Bank,[1014] etc.

1028. Sections 29 and 30 require the banks to prepare a balance sheet and profit and loss account on the last working day of the year in the form set out in the third schedule and to have it audited by a person duly qualified under any law for the time that it is in force.

§3. Foreign Exchange Dealings

1029. The Reserve Bank of India has been authorized to control the transactions in a foreign exchange, gold coin and bullion under the Foreign Exchange Regulation Act, 1947. This act was replaced by the Foreign Exchange Regulation Act, 1973 wherein, the Reserve Bank was authorized to control and regulate dealings in foreign exchange, payments outside India, export and import of currency notes and bullion,

1011. Banking Regulations Act, 1949, s. 12.
1012. Banking Regulations Act, 1949, s. 17.
1013. Banking Regulations Act, 1949, s. 12.
1014. Banking Regulations Act, 1949, s. 42.

transfer of securities between residents and non-residents, acquisition of foreign securities and acquisition of immovable property by foreign citizens in India. With the financial reforms introduced by the Government of India in 1991, the Act of 1973 was amended in 1993 and later replaced by the Foreign Exchange Management Act, 1999 (FEMA), which aims to facilitate external trade and payments and promote the orderly development and maintenance of foreign exchange markets in India. FEMA aimed at consolidating and amending the laws relating to foreign exchange with the objective of facilitating external trade and payments and for promoting the orderly development and maintenance of foreign exchange markets in India. Emphasising the shift in focus, the Reserve Bank in due course also amended (since 31 January 2004) the name of its department dealing with the foreign exchange transactions to Foreign Exchange Department from Exchange Control Department.

I. Foreign Investment

1030. Foreign investment comes into India in various forms. Following the reforms path, the Reserve Bank has liberalized the provisions relating to such investments:

(1) The Reserve Bank has permitted foreign investment in almost all sectors, with a few exceptions. Foreign companies are permitted to set up 100% subsidiaries in India.
(2) In many sectors, no prior approval from the Government or the Reserve Bank is required for non-residents investing in India.
(3) Foreign institutional investors are allowed to invest in all equity securities traded in the primary and secondary markets. The total investment by all the foreign institutional investors put together should not exceed 24% of the issued and paid-up capital of a company which can be raised up to the level of the prescribed sectoral cap by the respective companies by passing a special resolution to the effect.
(4) Foreign institutional investors have also been permitted to invest in Government of India treasury bills and dated securities, corporate debt instruments and mutual funds. The NRIs have the flexibility of investing under the options of repatriation and non-repatriation.
(5) The Government allows Indian companies to issue Global Depository Receipts (GDRs) and American Depository Receipts (ADRs) to foreign investors The GDRs/ADRs issued by Indian companies to non-residents have free convertibility outside India.

II. Indian Investment Abroad

1031. Any Indian entity can make investment in an overseas joint venture or in a wholly-owned subsidiary, up to 400% of its net worth.

§4. The Financial Corporation Act, 1974

1032. In order to finance the industries, certain financial institutions have been established, viz., the Industrial Finance Corporation of India, the Industrial Credit and Investment Corporation of India Ltd., the Industrial Development Bank of India, the Small Industrial Development Bank of India, the Industrial Reconstruction Bank of India, the Export Import Bank of India, the Securities and Trading Corporation of India, the Stock Holding Corporation of India, the National Housing Bank, etc. The Reserve Bank has the power to oversee these institutions and require the financial institutions to submit prescribed returns on liabilities/assets, source and deployment of the funds, etc. on a quarterly basis. These help the bank formulate a monetary and credit policy. In 1995, the Board for Financial Supervision was constituted under the aegis of the Reserve Bank of India, which supervises banks, financial institutions and NBFCs.

1033. The State Financial Corporations Act, 1951 was passed under which state financial corporations may be established for the purpose of promoting and developing small-scale and medium scale industries in the state with a special focus on spreading the industrial culture in the rural, semi-urban and backward areas of the state.

§5. State Banking

1034. There is nothing like state banking. All the banks are registered companies under the Indian Companies Act, 1956 and are regulated and supervised by the Reserve Bank of India.

I. Insurance Business

A. General

1035. The hazards of trade and commerce and the increasing complexities of life in recent years have made a precise knowledge of laws of insurance, as codified in India, very important. Urge to provide protection against the loss of life and property prompted people/groups to make some sort of sacrifice willingly in order to achieve security through collective cooperation. The story of insurance is as old as the story of mankind. The biblical story of Joseph or the Islamic story of Yusuf during famine in Egypt has been cited as the first insurance plan in recorded history.[1015]

1036. Insurance performs multiple functions all of which contribute in vary degrees to social and economic management today. Insurance offers security to individuals and transactions; it is a growing business to many others; and it is a legal device to distribute risks and make development possible to the society at large. Given the expansion to insurance into almost all aspects of life in recent times, one can expect

1015. Dharmendra Kumar, *Indian Insurance: The Historical Perspective*, in *India Insurance Report-Series I* (H. Chaturvedi, Dharmendra Kumar & Rahul Singh eds., Allied Publishers Pvt. Ltd. 2010).

the subject to assume great importance in the spheres of commerce, law, management and government. State control of insurance has been a subject of controversy in India after the Independence of the country. However, provision of adequate security to life and property is a fundamental duty of civilized society. This has been well considered by the government. Present day conditions have made it necessary for man to face many hazards and undertake risks in day-to-day life. Different types of private and public organizations including the governments themselves have undertaken, in different countries, the responsibility of providing many forms of cover to the individual from the possible results of accidents to his/her person involving even death and to his/her property.

1037. In India, the majority of the population is far from affluent. Therefore, the benefits which good insurance schemes can provide are of vital importance to the Indian people. Insurance is a comprehensive term susceptible of varied meanings. It is a contract of indemnity for the benefit of the insured and those in privity with him. The word 'assurance', which formerly did duty for 'insurance' in its modern sense, particularly in English maritime law, has now fallen into desuetude. Insurance now covers a multitude of risks and, therefore, there are many kinds of insurance. It is, however, mainly of four kinds: life, marine, fire and accident. The first Act in India dealing with insurance was the Indian Life Assurance Companies Act, 1912, which was based mainly on the English Assurance Companies Act, 1909. It was applicable to only to life insurance companies and did not affect companies doing other kinds of insurance business. The need for a comprehensive Act relating to the business The need for a comprehensive Act relating to the business of insurance was answered by enacting the Insurance Act, 1938. This Act was subject to several amendments from time to time., the most extensive of these, being the Insurance (Amendment) Act, 1950. Next time the Life Insurance Corporation Ac, 1956, providing for the nationalization of life insurance business. This was later followed by the Marine Insurance Act, 1963, dealing with marine business. Before 1956, the whole insurance sector was in the hands of private sector companies. A number of insurance companies became bankrupt and could meet their public obligations. Moreover, there was the temptation in take over the life insurance business of ghost companies. While the public was saved from burden of bubble companies, people had to put up with loss of bonus and low dividends at the government insurers. On the formation of the Life Insurance Corporation, the provisions of the Insurance Act, 1938 applied to life insurance business only as modified by section 43 of the Life Insurance Corporation Act, 1956. These provisions apply to regulate the working of the Life Insurance Corporation (LIC), e.g., all receipts in respect of life insurance business should be carried out and form a separate fund called the 'life insurance fund' which must not be applied directly or indirectly for any purpose other than those of the life insurance business.[1016] The LIC must prepare a balance sheet and profit and loss account every year in a prescribed meaner.[1017] Once at least in every three years, an investigation into the financial condition of the business, including the valuation of its liabilities by an actuary, must be made.[1018] Once in every two years, the LIC must submit copies of statements, abstracts referred to in sections

1016. Insurance Act, 1938, s. 10.
1017. Insurance Act, 1938, s. 11.
1018. Insurance Act, 1938, s. 13.

11, 13 and 18 of the Insurance Act, 1938 and also a return of investments made out of the controlled fund under section 27A of the said Act to the Insurance Regulatory Authority.[1019] Every return furnished to the Authority is open to inspection by the public and copy may be obtained on payment of fee.[1020]

1038. Controller of Insurance and his powers: The central government constituted under section 3 of the Insurance Regulatory and Development Authority Act, 1999(IRDA). It shall appoint a Controller under section 2B of the said Act. The IRDA administers the functions assigned to it under the Act. The IRDA administers the functions assigned to it under the Act. This Authority may require LIC to supply it with any information relating to the insurance business.[1021] If any return furnished appears to the Authority to be inaccurate or d effective, may decline to accept it unless it is rectified or any deficiency is made good, and for that purpose may call for and inspect any books of account or other document or examine any officer of the insurer on oath.[1022] the Authority may also order an investigation and valuation to be made again at the expenses of the usurer, by an Actuary appointed with its approval, if it finds that a faulty basis has been adopted in the valuation already made.[1023] The Authority or an officer authorized but it can grant licences for persons to act as insurance agents.[1024] Any dispute relating to the settlement of a claim on a life insurance policy for a sum not exceeding INR 2 million may with the option of the claimant, be referred to the Authority for decision, and the decision thereon cannot be called in question any court and is executable as decree of the Court.[1025]

1039. Powers of Authority: The Authority is empowered to order investigation of the affairs of an insurer by an investigating authority and to take suitable action.[1026] The central government is required to publish every year a summary of the various returns furnished to the Controller during the previous year.[1027]

B. General Insurance

1040. In 1960, there were ninety-nine Indian and nearly the same number of non-Indian companies engaged in general insurance business. In 1957 the first Indian Reinsurance Corporation of India was established. It was formed with a view to stopping of heavy drain of India's foreign exchange resources, as all reinsurance was being effected with foreign concerns. In 1968, drastic amendment of the Insurance Act, 1938 provided for more effective supervision and control over insurers doing general business, requiring increased deposits from them, giving the Controller of Insurance more powers to inspect and issue directions to insurers on all matters including the appointment and removal of their directors, constituting a TAC to fix, control and

1019. Insurance Act, 1938, s. 28A.
1020. Insurance Act, 1938, s. 28.
1021. Insurance Act, 1938, s. 110C.
1022. Insurance Act, 1938, s. 21.
1023. Insurance Act, 1938, s. 23.
1024. Insurance Act, 1938, s. 42.
1025. Insurance Act, 1938, s. 47A1.
1026. Insurance Act, 1938, s. 33.
1027. Insurance Act, 1938, s. 116-A.

regulate the premium rates and conditions of policies, etc. In spite of such control, there was persistent demand for the nationalization of general insurance business, so that there could be no concentration of wealth in the hands of a few insurers. In order to meet with the demands of the people the General Insurance Business (Nationalization) Act, 1972 was enacted. The Act was to provide for the acquisition and transfer of shares of Indian insurance companies and undertakings of other existing insurers in order to serve the needs of the community better and to ensure that 'the operation of the economic system does not result in the concentration of wealth to the common welfare, for the regulation and control of business to the common detriment' as required by Article 39(c) of the Indian Constitution. By sections 4 and 5 of the 1972 Act, all shares in the capital of every Indian insurance company free from all trusts, liabilities and encumbrances affecting them and the undertaking of every existing insurer which was not an Indian insurance company stood transferred to and vested in the central government from 1 January 1973. The central government under section 9 of the Act formed the GIC as a Government company. There is a difference between the LIC and the GIC: the former is a statutory corporation whereas the GIC is a company registered under the Companies Act. By section 10 of the Act, on the formation of the GIC, all shares which stood vested in the central government, except for a few shares, were vested in the GIC. All the insurance companies were thereafter merged into four 'acquiring companies': the New Indian Assurance Company Ltd., the United India Fire and General Insurance Co. Ltd., the Oriental Fire and General Insurance Co. Ltd. and the National Insurance Co. Ltd. from 1 January 1974.

C. Functions of the GIC

1041. The functions of the GIC according to section 18 of the Act include:

(a) carrying on any of the general insurance business if it thinks it is desirable to do so;
(b) aiding and advising the acquiring companies in the manner of setting up standards of conduct and sound practice in general insurance business and rendering efficient service to their policy-holders;
(c) advising them in the matter of controlling their expenses including payment of commission and other expenses;
(d) advising them in the matter of investment of their funds; and
(e) issuing directions to them in relation to the conduct of general insurance business.

1042. In all these functions, the corporation should keep in mind the desirability of encouraging competition among the acquiring companies as far as possible in order to enter their services more efficient. The amendment of 2002 has added a provision to section 18 of the Act, whereby the functions of the Corporation shall be performed by the central government. At present the Corporation is undertaking reinsurance business in India and also underwriting general insurance business in civil aviation and crop insurance.

D. Functions of Acquiring Companies

1043. Section 19 of the Act lays down the functions of the acquiring companies to be (a) to carry on general insurance business and to develop it to the best advantage of the community, subject to the rules if any made in this behalf by the central government under section 39 of the Act and subject to its memorandum and articles of association; and (b) to act so far as may be on business principles and in conformity with any directions that may have been issued to it by the GIC. Section 19(4) clarifies that the GIC and the acquiring companies may enter into reinsurance contracts or treaties for the protection of their interests, subject to rules if any made by the central government in this behalf.

E. Powers of the Central Government over the GIC

1044. Section 23 of the Act lays down that the GIC and every acquiring company shall be guided in the discharge of its functions by such directions as the central government may give in regard to matters of policy involving public interest. Rule 6 of the Central Insurance Business (Nationalization) Rules, 1972 in exercise of the powers conferred by section 39 of the Act requires the GIC to prepare and submit to the central government a report reviewing the working and administration of the Corporation during the year, as soon as may be after the end of each calendar year, and also appended to the report a similar report relating to each of its subsidiaries for the same year. The central government under section 35 of the Act is empowered to specify by notification the exceptions, restrictions and limitation, if any, subject to which the Insurance Act, 1938 shall apply to or in relation to the GIC and every acquiring company. Section 39 of the Act empowers the central government to make rules to carry out the provisions of the Act.

F Insurance Act, 1938 and the GIC

1045. The elimination of many private insurance companies made many provisions of the Insurance Act, 1938 redundant. Thus, under section 35 of the Act, the government of India by notification on 29 December 1972, required the four acquiring insurance companies on 1 January 1273:

(i) to keep separate accounts in respect of each class of insurance business under section 10 of the Act;
(ii) to prepare, at the expiration of each calendar year, with reference to that year audited balance sheet, profit and loss account, revenue account, etc. in prescribed forms under sections 11 and 12;
(iii) to maintain register of policies and of claims and of insurance agents under sections 14 and 43;
(iv) to furnish to the Controller, printed copies of revenue accounts, etc. as returns and of every report made to the members or policy-holder as well as a report of all general meetings held under sections 15,18 and 19;

(v) not to pay by way of remuneration or reward for soliciting or procuring business to anyone other than an insurance agent under section 40;

(vi) not to make any investment other than in approved investments under section 27B and within thirty-one days of the beginning of a year make a return to the controller, of all investments and the changes made therein during the previous year.

1046. The Controller of Insurance (now Authority) under section 21 of the Act may have any return which appears to him to be incorrect or defective, duly corrected and supplemented and may inspect any books of the insurer or examine any officer in connection with the return or decline to accept any return for sufficient reasons. All returns submitted to the Controller are open to inspection by the public and they can obtain certified copies thereof on payment of prescribed fee. Under section 42 of the Act, the authority or any other officer authorized by him may grant and renew licences for persons to act as insurance agents. The central government may direct the authority or any other specified person to investigate the affairs of the insurer and made a report and make suitable orders thereon. The manager and every officer of the insurer must provide all facilities for such investigation.

G. The TAC

1047. The TAC was established by an amendment in 1968 to the Insurance Act, 1938 to control and regulate the rates, advantages, terms and conditions that may be offered by insurers in respect of general insurance business. The committee under section 64U is a body corporate having perpetual succession and a common seal and with power to hold and dispose of property and to contract and to sue and be sued. The TAC consists of fifteen members nominated by the GIC with the prior approval of central government. Under section 64UA its chairman was to be the chairman of the Authority or a member of the TAC to be nominated by him and the secretary of the committee was an officer of the office of the authority nominated by the authority. The TAC is empowered to constitute regional committees and sub-committees and to make regulations for their working. Each regional committee shall consist of not more than seven persons nominated by the TAC under section 64UJ on questions connected with the fixation of rates, advantages, etc. for risk in its region and perform such other functions as may be assigned to it. The TAC under section 64UE may require the insurer furnish such information or statements periodically or ad hoc as may be necessary to discharge its functions and the insurers are bound to comply with such requirements. The TAC may from time to time and to the extent it deems expedient control or regulate the rates, advantages, etc. in respect of risks or classes of risks which in its opinion is proper to control and regulate. Any such rates, etc. regulated by the TAC are binding on the insurers and their contravention is punishable under section 64UC. In fixing or modifying the rates, etc. the TAC should regard and make suitable allowances for past loss experience and for future fluctuations and unforeseen future contingencies including hazards or catastrophes. The TAC constituted under section 64U of the Insurance Act, 1938 is a statutory body empowered to fix rates, etc.

from time to time. Its instructions have the force of law and are binding on all the insurers and their contravention is punishable.

H. Further Development

1048. The decade of the 1990s witnessed a wave liberalization sweeping through all the sectors of economy. The insurance sector was no exception. In 1993, therefore, the government appointed a committee on reforms in the insurance sector, the Malhotra Committee, headed by a former Finance Secretary, to evaluate the Indian insurance industry and recommend its future direction. The committee submitted its report in 1994 and recommended many improvements in the companies in order to Improve their performance and enable them to act as independent economically motivated companies. For this purpose it also recommended the setting up of independent regulatory body. Some of the recommendations are as follows:

(i) The government stake in the insurance companies should be reduced to 50% and they sold take over the holdings of the GIC and its subsidiaries so that these subsidiaries could act as independent corporations with greater freedom to operate.
(ii) Private companies with a minimum paid-up capital of INR 7 billion should be allowed to enter the industry. No company should deal with general and life insurance as a single entity. Foreign companies in collaboration with domestic ones are allowed to enter the industry. Postal life insurance should be allowed to operate in rural areas and one state-level life insurance should be allowed to operate in each state.
(iii) An insurance regulatory body should be set up and the Controller of Insurance should be made independent.
(iv) Mandatory investments of the LIC fund in government securities should be reduced from 75% to 50%.
(v) In order to improve customer services and increase the overage the insurance industry should be opened to in competition. For this reason, it was desirable that the LIC should pay interest on delays in payments beyond thirty days and that insurance companies should be allowed to set up unit linked pension plans.

I. Insurance Regulatory and Development Authority

1049. The Insurance Act, 1938 even after amendments since its enactment has retained in basic structure. The last exercise undertaken in 1999 and some modifications in 2002 did leave an imminent need to made a thorough review of the Act for the removal of perceived incongruities and inconsistencies and come up with a possible integrated set of provisions to take in what had been separately legislated for in the Insurance Regulatory and Development Authority Act, 1999. The IRDA since its incorporation a statutory body in April 2000 has fastidiously stuck to its schedule of framing regulations and registering private sector insurance companies. Since being set up as an independent statutory body the IRDA has put in place a framework of globally compatible regulations. In the private sector twelve life insurance and six general insurance companies have been registered. The insurance sector has been liberalized for six years. This has enabled many new players to set up new companies to compete with the well-established public undertakings in both the life and non-life sectors. These new companies have introduced many new products and this has provided an opportunity for customers to make a choice. At the same time lot of awareness has been created which helped this sector to grow. In these six year period there has been a tremendous growth in the volume of business both in the life and non-life sectors. Private insurance companies are consolidating their position on the market and at the end of financial year 2005–2006, they had captured about 22% of the market share of life business and in the next five years their aim is to increase their market share to 30%. On the non-life front, the situation is more critical as the market share of private companies is around 27%.

Chapter 3. State Incentives for Economic Activities

§1. General

1050. In the era of globalization Foreign Trade has become the lifeline of any economy. Its primary purpose is not merely to earn foreign exchange, but to stimulate greater economic activity. India's economic structure today presents a distinctly different picture from what it was in 1991 when economic reforms started. India has dismantled its quantitative restrictions, partially liberalized its exchange rate and reduced the rate of customs duties. The Government has announced various export promotion measures and incentives. The laws and facilitations announced by the Government were not only related to export and import of goods and services, but were also directed to up gradation of technology and integration of all the departments by using latest technologies available. Most areas, where earlier only government participation was allowed, have been opened for private participation.

§2. Foreign Trade Policy

1051. The foreign trade policy enumerates various measures and schemes to increase India's share of world trade and to act as an effective instrument of economic growth by giving a thrust to employment generation. In furtherance of this objective, the government offers various incentives to economic players in order to promote exports. Earlier the government used to notify the import and export policy every year. Later since 1992 the tenure of the policy was made five years in order to provide stability and thereby minimize the uncertainties for exporters and importers. In exercise of the powers conferred under section 5 of the Foreign Trade (Development and Regulation) Act, 1992 (No. 22 of 1992), the central government notifies the foreign trade policy for the next five years, and this notification also incorporates the yearly export and import policy. The government may make any amendment by notifications to the policy as it deems fit. Certain key sectors requiring growth are identified in each policy and initiatives are offered through various schemes (e.g., Vishesh Krishi and Gram Udyog Yojana[Special Agricultural and Village Industry Scheme]) for promoting the export of fruits, vegetables, flowers, minor forest produce, dairy, poultry and their value added products). Other specific sectoral strategies are notified from time to time. Incentives include the exemption from the basic customs duty, duty free import entitlements, the establishment of special economic zones (SEZs), the facilitation of imports of required inputs, providing exemptions for various taxable goods under the Income Tax Act, giving service tax/CENVAT credits. Additionally, units in an SEZ are usually exempted from a service tax. Development of special economic zones (SEZs) is a major initiative of the government. This is aimed at generation of additional economic activity; promotion of exports of goods and services; promotion of investment from domestic and foreign sources; creation of employment opportunities and development of infrastructure facilities. Tax exemptions in duties and taxes are enumerated under the relevant schemes. Besides other measures, the important initiatives announced in the policy (2009–2014) include strengthening the Focus Market Scheme (FMS) and Focus Product Scheme (FPS) by increasing the incentives available under the schemes and bringing more products and markets under these schemes; extending the Duty Entitlement Passbook (DEPB) scheme till 30 September 2011 and Duty Drawback Scheme afterwards; extending interest subvention scheme of 2% till 31 March 2013; continuing the income tax exemption to 100% EOUs and STPI units for the financial year 2012–2013 and introduction of EPCG scheme at zero duty and 1% duty credit scrip for status holders with a view to aid technological up gradation of our export sector.[1028]

§3. Incentives

I. Tax Incentives

1052. The following are some of the important tax incentives offered, which significantly reduce the effective tax rates for the beneficiary companies:

- five year tax holiday for: (a) power projects; (b) firms engaged in exports; (c) new industries in notified states and for new industrial units established, in electronic hardware/software parks; (d) export oriented units and units in Free Trade Zones; and seven years in case of oil exploration and refinery business;
- tax deductions of a certain percentage of export profits;
- deduction of a fixed percentage of net (total) income for ten years for new industrial undertakings (the time period of ten years may be revised);
- deduction of a fixed percentage on foreign exchange earnings by construction companies, hotels and on royalty, commission, etc. earned in a foreign exchange;
- deduction in respect of certain inter-corporate dividends to the extent of dividend declared;
- weighted deduction of 200% for in house research and development expenses, including capital outlays (other than those for lands) in the year incurred. Companies can also claim a deduction for expenses incurred in the three years immediately preceding the year in which the company commences business;
- accelerated depreciation for certain categories, such as energy saving, environmental protection and pollution control equipments.

II. Other Incentives

1053. Some of the policies under which the incentives are offered are: (a) the new industrial policy and other concessions in the North Eastern Region; (b) the incentive scheme for the reimbursement for acquiring a quality management system

1028. Annual supplement 2012–2013 to Foreign Trade Policy 2009–2014.

(QMS) ISO 9000/environment management system (EMS) ISO – 14001 certification; (c) investment aids and incentives for non-resident Indians; and (d) the Development of backward areas and an incentive package for special category states; (e) set up a special purpose tea fund (SPTF) in to cover INR 2.12 lakh hectares of plantation over a fifteen-year period; (f) launch of a Price Stabilization Fund (PSF) Scheme in April 2003 against the backdrop of decline in international and domestic prices of tea, coffee, rubber and tobacco. The objective of the Scheme is to safeguard the interests of the growers of these commodities and to provide financial relief when prices fall below a specified level; (g) a Personal Accident Insurance Scheme is under implementation by PSF through National Insurance Corporation Ltd. The scheme covers growers in the sectors of Tea, Coffee, Rubber and Tobacco and Spices (chillies, cardamom, ginger, turmeric and pepper) having plantations up to 4 hectares only. The Scheme envisages an insurance cover up to INR 1.00 lakh per person.

1054. The Electronic Trade Project (eTRADE) is a major initiative aimed at promoting e-delivery of services by various regulatory/facilitating agencies like Customs, Sea Ports, Airports, Directorate General of Foreign Trade (DGFT), Container Corporation (CONCOR), Export Promotion Organizations, Exporters, Importers, Agents and Banks. The services covered under the project include electronic filing/clearance of export/import documents by the stakeholders (exporters, importers, agents to Customs, Seaports, Airports, CONCOR, DGFT, etc.), e-Payment of duties, charges (handling/freight, etc.) and the electronic exchange/clearance of documents between community partners. The project has helped the trade and industry in easy and quick filing/clearance of import/export documents, easy and faster payment of charges/duties, faster and transparent clearances and faster receipt of incentives/drawback.

1055. e-Procurement has been integrated as computerized online comprehensive process covering the identification of buyer requirements and requisition processing, soliciting and receiving bids of all sorts, negotiating and establishing contracts and processing overall purchases and also undertaking vendor registration and inspection of stores to ensure quality. DGS&D has implemented e-procurement for most identified rate contract items which is an important part of the 'Mission Mode Project' under the National e-Governance Plan (NEGP). With effect from 1 October 2008, all supply orders against the Rate Contract must be placed by Direct Demanding Officers online through the DGS&D website only (www.dgsnd.gov.in). Over 42,000 supply orders have been placed online through the DGS&D system.[1029]

1056. India also has a comprehensive structure for economic development at the state level. The government of each state is responsible for the implementation and promotion of various incentive packages through use of these policies. The policies are formulated in furtherance of powers endowed on various agencies of the respective state government. In most states, the organizations present to assist and promote economic activity through the various incentives mentioned are:

- Investment Promotion Agencies (IPA).
- State Industrial Development Corporation (SIDC).
- Small-Scale Industries Development Corporation (SSIDC).

1029. Outcome Budget 2010–2011, Department of Commerce, Ministry of Commerce and Industry, Government of India.

- State Financial Corporation (SFC).
- District Industries Centre (DIC).
- Single Window Service and Escort Service.

§4. Subsidies

I. General

1057. The central and state governments also offer various subsidies to economic players through various subsidy schemes, which are provided for as part of the governmental policies. For example, the transport subsidy scheme was introduced in July 1971 to promote industries in hilly, remote and inaccessible areas. The North Eastern Development Financial Corporation (NEDFC) has been designated as a nodal agency to give subsidies to the eligible units on the basis of recommendations of the state-level committee. This scheme is part of the 'New Industrial Policy and Other Concessions in the North Eastern Region'. Under the same policy (as amended from time to time), the Capital Investment Subsidy Scheme 1997 has been introduced and ratified on 6 January 1998 under the Prime Minister's new initiative for the North Eastern Region. The scheme operates through the state governments.

II. Electric Policy

1058. In compliance with section 3 of the Electricity Act, 2003 the central government notifies the National Electricity Policy, according to which state governments can directly subsidize the marginal consumer category, and allocate substantial sums towards a direct subsidy.

III. Other Subsidies

1059. Other subsidies may include the stamp duty and registration subsidy, i.e., exemption on stamps duty and registration fee for registering documents within the state, the pollution control equipment subsidy for the installation of pollution control and monitoring equipment, interest subsidy, captive power generating subsidy and the like. Some states extend other incentives to small-scale units or priority industries as defined in their industrial policy statements. Such incentives include concessional loans granted by state financial corporations, price preference on goods made by small-scale industries (SSIs) in purchases made by the government and semi government organizations, exemption from the payment of octroi (entry tax) for a certain specified period, preferential allotment of land and sheds in industrial areas to SSIs and grant of interest free loans in lieu of deferred sales tax.

§5. Public and Private Participations (State as a Shareholder)

I. General

1060. Traditionally, most sectors were fully controlled by the government. The development of these sectors was purely dependent on the availability/allocation of funds out of the budget of the government. However, over the past decade, the government has encouraged domestic and foreign players to participate in the development of virtually all sectors (except certain sensitive sectors like defence, opened to a limited extent). This not only provides an alternative and innovative means of financing, thus – essential for rapid growth and development.

II. Development of Roads

1061. The development of roads in India is a notable example of such a venture. With a view to attract private investment in road development, maintenance and operation, the National Highways Act (NH Act) 1956 was amended in 1995. Now, private players can invest in the NH projects, levy, collect and retain fees from users and is also empowered to regulate traffic on such highways in terms of provisions of the Motor Vehicle Act, 1988. At present, National Highway network of about 71,772 km comprises only 1.7% of the total length of roads, but carries over 40% of the total traffic across the length and breadth of the country.

1062. Considering the target growth rate of about + 9%, it is estimated that the total target NH network of about 85,000 km may be considered as reasonable for the 12th Five Year Plan, for the development of the regions which are not connected by NHs.

1063. The private sector has, traditionally, played a fairly significant role in the provision of transport services such as bus services, road freight services, etc. Currently, more than 50% of passenger movement by road is undertaken by the private sector (varies from state to state) while nearly all the freight movement is in private hands. But in the provision of basic infrastructure like Road, the state has played an overwhelming role in the provision of these facilities in the past. In these transport infrastructures, new forms of public-private mix have recently been tried out in India. The government, in order to attract private sector participation and foreign direct investment, announces, from time to time, various incentives and schemes, which include the following:

(1) the government provides various incentives for private and foreign sector investment into roads. 100% foreign direct investment (FDI) under the automatic route is allowed for support services to land transport like operation of highway bridges, toll roads, and vehicular tunnels; services incidental to transport like cargo handling is incidental to land transport; construction and maintenance of roads, bridges; and construction and maintenance of roads and highways offered on build-on-transfer (BOT) basis, including collection of toll;
(2) government to bear the cost of:

- project feasibility study;
- land for the right of way and way side amenities;
- shifting of utilities;
- environment clearance, cutting of trees, etc.

(3) foreign direct investment up to 100% in certain sectors;
(4) provision of subsidy of a fixed percentage of a project cost to make projects viable. The amount of the subsidy is to be decided on a case-to-case basis;
(5) tax exemption of a specific percentage in any consecutive ten years out of twenty years following the commissioning of the project;
(6) duty-free import of high capacity and modern equipments;
(7) declaration of the sector as an industry (Infrastructure as defined in section 18(1)(12) of the Infrastructure Act includes, e.g., roads);
(8) easier external commercial borrowing norms;
(9) right to retain tolls and other charges, which are indexed to the wholesale price index;
(10) full exemption from basic customs duty to bio-asphalt and specified machinery for application in the construction of national highways.

Chapter 4. Competition Law

§1. Antitrust Law

I. Restrictive Practices

A. General

1064. The competition law has been in place in India since 1969. The Monopolies and Restrictive Trade Practices Act, 1969 (hereinafter written as MRTP Act, 1969) was enacted for the purpose of controlling monopolies and the concentration of economic power to a common detriment. Change in the economic scenario during the 1990s, mainly by reason of globalization, deregulation and privatization of the economy, made it indispensable to review the effects of the MRTP Act, 1969. It was found that the above Act was inadequate to meet the challenges of the new economic order. Therefore, a new law called the Competition Act, 2002 (hereinafter written as the 'Act 2002') was enacted. Section 66 of the Competition Act provides for the repeal of the MRTP Act and for connected matters. The purpose of the new Act is to promote competition so as to achieve efficient allocation of resources, to protect consumer interests and to ensure freedom of trade to the participants in the market. The Act was subsequently amended by the Competition (Amendment) Act, 2007. In accordance with the provisions of the Amendment Act, the Competition Commission of India and the Competition Appellant Tribunal have been established. The provisions of the Competition Act relating to anticompetitive agreements and abuse of Dominant position were notified on 20 May 2009.

B. Sources of Competition Law

1065. The antitrust law (as it is commonly called in the United States) of India is primarily found in the recently enacted Competition Act, 2002. As mentioned earlier, the Act is preceded by the MRTP Act, 1969 (now repealed), which was in existence for more than three decades. The case law developed during this period may also be relied upon in case of any ambiguity. These decisions would have persuasive value and act as a guiding post. The jurisprudence developed during this period would, indirectly, form part of the competition law.

1066. In addition to the Act 2002, certain provisions of the Companies Amendment Act, 2002 such as the Takeover Regulation issued by the SEBI in 1997 and the Consumer Protection Act, 1986, also form part of the competition law in India.

1067. This ensures transparency and fair play in the market. The purpose of the code is to prevent distortions in the market situation caused by symmetric information available to the other players and stakeholders. The Consumer Protection Act, 1986 provides the proper forum for consumers for redressal of their grievances against unfair practices by the companies.[1030] The Competition Amendment Act, 2009 provides that investigations or proceedings relating to unfair trade practices pending before the National Commission are, from its enforcement date, to be transferred to the Appellate Tribunal to be conducted by it, as it may deem fit.

C. Scope of the Competition Law: Exemptions from Competition Act

1068. The territorial scope of Act 2002 extends to whole of India except the state of Jammu and Kashmir. However, the statement becomes shallow in view of the fact that the act recognizes the 'effects doctrine'. According to this doctrine, the effect of the actions or behaviour, would determine whether the action or behaviour is anticompetitive and comes within the mischief of Act 2002. The Competition Commission established under Act 2002 has jurisdiction even over foreign players if the effect of their anticompetitive behaviour is felt in India.

1069. Competition Act, 2002 may be enforced against any enterprises except as exempted specifically by the central government under section 54 of the act. The central government may by notification exempt any enterprise if it is in the interest of security of the state or public interest or any practice or agreement if such practice or agreement arises from any obligation assumed by India under any treaty, agreement or convention with any other country or any entrepreneur, performing sovereign function on behalf of the government.[1031]

1070. No extra-territorial operation: An agreement between parties operating outside India for supply or distribution of goods in India did not require registration. Float glass could be imported into India on payment of customs duty. Hence, such import could not be prohibited.

1071. In addition, the activities carried on by the departments of the central government dealing with: (1) atomic energy; (2) currency; (3) defence; and (4) space are also outside the purview of Act 2002.[1032]

D. Competition Commission of India

1072. The act provides for the establishment of the Competition Commission of India (CCI) to carry out the purpose of the act.[1033] The primary duty of the CCI is to promote and sustain competition and to eliminate the practices having adverse effects on competition in the India market. The commission has been assigned regulatory, investigative, inquiry, adjudicative and advisory functions. The functions of the commission are related to three main areas: prohibition of anticompetitive agreements; prohibition of abuse of a dominant position; and the regulation of combinations. The following are the main powers and functions of the commission:

- *Inquiry/Investigation*: The commission may inquire into: (1) agreements that are specifically barred by the act if they have adverse effects on competition; (2)

1030. SEBI (Substantial Acquisition of Share and Takeover) Regulations, 1997.
1031. Competition Act, 2002, s. 54.
1032. Competition Act, 2002, s. 54.
1033. Competition Act, 2002, s. 7.

instances of abuse of the dominant position; and (3) combination having adverse effect on competition.[1034]

- *Regulator*: The Commission is to act as a regulator in the market to ensure fair competition and give impetus to the quality of products and services. It regulates acquisitions and mergers coming within the threshold limit and prevents the abuse of dominance.
- *Adjudication*: The Commission is made the sole recipient of all complaints against the infringement of Act 2002 from any source whatsoever and is authorized to adjudicate the matter thereupon.
- *Order*: The Commission may pass an appropriate order if any agreement is entered into which is barred by the act, or if the dominant position is abusive or if a combination has been formed having adverse effect on competition. It may also award *compensation* to the affected party.
- *Enforcement*: The Commission has the power to enforce its own orders.
- *Advocacy*: The Commission may give its opinion on references made by the central government regarding the policy on competition. The advocacy role impacts into the realm of policymaking.
- *Regulations*: The Commission may make regulations to carry out the purposes of this act.

E. Appeal

1073. Any person, central government, state government or a local authority or enterprise, aggrieved by any decision or order of the Commission may file an appeal before the Appellate Tribunal as mentioned under section 53-A of the Act. An appeal has to be filed within the period of sixty days. Parties aggrieved of the orders of the Appellate Tribunal may file an appeal to the Supreme Court within sixty days from the date of communication of the decision or order. This provision excludes the judicial review by High Courts by way of appeal. However, it may be noted that the High Courts still retain writ jurisdiction. It may be argued that this provision is against the basic structure of independence of the judiciary, as it tends to bypass High Courts. So far, the government has not taken any concrete steps in this direction.

F. Theoretical Underpinning of the Competition Act

1. In General

1074. Act 2002, after being enacted by Parliament got assent by the President of India. It has to come into force in three phases. In the first and second phases, the majority of the sections have come into force, but the main operating portion is yet to come into force.

1075. Act 2002 strives to promote and sustain competition in the market place. This is based on the philosophy that as long as markets are 'contestable', the right product of the right quality at the right price in an adequate quantity may be guaranteed

1034. Competition Act, 2002, s. 19.

to the consumers. When players in the market contest on merits, they also maximize their profits in the long run.

1076. The present act encourages the entrepreneurship and creation of wealth by emphasizing the regulation of monopolies and prohibition of abuse of the dominant position. This is a point of departure in the approach of the new act. In the earlier times, the old Act concentrated mainly on the control of monopolies whereas the new act stresses the abuse of monopolies/dominance.

1077. The Competition Commission under Act 2002 is conferred powers, wider in scope and extent than that of its predecessor, the MRTP Commission. The present Commission is empowered to stop the activity having adverse effect on competition and can also order payment of compensation to offset business losses of the affected parties. The emphasis of the Act is shifted from the size and place to the behaviour and effect. Act 2002 recognizes the 'effects doctrine' and entitles the domestic industry to seek redressal from the Commission against the anticompetitive behaviour of the foreign dominant players. The Commission has been conferred extra-territorial jurisdiction.

1078. The focus of Act 2002 is on three areas: (1) prohibition of anticompetitive agreements; (2) prohibition of abuse of dominance; and (3) regulation of combinations.

1079. The objectives of the Competition Law were highlighted by the Supreme Court in its decision in *Competition Commission of India v. SAIL.*[1035] The rational of free market economy is that competitive offers of different suppliers allow the buyers to make the best purchase. The motivation of each participant in a free economy is to maximize self-interest, but the result is favourable to the society. The main objective of the Competition Law is to promote economic efficiency using competition as one of the means of assisting the creation of market responsive to consumer preferences.

1080. Before examining specific provisions covered under Chapter II of the act, it is important to look into some of the definitions as they have a bearing on the subject.

2. Definition of Agreement and Cartel

1081. 'Agreement includes any arrangement or understanding or action in concert whether or not, such arrangement, understanding or action in concert is formal or in writing; or whether or not such arrangement, understanding or action in concert is intended to be enforceable by legal proceedings'.[1036] It is an inclusive and comprehensive definition, which includes not only written agreements having the force of law but covers any 'arrangement', 'understanding' or 'action in concert' between the parties. The term 'agreement' essentially involves express or overt meeting of minds and acceptance of the restrictions. The different expressions: 'arrangement'; 'understanding'; and 'action in concert' amplify the scope of the term of the agreement. The definition under the MRTP Act, 1969 was modelled on the basis of section 6(3) of the Restrictive Trade Practices Act, 1976 of the United Kingdom.

1082. The 'Cartel' includes an association of producers, seller, distributors, traders or service providers who, by agreement amongst themselves, limit, control or

1035. (2010) 10 SCC 744.
1036. Competition Act, 2002, s. 2(b).

attempt to control the production, distribution, sale or price of, or, trade in goods or provision of services.[1037]

3. Definition of Market

1083. The Competition Act does not define 'market'. However, the act specifies the method to determine the 'relevant market'. It says, '"relevant market" means the market, which may be determined by the Commission with reference to the relevant product market or the relevant geographic market or with reference to both markets'.[1038]

1084. The major elements for determining a 'relevant market' are a product market and geographical market. These, too, are defined in the act as a 'relevant geographic market' under section 2(s) and means a market comprising the area in which the conditions of competition for supply of goods or provision of services or demand of goods or services are distinctly homogenous and can be distinguished from the conditions prevailing in the neighbouring areas'.[1039] The expression 'relevant product market' is also defined under the Act and it means a market comprising all those products or services which are regarded as interchangeable or substitutable by the consumer, by reason of characteristics of the products or services, their prices and intended use.[1040] The definition of the relevant market is crucial for the purpose of appreciating the effect of anticompetitive behaviour. With reference to these two markets, the effect of anticompetitive behaviour or action, in a particular relevant market may be determined.

4. Definition of Competition

1085. The Competition Act, 2002 does not define 'competition'. This word will have to be given an ordinary meaning. Section 3 of the act, however, lays down that 'no enterprise or person or association of persons shall enter into any agreement in respect of production, supply, distribution, storage, acquisition or control or goods or provision of services, which causes or is likely to cause an appreciable adverse effect on competition within India'. Subsection 2 declares that any agreement entered into in contravention of the provisions contained in subsection 1 shall be void.

5. Definition of Enterprise

1086. The expression 'enterprise' has been defined in section 2(h). It means either a person (including a company) or a department of the government. Such entities come within the definition when they are engaged in any of the two kinds of activity, namely, either in reference to commodities or investments. In other words, operatives in the commodity or investment markets. The subsection says that any of them comes within the definition when it deals with any activity relating to articles or goods, namely, activity relating to production, storage, supply, distribution, acquisition, or

1037. Competition Act, 2002, s. 2(c).
1038. Competition Act, 2002, s. 2(r).
1039. Competition Act, 2002, s. 2(s).
1040. Competition Act, 2002, s. 2(t).

control of articles or goods or provision of service of any kind. The investment market would include the business of acquiring, holding, underwriting or dealing with shares, debentures or other securities of anybody corporate. The dealing may be done either directly or through any one or more of its units or divisions of subsidiaries. Such units or subsidiaries may be located at the place where the enterprise is located or at different places. The activity covered by the Act would not include working of the government relating to its sovereign functions, including activities carried on by departments dealing with atomic energy, currency, defence and space.

6. Conduct Regulated by Chapter II of the Competition Act

1087. Moving from general theoretical underpinnings of the Act to more specific conduct sought to be prohibited by the Competition Act, 2002. The focus of the Competition Act is on three areas: Prohibition of anticompetitive agreements; Prohibition of abuse of a dominant position and regulations on combinations.

II. Monopolies and Abuse of the Dominant Position

A. Anticompetitive Agreements

1088. Section 3 of the Competition Act, 2002 prohibits an enterprise or a person or any association of enterprises or persons from entering into anticompetitive agreements. The section declares such agreement to be void. The section covers agreements in respect of production, supply, distribution, storage, acquisition or control of goods or provision of services which cause or are likely to cause an appreciable adverse effect on competition within India. Any agreement entered into in contravention of the provisions contained in subsection (1) of section 3 shall be void.

1089. Horizontal Agreements: Horizontal agreements of a specified category are presumed to have an appreciable adverse effect on competition and shall be void. The rule of per se is made applicable to horizontal agreements. The horizontal agreements presumed to be having adverse effect on competition are under agreements that: (1) directly or indirectly determine the purchase or sale prices;[1041] or (2) limit or control the production, supply, markets, technical development, investment or provision of services;[1042] or (3) share the market;[1043] or (4) result in bid rigging or collusive bidding.[1044]

1090. The existence of a restraint in a licensing arrangement that affects parties in a horizontal relationship does not necessarily cause the arrangement to be anticompetitive. As in the case of joint ventures among horizontal competitors, licensing arrangements among such competitors may promote rather than hinder competition if they result in integrative efficiencies.[1045]

1041. Competition Act, 2002, s. 3(3)(a).
1042. Competition Act, 2002, s. 3(3)(b).
1043. Competition Act, 2002, s. 3(3)(c).
1044. Competition Act, 2002, s. 3(3)(d).
1045. Competition Act, 2002, s. 3(3) proviso.

1091. Vertical Agreements: However, vertical agreements entered into at different stages or levels of the production chain in different markets shall be void only if they have an appreciable adverse effect on competition. There is no prima facie presumption that vertical agreements have an appreciable adverse effect on competition. Those vertical agreements include: (1) tie-in agreement;[1046] (2) exclusive supply agreement;[1047] (3) exclusive distribution agreement;[1048] (4) refusal to deal;[1049] and (5) resale price maintenance.[1050]

1092. In addition, bid rigging and predatory pricing are also agreements or arrangements of the same nature. The Competition Act would have no application to an agreement about a subject matter which requires a licence and an application for the licence is still pending.

1093. Appreciable Adverse Effect: Act 2002 states the factors to be taken into consideration by the Competition Commission for determining the appreciable adverse effect of anticompetitive agreements. It is mandatory to look into these factors while inquiring into the allegations of contravention of provisions concerning anticompetitive agreements. These factors include: creating barriers to new entrants; driving existing competitors out of the market; foreclosure of competition by hindering entry into the market; accrual of benefits to consumers; improvements in production or distribution of goods or provisions of services; and promotion of technical, scientific and economic development by means of production or distribution of goods or provisions of services.[1051]

1094. Exemptions: The Competition Act, 2002 carries its exceptions[1052] indicating the exceptional situations in which the section would not apply. The subsection says that the provisions of the section are not to restrict the right of any person to restrain the infringement of any of his intellectual property rights (IPRs) and his export rights. His rights to protect his intellectual property rights cannot be taken away. The section gives the list of Acts in which such rights are enshrined. These Acts includes Copyright Act, 1957; Patent Act, 1970, Trade and Merchandise Marks Act, 1958 and Merchandise marks Act, 1999, Geographical Indications of Goods (Registration and Protection) Act, 1999, Designs Act, 2000, Semi-Conductor Integrated Circuits Layout-Design Act, 2000.[1053]

1095. The ambit of the Competition Act is not such as to include all agreements. Thus, agreements which are entered into in respect of various types of intellectual property rights and recognize the proprietary rights of one party over the other in respect of trademarks, patents, copyrights, GIs, industrial designs and semi-conductors have been withdrawn from the purview of ‘anticompetitive agreements’. They are inherently monopolistic rights which are created in favour of bona fide holders of various forms of intellectual property and have been treated as sacrosanct.

1046. Competition Act, 2002, s. 3(4)(a).
1047. Competition Act, 2002, s. 3(4)(b).
1048. Competition Act, 2002, s. 3(4)(c).
1049. Competition Act, 2002, s. 3(4)(d).
1050. Competition Act, 2002, s. 3(4)(e).
1051. Competition Act, 2002, s. 19(3).
1052. Competition Act, 2002, s. 3(5)(i) & (ii).
1053. Competition Act, 2002, s. 3(5)(i) & (ii).

1096. Any agreement relating to the production, supply, distribution or control of goods or provisions of services for the purpose of protecting rights to export are exempted from being considered as anticompetitive agreements.[1054]

1097. Issue of jurisdiction can be decided by Commission.

B. Abuse of the Dominant Position

1098. Abuse of the dominant position by an enterprise is a serious offence under the Competition Act, 2002.[1055] This subsection identifies five kinds of abusive use of dominant position, which includes: (1) unfair or discriminatory trade practices; (2) limiting or restricting production or technical or scientific development; (3) denial of access to market, barriers to entry and expansion; (4) imposition of supplementary obligations; (5) protection of other markets.[1056]

1099. Dominant Position: Under the MRTP Act, 1969 'dominant undertaking' was defined as an undertaking that either by itself or along with the interconnected undertakings, produces, supplies, distributes or otherwise controls not less than one-fourth of the total goods produced, supplied or distributed or services rendered in India.[1057] The concept of 'dominant position' has been explained in the Explanation appended to the section.[1058] Dominant position means the strength of an enterprise in the relevant market in India which enables the enterprise: (i) to operate independently of competitive forces prevailing in the market; (ii) to affect the consumers or competitors or the market in its favour.

1100. The present definition is closer to the practice followed under the European Union law. Under the law of the United States, to monopolize or attempt to monopolize, is illegal. There is no criterion to determine monopoly. The practice, however, indicates that there is mingling of the concept of monopoly with the dominant position. Accordingly, the basic criteria to determine monopoly, is to see whether one has dominant market power or control in a relevant market. Again no limit as to the market share or control has been prescribed.

1101. Important Factors: In considering whether enterprise enjoys a dominant position, the Commission has to have regard to all or any of the following factors:[1059] (a) market share of the enterprise; (b) size and resources of the enterprise; (c) size and importance of the competitors; (d) economic power of the enterprise including commercial advantages over competitors; (e) vertical integration of the enterprises or sale or service network of such enterprises; (f) dependence of consumers on the enterprise; (g) monopoly or dominant position whether acquired as a result of any statute or by virtue of being a government company or a public sector undertaking or otherwise; (h) monopoly or dominant position whether acquired as a result of any statute or by virtue of being a government company or a public sector undertaking or otherwise; (i) entry barriers including barriers such as regulatory barriers, financial

1054. Competition Act, 2002, s. 3(5)(i) & (ii).
1055. Competition Act, 2002, s. 4(1).
1056. Competition Act, 2002, s. 4(2).
1057. Monopolies and Restrictive Trade Practices, Act, 1969, s. 2(d).
1058. Competition Act, 2002, s. 4(2) Expl. (a).
1059. Competition Act, 2002, s. 19(4).

risk, high capital cost of entry, marketing entry barriers, technical entry barriers, economies of scale, high cost of substitutable goods or service for consumers; (j) countervailing buying power; market structure and size of market; (k) social obligations and social costs; (l) relative advantage, by way of the contribution to the economic development, by the enterprise enjoying a dominant position having or likely to have appreciable adverse effect on competition; and (m) any other factor which the Commission may consider relevant for the inquiry.

III. Mergers and Acquisitions

1102. The term 'merger' has not been defined under the Companies Act, 2013 (the 'Companies Act'), the Income Tax Act, 1961 (the 'ITA') or any other Indian law. Simply put, a merger is a combination of two or more distinct entities into one; the desired effect being not just the accumulation of assets and liabilities of the distinct entities, but to achieve several other benefits such as, economies of scale, acquisition of cutting edge technologies, obtaining access into sectors/markets with established players, etc. The provisions relating to the regulation of combinations be it a merger, amalgamations, acquisition of shares or controlling interest, are spread out in three statutes, viz., the Companies Act; Competition Act and Takeover Regulations. The entire scheme relating to combinations, under various statutes in India, is regulatory in nature. The provisions under the Competition Act, 2002 generally prohibit any combination that has appreciable adverse effects on competition in India. The Companies Act, 2013 restricts the acquisition or transfer of shares or controlling interest beyond a threshold without the prior approval of the central government. The Competition Act does not prescribe any such threshold limit beyond which acquisition cannot take place and would strike at any such acquisition if it has an appreciable adverse effect on an amalgamation. Under the 'takeover code', the following inferences may conveniently be drawn from these provisions:

- Any acquisition with the approval of the central government even beyond the threshold limit prescribed under the Companies Act, can be struck down even if it is likely to cause an appreciable adverse effect on competition.
- Acquisition under the threshold limit does not require governmental approval to be given in the case of mischief of the Competition Act if it is likely to cause an appreciable adverse effect on competition.

A. Competition Act, 2002

1103. Amalgamations: The Competition Act is also designed to regulate the formation of 'amalgamations'. (1) Section 5 of the Competition Act, 2002 deals with 'Combinations' which defines combination by reference to assets and turnover: (a) exclusively in India; and (b) in India and outside India. Section 5 also provides the framework for the amalgamations. According to section 5, amalgamations include:

- acquisition by persons to control shares, voting rights, or assets of other enterprises;

- acquiring of control by a person of an enterprise engaged in an identical business when the acquirer has control over the similar business and the enterprise; – merger or amalgamations of enterprises.

1104. A merger is a combination of two or more businesses into one business. Laws in India use the term 'amalgamation' for merger. Section 2(1A) of 'The Income Tax Act, 1961' defines amalgamation as the merger of one or more companies with another or the merger of two or more companies to form a new company, in such a way that all assets and liabilities of the amalgamating companies become assets and liabilities of the amalgamated company and shareholders not less than nine-tenths in value of the shares in the amalgamating company or companies become shareholders of the amalgamated company. According to the Competition Act, 2002, the following Merger or Amalgamation will constitute a combination in which:[1060]

(i) the enterprise remaining after merger or the enterprise created as a result of the amalgamation, as the case may be, have:

(A) either in India, the assets of the value of more than INR 1,000 crores or turnover more than INR 3,000 crores; or
(B) in India or outside India, in aggregate, the assets of the value of more than USD 500 million, including at least INR 500 crores in India, or turnover more than USD 1,500 million, including at least INR 1,500 crores in India; or

(ii) the group, to which the enterprise remaining after the merger or the enterprise created as a result of the amalgamation, would belong after the merger or the amalgamation, as the case may be, have or would have:

(A) either in India, the assets of the value of more than INR 4,000 crores or turnover more than INR 12,000 crores; or
(B) in India or outside India, in aggregate, the assets of the value of more than USD 2 billion, including at least INR 500 crores in India, or turnover more than USD 6 billion, including at least INR 1,500 crores in India.

1105. Regulation of combination: Section 6 of the Competition Act, 2002 states that, no person or enterprise shall enter into a combination which causes or is likely to cause an appreciable adverse effect on competition within the relevant market in India and such a combination shall be void.[1061] All types of intra-group combinations, mergers, demergers, reorganizations and other similar transactions should be specifically exempted from the notification procedure and appropriate clauses should be incorporated in sub-regulation 5(2) of the Regulations. These transactions do not have any competitive impact on the market for assessment under the Competition Act, section 6.[1062] No

1060. Competition Act, 2002, s. 5(c).
1061. Competition Act, 2002, s. 6(1).
1062. Competition Act, 2002, s. 6(4).

combination shall come into effect until two hundred and ten days have passed from the day on which the notice has been given to the Commission. The Commission shall, after receipt of notice under subsection (2), deal with such notice in accordance with the provisions contained in sections 29, 30 and 31. The provisions of the section 6 shall not apply to share subscription or financing facility or any acquisition, by a public financial institution, foreign institutional investor, bank or venture capital fund, pursuant to any covenant of a loan agreement or investment agreement.

1106. Inquiry, Investigation and Penalty by the Commission: The Central Govt. shall establish a 'Competition Commission of India'.[1063] The commission shall consist of a Chairperson and not less than two and not more than six other Members to be appointed by the Central Government.[1064] The Chairperson and every other Member shall hold office as such for a term of five years from the date on which he enters upon his office and shall be eligible for re-appointment. But the Chairperson or other Members shall not hold office as such after he has attained the age of 65 years.[1065] The Competition Commission has the power to inquire into the amalgamations upon its own knowledge or information to determine whether such an amalgamation has caused or is likely to cause an appreciable adverse effect on competition in India. It is not mandatory for the enterprises to give notification about the amalgamation to the Commission. Where the Commission is of the opinion that an amalgamation is likely to cause or has caused an appreciable adverse effect on competition within the relevant market in India, it may start investigations into such an amalgamation. After investigation, if it reaches a conclusion that the amalgamation has caused or is likely to cause adverse effect on competition, it shall direct that the amalgamation shall not be formed. If there is any contravention of the orders of the Commission, the person concerned may be detained in a civil prison for a term, which may extend to one year and shall be liable to a penalty not exceeding INR 1 million.

B. Companies Act

1107. Restrictions on Acquisitions: Sections 108A–108I were retransferred to the Companies Act, 1956 in the year 1991.[1066] The clandestine takeovers adversely affect the interests of non-controlling shareholders, particularly financial institutions, who are kept in the dark while secret negotiations are entered into with those having control of a company. The increasing damage of such takeovers is the raison d'être for the implementation of these provisions. These provisions purport to bring about fair play and transparency in the market place.

1108. All of these provisions and sections are applicable to dominant undertakings. Section 108A makes it obligatory on an undertaking to receive the prior approval of the central government before acquiring more than 25% of the paid-up equity share

1063. Competition Act, 2002, s. 7.
1064. Competition Act, 2002, s. 8.
1065. Competition Act, 2002, s. 10.
1066. The provisions of s. 108A–108H of the Companies Act were omitted and incorporated in Ch. IIIA of the MRTP Act, 1969 by the MRTP (Amendment) Act, 1984 as recommended by the Sachar Committee. The MRTP Act was further amended to restructure and the provisions of Ch. III-A have been retransferred to the Companies Act, 1956 as s. 108A–108I.

capital of a public company or a private subsidiary company of a public company. The provision applies only if the enterprise is the dominant undertaking or would become one, on such an acquisition. While section 108A applies to an acquirer or transferee, section 108B and 108C apply to the dominant transferor holding 10% or more of the total of the share capital of a company. Such transferor needs to give intimation to the central government of its proposal to transfer such a share along with the required particulars. The same is applicable to the transferors holding 10% or more in the foreign companies. Where the central government is satisfied that as a result of the transfer or any share, or block of shares of a company, a change in the controlling interest of a company is likely to take place and that such a change would be prejudicial to the interests of the company or the public interest, it may direct that such transfer not take effect.

1109. Tthe 'merger provisions' of the Companies Act govern a merger of two or more companies under Indian law. The merger provisions are in fact worded so widely, that they would provide for and regulate all kinds of corporate restructuring that a company may possibly undertake; such as mergers, amalgamations, demergers, spin-off/hive off, and every other compromise, settlement, agreement or arrangement between a company and its members and/or its creditors. Terms 'proceedings' in section 391(6) of Companies Act does not include within its ambit criminal proceedings against company and its directors.[1067]

C. Takeover Regulations

1110. The SEBI is the nodal authority regulating entities that are listed on stock exchanges in India. The SEBI is empowered to regulate the securities market so as to protect the interests of the investors in securities and to promote and develop the securities market. In exercise of this power, the SEBI has issued regulations governing takeovers in India. The primary purpose of these regulations is to bring about transparency and fair play in the market.[1068] The SEBI (Substantial Acquisition of Shares and Takeovers) Regulations, 1997 (the 'Takeover Code') restricts and regulates the acquisition of shares/control in listed companies. Generally, if an acquirer acquires 15% or more of the shares or voting rights of a listed company, the acquirer would be required to make an offer to the public to acquire at least 20% of the voting capital of the company.[1069] However, Regulation 3(1)(j) of the Takeover Code provides that Regulations 10, 11[1070] and 12[1071] would not apply to any transfer or acquisition of shares or voting rights pursuant to a scheme of arrangement or reconstruction, including amalgamation or merger or demerger, under any law or regulation, whether Indian or

1067. *G.E. Capital Services India v. Sharp Industries Lts.*, II (2005) BC 373 (Bom).

1068. *See* generally, N.L. Bhatia & Jagruti Sampat, *Takeover Games and SEBI Takeover Regulations* (Taxman Allied Services 2002).

1069. Regulation 10 read with Reg. 21 of the Takeover Code.

1070. Regulation 11 deals with consolidation of holdings by a shareholder holding between 15% and 55% of the shares of a company, and provides that such a shareholder cannot acquire more than 5% of the shares of the company in a financial year without making a public offer.

1071. Regulation 12 provides that if there is an acquisition of control of a company, whether or not by the acquisition of shares/voting rights, the acquirer is required to make a public offer.

foreign. Therefore if a merger is sanctioned by the Court under the Merger Provisions, the above-mentioned provisions of the Takeover Code would not be applicable.

1111. Disclosure requirements under the Takeover Code: It must be noted that Regulations 7 and 8 of the Takeover Code would continue to be applicable to a merger involving a listed company.

Disclosures on certain acquisitions. Regulation 7 requires an acquirer to make disclosures of the aggregate of his shareholding if the acquirer acquires more than 5%, 10%, 14%, 54% or 74% of the shares/voting rights of a company. Such disclosures must be made at each stage of acquisition and are to be made to the company and to the stock exchanges on which the shares of the company are listed. Regulation 7 further provides that an acquirer, who has acquired shares/voting rights under Regulation 11 (Consolidation of holdings), must disclose purchase or sale of 2% or more of the share capital of the company, to the company and to the stock exchanges on which the shares of the company are listed. The disclosures mentioned above are to be made within two days of: (i) the receipt of intimation of allotment of shares; or (ii) the acquisition of shares or voting rights, as the case may be. The company whose shares are acquired must also disclose to the stock exchanges, the total number of shares held by the acquirers mentioned above.

Continual disclosures. Regulation 8 requires a person holding more than 15% of the shares/voting rights of a company to make annual disclosures to the company (within twenty-one days from the financial year ending 31 March) in respect of his holdings as on 31 March.

§2. Law of Restrictive and Unfair Trade Practices

1112. The industrial revolution and the development in the international trade and commerce has led to the vast expansion of business and trade, as a result of which a variety of consumer goods have appeared in the market to cater to the needs of the consumers and a host of services have been made available to the consumers like insurance, transport, electricity, housing, entertainment, finance and banking. A well-organized sector of manufacturers and traders with better knowledge of markets has come into existence, thereby affecting the relationship between the traders and the consumers making the principle of consumer sovereignty almost inapplicable. The advertisements of goods and services in television, newspapers and magazines influence the demand for the same by the consumers though there may be manufacturing defects or imperfections of short comings in the quality, quantity and the purity of the goods or there may be deficiency in the services rendered In addition, the production of the same item by many firms has led the consumers, who have little time to make a selection, to think before they can purchase the best. For the welfare of the public, the glut of adulterated and sub-standard articles in the market have to be checked. In spite of various provisions providing protection to the consumer and providing for stringent action against adulterated and sub-standard articles in the different enactments like Code of Civil Procedure, 1908; the Indian Contract Act, 1972, the Sale of Goods Act, 1930, etc. very little could be achieved in the field of consumer protection. In order to provide for better protection of the interest of consumer the Consumer Protection

Act, 1986 was enacted. The purpose of the Act is to protect consumers against the marketing of goods that are hazardous to life and property. Under this Act, the right of the consumer to be informed about the quality, quantity, potency, purity, standard and price of goods, is sought to be protected. Besides, the Consumer Protection Act provides for a separate and specialized forum for the effective and efficient redressal of grievances of the consumers.[1072]

1113. The act was amended in the year 2002, which extended the provisions of this act to service providers indulging in unfair and restrictive trade practices or offering services, which are hazardous. This amendment also brought the sale of spurious goods or services within the meaning of unfair trade practices. However, the Act is not applicable to commercial purposes. The restrictive trade practice has been defined[1073] as any trade practice, which tends to bring about the manipulation of the price of goods or services or their conditions of delivery or flow of supplies. The definition specifies certain practices as restrictive trade practices, which come within the mischief of the act. Similarly the Act defines unfair trade practices[1074] as an unfair or deceptive method or practice used for promoting the sale or supply of goods or services at the detriment of the consumers. Unfair trade practices not only relate to the purchase of goods but also to hiring services.[1075] The admission of students by the institution in addition to the quota approved by the authorities' amounts to an unfair trade practice.[1076] Similarly, intentional delay in delivery of any goods to the consumers amounts to an unfair trade practice.[1077]

1114. The whole topic of law of consumer protection has been dealt with in detail in the following chapter relating to State Regulation of the Conditions of Commercial Transactions.

1072. *See* generally, S.K. Verma & M. Afzal Wani, *A Treatise on Consumer Protection Laws* (Indian L. Inst. 2004).

1073. Consumer Protection Act, 1986, s. 2(1)(nnn).

1074. Consumer Protection Act, 1986, s. 2(1)(r).

1075. *Mantora Oil Products (P) Ltd. v. Oriental Insurance Co. Ltd.*, 1991 (1) CPJ 326 (NC).

1076. *Akhil Bhartiya Grahak Panchayat v. Secretary, Sharda Bhawan Education Society*, 1994 (2) CPJ 283 (NC).

1077. *Om Prakash v. Assistant Engineer, Haryana Agro Industries Corporation Ltd.*, 1994 (2) CPJ 1 (SC).

Chapter 5. State Regulation of the Conditions of Commercial Transactions

§1. Price and Supply Regulation

I. General

1115. India has, in the pursuit of globalization responded to up its economy, removing controls and resorting to liberalization. For ensuring the availability of essential commodities at fair prices. It is necessary to curb the hoarding and black marketing of, and excess profiteering in such commodities. In order to deal with more effectively with persons indulging in such anti-social activities and the evil of vicious inflationary prices, commodities and goods which are very essential for general life must be within reach of the general public in the interest of natural justice.

II. Regulation of Prices of Essential Commodities

1116. Article 369 of the Constitution of India empowers Parliament to make laws with respect to trade and commerce and the production, supply and distribution of certain essential commodities.

1117. All essential commodities are included in Entry 33 of the List III, i.e., 'Concurrent List', certain state governments have promulgated ordinances or taken legal actions for controlling in respect of such commodities which could not be included in the central law. In order to further this concept and spirit, in the interest of general public, for control of the production, supply and distribution of, and trade and commerce, in certain commodities, as price regulation rests on all these grounds, i.e., control of production, supply and distribution, and trade and commerce, the Essential Commodities Act, 1955 was enacted.

III. Definition of the 'Essential Commodity'

1118. The Essential Commodities Act, 1955 defines the term 'essential commodity'. It means:

(1) cattle fodder, including oil cakes and other concentrates;
(2) coal, including cake and other derivatives;
(3) component parts and accessories of automobiles;
(4) cotton and woolen textiles;

(5) drugs – 'meaning of drugs' – as defined in clause (b), section 3 of the Drugs and Cosmetics Act, 1940;
(6) food stuffs, including edible oil seeds and oils;
(7) iron and steel, including manufactured products of iron and steel;
(8) paper, including newsprint, paper board and straw board;
(9) petroleum products;
(10) raw cotton, whether ginned or unginned and cotton seeds;
(11) raw jute; and
(12) any other class of commodity which the central government may, by notified order, declared for the purposes of this Act, being a commodity with respect in which Parliament has power to make laws by virtue of Entry 33 of List III of the Seventh Schedule in the Constitution of India.

IV. Section 2(b) of the Essential Commodities Act, 1955

1119. Section 2(b) of the Essential Commodities Act, 1955 has the power to control production, supply, distribution, etc. of essential commodities or for securing their equitable distribution, etc. of essential commodities or securing their equitable distribution and availability at fair prices.

V. Section 3(1) of the Essential Commodities Act, 1955

1120. Section 3(1) of the Essential Commodities Act, 1955 sets out:

Regulation of licences, permits, or other the production of any essential commodity. The central Government, if deems fit, may by order provide for:

(1) Controlling prices at which essential commodities may be bought or sold.[1078]
(2) Production or manufacture of any essential commodity.[1079]
(3) Storage, transport, distribution, disposal, acquisition, use or consumption of any essential commodity.[1080]
(4) Prohibiting the withholding from ale of any essential commodity.[1081]
(5) Requiring any person holding in stock, or engaged in production, or in the business of buying or selling, of any essential commodity.[1082]

1078. ECA, s. 3(2)(c).
1079. ECA, s. 3(2)(a).
1080. ECA, s. 3(2)(d).
1081. ECA, s. 3(2)(e).
1082. ECA, s. 3(2)(f).

VI. Section 3(2)(I) of Essential Commodities Act, 1955

1121. The central government my make or pass any order for regulating or prohibiting any class of commercial or financial transactions relating to food stuffs or cotton textiles which unregulated are likely to be detrimental to the public interest.[1083]

1122. When a person sells an essential commodity and he has to comply with an order made with reference to section 3(2(2)(f), the price that may be paid to him, will be determined as per the following provisions:

(a) Where the price can be consistent with the controlled rice, if such is the case, as fixed under this section can be agreed upon, then the agreed price.[1084]
(b) When no such agreement can be reached, the price is to be calculated with reference to the controlled price, to the extent that it exists.[1085]
(c) Where neither clause (a) nor clause (b) of section 3 applies, the price is calculated at the market rate prevailing in the locality at the date of sale.[1086]

1123. In case the central government is of the opinion that it is necessary to do so for controlling the rise in prices, or preventing the hoarding of any food stuff in any locality, it may, by notification in the official gazette, direct that the price at which the food stuff shall be sold in the locality shall be regulated in accordance with the provisions of this subsection.[1087]

1124. An authorized controller has to exercise functions of control in accordance with the stipulations of the central government as it concerns the production and supply.[1088]

VII. Penalty

1125. For making a false statement, the law provides imprisonment for a term which may extend to five years or with a fine, or both.[1089] Prior to the enactment of the Essential Commodities (Second Amendment) Act, 1967 provided imprisonment for three years.

VIII. Essential Commodities (Special Provisions Act), 1981

1126. The Essential Commodities (Special Provisions) Act, 1981:

1083. ECA, s. 3(2)(g).
1084. ECA, s. 3(3)(a).
1085. ECA, s. 3(3)(b).
1086. ECA, s. 3(3)(c).
1087. ECA, s. 3(3).
1088. ECA, s. 3(4).
1089. ECA, s. 9.

(1) Makes certain special provisions by way of amendments to the Essential Commodities Act, 1955 for a temporary period dealing with more effectively with persons indulging in hoarding and black marketing of, and profiteering in, essential commodities and with the evils of vicious inflamatory prices and for matters connected therewith or incidental thereto.
(2) In order to ensure the availability of essential commodities at fair prices, it was necessary to prevent the hoarding and black marketing of, and profiteering in such commodities.

1127. In order to provide for detention in certain cases for the purpose of prevention of black marketing and maintenance of supplies of commodities essential to the community and for matters connected therewith, the Prevention of Black Marketing and Maintenance of Supplies of the Essential Commodities Act, 1981 was also enacted by Parliament.

§2. Consumer Law

I. General Principles

1128. In the early law, the principle of 'caveat empor' i.e., 'let the buyer beware', was the philosophy of the law of sales. He is supposed to be knowledgeable and well informed. This was true 100 years ago, when both buyer and seller were on equal footing. As organized manufacturing activity increased, sellers became bigger and better organized, while the buyer continued to be unorganized and weak. The buyer could be easily misled and duped. In the present scenario, consumer need for support and protection from unscrupulous sellers and as such, today it has been replaced by 'let the sellers beware'. As a result of this change in the outlook, business is being heavily regulated on behalf of the consumers.

1129. The United Nations, in order to protect the interest of consumers, adopted guidelines for the protection of consumers on 7 April 1985. All countries are expected to take suitable legislative measures in this direction. Accordingly, to fullfil this object, Parliament of India enacted the Consumer Protection Act, 1986.

II. Consumer Protection Act, 1986

1130. In India, consumer protection is predominantly governed by central legislature, i.e., Parliament. The most important statutory schemes of consumer protection in India, besides the Consumer Protection Act, 1986, are the Sale of Goods Act, 1930, Essential Commodity Act, 1955 with amendments from time and again, Weights and Measures Act, Competition Act, 2002, etc. Many private consumer protection organizations or so-called non-government organizations are involved in spreading the spirit of consumer protection through the media and different projects.

1131. The main object of the promotion and development of consumer protection theme and spirit 'is to provide for better protection of interests of consumers'.[1090]

III. Definitions

1132. The terms which are mostly common in consumer affairs have also been defined in the Act.

A complaint 'is any allegation in writing made by a complainant'[1091] that:

(i) unfair trade practices or restrictive trade practices have been adopted by any trader; or services provider;[1092]
(ii) the goods bought by him have one or more defects;[1093]
(iii) the services suffer from deficiency in any respect;[1094]
(iv) a trader or service provider has charged a price in excess of the price fixed under any law or maximum displayed price or as agreed between the parties;[1095]
(v) goods which will be hazardous to life and safety when used, are being offered for sale to the public[1096] '(a) in contravention of any standard relating to the safety of such goods as required to be complied with, by or under any law for the time being in force;[1097] or (b) if the trader could have known with due diligence that the goods so offered are safe to the public;[1098] or
(vi) services which are hazardous or likely to be hazardous to the life and safety of the public when used, are being offered by the service provider which such person could have known with due diligence to be injurious to life and safety.[1099]

1133. Any of the following persons (complainant) can file a complaint:[1100](i) a consumer;[1101] (ii) any voluntary consumer association registered under the Companies Act, 2013 or under any other law;[1102](iii) the central government or any state government;[1103] (iv) one or more consumers where there are numerous having the same interest;[1104] and (v) legal heir or representative of the consumer who has made a complaint.[1105]

1090. Consumer Protection Act, 1986, Preamble.
1091. CPA, s. 3(C).
1092. CPA, s. 3(c)(i).
1093. CPA, s. 3(c)(ii).
1094. CPA, s. 3(c)(iii).
1095. CPA, s. 3(c)(iv).
1096. CPA, s. 3(c)(v).
1097. CPA, s. 3(c)(v)A.
1098. CPA, s. 3(c)(v)B.
1099. CPA, s. 3(c)(vi).
1100. CPA, s. 2(b).
1101. CPA, s. 2(b)(i).
1102. CPA, s. 2(b)(ii).
1103. CPA, s. 2(b)(iv).
1104. CPA, s. 2(b)(iv).
1105. CPA, s. 2(b)(v).

1134. The Act has provided a very wide definition of the term 'consume' in the act, e.g.: (a) any person who buys the goods for a consideration for any purpose except commercial purpose;[1106] (b) any person who hires or avails any service for any purpose except a 'commercial purpose.[1107] It is, however, pertinent to point out that commercial purpose does not include use by a person of goods bought and used by him and services availed by him exclusively for the purposes of earning his livelihood, by means of self-employment.[1108]

1135. 'Consumer dispute' means a dispute where the person against whom a complaint has been made denied or dispute the allegations contained in the complaint.[1109]

1136. Similarly, 'defect'[1110] 'deficiency',[1111] 'district forum',[1112] 'goods',[1113] manufacturer,[1114] 'member',[1115] 'National Commission',[1116] 'restrictive trade practices',[1117] 'service',[1118] 'spurious goods and services',[1119] 'state commission',[1120] 'trader',[1121] 'unfair trade practices',[1122] etc. have been defined in the Act.

IV. Consumer Protection Councils

1. Central Consumer Protection Councils

1137. The Central Council has to be established to promote and protect the rights of the consumers who have been described earlier. The Central Council shall consist of the following members:

(i) The minister in charge of the consumer affairs in the central government who shall be its chairman.[1123]

(ii) Such number of other official or non-official members representing such interests as may be prescribed.[1124]

1106. CPA, s. 2(d)(i).
1107. CPA, s. 2(d)(ii).
1108. CPA, s. 2(d)(iii).
1109. CPA, s. 2(e).
1110. CPA. s. 2(f).
1111. CPA, s. 2(g).
1112. CPA, s. 2(h).
1113. CPA, s. 2(i).
1114. CPA, s. 2(j).
1115. CPA, s. 2(jj).
1116. CPA, s. 2(k).
1117. CPA, s. 2(nn).
1118. CPA, s. 2(o).
1119. CPA, s. 2(oo).
1120. CPA, s. 2(p).
1121. CPA, s. 2(q).
1122. CPA, s. 2(r).
1123. CPA, s. 4(2)(a).
1124. CPA, s. 4(2)(b).

The central consumer protection council shall hold at least one meeting every year.[1125]

2. *State Consumer Protection Council*

1138. Section 71 of the Consumer Protection Act, 1986, enjoins upon every state to establish a state consumer protection council within the territory of India. The functions, objects and procedure of it are the same as that of the central council. Two meetings are to be held every year at the designated appointed time.[1126]

3. *The District Consumer Protection Council*

1139. The state government is required to establish for every district a council to be known as district consumer protection council.[1127] The district consumer council shall consist of the following members, viz., the collector of the district, who shall be its chairman,[1128] and such other number of other official and non-official members representing such interests as may be prescribed by the state government.[1129] The district council shall meet as and when necessary but not less than two meetings shall be held every year.[1130]

V. Agencies for Redressal of Consumer Disputes

1140. The Consumer Protection Act, 1986 envisages a three-tier grievance redressal system. The following agencies are established for the purpose of the redressal of consumer disputes:

(1) the state government have to establish a 'district forum' in each district of the state; it is also provided that the state government may, it deems fit, establish more than one district forum within a district;[1131]
(2) the state government is required to establish a state commission;[1132]
(3) the central government shall establish a National Consumer Disputes Redressal Commission.[1133]

1141. Jurisdiction shall also be exercised by these redressal agencies. The district consumer protection Forum shall have jurisdiction to deal with complaints where the

1125. CPA, s. 5(2).
1126. CPA, s. 7(4).
1127. CPA, s. 8-A.
1128. CPA, s. 8(2)(a).
1129. CPA, s. 8(2)(b).
1130. CPA, s. 8(2)(4).
1131. CPA, s. 9(a).
1132. CPA, s. 9(b).
1133. CPA, s. 9(C).

value of goods or services and the compensation does not exceed INR 20 lakhs (equivalent to INR 20 million).[1134]

1142. The state consumer redressal commission has jurisdiction to decide the cases where the value of the goods and services plus compensation is over INR 20 lakhs or 2 million, but not over INR 1 crore or 10 million. In addition, it also decides appeals against the orders of the District forum.[1135] The National Commission has both original and appellate jurisdiction. Where the matter exceeds INR 1 crore or 10 million, a complaint can be filed before it directly in its original jurisdiction. It also hears appeals from orders of the state commissions.[1136]

1. Circuit Benches

1143. Ordinarily, the National Commission shall perform its function at New Delhi and at such other places as the central government may, in consultation with the National Commission notify in the official gazette, from time to time.[1137]

2. Appeal Against the Orders Made by the National Commission

1144. Any person aggrieved by an order made by the National Commission in exercise of its powers conferred by section 21(i)(a) may make an appeal to the Supreme Court within a period of thirty days from the date of the order.[1138] The Supreme Court, however, can permit a delay, if it is satisfied that there is a sufficient cause for it.

VI. Administrative Control of These Redressed Agencies

1145. The National Commission shall have administrative control over all the state commissions in the matters of disposal and pendency of cases[1139] as well as the issuance of instructions regarding the adoption of uniform procedure.[1140] Generally, overseeing the functioning of the state commissions or the district forms to ensure that the objectives and purposes of the Act are best served without in any way interfering with their quasi-judicial freedom.[1141] The state commissions shall also have administrative control over all the district forums within their jurisdiction in all matters referred to in subsection (1) of section 24B.[1142]

1134. CPA, s. 11(1).
1135. CPA, s. 17.
1136. CPA, s. 21.
1137. CPA, s. 22C.
1138. CPA, s. 23.
1139. CPA, s. 24B(1)(i).
1140. CPA, s. 24B(1)(ii).
1141. CPA, s. 24B(1)(iii).
1142. CPA, s. 24B(2).

VII. Manner in which the Complaint Shall be Made

1146. Section 12 of the Consumer Protection Act, 1986 provides the manner in which a complaint can be filed. This complaint in relation to any goods sold or delivered or services rendered may be filed with the district forum, or state commission, or the National Commission as the case may be: (i) by consumer himself in respect of the goods sold, delivered or the service rendered; (ii) by any recognized consumer association – 'recognized association' means any voluntary association registered under any applicable law; (iii) any one or more consumers, where there are numerous consumers having the same interest with the permission of the district forum, on behalf of or for the benefit of the consumers so interested; or (iv) by the central or state government.

VIII. Procedure on Receipt of a Complaint

1147. The Consumer Protection Act, 1986(CPA) provides a definite procedure for declining with a complaint. It has taken adequate care to see that the complaint is decided within a specified period so as to avoid delay in the submission of the reply by the opposite party:

(1) The district forum has to observe the procedure as provided under section 13 of the CPA, i.e., it says that the district forum shall on receipt of a complaint, if it relates to any goods:

(a) refer a copy of the complaint to the opposing party mentioned in the complaint directing him to give his version to the case within a period of thirty days or such extended period granted by the district forum not exceeding fifteen days;
(b) where the opposing party on receipt of the complaint, or omits or fails to take any action to represent his case within the time given by the district forum, the latter shall proceed to settle the consumer dispute in the following manner, i.e., clauses (c) and (d);
(c) where the complainant alleges a defect in the goods which cannot be determined without proper analysis or examination of the goods from the complainant, seal it and authenticate it in the manner prescribed and refer the sample so sealed to the appropriate laboratory along with a direction that such laboratory make an analysis or test, as necessary, with the view of finding out whether such goods suffer from any defect alleged in the complaint or suffer from any other defect and to report its findings thereon to the district forum within a period of forty-five days of the receipt of the reference or within such extended period as may be granted by the district forum;
(d) before any sample of goods is referred to any appropriate laboratory, the district forum may require the complainant to deposit to the credit of the forum such fees as may be specified, for payment to the appropriate laboratory for carrying out the necessary analysis or test in relation to the goods in question;
(e) the district forum shall remit the amount deposited to its credit under clause (d) to the appropriate laboratory to enable it to carry out the analysis or test

mentioned in clause (c) and on receipt of the report from the appropriate laboratory, the district forum shall forward copy of the report along with such remarks as the district forum feels appropriate to the opposite party;

(f) if any of the parties dispute the correctness of the findings of the appropriate laboratory, dispute the correctness of the methods of analysis or test adopted by the appropriate, the district forum shall require the opposing party or the complainant to submit in writing their objections in regard to the report made by the laboratory;

(g) the district forum shall thereafter give a reasonable opportunity to the complainant as well as the opposite party being heard as to the correctness or otherwise of the report made by the appropriate laboratory and also as to the objection made in relation thereto under clause (f) and issue an appropriate order under section 14.

(2) The district forum shall, if the complaint received y it under section 12 relates to goods in respect of which the procedure specified in subsection (1) cannot be followed, or if the complaint relates to any services:

(a) refer a copy of such complaint to the opposing party directing him to give his version of the case within a period of thirty days of such extended period of time not exceeding fifteen days as may be granted by the district forum;

(b) where the opposite party, on receipt of a copy of the complaint, referred to him under clause (a) denies or disputes the allegations contained in the complaint, or omits or fails to take any action to represent his case within the time given by the district Forum, the latter shall proceed to settle the consumer dispute on the basis of:

(i) evidence brought to its notice by the complainant and the opposing party, where the opposing party denies or disputes the allegations contained in the complaint;

(ii) evidence is brought to its notice by the complainant.

1148. Where the opposing party omits or files to take any action to represent a case within the time given by the forum:

(3) No proceedings complying with the procedure set out in sub-section (1) and (2) shall be called in question in any court on the ground that the principles of natural justice have not be complied with.

IX. Powers of the Civil Court for Certain Purposes

1149. Section 13(4) lays down that, for the purposes of its proceedings, the district forums have been vested with the same powers as are vested in a civil court under the Code of Civil Procedure, 1908. Such powers are enjoyed by the forum in respect of the following matters:

(i) the summoning and enforcing of attendance of any defendant or witness and examining the witness on oath;
(ii) the discovery and production of any document or other material object producible as evidence;
(iii) the reception of evidence on affidavit;
(iv) the requisitioning of the report of the analysis or test concerned from the appropriate laboratory or from any other relevant source;
(v) issuing of any commission for the examination of any witness; and
(vi) any other matter which may be prescribed.

X. Enforcement of Orders

1150. Section 25(1) lays down that where an interim order made under the provisions of the Act is not complied with, the district forum, or the state commission, or the National Commission, as the case may be, may order the property of the person, not complying with the order to be attached. Under section 24(2), however, no attachment so made shall remain in force for more than three months, at the end of which, if the non-compliance continues, the property so attached may be sold and from the proofs any of the concerned authorities may award damages to the complainant and shall pay the balance, if any, to the party entitled thereto.

1151. Where any amount is due from any person under an order made by a district forum state commission or National Commission, as the case may be, the person entitled to the amount may under section 25(3) of the order, issue a certificate of the said amount to the collector of the district who shall proceed to recover the amount in the same manner as arrears of land revenue are recovered.

1152. The CPA for the non-compliance of the order of the district forum, state commission or the National Commission provides the provision of penalties. Under section 27, where a trader or a person against whom a complaint is made (or the complainant) fails or omits to comply with any order made by any of these concerned authorities, he shall be punished with imprisonment for a term which shall not be less than one month but which may extend to INR 10,000, or both.

XI. Limitation Period

1153. Section 24(A) lays down the period within which a complaint can be filed. According to it, the district forum, the state commission or the National Commission shall not admit a complaint unless it is filed within two years from the date from which the cause of action has arisen. However, this delay can be condoned, if the complainant showed sufficient cause for not filing within two years from the date from which the cause of action has arisen. The National Commission, the state commission or the district forum, as the case may be, records its reasons for condoning such things.

XII. Frivolous or Vexatious Complaints

1154. Section 26 of the Act lays down that when a complaint addressed before the consumer redressal agency is found to be frivolous, it shall for reason to be reduced in writing, dismiss the complaint and make an order that the complainant shall pay to the opposing party such cost, not exceeding INR 10,000.

XIII. Orders that Can Be Issued by the Redressal Agencies

1155. After conducting the proceedings in accordance with the provisions of section 13 of the CPA, 1986, the redressal agency, if satisfied that the goods complained against suffer from defects or that allegations regarding deficiency in service are proved, it shall issue an order to the other party, directing him to do or not to do any of the following:[1143]

(i) to remove defects pointed out by the laboratory;
(ii) to replace goods with new goods free of charge;
(iii) to refund the price of the goods or charge of services paid by the complainant;
(iv) to grant compensation for loss or injury suffered by the consumer due to the negligence of the opposite party; in addition, punitive damages can also be granted;
(v) to remove defect in the goods or deficiencies in services in question;
(vi) to order the discontinue of unfair trade practice or restrictive trade practice and that they should not be repeated;
(vii) not allowing hazardous goods for sale;
(viii) to order the withdrawal of hazardous goods from being offered for sale;
(ix) to cease manufacture of hazardous goods and to resist from offering services which are hazardous in nature;
(x) to pay such sum as determined by the redressal agency if it is of the opinion that loss or injury has been suffered by a large number of consumers that cannot be easily identified. It is also provided that the minimum sum so payable shall not be less than 5% of the value of such defective goods sold or service rendered, as the case may be, to such customers;
(xi) to issue a corrective advertisement so as to neutralize the effect of the mislealding advertisement, and this should be at the cost of the opposing party responsible for issuing the misleading advertisement;
(xii) to provide for adequate costs to the parties.

XIV. Compensation

1156. Compensation for the loss or the injury caused to the consumer is not only the most important aspect of the relief provided under the Consumer Protection Act, 1986, but rather a basic feature of the relief to be provided under the said Act. It

1143. CPA, s.14(I)(a)–(I).

is this aspect that differentiates between the relief provided under the ordinary and common civil law. Fixation of the appropriate figure of compensation is bound by the principles of the subject under which the claim arises, e.g., the principles of the law of contract and also of tort. The consumer forum too, however, must follow those principles laid down under the law of contract and the law of tort up to a certain extent, meaning that compensation cannot be allowed for remote or indirect losses or injuries. But these principles may have to be departed or modified in certain consumer cases where redemption of consumer sufferings may not be possible by resort to typical legal and business approaches. The approach of the consumer redressal agencies and also of the Supreme Court of India will be noted in some of the following cases.

1157. In many tort cases, the amount of compensation varies with the status of the complainant. For example, in an action for defamation, much greater money has been ordered to be recoverable by a man of status in the society than from the share of an ordinary man. With contract also, the courts take the social status of the claimant into account. In *Dharni v. Dharni*,[1144] a band which was booked in advance, failed to appear at the wedding reception. The court took into account the estimation of the aggrieved father held by his social and business friends. In consumer cases, however, this has not been the case. In *G.M., South-Eastern Railway v. Anand Prasad Sinha*,[1145] the state commission awarded high compensation to a passenger of status for a deficient railway service. The National Commission reduced INR 10,000 to only INR 1,500 representing the amount which would have been payable to an ordinary person.

1158. In *Coal India v. Ram Luthra*,[1146] an air-conditioner of a customer was damaged resulting in a total loss in the workshop and replacement was assessed in the amount of compensation, but when the matter was still at the appeal level, excise cuts were announced. It was held that the consequential reduction in prices could be taken into account at the appeal level for the purpose of adjusting the amount of compensation to the new price structure. In keeping with the ordinary principles, the complainant would have to discharge the initial burden of showing the nature of the loss or injury which has been caused to him under the consumer transaction. He will have to show the manner of the loss or injury and its extent in terms of money.[1147] If the source of injury is negligence on the part of the opposite party, some evidence of the degree and type of negligence would have to be shown.[1148] Where a bank could not attend to its customers because of striking employees and there being no negligence on the part of the bank, no liability arose as to any inconvenience or loss.[1149] Unlike civil courts, In matters relating to the Consumer Protection Act, 1986 parties can submit evidence through the use of affidavit not only as no question of evidence in service but also on the subject of determination of damages on compensation on account of the loss of goods, harassment and agony caused to the complainant.[1150]

1144. Current Law Year Book, (1988), p. 409.
1145. 3 Comp. Law Year LJ, 269 NC (1989).
1146. (1995) I CPJ 403 New Delhi.
1147. *Commercial Officier v. Telecom v. Bihar State Warehousing Corp.*, (1991) 1 CPJ 42(NC).
1148. *Indian Airlines cp. v. Rajesh Kumar Upadhyaya*, (1991) 1 CPJ 206.
1149. *Consumer Unity and Trust Society v. Bank of Baroda* (1992) 1 CPJ 18 (NC).
1150. *Prem Prakash Mehra v. Oriental Ins. Co.*, (1995) 3 CPJ 407 Punj.

1159. Where compensation is claimed for harassment, some proof of the fact of it would be necessary. Where an overcharged tractor price was ordered so to be refunded with interest, the National Commission upheld award of the state commission but rejected the award of INR 8,000 for harassment, finding that there was no proof of it nor any discussion in the judgment of the state commission.[1151] Similar has been the approach of the National Commission in *Indian Airlines v. S.N. Sinha*[1152] where the complainant while travelling with Indian Airlines was insured in his gums by a metallic wire piece from the food served by the airline. His outrageous claim of INR 50,000 for pain and shock and INR 10,000 for injury was reduced to INR 2,000 only on the plea that he could not substantiate his other losses. Unfortunately, neither the state commission nor the National Commission has been able to understand the philosophy of consumer protection. They are slow and hesitant as are other civil courts in India in awarding compensation for mental pain and suffering. Their approach is very conservative even though in some cases the district forum or the state commission has granted compensation for mental harassment. The National Commission reduced it to a very petty amount. A state commission awarded a medical practitioner for poor telephone service INR 1,000 for loss of his practice and INR 5,000 for mental injury. The National Commission maintained the figure of INR 1,000, but reduced the figure for mental injury to INR 200 only.[1153]

1160. The approach of the Supreme Court, however, is different from those of the state commissions and the National Commission. In *Lucknow Development Authority v. M.K. Gupta*,[1154] the Supreme Court granted compensation against the government officers for mala fide action, and held that under the Indian Constitution, sovereignty vests in the people. Every limb of the constitutional machinery is obliged to be people oriented. No organ in exercise of statutory powers can claim immunity, except to the extent that it is protected by the statute itself.

1161. The Supreme Court of India has departed from the approach of the national and state commissions. In *Charan Sing v. Healing Touch Hospital*,[1155] the appellant went to the respondent hospital for treatment for his stomach ache and burning sensation while urinating. On account of the negligence by the doctors of this hospital while conducting the operation, the body of the appellant became paralyzed. Not only was his kidney removed, but also he lost his job and had to spend a fortune paying the exorbitant medical bills as well as for medicines, tests and his up keep. He filed a claim of INR 34 lakhs (3.4 million) before National Commission for compensation. The Commission dismissed his claim as ‘excessive’ or ‘exaggerated’ and directed the appellant to make a ‘realistic claim’. He appealed to the Supreme Court which while accepting the appeal observed:

> While quantifying damages, consumer fora are required to make an attempt to serve ends of justice so that compensation is awarded, in an established case, which not only serves the purpose of recompensing the individual, but which

1151. *Bharat Tractor v. Ramchandra Pandey*, (1991) I CPJ 152(NC).
1152. (1992) I CPJ 62 NC.
1153. *Union of India v. Satya Bhama Thakur* (DR), (1991) 1 CPR 43 NC.
1154. III (1993) CPJ 7 (SC).
1155. III (2000) CPJ 1 (SC) 1.

also at the same time, aims to bring about a quantitative change in the attitude of the service provider.[1156]

1162. It further observed:

The legislative intent, for enacting the legislation, of a speedy summary trial, to settle the claim of the complainant (consumers) has been overlooked and its object frustrated by non-suiting the appellant in the manner in which it has been done by the National Consumer Forum.[1157]

1156. *Ibid.*, Art. 4.
1157. *Ibid.*, Art. 5.

Selected Bibliography

Agarwala A.N. *Introductions to Economics.* Vol. 11, Allahabad: Kitab Mahal, 2011.

Ahuja, V.K. *Intellectual Property Rights In India.* 2nd edn. Delhi: Lexis Nexis, 2015.

Ameer Ahmed H.B.I. 'Copyright Law in National and International Evolution'. *Legal News and Views* 26, no. 2 (February 2012).

Austin, Granville. 'Working of Democratic Constitution A History of the Indian Experience'. Oxford India Paperbacks, 2016.

Avtar Singh & Kaur Harpeet. *An Introduction to Labour and Industrial Law*. Nagpur: Butterworth Wadhwa Case, 2012.

Avtar Singh. *Company Law.* 15th edn. Lucknow: Eastern Book Company, 2013.

Avtar Singh. *Contract and Specific Relief.* 11th edn. Lucknow: Eastern Book company, 2013.

Bailey David, Whish Richard. *Competition Law*. 17th edn. London: Oxford University Press, 2009, ISBN 978-0-19-958655-4.

Bangia, R.K. *Company Law I.* 6th edn. Allahabad: Allahabad Law Agency, 2009.

Basheer Shamnad. *Overlapping Intellectual Property Rights*. India: Oxford, 2012.

Basu, D.D. *Commentary on the Constitution of India*. New Delhi: Lexis Nexis, 2016.

Bhashyam & Adiga. *The Negotiable Instruments Act*. S.N. Gupta rev. 16th edn. New Delhi: Bharat law House, 1997.

Chaturvedi, R.G. *Securitisation & Reconstruction of Financial Assets & Enforcement of Security Interest.* 4th edn. Jaipur: Bharat Law House, 2012.

Chauhan S.P. *Sources & Framing of the Constitution of India with Special Reference to Vedic Governance*. New Delhi: Universal Law Publishing Co., 2015.

Comish, W.R. *Intellectual Property, Patents, Copyrights, Trade Marks and Allied Rights.* 2nd edn. London: Sweet and Maxwell Publications, 1995.

Darashaw Vakil. *Commentaries on Transfer of Property Act, 1882.* 3rd edn. Nagpur: Lexis Nexis Butterworths, 2009.

Desai, T.R. *Partnership in India.* 7th edn. Napur: Lexis Nexis Botterworths, 2009.

Ghosh, K.M. *Company Law.* 14th edn. Delhi: Bharat La House, 2010.

Gordon, Wendy J., 'A Property Right in Self-Expression, Equality and Individualism in the Natural Law of Intellectual Property'. *Yale Law Journal* (1993): 102.

Gower. 'Principles of Modern Company Law'. In *Law of Library and Framatic-Copyright in a Nutshell*, edited by Rustom R. Dadachanji. 3rd edn. Bombay: N.M.Tripathi Pvt. Ltd., 1960, 1069.

Gower. 'Principles of Modern Company Law'. In *Law of Library and Framatic-Copyrifhtr in a Nutshell*, edited by Rustom R. Dadachanji. 3rd edn. Bombay: N.M.Tripathi Pvt. Ltd., 1960, 1069.

Gupta, S.N. *Dishonour of Cheques.* 3rd edn. Delhi: Universal Law Publishing Co. Pvt. Ltd., 1997.

Joshi, J.V. 'Copyright as an Intellectual Property and Information Technology'. In *Intellectual Property Rights and Copyrights*, edited by S.P. Satakar. New Delhi: Ess Ess Publications, 2003.

Khergamvela. *Negotiable Instruments Act.* Nagpur: Lexis Nexis Butterworths, 2009.

Lionel Bently, Jennifer Davis & Jane C. Ginsburg. *Trade Marks & Brands An Interdisciplinary Critique.* UK: Cambridge University Press, 2011.

Maheshwari R.P. & S.N. Maheshwari. *Mercantile Law.* 3rd rev. edn. Delhi, India: National Publishing House, 1975.

Majumdar, P.K. *Law Consumer Protection in India.* 6th edn. Nagpur: Lexis Nexis Buttewoths, 2012.

Manekar Prachi, *Insight into the New Company Law*. New Delhi: Lexis Nexis Butterworths Wadhwa, 2013.

Markanda, P.C. *The Law of Partnership.* Nagpur: Lexis Nexis Butterworths, 2010.

Mitra, S.C. *Law of Contract and Tenders.* 3rd edn. Allahabad: Orient Publishing House, 2012.

Mulla, D.F.D. *The Code of Civil Procedure*. New Delhi: Lexis Nexis, 2013.

Mulla, D.F.D. *The Indian Contract Act.* 13th edn. Nagpur: Lexis Nexis Butterworths Wadhwa, 2011.

Mulla, D.F.D. *Transfer of Property Act 1882*. 10th edn. Nagpur: Lexi Nexis Butterworth, 2006.

Muragendra B. Tabake. 'The History and Development of Trade Marks Law', *Legal News and Views* 26, no. 9 (2012).

Pollock & Mulla. *Indian Contract and Specific Relief Acts.* 14th edn. Nagpur: Lexis Nexis Butterworhs, 2012.

Poonam Pradhan, S. *Property Law.* Wadhwa, Nagpur: Lexis Nexis, Butterworths, 2011.

Ragavan Srividhya. *Patent and Trade Disputes in Developing countries*. India: Oxford, 2012.

Ramaiyya, A. *Guide to the Company Act*. Part-II, 14th edn. New Delhi: Wadhwa and Company, 1998.

Ravinchandran, KS. *Corporate Social Responsibility Emerging Opportunities and Challenges in India*. New Delhi: Lexis Nexis Butterworths Wadhwa, 2016.

Selected Bibliography

Roy Chaudhary S.K. & H.K. Saharay. *Dutt on Contract, The Indian Contract Act, 1872.* 8th edn. Calcutta: Eastern Law House, 1994.

Rustom R. Dadachanji. *Law of Library and Dramatic – Copyright in a Nutshell.* Bombay: N.M. Tripathi Pvt. Ltd., 1960.

Sanjeev Agrawal & Rohni Aggarwal. *Limited Liability and Partnership – Law and Practice.* Nagpur: Lexis Nexis butterworths, 2009.

Sethna, M.J. *Law Relating to Negotiable Instruments.* 6th edn. Allahabad: Orient Publishing House, 2012.

Verkey Elizabeth. *Intellectual Property Law & Practice*. Lucknow: Eastern Book Company, 2015.

Wadhawa, D.P. & N.L. Rajat. *The Law of Consumer Protection.* 2nd edn. Nagpur: Lexis Nexis Butterworths, 2009.

Table of Cases

A.C. Lakshmipathy v. A.M. Chakrapani Reddiar, AIR 2001 Mad 135

A.L. Mudaliar v. Life Insurance Corporation of India, AIR 1963 SC 1185

Abdul Azeez v. M.K.P. Kadar Mohideen, AIR 1963 Mad 428

Abdul Aziz v. M. Maniyapa Setty, AIR 1989 SC 553

Afzal v. Ram Kumar Bhurdra, ILR S 1886 12 Cal 610

Agarwalla Air Transport v. Md. Nasarutulla, AIR 1959 Cal 755

Agrenath v. Ram Ratan, 1958 ALJ 854

Akhil Chandra v. LGN Rly. Co., IR 1916 Ca 647

Alco Chem Ltd. v. Hyderabad Chemical Pharmaceutical Works Ltd., 2003 3 BC 508 (AP)

Alcove Industries Ltd. v. Oriental Structural Engineers Pvt. Ltd., AIR 2005 Del 173

Ali Mohamad v. G.P.P. Railway Co., AIR 1915 Nag 6

All India Bank Officers Confederation v. Dhanlakshmi Bank Ltd., 1997 90 Com Cas 225

Anil & Co. v. Air India, AIR 1986 Del 312

Annaji v. Ragubai, 6 MHCR 400(1871)

Anwarali Bepari v. Jaminilal Roy, AIR 1940 Cal 89

Army Welfare Housing Organisation v. Sumangal Services (P) Ltd., AIR 2004 SC 1344

Ashok Kumar J. Pandya v. Suyog Coop Housing society Ltd., AIR 2003 Guj 118 (NOC): 2002 AIHC 3401

Associated Cement Ltd. v. Their Workmen, AIR 1960 SC 777

B.A.Chopra v. New Zealand Insurance Co., Ltd., AIR 1967 Cal. 35

*B.S.N.L. v. Motorola India (P) Ltd., (*2009)2 SCC 337

Backer Khorasain v. Ahmed Ismail, AIR 1928 Rang 28

Balkesserbai v. Naranaji, ILR (1880) 4 Bom 352

Banarsidas v. Kansi Ram, AIR 1963 SC 1165

Banarsidas v. Kansiram, AIR 1961 SC 1165

Bank of Baroda v. Nanital Seeds Corpn, AIR 1971 SC 1210

Bank of Baroda v. Nanital Seeds Corpn, AIR 2008 Utt 22

Bank of India v. Binod Steel Ltd., AIR 1977 MP 188

Bank of India v. Grains and Gummy Agencies, AIR 1989 MP 28

Bank of India v. Nangia Construction (I)(P) Ltd., (2008) 7 SCC 290

*Bank of Nova Scotia v. Hollenic War Risks Assn (Bermuda) Ltd., (*1992) 1 AC 233

Bank of Rajasthan Ltd. v. Hajarimal Milap C. Surana, (2005) 10 SCC 238

Banwari Lal v. Punjab State Cooperative Supply and Marketing Federation Ltd., Chandigarh, AIR 1982 Del 357, 360

Basant Kumar Mitter v. Kusum Kumar Mitter, (1900) 4 CWN 767

Bechu Singh v. Baldeo Prasad, AIR 1933 Oudh 132

Belgaum Pioneer Urban Coop. Credit Bank v. Satyapromoda, AIR 1960 Mays. 48

Bellachi v. Pakeeran, AIR 2009 SC 3293

Bhagwandas v. Girdhari Lal, (1966) 1 SCR 656

Bhai Mehar Singh Kishan Singh v. Union of India, 1980 ACJ 110 Del

Bharat Glass Tube v. Gopal Glass Works, AIR 2008 SC 2520

Bharat Tractor v. Ramchandra Pandey, (1991) I CPJ 152(NC)

Bhola Nath Shankar Das v. Lachmi Narain, (1931) 29 ALJ 84

Bhoneswar Ram v. Ram Khelawan, 12 CLJ 137

Bikroo v. Anant Bahadur Singh, AIR 1921 Oudh 167

Bina Murlidhar Namdev v. Kanhaiyababu Lokdev, AIR 1999 SC 2171

Birdhi Chand v. Assam Travels, AIR 1954 Cal 170

Bishwanath Prasad Radhey Shyam v. Hindustan Metal Industries, AIR 1982 SC 1444

Bishwannath Agarwala v. State Bank of India, AIR 2005 Jhar 69

Blower v. Great Western Railway, (1872) LR 7 CP 655

Bombay Steam Navigation Co. Ltd. v. Vasudev Babu Rao Kamat, AIR 1958 Bom 5

Bombay Steam Navigation Co. v. Vasudev Baburao, AIR 1928 Bom 5

Bras v. Maitland, 119 ER 940

British Airways v. Art Works Export Ltd., AIR 1986 Cal 120

British India Steam Navigation Co. Ltd. v. Shanmugavilas Cashew Industries, (1990) 48 ELT 481 (SC)

*Bros. Exim International Ltd. v. Best Roadways Ltd. Nath, (*2004) 4 SCC 553

Bsanti Lal v. Phaphi, AIR 2008 Raj 72

C.K. Aboobacker v. K.P. Ayishu, AIR 2000 NOC 29 (Kerala)

C.T. Joseph v. I. V. Phillip, AIR 2001 Ker 30

Canara Industrial and Banking Syndicate v. Ramchandra, AIR 1968 Mysore 133

Carew & Co. Ltd. v. North Bengal Sugar Mills Co., ILR (1951) 2 Cal 386

*Delhi Development Authority v. Skipper Construction Company Pvt. Ltd., (*1997) 11 SCC 430

Deok, Rajgariah v. Anar Dai Poddar, AIR 1999 Pat 22

Deokar Exports (P) Ltd. v. New India Assurance Co. Ltd., (2008) 14 SCC 598

Deokar Exports (P) Ltd. v. New India Assurance Co. Ltd., AIR 2009 SC 2026

*Deputy Commissioner v. Cherian Transport Corp., (*1992) 74 Com Cas 563

Dev Sharma v. Laxmi Narain, AIR 1956 Punj 49

Devidas Jagjivan v. Pirjada Begum, ILR 8 Bom 377

Dhaesa v. Bandagisab, AIR 1999 Kan 190

Dhotha House v. S. K. Maingi, AIR 2006 SC 730

Dinshaw Maneckjee Patil, Re, AIR 1927 Bom 37

*Draupadi Devi v. Union of India, (*2004) II SCC 425

Duli Chand v. C.I.T,. AIR 1956 SC 354

*Dy. Commr. I.T. v. Cherian Transport Corpn. Ltd., (*1992) 74 Com Cas 563 Mad

E.H. Parakh v. King Emperor, AIR 1926 Sind 225

Eduljee v. Café John Bros, AIR 1943 Bag 249

Electronics Corporation of India v. Secretary Revenue Department, Government of Andhra Pradesh, AIR 1999 SC 1734

Elsa Tony Philip v. LIC, (1909) 2 K.B. 288

Epoch Enterprises v. MV Won Fu, AIR 2003 SC 24

Ethirington and Lanclashire and Yorkashire Accident Ins. Co. Re, (1909) 1 KB591

Europa', The, (1904-7) All ER Rep 387

Fattersal v. National S.S. Co., (1884) 12 QBD 297

Floating Services Ltd. v. M. V. San Fransceco Dipalola, (2004) 52 SCL 762 (Guj)

*Foley v. Hill, (*1848) 2 HLC 28

G.M. Roadways Co. v. P.G. Industries, AIR 1971 Cal 494

Galliora v. U, Thet, AIR 1929 Rang 117

Ganesh Trading Co. v. Moji Ram, AIR 1978 SC 484

Gas Authority of India Ltd. v. Official Liquidato, (2004) 4 BC 306 Ibom

Geigy SA's Patent, 1964 RPC

*General Accident Insurance v. Crank, (*1901) 17 T.I.R. 233

General Assurance Society v. Chandmull, AIR 1966 SC 1644

General Insurance Society v. Chandmull, (1966) 36 Com Cases 468 (SC)

General Traders Ltd. v. Pierce Leslie (India) Ltd., AIR 1987 Ker 62

Gherulal Parekh v. Mahadevdas, AIR 1959 SC 781

Table of Cases

Ghulam Ahmad v. Gulam Quadir, AIR 1968 J & K 38

*Glyn, Mills & Co. v. East and West India Dock Co., (*1882) 7 App. Cas 591

Gokeda Latcharao v. Viswariadhan Bhimayya, AIR 1956 AP 182

*Gopalpur Tea Co. Ltd. v. Penhok Tea Co. Ltd., (*1982) 52 Com Cas 238 Cal

Gopisetti Venkata Lakshmi Narasimharao v. M/s. Sri Satya Financial Services, 2010 (3) ALT 325

*Gujarat Bottling Co. Ltd. v. Coca Cola, (*1999) 5, SCC 545

Gurden Krishna Reddy v. Union of India, AIR 1965 AP 263

Gwalior Rayon Silk Mfg (Weaving) Co. Ltd. v. Union of India, 1985 ACJ 739

Hanil Era Textiles (P) Ltd. v. Puromatic Fitnes (P) Ltd., AIR 2004 SC 2432

Har Bilas v. Mahadeo Prasad, AIR 1931 All 539

Hari Prasad Jayantalal & Co. v. I.T.O. Ahmedabad, 1966 Comp LJ 320

Haribhai v. Sharaf Ali, ILR, (1897) 22 Bom 461

Harry & Genny v. Export Credit Guarantee Corporation, 1999 (97) Com Cas 663

Hastimal v. P. Tej Raj Sharma, AIR 2007 SC 3246

Hinduistan Club Ltd. v. Pawan Kumar Jain, (2006)129 Comp Cas 171Cal

Hiralal v. Tripura Charan, ILR 40 Cal 650

Holmes v. Bangladesh Biman Corp., [1989] 1 All ER 759

Holmes v. Bangladesh Viman Corp., 1989 AC 1112

Hugglunds Drives AB v. National Heavy Engineering Coop. Ltd., AIR 2002 Bom 305

Hukum Chand v. Jaipur Ice and Oil Mills, AIR 1980 Raj 155

Hussain Abdul Rehaman & Co. v. Lakhmichand, AIR 1925 Bom 34

Hussain Kazi v. C.I.T., (1941) CWN 629

Hussainbhai v. Motilal, AIR 1963 Bom 208

Ibrahim Ispahan v. Union of India, AIR 1966 Guj 6

Ind. Contract Act, 1872, Sec. 68

Inder v. Raghubir Singh, ILR (1930) 5 Luck 545

India General Navigation & Rly. Co. v. Dekhari Tea Co., AIR 1924 PC 40

Indian Airlines cp. v. Rajesh Kumar Upadhyaya, (1991)1 CPJ206

Indian States Bank Ltd. v. Kunwar Sardar Singh, AIR 1034 All 855

Industrial Finance Corpn of India Ltd. v. Connanore Spg and Wvg Mills Ltd., (2002)5 SCC 54

Irrawaddy Flotilla Co. v. Bhagwan Das, (1891) 18 IA 121, p. 127

J.B. Exports Ltd. v. BSES Rajdhani Power Ltd., AIR 2006 Del. 317

Table of Cases

Kumari Shahnoor Md Tahssen v. State of U.P., AIR 2007 (NOC) 437 (All)

Kundan Mal v. Nand Kishore, AIR 1994 Raj. 1

L. Mudaliar v. Life Insurance Corporation of India, AIR 1963 SC 118

Lachhman v. Naina, AIR 1940 Lah 40

Lachmi Narain v. Beni Ram, AIR 1931 All 327; ILR 53 All 479(1931)

Lake v. Simmons, (1927) AC 487, 508

Lakhwinder Singh v. Paramjit Kaur, AIR 2004 P&H 6: (2004) I ICC 151

Lakshmi Chand Textiles v. Union of India, AIR 2005 Del 2

Lakshmi Insurance Co. Ltd. v. Bibi Padmawati, AIR 1961 Punj 253

Lal Chand v. Hussaini, (1927) 97 I.C. 257

Lalchand Madhav Das v. Union of India, AIR 1986 Del 29

Lalchand Ramchand v. Pyare Dasrath Chamar, AIR 1971 MP 245

Lallan Prasad v. Rehmat Ali, AIR 1967 SC 1322

Lalman Shukla v. Gauri Dutt, (1913) 11 All L J 489

Laxmikant V. Patel v. Chetanbhat Shah, AIR 2002 SC 275

LIC v. Permanent Lok Adalat, AIR 2009 (NOC)467 (P&H)

Life Insurance Corporation of India v. Asha Goel, (2001) 2 SC 160

London and Lancashire Fire Ins. Co. *v. Boland, (*1924) AC 836 HL

Lucknow Development Authority v. M.K. Gupta, 1964 RPC 391

*M. Rangasamy v. Rengammal, (*2003)7 SCC 683

*M.S.Madhusoodhanan v. Kerala Kaumudi (p) Ltd., (*2004) 9 SCC 204

*M.V. 'Dong Do' v. Ramesh Kumar & Co. Ltd., (*2002) Com Cas 450 Cal

M/s Basanti Polymers v. State Chemical, etc. Corp. of India, AIR 1986 Raj. 1

M/s. Dale & Carrington Invt (P) Ltd. & Another v. P.K. Prathapan & Others, 2004 (7) Scale 584, 2005 AIR (SC) 1624, 2004 (122) CC 161, 2004 AIR(SCW) 5143

Madan lal Sobti v. Rajasthan State Industrial Development and Investment Corporation, AIR 2007 (NOC)638(Dwl)

Madhukar Goel v. M. S. Goel, AIR 1998 Del. 257

*Madhusoodhanan v. Kerala Kaumudi (P) Ltd., (*2004) 9 SCC 204

Mahendra Kumar Chandulal v. CBI, AIR 1984 Guj (NOC) 53

*Mahesh Chandra Basu v. R. K. Bhattacharjee, (*1908) 12 CWN 28

Malabar Steamship Co. v. Central Bank of India, AIR 1939 Sind 225

Manik Chand v. Ram Chandra, AIR 1981 SC 591

Marico Limited v. Raj Oil Mills Limited, 2008(37) PTC 109

Maritime Co. v. Gibbon, [1954] 1 QB 88, [1953] 2 ALL ER 1086

Table of Cases

*Oriental Road Lines v. Mohammed Hassan Sahib & Co., (*1988) 2 KLT 619

P. Archana v. Varada Siva Rama Krishna, AIR 2008 AP 216

*P. Sukhadev v. Commr of Endowments, (*1998)1 BC (DB 403 (AP))

*P.C. Chako v. LIC of India, (*2008) 1 SCC 321

*P.J.Johnson v. Astfro fiel Armodadorn, (*1989) 3 Comp LJ 5, 10 Ker

P.K. Kalasami v. K. Pannuswami, AIR 1962 Mad 44

Palaniappa v. Official Liquidator, AIR 1942 Mad 470

Palaniappa v. Pasupati Bank, (1942) 1 MLJ 425

Parasram perumal v. Air India Ltd., (1956) 56 Bom LR 944

Parasullah Malik v. Chandrakanta Das, (1917) 21 CWN 979

Patel Roadways Ltd. v. Birla Yamaha Ltd., (2004) 4 SCC 91

Patricia D'Furlong v. MD, East West Airlines, (2004) 2 CPR 60 (Hyd)

Pawan Nandlal Agarwal v. Asian Dye Chemicals, AIR 2008 (NOC) 804 (Bom)

Pearl life v. Johnson, AIR 2009 (NOC) 785 (NCC)

Prabhakaran v. M. Azhagiri Pillai, AIR 2006 SC 1567

Pradeep Oil Corpn. v. Municipal Corpn. of Delhi, AIR 2011 SC 1869

Prakash v. Mukhtar, AIR 1940 Lah 486

Pratap Bahadur v. Gajadha, ILR (1902) 24 All 521

Prem Prakash Mehra v. Oriental Ins. Co., (1995) 3 CPJ 407 Punj

Prithvi Singh v. Haji Hassan Ali, AIR 1951 Bom 6

Prudential Insurance Co. v. Inland Revenue Commrs, (1904) 2 KB 628

Punjab National Bank v. Beniprasad Maheshwari, AIR 1981 MP 95

Punjab National Bank v. Satyapal, AIR 1956 Punjab 118 at 120

Pure Helium (I) Ltd. v. ONGC, (2003)8 SCC 593

Purushottam Das Banarsi Das v. Union of India, AIR 1967 All 549

R. Lilawati v. Bank of Baroda, AIR 1987 Kant 2

R.D. Saxsena v. Balram Prasad Sharma, AIR 2000 SC 2912

R.R. Sarna v. Ruben, AIR 1946 Oudh 68

R.R.N. Ramalinga v. Narayana, AIR 1971 Ker 197

Radehey Shyam v. Official Liquidator, AIR 1968 Raj 220

Raghumal v. Official Assignee, Calcutta, AIR 1924 Ca. 424

Raghunadhan v. Harinasji, AIR 1927 Bom. 187

Raj Kishore v. Prem Singh, AIR 2011 SC 382

Rajasthan Handicrafts Emporium v. P.A. World Airways, AIR 1984 Del 396

Table of Cases

Shanti Devi v. Nand Lal, AIR 2005 Raj 218

Sharad Vasant Kotak v. Ramniklal Mohanlal Chawda, (1998) 2 SCC 171

Shashi Kapila v. R.P. Ashwain, 2002(1)SCC 583

Shital Kumar Saini v. Satvir Singh, (2005) 1 CPR 401

Shri Gopal Jalan & Co. v. Calcutta Stock Exchange, AIR 1964 SC 250

Shyama Charan Mal v. Chaudhary Deby Singh, ILR (1884) 21 Cal. 872

SICOM Ltd. v. Harjinder Singh, AIR 2004 Bom 337

Simrathmjull v. Nanja Lingiah, AIR 1963 SC 1182

Sinaya v. Munisami, (1899) ILR 22 Mad 289

Sir Mahomad Akbar KIan v. Attar Chand, 38 BLR 739

Sk. Md. Illiyas v. Narayan Sah., AIR 2009 Pat. 17

Snow White Food Products (P) Ltd. v. Sohan Lal Bagla, AIR 1964 Cal 204 at 214

Snowcem India Ltd. v. UOI, (2005) 124 Com Cas 161

Somasundram Mudaliar v. Ranjappa Mudaliar, AIR 1927 Mad 369

South Easter Carriers P. Ltd. v. Oriental Fire & General Insurance Co., AIR 2004 Ker. 139

Sriram Finance Corp. v. Yasin Khan, AIR 1989 SC 176

State Bank of India v. Dipak Malviya, AIR 1966 All 165

State Bank of India v. G.J. Herman, AIR 1998 Ker 161

State Bank of India v. Prem Dass, AIR 1958 Del 49

State of Karnataka v. Shreyas Papers Pvt. Ltd., (2006) 1 SCC 615

State of Kerala v. Cochin Chemical Refineries, 1968 SC 1361

State of M.P. v. Kaluram, AIR 1967 SC 1105

State of Punjab v. Labb Singh, (1985) 4 SCC 52

State of Rajasthan v. Mehta Transport Co., AIR 2002 Raj 17

Subha Naidu v. Haji Badsha Sahib, ILR (1902) 26 Mad 168

Subhendu Banerjee v. The CESC Ltd., AIR 2002 Cal 242

Sugar Warehousing Corpn v. Pawan Hans Helicopters Ltd., AIR 2009 Del 8

Sunrise Association v. Govt. of NCT of Delhi, AIR 2006 SC 1908

Suraj Narain v. Sukhu Ahir, ILR (1928) 51 All 164

Suraj Nath v. Union of India, AIR 1972 Cal 203

Surya Investment Co. v. S.T.C., AIR 1987 Cal 46

Swadeshi Chemicals Ltd. v. Kothari Industrial Corpn. Ltd., (1995), 18 Corpt L A 23 Mad

Syndicate Bank v. Estate Officer and Manager, APIIC Ltd. (2007)8 SCC 36

*Syndicate Bank v. Estate Officer, (*1862) 8 MIA 307

Syndicate Bank v. Official Liquidator, AIR 1985 Del 256

Syndicate Bank v. Wilfred D'Souza, AIR 2003 Kant 337. AIR 2003 Kant 337

T. Lakshmipathi v. P. Nithyananda Reddy, AIR 2003 SC 2427

T.C. Mathai v. District & Session Judge Thiruvananthapuram, AIR 1999 SC 1385

Tarun Bhargava v. State of Haryana, AIR 2003 P&H 98

The Almak, [1985] 1 Lloyd's Re 557

The Opium Case, 4 Ind Dec (O.S), 205

The Pilot Pen Co (India) Private Ltd. Madras v. The Gujarat Industries Private Ltd., Bombay, AIR 1967 Mad. 215

Tikkilal v. Komal Chand, AIR 1940 Nag 327

Traders Syndicate v. Union of India, AIR 1983 Cal 337

Transport Corp. of India v. Indian Rayon Corp., Veraval, (1992)1 Guj Law Herald 277 Guj

Tugun Ram v. Dominion of India, AIR 1966 Nag 260

*U.P. Coop Cane Union Federation v. West U.P. Sugar Mills Assn., (*2004) 3 SCC430

*U.P. State Sugar Corpn v. Mahalchand M. Kothari, (*2005) 1 SCC 348

Ulhanan Rajan v. Union of India, AIR 1992 Ker 230

Uniliver Australia v. Shingar Cosmetics Pvt. Ltd. and Ors., AIR 2011 Kant 30

Union of India v. ADJ, Kheri, AIR 2010 (NOC)742 (AllS

Union of India v. Azadi Bachao Andolan, 2003 (56) CLA 344

Union of India v. B. Prahlad & Co., AIR 1976 Del 236

Union of India v. Deoria Sugar Mills, 1980 ACJ 140

Union of India v. Endupadi Narasimhan & Sons, AIR 1964 Ori 34

Union of India v. Gajanand Oil and Dal Mill, [1984] 1 ALT 284

Union of India v. Gosalia Shipping (P) Ltd., AIR 1978 SC 1196

Union of India v. Hafiz Bashir Ahmed, 1988 Supp SCC 174 (2000) 4 SCC 553

Union of India v. Mulko Bai, AIR 2000 MP 22

Union of India v. Orissa Textiles Mills Ltd., AIR 1979 Ori 165

Union of India v. R. Gandhi, [2007] 76 SCL 350 (SC)

Union of India v. Satya Bhama Thakur (DR), (1991) 1 CPR 43 NC

Union of India v. Sugauli Sugar Works, (1976) 3 SCC 32

Union of India v. Universal Traders Corn, AIR 183 Ker 173

Union of India v. West Punjab Factories, AIR 1966 SC 395

*United India Insurance Co Ltd. v. M. K. J. Corpn., (*1996)6 SCC 428

Table of Cases

*United India Insurance Co. Ltd. v. Manubhai Dharmasinhbhai Gajera, (*2008) 10 SCC 404

United India Insurance Co. Ltd. v. Mauthulalakshmi, AIR 2003 Mad 284

*Usha Chopra(Dr) v. Chopra Hospita(P) Ltd., (*2006) 130 Com Cas 483 CLB

Vadalparty v. Appalanarasimhulu, (191)41 Mad LJ 563

Vaithelinga v. Saminada, ILR (1872) 2 Mad 44

Vakil & Co. v. Mahanarain, 1937 AMLJ 56

Vancouver Malt & Sale Brewing Co. v. Vancouver Breweries Ltd., AIR 1934 PC 101

Varghese Paul v. Narayana Naik, (1999) 2 Ker LT 571

Veerappa Chettiar v. Viswanath, AIR 1916 Mad 873

Vela Partha Garasia v. Ms Kusum M Shah, For decided on 2 September, 2011, in the High Court of Gujarat

Verda Seth Sam v. Lauckputty, (1862) 8 MIA 307

Vidya Ratan v. Kota Transport Co., AIR 1965 Raj 200

*Vikram Greentech (I) Ltd. v. New India Assurance Co. Ltd., (*2009)5 SCC 599

*Vinod Kumar Mittal v. Kaveri LimeIndustries Ltd., (*2000)2 Comp LJ 154 CLB

Virendra Dresses v. Virendra Garments, AIR 1982 Del 482

Waghela Rajsonji v. Shekh Masludin, (1887) 14 I.A 89

Walter v. Lane, 1990 AC 539

Yangtze Assurance v. Indemnity Marine, (1908) 2KB 504

Yarlagaaddav Devata China Yerakayya, AIR 1966 AP 151

Yashwani v. Vithal, ILR (1897) Bom 267

Index

The numbers here refer to paragraph numbers.

Index

Index

Index

Index

Index

Index

Made in United States
Orlando, FL
04 November 2026

90201251R00243